Making The Missouri Synod Functional Again

Waldo J. Werning

Biblical Renewal Publications
1914 Wendmere Lane
Fort Wayne IN 46825

Scripture quotations are from
The King James Version of the Bible

The Holy Bible, NEW INTERNATIONAL VERSION
Copyright 1978 by the New York International Bible Society,
Used by permission of Zondervan Bible Publishers.

Revised Standard Version of the Bible,
Copyrighted 1946, 1952, 1971, 1973.

New Evangelical Translation
Copyright 1991 by God's Word To The Nations Bible Society
Used by permission of NET Publishers.

Cover art by Jonathan Werning

Biblical Renewal Publications, Fort Wayne, Indiana
Copyright 1992 Biblical Renewal Publications
Printed in the United States of America

Library of Congress Cataloging pending.

ISBN 0-9632650-0-8

CONTENTS

i

FOREWORD

The world has undergone revolutionary changes over the course of the past half-century. These changes have affected not only society in general but also the church. In this age of challenges as well as opportunities for service, how has The Lutheran Church—Missouri Synod fared? A number of histories have been written recounting the opportunities and successes of the past.

This volume, however, differs from the books and other published materials that are already on the market. The author brings the history up to date, recounting and examining the events and tensions of the more recent past — especially events where, in his opinion, not all the facts have been told or where they have been distorted. After establishing the facts with documented proof, Dr. Werning then analyzes them and calls for true repentance.

In his analysis he also answers the basic questions: why did The Lutheran Church—Missouri Synod have to face conflict in its own ranks twice during the past three decades? And how could the LCMS have avoided much of the trauma that it suffered again in the 1980 and the early 1990's? The author suggests that while the church did sense the dangers that threatened its Scriptural and confessional unity in the '60's and '70's, it made the unfortunate mistake of continuing to follow a "managerial" approach as it sought to carry on the Lord's work, instead of following the Biblical and Confessional pattern outlined in Scripture. Thus it was destined to repeat its mistakes.

Dr. Werning maintains that "there is a world of difference between **institutional religion** and **Biblical spirituality**." He holds that only too quickly the Biblical church form and function can be disformed and so be in need of reform. He maintains that we have inherited institutional forms of religion that obscure Biblical spirituality. The major battle today is in the area of sanctification, Christian life and service. He asks the church to face this question squarely: "Does God's Word direct, empower, and rule our lives?" Is Christ the Head of the Church also as far as its life and work are concerned? He sense that we have church rituals and a large "spiritual nursery, and churches that need to hear the message of Revelation 2 and 3 and Titus 1:5: 'Correct what needs to change.' "

While the LCMS was facing some of its most traumatic challenges in the 1960's and '70's, Dr. Werning was serving in strategic posts where he could observe first-hand the effects of what was happening. When Synod's attention was focused on the faculty at Concordia Seminary in St. Louis and its doctrinal struggles, Dr. Werning was serving as Chairman of the Board for Missions where he could observe how these doctrinal disputes affected the church's mission.

The author brings many qualifications to his task as author of this book. He has worked in the area of Evangelism, Missions, and Stewardship during most of his ministerial life and continues to lecture on these subjects not only in the United States but also in foreign countries where the LCMS is active in missions. He has also served on numerous Synodical and District boards and committees and has taught at Concordia Theological Seminary in Fort Wayne a number of years.

No doubt this book will be received in Synod with varying degrees of enthusiasm. One may not agree with all of Dr. Werning's assessments of those in leadership roles, but it is apparent that he has sought to be fair at all times, and evangelical as he searches for facts. He is a voice calling out to the church to change its direction and start anew. His desire is to build functional Christians and a functioning church in a dysfunctional world.

Howard W. Tepker, Th.D.

vii

MAKING THE MISSOURI SYNOD FUNCTIONAL AGAIN

Waldo J. Werning

INTRODUCTION

"Who do you think you are, writing a book which suggests that the Missouri Synod is not functional?" That's a valid question. The circumstances and the nature of the book will help provide a documented answer. Anyone who would attempt to write a book such as this one must have determined that the situation is desperate, and must love and care deeply for his church.

By the grace of God, I owe deep gratitude to The Lutheran Church-Missouri Synod for a doctrinal heritage which is priceless. The value of my spiritual legacy from the Synod cannot be adequately calculated, as it numbers a father and mother, four grandparents (Werning, Rinderknecht, Dornseif and Gunther), and eight great-grandparents - all pious Christians and faithful members of The Lutheran Church-Missouri Synod. My devoted wife, Ruth, with her rich family heritage has been a very strong spiritual partner and has constantly enhanced my spiritual life and my ministry in the Gospel.

All of this still does not make me worthy of undertaking a task as monumental as this one. However, the growing dysfunction of the Missouri Synod during the past 30 years and its inability to accept the serious reality of the deep hurt experienced by a growing number of pastors and members alike cannot be ignored. The dysfunctional situations in many congregations and in the Synod have raised many agonized screams to heaven which all of those of us who have sensitive spiritual ears no longer find acceptable. Explanations, new planning processes and programs, rationalizations, excuses, justifications, will no longer keep the silent majority from voicing what many are thinking.

I believe that I represent many who have tuned out and tuned in whenever necessary because there is no other choice, as we cry out, "It's time to communicate with each other and stop playing games!"

I realize fully that one dare not talk, feel or trust in a dysfunctional family, but families remain dysfunctional as long as they are in denial. Only when tough love and intervention is practiced is there hope for healing and normalcy. But who dares to be vulnerable and speak the truth as many see it, because making oneself wide open is very dangerous. However, the greatest hazard in life is to risk nothing in the midst of a life-threatening crisis. Those who avoid risk may avoid personal suffering, but they also avoid a responsibility for bringing healing and health to those in need.

Writing a book about the dysfunctions of a church body, its congregations, pastors and members is no more enjoyable than undergoing major surgery or getting hit over the head by a two-by-four. Let it be said at the outset that this is a book that protests the brutalizations caused by those on the political left and political right who wield spiritual, psychological and emotional two-by-fours. I also grieve over the "do-nothing" and "look-the-other-way" of the listless middle-of-the-roaders. My book aims to identify all distortions of the true Biblical identity and process.

Admittedly, I am going way beyond my "comfort zone," as I invest the capital of my 47 years of pastoral experience and executive service into this moment of Missouri Synod history. I have no special intelligence to offer, but only a deep and abiding trust in the holy and eternal Word, and the Holy Spirit who inspired it and who promises to guide those who trust Him implicitly. For those who want to analyze the author's motives, I doubt that there is any purpose for that kind of useless activity. For those who want to throw bricks, let him who has no fault throw the first one. We are called to build, not tear down or apart.

My spiritual heritage from the Missouri Synod came from eight years of parochial school at Newhall, IA, six years at the Academy and Junior College at St. Paul, and four years' seminary training in St. Louis. Congregations in Missouri and Oklahoma provided seven years of valuable pastoral experience. I entered the pastoral ministry with a strong commitment to the complete adequacy of God's Word, the unique authority of Christ and His church, and a ministry of Word and Sacrament leading to functional individual Christian and congregational lives by the balanced use of Law and Gospel. As this book reveals, I soon gained a dedication to the church as the body of Christ in which there is no substitute for Matthew 18 or for "speaking the truth with love" (Eph. 4:15).

The call to serve as Assistant Stewardship Counselor of the Synod came as a surprise, and changed the direction of my life substantially. The four and a half years in St. Louis with Dr. John E. Herrmann as my mentor gave me a life-long understanding and commitment to the fullness of God's grace. Through this experience together with the opportunity to practice the grace approach in church life in the Southern Nebraska and South Wisconsin Districts (and the annual reading of Walther's Law and Gospel for a number of years), made me increasingly aware of various legalistic, moralistic, grossly institutional and bureaucratic methodologies and practices in the church.

Beginning service to the Synod as an Executive in 1952 under the presidency of Dr. John W. Behnken and knowing and working with most leaders of the Synod in 40 years of Executive and consultant work, I became intimately acquainted with the strengths and the weaknesses of The Lutheran Church-Missouri Synod, of its leaders and its members. Ten years as Chairman and Secretary of the Mission Board, nine years as Topic Editor of the International Lutheran Women's Missionary League, and almost 20 years as Chairman and Vice-Chairman of Lutheran Bible Translators - all positions which I did not seek or expect - provided contact with the various levels of the Synod and gave insights into emerging problems which are covered in this book. These years have taken me to all 50 states and five provinces of Canada, many with seminars and area meetings. About 250 LLL seminars were conducted over a number of years when they were popular, and about 400 seminars during the past 12 years in my own stewardship/renewal leadership work in North America.

I have been in more than 1000 congregations of The Lutheran Church-Missouri Synod during these years. Without costing the Synod one penny and without personal financial resources, but with the aid of other private funds or gifts, I have visited 80 nations and most of the LCMS mission fields at least two times, and Nigeria nine times. Stewardship part-time consultant work has been provided for 10 LCMS Districts, 13 congregations, and for 13 Lutheran churches overseas besides the United States and Canada. God graciously provided contacts and fellowship with many pastors and laymen who have enriched my life substantially with their theological and practical spiritual insights. A number of these, especially some deeply spiritual confidants, have been helpful resources to make me spiritually wealthy beyond calculation.

All of this has given me an understanding of my own fallibility and weaknesses and constant need of God's grace for every moment and task. This has also led to great respect and strong love for people everywhere, especially those who have become victims of church politics, bureaucracies, institutional conflicts and any other aberrations. This is what has brought me to be the first to fly into a vacuum which needs to be filled. I am no prophet, yet feel impelled to raise a prophetic voice. I am expendable, yet I am compelled by Christ's love to utilize this moment of grace to utter sounds of Law and Gospel at a desperate moment in our Synod's history. When political parties naively assume that they accurately reflect eternal truth and are disrupting the Synod with destructive conflict, someone must step out of the ranks to raise a voice of concern. The first to fly is very lonely and an easy target.

Many have come to the conclusion that most leaders, pastors and members of the Missouri Synod do not know how to handle conflict but rather try to control the noise level of the screams of agony from the multitude of victims on all stratums. The sounds of the screams are muffled by political and bureaucratic tactics and offset by public relations maneuvers to distract from the painful cries or to pretend as though everything is normal.

Twenty years ago it was the party of the left which held the Synod hostage and caused many wounds. This book will show that in 1992 the party of the right identified with the Robert Preus party with their campaign is holding the Synod hostage by the use of the same tactics which the party of the left used. We can no longer tolerate plundering in the name of "pure" doctrine by legalists nor allow the destruction of our mission through reinterpretation of the holy Word by antinomianists. It is time for all with their personal agendas to lay aside their own ideas and perceptions, and let God rule by His infallible Scriptures.

"The Sound of a Scream" was the classic article written by O. P. Kretzmann, former President of Valparaiso University in his *Campus Commentary* of Sept. 1973. While seeming not to be in sympathy with the direction of the New Orleans Convention that year, he sympathized with all those who were crying out in pain.

Kretzmann wrote, "However else the sound from Rivergate is interpreted, it needs to be heard as a scream. The pain had become unbearable. Oppressed brethren answered in the only way they could. 'Get off me, you are crushing me!' The screams sought relief - and with it a pardonable sense of momentary vengeance. Let somebody else do the screaming for a change!

Together with the great 'credibility barrier', the 'scream' is a phenomenon to be reckoned with. It can be explored by conversation with brethren who participated in it and felt the relief. The voice is there, ready to interpret. It says things like these:

I am only a simple pastor, trying to do my work. The Seminary does not care about me. It talks down to me, makes me feel like a fool. The CTM is too hard to read, not worth the effort. Even if I had time to read it, it gives me nothing I can use where I am. It disturbs me, but fails to comfort me.

Again, when the Seminary says, 'un-Lutheran' to President Preus (Jack), it says 'un-Lutheran' to me. I identify with him, belong to the Missouri he describes. To attack him is to attack me. I stand accused, but cannot comprehend the accusation.

The Scream continues, the Seminary has had it all its own way. Professors have felt free to pursue their exotic learning, to delight in new knowledge. But they are totally out of touch with me. They have no feeling for the church as I know it...

And again, the Seminary has not been honest with me. It calls me, 'unLutheran', yet insists nothing has really changed. Well, I know that I have not changed! I am preaching and teaching faithfully the way the Pastor did who confirmed me, the way I was taught. If the Seminary cannot even realize that it has changed, it is either blind or dishonest.

...The voice says, you talk of suffering, of persons and families who will suffer. Have you no feeling for that minority in the Seminary faculty, for their pain...Their pain is my pain. If they could not be loved and heard in the fellowship of the whole faculty, how can I expect to be loved and heard from where I am?

Therefore, the Scream is more than theological. It is from brethren of ours deeply

3

wounded. If that Scream can be heard now, and even welcomed for what it is telling us, that in itself could be seen as a gift of divine and necessary grace - and a little sign of hope for our beloved church's tomorrow."

This book is nothing if it is not an agonizing Scream from a representative of a multitude of disregarded, forgotten or mutilated faithful members of The Lutheran Church-Missouri Synod, who have been beat on by the party of the left 20 years ago, and the party of the right today, and deserted by the party of the middle. We ask, "Is anyone listening? Does anyone care?" Whoever speaks to us, let it be only a Word from God!

The Scream of 1992 comes from a wounded healer, a seeking servant! I pray that the reading of this book will provide adequate proof of being such a healer and servant. This book is written as my contribution that soon we may all together once again be able to talk and to feel as a spiritual family, and once again to trust one another. Trust has been absent already a long time ago because there has been no room allowed for talking and feeling.

We are a church in denial as surely as the family with an alcoholic member. As such a family finds its members dysfunctional and co-dependent, so most of us in the Missouri Synod are dysfunctional and co-dependent. We are experiencing major spiritual trauma. We are a pre-occupied church family, which needs treatment for more than symptoms. Who will not acknowledge that he or she has not been made dysfunctional in the Synod, even possibly in one's own congregation? For over 30 years we have basically not talked to each other but "told it to the press" and held "public court" instead of pursuing Biblical procedures; various congregations, pastors or District and Synodical leaders have simply ignored the Scream in whatever forum it was heard by rationalizing it, excusing it, denying it, justifying it, attempting to control it, or simply by walking off. Sometimes, there are antinomian tendencies, and at other times legalistic. Symptoms have been treated while the disease rages on.

The only reason that this book is published is that the members of the Synodical Commissions on Appeals, and to some extent the Commission on Adjudication also, have corrupted the process. Regardless of the pain I experience in telling the truth - and pain may be experienced by some of the guilty persons in having their sins named publicly - a person with a Biblical orientation and a shepherd's heart has no choice but to help alleviate the pain of the unnumbered victims in the Synod who have no place to go for adjudication, because the men entrusted with that responsibility have perverted the system and made it impossible to achieve the justice and mercy which God wants them to have through their church.

I realize that this book will make me seem to be a hero to many, but a truant to a few others. I will not accept either role, but only that of a wounded healer and a seeking servant. Whatever the cost, my book is written to help bring healing in a badly divided church, one which is not able to discern Biblical procedures in the midst of conflict. I join many others who do not want to go to the Pittsburgh Convention to face shouting partisans of the right or the pretenses of those who may be on the left but speak as though they are orthodox or in the middle. The greatest hazard at this time is to seek to avoid risk but simply hope that somehow we can ride out the impending storm at Pittsburgh by preparing clever arguments and tactics and expressing prejudiced views which are not based on evidence or facts. My friends who are Synodical veterans join me in the belief that there is nothing on the horizon to give hope that there can be rational communication with the party of the right with its blind following of Dr. Robert Preus or of any other individuals and parties whose plans may be disguised. All I know is that if we keep on doing what we are doing, we will keep on getting what we are getting!

At the same time, I proclaim and affirm the great Biblical and Gospel heritage which is ours in the Lutheran Confessions. As will be shown in this book, we have a rich legacy of Biblical doctrine and practice which has been attacked by some from time to time, which the majority of us in the Synod say will not be bartered at any price.

By God's grace, our future is rooted in our great Biblical and confessional heritage. Proposals for tapping these rich resources of our tradition will be offered for what appears to be some hopeless enigmas through the Pittsburgh Convention. We will be challenged both to thank God for the benefits from our entire heritage and also to step boldly to demonstrate full Christ-likeness while "speaking the truth in love." Let all those who enter the discussion or claim the privilege to be heard speak God's Word so that all may hear the voice of the Lord, not the utterances of political partisans.

I desire intensively to see the Synod reach the noble objectives set forward by the Synod Board of Directors in its Dec. 4-6, 1991, meeting in which the following goals were adopted for its work:

"Help the Synodical President and Planning Council provide a 'big picture' vision of the Synod that is congregation-centered and outreach-oriented, and help the Synod be a 'world church' modeled after the early church in Acts and a church body where members trust one another.

-Provide leadership to the Synod's Council of Administrators, program boards and commissions, and the Commission on Structure, as they work on converting vision to action, provide better use of people and material resources in order to meet the diverse needs of congregations; and help the church be mission-driven rather than dollar-driven, at all levels, with congregations in the front lines of outreach.

-Provide shared leadership in refining the Synod's system of college and seminary education.

-Provide shared leadership in 'creating an atmosphere whereby every congregation is a mission congregation, every member is a missionary, and every activity of the church is evaluated as to how it contributes to the mission,' seeking ethnic involvement in this process and helping to develop a 'comprehensive mission-support structure.'

-Clarify its responsibilities and emphasize its coordinative role between boards and commissions, including its role in quickly resolving conflicts within boards."

This book challenges Synod leaders and members to work hard to make all this possible by the Holy Spirit. But we will not experience it unless and until we tell ourselves the truth about ourselves and our spiritual delinquencies, and to assess our situation on the basis of Biblical terms, not by political expediency. This book is offered to leaders and members of the Synod with the earnest prayer that our Synod may in doctrine and practice be truly Biblical, evangelical, confessional, pastoral, truthful, loving, trusting, and filled with a strong mission spirit.

When we get beyond labels and obediently live out our faith Biblically, we will manifest our rich Biblical and confessional heritage, and we will not need a public relations firm to inform the world or to prove it. This liberating vision from the Gospel itself is uttered in the hope that all of us will be seeking servants under the Word so that in the future all problems will merely be stepping stones for greater faithfulness to Christ and greater service in His Kingdom.

About the Manuscript

Please accept my apologies for any irregularities in the quality of scholarship in this book. There are a number of normal procedures, including the Endnotes, which simply cannot be completed under the pressure of time to meet the publishing date. In a number of cases, the Endnotes in reproduced essays were placed at the appropriate place in the text in order to facilitate easier reading. I did not touch or change these Endnotes. However, the Bibliography contains the full information about the books which are involved.

If there is a lack of cohesion at a few spots, this is because a number of essays which I presented for various occasions have been edited to shorten them for the purpose of this book. It was sometimes difficult to build proper bridges in the time available.

A large volume of evidence in my files could not be used in many of the accounts listed in this book simply because the book is already too long. Readers should be aware that in December I ransacked more than 12 boxes or file drawers of primary materials and reduced these to 3 large boxes (involving over 6000 pages), plus 40 books. I trust that no one will question the summary of some of this evidence and thus force the release of more evidence which is available in all cases that are shared. It should be noted that all these files will be in the possession of the Concordia Historical Institute in St. Louis already during my lifetime, and they will not be sealed.

This impossible task was undertaken at a time that found me away from my office for five weeks during the first two months of this year - twice outside of the United States and three more times to conduct seminars in different parts of our country. It is obviously only by God's rich grace that this monumental task was completed by this date.

The first part of the book presents what I believe to be the true identity of the Biblical Christian and Biblical church. The rest of the book gives an account of the distortions caused by personal and political enterprises which have been intruded by party interests into the life of our Synod to obstruct our true Gospel mission. The last chapter presents recommendations for forgiving, healing, rehabilitating, edifying, loving, bearing one another's burdens, stirring up one another to good works, and marching together in a great mission adventure. May God bring us all together once again to give all of our energies to that great Gospel task!

Waldo J. Werning
Fort Wayne IN

Chapter 1

CONFLICTING PARADIGMS: INSTITUTIONAL LUTHERANS OR BIBLICAL LUTHERANS?

Beliefs are vitally important because they lead us to what we say and do. Our speech and actions have either good or bad consequences. Clinging to erroneous convictions is dangerous, and can be spiritually fatal. What we do and where we go depends upon our beliefs about Him who created and redeemed us and about ourselves. These beliefs can be termed our paradigms.

A paradigm is another name for a model, viewpoint, world view or pattern of how we look at or perceive truth - the truth about ourselves, the world and God. There are all kinds of paradigms, bad ones and good ones, wrong ones and right ones. Paradigms are our mental filtering systems which consist of our personal basic beliefs about life and its spiritual realities which guide our actions and reactions to every situation which we face.

Being able to recognize Biblically precise paradigms is necessary for spiritual health and survival. Failing to pursue proper paradigms happens when there are deeply rooted or unquestioned beliefs and practices of traditionalists or of those who do not have a high regard for God's Word. Those who debate the authority of God's Word and tolerate human interpretations possess beliefs that are in opposition to eternal paradigms. The past several decades have been marked by great missed mission opportunities because of paradigm paralysis, or confusion, especially in major matters related to institutional requirements, church authority, political power, church discipline, sanctification and stewardship.

Discussion of paradigms is vital because the direction of our lives and our churches is determined by whether our minds are set on the things of the world or on the Word of God. Only the Biblical paradigm can guide us to see the divine pattern with its capacity for transformation, renewal, improvisations, and new beginnings.

The importance of a Biblical mindset or paradigm is told in Rom. 12:2, "Do not conform any longer to the pattern of this world, but be transformed by the renewing of your mind. Then you will be able to test and approve what God's will is - His good, pleasing and perfect will." Eph. 4:17 tells how our attitude or mindset is strategic for directing our lives, "So I tell you this, and insist on it in the Lord, that you must no longer live as the Gentiles do, in the futility of their thinking." The importance of a Biblical paradigm is also seen in Col. 3:2, "Set your mind on things above, not on earthly things."

Those who cannot get excited about mental screens or paradigms can learn the consequences of paradigm paralysis or to recognize the difference between truth and error in Rom. 8:5-9a, "Those who live according to the sinful nature have their minds set on what that nature desires; but those who live in accordance with the Spirit have their minds set on what the Spirit desires. The mind of sinful man is death, but the mind controlled by the Spirit is life and peace; the sinful mind is hostile to God. It does not submit to God's law, nor can it do so. Those controlled by the sinful nature cannot please God. You, however, are controlled not by the sinful nature but by the Spirit, if the Spirit of God lives in you."

Two Christians can be in identical situations but react in opposite ways. It all depends upon whether they have an attitude of fear or faith, doubt or hope. The mindset of distrust in Biblical matters shows in unwillingness to accept divine truth, whereas the attitude of trust by the Holy Spirit leads to acceptance of the truth about ourselves as being sinners and being saved, that we are regenerated through baptism in Jesus Christ, and that by the power of the Holy Spirit the new nature in Christ is victorious over the old nature.

When Biblical paradigms or beliefs direct us, various changes can be made. The Holy Spirit will empower a shift away from being guided by man-centered majority votes to a living God-centered cosmology, from bits and parts mentality to spiritual wholeness, from rationalizations to faith, from religion to true spirituality. Patience is needed to translate Biblical paradigms into reality to reach a majority of members.

Finding the Biblical Paradigm

Gaining a realistic paradigm and belief system to put into practice is not easy. Minds easily become bewildered by misconceptions, traditions, illusions and falsehoods. Only a Biblical paradigm gives us a realistic view with which to negotiate the landscape of life. The wrong pattern will make our destination a fantasy.

Possibly the biggest barrier to adoption of Biblical paradigms is thinking that we have learned all that there is to know, that we are confessional Lutherans and therefore immune from faulty statements and practice. We may believe that we could never have modern cultural heresies which dilute truth. But our viewpoints and paradigms need constant assessment and refinement in order to clear out cultural perversions in the light of God's Word. The Word, unlike the world, is constant. It forces us to recognize that some of our human views are wrong, and that the cultural paradigms need to be greatly changed. The Word takes away every reason to defend or depend upon a purely secular view of the world. Commitment to the divine paradigm of eternal Truth requires continuous and never-ending self-examination.

We are constantly confronted with competing world views, even in the church. All the ideologies that plague modern society are based on tentative world views, many of them false. Human paradigms cannot measure spiritual forces which break through natural expectations.

The entrance of Christ into the world as Savior and Lord, and the presence of the Holy Spirit forces a paradigm shift in the understanding of a person's life. God's redemptive act radically changes the picture. The effect of this spiritual shift is incalculably vast and profound for the spiritual model which provides the realities of the Christian's pursuit of happiness.

A Biblical paradigm leads Christians to live very different than religious moralists and legalists. Some perceive Christianity as merely a system of beliefs to adhere to or a set of theological propositions to live by, rather than faith in and a relation to the God-man, Jesus Christ. Biblical paradigms show us how our lives and lifestyles are to be connected to the Creator, Redeemer and Sanctifier. We are to avoid paradigms which allow forms to be sacred, while authentic spiritual functions are neglected. The temptation always is to work at revived traditionalism rather than Biblical church renewal.

Institutional Lutheran or Biblical Lutheran

Institutional Christianity and Biblical Christianity are two different worlds. If the church and its members are to have integrity in following God's eternal plan, they must understand His purpose for them and the earth they are to manage. They are to comprehend the true nature of the church, and their call as Christians to move in the direction revealed in God's divine Master-Planbook.

Christ builds His Church, and we are to organize churches to bring direction by the Word out of chaos in human society, taking dominion under His authority. Basic issues of Biblical purpose must be addressed by God's people if they are to demonstrate a Kingdom mentality which transcends human limitations and confusion, in a particular generation.

Human nature consistently tries to confine religion to buildings or rituals. Human instinct ordinarily deals with the urgent and what can be seen, handled and controlled. This tendency is also strong in the church, which is easier to understand and direct in its institutional form than in its more abstract spiritual reality as the body of Christ. Thus the church is sometimes erroneously seen as a spiritual association in human form and organization, where members run the institution while God handles the faith matters. Consequently, Christ's kingdom is often perceived as inside the boundaries of the organization and the church building. Many do not have the proper understanding of the church as the Biblical "ecclesia" (called out ones), but they see it basically in its organizational and institutional form. In that sense, they have become Church Christians or Lutherans (institutional members), instead of being Biblical Christians (called out ones).

The goal of this chapter is to show how human institutional and organizational traditionalism generally hampers the church in carrying out its mission, while we point to the way to be Biblical Lutherans. There have been obstacles to obtaining spiritual creativity and freedom, and to exercising our faith under grace without the restraints of traditionalism. Ecclesiastical programs and membership promotions are easily mistaken for fulfilling the Great Commission. The institutional church has created its own crises through managerial-political ways that have interfered with true pastoral leadership and the activity of laymen in exercising their God-given positions and tasks effectively.

It is time to go back to basics and to ask the primary questions: What does it mean to be Christian? What does it mean to be church?

This is the moment to be Biblically revolutionary and once again face and apply the obvious. George Orwell has been reported to have said, "We have now sunk to a depth at which a restatement of the obvious is the first duty of intelligent men." If naïve or timid church leaders and passive church members are to awaken from their slumber, obvious Biblical truths must be declared and applied so that the church is shaken at its very foundation. The integrity of the church's mission is at stake. When the church stops servicing the whims and selfish desires of institutionalized Christians, then pastors and lay leaders can be loosed from ecclesiastical busy work to be free to be active Biblical Lutherans.

By charting the attributes and qualities of the Institutional Lutheran and the Biblical Lutheran, we can gain a clear perspective of the issues involved in a Biblical paradigm of the Christian life and of the church. This will help us to focus on weaknesses and barriers which we should avoid, and to make proper adjustments to pursue the truly divine plan for each believer.

Ralph W. Neighbour Jr. states that since the time of Constantine in the 4th century the church has functioned primarily as a "cathedral," being identified with these elements: a building, a special day (Sunday), a professional leadership, services performed for the people, and a way to maintain itself (offerings); the "cathedral" church finds itself isolated from the society around it, is not relevant to all the needs which Christ identified, and is materialistic and often political. [1]

In contrast to the "cathedral" church, the Bible presents a called-out Christian community, the body of Christ manifesting itself not only in corporate worship, but also in frequent Bible study, meeting not only at church but also in homes on any day of the week. Unlike the "cathedral" which draws its church staff almost exclusively from the seminary and the church college, the body of Christ-Christian community draws its church staff also from the congregation. When members of the "cathedral" church have a problem, they see the pastor, whereas members of the New Testament style church build up one another through interpersonal relationships by speaking the Law and Gospel to each other

9

as Eph. 4 requires.

The cathedral church pressures leaders into programs to seek to keep members awake and active, while the Biblical church by the Spirit's work equips every believer to do the works of service which God has prepared for him to do (Eph. 2:10; 4:7). The key words heard in the cathedral church are, "Come to church," while the Christian Community church continually repeats, "Go and make disciples." The cathedral church stresses confession of the distinctive beliefs of the church at the expense of knowing and applying the Scriptures to daily relationships and actual spiritual needs.

The day of the Biblical Christian and the priesthood of all believers is here and should always have been consistently practiced in the Lutheran Church. Those who do not recognize this are the ones who have invested much in limited dogmatic and 16th Century liturgical structures, and in the bureaucracy status quo. The program-based church that draws people to a building to serve the church is no substitute for the Body-life inaugurated by Jesus, the Builder of the Church, and the Holy Spirit, its sustainer and strength.

The following pages show the paradigm shift required if we are truly to be the New Testament church, not to enlarge the institution and its programs, but to increase the kingdom of Christ and gain unity of faith and maturity through Christian community(Eph. 4:1,7-16). Reformation is proposed for those churches which have only fragments of Churchianity that have tainted true Christianity.

INSTITUTIONAL LUTHERAN

Churchianity (Religion)

BIBLICAL LUTHERAN

Christianity (Spirituality)

The Institutional Lutheran focuses on church rituals, rules and regulations which are to be kept. He is geared to religious rites and observances, such as attending worship services periodically in order to stay in favor with God. He acts because it is a required function of the Christian. He is tied to doctrines to hold and keep for their own sake, and emphasizes knowledge and the cognitive more than the practice of the faith in daily life. He intellectualizes the faith and fails to understand its relational nature. He sees his task only as proclamation, not as communication.

The Biblical Lutheran, on the other hand, centers on spirituality which involves relationships - a living relationship with the living God, and then with fellow Christians and all people. He studies the Bible in order to grow in grace, knowledge and faith that results in true worship as a proper response to God's love in Christ Jesus. His emphasis is on internal matters more than externals. His focus is on how God initiates faith and action by His grace, and how by grace the believer is empowered to respond through all of life.

Institutional Maintenance

Mission Outreach

The Church or Institutional Lutheran is concerned with organizational maintenance and regularly asks, "What does the church need?" He wants church leaders to tell him what is expected and what to do so that the church can be maintained at a respectable level.

The Biblical Lutheran is geared to the Great Commission and mission outreach, asking, "What is life's purpose? What is God's call and assignment to me?" He is directed by Biblical principles which guide the sanctified life, wanting to know the will of God rather than what the institution desires.

Convert   Disciple

The Church Lutheran thinks in terms of converts, who are saved, seeing the function of the church and of individual Christians mainly in terms of winning souls. He concentrates on seeking converts and gaining more church members, but does not view the church as the body of Christ, only as a divine institution.

The Biblical Lutheran sees every believer as a disciple of Christ, recognizing that conversion by the Spirit is but a first step to be followed by a lifetime of Christian growth. He sees Christian nurture and education as an essential part of life. God's grace pulls him beyond conversion to be a disciple who seeks to learn and become mature.

Managerial   Pastoral

The church will be paralyzed by institutionalism when it features structures, supervision, bureaucratic regulations and various types of legalism in the place of or over the pastoral approach which stresses the all-sufficiency of Christ through Bible study. The last decades have given us a managerial style of church work in which pastors become professionals and members become supporters.

The managerial style and institutionalism are present when the form, structure and organization become more important than the people, who begin to function like cogs in a machine; when an exchange of Biblical theology of grace is made for the practice of pragmatism; when relationships are secondary to program needs; when communication breaks down because of red tape; when people become prisoners of church procedures; when pious thoughts or political ways take precedence over Biblical priorities; when nonessentials are allowed to become absolutes; when orthodoxy and doctrinal statements compete with or are substituted for spiritual vitality and reality; and when people want to be served rather than to serve.

The result of all this is that the policy manual and church regulations become the driving force. Then a hierarchy of leadership develops, increasing the problems of communication from the leaders to the people, and the people to the leaders. Members support the institution rather than the purpose for which the church exists.

The managerial style majors in oiling the organizational wheels to work in harmony so that leaders may lead and followers may goose-step in peace, as the pastor becomes a "pastoral director." Little tasks receive meticulous attention while spiritual needs are easily ignored. People are called out of the sinful world only to have their spirits broken in the church with an avalanche of worldly work.

Managerial organizationalism allows people to be invited to exalt Christ but then are led to exist with comfortable church membership, cultural ethics and morality, and "salvation" by grace through faith plus performing the right rituals. Members who are called, "Come unto Me all you with heavy burdens," are sent into kitchens to feed church people, and into committee rooms to run church affairs. They are served spiritual verbal tranquilizers so that they can endure fatigue and aimlessness with little sense of God's call. The problem is alsoseen in people who bring the "world" into the church through their ways of believing and ways of achieving self-worth and joy. Such people are running around to get scraps of wood to throw on the altar of church devotion in order to keep the religious pot boiling.

The life of the Biblical Lutheran is loving and caring, setting aside lesser agendas and seeking pastoral feeding and leading with God's purposes being his purposes.

People are to be fed and led by the Word, directed toward a Biblical vision for mission to respond creatively out of God's love for them and all people.

Reactive (Motivated by Crises)	Pro-active (Directed by Biblical Principles)

The entire institutional system is basically built upon reaction to circumstances, especially to correcting problems which regularly arise. Cultural Christianity reacts to church conditions and responds to the ecclesiastical environment, preoccupied so much with the church "forest" that it reacts only to what tree is closest.

The Biblical Lutheran is pro-active, instructed by Scriptural principles and strengthened for creative tasks by the Word. He responds on the basis of divine imperatives and is guided by the will of God, not the will of the church majority or a clique in the church. He is not the helpless victim of church conditions or members who insist that "We never did it that way before." He does not offer servile obedience to short-range programs which are designed to overcome emergencies until the next crisis erupts.

Immobilized .... Mobilized

Church Lutherans find themselves paralyzed by a variety of obstacles: by being TV addicts, by sports and spectatoritis, by enslavement to hobbies which make demands beyond reason, or by spending many idle hours with the same friends. They may be immobilized in church meetings where little more happens than discussion and planning of programs which go nowhere, and plans that are not enacted. We are the most mobilized civilization in the history of the world, yet it appears that we are more immobilized as Christians and as churches than the Christians in Paul's day.

The Biblical Lutheran is not restrained by any cultural barriers or church structures, but is mobilized to go, proclaim, teach, baptize - witnessing of Jesus Christ on the basis of Acts 1:8. He devotes much time to Bible study and to implement the Great Commission, not getting lost in "housekeeping" responsibilities and spinning of organizational wheels. He uses the home base as the launching pad to go into the entire world aggressively.

Tell .... Teach

Institutional Lutherans ordinarily do not move or respond until they are told of the expected performance through church programs. They inquire, "What are you asking us to do?" They are reactors to programs, not initiators on their own on the basis of the Christian calling. A major characteristic of telling is voicing regular exhortations with considerable urgings to measure up to needs as portrayed by the leaders.

Only an effective approach will ensure the spiritual depth of character from which to draw strength for generous service and gifts to the Lord. Sound Biblical teaching of sanctification alone meets the need of deprogramming of the Church Christian who must unlearn the superficial Christianity which is allowed in the maintenance church.

Fruits .... Roots

Churchianity is greatly concerned with fruits, as there is much shaking of the financial tree by fruit pickers who are starving for the dollars and service required for church survival. There is a pressure-cooker attitude which panics at the very thought of not meeting the man-made goals and budgets or in filling positions and completing the tasks of the organizational church.

Biblical Lutheran leaders concentrate on the roots like Jesus did, holding themselves responsible to dig, fertilize and water. They recognize that there can be no healthy and abundant fruit without nourished roots. We are to be involved in a process of discipleship which builds a healthy tree before adequate fruit is expected.

Instant Results (Event)　　　## Natural Results (Process)

The Institutional Lutheran has a microwave mentality by which a button is to be pushed within the church, and one hour later a successful program should be completed. This puts pressure on leadership to contrive events and success programs rather than on an educational process which effectively penetrates minds and hearts, and ultimately the entire world for Christ.

A culture which demands instant gratification wants to see a better church and a better world quickly through one event, failing to recognize that it may take two, three, or five years and more to establish a Biblical discipleship process and to experience fruit within the church. Many orthodox leaders, too, have lost the will and courage to go beyond the quick-fix or microwave mentality which expects full results in one event.

The Biblical Lutheran is not tempted to be a secular pragmatist, but commits himself to Biblical convictions, and avoids superficial Christianity and a cut-flower commitment. He looks for spiritual results through spiritual seedtime and harvest.

Good Church Members　　　## Growing Christians

Church Christians make a strong emphasis on being good church members. But what is a good or a bad church member? This kind of accent on church membership punctuates doing and activities to the detriment of spiritual quality, with the result that members are satisfied to belong to the church club without having acquired spiritual growth. The Scriptures place the accent on Biblical Christians who grow and mature, not on performance in order to be a member in good standing.

An Examination of the Institutional Lutheran-Biblical Lutheran Tension

Though sincere and faithful to what he knows, the Institutional Lutheran is in bondage and slavery to rituals, regulations and traditions, no matter how orthodox his theology. The Biblical Lutheran is emancipated from such servitude and has freedom to obey Christ and His Word. This is no time for doctrinaire answers or cognitive abstract statements without application, or not relating theology to practice.

God is not anti-tradition or anti-institution, but our practices can replace Him with traditionalism and institutionalism. These are a decapitated Christianity in which Christ is not allowed to be Head of the church, and where the mind of the majority replaces the mind of Christ.

The only traditions which Christians are obligated to keep are those contained in the Scriptures, but there are good church traditions that may be incorporated into church life as long as they do not detract from the Gospel mission of the church.

There are also bad traditions as illustrated in Mark 7:1-5, where Jesus criticized the Pharisees for their traditions which became vain worship, for their teachings were rules taught by men.

Traditions are wrong when they set aside the truth of God's Word or obscure its meaning, when they set aside God's will, when they exalt man's ideas as equal with God's, and when they replace spiritual devotion with mere ceremonies. Tradition was an immediate problem in the early church as the Pharisees confronted Jesus with the question, "Why do your disciples break the traditions of the Elders?" (Matt. 15:2). Jesus came to change their Old Testament traditions and oral laws, and to usher in the Kingdom of grace and freedom based upon justification by grace through faith in Jesus Christ. Jesus cut through the confusion by asking, "Why do you break the command of God for the sake of your traditions?"

Being creatures of habit, members in churches can easily find themselves in the same predicament. They may have traditions which result in not being able to hear or do what the Word requires. In fact, most church members who have an obsession with tradition will fight if a Biblical procedure is introduced which, as they see it, is in conflict with their routines and rituals.

When we have Biblical habits, this is good. But institutional habits which conflict with God's Word are hard to break. All who have an obsession with traditions which hamper Biblical procedures are guilty of traditionalism. It is beneficial to have good traditions, but traditionalism is a hardening of the form, rituals and institutions which does not allow the change which the Scriptures dictate.

The maintenance approach to church work has become an institutional tradition which conflicts with the mission call from God. The maintenance mentality reacts basically to situations, especially crises, while the mission mentality acts on God's Word.

Maintenance churches concentrate their resources considerably on member-related activities, losing touch with the Christian community and world mission responsibilities. They have been conditioned to attempt only what is predictable and achievable, measuring efforts and success mainly by statistics. Maintenance groups look at their work basically as performance, while mission congregations find Christianity a spiritual experience with a living God and loving relations with others.

True Christian tradition finds us seeking to be the church for no other reason than that this is our calling from God. The Bible, not the world, sets the agenda for the faithful church. We seek to be distinctively and unapologetically the church in obedience to Christ, and to transcend culture.

Christian tradition is the living faith of the Biblical church and Biblical Christians, shared faithfully from generation to generation. Traditionalism (not traditions) is a dead faith of the institutional church and Church Christians. Tradition involving good values is good. Churches need tradition in doctrine and practice, but this causes distress and malfunctions when they becomes rituals for their own sake and becomes traditionalism.

Building functional churches is harder than merely replacing or rearranging old programs. Reforming a church means dropping or destroying old methodologies as well as developing new structures and approaches based on Biblical truths and principles. It is very difficult to detect and admit the slow deterioration of vision and the gradual death of faith, which should be venturing courageously and obediently to the tune of heavenly music of the Gospel.

Levels of Satisfaction and Dissatisfaction

Biblical Lutherans are concerned about raising levels of spiritual satisfaction, while Church Lutherans center on wanting levels of dissatisfaction lowered. This is an essential consideration for aggressive mission churches. Kennon L. Callahan provides some interesting conclusions on the basis of 23 years of experience in over 750 churches. He writes, "Over these years of research and consultation, twelve factors have emerged persistently as the central characteristics of successful mission churches. These twelve fall into two categories: six are relational characteristics and six are functional characteristics. Generally speaking, effective, successful churches have 9 of these 12 central characteristics. Moreover, the majority of the 9 are relational rather than functional. Tragically, too many churches have centered on the functional rather than the relational factors that contribute to missions and success." [2]

Callahan names the relational characteristics that a diagnostic approach takes seriously: "1. Specific, concrete mission objectives. 2. Pastoral and lay visitation. 3. Corporate, dynamic worship. 4. Significant relational groups. 5. Strong leadership resources. 6. Streamlined structure and solid, participatory decision making." [3]

He provides the functional characteristics to take seriously: "7. Several competent programs and activities. 8. Open accessibility. 9. High visibility. 10. Adequate parking, land and landscaping. 11. Adequate space and facilities. 12. Solid financial resources." [4]

Callahan affirms that the central relational characteristics are the key sources of satisfaction and well-being in a congregation. The more these relational characteristics are present, the higher the level of satisfaction. He states that the more the functional characteristics are present, the lower the level of dissatisfaction in the congregation. He concludes, "The level of satisfaction needs to be higher than the level of dissatisfaction in order for the congregation to have a sense of confidence and competence about its mission. Congregations in which the level of satisfaction is higher than the level of dissatisfaction generally have a stronger sense of intentionality and well-being about their life in mission; they possess a sense of their own strength and a responsible hope that they can accomplish the mission to which God calls them." [5]

Unfortunately many pastors and congregation officers focus their ministry and work on lowering the level of dissatisfaction while neglecting to work at the points which raise the level of satisfaction. In order to manage the noise control of pain when it is present, even pastors who are caring persons usually are much more attuned to a level of dissatisfaction around them than focusing on raising the level of satisfaction. They are reactors, responding to complaints and gripes, reacting to signals of dissatisfaction rather than acting with strategic long-range Biblical planning to raise the level of contentment. They also make the mistake of trying to relieve discontent quickly and so are perceived to use pressure tactics. Their guilt causes them to work harder, not smarter, preoccupying themselves with the symptoms of dissatisfaction.

When we preoccupy ourselves with certain activities and functions to lower th level of discontent, we have neglected some of the central relational characteristics which raise the level of satisfaction, beginning with the development of significant relational groups. By the time that a pastor and several of his church leaders have worked hard at programs to maintain the church and efforts at increasing the financial support, they often are too tired or have run out of time to train more Bible class teachers and to plan intensive Bible study for all members, and to organize relational groups in which the Word helps people in their spiritual growth. Some will spend most of their efforts on a liturgy and a Sunday experience for helping various members to go through their weekly rituals rather than pursuing an Ephesians 4 model of Christian community and a Book of Acts pattern of encouraging house to house gathering for Bible study and fellowship. In our chapter on building Christian community, we will present a strong emphasis on small group fellowship in the congregation under the direction of the pastor and the elders and their assistants. Traditional approaches which center on rituals, Sundays, committee work and church buildings simply do not pass the scrutiny of New Testament models. Callahan reminds us that some churches become so involved in sponsoring a vast array of programs and activities that they lose sight of the people these functions allegedly serve. People are more important than programs, and programs are not that vital if they do not help people.

Confusing Substance and Style

We have heard much about substance and style in the past several years, some of it good and some of it a bit of non-sense. Substance involves the theology and beliefs of a church, which is its vision. The style and manner in which the church does its work is the concern of communicating the message or how it performs its mission or follows its vision. A study of substance and style is vital for a proper self-assessment of churches and of appraising what is happening in other congregations.

The character or substance of a church is determined by its doctrines, and faithfulness to God's Word. The style is the ways and methods by which the message is disseminated or transmitted. One is the belief, and the other is the doing. One is the vision, and the other is the mission activities and ministry services.

This matter can be compared to the human body and its functions. The body needs to be complete and whole to function effectively. The body is the substance, and the function is the style. First there must be an understanding and commitment to Biblical truth that the Christian is complete in Christ, and no performance or functions add to the substance or character. The believer may negate his life purpose by failing to function, but that is a problem of frustrating his mission, not of having a complete body.

This is very vital because there are always activists who look at actions and style, mistaking them for substance, and believing that if they do what another church does in order to get many people to attend that they also will succeed to get bodies out. The fact is that usually crowds of people can be gathered by giving them a style that they want just so they feel good.

The communication through style and marketing is exceedingly important for the reason that people respond basically on the basis of their perceptions, impressions or if there is effective communication with them. This means that once we are committed faithfully to the Biblical substance, then we must find a style, communication or marketing form that will break through cultural transmission barriers and not drive away those we are trying to reach. If the targets of our Biblical ministry are annoyed or turned off by some communication obstacle or unnecessary style, then they will not even want to hear our message. Even though in their hearts they want to go to the same destination we do, they will reject our Biblical paradigm because they are convinced we have nothing to offer or we have given a negative image to a positive message. We will be total foreigners to them, having failed to bridge cultures or to gain interest from them so that they have an opportunity to exchange their old paradigm for a new one by God's grace that will get them to their destination.

One of the great negatives in church life is the failure to recognize the full Biblical paradigm together with the communication style in proclamation and church activities which the divine plan imposes upon us; and sometimes their distinctives are confused. Because of the institutional and maintenance model broadly endured in Christianity today, many leaders do not recognize that their paradigm is made of selected bits and pieces which they inherited without asking the right questions or making intensive study of it. What they have is what works from the experience of the past which involves doctrinal formulations without their practice, as they do not acknowledge the shortcuts taken or how the Christian life and the church have been segmented.

In a market-driven environment, the church must avoid being itself market-driven in the sense that style distorts substance. However, many orthodox Christians are plagued with the false paradigm that market orientation is somehow unBiblical. Marketing means meeting the real needs of the people; and the church is in the business of providing what God has to offer through the Gospel in a style which delivers that message of God's grace

16

without any distortion. Jesus proved that in His ministry. That's what I mean by market orientation, which offers a style that reaches congregation and the community in a relevant way. Opponents fear that the wrongs that accompany secular marketing will infect the church, but that is a legalistic or even a pietistic fear which has no basis in fact. The question is whether the substance is Biblically authentic or not. The substance remains the same in a true market-oriented church: Biblical truth is the source of Biblical messages, meeting the spiritual needs of all members through a grace-based, Word-Sacrament ministry, focusing on people not programs, while utilizing the resources of all members for reaching the community and the world. Style follows substance, as practice comes after principle, and prescription after description. The big problem arises when we become overly style or technique oriented, or when we insist that the style be only the same as 16th century German, which can happen to orthodox Christians as well as any other.

Market orientation takes into consideration the fact that the Boomer population must hear the Word as it continues to search for meaning in life, is in pursuit of belonging and is seeking to establish ties that help them to plant roots and feel secure. Many seek the church as a means of inculcating acceptable social values in their children. Others are committed to a fast-track lifestyle. All need to find their identity and meaning in Jesus Christ, the substance in the fullness of the Gospel. Those who confuse the issue by trying to fuse style with substance are attempting to give us a culture-Christianity, which the Gospel does not allow.

Keep The Message and The Mode of Communication Separate

God is a communicator. The one who represents God in preaching and teaching must transmit God's message clearly so that it can be received by the ear and mind before the Holy Spirit does His work. It is significant that God wraps His message in human beings to be delivered to other human beings. God first embodied (incarnated) His message in the person of His Son, Jesus Christ. Thus God's basic message of communication is incarnational, as Christ became a human being to be understood by human beings. God moves into the receiver's frame of reference by using the language thought patterns of those to whom He spoke. Jesus is His message, and communication is His style. God invites the listener to identify with Him by the message He gives through the messenger He sends. God takes the initiative in the communication of His love for all people with the purpose to meet the real not just the felt needs of the receptors.

God wants to be understood and seeks a response from the hearer. Enlightening of the mind and a proper attitude are the work of the Holy Spirit. However, if the messenger and the style communicates unintelligible words and ideas from another culture or another century, there is no message which the Holy spirit can use to enlighten. Response, like understanding the message, is also the work of the Holy Spirit. However, the communicator, as St. Paul, is required to communicate clearly and faithfully the Biblical principles and the will of God which is to be lived by the Christian.

The communicator's role is to disclose the message so clearly that the hearer receives the knowledge of the subject matter and the facts are identified. After that, it is the Holy Spirit's task to enlighten the mind to give the right attitude and proper action.

One of the greatest barriers to gaining understanding of divine Truth is a traditional and human mindset which holds to paradigms which are in conflict with or distort Biblical ones. If the communicator does not recognize the problems and barriers to effective communication because of faulty paradigms, the receiver will filter what he hears through those wrong mental models and not get the message God wants to deliver.

The only barrier or stumbling block to the preaching of the Gospel and evangelizing should be the Gospel itself. However, styles which offer the Biblical message in 16th century German style to those who are attuned to 20th century American terminology will not be heard. Confessional Lutherans dare not misread this situation by saying that the hearers are not then interested in the Gospel, for actually the Gospel is not being transmitted in intelligible words and style. We have mistaken substance for style if we insist that all new members must be just like German Lutherans culturally. Often, when unchurched people say that they find the church strange, they are not referring to the Gospel but to the habits and traditions of another culture and another time which they are asked to embrace together with the Gospel. Unless the institutional church removes unnecessary barriers of culture which give the non-Lutheran a view of the church as irrelevant because of its style, these people will not give us the time of day or believe that we have anything to offer them.

Another confusion of substance and style is the addition of rituals, rules and regulations which have become part of the church tradition, identifying this style of doing things as making a person Christian and that one cannot be Lutheran without following those specific rituals in their old traditional forms. Such legalisms and moralisms have become a distinct barrier to having a living relationship with Jesus Christ and acceptance of the Gospel as the only condition for being a Christian. Sometimes, we assess a person as a good confessional Lutheran simply because he or she can recite the doctrinal formulations and do the expected ancient rituals without that person having any spiritual understanding or depth about him. Confusion has entered this arena because some have mistaken a different style for being disloyal to the substance.

Emphasizing Information at the Expense of Spiritual Formation

The issue of substance and style, as well as doctrine and practice, are also urgently related to the use of God's Word as information and spiritual formation. Many leaders and members do not realize how much their educational programs center on conveying information more than spiritual formation by the Holy Spirit. Spiritual growth is not produced by the transfer of information for its sake, but for the sake of a faith relationship with Christ. Using the Bible merely as a source of information for salvation quickly produces pride, causing us to focus on something outside of ourselves - our actions. Then growth is seen as obedience to a set of rules to be followed and a pietistic path to be mastered. Religious self-centeredness will be the result. But spiritual formation focuses inside, not only to gain redemption, but also to produce spiritual health and growth for maturity.

The Biblical paradigm reveals that the purpose of God's Word is for information and spiritual formation, for doctrine and practice. The failure to recognize this can quickly lead to Christianity which is cocooned in the head where the Christian facts are received by the ears and spoken and sung by the mouth in worship services, but it never touches the heart, hands and feet. This cocoon type of faith is unrelated to spiritual reality, as it centers on salvation in which daily life is concerned with preserving the faith to the exclusion of sanctification and at the expense of expressing the faith. Cocooned faith often isolates itself from the realities of the struggles and conflicts of faith in this world.

How are information and spiritual formation related? Information is the Biblical model, while spiritual formation is the use of the model in the walk of life. Information provides the mental model which shows what the Christian faith is all about. Spiritual formation produces a faith which puts that Biblical model to good use as the Christian follows the road to travel. Spiritual formation is not a doctrinal system, but a Spirit-powered faith venture.

Information can be compared to the recognition of the existence of a tree, whereas spiritual formation shows that the truly righteous person is "like a tree planted by streams of water, which yields its fruit in season and whose leaf does not wither. Whatever he does prospers" [Ps. 1:3]. Jesus, as the true Vine, associated believers with a branch of Himself, showing that unproductivity is contrary to existence in Him.

When we see God only through the medium of theological concepts or doctrinal formulas, we see Him as separate from ourselves rather than living in us. His Word shows that we are intimately and eternally related to the extent that Christ as the Vine produces the fruit, and we as branches bear the fruit (John 15).

There is no life in dead orthodoxy, or mere mental assent or head knowledge, but only in the expression of our faith. Informational reading of Scripture can result in merely tinkering with our doctrinal system, rearranging current structures of life, and modifying our paradigms to meet our mistrusts or prejudices, thus locking us into our old self-generated sinful identity and removing the possibility of miraculous spiritual formation. Unfortunately, information-seeking and behavioral dynamics are so deeply ingrained in the whole fabric of our human nature that they automatically take over and can blind us whenever we open the Bible, hear a truth, or face a spiritual task.

Church traditions and even cultural patterns easily become the interpretive principle when people read the Bible. We must expect spiritual formation through being shaped by the Word because we have been misshaped by the world. This is urgent because our interpretive eyes are strongly influenced by our old nature and culture, which wants the rights of the Kingdom without obedience to the King.

Information may include doing to the extent that the performance is part of the information system for acceptable behavior to be considered a "good confessional Lutheran." Thus informational modes of the human paradigm facilitate regulation and control of life in man's own way and on his own terms. God's grace seeks to liberate us from this destructive bondage, as the Holy Spirit seeks to recreate and form in us not only a maturing character, but also a whole new structure of attitudes, relationships, habits and responses to His Word.

The old nature influences us to file the Word of God into neat systematic categories which offer partial information or even accept misinformation that is actually a denial of the whole will of God. Therefore, our primary focus of reading the Word of God must be God Himself, not on truth about God.

To the extent that any Lutherans see and use the Bible as mere information to be accepted and obeyed, the Biblical paradigm has been distorted and misused. Leaders should make certain that their communication is clear and that their Biblical paradigm presents God's way as a transforming force in the life of each Christian by His grace.

The goal of spiritual formation is that by grace each Christian may be a mind through which Christ can send His thoughts, a mouth through which His words can be heard, a heart through which His love can be expressed, hands through which He reaches those in need, feet which will go where His peace and help are required.

The New Testament emphasis is on transformation, not mere information, which overcomes spiritual bankruptcy, bondage, disease, dullness and poverty, showing that not only souls are saved but characters are transformed.

Christ and the Gospels specifically emphasize loving relationships with others, obedience to Jesus' Word, taking up one's cross, being a servant and a fruit-bearer. Paul and the Epistles emphasize caring fellowship, putting off the old and putting on the new man, walking worthy of God's call, and managing all resources for God.

Objectives of Communicating the Word

The purpose of communicating God's Word is for each believer to gain adequate Christian knowledge, understanding, attitude and action. Information is to be imparted by the teacher, and spiritual formation is to be experienced by the Holy Spirit. What is man's task and what is the Holy Spirit's task?

Man's Task (Information)   **Knowledge**

Holy Spirit's   **Understanding**
Task (Spiritual Formation)   **Attitude**
                                            Action

God's messenger has but one task, and that is to impart Biblical knowledge to the hearer. The church's educational and programmatic responsibility is to provide sufficient information in ways that the mind or intellect might find it possible to grasp accurately the facts of what is being presented. Man's reason must know the details and truths of the subject to be conveyed. Without knowledge of the content of the Word (Law and Gospel), the reality of hearing has not happened.

The necessity of conveying the Word intelligibly is seen in Rom. 10:14, "How can they believe in the One of whom they have not heard? And how can they hear without someone preaching to them?" Reasoning and sorting out the facts happens in the mind of the unbeliever as well as the believer. However, the results in understanding, attitude and action are all the work of the Holy Spirit in the believer. Eph. 1:18 is a prayer "that the eyes of your heart may be enlightened in order that you may know the hope to which He has called you.." This is a move away from mere knowledge of Biblical facts to word expression of the Christian faith by the Holy Spirit.

Chapter 2

THE BIBLICAL LUTHERAN SEEKS GRACE-POWER FOR JUSTIFICATION AND SANCTIFICATION

God's grace is not only for saving us, but also for sanctifying us. Grace will never be understood unless we understand God. What is meant by the God of Justice-God of love? What are the uses of Law and Gospel? Why emphasize repentance and forgiveness? Why not keep it simple and say no more than, "Believe on the Lord Jesus Christ, and you shall be saved?"

God of Justice-God of Love

Why do so many people believe that God sometimes is not fair? Why do they become confused about the goodness of God in their own situations or in world catastrophes? If God is love, why are so many people hungry and why are they out of work?

Far too many Christians hold a superficial view or understanding of God. They have more of a human and cultural paradigm of God than a Biblical one. Too few know the real and living God - the God of Justice-the God of Love.

Everything in the world is derived from God and dependent on Him. He has roots only in Himself, and everything else springs from Him and has its source in Him. Everything originates from Him and has no life or livelihood apart from Him. He is able to explain all things, whereas we are incapable of fully explaining or understanding ourselves and our existence. Our mental limitations prevent us from fully comprehending God or discerning His justice or His love, and His dealings with us.

God is just and holy. God cannot be understood in human images or concepts. We tend to think more of Him by His actions than by His attributes. We think of Him vaguely guiding, loving and comforting His people, but may wonder where He is when we are suffering and in need. The natural tendency is to think of God in abstract terms, and then get angry at Him if He does not control earthly affairs the way we want them to happen. But He is the Living God, a personal God, whose nature is revealed in His relationship to us. He is not far off. He is here.

His grace, love and goodness, as well as His wrath and judgment, are personal qualities expressed in personal actions: "We know that God's judgment against those who do such things is based on truth...Or do you show contempt for the riches of His kindness, tolerance, and patience...?" (Rom. 2:4); "Consider therefore the kindness and sternness of God.." (Rom. 11:22).

God's holiness separates us totally from Him, and does not allow Him to tolerate our sin. There is a purity behind God's anger, too intense to ignore evil. He cannot pretend that the wrong is not there. His justice is too true to let sin go unchecked and unpunished, so we experience floods, earthquakes, sickness and more as reminders of our inherited sin. We even experience broken relationships and false doctrine. God can never tolerate or overlook such sin. He will not overlook the evidence because that is against His own holy nature. At the same time, God's wrath has none of the sinful associations that are attached to human anger. God's verdict rests on divine justice, not on human standards.

Why is sin so serious? It is rebellion against God, the Creator, and is incredibly monumental because it is committed by ones who are made in His very image. Sin is important to acknowledge and face because man is important.

God's power embraces His justice, anger over sins, control of all things, benevolence, love and saving grace. He is limited only by the limits He sets upon Himself. Being righteous, God can frighten us because of our sins, but His love calms us as He assures us that He is our merciful God in Christ Jesus, able and willing to save us and lovingly care for us.

God looked at His human creatures in their sinful rebellion and saw that He had to punish them. The ultimate question requires an understanding of how God can be merciful without compromising His justice. How does a Holy God declare His Holy Justice and still express His Holy Love. His love is too honorable, just, pure, and gracious for Him to ignore what corrupts and destroys.

It is important to understand clearly God's wrath and His judgment, for the very idea is naturally offensive to us. It seems barbaric, belonging to times when people demanded retribution. But these are not just Old Testament ideas which Christ made obsolete or are outdated by modern culture. The reality of absolute right and wrong, justice and guilt are not canceled in the person of the loving Jesus, nor is divine wrath. Indeed, Christ taught it most clearly as He told what happened to Sodom and what will happen to those on the Last Day who reject God and His will.

The exciting thing is that God does not withdraw His love from His people when their lives are not what they should be, or when they sin, for the God of Justice-God of Love is the God of Grace.

God's love permeates His nature and character, for His love in Christ Jesus has satisfied His justice that had to be expressed against sin. Thus the Scriptures speak of His unfailing, tender and enduring love. He loved us so much that He could not tolerate our destruction, but designed a way that we might be saved eternally and experience His love in the midst of strife on earth. The just God is also a loving God. Jesus confirmed this love for us, "As the Father has loved Me, so have I loved you" (Jn. 15:9).

Even in His justice, His love was dominant and His desire was not to want to destroy those He had created and loved. His love drove Him to find a way so that sinful human beings could escape His anger and condemnation. A sacrifice had to be made to pay the penalty for sin. The sacrifice had to be both divine and human - divine to be adequate to carry the full payment for sin and take the condemnation fully, and human in order to experience the suffering necessary to be a substitute for the sinners themselves.

The God of Love did not spare His own Son, but gave Him up for us all (Rom. 8:32). "Therefore, there is now no condemnation for those who are in Christ Jesus.." (Rom. 8:1). Now there is no condemnation against us, and we have peace with God (Rom. 8:1; 5:1). Now no one can any longer charge us or condemn us to Hell because Jesus Christ has taken our condemnation on Himself.

God Communicates Through Law and Gospel

Our just and loving God has provided the killing power of the Law and the reviving power of the Gospel to produce healthy Christians. The failure to understand or to distinguish between Law and Gospel creates spiritual patterns that are humanistic, fearful, frustrating, or legalistic.

There is nothing so sick about a Christian's life or a congregation's existence that a proper distinction and use of the Law and Gospel cannot cure. Many Christian lives are shapeless or weak because they have not experienced the exposure of the Law or the healing power of the Gospel.

To use the Law only to urge a person to do loving acts is like telling a soldier whose legs have been shot off to get up and march. To use only the Gospel to send Christians

22

on God's mission when they do not recognize their diseased lives is like trying to communicate with people whose minds are drugged.

The Law is God's sharp and straight edge to show us how crooked and ragged we are, not a motivation for getting people to act as Christians. The Law corrects, angers, and frustrates. It never gives an inch. The Law is a mirror to show man's true condition. The Law just stands there nagging, but provides no power or willingness to do what it demands. The Law condemns, and presents no way for escape from justice.

There is a third function: to reveal the will of God and what is pleasing to Him. The use of the Law as a guide for Christian action is called the Third Use of the Law, which is only for the Christian who is able to serve God by grace. In this sense, the Law is a standard of God-pleasing behavior to be achieved by the Spirit's strength. While the Ten Commandments do not have the same function as in the Old Testament, they are valid for use in the New Testament to show what God wants.

The Bible presents the will of God as the ethical basis of behavior and prescribes what is right and wrong. Obedience to God's Law is in harmony with grace and saving faith when one acts in faith by the Holy Spirit as a result of being justified.

There are general misuses of the Law and extremes to be avoided:

1. Various forms of *antinomianism*, which is a confusion of the Law and Gospel, or teaching and using the Gospel without preparation provided by the Law. The fact that we are not under Law as a means for being justified does not imply that the Law is not a guideline for leading a godly life for the Christian. Erasing the guideline displaces lawfulness with lawlessness, and obedience with disobedience. The object of the Christian life is the rule of Christ, which means the denial of self-rule - or as St. Paul said, we are not to live under the rule of the Old Man, but "live by faith in the Son of God" (Gal. 2:20).

Jesus said, "If anyone loves Me, he will obey My teaching" (Jn. 14: 23). This means a teaching of sanctification - living the Christian live - and the Third Article of the Apostle's Creed.

The avoidance of Law or considering Law to be relative or setting aside all absolute Law leads to justifying one's continuing in sin in some way. To avoid antinomianism, both Law and Gospel are to be used side-by-side in proper order and with proper distinction.

2. Attempts to use Law to produce change in the Christian's life - legalism. The Gospel alone by the Spirit will yield faith, love, patience, joy and generosity. There is always the temptation to use the Law as a club when there is poor Christian behavior. The user of the club forgets that Christian behavior is the fruit of Christian faith by the Gospel.

Legalism can never break the mastery of sin. It works primarily through fear of punishment and desire for reward. Legalism insists on conformity to man-made religious rules and requirements, which are often unspoken but nevertheless very real. We may even attempt to bind the consciences of others with our private convictions or our rules of conformity to a particular style of culture or religious tradition rather than to Christ Himself. We may force legalism on others, allow others to force it on us, or even force it on ourselves. There may be occasions when we let our rules or traditions in practice to be more important to us than God's will.

Legalism is a form of spiritual abuse through manipulation by subtle human standards. The right words are used, but the tactics are wrong, as God's name is attached to all sorts of organizational programs and doctrinal formulations placed before people in the name of Christ. Then people's spirituality is measured by the extent of their participation in programs or as loyal Lutherans rather than the full expression of personal sanctification by grace. It is easy then to descend into a legalism which pressures people to be involved in the church, controlling and condemning in a way through the unwritten codes that actually wound believers' spirits and keep them from the joy of their resurrection and victory in Christ. Legalism gives birth to abusive spiritual dynamics within the church.

3. Moralism is using the Gospel rather than the Law as a guide to teach ethics and morals or to allow the impression that Christianity is merely a matter of how we act. Moralism causes each Gospel story to become a moral to teach, and therefore each good Biblical character becomes only a moral model to be copied. This process slowly drains life from the Gospel until it emerges only as a model in a morality play. Moralism leads to the establishment of new codes as laws of life and of the church. Then church members will be tempted to trust in their own supposed goodness.

The Gospel is so complete that it asks for no meritorious good work from anyone in order to gain salvation. It produces and empowers for good works, but does not demand them for anyone to be justified before God.

Human beings want to provide a deposit for their credit and thereby attempt to satisfy the demands of God. But the Gospel informs us that God already has on deposit the riches of His grace for our spiritual poverty. The Gospel is God's "drawing power" - not only drawing believers away from sin, sinful and earthly pleasures, but also drawing them to Himself and all that He wills.

The cross of the Lord Jesus is God's greatest demonstration both of His Law (justice) and His Gospel (love). The Law prepares the soil of the heart for the Gospel seed of God's mercy, while the Gospel is the seed and fertilizer to produce a righteous harvest.

The New Testament process for the Christian life is both practical and simple: the growth and development of God's people according to God's design based on a balanced use of Law and Gospel, making proper distinctions in their use.

Application of Law-Gospel For the Old Man-New Man

A disastrous paradigm confusion exists in Christianity worldwide regarding the new nature and old nature of Christians, including also Lutherans. Forty years of observations in the United States and in various areas of the world have caused me to reach the conclusion that over half of all Christians, including Lutherans, do not have a clear knowledge or accurate understanding of the new man's victory over the old man through Christ. This means that the majority do not know who they are or realize the true nature of the spiritual struggle which they face. Needed is a Biblical paradigm of the dual nature of the Christian, and how life's battles are fought and won.

We look first at the descriptions of the old and new natures, the various names by which they are known, and the distinctions between the two.

Old Man	New Man
Old Self	New Self
Old Nature	New Nature
Flesh	Spirit
Sinner	Saint
100% Spiritual Being	100% Spiritual Being
100% Sinful (Rom. 7:18)	100% Holy (Eph. 4:24)

In the left column the various names are equivalent to the Old Man, while the same is true in the right column of the New Man. Paul in Galatians calls them flesh and Spirit, while Martin Luther's favorite name was sinner and saint.

What is the origin of the old self? We were born as the old nature, 100% sinful as Paul tells, "I know that nothing good lives in me, that is, in my sinful nature" (Rom. 8:17). The old self is a total corrupt spiritual being in conflict with God. The new self is also a total holy spiritual being, not a half one. He is 100% righteous: "Put on the new self, created to be like God in true righteousness and holiness" (Eph. 4:24). The Bible tells that the new nature was created in Christ Jesus and came into being when we were baptized into Christ.

The old self is an unreformable rebel, thoroughly corrupt and full of deceit. He is dangerous, deadly, and destructive of true spirituality. He stands before God empty-headed and empty-handed. He has neither word or deed which can be accepted by God. He is conceited, arrogant and perverse.

The new self is born of God - righteous and holy. Just as a carpenter cannot build a tree, so we cannot by human efforts become children of God, but must experience the new birth by baptism. The new nature in us is the very life of Christ, which is dead to the things of the world and alive to Christ.

Note what four New Testament Chapters teach: Colossians 3:2, 5, 8-15: in reference to the Old Self, "Do not set your mind on earthly things...put to death whatever belongs to your earthly nature...rid yourselves of such things as...do not lie to each other.."; concerning the New Man, we read, "Set your minds on things above...put on the New Self...clothe yourselves with compassion, kindness, humility, gentleness and patience...put on love...let the peace of Christ rule in your hearts."

Eph. 4:22-25,29, and 31-32 tell, "Put off your Old Self which is being corrupted by its deceitful desires, put off falsehood, do not let any unwholesome talk come out of your mouths, get rid of all bitterness, rage and anger...Be made new in the attitude of your minds, put on the new self, speak truthfully to your neighbor, be kind and compassionate to one another."

Gal. 5:16-26 teaches: "Do not gratify the desires of the sinful nature, the sinful nature desires what is contrary to the Spirit, they are in conflict with each other. The acts of the sinful nature are obvious, crucify the sinful nature with its passions and desires, do not become conceited, provoking and envying one another...live by the Spirit, the Spirit desires what is contrary to the sinful nature. They are in conflict with one another. The fruit of the Spirit is love, joy, peace, patience, kindness, goodness, faithfulness, gentleness and self control. Since we live by the Spirit, let us keep in step with the Spirit." Verse 17 tells how a civil war is being fought in us between the old and new beings. Every time the Word of God is read or heard, the old nature battles and tries to stop the believing and doing of it, and wants to immobilize the new nature.

Galatians 6:8 reveals what the rewards of the old and the new natures are: "The one who sows to please his sinful nature, from that nature will reap destruction; the one who sows to please the Spirit, from the Spirit will reap eternal life."

Rom. 6:6, 11-13, 22 teach, "Crucify the Old Self, no longer be slaves to sin, count yourselves dead to sin, do not let sin reign in your mortal body, do not offer the parts of your body to sin as instruments of wickedness, sin shall not be your master, the wages of sin is death...count yourselves alive to God in Christ, offer yourselves to God, offer the parts of your body to Him as instruments of righteousness, you have been set free from sin and have become slaves to God, the benefit you reap leads to holiness, and the result is eternal life."

The old and new coexist; the old must daily be put down with the Law. The believer, in whom the new man reigns, is empowered by the Gospel to be a functioning member of the body of Christ.

Luther says: "To be both old man and new means to be one who is sick, in whom illness and health contend," and uses the phrase "righteous and sinful at the same time."

25

We live on resurrection ground. On that grace ground we can face any temptation; we can patiently bear any privation; we can cope with any task or difficulty. The "Civil War" is won! To be sure, grave battles are to be faced in our struggles, but we are working from victory, not for victory. (Rom. 7:18-31,37)

What is the secret of winning the spiritual civil war? It all depends upon which nature we starve and which one we feed! Unfortunately, far too many Christians feed the old self with the influence of bad companionship, evil videos and TV shows, and harmful magazines, while their Bibles are closed and their worship of God is infrequent. Rather, the design for victorious Christian living embraces generous feeding of the new self and starving of the old self. Whichever one is fed will be strong, and whichever one is starved will be weak.

Finding Self-Worth and Self-Esteem

Self-esteem has become a somewhat badly used and maligned concept or paradigm because of a failure to distinguish between the old and new natures. In our old self, there can be no self-esteem or worth. Worth is gained only in the new nature in Christ. The Christian's righteousness, in which the Christian is clothed by faith in Christ's redemption, is always entirely an imputed or credited righteousness, which is our real worth.

There are two ways in which people may attempt to gain self-worth or acceptance by God and others: either in their person or in their performance, either in what they are or what they do. Christians have a choice: either try to find their self-worth or acceptance in Christ's righteousness or in man's righteousness.

The old nature seeks to gain self-esteem and acceptance through performance, believing that the more one does, the greater worth he has, and the more he will be accepted by God and others. But how much performance is necessary? Who sets the standards, and how will the performance be measured? Will the yardsticks be changed sometime? How long will today's performance be remembered or counted for my credit? The only answer to these questions are despair and surrender that leads to low self-worth and the conviction that no one can ever be accepted by God or others - and that one never does enough. The whole matter is really a form of "salvation by works," and is totally destructive of self-esteem.

The performance trap is a deception that deceives us in believing that our salvation, status, and relation with God and others depend on how well we perform. Human nature insists on mixing performance with grace. But when we depend on performance, we cannot feel good about ourselves regardless of what we have accomplished. Performance-based Christianity allows continued feelings of guilt and condemnation and a sense of worthlessness and low self-esteem. There will be self-belittling and despair, not knowing whether our performance is accepted or sufficient. Self-performance leads to condemnation.

Performance-based acceptance and self-esteem contradicts Eph. 2:8-9, "For it is by grace you have been saved through faith - and this not from yourselves, it is a gift of God - not of works, so that no one can boast." Grace and grace alone is the only basis of our right relationship with God. It is undeserved, for if we deserved it, it would not be grace. It cannot be repaid by works or the grace-base would be changed into a performance-base.

True value is not only traced back to the heart, but it is derived from God Himself. We have value, and our time and possessions have value, because they originated from God, who is the ultimate Value. His justice and love form the conditions and the boundary of all true value. Why then do we tend to place more value on things than on God?

Devaluation of ourselves begins with the devaluation of God. Distorted identities come from distorted faith. Christ's love in giving His life for us is the measure of our value.

26

God accepts us unconditionally because Christ washed all our sins and guilt away to give us His goodness.

What we believe about God and ourselves affects our lives. When we see ourselves through God's eyes instead of the eyes of others, or experiences of fear, failure or abuse, God's grace gives us strength to rise up and live the abundant life He has planned for us.

Performance and works so dominate people's search for value and esteem that it is hard to make the distinction between our identity and the way we behave. Our true worth is based upon what God's Word says is true of us, and what Christ did. There are no human standards which can make us feel good about ourselves. There is no need for perfectionism, withdrawal from risks, or manipulation of others to help us succeed because we are already justified, completely forgiven and fully pleasing to God in our new nature in Christ.

Neither do we need the approval of others to feel worthy or to please others at any cost, because as God reconciled us in Christ, we need to be reconciled to others. We can be willing to be open and vulnerable, willing to be criticized and at the same time please God no matter what others think. We are deeply loved by God, and can have patience and kindness toward others because Christ made satisfaction for our sins.

The Scriptures do not allow any dependence upon feeling to give assurance of salvation or whether God loves us or not. We are not to go to church because it feels good, and it make us happy. Feeling good and being happy is important! However, people can feel good when they are complimented by someone or when someone has done them a favor or hugged them. All these are important from a human psychological or emotional perspective, but they can give no assurance for salvation, nor are they power for living the faith. Salvation and sanctification are assured only by the objective truth of God's Word that He loves us despite our unlovableness, and that He meets our needs in Christ whether we feel it or not. It is a terrible thing to substitute our feelings for the eternal truth of God's action of regeneration and indwelling by the Holy Spirit.

Feelings will give us highs and lows related to self-worth. The righteousness of Christ which is ours by faith is what determines our worth. Our feelings, then, should be based upon God's historic love action for us, and the indwelling Christ, not whether we feel His presence.

Those who have been hurt and scarred by a sense of low self-worth caused by their own or others' false assessment of themselves by human standards no longer need say, "I am hopeless, and I cannot change. I have no worth." Such defeatist attitudes and inferiority feelings are resolved by God in our regeneration, where we are made new and complete in Christ.

This leads to the question: What is our real identity? Who is the real me? Where do I get my self-worth or self-esteem? It all depends on whether the new man or the old man is in control. By God's grace, all Christians should be victorious amidst even the most difficult struggles in life by knowing that the new man is being fed by the Gospel and the Word to be strong; at the same time, the old man is being starved and shackled - indeed, sat on - because the new creation in Christ is in charge by the Holy Spirit.

There is no greater worth in the world than Jesus Christ, the Son of God and Man, our Savior, who lives in us by faith. His worth is now ours! Nothing can be added to give us more esteem or worth! Nothing in the world is even in the same ball park when worth is measured.

By imputing His righteousness to us, God attributes Christ's worth to us. He has given us complete self-esteem totally apart from our ability to perform. Christ's righteousness is our worthiness to stand in God's presence without fear of condemnation. Our esteem is established in the gift we have received: "To each one of us grace has been given as Christ apportioned it" (Eph. 4:7).

Think of the worth which the grace-filled Christian brings to the world and his fellow man through his in-Christness: through the new creation God wants to reveal His holiness (Is. 6:3); He displays His faithfulness (1 Cor. 1:9); He manifests forgiveness (Col. 3:13); He demonstrates grace (Tit. 2:11); He wants to show His love (1 Jn. 4:11); God demonstrates patience (1 Cor 13:4); He wants to give comfort (2 Cor. 1:4).

Having established the Biblical paradigm of self-worth or self-esteem, we need to perceive the distortions, misrepresentations or misinterpretations of the use of these terms. There are those who badly misuse the matter of self-esteem by crediting sinful man with worth in and of himself. Man has intrinsic value as a creation of God, but any attempt to attain high self-esteem on that basis alone inevitably drives a person towards performance-based acceptance. To make a person feel good by telling them, "You are worthy and should hold yourself in high esteem," is confusing and inaccurate. On the other hand, simply to tell a person, "You are a wretched, miserable person," without any reference to sin and grace, or the old and new nature, is a total law approach and can be very damaging.

Satan's lies cause us to have a low self-worth which says, "I must meet high standards or be perfect, and I must be approved by others to feel good about myself. When I fail, I am unworthy of God's love and deserve to be punished. I am what I am and cannot change. I am hopeless."

A high self-worth is gained when we listen to God's Word, "I am totally accepted by God" (reconciliation) - "He has reconciled you by Christ's physical body through death to present you holy in His sight..." (Col. 1:22); "I am completely forgiven by God" (justification) - "Therefore, since we have been justified (declared righteous) through faith, we have peace with God through our Lord Jesus Christ" (Rom. 5:1); "I am deeply loved by God" (propitiation) - "This is love: not that we loved God, but that He loved us and sent His Son as an atoning sacrifice (propitiation) for our sins" (1 Jn. 4:10); "I am a new creation, complete in Christ" (regeneration) - "Therefore, if anyone is in Christ, he is a new creation; the old has gone away, the new has come" (2 Cor. 5:17).

The Flow Of Grace (Gospel Power) For Salvation and Sanctification

Amazing grace! Do we really grasp its full dimensions? But what about grace abused, grace under-used, grace disregarded, neglected, and misunderstood?

Grace first means God's unmerited love and mercy in Christ Jesus. Grace reveals the very being of God. It faces us with the mercy and power of God. Grace focuses on God and what He has done to save us and to empower us for Christian living, and takes the spotlight off of ourselves. It liberates us not only from eternal damnation, but also from enslaving sinful habits.

We have looked at the richness of grace in giving the believer unconditional love and forgiveness in Christ. But grace is not limited to salvation alone. There is a flow of grace and Gospel-power that continues in the Christian's life after justification which must not be ignored. Some restrict grace to unlimited love and salvation, making a grace-cocoon in which the Christian is to go through life simply holding on to his faith until the last day, while failing to accept grace for the sanctified life. Any restriction of divine grace which excludes Gospel power for doing good works puts restraints on the effect of grace in our lives which has a terribly negative influence.

Marvelous is the flow of grace and the Gospel power which begins in salvation and continues in doing good works and living for Christ. Various Scriptures propose grace to describe the spiritual gifts and excellences which God works in all believers to provide willing and faithful service: "Each one should use whatever gift he has received to serve others, faithfully administering God's grace in its various forms" (1 Pet. 4:10).

Our service is in the strength of God by grace. Other Scriptures show this flow of grace, beginning with the strategic Ephesians 2:8-10 where we not only learn that we are saved by grace through faith, not by works, but that grace flows into sanctification by grace: "We are God's workmanship, created in Christ Jesus to do good works, which God prepared in advance for us to do" (v. 10). 1 Cor. 3:10 shows grace from God to be the power for Paul to lay a foundation, and someone else to build on it.

There are no more superlatives in any verse in the entire Bible than those applied to grace in the sanctified life than in 2 Cor. 9:8, "God is able to make all grace abound to you, so that in all things at all times, having all that you need, you will abound in every good work." Simply astounding! Being aware that grace is the only reason for our redemption, we are here informed that grace-Gospel power is the only source for our serving God and our fellow man. The same flow of grace is seen in Acts 4:33, "With great power the apostles continued to testify to the resurrection of the Lord Jesus Christ, and much grace was upon them all" (Acts 4:33). Great grace results in great witness!

Unfortunately, many Christians appear to be uninformed and unaware of the promise of grace for the sanctified life, and so use excuses about their weaknesses and lack of abilities while overlooking the fact that their good works are performed only by the grace of God which He has promised to them. Thus there is a need for a paradigm shift by Christians to see grace as 100% operative in their good works as well as in their on-going rescue from guilt and sin.

Indeed, 2 Cor. 12:9 focuses directly on this issue: "My grace is sufficient for you, for my power is made perfect in weakness." When someone responds to a stewardship challenge by saying, "I cannot do that. I do not have it in me," God could reply, "Of course, you do not have it in you. My grace is given exactly for your situation. Only when you recognize your personal weakness will My grace be the strength to perform the task no matter how challenging it is." That's how Paul responds to show what grace means for the Christian life: "That is why, for Christ's sake, I delight in weaknesses,...in difficulties. For when I am weak, then I am strong" (2 Cor. 12:10).

2 Thes. 2:16-17 utilizes divine grace in its double purpose in the expression of hope that our loving God who first "by His grace gave us eternal encouragement and good hope," and then may "encourage your hearts and strengthen you in every good deed and word."

Paul's letter to Titus offers the two dimensional benefit of grace: "The grace of God that brings salvation has appeared to all men. It teaches us to say 'no' to ungodliness and worldly passions, and to live self-controlled, upright and godly lives in this present age...to purify for Himself a people that are His very own, eager to do what is good" (2:11-12, 14). 1 Pet. 4:10 shows that grace is not to be hoarded or unused, but shared: "Each one should use whatever gift he has received to serve others, faithfully administering God's grace in its various forms." Thus grace is to be received and lived to the fullest. Grace received but not expressed is what has been correctly termed, "cheap grace."

What is the practical application of the Biblical flow of grace and Gospel power from justification to sanctification? It first has special relevance to pastors in preparing and delivering their sermons, and also for worship services that sanctification should receive equal concern as justification. There must never be any minimizing of God's grace for justification, but there must be an awareness that grace in sanctification has been sadly neglected. Lives are being torn apart by fear, pride, selfishness, gossip, greed, sexual sins and infidelity, lovelessness, and many other sinful habits, which will not be overcome by simply assuring people that God's grace makes their salvation certain. Repentance is to be sought with assurance that forgiveness is offered by the God of grace together with the power not only to overcome but to substitute positive actions for the sinful ones.

Look at the themes which Jesus presented in the Sermon on the Mount in Mt. 5-7, all of which deal with living the Christian life and to seek righteous living. He speaks of wise and foolish builders. Search Romans 6-8, and find the secret for victorious living, of the new man's victory over the old man, of being conquerors here on earth and for eternity - the Spirit giving us strength. Read Paul's two letters to the Corinthians and see constant notes of sanctification, never forgetting assurance of salvation, but pointing to God's grace and Gospel power for righteous acts, and for keeping faithful to the One who has called us.

When people's hurts and sinful habits are not addressed, they may easily conclude that God simply is interested in saving souls for eternity, but He does not identify with their human pains, doubts, depressions, fears, temptations, and struggles. As grace and Gospel power need to be constantly applied to justification, so it needs constantly, week after week, to be applied to sanctification and holy living. My observation is that there has been a broad ignoring of the application and flow of grace to sanctification.

Grace links us with God's supply line. When we live in God's grace, we will not have confidence in the flesh or in human ingenuity. We can express grace, but we cannot dispense it, because that is God's task. Grace alone is the reason for our sanctification. Grace frees us from institutionalism's "do's and don'ts" and the intimidation of others' demands and expectations. In our day, grace needs to be rescued from its one-dimensional application in justification, to flow smoothly and fully from salvation to sanctification, from justification to good works. Grace also needs to be rescued from its assassins: legalism, moralism, institutionalism, traditionalism, fear, manipulation, and human regulations and control. These are some of the "grace-killers."

Grace is not a legalistic push, but a Gospel pull. Grace is discredited when institutional approaches and church traditions turn it into a doctrine to hold or a system to follow. Any time that believing is separated from obeying, grace has been abused. Grace involves not only a change of mind and heart, but also a change of conduct. Grace has two dimensions - a flow from justification to sanctification.

Unfortunately, the second dimension of grace has not been manifested in our sermons and presentations adequately nor has it been understood effectively by the laity of our church. The result is that even sanctification presentations end with the simple assurance that we are saved by God's grace and all is well, and our laity look at their failures in Christian living and take comfort in the fact that they are saved as bad as they are in their stewardship life, but there is little they can do about it. The result is that God's Supply House of Grace is often untapped, while people live in a legalistic and moralistic life.

Needed is a Second Reformation - One in Sanctification

Sanctification, the practice of the Christian faith or of active Christian living, has always been a major problem. The Gospels and Epistles are filled with exhortations to do good works, while at the same time presenting examples of churches and Christians who are complacent or even disobedient to the will of God.

Will churches and their leaders recognize the great crisis in sanctification caused by the failure of most Christians to live lives consistent with their confessions? Is it an overstatement to declare that the Christian church worldwide requires a second reformation - this time clarifying and defining sanctification?

The situation varies from congregation to congregation, and from Christian to Christian. Institutional practices of the church often are the reason for bad sanctification among the members. Possibly, the greatest offender is the church itself by maintenance and organizational stewardship practices. Sanctification is side-tracked first by the church's use of its institutional goals for members to respond rather than to face God's will as seen in Biblical principles for service and giving.

Are churches and pastors fully aware of the bad situation in sanctification among the members? Most members' response for service is based upon stated needs rather than God's call to fulfill their purpose and ministry based on God's gifts to them. About 60%-70% of most churches provide no service through the church, and possibly 50% do not provide care to others who are in need. It should be said that service to God as His priests and servants involves not only church work but also to give good value at daily work and also to serve fellow man in need.

The biggest problem in the church's practice of sanctification is found in the legalistic and moralistic attitudes of Christians, which negate not only God's grace working in them by the Spirit through sanctification, but also in justification itself.

Legalistic, moralistic and pietistic distortions come sometimes from the pulpit, and sometimes from the pew, and at other times are found in the pulpit and the pew. These are seen mostly by their behavior and outward action, first and foremost by keeping scores, and by judgments related to the right or wrong kind of behavior. People are then assessed more by church attendance and participation in church affairs than in their devotion to God and their spirituality.

It is tragic to observe that sincere, well-meaning Christians world-wide in many small and large churches are judged more by their performance or lack of it than by their relationship to God and their fellow man. When they meet the requirements of the "church club," they receive a passing grade as a good Christian, without a real consideration of having a living relationship with God and their fellow men. This problem not only involves legalistic postures related to wrong use of the Law, but especially the making of human laws and requirements either of what must be done or what must be avoided. In those church camps, Christians are identified not by their faith in Jesus Christ but by their refusal to wear cosmetics or certain clothes, dance, drink, or some other "worldly activity" as they define it. I am not saying that the actions against which Paul speaks in his Epistles as sins are not to be identified (for they are), but that the avoidance of them is an expression of Christian faith in putting down the old nature, not a rule to keep in order to be a good church member.

Sanctification is the condition into which God has called believers by grace to live a holy life according to His will. It involves the killing of sinful actions and of growth in holiness. It is the spiritual process of walking with God. While justification is standing before God through His declaration of our being righteous, sanctification is our expression of faith and manifestation of the righteousness of God by the conduct of our lives through the guidance and power of the Scriptures, "It is God who works in you to will and to act according to His good purpose" (Phil. 2:13).

Some of the examples of God's encouragement to us to live the sanctified life are: "...Do not conform any longer... but be transformed..." (Rom. 12:2); "...Flee these things and pursue righteousness..." (1 Tim. 6:1); "...live a new life..." (Rom. 6:4); "...Participate in the divine nature and escape the corruption in the world..." (2 Pet. 1:4); "...Purify ourselves from everything that contaminates body and spirit, perfecting holiness out of reverence for God..." (2 Cor. 7:1).

Sanctification is the will of God, as God sets us apart for Himself and His service. Indeed, we are to give an account to God(Rom. 14:12). 1 Thessalonians presents a strong message for Christian living: "...We instructed you how to live in order to please God...we ask you and urge you in the Lord Jesus to do this more and more. For you know what instructions we gave you by the authority of the Lord Jesus. It is God's will that you should be sanctified; that you should avoid sexual immorality; that each of you should learn to control his own body in a way that is holy and honorable, not in passionate lust like the heathen...for God did not call us to be impure, but to live a holy life. Therefore, he who rejects this instruction does not reject man but God, who gives you His Holy Spirit" (4:1-8). God reminds His people that they are His and are to be obedient to Him.

The only means of sanctification is the Word of God: "...Sanctify them by the truth; your Word is truth.." (Jn. 17:17); "...To make her holy, cleansing her by the washing with water through the Word.." (Eph. 5:26).

The agent of sanctification is the Holy Spirit, our Sanctifier, who initiates and cultivates our sanctification: "...The Word of God, which is at work in you who believe" (1 Thes. 2:13); "...Who are chosen according to the foreknowledge of God the Father, by the sanctifying work of the Holy Spirit" (1 Pet. 1:2). The holiness of God is reflected in the life of the sanctified Christian only by the help of the Holy Spirit. Because of the old nature in us, we will never achieve sinless perfection, but there is to be growth, as the will of God for each of us is our sanctification (1 Thes. 4:3). Sin is not to rule our hearts.

When Paul stressed to Pastor Titus that we are justified by God's grace, he continued, "I want you to stress these things so that those who have trusted in God may be careful to devote themselves to doing what is good" (Tit. 3:8). Insistence on good works by God's power will not crowd out the central position of the doctrine of justification without works. Only if one does not really know the Biblical truth of justification by faith will he be timid in teaching about doing good works. There is no other incentive or power for good works other than by the pure grace of God.

Adolf Koeberle has a very helpful explanation of God's part and man's responsibility in sanctification: "The paradox of God's sole activity and man's responsibility which is found in sanctification as well as in justification, brings with it an entirely new conception of the New Testament imperatives whose importance and frequent occurrence cannot be emphasized strongly enough...The numberless exhortations of the Epistles are not in the first place addressed to unbelievers who are thus to be driven to a decisive ethical choice. They are actually addressed to those who are baptized, to the regenerate and to those who have become members of Christ and His Church, who on the basis of their communion with Christ already possess what is being required of them. For men who are in the unregenerate state of the natural man the high points of St. Paul's exhortations are as unintelligible as they are unattainable. Without the reality of the presence of the Holy Ghost, such commands would be utterly meaningless. But since God has turned tasks into gifts in the Gospel, the believer can understand and accept such great things." [6]

The impulse which the Gospel gives to expressing faith is described by Koeberle in this way, "The absolutely indispensable significance of sanctification for a Christian faith can be described in these statements: 1) Faith that does not heed nor use this divinely given gift of renewal perishes through its self-imposed poverty. 2) Faith that proves its vitality in sanctification grows thereby in strength and constancy. 3) Faith that exercises self in holiness is just the faith that turns men to repentance and teaches the one who is doing good works to seek after the promises of forgiveness." [7]

The Holy Spirit through the Word does not allow for paralytic Christianity, but enables us to experience the reality of Christ's love and power by producing fruit in us (Jn. 15:1-8) and by helping us to honor Christ in our circumstances, deeds and relationships.

Chapter 3

BIBLICAL LUTHERANS FORM ACTIVE CHRISTIAN COMMUNITIES

The historic struggle of the church related to function and form since Paul's day has been the tension between the body of Christ and its institutional form, between building a church or a Christian community. Form must follow function just as surely as there must be some form to hold or convey water.

This chapter will confront many of the troubling issues related to the distinctions and balance between the body of Christ and its organizational structure. It deals not only with identity, but also with purpose related to the paradigms or models we use in our churches.

God has called us together in Christ, "...Being built up as a spiritual house or holy priesthood, ... through Jesus Christ" (1 Pet..2:5). The New Testament tells much about a body of believers and a people of God, having little emphasis on buildings. Jesus called a group of men who walked with Him, whom He prepared together for the ministry of building His Church. God sent Paul out in his ministry from a church, traveling with a group of workers who shared with him in the work which God had entrusted to them. There were teams of elders, deacons, and church councils working together as one body in Christ, and members of one another.

Ephesians 4 - A New Testament Model

Aside from the centrality of the Word and Sacraments, what are the essentials for shaping the church? What are its functions and what should its form be? Ephesians 4 presents decisive direction in determining the goals and activities for developing a strongly operating church. It offers broad terms for the position and the work of the pastor and the priesthood of all believers.

In Eph. 1:4 and 18, Paul reminds that God chose us in Christ before the creation of the world, and he prayed that we may be enlightened in order that we may know the hope to which God has called us. In 4:1, he exhorts, "I urge you to live a life worthy of the calling you have received." Following God's will, we are not members of the church because we decided to be on our own terms and desired to follow Jesus. Ours is a solemn call not merely to exist spiritually, but to fulfill the purpose of God's call to us.

This call is not one to merely occupy pews in a church building or endure regular rituals and ceremonies which are necessary for church membership, or to agree to affirm certain doctrines in order to prove acceptable or worthy. Already Paul reveals in 4:2 that the church encompasses vital relations with people humbly and gently in the context of encouraging relationships: "...Be patient, bearing with one another in love." Relationships that neglect the truths of Biblical directives to affirm others will not promote godly character. Maximum growth in Christian maturity occurs when truth is presented in the context of relationships.

These relationships are seen as each member functions as a part of the body of Christ: "There is one Body and one Spirit - just as you were called to one hope when you were called - one Lord, one faith, one baptism; one God and Father of all, who is over all and through all and in all" (v. 4-6). Paul provides a clear picture of this by comparing the church to the human body in Romans 12: "Just as each of us has one body with many members, and these members do not all have the same function, so in Christ we who are many form one body, and each member belongs to all the others" (v. 4-5). In 1 Corinthians 12:18, Paul makes an application to individuals: "In fact, God has arranged the parts of the body, every one of them, just as He wanted them to be."

In order to make it possible for each Christian to function effectively in the body of Christ, Christ has supplied every member with gifts to utilize in the church: "To each one of us grace has been given as Christ apportioned it" (4:7). Grace or gifts were not given to some of us, every other one of us, most of us, or even only to 99% of us. Each one of us has been "gifted" or "graced." The only question is whether the grace and gifts have been discovered, and then used. This is the divine plan, not just some grand stewardship idea concocted by activistic pastors or church elders.

How many members of congregations recognize what they are good for, to what they have been called, and are they walking worthy of that call? The issue is that when they were saved by grace through faith in Jesus Christ, God also called them to walk worthy of this great salvation. Christ distributed grace and gifts to them to fulfill their purpose. Christians are not on their own without grace or gifts which they must somehow work up within themselves. In a real sense, they are already prepared to fulfill their purpose because Christ gave grace and gifts by the Spirit.

This same Christ gave church ministries for some to be pastors and teachers who are to feed and teach the members of the church (v. 11). What are the pastors to do besides proclaiming the Word and administering the Sacraments? What is expected of the teachers? "To prepare God's people for works of service, so that the body of Christ may be built up" (v. 12). Preparing the people for service or works of ministry should result in the members speaking the word of Law and Gospel to each other so that all the members of the Body may be built up. This requires Bible study and training sessions where the preparation is happening. It necessitates participation of all Christians in studying the Bible together by which they can be equipped for the work that they are to do (v. 12) on the basis of the grace and gifts which Christ has given (v. 7). The divine system is that everyone is to minister according to the gifts he has received.

How long should this continue? "Until we all reach unity in the faith and in the knowledge of the Son of God and become mature, attaining to the whole measure of the fullness of Christ" (4:13). God's Word alone will give us unity in the faith and help us dispel all human notions about the Christian faith and the church. Certainly, the unity of faith has not even been reached in most congregations for the reason that many of its members are not present where the preparation by the teachers of the Word is being offered. The church will be impaired by disunity of faith as long as there are a substantial number of members who are unwilling to be Biblically equipped.

How long is the preparing to go on? "Until we all become mature, obtaining the whole measure of the fullness of Christ" (v. 13). As long as there are members who fail or refuse to participate in the Bible training, there will continue to be spiritual infants and a big spiritual nursery of ones who are blown here and there by every wind of teaching and will be deceived (v. 14). Obviously, members are not to stop learning when they have merely learned the basics of the Christian faith, but they are to be spiritually developed with the expectation that they are willing to reach the full height of Christ. I have not heard of any Christian, even among the giants of the faith alive in our time, who will admit to having attained the full measure of the fullness of Christ. So why are so many members sitting with their Bibles closed? Are they watching their TVs and VCRs while being spiritually immature? Obviously, because they do not know the divine plan and the call to which they have been called.

Verse 15 reveals how spiritual growth happens: "Speaking the truth in love, you will in all things grow up in Him who is the Head, that is Christ." The Biblical formula for unity of the faith and growing to maturity is a church where the truth is spoken in love. Some speak the truth, but legalistically, and not in love. Some do everything in love, but fear to speak the truth. The divine procedure is to speak the truth in love. The result is spiritual maturity, for then "We will in all things grow up into Him who is the Head, that is, Christ."

The divine plan is presented in all its simplicity in verse 16: "From Him (Christ) the whole body joined and held together by every supporting ligament, grows and builds itself up in love, as each part does its work." Here is the key to the successful functioning of the church. Christ, who is the source of forgiveness of sins and has given grace and gifts to each believer in the Body. An amazing truth is expounded here: the whole Body is joined and held together by every supporting member; every member has been given grace and gifts for being joined together and held together in the church. Then why are so many churches disjointed or disunified? Because too many members are not using their verse 7 grace, and thus each part is not doing its work. That work is not determined by church needs for workers or money for church budgets, but by the grace and gifts which Christ has apportioned to each one. When each one functions worthily according to his call, the Body (the church) "grows and builds itself up in love."

The divine system is one in which everything depends upon Christ, and nothing depends upon the believer except to trust and receive God's grace in order to be able to respond to the call. Why is this divine plan such a mystery among the majority of Christians? The plan of God has often been so segmentized and fractured by bits and pieces of exhortations to people to support church maintenance plans rather than showing them the heavenly blueprint for operating effectively by God's grace.

If God's people are to comprehend the fullness of God's plan displayed in Ephesians 4, further attention is required regarding such basics as the body of Christ, the nature of the church, how Christian community is established and maintained, the role of the pastor and the laity, and authority in the church. Confusion of the body of Christ by traditions and practices of the organized church must also be addressed. What are the issues of the church, the body of Christ, the community, and ministry as we seek to gain a Biblical map in building the church and Christian community?

Body of Christ

The church known in its invisible nature is named the body of Christ: "God placed all things under His (Christ's) feet and appointed Him to be head over everything for the church, which is His Body..." (Eph. 1:22-23); "...For the sake of His Body, which is the Church" (Col. 1:24). Paul speaks about weak believers with unspiritual minds who have lost connection with "the Head, from whom the whole body, supported and held together by its ligaments and sinews, grows as God causes it to grow" (Col. 2:19). This is the invisible Church which consists of true believers known only by God. This differs from the visible church or congregation, where members can be identified and counted. When Jesus says, "I will build my Church" (Mt. 16:18), He is referring to the invisible Church, which is His bride. Paul said, "...I promised you to one husband, to Christ, so that I might present you as a pure virgin to Him" (2 Cor. 7:2). Paul reminds us that we are members of Christ's body (Eph. 5:30). True believers are also identified with the family of God: "I will be a Father to you, and you will be My sons and daughters, says the Lord Almighty" (2 Cor. 6:18); "You are no longer foreigners and aliens, but fellow citizens with God's people and members of God's household" (Eph. 2:19).

Our highest title is not "church members," but children of God: "To all who received

35

Him, to those who believed in His name, He gave the right to become children of God" (Jn. 1:12); "How great is the love the Father has lavished on us that we should be called children of God! And that is what we are! The reason the world does not know us is that it did not know Him" (1 Jn. 3:1).

Each member of the body of Christ has high value, and is interdependent upon one another. Committed to truth, united by the Spirit, motivated and filled by Christ's love, and equipped to serve, each member of the Body functions according to its sanctified design. The Church as the body of Christ is the fullest expression of the person of God in the midst of His creation. This is the Church which is a refuge for our life in this world. The denial of the intimate body relationships through independence and individualism of church life is deadening to our body of Christ function. God's design is that we show before the world the "one another" relationship and service, functioning as a body to share life together as members of each other.

No member or no part of the Body in any local place in the world should live or work in such a way that it appears to be totally consumed with, by and for itself. We are part of the Body on earth, with mutual responsibilities to one another before God. To be true to the Head, we cannot live as though we are the whole Body, all there is, and be unaware of our brothers and sisters in the congregation and around the world, and be uninvolved in their needs and their suffering. Resources which God has given to us individually are not to be consumed for our own benefits while there is spiritual need elsewhere.

Individualism may exist in the institutional system, and selfish independence may rule in the hearts of church members, but this is a denial of the body of Christ which exists for mutual relationships and submission to one another. Submission is offered to one another as we hear in each other's voice God's Word, which gives us direction, strength and hope. God has provided a sanctuary in the Body where we are secure and free, a place where God reigns and His life is shared fully with one another.

Besides being overly independent, some insist on a private faith, insisting that they will keep to themselves and do their own thing. Privatizing faith in such a manner is depreciating and devaluing it. In such an atmosphere, edification will not only be hampered, but will soon be non-existent. Our Christian faith is not to be understood as being private and individual, as though we can cut ourselves off from accountability to others in the Body. A faith that is secluded or isolated is a distortion of the Biblical witness. Not only is individualized Christianity an evasion of sharing within the Christian community, but it is also a withdrawal from public life where a Christian witness must be given by each one. No stepping outside of community can be allowed if it is to remain a healthy and safe place to be.

The mutual responsibility and interdependence of individual members of the body is best seen and understood in a survey of the "one another" exhortations of the Epistles. Believers are informed how to live in view of their relation to Christ:

"Spur one another on toward love and good works" (Heb. 10:24)

"Love one another, even as I have loved you" (John 13:34).

"Each member belongs to all the others" (Rom. 12:5).

"Be devoted to one another in brotherly love" (12:10a).

"Honor one another above yourselves" (12:10c).

"Live in harmony with one another" (12:16a).

"Accept one another, then, just as Christ accepted you" (15:7).

"Instruct one another" (15:14).

"Greet one another" (16:16).

"Have equal concern for each other" (1 Cor. 12:25).

36

"Serve one another" (Gal. 5:13).
"Carry each other's burdens" (6:2).
"Be patient, bearing with one another" (Eph. 4:2).
"Submit to one another" (5:21).
"Bear with each other and forgive whatever grievances you might have against one another" (Col. 3:13).
"Teach and admonish one another" (3:16).
"Encourage one another and build each another up" (1 Thes. 5:11).
"Confess your sins to each other and pray for each other" (James 5:16).

These "one another" functions are to be enacted by all members of the body of Christ, not just by a few or only those who are especially gifted or who are most enthusiastic. God intended that each Christian, no matter how weak or strong, is to be such a functioning part of the Body. The very nature of the body of Christ reveals that each member is to function and contribute to the process of edifying or building up each other. God made us dependent upon each other. The Biblical emphasis is upon the importance of becoming mature in Christ, both as individual believers and as a corporate body. We are not given the choice of whether or not we want to function.

Building A Christian Community

Christians in community might be defined as the redeemed people of God called together by the Holy Spirit to use all of their spiritual and material resources for building each other up in faith through mutual teaching and caring, and to share the saving Gospel of Jesus Christ with those who do not know and experience His love and mercy. No person is complete, and no one has been entrusted with all. Completeness is found only in mutual sharing and caring of Christian community. In Christ we are brought into this community through the Word and Gospel, through which He imparts, increases and strengthens faith. Jesus at the time of His Ascension went to the Father to make it possible for all believers to be incorporated into the we-community of eternal trinity - God's own eternal love circle.

God has become real to us as Christ is incarnate in His body where He is the head, and we are its members fit and joined together. Thus we become all God intends us to be only as we function together. Every Christian needs the Body environment if he is to be truly strong, where people can interact on a daily basis.

God has directed that salvation is gained through Christian community. The Body is His chosen instrument to convey the message of redemption and reconciliation to alienated people in a dysfunctional world. Yet very few ever experience true community or have a vision of an authentic Christian community.

Many do not even know how to communicate God's Word to their own family or the simple Gospel to their neighbor. The proper task of communication is to create love and harmony through the Gospel. The purpose of communication at all times should be reconciliation.

How is the Christian community - koinonia, both horizontal and vertical - created? What is its true nature, and what are the dynamics of maintaining community? What are the barriers to community building?

The true Christian community does not function well where people only feel good or where they smile and express much joy while their spirituality is paper thin. The picture of many people sitting in pews and then bustling about working in church sales and bazaars, active in church athletic events and filling an ecclesiastical edifice with people does not prove the existence of true Christian community. The words fellowship and community are too often used loosely when groups of church people get together for an event, for those activities can be shallow and meaningless when evaluated from the vertical perspective rather than the horizontal. People can be very isolated and fragmented even though they are getting together in churchly activities. People are often together without any actual spiritual intimacy.

Most fellowship and attempts at community are built upon hearing only good news and what people want to hear. One of the proofs of genuine community is the ability to listen to bad news about oneself and of others, about accepting law and judgment, confessing sins to one another and receiving the assurance of absolution, and then gaining relief through the good news of forgiveness of all our sins. True community does not allow denial or rationalizing of sins, shallow spirituality or scapegoating, but insists on loving confrontation by the Law and Gospel.

True community does not allow unloving confrontation or insensitive relations, but is committed to feeling that overcomes loneliness and alienation. Here people are called to wholeness even while simultaneously they recognize their incompleteness. They are invited to power while acknowledging weakness. They are summoned to independence and interdependence at the same time, as rugged individualism is denied. Lack of community encourages us to hide our weaknesses and failures, and teaches us to be ashamed of our limitations, driving us to be super-people in the eyes of others.

While the hearts of many are breaking for real community, few find a level of trust, vulnerability and intimacy that offers God's Gospel strength. The result is that many are hidden behind masks of fear and pretense or where they share only what is not threatening to them. They cannot share freely the things they have in common - inadequacies, imperfections, and incompleteness. True community is where Christians can communicate honestly with each other, whose relationships go deeper than the veils which hide the reality of their condition.

The Christian community built upon the body of Christ is and must be inclusive of all repentant sinners. Being exclusive violates the nature of Christ's community. Any exclusion or any cliques are enemies of community, where repentance and forgiveness must be central. Thus the Christian community should ask, "How can we Biblically justify accepting this person?" rather than raising the question, "Can we justify keeping this person out?" This is an issue not just of church membership, but of building community within the body of Christ.

Where Biblical realism exists so that the word of Law and Gospel is spoken to each other lovingly, there is true community. Such community examines itself faithfully. This is important because no community can ever be 100% healthy, having no spiritually sick members. Thus if the Christian community is to be a safe place for even the weakest, such questions must be regularly asked as, "Are we a healthy group? Are some sin-sick? Are we on target? How are we doing?" This will help assure that our Christian community is a safe place, where weaknesses are admitted and not denied, and where people are accepted and cared for.

It takes a great deal of work for Christians to achieve safety of true Christian community. There will be freedom to seek spiritual health, to be a functioning member of the body of Christ and be free to relinquish all disguises and facades. This requires vulnerability not only from the members but also from the leaders. None of this can be accomplished by human effort, but only by the Holy Spirit through the Gospel of reconciliation. Openness to each other requires that we be vulnerable, having the willingness even to be wounded, to cry with those who cry, and to hurt with those who hurt. The greatest vulnerability is always the public recognition that we are sinners not only in our origin but also in daily lives. Thus we do not give the impression that we are without fault or without weaknesses, for we are not. Healers filled with love let themselves be wounded, and they can help heal others.

A characteristic of the community is that it communicates, that each has mutual access to each other without restrictions. Thus the standards of good communication are the basic principles of community-building. Good communication means that there is an open door to each other, and that there are no locks on these doors or doors slammed in faces. There is freedom to listen and also to speak. All must be free to do both without fear of some authorities retaliating.

Some who come to the community or are in the community are hurting so badly that reality escapes them, and they cannot communicate accurately but try to fake it. People who are in denial will naturally play the game of "let's pretend," but the strong are to bear the infirmities of the weak and learn to minister to them. If the community is not capable of helping those hurting in this way, it is not functioning according to God's design, for Jesus alone can meet their needs. Any attempt to avoid conflict which is necessary for healing will weaken the community. At times there is a need to struggle lovingly. Issues are always to be confronted openly, not put under the table. Disagreements are inevitable and sometimes painful, but it is necessary to face them realistically rather than pretending that there are no fractured relations or divisions.

Another thing that can hurt or destroy a community is to allow false expectations. Only Biblical standards are to be taught and allowed, while all human assumptions and outlooks are to be avoided. It is crucial to be aware of the preconceptions that people bring to community, the ones who bring traditional prejudices that fit dogmatic institutions or rigid organizations more than a Biblical and loving Christian community. Some may even be looking for a shallow fellowship without any appreciation of orthodox Christian doctrine. They bring sentiments about caring for one another without bringing faith in the One who set the standards for community. So all who come to and are members of the community must empty themselves of their organizational propositions and proposals or traditional expectations and accept God's Word as the common basis for community. The first order is to be humble and obey God in His Word by His Spirit. Without that, community cannot survive.

The Christian community is strengthened when its individuals die to themselves, as Jesus suggests. This requires emptying of ourselves, our carnal wills. Strength is gained only when we recognize our brokenness, our own death to selves. The tendency is always for us to insist on being full and to refuse to empty ourselves. Yet emptiness clears out the debris which stops building the right foundation for Christian community. The temptation is always there to avoid emptiness and brokenness by fleeing into rationalizations or into church organization with its rules, rituals, legalisms and institutionalism. Institutionalism and traditionalism is always a flight away from community building.

Christian community is maintained through gathering around the Word and the sacraments and by gathering in church family groups as the New Testament church, which then leads to edifying and evangelical church discipline. Tensions will always exist because of authority, structure, commitment, individuality, and difficult decisions as to what to include or to exclude. These are all part of attending to community health and strength. Pressures will often invite us back into traditional ways of behaving to maintain respectability and the peace of the institution.

We cannot properly maintain the community unless we regularly contemplate ourselves as a body or organism, not as an organization or the institutional church. Yet so many churches do not achieve such community. Aspirations of individuals are to be considered alongside the building of community. Spiritual transformation happens most compellingly and completely in the context of Christian community. As taught by Jesus and Paul, community is not optional, but a normal expectation. Disciples do not live and work apart from community. Yet we have usually substituted attendance at worship services or of certain levels of participation in the institutional church for Christian community.

The Book of Acts shows the early church as having great quality of its community. Love was expressed, sins and problems were faced, reconciliation was occurring, and people were not divided between Jew and Gentile, slave and free, male and female. A little Jesus veneer on the institutional church is not the Biblical answer and does not enrich the lives of people.

Reviewing the broad range of considerations to develop close personal relationships and Christian association, the Scriptures show us that every individual Christian should participate in creating unity in the Body, and that no one is more important than another. We are to value ourselves only as God values us: "Do not think of yourself more highly than you ought, but rather think of yourself with sober judgment, in accordance with the measure of faith God has given you" (Rom. 12:3). The main ingredients of Christian fellowship is to communicate, to learn and understand, to forgive, to cherish and prize, to maintain unity, and to share resources with others.

Another aspect is approaching matters from others' point of view, where with empathy we learn to understand their situation. Here we recognize the differences between us, the dangers of differences when they relate to substance and doctrine, and accepting differences when they concern cultural style and practice. We accept the teaching of Paul to become all things to all people so that we may win them, not to self or institution but to Jesus, learning to accommodate in non-essentials. Great discernment will be used in being critical and judging others, recognizing the difference between perception and reality. Each should learn to cultivate a sensitive spirit towards those who have spiritual struggles, and minister God's grace to those needs.

Another basic is not to allow any barriers to a relationship because of an unforgiving spirit. Clarity is required to accept the Biblical conditions for forgiveness and its cost. We will submit to God's control, and accept injustices if necessary like Joseph did so that God can accomplish His work through us. It will be necessary to understand the nature of giving and taking offense, and how to avoid and overcome offenses. All should understand that the results of an unforgiving spirit are denial or excusing of sins, anger, animosity, hate, spite, vengeance, slander, and bitterness.

Fundamental, too, is the sustaining of the oneness God gives us with others by maintaining unity of faith (Eph. 4:13), and to nurture unity in doctrine and practice in the local church through a dynamic fellowship. Unity in marriage and of the family is fostered to keep strong the basic social and Christian unit God has created.

Inherent in Christian association is serving one another in the role of a servant. Every opportunity and challenge will be utilized to be salt and lights, to use spiritual gifts, and to help others fulfill their potential in Christ. The principle of sowing and reaping, of giving and receiving, will be practiced. Responsibility and accountability will be accepted. Above all, all will see their sufficiency in Christ alone, as each contributes the grace he has been given for the building up of the Body both through inreach and outreach.

Building Christian community will result in the church becoming a serving institution. If the institutional church is to achieve servanthood, it will be committed to a Word-process with effective teaching and learning, leadership and followership, in which everyone is being uplifted in some way.

Small Group Fellowship and Support System

The first-century church did not depend on wholesale methodologies in their communication, but rather used small group dynamics and a person-to-person approach. Peter went to the house of Mary, where many people had gathered (Acts 12:12); "Taught you publicly and from house to house" (Acts 20:20); "Greet the church that meets at their house" (Rom. 16:5); "The church that meets at their house" (1 Cor. 16:19); "Nympha and the church that meets in her house" (Col. 4:15); "To the church that meets in your home" (Philemon 2).

One of the strengths of the Early Church was their togetherness, and explosive dynamic:

They prayed together (Acts 1:14);
They were all together in one place and were empowered by the Holy Spirit (2:1-4);
They taught the Word together (15:35);
They suffered together (16:22);
They sang together (16:25).

The Early Church was not an impersonal institution, but a place where the message penetrated all homes through interpersonal relationships. There was effective ministry to each other centered in the use of the Word to nourish and strengthen faith in the hearts of people.

There are many good Biblical and practical reasons for providing care groups as support systems in congregations. They assure that members are vitally connected to the church, while they provide multiple points of entry into the church membership. There is no better way to care for the people, and to be accountable for their spiritual welfare. Fellowship groups are a place to provide safety and security. They are a center for experiencing community at its best. Here's where vital Christian fellowship is offered.

Small groups aid in personal spiritual growth, where individuals can speak fully and openly and find Biblical direction for their problems, frustrations, joys, sorrows, and needs. Relevant Bible study and discussion is an essential part of the program. Opportunity is provided for personal exploration and application of the Word to personal faith for learning and growing. The pastor and elders use a variety of Biblical resources that will deepen understanding of God's Word and will.

Small groups are to help others, "Encourage one another daily" (Heb. 3:13). They are a laboratory to learn how to share love by Law and Gospel. By caring and encouraging one another through the Word, individuals are ministered to and will especially be aided to meet crises which arise from time to time. This loving support includes sending cards for encouragement, baby-sitting for one another's children, sharing the happy and sad experiences of each other's lives, providing meals for the sick, and visiting and phoning when some are hurting. This is a place to know and be known in a supportive environment as we struggle, make decisions, and overcome difficulties.

Small groups help mobilize Christians for commitment and ministry. This is an effective way to shift the work of the church to the people, and to help follow the Eph. 4 model. Unlimited opportunities for meaningful service are provided, also for developing new ministries. An environment for developing abilities and spiritual gifts is offered.

Small group fellowship is an effective method of renewing nominal members and for assimilating new members. Isolation is a great danger for those who are new in the faith and for those whose faith has weakened. Such people need more than merely attend worship services, but require contact with fellow Christians in Body-action.

Ingredients for effective small group operation and planning begin with reliance on the authority of God's Word as the check point for the purpose and program of the groups. These are not to become churches within the church or small independent churches, but the pastor is to exercise his office through selection of study resources and careful training of group leaders. A vital link with the pastor and elders is to be maintained at all times, for this is the ministry of the entire church. Renewal of the church is to be related to the renewal which is experienced in small groups, which can be the beginning of the spiritual awakening in the congregation. As there is accountability between the members of the group, it is also true of the pastor and elders as well.

Each group should be kept as small as possible and as large as necessary. The smaller the group, the greater the interaction and discussion. Ordinarily the number might involve 10 - 15 persons. They work best in geographical areas so that close contact can be maintained. However, there may also be special support groups which embrace people who have specific needs. Groups may begin meeting on a monthly basis but, as they grow through experience, they may meet bi-weekly. In highly developed small group programs, some may be mature enough to meet weekly. Encouragement should be given to participants to prepare Bible studies before each meeting. A clear purpose for the small groups and the commitment on the part of participants should be presented. The times, places and purposes of the meetings should be clearly communicated by the leaders. Attendance records should be kept and even visits by the leader or members of the group should be made on absentees.

Honesty and openness are to be encouraged in an atmosphere of trust. This means that the leader should not be judgmental, harsh, or highly opinionated, or overly reactive when things do not go as he wishes. No one should be allowed to dominate the discussion. People should not be allowed to confess anyone else's faults but their own. Specific personal problems ordinarily are to be avoided in the group except when a personal visit has already taken place and the individual wants support from the group. A disturbed person cannot be allowed to become the center of the group. No "dumping" should be allowed.

Confidences should be kept even while personal matters which require private attention should be avoided. At the same time, all members should be encouraged to have a confidant or person with whom they can meet privately on a regular basis for Biblical encouragement and accountability. It is wise for everyone to find someone to ask private and difficult questions, to help live through deep hurts or the pain of being isolated or even different. Two are always better than one, and Christian teammates are valuable assets. The Scriptures certainly show the value of having a person besides the pastor to which to confess one's sin, to hear forgiveness, and to be strengthened through the Word and prayer. Confidants should meet on a regular basis to pray for spiritual healing wherever necessary, rejoice in victories, and to encourage one another.

Fellowship groups can become fertile soil in which leaders develop and flourish, as members are entrusted with responsibility and allowed to gain confidence while learning leadership skills. They provide the basic environment for both training in godliness and corrective discipline. No pastor, however talented, can care effectively for more than a small number of families. Small groups provide a realistic solution to the congregation's need for ministering to all people.

In a LEADERSHIP magazine survey of 500 leaders, almost half reported that they believe that the recovery movement plays a significant role in American churches to help people deal with emotional, mental or physical health needs. Three out of five churches have at one time or another offered at least one kind of support-group ministry, the most popular being: single parents (31%); recovering alcoholics (28%); grief recovery (23%); divorce recovery (22%); substance abuse(18%); eating disorders (18%). Also important was assistance to victims of one kind of abuse or another. Three-fourths of the church leaders were favorable toward the recovery ministry through support groups. Unwarranted negative opinions are held by some Missouri Synod pastors, which are untenable. These will be considered later when a Christian approach to the AA Twelve Steps is considered.

Recently I noted that Nigeria is a culture which is built upon family solidarity and support. Nigerian pastors and members alike who have full and abiding support through their blood family are basically deserted by their spiritual family and must often carry their burden by themselves within the church. The best that our Lutheran church could do was to give them their spiritual lift and encouragement by sitting in pews in a church looking at each others' backs and listening to a pastor proclaiming the precious Word, but that dynamic Word has not entered the community of Christians in their daily lives as we see it in the Book of Acts. The same is true of most congregations and most members of The Lutheran Church-Missouri Synod, whose spirituality is measured by how often they occupy space in the church building for one hour each week rather than by the pursuit of their privileges and responsibilities according to the Ephesians 4 model of the body of Christ-church or the priesthood of all believers.

When will we stop the mouths of the detractors who sling mud at the Ephesians 4 model by glibly calling the small spiritual family groups a "church within a church"? Already early in my pastoral ministry I heard this thoughtless criticism. Yet in my second congregation I helped initiate geographical zones or shepherding groups, which were spiritually productive. I carefully taught the elders and leaders who led these groups, and I always remained responsibly in charge. I could rest much more securely in the knowledge that my ministry in the Word was being extended through the life of the spiritual leaders of the congregation to all the members according to the New Testament model, not the cathedral model.

Shepherding and support groups are based upon the Scriptural concept of Christian community which penetrates deeply into the congregation to build interpersonal relationships. For those who want details on the organizing of shepherding groups, information is provided in Chapter 7 of my book, *Vision and Strategy For Church Growth*. [8] It contains important information for those who are not imprisoned by the past cathedral style, which is institutionally program-based, and is antithetical to the people-based church.

It is more accurate to see the New Testament church as "living stones" which are being built up as a "spiritual house" (1 Pet. 2:5). The church today should not be seen as an edifice made by joining stones and bricks by mortar, but by joining human lives by the Holy Spirit. Can we be sufficiently honest to admit the inefficiency of the program-based church with its buildings standing empty except for a few hours each week for the spiritual specialists to serve the people while only a small percentage of the members are involved in the people-based service tasks, trying to reach the large group of hopeless inactives. The program-based edifice church competes within its own membership for people to fill the program positions while the pastor is the officiant of the rituals that are to be kept by the members, and the members remain basically unattached relationally.

The Ephesians 4 relational church has clear directions set by the pastor with a clear focus of God's people who are to be prepared for their works of service to edify the body of Christ (Eph. 4:12). Some leaders with Biblical and contextual insights have stated that those churches in the 21st Century which are not built upon this small-group model will basically be irrelevant to the people they are to reach.

To summarize, small group shepherding support systems shift the work of the church to God's people and fulfills Ephesians 4. This provides multiple points of entry into the church, and is the best way to care for the people. It gives one-on-one loving care between members. It provides application of the Bible to daily life through development of unity and true spiritual fellowship; it aids in spiritual and personal growth. Shepherding groups also mobilize the members for commitment and meaningful service. It also allows for non-threatening friendship evangelism and the discipling of new converts. It also encourages renewal of inactive and nominal members.

Evangelical Church Discipline and Community Health

The purpose of being joined together in the body of Christ and in Christian community is to keep us strong in the faith and to express it consistently in our sanctified life. Failure to edify fellow Christians and to observe loving and Biblical discipline(which is a part of discipling) toward one another results in weakened relationships and strife in the Body. Careful Biblical discipline produces loving relationships. Corrective church discipline may seem distasteful, but it actually heals the erring and spiritually crippled brothers and sisters in Christ. Only the exercise of the costly love of such discipline can assure health for all within the Body.

Some believe that discipline is simply removing an individual from the church. However, church discipline is both formative(as it deals with the problem before it gets too serious), and it is reformative(as it deals with the problem if the person becomes somewhat hardened). Formative church discipline is really edification which demonstrates love to one another in order to prevent problems or stop them from growing. Formative discipline is helping one another through the use of God's Word so that people develop spiritually in a healthy way.

One big reason why there is so little renewal in many churches is because leaders fail to pursue Biblical procedures that require reformative discipline. Recovery of evangelical discipline is the only hope for aggressive renewal in the Missouri Synod. Such discipline is not a stiffening of the Law or a reinforcement of authority, but rather applying the grace of the Gospel.

There are two extremes: 1. legalism, which adopts an assortment of rules and policies to be used for "codifying sins" and "giving sentences" against wrongdoers; 2. "cheap grace" which relativizes Biblical truth and ends up with tolerance, false humility, flexibility, and false love.

To abandon discipline because it has sometimes been badly administered is unwarranted. The answer to bad church discipline is Biblical church discipline, not "no discipline." Evangelical discipline is a solution to today's failure in churches and is urgent, as it has far-reaching significance for Christian life that has been impoverished as a result of its lack.

The Keys of the Kingdom is the mandate for discipline given by God (Mt. 18:15-18). This authority forgives and retains sins by use of Law and Gospel.

The church will always be tempted to avoid the responsibility of evangelical discipline, rationalizing and pretending the problem will somehow go away by itself. Such failure represents a breakdown of grace and a departure from the Gospel. Final excommunication is the forum under which the church continues to make grace available to the unrepentant, because it has not been accepted inside the church. It is the only loving and redeeming course of action possible in certain circumstances. Love will not allow a person to destroy himself without being warned in a merciful but shocking manner. The church uses evangelical discipline to safeguard the Gospel by which alone people can be saved.

The practice of evangelical church discipline embraces four objectives: restoration of the sinner to righteousness, reconciliation to God and fellow Christians, the purity of the church, and freedom from the bondage of sin.

1. **Restoration** of the sinner to righteousness. Restoration of the sinner is the way to end alienation from God by taking away the guilt of sin. This shows that the members of the Body care enough to correct the one who sins. It shows strength in members who want to restore the community, not to protect its weaknesses. It says that we are serious about the Gospel we confess. Christian community exists to be an environment where healing and restoration are provided continually for those in need. Jesus encouraged the disciples to care for each other and to protect each other as He revealed in His account of one sheep that had gone away, which prompts the shepherd to leave the 99 and seek the one in trouble (Mt. 18:12-13). In Mt. 18, Jesus tells specifically about restoration within the body of

Christ. Lack of concern for restoration reflects shallowness of relationships. Restoration is completed through the forgiveness of sins when the person repents.

2. **Reconciliation.** True reconciliation never takes place without change of heart in the parties involved. Like restoration, reconciliation lies at the heart of the Gospel for God has committed to us the "ministry of reconciliation" (2 Cor. 5:18-19). Reconciliation replaces a condition of conflict with one of peace, ending hostility and restoring harmony. The result is peace with God, ourselves and our neighbors. Restoration is regained only when we deal with sin.

Everyone in the church ultimately shares responsibility for the reconciling approach, beginning with anyone who is aware of the event. It does not tell us to call the pastor and let him initiate the steps, but it involves others in the Body also. Spiritually mature believers are especially responsible (Gal. 6:1).

3. The **purity** of the church. "...As Christ loved the church and gave Himself up for her to make her holy...and to present her to himself as a radiant church, without stain or wrinkle or any other blemish, but holy and blameless" (Eph. 5:25-27). The reference is to the body of Christ, the invisible church, but corrective discipline is required in the institutional church and in the visible community if it is to be purified. It seems that holiness has become an empty word in many places. Other goals supersede the purity of the church. We become preoccupied in making annual budgets, programming of all kinds, building programs, and whatever we think works.

People tend to try to hide impurity and sin, forgetting how important purity is to God, who sees all. Impure members poison the Body, for "a little leaven leavens the whole lump" (1 Cor. 6:6-8). Good can and will be corrupted by the constant company of the bad. Because the church is Christ's, its purity is a valuable goal in its own right, also protecting the reputation of the church before the outside world.

Areas in need of purity are our message, our methods and church practice, and the moral lives of individual members. God accepts us where we are, but does not leave us where we are. Faithful members have a right to expect purity from their church. The practical demonstration of love and obedience to truth require a loving confrontation with evil wherever it may be found in the Christian community. There are three possible responses: no confrontation because we are peace-keepers, unloving confrontation with Law and legalistic tactics, or loving confrontation with a clear and distinctly Biblical approach through the Gospel.

4. **Freedom** from the bondage of sin. "...Where the Spirit of the Lord is, there is freedom" (2 Cor. 3:17). The "freedom that Christ has set us free" (Gal. 5:1) is not only a freedom from the guilt of sin, but also from the slavery to habitual sins, those that arise from specific spiritual weaknesses. Evangelical discipline is the only hope in the community for those who gossip, are untruthful, alcoholics, bitter, angry, promiscuous, porn-addicted, drug-addicted, and overindulgent. They may only find victory if members of the community speak the Law and Gospel to them so that they might be free. We dare never underestimate the power of sinful habits in believers' lives. The role of ordinary Christians by the Spirit's power cannot be overestimated in helping those enslaved to sin to find the way of freedom.

The Biblical revelation of church discipline is God's loving plan for keeping or restoring believers to fellowship with Himself within the body of Christ. This involves not only proclaiming pure doctrine and administering the Sacraments, but also exercising God-pleasing church discipline in the congregations. Church discipline grows out of the responsibility to nurture.

Many people want to avoid discipline because they say it will cause division and disunity. The opposite is true, for disunity is found where doctrine is ignored and unspiritual practices are allowed while outwardly maintaining peace. Real disunity is caused by disobedience to God's Word, not by obedience to it. The question really centers on whether we will merely be peace-keepers or be spiritual healers.

The New Testament contains abundant evidence of the practice of discipline by the church (Mt. 18:15-20; Acts 5:1-11; 1 Cor. 5:1-5; 2 Cor. 2:5-11; Gal. 2:11-14; 6:1; 2 Thes. 3:6-15). Continuation in sin was taken very seriously, and discipline was practiced.

Paul rebuked the Corinthians for their lack of discipline, as they were so blinded by their pride that they could not recognize the ugly problems that had developed in their midst. Insensitivity to one moral issue led to compromise on others. Its neglect was followed by a host of spiritual failures.

Thyatira was a rugged testing ground for the Christian Gospel of grace. The church at Thyatira was infected by a complacent neglect of immorality in its midst. Social and economic influences tempted the members to soften the spiritual line. Because the church didn't discipline the members, the Lord warned that He would discipline them (Rev. 2:22-23).

The result of neglecting discipline is not only a lack of doctrinal and spiritual purity, but also a lack of power in the church community, and a lack of progress in the mission of the church. Sin stops the flow of blessings from God and causes judgment upon us. Those who observe sin and fail to warn the guilty of its consequences shall be held to account (Prov. 24:11-12; Ezek. 3:18; 33:1-16).

The authority for church discipline comes from Christ in Matthew 18 in which He tells that what the church binds on earth shall be bound in heaven and whatever is loosed on earth shall be loosed in heaven. This is an awesome responsibility which will be sidestepped only to the detriment of the church and its members.

In Matthew 18:15-18 Jesus gave guidelines about how a believer who has committed a fault should be treated. When it is possible, the difficulty should be corrected privately by a member who is aware of the problem or between persons who are involved. If this personal encounter does not solve the difficulty, two or three others should be requested to help get to the root of the matter. If the offending person still refuses to repent, the matter should be brought to the attention of the church. If the person still does not change and seek forgiveness, he must be removed from the fellowship of the group in order to arouse his conscience, remind him of how serious his situation is, and to win him back. A church that compromises at this point denies the perfect character of God and does not fulfill God's purpose for the church's own members.

The purpose of discipline is: 1. to restore a person who either in word or action is denying the Word of God and giving offense (Gal. 6:1; Mt. 6:14-15); 2. to correct a wrong situation where offense needs to be removed (1 Cor. 8:9); 3. to maintain the Christian testimony of the church (1 Tim. 3:7); 4. to encourage all members to remain faithful in their witness (1 Cor. 5:6-7).

In Hebrews 12, the renewal of spiritual vitality (v.12-17) follows the discipline of God (v. 4-11). Here we see the loving motive, the link between love and discipline. We also see the family relationship, concern for weak brothers and sisters in the family of God. Hebrews 12 also shows the wholesome benefits by a proper response. Loving discipline reveals to the congregation and its neighbors, the strong disapproval of God.

Many agree that there are various situations where discipline is needed but no action is taken because of fear of consequences or preference for avoiding problems. Fear for the outcome of church discipline is a real issue for many. However, if problems are ignored, they will be assimilated into the character and tradition of the church. They will continue to haunt church leaders and the members. Leaders who avoid confrontation will afflict that church unless and until the problem is dealt with scripturally. Ultimately, these leaders andcongregations develop an unbiblical attitude toward church discipline, and they will face the judgment of God.

The situations and sins which necessitate church discipline involve the following: not using the Means of Grace diligently or habitually disregarding Christian practice; not leading a godly life in conformity to the will of Christ, not accepting the doctrines of the Bible; being wrapped up in self and materialism with no interest in evangelism or stewardship; not accepting brotherly admonition; and violations of Christian love, unity, and truth.

The breakdown of sanctification and the lack of edification between members have produced the general breakdown of church discipline in most churches. Churches have been guilty of the fallacy of thinking that pure doctrine will automatically produce good works in people's lives and have been led to deal softly with the practical implications of those doctrines.

The church that neglects to lovingly confront and to correct its members is not being kind, generous or gracious. Such a church is hindering the Lord's work and the advance of Christ's kingdom. The church without discipline is a church which is losing its purity, power and progress.

Beyond church discipline of members, churches must take the opportunity to deal effectively with the pastors who have evidenced offensive habits or have shown ineffectiveness in a grave manner, and have failed to recognize this or to deal with it in a forthright manner. One of the evangelical churches includes the following reasons in its constitution and bylaws for dealing with pastors: any conduct unbecoming a minister or indiscretion involving morals; recognizable general inefficiency in the ministry; a failure or inability to represent the true doctrine or a declared change in doctrinal views; a contentious or non-cooperative spirit; assumption of dictatorial authority over a congregation; arbitrary rejection of District counsel; a habit of running into debt which brings reproach upon the church; a marriage in violation of its position on marriage and divorce; and improper attitude toward those dismissed from their fellowship. Of course, legalism is to be avoided, while love prevails.

The task of evangelical discipline is not to "clean house," but to clean up; not to purge, but to purify; not to annihilate, but to rehabilitate.

There may even come a time that a Nathan is needed, as the Lord sent Nathan to David (2 Sam. 12:1) to discipline David. Armed with God's wisdom, Nathan told a story which caught David's interest and judgment against a perpetrator of a crime. Nathan told David, "You are the man"(2 Sam. 12:7). The truth was expressed plainly, openly, and boldly, yet with humility. The bold words had a saving effect. As a result, we read the beautiful Gospel messages of forgiveness in Psalm 32 and Psalm 51. Periodically, the Christian community needs a Nathan for one of its members, possibly even a prominent one. Are we strong enough to be a Nathan? Do we love enough? Do we care enough?

Critics and fence-sitters will always be present to dissuade us from obedience to the Gospel. How often we are lacking the Christian courage and love that will meet the needs of one enslaved in sin! Let our compassion be stronger than their criticism. Unless we can see beyond the human situation to the spiritual conflict which needs to be won by encouraging, exhorting, correcting, and loving one another, healing will not be brought to the sinful slave or to the community. We can repeat the theological formula about human sin, but blur the truth of how God uses the minds and mouths of His redeemed to present the message of reconciliation even in tough situations. The authority to speak and act is the authority of Christ Himself: "As the Father has sent Me, I am sending you...If you forgive anyone his sins, they are forgiven; if you do not forgive them, they are not forgiven" (Jn. 20:21-23). Ours is a divine mission empowered by the Holy Spirit.

As the immune system prevents infection from invading the body, so evangelical church discipline stops various spiritual viruses from inflaming spiritual life. When the spiritual immune system breaks down through inactivity or by forcing the pastor and the elders to be the sole protectors of poisonous invaders of the Christian community, then vain philosophies and innovative doctrines can easily enter the community even though there might be a few members who complain but do nothing about it.

The breakdown of the spiritual immune system by the failure to exercise and care for those who are spiritually sick, I believe, is one of the crises of our Missouri Synod. We may talk about these people and complain about how bad things are, and why doesn't anyone do something about it, but we fail to apply the Lord's way of preventing spiritual poisons from entering the Christian gathering. One of the tragedies is that churches will finally use corrective discipline in a catastrophic situation when something very wrong takes place, but they will not utilize preventive discipline, which is inherent in the spiritual immune system of God's approach.

What is the beginning of the breakdown of the spiritual immune system? When the church fails to pursue the Ephesians 4 body model of teaching and expecting every member to walk worthy of their call from God and to recognize and utilize the grace which Christ has apportioned to them (v.7), then the body is crippled to such a large extent that major paralysis exists. Any human body in which 60%-70% of its organs and members do not function is dead. The spiritual body has a phenomenal ability by the Spirit of God to exist with many weak and paralyzed parts, clinging almost as appendages rather than organic members.

If we are to experience healing from this paralysis of the Missouri Synod Christian community and of the failure of the spiritual immune system to operate in a healthy manner, the first step is to recognize not only the symptoms but also the disease itself. The institutional and human paradigms simply must be discarded, and then the Biblical blueprints studied and ultimately adopted faithfully so that spiritual health can be gained not only in individual members, but in the entire body of local believers. Each one of us faces the question whether there is a need for a paradigm shift in our congregation, and how it can be achieved.

Dictionary meanings that are helpful at this point are that discipline means instruction or also to bring under control. Hebrews 12 indicates that the living of the Christian faith also involves throwing off anything that hinders and the sin that so easily entangles so that we can run with perseverance the race marked out for us. Focusing on Jesus, who began and perfects our faith, we are to be reminded that life is a struggle that includes discipline.

We are told that as a father instructs and disciplines his sons for their own good, God does the same for His spiritual children. God does it to keep us focused, and it actually should produce a harvest of righteousness and good deeds. To indicate how important discipline is for maintaining Christian community, God says that it is to be exercised so "that we may share in His holiness" (Heb. 12:10). Christ is not only dishonored but the body is made dysfunctional when the community fails to exercise evangelical discipline. Rather than driving away and creating fear and alienation, discipline is intended to draw us close and motivate to goodness and obedience.

Learning Happens Best in Community

Unfortunately, many Bible classes are little more than lectures with an opportunity for the more interested and enlightened participants to speak up or ask a question from time to time. Such situations are signals that the goal of that Bible study is basically head knowledge. But we are not only to "get it right," but also to "get it out" in our lives in our daily activities. The notion that the pastor or the Bible class leader is the "answer man" is totally unacceptable. The habit of allowing Bible study members to come just

48

to listen is intolerable. Maximum learning happens when participants are involved in studying the Scriptural questions and lessons beforehand and sharing what they have found in their homework. Such community study is central for Christian growth. Bible study should be Body study. There is one teacher, but there are as many communication points and lines as people in the class. This is necessary for healthy body relationships.

Bible study in Christian community means relational activity, gathered to share God's Word, not just ideas about the Word. We are not just individuals, but a family of believers who are to learn from each other, where we teach each other and hold ourselves accountable to each other - all under the authority of Christ and of the ultimate responsibility of the pastor.

Many have not recognized that the first of the two commands of the Great Commission is to teach or edify: "Teaching them to observe all things that I have commanded you!" (Mt. 28:20). People cannot tell what they do not know. The great weakness of evangelism among Christians and churches is that people's knowledge of the Word is very shallow. The reason for this is that only a minority of members are where the teaching is taking place for maturity.

Educating Christians For Maturity

John Naisboth in *Megatrends* told how U.S. society changed over the course of time from being centered in agriculture, to industry, and finally to technology. He told of a major adjustment that our culture made to be an information society, centering on education which utilizes computers.

While reading *Megatrends*, I considered the situation in a majority of our Lutheran churches related to their main methodologies to accomplish their mission. Historically, our church has been worship-centered, adding teaching and education in varying degrees. The majority of church members have been given the impression that the primary activity is worship, and that group study of the Bible is optional. Various churches have had strong emphases and even special programs to enlarge Bible study on the part of their members, but teaching and education still remains a secondary activity on the part of most members. For example, in my own denomination when I entered the ministry 47 years ago about 6% of the adults were in Bible classes, and it has plateaued at about 20% during the last 15 years. We are still a worship-centered church, as are most others.

A major adjustment is needed to achieve an education-worship model. Another adjustment required is to get away from child education at the expense of adult education. Many Christians have the habit of sending their children to Sunday School and hold the church responsible for the education of their children, believing that they are supporting the church in its responsibility. The fact is that God holds the parents responsible for the spiritual training of the children and that the church is supporting them. A major change in paradigms is necessary to lead people to understand that Bible study and spiritual nurture is a life-long process, never ending for all members.

Indeed, rather than inviting inactive members to attend worship services, church elders should be trained to share selected Bible studies with these lethargic members. Worship services are not the best approach for gaining back dormant members or even to win the unchurched, because it is almost impossible for one sermon to communicate the message which is required for the variety of spiritual needs of the inactives and non-Christians. Each person comes with individual understandings and spiritual inadequacies which should have more than a shotgun approach to target their spiritual demands.

Worship is intended to be a celebration of an active Christian faith. It is very difficult for people to worship Someone they hardly know of or whom they really don't know at all. How can you worship a God with whom you are not really acquainted? Special Bible study in the homes by elders and evangelism callers is designed to help them know the true God, with the prayer that they will then be eager to worship Him.

The Great Commission command to teach is the foundation of the church's responsibility to edify and to evangelize. The New Testament model for reaching all people through Christian nurture is seen in 2 Tim. 2:2, "The things you have heard me say in the presence of many witnesses entrust to reliable men who will also be qualified to teach others." Paul told Pastor Timothy that the Word of God which he had heard from Paul was to be taught to reliable-faithful men who would be able to teach other Christians. Teachers are to be multiplied for the nurturing of all members. I know that the interpretation by some well-known exegetes indicate that 2 Tim. 2:2 applies to "seminary" training of pastors. However, we have no official interpretation which would allow this verse not to apply to pastors instructing elders and leaders in order to lead Bible study on a mature level. This is a model for training lay people, too, under the supervision of the pastor.

This is a model that has been neglected by most churches. This teaching is to focus on spiritual formation of the Christian which involves a growing knowledge, understanding and relationship to Christ and to fellow men, as believers learn Christ's plan for their lives. This is more than a general Bible study for establishing Christians in the faith. Renewal of the church will not just touch up its fading image or repair a few minor cracks. True renewal will concern itself with the spiritual health of every individual member. This is a matter of making mature disciples.

There are four levels of spiritual development for Christians: 1) being evangelized, which ends when faith in Jesus is established; 2) being grounded or established in the faith, which involves ordinary Bible study; 3) being nurtured for maturity, which is accomplished by self-discovery and group-discovery Bible study approaches, and applicational and relational courses for spiritual formation; 4) being a discipler or teacher. The fourth level is where spiritual multiplication and reproduction of believers is taking place - building disciples.

The priority of the congregation is to be a teaching center, taking drastic steps in disciple formation classes to draw members into spiritual formation forums which catch their full attention to study all the spiritual questions of life. Pastors are to nurture or disciple key leaders, who will be able to teach other members so that a maximum number of members are in Bible study. "...The things you have heard me say...entrust to reliable men who will also be qualified to teach others" (2 Tim. 2:2). The health and strength of the church is dependent upon having a core group of mature leaders who have been educated intensely and are capable of providing mature leadership through teaching.

This process of disciple-making of level three (2 Tim. 2:2) is the basic approach which is to be the foundation of all other church activities. Disciple-making is spiritual multiplication, the process of building scriptural truths and pass-on-able skills into other lives so that they will be able to do the same for others. Just as Jesus poured His life into His disciples, so teachers today are to do the same.

Goals of such level 3 education for maturity are:

1. Develop a comprehensive plan of education, based on the Matthew 28:20 and 2 Timothy 2:2 model to make mature Christians (Eph. 2:12-15) who are strong to edify fellow Christians and to evangelize non-Christians.

2. Build a strategic plan of discipling which encourages Christian disciples to learn, grow, mature and shape in the image of Jesus Christ by keeping strong in God's Word.

3. Utilize Biblical information and power for the spiritual formation of the believers, going beyond the cognitive to functional Christian life.

4. Provide the whole counsel of God in a simple and uncomplicated study course, being pro-active rather than reactive, preventative instead of merely curative.

5. Change the world view and value systems of Christians from moralism-legalism to grace, from maintenance-needs-institutional to Biblical body of Christ principles.

6. Construct a whole congregation approach, targeting every potential learner for being established in the faith and for being educated for maturity.

7. Mobilize the entire church by equipping all Christians for their works of service (Eph. 4:12) through an intensive educational curriculum, activating the priesthood of all believers in the most Biblical and practical form.

The model for discipling members is seen in 1 Thes. 2:7-13, where Paul shows why and how he taught them: "But we were gentle among you, like a mother caring for her little children. We loved you so much that we were delighted to share with you not only the Gospel of God but our lives as well, because you had become so dear to us. Surely you remember, brothers, our toil and hardship; we worked night and day in order not to be a burden to anyone while we preached the gospel of God to you. You are witnesses, and so is God, of how holy, righteous and blameless we were among you who believed. For you know that we dealt with teach of you as a father deals with his own children, encouraging, comforting and urging you to live lives worthy of God, who calls you into his kingdom and glory. And we also thank God continually because, when you received the word of God, which you heard from us, you accepted it not as the word of men, but as it actually is, the word of God, which is at work in you who believe."

Here Paul showed the "what, how, and why" of discipling. What? He showed care, shared the Gospel and himself, encouraged, charged, reproved, and thanked God. How? He did it very gently, with delight, like a father, and worked zealously night and day. Why? He did it that God might be glorified, because they were dear to him, and that they might lead a life worthy of God. Paul showed that the discipler should tell the disciple why, show him how, get him started, keep him going, and teach him to reproduce himself. His basic principles were concentration on God's Word, development of relationships in a spiritual climate, gaining commitment, and taking time.

Paul's joy of spiritual parenting is very apparent. He discipled leaders so that they in turn could become responsible, trained and equipped teachers for ministry. It was obvious that it was his aim to see disciples learning, growing, maturing and shaping in the image of Christ in order to edify and to evangelize.

"21st Century Discipling" Course

21st Century Disciples With a 1st Century Faith is a special discipling course for Lutherans which is ready for publication. It has been submitted to the Board For Parish Education Services of the Synod and Concordia Publishing House for publication. [9] While traditional Bible courses usually focus on knowledge and the cognitive as the main goal, these two goals are assumed in this course, and the subject and the subject matter are covered to gain a wholistic understanding of the Christian faith. The method is interpersonal discipleship as contrasted to individual involvement in a Bible class where listening is the main responsibility.

This 26-week course has three components: the Student's Course Book, the Student's Workbook with questions and discussion, and a Teacher's Guide. The students are to prepare for five to ten hours each week and come to the two-hour class with the answers all written out. Instead of lecturing, the leader requests all participants to share their answers. This allows through maximum learning through self-discovery and then group-discovery. It is the leader's responsibility to allow all members of the group to gain a mature understanding of the Christian faith through applicational and relational teaching.

The course study book, *21st Century Disciples With a 1st Century Faith*, includes five chapters: Living with God; Living with Myself; Living with My Family and Fellow Man; Living with My Resources; Living in the Body of Christ and in the Church. It is a basic Bible study which summarizes the entire Christian faith in 21st century terms with fidelity to the 1st century truths.

The target is those who have already been established in the faith and show security in Christ and a willingness to grow and mature. They need not be those who already are showing and experiencing their potential, but also those who have an unrealized aptitude and who have the desire and willingness to grow. They should also have the ability to become disciplers when their training is ompleted. Church elders should be involved. Adult confirmands who have inished the basic course of doctrinal instruction should be challenged to enroll in this course as the first step of study after their confirmation.

The process of disciple-making is the basic approach on which all other church activity revolves. Disciple-making is spiritual multiplication and reproduction of believers, not just adding members to the church. Believing that the maturing of disciples is part of the Great Commission, we will determine by God's great grace to develop disciples who are sufficiently strong to be able to multiply themselves spiritually through others.

This course follows the same methods which Jesus and Paul employed through inspiration, instruction and involvement. Both trained those who followed them. They poured their lives into these men and extended themselves through them. These discipled men did the same. The process was repeated again and again as people learned the truth, and vital relationships were established. The key was to get away from simple doctrine and cathedral preaching as the sole goal of the Christian's faith toward a mature faith shared in lively community. Paul said, "Let us leave behind the ABC's of Christ's teaching, and let us rush on to maturity..." (Heb. 6:1, NET). Each student is to be given the opportunity to develop the qualities, habits and discipline that mark him or her as a servant of Christ, revealing maturity in relationship with God and with other people.

Chapter 4

BIBLICAL LUTHERANS ARE EVANGELICAL AND CONFESSIONAL IN DOCTRINE AND PRACTICE

An historic battle has been waged in Lutheranism in Europe and America related to being truly evangelical and confessional in two basic areas: there is the constant battle to adhere to pure Biblical doctrine and at the same time to have integrity in all church practices. Ever since the "new theology" and "new hermeneutics" have been introduced by their enthusiasts as an option to Biblical truth, Lutheran churches have had to confront various attempts to subvert confessional doctrine and practice. An incredible amount of time and published materials have been invested in this battle for the Bible and for the church at the expense of its Gospel mission.

As a Synodical and District Stewardship leader, I came to the realization in the early '60's that the very Word and Gospel which is the basis of stewardship theology was being torn away and shredded by some who had been called by God to hold true to the Word and to their ordination vow. A majority of the District Presidents became alarmed to one degree or another, and several other District Stewardship leaders and I concluded that the Biblical foundation of the church was being attacked.

In August, 1964, Dr. Gustav Lobeck, then President of the Iowa West District and his Stewardship Executive, Dr. Ellis Nieting (later President of that District) and I were visiting at a motel in Seward, NE, when a Southern Nebraska District meeting was being held at the college. Lobeck informed us of the seriousness of the doctrinal problems in the Synod which were discussed by the Council of Presidents, and that he felt it was already too late. From my observations, I believed that the situation was serious, but not that bad. Lobeck insisted that it was already so bad that he questioned whether the Missouri Synod could retain its orthodoxy. I said that I found this situation totally unacceptable, and that something must be done about it. Lobeck replied that he would give support to whatever efforts would be made to make a positive witness in this dangerous situation. He, Nieting and I agreed that we would wait for the fall meeting of the Council of Presidents to see whether any progress would be made to correct this condition. But nothing happened in that meeting to change anything.

At that, we agreed to make plans for the February 1965 COP meeting in St. Louis, and that we would gather a representative group of people at a meeting on the night of the close of the COP meeting. About 25 people attended the meeting on February 18, 1965 at Epiphany Lutheran Church in St. Louis, including pastors, laymen, Seminary professors, and Synodical officials and staff. Lobeck reported that there was a total stalemate in the COP and that no effective thing was planned to counteract the false doctrine that was creeping into the Missouri Synod. It was decided by the group to proceed with what developed into the "Faith Forward - First Concerns" movement. This was followed by a meeting of 20 representative leaders at Downer's Grove, IL, on Feb. 26, 1965, where a commitment to proceed was then made.

When then President Oliver Harms visited Nebraska several weeks later, I visited with him personally to inform him about what was happening and that a number of District Presidents requested a meeting with him in late April after the next COP meeting. On April 29-30, 1965, about 70 representatives met in St. Louis from all over the Synod, including institutional presidents, district presidents, Synodical staff, a Synodical Vice-

President and others, at which time a series of essays were presented related to evangelical and confessional responsibilities in institutions, Synod, districts, congregations, education and evangelism. This group sent six District Presidents to President Harms to assure him of complete loyalty to the Synod and whole-hearted support to him in whatever action was necessary to stop the theological disintegration in doctrine and practice. The response of President Harms was one of gratitude and support but he wished that he could know that he had the full support of the Synod in any attempt to act resolutely in this matter. This meeting was reported by then President Harms in his May 1965 "Memo to My Brethren." These Presidents shared with Harms the problems they faced in their Districts because of unsettled theological issues, that the church was a divided church with ten's of thousand's offended, and that idle assurances would not settle the issue. The District Presidents stated that they represented a good number of district presidents, college presidents, executives, professors, pastors, teachers, and laymen.

At that time, the "Faith Forward - First Concerns" document was finalized and circulated to all the pastors of the Synod with an accompanying letter with the names of about 10 pastors, and 10 District Presidents. About 140,000 signatures were gained during the next months from people throughout the Synod. This document, for which I was privileged to be the editor and the main writer, is now in the Concordia Historical Institute in St. Louis. As you read the attending letter and the document itself, you will observe the places where Lutheran evangelical doctrine and practice were being eroded.

*　　　　*　　　　*　　　　*　　　　*　　　　*

1965

FAITH FORWARD - FIRST CONCERNS

1317 Tower Drive - Fort Dodge, Iowa 50502

Dear Brother in Christ:

Are you disturbed by the doctrinal unrest in our Missouri Synod? Do you agree that there is harmony between the old and new schools of Biblical interpretation, as the February 1965 CTM editorial claims, when it says that both schools "often fail to see that they are singing the same hymn of adoration to the incarnate and crucified Savior, even though they are using different words and melodies?" Or do you feel that the two systems of interpretation represent two totally different melodies which are not in harmony with each other?

We, the undersigned executive committee, represent over 100 professors, pastors, teachers, laymen and executives — many holding prominent positions — who are greatly concerned about the chipping away at the foundation of the Word in the name of theological progress. This is a totally positive action by a large community of interest (not an organized group), who seek to dramatize our support of our Synodical President in his efforts to supervise doctrine and practice in our midst. We expect the public doctrine of Synod based on the Scriptures to be reflected as faithfully as possible by all Synodical Institutions, agencies, departments, as well as auxiliaries and affiliates — a goal toward which we are confident the praesidium is working. We seek to stop the subversion of our fellowship by the independent action of those who would impose the so-called "new hermeneutics" upon us.

We approve and applaud many of the curricular changes and innovations which have been introduced in the Synod's program of ministerial training in recent years. We believe it is good that the professional ministers of the Word are not simply assuming, as many did a generation ago, that the opinions and conclusions of men, even of the most prominent scholars, were always right, but are seeking to assure themselves of the correctness of the same through earnest questions and serious study. At the same time we are concerned that the plenary, verbal inspiration of the Scriptures continue to be forthrightly — publicly and privately — upheld by every member of The Lutheran Church - Missouri Synod and that the authenticity of all Canonical Books of the Bible and particularly also the historicity of the first chapters of Genesis are accepted. We are also determined that every member of the Synod let the Bible speak as the final authority in every matter of doctrine and practice among us.

We are not alarmists and we are not in sympathy with those groups within Synod that are resorting to bitter and uncharitable attacks of brethren through the printed page. We have, however, come to the realistic conclusion that there are some pastors, some teachers, some faculty members at our colleges and seminaries, and some authors who either by deliberate intent or through unclear and indefinite statements, and sometimes by careless comments and innuendoes, perhaps even unintentionally, are causing confusion among us regarding the inspiration, authenticity, and authority of Scripture. It is also our impression that some of these men are uncharitably belittling the writings of some of the past leaders and scholars of our Synod.

There is a ground-swell of feeling among our brethren that the hour is late, and it is now time to demonstrate the support and unity of the great majority of our Synodical membership who seek to keep faithful to the Scriptures and the Confessions. We want to support the elected leaders of our Synod in every effort of exhortation and discipline toward those who are causing the above-mentioned confusion. Do you feel as we do concerning this? If you do, sign this letter and return it to us at once, with the request that your convictions be conveyed to President Harms in person within the next month. You may wish to encourage other pastors, teachers, and laymen in your area also to sign this letter. We seek the names only of men who are of positive temperament — not identified with any "anti-group." Concerned lay leaders, especially those with high scholastic achievement, ought to be encouraged to express their concern, too. These letters should be returned to us by April 10.

We seek only to edify — to show kind concern both for the many offended ones and for those who are giving offense — and to call vigorous attention to the sad future we face if we continue down the road of religious propositions instead of declaration of God's truth. We invite you to join us in the expression of our spiritual unity as we pray that God's name may be hallowed by our Synodical doctrine and practice: "When the Word of God is taught in its truth and purity, and we as children of God also lead a holy life according to it. This grant us, dear Father in heaven. But he that teaches and lives otherwise than God's Word teaches, profanes the name of God among us. From this preserve us, Heavenly Father."

(Signatures of 10 parish pastors and 10 District Presidents)

FAITH FORWARD — FIRST CONCERNS

A PLEA OF CONCERN IN CHRISTIAN LOVE

1. WE WHOLEHEARTEDLY SUPPORT OUR SYNODICAL PRESIDENT AND OTHER LEADERS WHO HOLD AND TEACH THE SCRIPTURAL AND CONFESSIONAL VIEWPOINT OF THE INSPIRATION OF THE BIBLE TOGETHER WITH THE HERMENEUTICAL PRINCIPLE OF "SCRIPTURE INTERPRETING SCRIPTURE."

Without question a very high percentage of Synod's membership reflects the public doctrine and position papers (chiefly the "Brief Statement") of our church body. We wish to voice that position and to express support of our leaders at a crucial period in our church's history.

2. WE ARE SADDENED BY THE ACTION OF INDEPENDENT GROUPS WITHIN OUR CHURCH WHO IN TAKING UPON THEMSELVES THE EXPOSE OF DOCTRINAL ABERRATIONS IN OUR MIDST ARE UNDERMINING THE WORK OF OUR SYNODICAL LEADERS! WE REGRET THE CONDUCT OF THESE CRITICS, EVEN THOUGH THEIR INTENTION MAY BE A CONCERN FOR TRUTH.

It is regrettable that some objectors have gone beyond the limits of ordinary alarm and have made rash and reactionary statements which have beclouded issues. We disassociate ourselves from such groups that have pointed to personalities as much as to basic issues.

3. WE REJECT AS UNFAITHFUL TO SCRIPTURE THE SO-CALLED "NEW HERMENEUTIC" WHICH WRONGFULLY REGARDS SOME HISTORICAL PARTS OF THE OLD TESTAMENT AS SYMBOLICAL, THUS DESTROYING THE FOUNDATION OF FAITH AND HUMANIZING GOD'S WORD. WE ARE ALARMED AT THE OBSCURANTIST POSITION OF THOSE THEOLOGIANS WHO ATTEMPT TO GIVE CREDENCE TO THEISTIC EVOLUTION AS TRUE WHILE KNOWLEDGEABLE SCHOLARLY SCIENTISTS REALIZE THAT EVOLUTION IS A THEORY, A POINT OF VIEW USED TO ORGANIZE, EXPLAIN, AND RELATE OBSERVED FACTS, AND AS SUCH SUBJECT TO MODIFICATION AND CHANGE. FROM A BIBLICAL VIEWPOINT, CHRIST AND THE NEW TESTAMENT TEACH THE CREATION ACCOUNT OF GENESIS AS HISTORICAL AND LITERAL.

WE REJECT ALSO THE **ABUSE** OF FORMGESCHICHTE WHICH INSTEAD OF IMPLEMENTING THIS APPROACH TO NEW TESTAMENT STUDIES AS A VALUABLE HEURISTIC (HERMENEUTICAL) DEVICE TO FIND OUT WHAT THE TEXT **MEANS**, EMPLOYS IT RATHER TO EXPLAIN THE **ORIGIN** OF THE TEXT IN A MANNER THAT EXCLUDES ANY NOTION OF INSPIRATION IN THE TRADITIONAL SENSE OF THAT TERM; WHICH REDUCES THE GOSPELS TO POST-EASTER PROPAGANDA DOCUMENTS CONSISTING OF ISOLATED "PERICOPES" TAKEN FROM VARIOUS ORAL TRADITIONS AND ARTIFICIALLY STRUNG TOGETHER WITHIN CONFLICTING CHRONOLOGICAL SCHEMES, THUS FRAGMENTIZING THE SCRIPTURES AND MAKING VIRTUALLY INAPPLICABLE THE PRINCIPLE THAT 'SCRIPTURE INTERPRETS SCRIPTURE'; AND WHICH QUESTIONS THE AUTHENTICITY OF MUCH OF THE CONTENT OF THE GOSPELS ON THE BASIS OF THE WHOLLY ARBITRARY CRITERION THAT IN ORDER TO QUALIFY AS GENUINE A "PERICOPE" MUST CONTAIN NOTHING THAT COULD HAVE BEEN DERIVED FROM "JEWISH APOCALYPTIC EXPECTATIONS" OF FROM "THE THOUGHT-WORLD OF EARLY CHRISTIANITY."

TO STATE WITH SOME NEW TESTAMENT CRITICS THAT CHRIST MERELY

"ACCOMMODATED HIMSELF" TO THE THINKING OF HIS TIMES IS TO OPEN UP THE FLOODGATES TO A CRITICAL EVALUATION AND EVENTUAL REJECTION OF ALMOST EVERYTHING HE SAID OR DID. TO INSIST ON A DETAILED STUDY AND UNDERSTANDING OF EVERY CIRCUMSTANCE OF THE DIVINE RECORD AND TO CATEGORIZE ITS FORM BEFORE ACCEPTANCE (OR REJECTION) IS TO DENY THE TIMELESSNESS OF GOD'S MESSAGE TO MEN AND REDUCE IT TO A MERE HUMAN LITERARY PRODUCT.

With our synodical leaders we adhere to the Lutheran Confessions which prescribe the use of Scripture in the theological quest in these words: ".... The **Word of God shall establish articles of faith and no one else, not even an angel**." "We pledge ourselves to the **prophetic and apostolic writings of the Old and New Testaments** as the pure and clear fountain of Israel, which is the **only true norm** according to which all teachers and teachings are to be judged and evaluated...."

The "new hermeneutic" is intellectually dishonest as it does not acknowledge the basic inconsistencies in doctrine, exegesis, and logic which it creates by attempting to synthesize Scriptural truths with popular scientific and philosophical propositions of our day. We are in danger of a naivete which mistakes much learned religious talk for spiritual reality and truth. A person cannot say "yes" and "no" at the same time to spiritual realities. By its attempt to be acceptable to human reason and current scientific theories, the "new hermeneutic" has violated what is basic to all valid exegesis of the Scriptures: the analogy of faith. The "new hermeneutic" proposes symbolical or "poetic" meanings outside of clear textual and contextual intent in violation of the analogy of faith. By that subjective method it is impossible to establish a single article of faith. Those who interpret the Word must speak as the oracles of God, and must speak faithfully without fear of a scoffing, rebellious world's wisdom. The Word, like the Gospel itself, need not be proven, but must be proclaimed in faith. The rationalizing of Scriptural evidence on the basis of human factors and theories is a fraud—a denial of faith.

It is only our concern for the Gospel which prompts us to challenge this unscriptural and un-Lutheran approach to Biblical interpretations. We are totally committed to the **doctrina evangelii** as based on Scripture and enunciated in our Lutheran Confessions. This is not only the one hope for sinful mankind but it is also the only message which will bring true unity to the church.

4. WE PLEAD WITH THOSE PROFESSORS, PASTORS, AND TEACHERS WHO ARE "TEACHING OTHERWISE" TO DESIST IMMEDIATELY FROM THEIR PROPAGANDIZING FOR THEIR "NEW SYSTEM." WE ASK THEM TO HONOR WITH INTEGRITY OUR SYNODICAL **POSITION PAPERS** ON THE SCRIPTURES AND TO AVOID SUBJECTIVE ARGUMENTATION AND HUMANISTIC THINKING. WE PRAY THAT THE HOLY SPIRIT WILL KEEP THEM FROM ELEVATING REASON WHERE FAITH MUST REIGN LEST THEY PLACE THEMSELVES IN THE UNTENABLE POSITION OF VIOLATING THE FOUNDATION OF FAITH.

There is no Scriptural or Confessional basis by which man by his own will or reason may declare symbolical or allegorical those historical portions of the Old Testament that may conflict with human reason or with scientific theories in any age. This does not suggest a wooden literalism that fails to distinguish between obvious figurative meanings and straight narrative and natural meanings. The rationalism of the allegorists puts God and His creation on the operating table of modern science. The science-picture of the world becomes more valid than the picture God gives in His own Word of supernatural activity in creation. If God is really God, He must be allowed to create the world instantaneously—as He said. The rationalists completely bypass the nature of God and His revealed Word if they think they can confine Him to the straitjacket of a world-picture or of Hebrew culture.

They picture the Creator as a master planner limited by scientific conceptions of time and space. Scripture is not to be interpreted in the light of what a majority of scientists or philosophers declare to be most reasonable, for the Word is independent of any scientific theory of the universe.

Luther's commentary on Genesis makes strong indictments against those who would allegorize such historical parts as the creation narrative because reason is unwilling to accept what must be accepted by faith. Theology does not concern itself with external evidences and credibility but accepts in **faith** the revelation God has given us in the Scripture. The "new hermeneutic" takes a basic step away from and is incompatible with the very fundamentals of the doctrine of inspiration and the principles of interpretation which are inherent in Luther's teachings, the Confessions, and the Expositions of Luther's Catechisms...

There is an arrogance which puts literal truths of the Bible and articles of faith under constant attack by the use of this-worldly principles fed on what appears to be the latest research of favorite or "super" theologians. To criticize their findings invites criticism of obscurantism and naivete. Their theme is that confessional theology is irrelevant and even is the reason for unbelief. There is an apparent arrogance that looks to those who reject the "new hermeneutic" as being benighted and naive, even though serious and scholarly study has been undertaken before rejecting this unfaithful hermeneutical method. The voices cry out that a new theology is needed for social relevance, giving the impression that only a new theology can rescue the Bible from hopeless irrelevance for the 20th century. They build and sustain the illusion that traditional, orthodox theology is growing more out of date because of new scientific discoveries. One is considered enlightened only if he changes his theology as he grows in scientific understanding. The impression is given that the whole world would like to become Christian if only theology would become "modern."

The apostles of the "new hermeneutic" adopt unproven axioms and then set them up as theological guides. Though much sound scholarship is a part of their endeavors, it sometimes seems more like theological propaganda. Often it is a reconstruction of Biblical truth instead of timely exposition. It is rather a tinkering with the Word as if the Word is believable only when synthesized with science and philosophy—an utterly impossible task. Unwarranted inferences are made which are truly alarming—inferences to the effect that Christianity must reject the outmoded world-picture of the Bible and embrace some currently proposed ontological scheme.

All the while the proponents of the "new hermeneutic" take pride in the fact that they have retained faith in Christ as Savior and the Bible as a source and record of God's great acts. They adopt the "new hermeneutic" fully convinced that Christ and the inerrant Word have lost no significance, yet they strip truths from our historic confessions in order to make our faith palatable to human reason. But the price is too high: It first costs us historic truths in Genesis, then it counts Jonah as a "fish story," after which messianic prophecies are discounted The New Testament is next in line. At this time we must be reminded of Luther's declaration: "If we tear out one thing, we treat out everything." The authority of Christ and the authority of the Scriptures in their entirety stand and fall together...

5. THE INDEPENDENT ACTION OF SUCH BRETHREN IS PERVERTING THE INTEGRITY OF OUR FELLOWSHIP TOGETHER IN A VOLUNTARY ASSOCIATION OF CHRISTIANS IN THE LUTHERAN CHURCH-MISSOURI SYNOD, WHICH TOUCHES ITS DEEPEST MEANING. THIS FACES US WITH A DEPARTURE FROM SCRIPTURAL DOCTRINE AND IMMINENT RUPTURE OF THIS BLESSED FELLOWSHIP.

Since the Confessions do not speak to every issue of every age, church bodies in declaring the basis of their fellowship in Christ and His Word may find it vital and necessary to adopt a confessional standard such as the Brief Statement on the basis of the Scriptures and Confessions without becoming a sect thereby. Members of a church body who have voluntarily joined such a church body must be expected to honor such public doctrine and confessional basis, and those who have a change of mind or disagree should be prepared to leave the fellowship voluntarily. Independent action that refuses to honor the church's confessional stand is foreign to this fellowship and its voluntary nature, and forfeits the sacred privileges of such a fellowship.

The ultimate end of speaking the Word together for edification of all members is for mutual binding and loosing — a mutual care based on a mutual agreement in the Word. On that basis the church must decide who will be counted as members, and it must make some judgments along the way which will only be erased finally on Judgment Day. The church must exercise its legitimate right of united defense against false doctrine and schism. We can no longer be detracted by those who belittle the church's responsibility to discipline those who betray our fellowship a expressed in the Confessions and our public doctrine.

6. WE EXPECT THE PUBLIC DOCTRINE OF SYNOD TO BE REFLECTED AS FAITHFULLY AS POSSIBLE AND WITH CONVICTION BY ALL SYNODICAL INSTITUTIONS, AGENCIES, DEPARTMENTS, AS WELL AS AUXILIARIES AND AFFILIATES.

Our synodical institutions, agencies, and departments are not tools for crusaders of "new hermeneutics" or of unionistic fellowship but they are God's instruments and the church's proper vehicles to serve the church faithfully for teaching and declaring God's truths. Men employed by a church to equip people for ministry are forced by common decency and honesty to abide by the public doctrine of the church. The church is not our servant, but we are servants of the church — and bound together in Christ through our common confession. This is the way in which our church will go forward in every aspect of its tasks, and the Kingdom through the Gospel will come to men.

7. WE EXPECT CAREFUL ATTENTION TO BE GIVEN TO THE INERRANT WORD AS THE SOURCE AND POWER FOR ECUMENICAL EFFORTS AND ATTEMPTS TO CREATE UNITY IN THE VISIBLE CHURCH. UNITY BETWEEN LUTHERANS SHOULD BE PURSUED AND SOUGHT VIGOROUSLY BY OUR CHURCH THROUGH HONEST DISCUSSION OF DIFFERENCES IN DOCTRINE, HERMENEUTICAL SYSTEMS, AND IN PRACTICE.

In the face of a false emphasis on ecumenicity, we declare that unity based on anything else than the inerrant and inspired Word together with true Biblical hermeneutics is dishonest. To discount doctrine and hermeneutics in the interest of the ecumenical movement is a violation of New Testament teachings. Our ecumenical efforts dare not ignore essential differences of faith and order but must seek to resolve them by honestly demanding a visible manifestation of true unity in the Word which also involves principles of interpretation by which the message is made clear.

8. WE ASK OUR THEOLOGIANS TO LEAD US AS AUTHENTIC LUTHERANS IN A CREATIVE EXPOSITION OF THE WORD (THE HOLY SCRIPTURES IN THEIR ENTIRETY) FOR THE PROBLEMS, OPPORTUNITIES, AND THEOLOGICAL CONCERNS OF OUR DAY. THE MISSOURI SYNOD WILL NOT SERVE THE GOOD OF THE KINGDOM BY ADAPTING ITS THEOLOGY TO THE CURRENT THEOLOGICAL CLIMATE, WHICH HAS BEEN CHEWED AND RECHEWED IN EUROPE FOR YEARS. OUR SYNOD WILL SERVE A GREAT PURPOSE BY THE POWER OF THE SPIRIT ONLY AS IT STANDS IN JUDGMENT OF ALL SYSTEMS BY THE WORD AND PROCLAIMS SCRIPTURAL THEOLOGY RELEVANTLY AND WITH TRUE INTEGRITY. OUR THEOLOGIANS WILL SERVE ALL LUTHERANS AND CHRISTENDOM IN GENERAL AS THEY GUIDE US TO A FAITHFUL UNDERSTANDING OF THE **NORMA NORMANS** PRINCIPLE OF BIBLICAL IN-

TERPRETATION. WE LOOK TO OUR COMMISSION ON THEOLOGY AND CHURCH RELATIONS TO PROVIDE POSITIVE LEADERSHIP THAT REFLECTS OUR PUBLIC DOCTRINE.

We are dismayed at the fearful frettings of some men about the Bible becoming a "paper Pope" that as a result some have seemingly lost their reliance upon the Word of God in its fullest authoritative sense. Rather than placing God's Word under man's microscope to dissect it by the use of reason and earthly wisdom, we must allow the Word — God's microscope — to search out our works and ways in order to direct us to man and his institutional paths, not judge and reform the Word by man's knowledge and wisdom. We do not stand above the Word, but beneath it. We are not lords but servants of the Word. Hermeneutical principles are not derived apart from the Word but from the Word itself without reference to the philosophies and theories of the world. Reason must become and remain captive of the Lord. The Bible provides its own hermeneutics, the hermeneutics of revelation.

The "new hermeneutic" is not new, as should be quite obvious. We seek to face 20th century issues by facing them creatively with the Word whereas the humanists in the 'new hermeneutic' attempt to pull us back to a 19th century liberal theology veneered thinly in modern dress.

Christianity Today (Jan. 1, 1965) in the article "Reflections on American Theology" stated: "...The 'growing edge' of Protestantism would seem to lie outside the circle of 'cooperative Protestantism.' The two major bodies that had striking records of growth during the 1940-54 period were the Southern Baptist Convention and The Lutheran Church-Missouri Synod, neither of which belonged to the National Council of Churches. From 1940 to 1954, the Southern Baptists increased from 4,949,174 to 8,163,562, a gain of 64.9 per cent in comparison with a population increase of 24 per cent. The Missouri Synod Lutherans during the same period increased from 1,298,798 to 1,932,000, for a gain of 48.9 per cent." (Page 165)

Dr. O. R. Harms wrote of the Missouri Synod (Concordia Historical Quarterly, January, 1964, p. 119): "The opportunity is ours, but we stand a good chance of making most serious and consequential errors. After the St. Paul convention, I believe it was, *Time* evaluated the doctrinal position taken by the Synod and, quoting a theologian of another body, said something like this: 'It is possible that the Missouri synod could sweep all of us along.' I believe this to be true even today. We have the theologians capable of doing it. Given the right guidance in this opportunity, they may do it. They will never do it if they fall in line with the 'liberal' theologians of our day. They will ever do it by studying and quoting theologians whose orthodoxy is questioned. They can do it by inquiring into all the facets of the answers given in the past. We must ask the question: 'How did we come to be what we are? What is it that makes the Missouri Synod 'tick'? Is it some form of activism? Or is it an activity motivated by the certainty that we have a Bible-based position which is correct? Congregations persuaded that the latter is the case, and moving out into the respective communities, will be a power in God's hands for the expansion of the kingdom.'"

9. WE INVITE OUR BRETHREN TO JOIN IN OUR SAVIOR'S DIVINE COMMISSION OF PROCLAIMING TO ALL NATIONS THE WORD WHICH WE ACCEPT TOTALLY AND IN ALL ITS PARTS TO BE GOD'S INSPIRED INERRANT WORD. THESE DAYS CALL FOR UNITED EFFORTS BASED ON A SOUND CONFESSIONALISM WHICH IS AT THE SAME TIME A DYNAMIC CONFESSIONALITY IN THE FORM OF GOSPEL PROCLAMATION TO THE HEATHEN MASSES, AND WE CAN ILL AFFORD DIVISIVE ARGUMENTS THAT NEITHER EDIFY NOR BUILD THE KINGDOM.

We affirm the necessity of creative initiative and forward movement in our evangelical theological voice as the Gospel is presented to a world in turmoil. We accept positive and correct exegetical insights of biblical scholarship wherever they may be found even though we are compelled to reject the presuppositions and methods of some of the exegetes. We look for scholarship that provides a dynamic confessionalism according to the norma normans principle of interpretation.

We believe our church should be involved in a process of creative study and planning in theological concepts related to issues of our day rather than reacting only to crises. Our church by an evangelical orthodoxy should seize every opportunity not only to take the Gospel to every corner of the earth but also to clarify through the Word the modern issues of ecumenicity, church unity, social problems, and hermeneutics to other Lutherans and to Christendom in general. Some of the leading theologians of the LCA and ALC have adopted the un-Lutheran stance of the "new hermeneutic," and unless the permissiveness in our Synod is brought to a halt we will complete one of the greatest doctrinal changes of historic proportions since Luther's day. Let those who would impose this fundamental change of doctrinal stance upon our fellowship join the groups which already allow such an opportunistic and relativistic confessional position.

It might be said that the Missouri Synod has been more relevant to the American scene than other Protestants in the past 20 years and continues to seek new forms of proclamation - yet critics within our church are parroting the same criticisms about supposed dead orthodoxy that outside critics threw at our church 30 years ago.

10. WE TAKE OUR STAND TOGETHER WITH THE VAST MAJORITY OF MEMBERS, PASTORS, PROFESSORS, AND TEACHERS OF SYNOD WITH THE PRAYER THAT WE MAY ALL BOW BEFORE THE WORD IN HUMILITY AND FAITH, NOT ADDING THERETO OR SUBTRACTING THEREFROM THROUGH THE USE OF LOGIC, HUMAN WISDOM, OR SEMANTICS.

We feel that the propagandizing for the "new hermeneutic" has gone far enough, and it is now time for decision by those who would continue to hold this position. We consider this new school of "Missouri Synod hermeneutics" to be a tragic distortion of truth. We question the factuality of the editorial of the February 1965 Concordia Theological Monthly about the harmony between the old and new schools of Biblical interpretations when it states that both schools "often fail to see that they are singing the same hymn of adoration to the incarnate and crucified Savior, even though they are using different words and melodies." They are two different hymns not in harmony with each other and with completely different treatments of the Word. We cannot be obscurantists and ignore centuries of doctrinal formulations and thus turn the 20th century into a period of conformity to new forms of old aberrations. The two schools of interpretation have been manifest in different forms in centuries past, and we will not serve our Savior by attempting the impossible through synthesizing the plain meaning of Scripture with the rationalistic form of the "new Hermeneutic." We do not need a new theology but a vigorous effort to help modern man to find and express the old "faith in a changing society."

We question the intellectual honesty of our "proponents of the new hermeneutic" and "prophets of ecumenism" whose ethics suggest remaining within our denomination while they work for "subversion, encirclement, and infiltration" as they "somehow telegraph to the world who it is they serve and where their loyalties already lie" until the church bows to the ecumenical movement (M. Marty, "Interim Ethics for Ecumenists" in *Christian Century*, Jan. 11, 1961). We ask for appropriate statements and apologies from the chief proponents of the "new school" to assure our Synod of their position regarding our public doctrine and basis of fellowship.

* * * * * *

61

Lawrence B.(Lorry) Meyer, who served the Synod's President and Board of Directors in varied capacities over the years and who helped initiate some of the very aggressive mission projects of the Synod, who had many friends among the left and the right, produced a private undated publication in 1969 entitled, *Missouri in Motion*. Meyer, who I believe was one of the unsung mission heroes in the Missouri Synod of this entire era, wrote a very fitting summary of the Missouri Synod's strategic mission progress and ended his book with an "EPILOGUE," which not only indicated a heavy heart about how the false doctrine and practice was harming the Synod, but in which he made a strong confession of his own faith related to Biblical inspiration and integrity. Meyer wrote:

EPILOGUE

Now that we've seen the Missouri Synod in Motion, we are seized with wonder and amazement at the greatness of the grace of God. Contrary to the predictions of certain failure for the founding fathers and all their works, the tiny synod they created has become a major force in the U. S. A. and beyond in maintaining the preaching of God's Gospel of Salvation clear and loud.

But what about the future of the Missouri Synod? There are those who say that its future is behind it, that in doctrine and practice it is going down the drain.

It must be admitted that the Missouri Synod, too, is afflicted with doctrinal blemishes, spots, and wrinkles and must ever be on the alert against false doctrine and practices ensuing.

Among the more serious diseases threatening the unity of our church and to which too many of our members are being exposed in one form or another is the so-called "new doctrine of inspiration." Sad to say, some of our people have been inoculated and are succumbing in various degrees to this so-called "new hermeneutics." This new approach to Scriptures and the doctrines as we have been teaching in our church on the basis of Scriptures and the Confessions is altogether at variance with the doctrine on the inspiration of the Bible taught and believed by the members of The Lutheran Church-Missouri Synod for these past 120 years.

Plenary and literal interpretation is set in juxtaposition to imagery and allegory — symbolic versus reality — non-fact versus fact — historic and higher criticism of the individual books of the Canon versus the authority of the text of the Bible itself. These are creeping cancers in our theological body today. Simile, metaphor, hyperbole, figurative language, versus a *literal* "thus saith the Lord" is beginning to gnaw away at the very vitals of our doctrinal body.

It is altogether inconceivable how anyone can apply the so-called "new hermeneutics" to, for instance, Genesis 1, 2, 3-11, Deuteronomy, Isaiah, Job, Jonah, etc., or to the total Old and New Testament Canon, and at the same time profess to believe in what The Lutheran Church-Missouri Synod throughout the years has called Plenary, Verbal, and Inerrant Inspiration. To be sure the same phraseology and words are used but with different meaning and connotations.

To apply the theories of this so-called "new hermeneutics" which have evolved in the past five decades in Europe and then transplanted to America as criteria to reject the Biblical statement that "all of Scripture is divinely inspired" and to put pagan mythology and dimmed history of four thousand years ago in juxtaposition to the WORD OF GOD is a wrong approach to God's Holy Word.

Unless this "new hermeneutics" is rooted out of our midst our orthodoxy of yesterday will degenerate into something tomorrow which will be an abomination unto the Lord. This is not merely a conjecture. It can be documented by the development of the history of most of the major Protestant church bodies in the world. And please note that history also documents that such unorthodox methods of using the doctrine of the "inspired Word" did not originate with the laity nor with the rank and file of the clergy, but in seminaries — beginning with Wittenberg immediately after Luther's death.

According to the Bible and the Confessions and teaching of great Lutheran scholars beginning especially with Luther:

We believe that Moses was the inspired author of the Pentateuch, and that Genesis 1-11 are literal historic facts...

We categorically reject the theory that the Creation Story in Genesis is to be interpreted as symbolic...

It is furthermore granted that in the course of the centuries modifications, additions, glosses, words from the other languages, errors by transcribers, etc. may have crept into the text. And when Jesus said to the Jews "they have Moses and the prophets" (Luke 16:31), he was referring to the text of the Torah as it was in the possession of the Jews of his day.

It is one of the mysteries of present day "new theology" how anyone who claims to believe the Bible can take a concordance and look up the name Moses and find approximately 150 references in the Old and New Testament to Moses and still deny the authorship of the Pentateuch to Moses.

It is an historical fact that all liberalism in the church today had its seed in the non-acceptance of the doctrine of plenary inspiration as we understand and teach it from the Bible and the Confessions. It is simply inconceivable that someone can make the statement "I believe that the Bible is the inspired Word of God" and then turn around and doubt the God-spoken authenticity of His Word in the Bible."...

If the story of Genesis can be demoted and reduced to a symbolic story of creation instead of accepting it as an historic happening, why should be dare to hope that the miracles narrated in both the Old and New Testaments, the story of the Virgin Birth, the resurrection of our Lord and the ascension of our Lord will not be presented as non-factual but as symbols, allegory, or hallucinations...

Unless some very drastic steps are taken to stop these "for discussion only" papers and essays which, however, present the subject matter as though it were Bible doctrine, we shall lose our orthodoxy and with it the theological leadership in the Protestant world which God has made us responsible for...

*   *   *   *   *

During the years from 1965 to 1969 when J. A. O. Preus was elected President of the Synod, I was leader of the "Conservative" movement or the party of the right. Some of the essays which are reproduced in this book with my documentation reveal that I worked very zealously to assure that we would be Biblical Lutherans and not institutional Lutherans in our activities to counteract the false doctrines and practices which were being brought into our Synod by the party of the left. During the course of this time, I was invited to present various essays in different places on specific occasions. One of these essays, *The Theological Task Today For The Church's Mission To Win The World For Christ*, was presented at a convocation at Concordia Theological Seminary in Springfield, IL, on Nov. 22, 1969, and presented to the Illinois and Wisconsin All-Lutheran Campus Pastors' Conference on Nov. 27, 1969, and printed at the request of the latter conference. Parts of this essay, which are still appropriate today are reprinted here:

THE THEOLOGICAL TASK TODAY FOR THE CHURCH'S MISSION TO WIN THE WORLD FOR CHRIST

The crisis of the church today requires careful scrutiny of how theology determines the mission and strength of the church. This treatise proposes some of the strengths and weaknesses of the theological enterprise in matters which weaken the church's mission to an already confused world. It also proposes how theology needs to concern itself with making practical contributions toward advance in the church's Gospel mission to the world.

The Christian believer lives **by faith**. His life is a venture of faith. His faith moves him to act or refuse to act. This centrality of faith to life is shown in Hebrews 11 (TEV): "It is by faith that we understand that the universe was created by God's Word so that what can be seen was made by what cannot by seen. it was faith that made Abel offer. It was faith that kept Enoch from dying. It was faith that made Noah hear God's warning. It was faith that made Abraham obey. It was faith that made Abraham able. It was faith that made Abraham offer. It was faith that made Isaac promise. It was faith that made Jacob bless. It was faith that made Joseph speak. It was faith that made Moses refuse. It was faith that made Moses leave Egypt. It was faith that enabled the Israelites to cross the Red Sea. It was faith that made the walls of Jericho fall down. What a record these men have won by their faith."

God claims to be the infallible Author of the Sourcebook, which He says is without error. Whether we believe that His revelation is with or without error, God's Word still stands that there exists Christian truth on one side and religious error on the other. It is accepted by faith.

In a day when absolutes are questioned or rejected by many, we should remind ourselves of the successful community which is one of the most narrow-minded communities on earth. Prejudiced so that they deal in absolutes in all they do, the scientific community produced the giant moon ships on their successful orbits. Truth is absolute. I insist my druggist must work by absolutes, for my life depends on it. Anyone who says that there are no absolutes already has an absolute. Absolutes are a fact of life, so is truth and so is error.

My religious life is affected by that fact, for the historical Christ Himself is an absolute. Though He were born a thousand times in Bethlehem, if he is not born in my heart by faith, His gift of salvation has been rejected, and I am lost eternally. That's a Biblical absolute. We are not discussing fake images of Christ - the Church's "Christ," a theologian's "Christ," but the Christ of the written Word. He is very exclusive. Most exclusive are the statements He made regarding the way of salvation and the path of faith here on earth. But he is also inclusive in that He shed His blood for **all** men, for He paid the inclusive price for all people's salvation. Yet He becomes exclusive when faith is demanded for the acceptance of the Gift of Salvation (Eph. 2:8-10). We have no other model than the Christ of the written Scriptures. His Word deals in absolutes. That doesn't mean that when we witness that we in our manner become dogmatic or bulldoggish in presenting Scriptural truths.

We dare not synthesize truth and error in the Christian faith. There is a synthetic cultural Christianity and a "New Theology" offered as a Christian option. There is a synthetic world religion, which some call the "New Humanism." Only certain doctrines and practices, however, qualify as Christian or Confessional, unless we prostitute those titles.

The "New Theology," of course, is not new at all, even though there are a few refinements from the past, mostly to make it more palatable. The "New Theology" is basically an attempt —

1) To relate God's redemptive deeds to history in such a way that there is no need to

64

try to establish the **facts** of history. The "facts" of history may lie forever hidden under subjective interpretations, but this does not threaten theology for the new theologians so long as by the "leap of faith" they believe that on a level, not subject to human investigation, a divine purpose is being realized.

2) To relate (tell, speak about, proclaim) God's redemptive activity in theological formulas, which because they are **all** ultimately only word-pictures of what God is doing, may differ greatly from each other so long as **somehow** a divine, saving intent is expressed.

Humanism is the appreciation of man and of the values in human life. The **"New Humanism"** is the opinion that **man** is the ultimate reality which needs to be expressed in theological formulas, and that such formulas do not in fact intend to make affirmations about **God**, but are actually articulations of **man's** understanding of his own existence (anthropology).

The new humanism seeks to unite theology and humanism in a synthesis in which the human conquers the divine - now they **celebrate** humanity rather than acknowledging the total depravity of the flesh which is conquered alone through the indwelling Christ. This synthesis between Biblical faith and humanism negates the tension between Christ and the world, the spirit and the flesh. This emancipation of man from divine rule and judgment is preceded by a rejection of the Holy Scriptures. Then, the new humanism claims that the weakness of the flesh or of human nature is derived from cultural characteristics that can be changed. It wants to give reason another chance. It has a passion for synthesizing the secular with the divine, and has a reverence for life that becomes idolatry. It is a big faith in a little god, a religion of humanity!

The theological task today means honest confrontation with the historical Christ, not to separate Him from His own history or His own life of acts and words here on earth, while thinking that we can retain Him as Savior. The mission of an authentic Lutheran Church to influence the world requires honest scholarship that refuses to accept mutually exclusive viewpoints at the same time.

The theological differences between evangelical theology and the "New Theology" are not just interpretations in small matters, but are differences concerning the very basics of the faith. Those who fail to recognize antitheses should realize there is a law of cause and effect. Logic reveals this to be the ultimate canon of the sciences. In every scientific investigation this truth is assumed. The truth of the law of cause and effect is seen in Rom. 1:18-32. Truly, the "New Theology" leads to the "New Morality."

We get the impression that the "cards are stacked" against orthodox views regarding the Scriptures and other basic doctrines by the "New Theology." The Missouri Synod itself admitted the existence of significant problems when in Denver Res. 2-27, it stated that "the Synod dedicate itself anew to the Word of God and the Lutheran Confessions that, under the guidance of the Holy Spirit, the Synod may also speak successfully to the **theological problems which beset it today,** resolve the **controversies which vex it,** and apply Christian discipline."

Dr. Paul Bretscher in his doctrinal essay at the San Francisco Convention stated, "In the life of Jesus we note both a very positive and negative concern about 'doctrine': a positive concern for **His doctrine** and a negative concern regarding all **false doctrines.**" He adds: "God was most jealous of His doctrine. Over and over again He spoke out through His chosen prophets against false prophets, false dreamers and their false prophecies and dreams, and He threatened them and their followers with fearful punishment (Deut. 18:22)." He concludes that in our prayers and hymns of our Christian heritage we confess: '(1) that there is such a reality as 'doctrine'; '(2) that there is 'pure doctrine'; (3) that there is 'false and pernicious doctrine,' 'corrupt teaching,' and that there are 'corrupters of God's Word'; (4) that there are those who have erred because they were ensnared by 'false doctrine'; (5)

that because of 'false doctrine' schisms exist in the church; (6) that Satan has a hand in 'false doctrine'; (7) that we recognize only Christ as our Master, our Teacher, in determining what is 'true' and 'false doctrine'; (8) that we need to pray for the gift and preservation of 'pure doctrine."'

The "New Theology" and humanism breeds what? It is my conviction that the "New Theology" has resulted in the following theological deviations:

1. Christian universalism. By that I mean that Christ in His redemptive act has saved all people - regardless of whether they believe or not. Universalism is the notion that ultimate reality is **process**, which by virtue of a built-in divine benign intent, will result in the redemption not only of individuals, but of all history and cultures, without benefit of the particular way his divine "grace" is expressed in the **Christian** gospel. Humanity is not saved **exclusively** by the **Christian** gospel — the Christian is gospel merely **one** way among **many** of expressing the conviction that humanity is being saved. It is our business now to bring this to the attention of people to give them a new humanity. We are to demonstrate it and to celebrate it because they are not aware of it. So-called Christian universalism is growing fast today in Lutheranism, also in orthodox LCMS congregations. Anyone who is not aware of it ought to do a little homework.

2. The "New Theology" breeds the new morality and an untenable situational ethics. Christian faith and Biblical truth have a quality of constancy and continuity which is denied by the relativism of the new morality. Disappearance of religious absolutes has encouraged man to deify himself. The establishment of man as a worthy authority means the disestablishment of God. This humanist position is unrealistic, for it does not take proper account of evil and the absolute depravity of human nature. In humanist thinking, a person must not think in moral or ethical absolutes and no extra-human source of power and standards which are at work in acknowledging and understanding right and wrong. The new morality views a man's life as restricted to his consciousness of the human situation, making him a prisoner of sinful nature. This offers no hope to the confused and weak as they are defeated by their own emotional conflicts and wanton desires.

3. The "New Theology" also produces the demand to accept theistic evolution as a viable option for the doctrine of creation in the Bible. Evolution has never been established by science as a law or fact. Science has three classifications of ideas: hypotheses, theories, and laws. Evolution is merely an unproven hypothesis. Darwin's "Origin of Species" is said to have 800 phrases like "Hence...let us suppose...it may be...let us conclude," etc., but others made a religion out of these hypotheses. The second law of thermodynamics insists on a universal tendency toward decay and disorder, not growth and development. Where is one instance in the history of man of some kind of macro-evolution? Where is there one example of the evolving of some organ like an eye, ear, reproductive organ, or a brain? Development of a wart or an example of micro-evolution proves nothing.

Some have shown the impossibility of survival of man, animals, insects, birds, and fish if evolution is to be taken seriously. Behind the existence of life on land and in the oceans is a Master Plan based on a unique series of food chains that preserve and sustain all of life on earth, and they are completely interdependent. There is a fantastic web of life of interdependence and absolute necessity of standard conditions and full development if plants, birds, animals, fish or man are to survive even for five minutes. Only a supernatural power could pressure these conditions. There are no intermediate steps possible, and no creature can survive in any partial stage of development or without all organs functioning completely. Evolutionists must honestly face these and related questions. They avoid these issues, and yet many dare to take unproven hypotheses and accept them as religious beliefs.

It depends upon where they place their faith.

Genesis gives the why and how of creation. Some say it doesn't give the how, but it does supply some basic facts. That does not make the Bible a textbook for science. There was only one scientist present at the time of creation, and his name was God. Genesis is His record of the beginning of our universe. All subsequent Biblical revelation presupposes a knowledge of the origin of the earth, of life, and man. Often throughout the Old Testament God is called the Creator of the heavens under the earth, and as such He is worshiped. The Gospel of John begins with the reaffirmation of the creative work of God. Romans opens by showing men that their ignorance of God is inexcusable, because the created universe which surrounds them should suffice as the revelation to them of the invisible things of the Godhead. Paul's Epistles exalt Christ as the One by whom the world were framed. Hebrews likewise places creation in a strategic place. Paul points to a faithful Creator as one to whom we can trustfully commit our souls. Destroy the reliability of the Genesis account of creation, and the great structure of New Testament truth is without foundation, including the origin of sin.

"By the Word of the Lord were the heavens made; and all the hosts of them by the breath of His mouth" (Ps. 148:5). "They purposely ignored as fact: Long ago God spoke, and the heavens and the earth were created. The earth was formed out of water, and by water, and it was by water also, the water of the Flood, that the old world was destroyed. But the heavens and earth that now exist are **being preserved**, by the same **Word of God...**" (2 Pet. 3:5-7). "It is by faith that we understood that the universe was created by God's Word so that what can be seen was made out of what cannot be seen" (Heb. 11:3).

Theistic evolution is unScriptural, contrary to Jesus Christ who created everything out of nothing, thus contradicting the Gospel itself. To maintain that it was created in another way than God's Word declares is placing more faith in another source than God's Word. It is an illogical and faithless concession to naturalistic humanism. The "New Theology" and humanism breeds this type of irrationality. True science does not contradict God's Word, but the Bible warns of "science falsely so-called." No LCMS pastor or lay members can justify belief in theistic evolution, for such would be hampering the mission of Christ. I hope the day is past when any LCMS members are embarrassed to embrace God's creation boldly, and no longer give credence to any kind of evolution. In the July 1966 LWML Quarterly I wrote a topic as LWML Topic Editor on the Bible against evolution ("The Bible and Science"), and some pastors wrote letters to condemn me for my Scriptural testimony as being obscurantist. I pray our Synod will leave such rebellion behind for all time.

4. The "New Theology" breeds false ecumenism. False ecumenism is the attempt to cultivate consensus without real agreement. Through organizational groupings a greater strength is expected. False ecumenism wants organizationalunity instead of Scriptural unity. This comes by synthesis of varying viewpoints as long as the simple Gospel is confessed. Divergences become pastoral concerns. The false ecumenical demand is that differences be overlooked in the interest of church union. Doctrinal indifference is one of the signs of the false ecumenical movement. Even though denominational differences are very serious and regrettable, they are not as much the scandal of Christendom as is the belittling of the great Christian doctrines on the authority and integrity of the written Scriptures. A scandal of Christendom is the tragic lack of convictions on the part of those who substitute outward organization for true spiritual oneness in God's Word.

5. The "New Theology" and New Hermeneutic also produces an attitude that shows

disregard for an absolute authority mediated by the errorless written Word. The book, "Christ: The Theme Of The Bible" by Norman L. Geisler [10] shows the authority, integrity, and unity of the Bible in all its parts. It shows how historical parts must be accepted on face value. Geisler says, "There are numerous individual citations which reveal that Jesus affirmed an authoritative collection of writings, divine in origin, and unimpeachable in their declaration. Compare, for example, the fact that (1) Jesus resisted Satan by three emphatic quotations of the Old Testament prefaced by 'it is written' (Matt. 4:4,7,10). (2) Jesus cleansed the temple on the authority that 'It is written, My house shall be called a house of prayer.' (Matt. 21:13). (3) He pronounced a woe on His betrayer, based on the fact that 'it is written' (Matt. 26:24). (4) Jesus rebuked religious hypocrisy, with 'as it is written' (quoting Is. 29:13 in Mark 7:6).(5) He affirmed His own Messiahship from 'the place where it was written,' 'The Spirit of the Lord is upon me...' (Luke 4:17-18). (6) Jesus answered the lawyer's question on how to inherit eternal life by saying, 'What is written in the law?' (Luke 10:26). (7) He based His own authority and identify with God on the basis of the fact that 'it is written in the prophets.' (John 6:45; cf. 10:34). (8) Jesus even affirmed the authority of what was written (in the Old Testament) despite the fact that the religious authorities of His day wished to kill Him for it. (cf. Luke 20:16-17)". [11]

Geisler continues, "Jesus often told them, as in Matthew 22:29, 'You are wrong, because you know neither the Scriptures nor the power of God.' Jesus personally verified the historical truth of (1) Adam and Eve (Matt. 19:4), (2) Abel's murder (Matt. 23:35); (3) Noah and the Flood (Luke 17:27); (4) Lot and the destruction of Sodom (Luke 17:29); (5) the existence of the patriarchs Abraham, Isaac and Jacob (Luke 13:28); (6) Moses and the burning bush (Luke 20:37); (7) the wilderness wanderings of Israel (John 3:14); (8) the story of Elijah and widow (Luke 4:25); (9) and of Naaman the Syrian leper (Luke 4:27); (10) David and the tabernacle (Matt. 12:41); (11) Solomon and the queen of Sheba (Matt. 12:42); (12) Jonah and Nineveh (Matt. 12:41); and (13) Daniel the prophet (Matt. 24:15). The events of the Old Testament were not only considered to be historical but many of them were supernatural in character. In effect, Jesus' references verify the miraculous nature of Old Testament events: 1. The world's destruction by a flood (Luke 17:27); 2. Lot's wife being crystallized (Luke 17:32); 3. The burning bush before Moses (Luke 20:37); 4. The healing of Israel from snakebites (John 3:14); 5. The manna from heaven (John 6:49); 6. The healing of Naaman the leper (Luke 4:26); 7. The miracles of Elijah for the widow (Luke 4:25); 8. The preservation of Jonah in the whale (Matt. 12:41).

The Gospel is denied in a substantial way if we deny Jonah as historical when Jesus used that account as predictive of His resurrection - or if we deny the Flood when it is used as predictive of the power of the Word for destroying the earth by fire on Judgment Day (2 Pet. 3:6-7). The New Hermeneutic and presuppositions of the higher critical method of interpreting the Scriptures allow for tearing Biblical history from Gospel truth, and so denies the Gospel in a substantial manner. It is ludicrous to tear history and the truths it teaches apart, whether it is Eisenhower and Kennedy or whether it is Christ, John, Abraham or Moses.

6. The "New Theology" brings a repudiation of the supernatural and miraculous. But if one link of the miraculous is broken, then all links are broken. If Christ was born of a virgin, if Christ rose from the dead, then Israel went through the Red Sea on dry land and was fed by manna from heaven in the wilderness; then Genesis 1 and 2 is history as God wants us to know it; then baptism and regeneration and the indwelling Christ are a reality; then the power of the Holy Spirit through the Word is available to win the world for Christ. Regarding the Christian faith, the question is whether a person will have faith

in Christ on a humanistic or Scriptural basis.

7. The "New Theology" also frees ego or big "I" to become the king of life. Then Christian truth is decided by majority opinion rather than clear Scripture. The in-group, and the avant-garde become directors as to what is to be considered viable options — resulting in decisions that are subjective and expedient. But we are to challenge religious opinions, not to revise the Word.

Proponents of the "New Theology" sometimes offer false options to the church today. We will isolate several that should be challenged in some degree:

1. They suggest a false option between Christianity and Confessionality. We live on two levels: First, Christian; second, Confessional and organizational. God alone knows who belongs to the first group. Men must decide by basic principles they adopt who is to belong to their specific grouping on the second level and by what criteria decisions are to be made. They may be challenged, but they have the right to organize in Confessional groupings without inferring that others are not Christian, or second-rate at best. When a Lutheran body takes a strong Confessional position against fellowship with another body, the question has been asked whether this means that we don't consider the others Christian, whereas it is a question of whether we agree on Confessional principles and practices. Sometimes these are treated as antitheses - Christianity and Confessionalism, but they are complimentary.

2. Another false option: Christ or the Bible. When we confess God's Word to be the inerrant, infallible written Word in the historical sense, some strongly criticize us of being guilty of bibliolatry or biblicism. Christ and the Bible are not antitheses. Recall the quotations from Geisler's book, especially, "You cannot separate the authority of Christ from the authority of the written Scriptures which reveal Christ." Some maintain that those who believe the Bible to be an errorless and infallible Source are worshiping the Bible. I haven't yet met a Lutheran pastor who worshiped the Bible. What I am concerned about is not bibliolatry but idolatry — idolizing man's mind and his notions over the Bible.

3. Two mutually exclusive religious positions are allowed to stand, one which denies Christian truth, and still they still want to call it a Christian Lutheran community. While they say they are overdoing uniformity, they have uniformity and unity all mixed up. We are speaking about basics and non-basics of Christian and Biblical truth. This is about fundamentals which God makes fundamentals, not which we would like to make fundamentals. Remaining vague about the meaning of unity, uniformity and diversity in relation to Biblical requirements, some keep the issue confused by refusing to give definitions and by retaining two mutually exclusive positions.

Some insist that "there needs to be diversity," and we must strive for a "willingness to recognize greater variety in theological statements and positions." It is not a sign of strength to have a babble of voices proclaiming varying basic theological viewpoints, some of which are in conflict with the Scriptural and Confessional voice. Rom. 15:5 and 6 ask us to have the **same point of view** among ourselves by following the example of Christ Jesus.

8. Another false option is to create a tension between the individual against the corporate group. Only a few things are more prejudicial than the individualism of the "New Theology" which does not regard the will of the Confessional group. Theological changes by some individuals are promoted privately until such a time that it is possible to come out in the open. This is not honest, nor brotherly. Love demands honesty, integrity and faithfulness to the Confessional commitment of the group. Such individualism results in anarchy both

in authority of God's Word and in morality. Ignoring or subverting Confessional norms of the group by an individual or a click makes the individual an enemy of the group and the group an enemy of the individual. The "New Theology" tends to promote such improper individualism.

9. Another false option is proposed between God's Word and love. Those who believe God's Word demand certain norms and evangelical discipline are sometimes considered legalistic and devoid of love. God's Word demands Confessional norms to be honored faithfully, and we must not fear criticism. Luther says, "The sin against doctrine is worse than those against love. There are two kinds of sins. The first is committed against the word of Christian doctrine and faith and the second against love. The sin against doctrine is in no wise to be tolerated, but we are to have patience with sin against love because by it we sin only against our neighbor without violating doctrine and faith. However, if anything is undertaken against the Word, faith and the honor of God, we are in no wise to preserve silence, and are to bear it far less patiently. Then we should offer stubborn resistance." (SL 19, 1182) Love honors God's Word. Love is the fulfilling of the law, not the breaking of it. Those who know Christian love will heed God's Word even when it is unpopular - and when some pit love against God's Word. Some act as though right belief excludes love. They are not antithetical or mutually exclusive.

10. A tragic option suggested by some is that we must change our message or lose our youth, students, and intellectuals. This is wrongly identifying the nature of the problem. Man doesn't want to hear what God's Word has to say. In the case of Jesus Himself we see that "He could not do many mighty works there because of their unbelief," and so we would not say the cause was in the impotency of Christ, but in the hardness and unbelief of His listeners. The Athenian University was the home of cool, cultivated, critical intellect, which had tried all things and found all wanting, and so few hearers had open ears for Paul's new teaching. The Gospel is an offense, but it cannot be changed. Man doesn't want to hear the truth, for it is an insult to the intellect to learn that some of earth's wisdom is trash. We are members of the Lutheran community, and that means we witness to Christ through the truths of God's Word which do not change with situations or the demands of the intellect.

11. Another false option is to allow two definitions of Biblical inerrancy at the same time. An inerrant, infallible autograph is the only view of the original Scriptures which is in accord with the nature of the Triune God, who declares that the Scriptures are completely true. Higher criticism brought a hostility to God's claim of Biblical inerrancy because belief in verbal inspiration is held to be incompatible with scientific claims. The ease with which contemporary theologians have dispensed with the infallibility of the Bible is surprising in view of the Bible's own claims. When theology cuts itself off from the control of the clear Biblical text and the Lutheran principle of "Scripture interpreting Scripture," it retreats from the plain sense of the text into the subjective wastelands of human speculation. The denial of objective and propositional revelation in Scripture results from denial of God's claims of perfect revelation. A century of disbelieving Biblical infallibility has created a climate in which the Bible provides the "themes" for theology, but not its "norms." But God's Word is a unitary product, and it does not recognize a dichotomy between history and salvation that the proponents of the "New Theology" would thrust upon it.

One of the very real problems of the "New Theology" has been the centering on personalities instead of issues in theological discussion. Evangelical spokesmen have been labeled as fundamentalists, even though they have been thoroughly biblical and have said no more or no less than God's Word itself states. The sweeping criticism is meant to destroy the effectiveness of the evangelical spokesmen by making him some sort of theological Neanderthal man. All discussion must center only on issues, not in personalities.

The "New Theology" becomes very dogmatic in its subjective interpretative method and in its relativizing of doctrine. This all gives a rudderless future — **anarchy** in authority and in morality. It reminds one of Is. 5:20, "Woe to them that call evil good and good evil."

This leap into irrational optimism might be compared to a person who is drugged, for this is a spiritual drug which causes the adherent of the "New Theology" to retreat from reality.

*   *   *   *   *   *   *   *

At the same time, other essays were presented, one which was printed and received wide distribution in 1970. Parts of this essay, which calls for integrity in practice as well as in doctrine are reprinted here:

TRUTH, UNITY AND THE CONFESSING CHURCH

For more than 400 years Lutherans have identified themselves and their beliefs to one another, to other Christians, and to the surrounding world by pointing to their great confessions of faith in the Book of Concord. The Lutheran Church-Missouri Synod, has always been known as a staunch confessional church. If we are to take the Scriptures, our Lutheran confessions, and our Missouri Synod heritage seriously, we must work to become a **confessing** church as well.

What is a **confessing** church? Such a church is one that lives what it believes, practices what it preaches, teaches what it professes, and actually uses the Word of God in its daily life as both a healing and motivating power.

The confessing church not only has a confessional basis in its written documents of the past, but actually confesses openly and vigorously the doctrine contained in these confessions. Confessing our faith in this way is not a matter of choice or indifference, but is of the very essence of Christianity. Our Lord reminds us that confessing Him before men is necessary, or He will not confess us before the Father in heaven. Our own Lutheran confessions were real acts of confession, often in the face of extremely trying circumstances. Confessing what we have heard and seen in Jesus Christ is the foundation, the life, and the activity of the **confessing** church. In fact, the "church" that is confessional without being confessing is not a true church.

There are times when the confessing church must be especially vigorous in its confessing. Such heroic confession is called for when the unity of the church is threatened or impaired by divisive forces. Such courageous confessing is essential when the presence of doctrinal error or apparent indifference to pure doctrine threatens the church's continuing commitment to the truth of God's Word. We in The Lutheran Church-Missouri Synod can no longer assume either the unity of our membership or its total commitment to the truthfulness and contemporary viability of our historic Lutheran confessional doctrinal position. For Lutherans who seek to preserve and extend their doctrinal heritage and their unity in the Gospel of Jesus Christ, the time has come to confess with courage and conviction. The **confessional** Lutheran church must in a specific way be a **confessing** church dedicated to the restoration, preservation, and extension of both its **truth** and its **unity**.

The fact that both the truth and the unity of the Lutheran Church are severely threatened today is very clear. Commentators in both the secular and religious press have repeatedly called attention to the divisions existing within our Synod, particularly since the Denver

Convention. President C. J. Lawrenz of the Wisconsin Synod Lutheran Seminary reported to his Synod's convention, "Manifest at Denver were two theological positions which cannot be harmonized and reconciled or stand side by side in one church body, if it is really to wear witness...The cleavage pertained most specifically to the authority of the Scriptures, to the principles of church fellowship and to the scope of the church's mission. The division was most pronounced on the first point, especially as it pertained to inerrancy." The *Christian Century*, for example, asserted that the divisions within the synod are deeper than those between the various synods. Our new president, Dr. Jacob Preus, has repeatedly expressed his desire to bring unity to our divided church on the basis of the confessions and our synod's doctrinal position.

For several years it has been evident to many pastors, teachers, and laymen that there are deep-seated and extensive differences and divisions within our beloved church body. Past assurances that such differences are insignificant or have been resolved have not been very convincing. Already the post-convention period has seen a divisiveness on the part of a few who have chosen to disagree publicly with a Scriptural pronouncement on Biblical inerrancy by President J. A. O. Preus.

If our Synod is to regain its unity and fraternity, it must first recognize the situation for what it is. We can't do anything about our disunity until we understand its nature and cause. Our Synod passed resolutions to assure a congregation of the Synod's intent to abide by its Scriptural basis (Denver Res. 2-30) and to affirm its wholehearted desire to follow orthodoxy in all its doctrines, teaching, and practice and to reject all heterodoxy (Res. 2-33). The Synod understands the meaning of orthodoxy and heterodoxy in convention, and now we assure our fidelity to the Synod to understand and practice after the convention. A convention resolution on doctrinal matters is like a good Sunday sermon that needs to be practiced by members from Monday to Saturday.

Why are we disunited? There have been several inaccurate answers to this question. Some writers see our disunity as the result of a bitterly fought presidential election or as the consequence of "conservative" political activity. Apart from the fact that this interpretation overlooks the political or promotional activity of "non-conservatives" and apparently regards such activity as unifying rather than divisive, this explanation is totally wrong.

The questions raised often are all **doctrinal**, directly or indirectly:

-Is Holy Scripture really God's inerrant and fully authoritative Word?

-Can members of organizations which deny the Lord Jesus Christ and His way of salvation also be members of the Lutheran church without compromising their faith or witness of their church?

-Can members of a confessing church be involved in ecumenical organizations which weaken or compromise the Christian faith and confession?

-Is it possible to formulate doctrinal statements correctly?

-Can the orthodoxy of a church body be established from its statements alone and without paying a great deal of attention to what is actually taught, preached, and lived by its members?

-Does the failure to exercise discipline with those who depart from the church's confessional position indicate anything about its confessional character?

That the differing answers in our Synod to these questions indicate the **doctrinal** nature of our disunity is rather obvious.

By now it has become apparent that Lutheran concern for the **unity** of the church is closely bound up with concern for the **truth**. Unity and truth go together: if we are to solve the problem of division and disunity in The Lutheran Church-Missouri Synod and beyond, we must first deal satisfactorily with the doctrinal issues which divide us, and which have become so evident to all of us in recent years.

Concern for doctrinal truth and integrity is no luxury, but a necessity of spiritual life. Doctrine is simply the verbalizing of our Christian faith on the basis of God's own Book, the Bible. If doctrine goes, our faith goes, too, for our faith **in** Jesus Christ and His Gospel is simultaneously faith **that** Jesus Christ did in fact live, die, and rise again for our justification and life eternal - and such faith is of its very nature **doctrinal**. Take away the doctrinal content of our faith, Jesus Christ and the Gospel, and you destroy the church as a divine institution. Take away the divine basis for all doctrine - Holy Scripture - and you reduce the faith of the church to wishful thinking and its certainty to a merely human one. According to our Lord, it is the Truth - not error or opinion - that makes men free. The Truth that liberates men comes only from continuing in His Word. For this reason our Lord and His chosen and inspired apostles warn the church again and again about the folly of forsaking the truth of the divine doctrine. Jude's admonition is the abiding watchword of the confessing church: "Contend for the faith which was once for all delivered to the saints."

It is the truth of the Gospel in its various forms - oral, written, or sacramental - that the Holy Spirit uses to create and sustain faith in men's hearts. With that gift of faith He creates the one holy Christian church, the community of believers. When the Augsburg Confession in article Seven links the unity of the church to the "doctrine of the Gospel," it is **not** giving us a minimal formula or program for the establishment of denominational fellowship, but reminding us that the true unity of the church is **spiritual**, that it is always found where faith and the fear of God exists in men's hearts (see Apology VII, 31: Tappert p. 174), that it is brought into being not by human ceremonies (not even by synodical resolutions) buy only by the use of the purely taught Gospel and rightly administered sacraments. A unity of Christians produced and maintained by anything else is not the true unity of the church, but the kind of outward harmony condemned by our confessions as "contrary to the truth and actually intended for is suppression" (Formula of Concord XI, 95; Tappert p. 632).

Can one still be a truly confessing Lutheran within the Missouri Synod, or must we withdraw from the Synod in order to make our witness heard and obey our Lord's will? Our fathers have taught us well in insisting that separation from a church body should occur only when the church body has become heterodox. Separation for any other reason is separatism, a sin of pride that truly destroys the peace and harmony of the church. Our *Brief Statement* wisely states: "A church body does not forfeit its orthodox character through he casual intrusion of errors, provided these are combated and eventually removed by means of doctrinal discipline." The question can thus be put very directly: Is the present situation in the Synod best described as "heterodoxy" or the "casual intrusion of error"? If it is the former we have no choice but to leave, and to leave in the name of God. But if it's the latter, then we must stay for the sake of our brethren and in order to carry on the proper doctrinal discipline. There are many reasons for arguing that our Synod as such remains truly orthodox, and that consequently we should remain **within** the Synod as we seek to be confessing, not merely confessional, Lutherans.

Consider the faithful testimony of hundreds of thousands of faithful members of The Lutheran Church-Missouri Synod whose voices are not heard in our public assemblies or periodicals, but who are well known to all of us; they too are living evidence that the Missouri Synod is an orthodox church today. Together we must make serious and strenuous efforts to carry on a proper and God-pleasing evangelical discipline with those who have erred. We must use every channel of the Synod in order to edify and correct - Circuit and District meetings and conferences, auxiliary organization activities, and publications. Members have all the organizations required in the Synodical channels to do what God requires.

Confession, not separation, is the answer. There are many forms this vigorous confessional activity should take. Consider participating in the following manner:

-Support the president and vice-presidents of the Synod in their efforts to supervise our doctrine and life, remembering them in our private and corporate prayers, and following their leadership in doing the work of the church.;

-Support officials on the local and district levels who provide positive confessional leadership for their constituency;

-Provide dedicated stewardship, missions, and evangelism efforts at home and abroad;

-Speak out for the truth of God's Word in local congregational assemblies, circuit meetings, district conferences and conventions, LLL and LWML meetings, and the various boards and committees to which we belong;

-Communicate with our leaders and editors of our publications with regard to our concerns, encouraging them for their faithfulness to the Lord, and by offering articles for publication;

-Alert others through regular channels in our parishes, circuits, and districts to the crucial needs of the church in this hour, and inviting them to be active confessors of the truth, and admonishing any who err so that they might repent and experience forgiveness in Christ;

-Encourage and participate in serious Bible study in our homes, schools, churches, and conferences to the end that we continue to learn the truth of God's Word and will for our lives;

-Urge our responsible leaders at every level to continue exploring the unresolved doctrinal problems within our synod.

Our theologians should lead us as authentic Lutherans in a creative exposition of the Word (the Holy Scriptures in their entirety) for the problems, opportunities, and theological concerns of our day. Our Synod will serve the good of the Kingdom by refusing to adapt its theology to the current theological climate which has been taken from a defunct European theology. These days call for a united effort based on a sound Confessionalism which is at the same time a dynamic Confessionality in the form of Gospel proclamation to the heathen masses, and we can ill-afford arguments that neither edify nor build the Kingdom. Thus we bow before the infallible Word in humility and faith, not adding thereto or subtracting therefrom by the use of logic, human wisdom, or semantics.

"THE CONFESSING CHURCH IN ITS SEMINARY & COLLEGE CLASSROOMS, PUBLICATIONS, DIALOGS & DISCUSSIONS, AND ALL OTHER OCCASIONS:"

The Confessing Church presents clearly the facts of God's Word, the testimony of its Confessions, and the position adopted in its constitutional and Synodical resolutions at all times under all situations. It does so evangelically, winsomely, and with love. It presents itself and its message with fidelity - clearly and unequivocally, not using words or phrases with dual meanings or coming to inconclusive decisions. It confesses its Confession.

It has become popular in many church circles to claim open-mindedness in presenting issues by portraying the "pros" and "cons" and then ending with a synthesis of ideas, leaving the reader or listener to make a choice. This will not be true of the Confessional or Confessing Church. The Confessing Church presents the theses and antitheses, and then speaks clearly her Confession on the basis of God's Word and makes plain the church's position on the basis of the true Biblical doctrine.

Fidelity is required in the church's classrooms: We dare not present opposing views of different scholars and then let the student make up his mind as to what he will accept, but rather learn why the church's Confession is true under all circumstances. A Confessing Church has a Confession to proclaim.

Fidelity is required in all dialogs, discussions, and in disciplinary cases; It is not a question or argument between two opposing viewpoints, but the church's Confession is brought to bear on every situation, difficult or easy. Until the church itself changes its position and Confession, a Confessing Church has a Confession to proclaim.

Fidelity is required on this basis in publications: Major doctrines dare not be discussed through "pro" and "con" viewpoints, ending in an inconclusive synthesis or a plea that we must keep an open mind.

That circumstances are never to be settled with "pro" and "con" viewpoints ending with a synthesis is evident from the Confessions themselves: "Such an explanation must be thoroughly grounded in God's Word so that pure doctrine can be recognized and distinguished from adulterated doctrine.." (FC Tappert, Preface, Page 13); "In order to preserve the pure doctrine and to maintain a thorough, lasting, and God-pleasing concord within the church, it is essential not only to present the true and wholesome doctrine correctly, but also to accuse the adversaries who teach otherwise.." (FC Tappert, Page 506:14); "...find in the previously mentioned writings what he should accept as correct and true in each of the controverted articles of our Christian faith, according to the prophetic and apostolic writings of God's Word, and what he should reject, flee, and avoid as false and wrong...Insure that the truth may be established the most distinctly and clearly and be distinguished from all error.." (FC Tappert, Page 507:16); "...since within the past 25 years a number of divisions have occurred among some of the theologians...We wanted to set forth and explain our faith and Confession unequivocally, clearly, and distinctly in theses and antitheses, opposing the true doctrine to the false doctrine, so that the foundation of divine truth might be made apparent in every article.." (FC Tappert, Page 507:19); "...We have no intention (since we have no authority to do so) to yield anything of the eternal and unchangeable truth of God for the sake of temporal peace, tranquillity, and outward harmony." (FC Tappert, Page 632:95); "We wanted to set forth our position so clearly that our very adversaries would have to confess that in all these questions we abide by the true, simple, natural, and proper meaning of the Augsburg Confession...We do not propose to look on idly or stand by silently while something contrary to the Augsburg Confession is imported into our churches and schools.." (FC Tappert, Page 633:6).

It may well be, of course, that the kind of "speaking the truth in love" we have described will be misunderstood or even challenged. Some may regard our positive activity on behalf of the truth and unity of the church as negativism, or "protest action", or even as reactionary divisiveness. To those who see our activity as negative we must make it clear that we are for the truth of the Gospel and the true unity of the church and that, if the word protest is used, we protest only those things which oppose Scriptural truth and unity. Our words and actions must constantly evidence our commitment to the primary objective of the Synod, namely, "the conservation and promotion of the unity of the true faith". To those who may regard our zeal for confessing the truth as a divisive action we must insist that confessing the truth promotes unity, not division.

Our Synod will not be truly united unless and until it is united in the TRUTH! To **recognize** disunity in an attempt to overcome and heal it is not to **cause** disunity or to be divisive, any more than the proper diagnosis of a disease is to be confused with its cause. Luther's Reformation resulted in a divided Christendom, but would any among us seriously maintain that Luther promoted divisiveness rather than true spiritual unity? The history of the church is filled with many such examples where Christians have deemed God's requirements for the truth and unity of the church to be more important that man's notions of ecclesiastical peace and harmony. In the church it is especially true that sociological and psychological factors can never adequately explain doctrinal divisions.

The ultimate end of speaking the Word together for edification of us all is for mutual binding and loosing - a mutual care based on a mutual agreement in the Word. On that basis the church must expect all of us to do what we have agreed to do and vowed, and the church must make some judgments along the way which will only be erased finally on Judgment Day. The church must exercise its legitimate right of united defense against unscriptural doctrine and schism. it dare not be detracted by those who belittle the church's responsibility to discipline those who betray our fellowship as expressed in the Confessions and our public doctrine. All members should insist that the public doctrine of our Synod will be reflected as faithfully as possible and with courageous conviction by all Synodical institutions, publications, agencies, departments, as well as auxiliaries and affiliates.

Finally, we should remind ourselves and others in the Synod that once before in the history of confessional Lutheranism there was a titanic internal struggle for the preservation of the truth and unity of the Lutheran Church. We are referring to the bitter struggles which were carried on in the German Lutheran Church from Luther's death in 1546 and until 1577 when the Formula of Concord was signed. This confessional document is the product of many years of intensive and courageous effort on the part of the loyal Lutherans like Chemnitz and Andreae. We need to read the Formula again in these days, particularly the Preface and introductory and concluding paragraphs, for here we will find confessional guidance for the confessing church. Listen to some of these statements as they might apply to today's need:

"From our exposition friends and foes may clearly understand that we have no intention (since we have no authority to do so) to yield anything of the eternal and unchangeable truth of God for the sake of temporal peace, tranquillity, and outward harmony. Nor would such peace and harmony last, because it would be contrary to the truth and actually intended for it suppression. Still less by far are we minded to whitewash or cover up any falsification of true doctrine or any publicly condemned errors. We have a sincere delight in and deep love for true harmony and are cordially inclined and determined on our part to do everything in our power to further the same. We desire such harmony as will not violate God's honor, that will not detract anything from the divine truth of the holy Gospel, that will not give place to the smallest error but will lead the poor sinner to true and sincere repentance, raise him up through faith, strengthen him in his new obedience, and thus justify and save him for ever through the sole merit of Christ, and so forth." (FC XI, 95 and 96; Tappert p. 632)

"We wanted to set forth our position so clearly that our very adversaries would have to confess that in all these questions we abide by the true, simple, natural, and proper meaning of the Augsburg Confession. And we desire by God's grace to remain steadfastly in our commitment to this Confession until we die. As far as our ministry is concerned, we do not propose to look on idly or stand by silently while something contrary to the Augsburg Confession is imported into our churches and schools in which the almighty God and Father of our Lord Jesus Christ has appointed us teachers and shepherds." (FC XII, 6: Tappert p. 633)

"We wanted to set forth and explain our faith and confession unequivocally, clearly, and distinctly in theses and antitheses, opposing the true doctrine to the false doctrine, so that the foundation of divine truth might be made apparent in every article and that every incorrect, dubious, suspicious,and condemned doctrine might be exposed, no matter where or in what books it might be found or who may have said it or supported it. We did this so that we might thereby faithfully forewarn everyone against the errors contained here and there in the writings of certain theologians, lest anyone be misled by the high regard in which these theologians were held." (FC Rule and Norm, 19; Tappert p. 507)

Our Fathers recognized that there could be no true or lasting concord that was not based on the truth of God's Word. Like them, let us dedicate ourselves to being a confessing church. God's truth and the unity of His church demand nothing less!

*　　　　*　　　　*　　　　*　　　　*　　　　*

Evangelical and Confessional Lutherans Avoid the Left, Right and Middle

The formation of parties of the left and the right in the Missouri Synod has inflicted enormous damage which is difficult to calculate. The remaining parts of this book will give a summary of how the Synod was held hostage by the party of the left during the 1960's and 1970's, and how it is being held hostage by the party of the right in the early 1990's. As the organizer of the party of the right in 1964-1965 and being intent to keep on a Biblical track as closely as possible in response to the synodical takeover by the left, I believe that I can fairly recognize guerrilla warfare where it is present. I doubt that it is an overstatement to say that the Missouri Synod has experienced a spiritual Nicaragua and El Salvador where both the left and the right have run roughshod over their countrymen. The warriors become so self-centered and fearful that they no longer recognize their excesses. As much blood was shed in these countries, much bleeding has been experienced in the Missouri Synod by many. The Koreans have a saying that when the whales fight, the shrimp get hurt. Tens of thousands of "shrimp" have been hurt in the Missouri Synod, which will be seen as the actions of the left and the right are chronicled.

But first, we need to study what the Scriptures and Confessions say about being Biblical Christians, avoiding the organization of parties of either the right or the left, or allowing some to think that they are in the middle. An essay which I wrote but which did not receive broad circulation was written and presented especially on this subject in the early 1970's. This is as practical and urgent today as it was at that time. It is mainly an enlarged outline, and the reader will have to study the references personally, since there is neither time nor space to print them out.

PARTIES OF THE "LEFT" AND THE "RIGHT" - WILL THEY SPLIT THE CHURCH?

I. God reveals what His Church should be.

A. God's revelation of His Word presents God as the God of Truth (John 14:6; 18:37), the One who decides what the divine Law is (Ex. 20; Mt. 22:37-40), the One who also decides what the Gospel is (John 3:16).

B. God is a jealous God: He permits nobody to usurp or to be given His glory, whether this be amending, improving, or abrogating His Law (Gal. 3:10; Rom. 6:23a) or the Gospel (Mt. 28:20; Gal. 1:8, 9; 5:9, 12).

C. God's revealed Word, accordingly, demands complete loyalty by His children:

1. There is no place for a right or a left party where loyalty to God is concerned, for He requires **one** mind, voice, etc. - Rom. 15:5-6; 1 Cor. 1:10; 2 Cor.13:11.

2. The weak (i.e., "left" or "right") are to be tolerated for a time when they are really or truly weak and not overthrowing either the Gospel by insisting on their own brand (Gal. 1:6-9; 3:3; 4:9; 2 Tim. 2:17ff.) or overthrowing Scripture by insisting on their opinions in opposition to clear Scripture (Eph. 2:20-22; 2 Tim. 3:16ff.).

D. It is God's will that the visible church have, teach, and confess the entire doctrine of the Word of God and administer the sacraments according to Christ's institution.

1. The important question: What message do we have for the world? What does the church say to the world? This has already been decided by Christ and God's Word. Men's words must be judged by God's Words. Importance of words: In life; in God's Word (Mt. 12:36 37; Mt. 22:29; John 12:48 49; John 17:17; Luke 4:32, 36; 1 Cor. 2:13; 1 Thes. 2:13; Jer. 16:2; Rev. 22:19). The Bible presents God as the One who reveals Truth (John 14:6; 18:37). Lutheran Confessions: The Word of God does not lie, can-

not fail (Tappert, 213:20; 444:13), the Holy Spirit knows what He has written (122:108), only through the Word does God make Himself known and understood (116:67; 217:17; 471:13) the devil and our natural disposition drives us to scorn the Word (302:2; 378:99; 434:104; 623:41).

2. We see this from the fact that God insists that His congregations have faithful pastors, and beware of false teachers, and on having His congregations maintain pure doctrine and practice, reproving those who depart from His Word.

3. Accordingly, the visible church can authorize and tolerate only one doctrine, the God-revealed doctrine (only one Gospel, the one taught in Scripture). The Evangelical Lutheran Church has one Gospel, the Scriptural Gospel, not added to, nor subtracted from. It requires a Gospel-believing, Scripture-obeying, group of people, united in confession of the faith and in practice. God requires one voice and one view and one mind in missions: Rom. 15:5-6; 1 Cor. 1:10; 2 Cor. 13:11; Gal. 5:10; Phil. 1:27, 4:2; 1 Pet. 3:8. No unity with diversity in doctrine! It is a mistake to assume that the position of the true visible church may well be a middle position between the party of the right and the party of the left. No middle position, only one position - the Scriptural position.

4. Christ's Word divides even as it unites - John 6:60-62, 66; Mt. 10:34-49; Mt. 12:30. The Bible is a book about polarization - resulting from conflicting attitudes about Christ, the Scriptures themselves, the Gospel, attitudes about the nature and mission of the church. Polarization is what the Christian message is all about - the contrasting positions of darkness and light, of death and life, of judgment and forgiveness, of despair and hope. Neutrality is impossible, for polarization is inevitable - either for or against the truth, Gospel, pure doctrine. Avoid divisions that are not of God or are mere quarreling.

E. The Evangelical Lutheran Church, where not degenerate, is not congenial to dissent from its doctrinal position, does not condone anybody who wishes to have the freedom to deviate from its confessions. Thus it cannot allow room for three parties: left, right and middle - only one position. The very thought of tolerating a position within the Synod other than the Scriptural position is repugnant to every faithful member in the LCMS, and he is supported in this attitude by the Confessions and LCMS constitution. God tells us that Satan will always attack His Word, cause uncertainty and confusion about the Word, even that there will be false teachers. How could the Missouri Synod be the one exception?

F. Today some are calling those who hold to the traditional LCMS position fundamentalists or Biblicists - that is, rightists. This cannot by tolerated. The church needs to be awakened to her dangers: to the sinfulness of sin; to the dangers of apathy and indifferences; to the dangers of loss of "first love" in doctrine and practice.

II. The Church cannot be split.

A. The **unity of the church** (die Einigkeit der Kirche, Unitas Ecclesiae) is a divine work. Men can neither create nor destroy (fracture) the unity of the church of which Augsburg VII speaks. This unity is created by the Holy Spirit when "He calls, gathers...the whole Christian Church on earth, and keeps it with Jesus Christ in the one true faith" (S.C. 3rd Article). In the unity created by the Spirit there is "no sect or schism" (Tappert 417:51). This true spiritual unity men cannot destroy - they are capable only of forsaking it, defecting in unbelief.

III. The unity in the church (die Einigkeit in der Kirche, concordia, consensus, tranquilitas

in ecclesia) **can be disrupted by dissension, controversy, discord**, and by political parties of the left or right.

(Note: When the Symbols refer to the **unity** of the church, they use the terms **Einigkeit** and **unitas** with the genitives **der Kirche** and **ecclesiae**. When the Symbols refer to concord in the church they use the term **Einigkeit** and Latin equivalents such as **concordia, consensio,** etc., with the prepositional phrase **in** der Kirche and **in** ecclesiae.)

A. Lutherans deplore discord (99:15-16; 195:90). They desire harmony and concord (25:2-4; 26:13; 222:52; 242-59). They deplore discord by reason of its **evil origin** - Satan, "foe of mankind" (Pages 3-4), and by reason of the **damage** it does:

1. Because it is never without offense (502:7-8).
2. Because it causes anguish (201:127-128).
3. Because it tears churches apart (140:232 and 236).
4. Because it obstructs the course of the Gospel, and the pure, unadulterated Word of God (Tappert, Page 4).

B. Lutherans do everything possible to settle controversy and to restore harmony (26:13).

1. Lutherans attempt to settle controversy **not** by agreeing to differ or by sanctioning diversity. They believe differences ought to be carefully and accurately explained (Page 6) and that error should not excused (503:9-5). They suggest love towards weakness in deeds (139:232; 141:243), but doctrinal errors are not to be tolerated.

2. They attempt to settle controversy by working for unanimity, and to this end they
   a. expose and refute error (Page 6; 506:14).
   b. patiently keep on repeating their confession in the hope that dissenters will be persuaded (Page 5-6; Page 12).
   c. recommend the use of "sound words" to avoid misunderstanding (557:36).
   d. suggest diligent visits to their schools and even censorship! (Page 14).

C. Lutherans, nevertheless, acknowledge that under certain circumstances, controversy is necessary - 1 Cor. 11:18-19 (503:9-10), and therefore the "Biblical Christian" in opposition to the party of the "left" or of the "right" will "split the church" in the sense of causing **necessary** controversy for political parties which have **already** disrupted the unity **in** the church. Censures and condemnations cannot be avoided (Page 11).

IV. Who is splitting or polarizing the church?

A. Professing and living by Biblical and confessional standards are not options, for we cannot tolerate them, for we must reject situations where the fundamental articles of faith are reinterpreted within the framework of process philosophy, and where having repudiated the notion of substance, they reject also Christ's essential deity, deny ethical absolutes, empty sin of guilt, make redemption a process, etc. Beware when some defend their theology and actions in the name of "reconciliation" and demand a "diversity" which God does not tolerate. This is not political or social, but the basic issue is **theological**. "Reconciliation" does not mean "capitulation" or "acquiescence" for a false unity in the church.

B. If we are true to the Scriptures and Confessions, we will sometimes be forced to say with Luther, "Expect no fellowship from me" (575:33). We cannot tolerate, therefore: those who **say** that they are faithful to the Scriptures and Confessions, but say and do things which contradict their confession; who call legalistic, loveless, biblicists and fundamentalists those who accept faithfully the truths of the Scriptures and the Confessions; those who are orthodox in doctrine by disobedient to the 8th Commandment and fail to practice the truth. **Honesty** insists that when the Synod has a **lodge** position (Handbook), no options are allowed. Errors are not to be allowed under any situation or at any cost (503:9).

C. If we are to be faithful, God allows us no options.

1. The battle is real, not imagined, and it is growing in intensity (Eph. 6:10-18).

2. The weapons are spiritual, not organizational; divine, not worldly or political (2 Cor. 10:3-5).

3. The battleground is for the minds of men that they may be obedient to the mind of Christ (2 Cor. 10:5; Rom. 12:2).

4. The issue is the truthfulness of the divine revelation as Christ has revealed in the Holy Scriptures, and God will not allow us to condone an errant inerrant Bible (2 Tim. 4:1-5; 2 Pet. 1:16-21; 2:1-3), or false practice.

5. Historic, Biblical Christianity is at stake, not only Confessional Lutheranism.

*   *   *   *   *

Politics and Influence in the Church

The LCMS Council of Presidents, on Nov. 18, 1988 issued a statement, *The Ministry of Influence in the Church* (commended by the 1989 Witchita Convention), which concluded that there is such a thing as wholesome politics as well as evil or destructive politics in the church. That document makes some important suggestions which the Biblical Lutheran needs to consider:

"To influence is a privilege, right and responsibility that every member, pastor, teacher, voter, delegate, etc., possesses...If properly understood and used, 'politics' is the **art** of influencing others...sharing or promoting an idea, philosophy, candidate, or opinion...It can thus be a wholesome responsibility to offer solutions for problems and to seek the support of and for others. Such a Ministry of Influence should both be encouraged and facilitated in the life of the congregation and its voters etc., as well as in the life of the district and Synod.

"...Responsible influence will bless and not curse and will seek to live in harmony. Such love in the Ministry of Influence will be careful to do what is right, wise, and helpful, will not use evil means to achieve its ends, will not repay evil for evil but will attempt to live at peace. (Romans 12:9-21) The Ministry of Influence in its purest sense cannot gloss over or tolerate wrong; it must instead strive to both possess and communicate the **truth**.

"Therefore, we are not to abuse this Ministry by acts of covetousness, by sins against the Fourth and Eighth Commandments, nor by demanding our own way, degrading another person and striving to get our own way (self-serving). Regardless of our desired ends, exalted as they may be, we cannot attempt to attain them through destroying, controlling, hating, promoting one at the expense of another or appealing to base human nature. We can also demean or seek self-serving control by accusing others of some destructive influence or activity when in fact **they truly may be acting responsibly**.

"A responsible Ministry of Influence will not seek to be 'a party of power' in the Church. Instead, it will seek to live under the only power, which is the Word...

"The power in the Church, therefore, is not, not ever shall be, politics, persons, programs, presidents, District or Synodical staff, political groups or cliques. It does not lie in the structures, societies, synodical headquarters or seminaries. The power is not in communication media, communication networks or communication tools.

"The Word of God is to be **the** influence in the Church and its life. It is **the** 'inflow' in the voter's assemblies, in meetings and in conventions...under the influence of the Word which shapes our own influence into a loving and caring exercise that is both responsible in itself and seeks to lead others to be responsible both to God and to one another. Any other influence needs to be resisted and uprooted in the church."

Additional suggestions in this document on the proper use of influence "means understanding of the deliberative process, includes the objective evaluation of all needs of a congregation or the Synod, which involves an awareness of and study of all the issues as we face them within the context of putting the best construction on everything under Christ. We must also realize that those who serve have the responsibility to serve in the best interests of the church and its purposes. This means that we welcome constructive criticism, rebuttal and open debate." The document rightfully warns against use of "election lists" which by inference means that people who are not on the list may be innocently associated as degradation of the election process and character assassination.

Regarding abuses, the document states that they "can occur when we **allow** people, friends and peers to believe things that are not true; when we judge and advise without having the jurisdiction to do so or when we judge or advise without the full facts; when we seek to influence by threats (such as withholding of money); when we supposedly are representing a 'great number' but in fact are representing only ourselves; when our own inflow keeps others from practicing their priesthood rights; when we seek to set the agenda for the Church instead of allowing the elected officials from carrying out their elected responsibilities; when we seek to control instead of influence; when we have a Church within a Church; when we meddle in the affairs of others or assume a charge or call that has not been given to us."

Seeking Renewal in Doctrine and Practice

The situation in the LCMS generally illustrates the need for two kinds of renewal: doctrinal and spiritual. Doctrinal renewal is a necessity for many more than we may realize because they have been caught in the web of the theological aberrations which infects our congregations through our culture. Spiritual renewal is a challenge because of various conditions that vary between congregations, such as activism, dead orthodoxy, lack of discipline, failure to disciple and edify, lukewarm evangelism, and maintenance stewardship.

Many Missouri Lutherans know things are not right, but they do not know the combination to the lock that opens the door to renewal. They hold an idealism without pursuing questions too deeply, so that ecclesiasticism or churchianity keep dissipating the roots and spontaneity of faith and vision. Many perceive an imbalance between form and living faith, doctrine and practice, and vision and reality, but they allow the urgent to crowd out the important because maintenance or survival demands immediate action.

Most people are inclined to the **status quo** and do not want to rock the boat. Many congregations do not seem to know how to untangle the web of wrong priorities. Most difficult is change in ourself. A mentality that allows mere maintenance salves consciences as another "quick fix" is used to keep the church going another month, another year.

From a human viewpoint, many face an enslavement to a pietism which confuses and improperly separates the spiritual and the physical, the perceived and reality, the internal and the external. Churches become deluded by statistics utilized in a way that soothes fretful minds and satisfies human expectations.

The struggle sometimes centers on some of the following issues:

1. Doctrinal relativism rather than Biblical integrity;

2. Obscurantism in communication rather than being relevant in life and practice;

3. Institutional self-centered rather than mission-centered;

4. Laity are **objects** of religious care and consumers of church resources rather than **agents** - servants and witnesses of God's saving love;

5. Leaders legitimatize and parcel out activities rather than disciple the members to be active in service and witness on the basis of 2 Tim. 2:2 and Eph. 4:12, 16;

6. Goal of better church members rather than stronger Christians.

Biblical history shows that renewal usually began in an individual servant of God, who then became God's instrument to stir up the people to become aware of their spiritual decline and the need for a closer walk with God. It rested on a powerful and clear proclamation of the prophetic Word of God. It was marked by genuine worship of God and the destruction of idols that blocked the acknowledgment of Him as the true and living Lord. Repentance of sin and separation from its control and slavery were followed by forgiveness, which then provided unbounded gladness and the joy of great service to God.

Before urging churches to have a five-year program or plan in hope to stir up the people, our leaders should place before the people the heavenly vision named in Prov. 29:18, "Where there is no vision (proclamation of the Word to God's people), the people perish (break away, cast off restraint, become unmanageable)." There should be no question that the Word works.

This vision and Biblical knowledge will center on pure theology and practice. Can we honestly face the fact that our Synod's problems are much deeper than personalities, procedures and protocol? As briefly and accurately as possible the tragic mistakes of our recent history are recounted in these pages: 1. disobeying Truth and Biblical principles; 2. forming and utilizing political organizations and activities which corrupt the Biblical system; 3. the Synod itself either through the bureaucracy or through being politically captured by an interest group fails to follow Scriptural precepts.

Dr. O. H. Pannkoke published his own story from Quitman, GA in 1966 under the title, *A Great Church Finds Itself*, which reveals one incident in the Synod's history which is not a happy one. His account and book cannot be dismissed simply as coming from some ecumenical liberal within our midst in the past. Dr. John C. Baur, long-time columnist for Christian News during the latter part of his life, wrote about Pannkokes' book, "It is good that you have taken time out to record the undertakings in which you have played a vital role, especially since some of them were inaugurated by you,...and the rest profited greatly by your intense drive for progress. It would be difficult to point to another man who has tackled more difficult tasks and succeeded in them as you have."

Pannkoke tells of reactionary forces within the Synod which failed to pursue proper policies and which showed partiality on the basis of personal biases. He obviously was very successful in fund-raising for various institutions in all Lutheran bodies. There may have been some legitimate concerns about statements or positions related to ecumenical relations or doctrinal differences with other Lutheran bodies, but these should be dealt with an evangelical Biblical manner, not high-handed as they seemed to be. Pages 239-243 record Pannkoke's story [12]:

"By a strange quirk of fortune I became the object of reactionary opposition again in the 30's. It brought me the bitterest experience of my life. Some of the leaders of reaction moved heaven and earth to excommunicate me...

"While my program to meet a changing world was little understood and untried in the early 20's, by the 30's it had proved itself in all the ventures described above. No argument remained whether it was right or not. The Missouri Synod, too, profited from my work. It faced identically the same problems as the other Lutheran synods. Especially the younger men, facing the changed church life of the cities, were impatient with the hostility toward new methods and toward other Lutherans. They were friendly toward my program and admired my achievements...

"The future looked bright, when, out of a clear blue sky disaster truck again. In 1933 I was sued for divorce. It was a personal tragedy, but the reactionary group used this tragedy to discredit and condemn me. Until 1947 I was under a relentless attack whose purpose was to excommunicate me. The issue against me in 1916 had been unionism, associating with other Lutherans. Unionism had lost its sting by the 30's. The new issue of the divorce was more promising. It could be used to ruin my character with those who did not know me and with those who knew me superficially, and so it was used for fourteen long years. It was only in 1947, after years of bitter heartaches, great expense, and endless fighting to clear my good name, that the Synod at the Centennial Convention was compelled to vindicate me and clear my name.

"The story of this development and the way in which it was used by the reactionaries is told in full in the five issues of *The Smith Case Reporter*. They were sent to every pastor of the Missouri Synod. It will suffice here to touch the high points.

"When the attack on me began, I faced it in the belief that justice would prevail. To my amazement, I soon discovered that no system of justice existed in the Missouri Synod. The church officials were the prosecutors, the judges, and the executioners. The very foundation of justice, judicial procedure, was unknown.

"Justice was completely political. One church official would mark a man and as a matter of comity, all other officials would support him, The machine closed ranks...

"When I realized this, it became clear to me that I had no chance unless a real system of justice were established in Synod. That was the purpose of *The Smith Case Reporter*. It was published in 1941 just before the Ft. Wayne Convention of the Synod...The upshot was that the Ft. Wayne convention adopted a system of justice and of fair judicial procedure.

"The highest tribunal in the new system was the general synodical Board of Appeals. I immediately presented my case to this board and in due course of time they completely vindicated me. According to the rules officially adopted at Synod in 1941 the decision of the Board of Appeals must be presented at the next Synod, which must elect a Committee of Review. This committee was to determine whether any procedural errors were made by the Board of Appeals and whether new evidence has been produced. If it reports negatively on both counts then the Synod must adopt the decision of the Board of Appeals and close the case."

An account is then given by Pannkoke that a Committee on Review was elected. It found no error in procedure and no new evidence, and reported this to the Saginaw Convention in 1944. Pannkoke's book tells how prominent officials took the floor and passionately supported a resolution to try the case again from the beginning, and the resolution carried, "The implication was clear that they wanted Pannkoke condemned and were willing to flagrantly violate the newly-established judicial system to achieve their ends. Who would not conclude that the defenders of orthodoxy forget all about justice and fair play when they are hunting down a 'heretic'?"

Pannkoke then tells about receiving a letter from the Chairman of the "unconstitutional rump Board of Appeals" requesting him to appear and defend himself. He replied that his case had been closed according to the Constitution, that their appointment was unconstitutional, and that if they insisted on proceeding, he would defend himself before the proper authority. He heard nothing further from anyone. Before the 1947 Convention in Chicago, he arranged for a prominent attorney to secure an injunction to prevent the Missouri Synod from any unconstitutional action against him.

Pannkoke writes, "Synod appointed a Committee to review the case. After bitter wrangling, the Committee reported that the Synod had erred in 1944 in appointing the rump Board of Appeals to retry the case from the beginning. It recommended that the decision of the Board of Appeals vindicating me be adopted. This was done."

He concludes his book by recording, "I have endeavored never to betray a friend, nor to turn my back on an enemy, to guard the sacredness of my word, to have the courage of my convictions, to be a free man."

The only reason for recounting this story is to emphasize the issue that the Synod's leaders have sometimes found it difficult to deal with members with whom they disagree and sometimes have found it difficult to deal with conflict. Conflict is to be expected, but we must also expect that we will know how to deal with it Biblically. As today, there have been times when we tended to try to annihilate rather than rehabilitate; indeed, sometimes we have failed to identify what the real issues are or to "speak the truth in love." Instead, we find it easier to attack people.

The rest of this book will deal with major events of the past 30 years which tend to find us allowing or getting into political fights and using clever tactics rather than keeping focused on Biblical procedures.

We will review the battles fought by the parties of the left and of the right, and we will propose deeper insights into the theology and practice related to politics in the church as they pertain to varying conditions, elections, controlling through politics, and perverting the system. We will look at how the Biblical system can easily be corrupted, and how Biblical Lutherans are to utilize their political influence within the system.

Chapter 5

THE PARTY OF THE LEFT HOLDS THE SYNOD HOSTAGE

THE PARTY OF THE LEFT CAPTURES THE ST. LOUIS SEMINARY, PUBLICA-TIONS, LUTHERAN LAYMEN'S LEAGUE, AND CONTROLS THE SYNOD'S ADMINISTRATION

Government in the church is necessary to organize activities which are necessary so that the Word of God may be proclaimed according to a pure understanding and the Sacraments rightly administered. While there are no divinely prescribed ways in which to organize such activities, the Synod provides adjudication policies to protect the rights of congregations, pastors, and others. As such, the Synod's Constitution includes as one of its objectives, "To provide protection for congregations, pastors, teachers, and other church workers in the performance of their official duties and the maintenance of their rights" (Const. III, 9).

The Synod is not merely advisory to the congregations, pastors and teachers in doctrine, but is given express authority to supervise the doctrine, life, and the administration of pastors and teachers (XII, 7), including the power to suspend and expel (XII, 8; XII, 3-4)

We properly expect our Synod to maintain the absolute authority of Holy Scripture as the only rule and norm for faith and life, and the acceptance of the Lutheran Confessions without reservation, as the true and correct exposition of the sacred Scriptures. We also expect the maintenance of the right of self-government of congregations in all matters not commanded or forbidden by the Word of God, and to provide judicial procedures for removal of those who are disobedient. Such administration at all times is governed completely by the Word of God, not by business administrative philosophies or political considerations.

Our historic Synodical and congregational polity or practice is built on an intense desire to be truly faithful to God and His Word as we know them also in the Lutheran Confessions. Though God expects us to be consistent in doctrine and practice, such dependability has been too scarce in some Districts and many congregations. A member of Synod cannot be assured in going from congregation to congregation or district to district that he will receive even-handed leadership and treatment in a dependable or consistent manner in keeping with Synodical policy.

My research reviewed the evidence and accounts of over 30 years of Missouri's history of conflict, ransacking very many full boxes and file trays of primary materials, and also rummaging through all issues of *Christian News*, *Missouri in Perspective*, and *Affirm* magazines. For one who cares for and loves his Synod, this was an extremely traumatic experience and caused considerable, emotional pain.

In order to provide a credible analysis and observations of the tragic Synodical conflicts, such probing was necessary. There is so much primary material that should be reported and summarized that it would take three or four books to cover it adequately. However, producing just one volume at this time forces summarization of evidence at most points. Obviously, it pays to keep accurate notes and files in all committee and church work, and this has become very helpful not only for writing this book, but also for the future if any protagonists wish to debate the accuracy of the facts or conclusions which are presented.

Chapter 4 presented the account of the action of the "Faith Forward - First Concerns" action of many of us in early 1965, and also of the beginning of the organization of synodical loyalists who were ready to take a stand against the intrusion of false doctrine and practice into our Synod. At this time, highlights of some of the events of those days will be recounted.

Two Laymen Share Their Concerns With The Synod

Roy H. Guess of Casper, Wyoming, sent a letter, "To All Missouri Synod Lutherans," in 1966 to all pastors in order to share his experience of liberal tendencies in the Methodist and Presbyterian churches from which he came, which he now recognized in his new LCMS church home. He warned that Missouri Synod Lutherans should not say that what happened in other Protestant churches cannot happen here, too. He had never been inside any Lutheran church before he visited Mt. Hope in Casper, and he wrote, 'We knew immediately that the Holy Spirit was truly in this church through the Word. We thought we had found the perfect church home. Today, our joy has turned to apprehension and sadness...yes, even frustration.'

Then he reports of his concerns in reading the *Lutheran Witness* and the *Reporter* of that day, noting that some of the same aberrations he experienced in the other churches were now appearing in Missouri Synod publications. He noted that the *Lutheran Witness* at that time was promoting one side of controversial issues while failing to confess the true Biblical truths. He complained about the ridicule of orthodox Lutherans and groups. His 17-page letter, which was also sent to thousands of laymen ended by encouraging everyone to be a "concerned Christian."

An address given by Marcus Braun of Kansas City at an LLL Zone Rally, at St. John's in Clinton, IA, on March 7, 1967, also received tremendous response throughout Synod, as did the letter by Roy Guess. Like Guess, Braun stated that he first became concerned about doctrinal deviations in the Synod when he read questionable articles in the *Lutheran Witness*. He told of a personal visit with a St. Louis Seminary professor at that time who preferred to believe that the Scriptures are true in the same sense that Aesop's Fables "are true" or Greek or Roman mythology "are true" since they demonstrate certain moral lessons for us to learn. This professor asserted that Genesis was not inerrant because a serpent has no vocal cords, and therefore could not speak to Eve. Braun challenged statements by this professor in the Sept. 1965, CTM (Concordia Theological Monthly) which stated, "It does not seem to this writer that we are serving the best interests of the church when either we continue formally to reaffirm the inerrancy of the sacred Scriptures or even continue to employ the term." He quoted a professor from River Forest who questioned the fact that Jonah was three days in the belly of a fish and that Moses wrote the Pentateuch. He also gave instances of professors proposing evolution.

The sad part of this is that even after various documents such as these were published with evidence of doctrinal deviations, the synodical administration together with the Council of Presidents were totally incapable or unwilling to bring the errant brothers back to a confessional Lutheran position.

Former President John W. Behnken Expresses Grave Concerns

The "Faith Forward - First Concerns" movement received broad participation from pastors and laymen on all levels of the Synod. These concerns came not from hearsay, but from actual experiences of people who had sons, relatives, or friends at the Seminary or who had heard Seminary professors speak at different conferences or meetings, or had read firsthand in the *Lutheran Witness* and *Reporter* what had been said. During 1966, former President John W. Behnken visited in South Wisconsin to make presentations for the Lutheran Church Foundation, which provided an opportunity for a number of personal visits with him. Some of these visits were in my office at the South Wisconsin District headquarters in Milwaukee. He told of his deep anxiety over the change of doctrine in the Synod and stated that he wished that he had known 8-10 years before what he knew at the present, because then he would have acted entirely differently in his presidency. He also stressed his conviction that he now believed that several prominent figures at the St. Louis Seminary (which he named) had lied to him.

In one of his visits with me in the South Wisconsin District Office, Dr. Behnken mentioned the questions which he had given to then St. Louis President Fuerbringer, but never received any answers. All he received was assurances that everything was well. Dr. Behnken indicated that he would like to send these questions to the Council of Presidents (District Presidents and Synod Praesidium), but he did not have a secretary or an office to do that. When I volunteered to help him get them mimeographed, he gratefully accepted the offer. His letter shows that I sent these for him to the Council of Presidents, the Boards of Control, the members of the theological faculties, and the Religion Departments at our Teacher's Colleges. On March 16, 1967, Dr. Behnken wrote me, "Let me assure you that I am glad that you saved the mimeograph stencils of the document, "QUESTIONS CONCERNING SOME STATEMENTS IN GOD'S HOLY WORD." He then made a request to have more copies printed and to send some to Dr. William A. Buege, who was to give them to the Valparaiso University Department of Religion. He sent this letter to the Council of Presidents and his 28 questions of the St. Louis Faculty which were never answered.

March 6, 1967

TO ALL MEMBERS OF THE COUNCIL OF PRESIDENTS

Dear Brother in Christ:

Enclosed you will please find a mimeographed copy of "SOME QUESTIONS CONCERNING SOME STATEMENTS OF GOD'S HOLY WORD."

After attending two meetings of the COUNCIL OF PRESIDENTS and the THEOLOGICAL FACULTIES I was troubled very much. I wrote down a number of questions and referred to the many passages of Holy Writ in which God gives His answers. Next I presented these to two good theologians of our Synod (not members of any faculties of our Seminaries or Colleges). These men urged me to proceed.

On August 6, 1966 I mailed the questions, as I am presenting them to you, to the President of the Seminary, Dr. A. O. Fuerbringer. We have had some correspondence about them. Dr. Fuerbringer stated that he wanted to assure me that the Bible account of creation is not to be judged in the light of the theory or philosophy of evolution, and that the text must be interpreted as it stands there. But he then referred to Joshua 10:12-14, pointing out that there we depart from the literal sense just because it does not fit the Copernican theory. He also sought to explain why some of the professors have spoken as they did. But we have come to no conclusion by this correspondence.

The President is informed about my intention to send copies of the questions to the COUNCIL OF PRESIDENTS, THE BOARDS OF CONTROL and the MEMBERS OF THE THEOLOGICAL FACULTIES, etc. I should have mentioned also the BOARDS OF CONTROL and the DEPARTMENTS OF RELIGION at our TEACHERS COLLEGES. I called attention to the fact that this is really a "public" matter which has been discussed rather publicly. Some of it has appeared in print. Furthermore, some of the men have spoken to conferences in different parts of our Synod.

On January 1, 1967 I informed our Synod's President, Dr. Oliver R. Harms, what I had done. I also mentioned my intention to send copies to the persons mentioned above. I assured him that I did not want to interfere with him and his work in the least. In fact, just the opposite is true. I had a very fine letter from him.

The above as well as the mimeographed questions indicate that I am very much concerned. I know that this is true also of others in many parts of Synod. Of course, I realize full well that I am not an **official** of Synod. But I am a **member** of Synod. As such I am deeply concerned. I sincerely hope that these questions, especially the Bible texts will be truly beneficial and of real service. May they move many to pray fervently and work earnestly and zealously that our Synod may remain unwaveringly faithful and unswervingly loyal to the precious, divinely inspired and hence infallible Word of God, and to our Lutheran Confessions as a correct interpretation of this Word of God. May God graciously grant it!

Wishing you God's choicest blessings

Yours in Christ,

John W. Behnken

-      -   -   -

SOME QUESTIONS CONCERNING SOME STATEMENTS IN GOD'S HOLY WORD

by Dr. John W. Behnken

Some present day theologians hold that God's account of creation is not to be taken literally, factually or historically, but must be understood as a legend, a parable, a symbol, a myth, etc. The term "Symphony of Creation" also has been used.

Some other accounts in Scripture, even Books of Scripture, have been subjected to similar treatment.

Modern discoveries, advanced learning in the natural sciences, the "refinement" of the term "evolution" to "theistic evolution" etc., are given as reasons for this new approach to the accounts in God's holy Word.

Then there are those who hold that where the traditional and the new interpretations of Scripture are in conflict with each other we must grant the new interpretations equal rights, regard them as optional, mere alternatives, and hence permissible.

In view of the above I have a number of questions concerning some of the accounts which God has given in the Pentateuch. I am especially eager to know what position the present day theologians of my dear Alma Mater, Concordia Seminary, are taking. My earnest request and fervent plea is that I be given frank, conscientious answers on the basis of Scripture, God's holy Word.

1) Must God's historical account of the world's creation in Genesis 1 and 2 be judged in the light of the theory of evolution? Or must the theory of evolution be judged in the light of Scripture? Is this an optional matter? If so, why? If not, why not? Please refer also to Ex. 20:11; Ne. 9:6; Ps. 19:1, 24:1-2, 33:6, 33:9, 95:3-6, 96:5, 102:25, 121:2, 146:5-6, 148:5; Is. 40:18-28, 45:12; Jer. 10:10-13, 32:17; John 1:3; Acts 4:24, 14:15, 17:24; Rom. 1:20; 1 Cor. 8:6; Eph. 3:9; Col. 1:16; Heb. 1:1-2, 1:8-10, 3:4, 11:3; Rev. 4:11.

2) Is God's account of man's creation, as recorded in Gen. 1:16-17 and Gen. 2:18-25 factual, or must it be interpreted in the light of "theistic evolution?" Or is this optional? If so, why? If not, why not? Please refer also to Gen. 5:1-2; Deut. 4:32; Job 33:6; Ps. 100:3;

Is. 51:13; Col. 3:10; James 3:9.

3) Did the devil actually speak through the serpent as recorded in Gen. 3:1-5? Cf. Rev. 12:9, 20:2. Or is this merely a legend: Is this optional and permissible? If so, why? If not, why not? - Is there anything to the argument advanced against the serpent's speaking: "The serpent has no vocal chords?" Did Balaam's ass, which had no human vocal chords, speak to Balaam as recorded in Numbers 22:28-30? Did God's angels, who are spirits and have no vocal chords, speak and sing to the shepherds on Bethlehem's plains as recorded in Luke 2:8-14? Did God, Who is a Spirit, (John 4:24) and has no vocal chords, speak to man again and again?

4) Did God actually plant a real "garden eastward in Eden" in which "He made to grow every tree that is pleasant to the sight and good for food" of which He said: "Of every tree of the garden thou mayest freely eat; but of the tree of the knowledge of good and evil, thou shalt not eat of it; for in the day that thou eatest thereof thou shalt surely die," Gen. 2:8-17? Please refer also to Gen. 3:23; Is. 51:3; Ezek. 28:13, 31:9, 36:35; Joel 2:3. Or is all this merely a legend? May the 'legend interpretation' stand alongside the clear statements of God's Word? Is this optional, permissible? If so, why? If not, why not?

5) Did Adam and Eve actually eat "of the fruit of the tree in the midst of the garden" (Gen. 3:3)and thereby bring sin, death and eternal damnation on all mankind? Please refer also to Gen. 3:19; Rom. 5:12, 6:23; 1 Cor. 15:21. Or is all this merely a legend? May the "legend explanation" stand alongside the clear Word of God? Is this optional? If so, why? If not, why not?

6) Is the Messianic prophecy in Eden, Gen. 3:15, factual, historical? Or is this merely a myth which must be demythologized, or merely a beautiful legend, or a part of the "Symphony of creation"? May both explanations stand side by side? Is this an optional matter? If so, why? If not, why not? Cf. Rom. 16:20; Heb. 2:14; 1 John 3:8.

7) Did Cain actually murder his brother Abel as recorded in Gen. 4:1-15? Please refer to Matt. 23:35; 1 John 3:12. Or is this a myth, a legend? May both interpretations be permitted? If so, why? If not, why not? If we permit such explanations of God's account in the foregoing questions, why not also here?

8) Is the account which God gives of the world's destruction by the flood in Gen. 7, actual history? Or is this merely a myth or a legend? Please refer to 1 Peter 3:19-22; 2 Peter 3:1-10. Are both interpretations permissible? If so, why? If not, why not? If we say, "It is optional" in answers to questions one to six, why not here?

9) Are the seven years of plenty followed by seven years of famine, as recorded in Gen. 41, history or legend? If the interpretation, "a myth, a legend" is permitted in answer to questions one to six, why not here?

10) Were Jacob and his sons and their cattle and their goods, which they had gotten in the land of Canaan, Gen. 46:5-7, actually brought down to Egypt because of the famine? id Joseph provide for them by speaking to Pharaoh to grant them the land of Goshen? Please refer to Gen. 45:16-28, 46:28-34, 47:1-12. Or is this merely a legend or a myth? May we permit the latter interpretation to stand alongside of God's inspired account? Is this interpretation optional? If so, why? If not, why not? Is not the answer, "It is a legend, it is a myth" just as proper here as it would be in questions one to six?

11) Did the children of Israel actually become slaves some time after Joseph's death, as recorded in Ex. 1:7-14? Or is this merely a legend? May the latter interpretation be accepted alongside of the account which God has given? If so, why? If not, why not? If we permit it in answer to questions one to six, why not here?

12) Is the marvelous deliverance which God provided through Moses, the so-called exodus, factual, historic? Please refer to Gen. 46 to Ex. 13. Or is this merely a legend or a myth? May the latter explanation be permitted alongside of God's account? If so, why?

If not, why not? If it is permitted in answer to questions one to six, why not here?

13) Is the account of Israel's passing through the Red Sea with the "waters a wall unto them on their right hand and on their left" because Moses, according to God's account "stretched out his hand over the sea", Ex. 14:15-22, as well as the other miraculous help which God granted them, e.g., the pillar of a cloud or the pillar of fire, real, factual, historic? Ex. 15. Or is this merely a myth or a legend? If so, why? If not, why not?

14) Is God's account of the daily manna and quail in the wilderness - except on the Sabbath - according to Ex. 16:11-36, factual, historic, or is this a myth or a legend? Is it actually true that when some gathered more than they needed, v. 20, it "bred worms and stank" except when on Friday they "gathered twice as much" v. 22, and on the Sabbath "it did not stink, neither was there any worm therein" v. 24, or is this a mere myth or a legend? Could the latter explanation be permitted to stand alongside of God's account? If so, why? If not, why not? If it is permitted in answer to questions one to six, why not here? Cf. John 6:31, 6:49.

15) What about water out of the rocks when Moses smote them with the rod, and the quantities sufficient for the people and the cattle according to Ex. 17:1-7 and Number 20:11? Please refer also to Neh. 9:15; Ps. 105:41, 114:8; Isaiah 48:21. Is this factual, historic, or merely a myth or a legend? May we permit the latter explanation to stand alongside to God's account? If so, why? If not, why not? If it is permitted to answer to questions one to six, why not here?

16) In Ex. 17:8-16 God gives His account of the battle against the Amalekites. Moses had the rod of God in his hand. When he held up his hand Israel prevailed. When he let down his hand the Amalekites prevailed. When his hands were heavy, Aaron and Hur stayed up his hands. Thus Israel defeated the Amalekites. Is this factual, historic, or is it a legend? May the explanation that it is a legend stand alongside of God's account? If so, why? If not, why not? If we permit it in answer to the first six questions, why not here?

17) Did God actually give the law as Ex. 19 and 20 have recorded it? Did God speak amidst lightnings and thunderings? Did the mountain smoke? (Ex. 20:18) Did the people stand afar off? (Ex. 20:21) Did God say, "Ye have seen that I have talked with you from heaven?"? (Ex. 20:22) Is all this factual, historic? Or may we call it legend? May both interpretations stand side by side? If so, why? If not, why not? If we permit it in questions one to six, why not here?

18) Is God's account of the very large cluster of grapes, which the spies brought back from Canaan's Brook of Eshcol, as recorded in Numbers 13:21-24, factual, historic, or is this merely a beautiful legend? May the latter interpretation stand alongside of God's account? If so, why? If not, why not? If we permit an optional interpretation in answer to the first six questions, why not here?

19) What about the forty years' wandering in the wilderness until all had died, who were twenty years old and upward at the time when the spies brought back their report, - all with the exception of Joshua and Caleb? Is this account which God has given in Numbers 14:21-34 factual, historic, or is it a legend? May the latter interpretation stand and be accepted alongside of God's account? If so, why? If not, why not? If we permit an optional interpretation in answer to questions one to six, why not here?

20) Did the ten spies, who brought back an evil report and caused the people to murmur against God and against Moses, actually die of a plague before the Lord as recorded in Numbers 14:36-37, or is this merely legend? May the two explanations stand side by side and let the reader have his choice as to what interpretation he wishes to accept? If so, why? If not, why not? If we permit the explanation of "legend" in answer to the first six questions, why not here?

21) Numbers 16:1-35 brings God's record of the rebellion of Korah and 250 princes of

90

the assembly. It states that "the earth opened her mouth and swallowed them up", and that "they and all that appertained to them, went down alive into the pit, and the earth closed upon them; and they perished from among the congregation." Is this factual, actual history, or a myth or a legend? May both intepretations be permitted? If so, why? If not, why not? If we permit the "legend of myth" interpretations in answers to questions one to six, why not here?

22) Did Aaron stay the plague, which took the lives of 14,700, by putting incense on the fire in the center, this making atonement for the people, as recorded in Numbers 16:46-50, or is this merely a myth or a legend? May the latter intepretation be permitted as optional? If so, why? If not, why not? If we permit the "legend or myth" interpretation in answer to questions one to six, why not here?

23) Did only Aaron's rod bud and blossom and yield almonds, as God has stated in Numbers 17:1-13? Was it kept for a token against the rebels? Or is all this merely a legend or a myth? If so, why? If not, why not? May both interpretations stand side by side? If not, why should be permit it in the answers to the first six questions?

24) Did Moses and Aaron, by smiting the rock instead of merely speaking to it, sin so grievously against God that they were not permitted to lead the children of Israel in Canaan, as God has stated in Numbers 20:7-13? Or is all this merely a legend or a myth? Is the latter interpretation permissible alongside of God's statement? If so, why? If not, why not? If "legend or myth" is permitted in answers to questions one to six, why not here?

25) Is the healing from the deadly bite of fiery serpents by a mere look at the brazen serpent which Moses had made and put on a pole, as recorded in Numbers 21:1-9 an actual historial fact, or is it a myth or a legend? May I accept either the one or the other explanation? If so, why? If not, why not? If we permit the "legend" or "myth" explanation as answers to questions one to six, why not here?

26) Did Balaam's ass actually speak as we read in Numbers 22:28-30, or is this myth or a legend? May I permit the latter interpretation to stand alongside of God's clear account? If so, why? If not, why not? Must I permit it here if I permit it in the first six questions?

27) Did Balaam actually speak the prophecy concerning the "star out of Jacob" and the "Sceptor out of Israel", as recorded in Numbers 24:17-19, or is this a mere myth or legend? If the latter, why? If not, why not? May I permit the latter to stand alongside of God's clear account? If I permit the "legend or myth" interpretation in questions one to six, why not here?

28) Did Moses actually see Canaan from Mt. Nebo? Did he die there though "his eye was not dim, nor his natural forces abated"? Did God actually bury him? Is this inspired record in Deut. 34:1-9 actual history, or is it a mere myth or legend? May both explanations stand side by side? If so, why? If not, why not? If we permit the "myth or legend" interpretation in the first six questions, why not here?

Other incidents, inspired accounts, might be mentioned from the Pentateuch and the same questions asked which I have asked above? In fact, this applies to every account of the Old and New Testaments, especially those where we find God's account of that which to us is most marvelous, yes, miraculous, which our reason simply cannot grasp. I am not a so-called "literalist" or "fundamentalist". I know that there are parables in Holy Writ. I know that there is poetry. However, I cannot agree that everything, which our reason cannot grasp or understand, must be placed into the category of "parables, legend, myth, etc." in an effort to make it understandable and acceptable to human reason. The miracles of the Old and New Testaments are simply beyond - not contrary, - to reason. This applies also to the miracles of our Savior. It applies to His coming into the world, to His life, His suffering, His death, His resurrection, His ascension into heaven. My reason asks:

How could God's Son be born of the Virgin Mary? How could God "lay on Him the iniquity of us all"? How could He make Him, Who knew no sin, to be sin for us? How could the God-man suffer and die for my sin? How could He say, "Destroy this temple, and in three days I will raise it up" and actually do this on Easter morning? How can St. John say of Him, "His is the propitiation of our sins, and not for ours only, but also for the sins of the whole world"? How can my Spirit-wrought faith assure me that Christ's perfect fulfillment of the law and His innocent suffering and death actually has reconciled me to God, that on account of it God forgives all my sins and makes me absolutely certain that I shall inherit eternal life? My reason does not grasp, nor can it explain these marvelous truths. I accept them and believe them because God's Word says so.

Should this submission to God's Word not apply to all parts of Scripture? Must I not be ready to say, "Thus saith the Lord"? Is this not true in every case unless Scripture itself compels us to interpet it otherwise? Must we not let Scripture interpret Scripture? Must we not accept the truths which God has recorded in Holy Writ as He has given them? Dare we, as one of the great theologians of our day has expressed it, "make a text of Scripture say what we want it to say?" God forbid! May we ever let God speak, let Him say what He wants to say, and wholeheartedly accept what He has said. God grant it.

J. W. Behnken, D.D.

*   *   *   *   *

On October 7, 1959, Dr. Behnken had already proposed an exhaustive list of questions for use in the interviewing of prospective instructors for the facilities at our colleges and seminaries. Some of these questions were then put into the above document. In 1959 Dr. Behnken prefaced his list by writing: "European theology is infiltrating the American churches, also Lutheran churches. We are not immune. Some of our men have studied at European universities where verbal or plenary inspiration of the Bible suffers severe attacks and where those who accept the infallibility and inerrancy of Holy Writ are classified as naive, old-fashioned, out-of-date obscurantists. Some have read and studied the theology of Aulan, Barth, Emil Brunner, Boltmann, and others, and unfortunately have absorbed some of it and have been influenced by it. Our Synod, having taught and teaching today that Holy Writ is divinely inspired in all its parts and hence the infallible and inerrant Word or God, cannot condone such teaching if it wishes to remain loyal to God, Who gave us the Holy Scriptures."

Various issues of former President Oliver R. Harms' Memo *To My Brethren* mentioned his concern as Synodical President about the teaching at the St. Louis Seminary about the basic doctrine of the authority of the Scriptures (February, 1963), the immortality of the soul (November, 1963), Old Testament interpretation (November, 1964), and that the Seminary "honor Synodical resolutions" (the Jonah question, August, 1965), etc. Unfortunately, nothing more was done by the Synodical President and Council of Presidents than raise the issues and receive general assurance that nothing different was being taught. There was a frustrating stalemate without any action based upon Biblical and constitutional requirements.

Shortly before the New Orleans Convention, Dr. Roland Wiederander, former First Vice-President of the Synod, described what happened to the church after he had presented a paper already in 1963 to the Council of Presidents and seminary faculties, stating the need for clear theology. That paper of December 2, 1963, said in part, "Despite repeated efforts, we have not dealt honestly with our pastors and people. We have refused to state our changing theological position in open, honest, forthright, simple and clear words. Over and over again we said that nothing was changing while we were aware of changes taking place. Either we should have informed our pastors and people that changes were taking place and, if possible, convince them from Scriptures that these changes were in full harmony with "this saith the Lord!" or we should have stopped playing games as we gave assurance that no changes were taking place. With increasing measure, the synodical trumpet has been giving an uncertain sound."

Dr. Wiederander then described the steps that occured over the following ten years: "Quite generally our pastors and almost entirely our laity became more and more confused. Confusion led to uncertainty. Loss of credibility destroyed the possibility for meaningful discussion. The loss of meaningful discussion set the stage for head-on collision."

Early in his presidency, J.A.O. Preus met with the St. Louis Faculty on November 18, 1969. After he had indicated some of the basic theological difficulties, he said, ". . .We have not faced this problem very well. We have not really come clean in the relationship of the higher critical theories to the divine inspiration of the Scripture. We need to give these matters our serious and earnest attention. . .There are really two ways to respond to resolutions of Synod that trouble us: one is to tackle the problem head on, and the other is to teach contrary to them in the classroom. Both of these approaches, of course, present problems. I would remind you that you have channels for change, if you feel that change is called for. In the meantime, we need to respect out Synodical statements, and it is my constitutional responsibility to see to it that Synodical resolutions are carried out. If you do not or cannot agree with these things, then I urge you to use the proper channels for changing them."

On May 17, 1972, Dr. J.A.O. Preus again addressed the Seminary faculty and gave clear information as to the specific doctrinal questions and deviations.

Four Books On The St. Louis-Synod Theological Problems

In early 1973, Rev. Tom Baker, graduate of the St. Louis Seminary in 1971, published a book, *Watershed at the Rivergate*, which presented confessional and Scriptural principles, the historical-critical method infiltration, the neo-liberal political organization, the media, and the future which was to be decided at the New Orleans Convention. It provides considerable evidence of the reality of the theological delinquencies of the St. Louis faculty.

In 1977, *Anatomy of an Explosion, Missour in Lutheran Perspective* written by Professor Kurt Marquart, was published as the Concordia Seminary Monograph Series, No. 3, by the Seminary Press in Fort Wayne. Professor Marquart presented the theological and historical rationale of the Missouri Synod conflict, the basic Biblical and confessional principles, the counterconfessional and ecumenical attack, and the counter-Biblical attack. This was mostly a theological treatise which was helpful to ascertain the real nature of the conflict, which was doctrinal, not procedural as the Saint Louis faculty propagandized.

St. Louis Seminary Professor Frederick W. Danker published a book [13] in 1977 entitled, *NO ROOM IN THE BROTHERHOOD, The Preus-Otten Purge of Missouri*. Unlike Baker's and Marquart's books which were theologically oriented, this book presented selected parts of the history of the conflict by centering on procedures. Oftentimes flippant and irreverent, Danker's book does provide some sequence of the battle, however subjective. If you believe his claim in his "Foreword" that the battle was between traditionalists and progressives, you will also believe his statement, "I can claim non-partisan objectivity." After that, you can also take the claim of "integrity" with a grain of salt. He tells of his reaction to the Fact-finding Committee appointed by Preus naming the Committee's criticisms as being "unLutheran and tenuous criticisms," and added, "the demonic, I pointed out, manipulates people behind a front of religious piety and endorses such manipulation through encrusted formulations." A frivolous attitude was shown when he wrote, "The Committee, however, appeared to have no interest in exploring the depth meaning of the Biblical accounts, and I heard the Lord in good humor say to me, 'I did, but I won't invite them to try it'...I was convinced on January 23, 1971, that the Holy Spirit did not have a ghost of a chance in Missouri." [14]

In response to "A Statement of Scriptural and Confessional Principles" which President Preus presented to the faculty and the Synod, he wrote about the perils of this rationalistic approach, and added, "Anyone who challenged his Statement would in effect be challenging the Synod. This was managerial efficiency with a vengeance." [15] He tells of the faculty response which declared, " 'A Statement' has a spirit alien to confessional Lutheran theology...We also said, the promulgation of 'A Statement' is divisive...All that mattered to Preus was answers, not questions or problems." [16]

After the New Orleans Convention, Res. 3-01 declared "A Statement" to be a "more formal and comprehensive statement of belief," and "in all its parts, to be Scriptural and in accord with the Lutheran Confessions, therefore a formulation which derives its authority from the Word of God and which expresses the Synod's position on current doctrinal issues." Danker referred to those loyal to the Synod's doctrine as "right-wingers" and to Preus as a "zealous wagon master defending his encampment against attacking Indians" and the Bibilical theology of "A Statement" as "paint-by-number theology." He called this a move toward sectarianism and told how 500 delegates and visitors at the New Orleans convention protested, singing, "The Church's One Foundation Is Jesus Christ, Her Lord." [17] Having been present and thinking about this demonstration even today, I find it bizarre for those who disagree violently with what Jesus taught as portrayed in a "A Statement" singing about Jesus being the only foundation of the church - when they had just displaced Him with rationalism.

Danker also tells about his and the faculty's reaction to the "Report of the Synodical President to The Lutheran Church-Missouri Synod" published on Sept. 1, 1972 (known as the Blue Book), writing that "this report was an ingeniously contrived literary guillotine," claiming that it was a prejudicial attack on the faculty. [18]

In Chapter 17, Danker gives his distorted view of the battles fought in the Mission Board and points to me (who became Chairman in 1971) as a "hard-line traditionalist." To show how the rebellious Mission staff and the St. Louis Seminary faculty considered the Mission Affirmations as license for "anything goes" theology and practice, here is a sample of what Danker wrote, " 'They rejoice over a universal redemption won for all in Jesus Christ'...such words made obsolete the favored illustration recited on Mission Sundays about the number of souls per minute going to Hell. This paragraph suggested that God might yet have mercy on those who died before the Missouri Synod or some other group could reach them. It was the first major blow that had ever been struck in Missouri for divine executive privilege...Most of the Synod's Mission staff have taken the document so seriously as to implement the resolves at every opportunity." [19]

Chapter 21 of Danker's book gives an account of the Seminary student moratorium and provides an account of the communication, rumors, and discussions that were going on, showing the games that the faculty and students were playing which gives the impression of being childish. The political campaign of these rebels was so active that a rumor center and service was organized including the provision of telephone contacts, which they claimed was necessary "for the maintenance of community cohesion in the face of divisive tactics by opposition forces." [20] The entire book is filled with such political tactics, procedural challenges, and dissemination of personal viewpoints for serious consideration even in theological matters contrary to Synodical positions. Although this book contains a number of historical documents, the flip and subjective commentary provides very interesting reading, but little else positive can be said about it.

John Tietjen provides a rather complete chronology of all of the events that took place during his St. Louis Presidency, but does not offer any of the historical documents. His book, *MEMOIRS IN EXILE, Confessional Hope and Institutional Conflict* [21], might be termed a blow-by-blow personal account of how he saw the conflict. He accounts for various personalities involved, offers considerable dialogue, and at times describes many anatomy positions - "lips pursed...furrowed brow...without a smile..."

Tietjen's "Chronology of Events" at the beginning of the book is very helpful, as it puts into perspective the procedural sequences. Tietjen was elected President of the St. Louis Seminary in May, 1969, and Dr. J. A. O. Preus was elected President of the Synod in July. On May 17, 1970, Preus announced his intention to take action against the St. Louis Faculty in view of stated deviations from the Synod's doctrinal position. This is the course of action during the following years:

9-9-70 - Preus announces appointment of a Fact-Finding Committee (FFC) to investigate the Sem Faculty.

12-11-70 - Interviews of Faculty by FFC begin.

1-5-71 - Faculty announces decision to continue participation in interviews under protest.

7-15-71 - Milwaukee Convention gives FFC Report to the Board of Control (BOC).

9-20-71 - BOC begins review of FFC Report.

12-13-71 - BOC declines reappointment of Faculty member Arlis Ehlen.

1-4-72 - Faculty requests meeting with Preus to challenge his ethics in the BOC's decision concerning Ehlen.

1-7-72 - Preus advises of impending disciplinary action against Tietjen.

1-18-72 - Tietjen and Preus meet to work out compromise.

2-18-72 - Preus withdraws from compromise agreement and gives the BOC "A Statement of Scriptural and Confessional Principles" to serve as standard for doctrinal review.

3-5-72 - Tietjen refuses to implement the Preus demand that Ehlen be barred from teaching courses.

9-1-72 - Preus issues his report "Blue Book," alleging that some faculty members are teaching false doctrine.

9-8-72 - Tietjen issues "Fact-Finding or Fault-Finding?" to criticize the "Blue Book."

9-20-72 - Council of Presidents (COP) announces controversy compromise.

10-26-72 - Preus finds COP compromise unacceptable.

1-15-73 - BOC completes interviews with faculty, clears all of the charge of false doctrine.

7-10-73 - New Orleans Convention confirms that convention-adopted doctrinal statements are binding.

7-11-73 - New Orleans Convention adopts "A Statement" as binding.

7-12-73 - New Orleans Convention condemns faculty for teaching false doctrine.

7-13-73 - Convention requires newly-elected BOC to deal with Tietjen.

7-23-73 - Faculty issues "A Declaration of Protest and Confession."

8-13-73 - BOC suspends Tietjen as President and faculty member, then delays implementation of its action.

8-28-73 - Evangelical Lutherans in Mission (ELIM) organized.

1-20-74 - BOC suspends Tietjen as President.

1-21-74 - Seminary student body announces moratorium on classes and faculty announces that they consider themselves to be suspended.

2-17-74 - BOC requires faculty decision to return to class or to be held in breach of contract.

2-19-74 - Students decide to join faculty in organizing "Seminary in Exile" (SEMINEX).

Many contradictory and illogical statements were made by the faculty and their supporters in the Synod related to their doctrinal position and the historic position of the LCMS. Consistently, they tried to show that solid Missourians were objecting to Synod's doctrine and practice being purified and for becoming more Biblical. Tietjen's book provides many evidences that this is not true. Indeed, the opposite is the case. His book provides such evidence as the following:

"I had expected to work closely with Harms. Now I was to work with a Presidency whose candidacy had been proposed by people within the Missouri Synod whose understanding of the church's theology and mission was different from mine. Some of these people were hurling heresy charges against faculty members..." (Page 4) "Observers described the Cleveland Convention as a turning point in the life of the Missouri Synod, signaling a move away from rigidity in theology..." [22]

I (Werning) had a very interesting experience during the early days of the Cleveland Convention when I was invited to meet with a number of the people who later helped form the party of the left, and who were allies of Tietjen. Basically, it was a meeting of writers, supporters, and friends of the American Lutheran Publicity Bureau and its magazine. Apparently, I was invited because I was the Evangelism columnist for the *American Lutheran* magazine, having served for about 10 years. There was no question about the different theological commitment of many of these people, which I reported personally to Dr. Oliver R. Harms after he was elected President at that Convention.

More than double-talk was evident in various discussions and situations reported by Tietjen in his book, which indicated that there was the introduction of a new and different theology than the clear and unambiguous doctrine which the Missouri Synod has historically held. Some of these examples from Tietjen's book follow:

1. Tietjen's statement to the FFC(Fact-Finding Committee): "To talk about the historical events as if they themselves were important is to miss the whole point of the New Testament. Even the disciples did not understand until they believed." After the FFC interviews, Tietjen told Andrew Weyermann, "You were eloquent in making it clear that it was the Scripture proclaiming the Gospel that was the only rule and norm. Zimmerman and his committee were working with a notion of Scriptural authority that separated the Scripture from the Gospel." Weyermann said, "When people want to throttle you with facticity and inerrancy, you have to insist on the gospel meaning in the facts as more important than the facts themselves. Only the Gospel saves, not the historical facts." [23] Here one has an example of placing historical facts in contradiction to the Gospel message, whereas both are the real essence of the Scriptures.

2. Tietjen recounts a discussion at the hotel during the Milwaukee Convention, in which

he said, "If they do succeed, church conventions will tell us what the Bible teaches about Adam and Eve and a six-day creation and Jonah and the whale and a lot more. You'll either have to agree, keep quiet or get out." He quotes Arthur C. Repp, "The Preus people have a very different different understanding of what Lutheran is...They think they know exactly what the Bible teaches and that they have a right to tell us what we have to believe and teach." [24]

3. Tietjen tells of the charges against the faculty as summarized in the *Blue Book*: "a. false doctrine of the nature of the Holy Scriptures coupled with methods of interpretation which effectively erode the authority of the Scriptures. b. a substantial undermining of the confessional doctrine of original sin by *de facto* denial of the historical events on which it is based. c. a permissiveness toward certain false doctrines. d. a tendency to deny that the Law is a normative guide for Christian behavior. e. a conditional acceptance of the Lutheran Confessions. f. a strong claim that the Seminary faculty need not teach in accord with the Synod's doctrinal stance as expressed in the Synod's official doctrinal statements and resolutions." [25]

4. The faculty published Tietjen's 35-page Response to the FCC Blue Book under the title, *Fact-Finding or Fault-Finding? An Analysis of President J. A. O Preus' Investigation of Concordia Seminary*, which presented their conclusions: "1. The fact-finding process was conceived as a prejudgement that has shaped the inquiry, predetermined its results, and subjected the seminary to treatment that is **unfair.** 2. The procedures employed by the Fact-Finding Committee have produced results that are **unreliable.** 3. The report is a strange blend of half-truths, misunderstandings, and distortions which makes the profile it presents **untrue.** 4. The views of Scripture interpretation which lie behind the investigation and shape its results are **less than Scriptural.** 5. The theology which lies behind the inquiry and the Report, by whose standard the theology of the faculty was measured is **unLutheran.**" [26] Thus the Synod's doctrine is called less than Scriptural and unLutheran.

5. Tietjen wrote, "There were two irreconcilable theologies in the Synod and the New Orleans Convention was going to have to choose one and reject the other." [27] Please recall that the Synod had been assured by the faculty that no new theology had been introduced by them.

6. Tietjen quotes Frederick Danker in a statement to the FFC, "God's activities are always much more than they appear to us; those who think they can film a miracle show that they do not understand what a miracle is..." Tietjen also recorded, "Arthur Repp was asked to clarify his statement to the FFC that the Creation account in Genesis was not intended to be a literal description of a one-time event. Repp pointed to the figurative expressions and the anthropomorphic language of Genesis 1. He called attention to the variations in the two creation accounts in Genesis 1 and 2. More important, he said, was the poetic, polemical and liturgical structures of these chapters which take them out of the category of straight reporting or history, and he described that structure in detail. Asked about his views on the book of Jonah, Alfred von Rohr Sauer pointed out that the Blue Book had dealt with his views under the rubric of an alleged permissive Christology...According to Sauer, it would have been possible for Jesus to infer that His stay in the grave would be like Jonah staying in the fish for three days without thereby asserting that the Jonah account is in fact historical..." [28]

7. Tietjen quotes pertinent parts of the New Orleans Resolution 3-09 that condemned the position of the faculty: "a. Subversion of the authority of Scripture (formal principle); b. 'Gospelism' over 'Gospel Reductionism' for by the authority of Scripture is reduced to its 'Gospel' contents; c. Denial of the third use of the Law, i.e., the function of the Law as guide for the Christian in his life...repudiate that attitude toward Holy Scripture...which reduces to theological opinion or exegetical questions matters which are in fact

clearly taught in Scripture." The Resolution lists examples of these matters: "facticity of miracle accounts and their details; historicity of Adam and Eve as real persons; the Fall of Adam and Eve into sin as a real event...; the historicity of every detail in the life of Jesus as recorded by the evangelist; predictive prophecies in the Old Testament which are in fact messianic; the doctrine of angels, the Jonah account." [29] It becomes very obvious now why former President John Behnken already in the late 50's and during the 60's did not receive any answer from the faculty under the presidency of Dr. Fuerbringer to his 28 questions. The New Orleans Convention showed that the faculty denied the historical records of the Scriptures on many questions which Dr. Behnken was asking.

8. After the New Orleans Convention, various faculty proposals were considered, including bluntly attacking the resolutions, demanding that the Synod right the wrongs committed at New Orleans, and forming a coalition of congregations within the structure of the LCMS to fight against it. "On one item everyone was agreed: a bold and public rejection of the New Orleans action was needed...On July 23 the faculty majority adopted 'A Declaration of Protest and Confession' and 51 members of the faculty and executive staff signed the document. After Chapel worship the next day, Richard R. Caemmerer read the document to the seminary community assembled in front of the statue of Martin Luther...Our church is in danger of losing its truly Lutheran character and of becoming a sect.." [30]

Clearly, the Synod's problems were not political, but theological! What many suspected or claimed in 1973 has now been confirmed by Tietjen in *Memoirs*.

The rest of the book continues to recount various tactics which the faculty and the Synodical President used to counter each other, and then it proceeds to tell about the Association of Evangelical Lutheran Churches (AELC) and the Evangelical Lutheran Church in America (ELCA). Some of the documents which ELIM and its supporters produced and circulated were also signed and supported by the faculty, and these will be presented later in this chapter. The Synod and its President responded with various documents to counteract those actions of ELIM, AELC and the faculty.

"Message of the Church" Document

On January 20, 1974, the office of the Synod's President sent a letter and other documents under the title, "Message to the Church." It presents the so-called "deal" as an act of conciliation, and also a January 22, 1974, letter from the faculty and executive staff presenting their ultimatum to be cleared of any charges of false doctrine.

One of the significant documents in this "Message to the Church" was a January 26, 1974, letter written by some students, which said, "Because of this climate it is imperative, at this time, that we, as students, withhold our names. However, our names are on file in the office of the Acting President of Concordia Seminary and this letter is being written with his authorization." The faculty and ELIM supporters tried to show that this letter had no validity, but the fact is that since that time some of these students had become pastors and professors. Today they confirm the truth of their statements at that time. They have in fact validated its accuracy.

These students wrote, "For years we have been harassed and bullied by those who call themselves evangelical. We have experienced **various acts of intimidation**. Here are a **few examples:**

1. A student was ejected from a class for refusal to accept the ideological orientation of the professors, being forced to take the course again the following term.

2. Students have failed classes or have had grades lowered for theological disagreement

with professors who were themselves engaging in doctrinal aberrations.

3. The former president of the Seminary told students (who are now in the fourth year class) that they would be taught the Historical-Critical Method despite the accepted position of the Synod. Students have been required to use this method if they wished to pass their courses...

6. Class time and even public chapel exercises have been consistently used for ridiculing the expected activities and accepted responsibilities of the synodical administration.

7. Students have been exposed to such aberrations as universalism, denial of a personal devil, the refusal to say that anyone will go to hell, etc. These aberrations have not been clearly and emphatically rejected...

9. Professors have frequently denigrated the traditional orthodox doctrine of the Lutheran Church as well as its heritage by snide remarks, cynical observations, and by broad innuendo. Classes in the history of Lutheranism have been often turned into parties of ridicule.

10. There has been an almost increasing ridicule of the simple child-like faith of the laity. In fact, the laity of the church is often described as being so ignorant that they become the pastors' adversary.

11. The counseling services of the Seminary have been used deliberately for purposes of brainwashing. For example, conservative professors have consistently been by-passed and have not automatically been given advisees. Therefore conservative students have risked labeling themselves by asking for conservative professors as advisors.

"During this current academic year many of the above mentioned practices of harassment have continued. Even in these last days we have experienced some incredible cases of intimidation. Here are just a few examples:

1) 'In a given course, the traditional orthodox doctrine of creation was ridiculed as being unscholarly, if not totally stupid. Proponents of the orthodox view were portrayed as being fearful to present their views for scholarly review.

2) 'During a recent presentation by the acting president to the student body, a liberal professor left his seat on the main floor of the chapel and proceeded to the balcony where it was generally known that conservative students sat. He proceeded to call the acting president obscene names.

3) 'In class the New Orleans Convention has been described as being devoid of the Spirit of God and conservative delegates were described as being barbaric.

4) 'Chapel exercises have been devoted perversely to such matters as compromising the prayer life of students by forcing them to participate without warning in prayers that violate their theological position. Devotional periods were turned into entertainment or political rallies...

6) 'Upon resumption of the classes this fall, a professor expressed refusal to abide by synodical resolutions passed at New Orleans and stated that those in disagreement should register for other classes.

7) 'The Gospel has consistently been turned into a new Law, destroying the Gospel which, in its Lutheran sense, is the pure proclamation of the forgiveness of sins...' "

"We could cite many more instances and are willing to do so upon request. We have set forth these items to give you an idea of the oppressive climate and theological perversion that has been promulgated under the guise of the Gospel at Concordia Seminary."

- - - - - - - - - - - - - -

Many parents, uncles and aunts, pastors of vicars, and pastors who knew St. Louis graduates in their circuits tell of many instances of doctrinal deviation among the men who studied at the seminary in those days. So it is not only former students, but also relatives and fellow members of the Synod who heard firsthand from the students about what was being taught at the seminary. Some agreed with their professors and some did not, but all agreed that a different theology was being taught. I personally had the misfortune of having to face some of these students as pastors or as college or seminary instructors and learned that they had absorbed the Historical-Critical Method with its doctrine and assimilated it into their theological system.

Richard E. Hoffmann

One of these men was Richard E. Hoffmann, who in 1965 and 1966 caused concern to some members of his congregation and to the Lincoln, Nebraska Circuit Pastoral Conference. As a member of that Conference and together with a Vice-President of the District, we were assigned by the Conference and then the District President the responsibility of meeting with Hoffman, which we did a number of times. Both in private visits and public meetings, Hoffmann said that physical suffering and death are not acts of God but are of the devil alone. When the Vice-President and I presented Scriptures like Hebrews 12 and many other Old and New Testament passages, he stated that if he had enough time to do the research that he could show that these passages do not apply.

Then we wrote a treatise on the subject. In a March 6, 1966, meeting at Trinity Lutheran Church in Lincoln, NE, Hoffmann stated that most of the Bible verses used in the treatise would have to be thrown out - some because of the context, some because of the English words, some because they are not clear, and some because of the original language. He said, "I have many, many questions about the Scriptures. The Scriptures are clear only when they speak about salvation. Until I can understand the Scriptures and Confessions, I will have to wait with my judgments on individual passages." On March 10, 1966, Hoffmann wrote the Circuit Counselor: "It would be useless to point out that I have cleared my paper with its conclusions with men of the Seminary...the burden is not mine; I teach as I have been taught. Nor is the task of instruction mine as far as my fellow pastors are concerned." Soon Hoffmann accepted a Call to the St. Louis area and became active in ELIM affairs, and then joined the AELC and ELCA.

Prof. John Elliott

When about 200 District and Synodical leaders met in St. Louis on August 29-September 2, 1966 at a Mission Institute sponsored by the Synod, Seminary instructor John Elliott was one of the presenters. Elliott disturbed a number of men with comments about two and three Isaiahs, and such words as the following: "We can speak neither of a uniform theology of the New Testament nor of a single kerygma but only of theologies, kerygmas, and varying expressions of good news adapted to specific audiences in specific situations..." In reference to the Trinity, Elliott told a story about asking a dying man, "Do you believe in the Father, Son and Holy Spirit?" The man responds, "Here I am dying, and you come to me with riddles."

Dr. Herman Gockel wrote a letter to object strongly to Elliott's theology which impacted upon the Gospel. I became involved in discussions with Instructor Elliott because during one noon meal some of us were discussing the doctrinal aberrations of Elliott's essay. When I voiced my objections, I was apparently overheard by some of Elliott's supporters. Later, at a recess some of his seminary supporters and Bill Irving(staff man from Lutheran Laymen's League) came to me and said, "We hear that you disagree with Elliott's essay." I stated that indeed I did, but what else is new? They asked me what parts I believed were wrong. I stated that I do not make it a practice to stand in hallways giving my impression of what I thought I heard an essayist say, but would be glad to respond if I were given a copy of the essay as presented. I was assured that I would receive a copy of the essay. When I did not receive a copy as promised, I approached them and Elliott but was told that the then President Fuerbringer made such decisions. I talked to Dr. Fuerbringer, and he stated that I would get a copy of the essay when it was revised. When I objected and stated that I had been promised a copy now, Fuerbringer said I would have to wait. I told Synod Pres. Harms about this problem and asked him to help. He assured me that he would get a copy for me, but ultimately he himself was not able to acquire a copy for me. However, I was able to get one from another source in St. Louis.

Elliott wrote me a letter in March 1967 about meetings between himself and me with Synod and seminary representatives present. He wrote that "one of the most important results (of these meetings) was the manifestation of two quite different, if not irreconcilable, approaches towards the understanding and interpretation of both the sacred Scriptures and the Lutheran symbols." This statement identified the seminary theology under the administration of Dr. Fuerbringer, more than two years before Dr. Tietjen and President Jack Preus came on the scene.

Prof. Walter Bouman

In 1967 it was announced that Professor Walter R. Bouman at River Forest was to be given tenure. Students and parents of students at Concordia, River Forest, who were members of the South Wisconsin District complained about the teaching of certain professors, including Walter R. Bouman because he would be given tenure. These students complained to South Wisconsin officials, including me because I was the Executive for the Student Aid Committee which was supporting them at college. On that basis, I wrote a letter to the Board of Control to object to giving Bouman tenure. This resulted in considerable correspondence and personal visits with him on May 9 and Aug. 13, 1969. It continued with correspondence to Bouman, the River Forest Board of Control, his pastor Dean Lueking and others. The theological concerns ranged about as broad as the questions as Dr. Behnken had asked of the St. Louis Seminary, where Bouman's theology obviously originated.

The file on Bouman includes the following bizarre statement which Bouman made in a conference essay at Des Plaines, IL: "When I was under attack from Waldo Werning, I went through all his articles in the old *American Lutheran* and picked out all of the heretical statements which he wrote in the *American Lutheran*. I compiled them and sent them to him as a way of getting him off my back. (laughter) I succeeded. (laughter) God help me, he turned his attention elsewhere, (laughter) and when I succeeded in getting him off my back I let it go at that, I didn't pursue it. I don't say these things as accusations. I may be accusing him, but I don't want to be." Bouman later apologized for making that statement and that he never did send me a list of heretical statements nor ever communicated this to me.

Despite all of the legitimate objections to Bouman's teaching in the River Forest classrooms, he was transferred to the LCMS Ohio District when he took a call to the ALC Columbus Seminary, as the RF Board of Control granted him a release but with the special communication to the Ohio District for responsible follow-up "for correction." One needs only to talk to Bouman himself today and others associated with him (students and colleagues) to know of his harsh anti-Missouri convictions and actions, which show him to be totally in opposition to what Missouri, the Lutheran Confessions and Bible teach.

Prof. Bruce Malkow

In 1971, some students of Concordia, Milwaukee, visited me in my South Wisconsin District Office to tell me that they were objecting to the unBiblical teaching of Professor Bruce Malkow. I asked them why they came to me. They stated that I was the District Executive for the Student Aid Committee and that the District was giving financial help to them. The students expected me to help them make the classrooms safe for other students to be taught nothing but true Biblical doctrine and not to hear false doctrine. I conferred with our District President. He said that I had the responsibility to pursue this matter, which I did. Later I was joined by the Rev. Dr. Ervin Lemke and Rev. Gerold R. Martin, pastors of the South Wisconsin District. Dr. Malkow exhibited the typical attitude toward the Scriptures and its doctrines, as he had learned at the St. Louis Seminary.

After two years of tedious effort, much stalling and various meetings, I presented the case for the three of us to the Board of Control with Malkow present. After presenting evidences of various kinds, this is a summary of my concluding report to the Board, showing how the destructive historical-critical theories of the theological "elite" impact upon and actually destroy the accuracy of the Biblical account and of the Gospel itself. I referred to 2 Pet. 3: 5-7, "They deliberately forget that long ago by God's Word the heavens existed and the earth was formed out of water and by water. By these waters the world at that time was deluged and destroyed. By the same Word the present heavens and earth are reserved for fire, being kept for the day of judgment and destruction of ungodly men." I asked Prof. Malkow, "Since the same Word affirms the destruction of the world by water through the Flood and the destruction of the world on Judgment Day by fire, will you agree that there was an actual flood?" He denied the historicity of the Flood. Then I quoted 2 Pet. 2:5, "If He (God) did not spare the ancient world when He brought the flood on its ungodly people, but protected Noah, a preacher of righteousness, and seven others," and asked Dr. Malkow, "In view of the fact that an individual historic person, Noah, and seven others are named in relation to the destruction of the world through the Flood, will you not in view of 2 Pet. 3 and now 2 Pet. 2:5 admit that at least there was a flood?" Malkow then retorted, "Yes, I will affirm that there was at least a flood." Thereupon, I asked him, "How did you come to the conclusion that there was a flood, and cannot accept the evidence of the text that there was **the** Flood?" Prof. Malkow indicated that the Scriptures which I had quoted caused him to rethink the matter. At this point in my report to the Board of Control in a February, 1973, meeting, Malkow broke in and told the members of the Board, "I have changed my opinion, and I do not believe that there was even a flood." Thereupon, I told the Board, "Our presentation is completed."

On June 12, 1973, the Board rendered its decision that Prof. Malkow had undermined the authority of Scripture by questioning the historical reality of Adam and Eve, Noah, Ruth, Esther, Job and Jonah. They declared that he was guilty of teaching false doctrine. Malkow, a 1965 graduate of the St. Louis Seminary, told me that I should be facing the St. Louis faculty members who taught him these theological insights, not him. At the New Orleans Convention, Malkow met with the President of the LCA and soon became a clergy member of that church body.

Lueking-Frey "Openness and Trust"

Support of the errant Seminary and its theology was orchestrated by a group under the leadership of Dean Lueking-Bertwin Frey, which became the ELIM organization. On Oct. 23, 1970, Lueking sent "A Declaration of Determination" by Frey with a cover letter from Lueking which said that Frey's statement is "spontaneous and unsolicited," - a very interesting claim. Frey complained about efforts "to lead the Synod in a new direction," which obviously was the opposite direction that the faculty was taking the Synod. He stated that they were "determined to resist the efforts to drive wedges between us" and to "keep the unity of the Spirit." He wrote, "We deplore the suggestion that our pastors and teachers should be required to teach in harmony with every resolution of our Synodical conventions," and they wanted "to follow the Spirit's leading" and to "keep Missouri truly Lutheran."

The document which shows the unBiblical doctrine of the faculty and its supporters is "A Call To Openness And Trust" adopted in St. Louis on Jan. 31, 1970. Among the more interesting and challenging statements of this document are: "Justification by faith demands diversity in unity...It seems necessary to ask basic questions and to answer them clearly and concisely once again...We see these confessional statements as setting forth a life of Christian freedom in the Gospel...Now is the time for openness and trust among brothers and sisters in Christ so that new structures and patterns may be shaped...We tend to make judgmental rules out of propositional theological statements rather than using such statements to free people. God makes men free to follow diversity in understanding Scriptures...In our time of increasing polarization, it seems important to recognize that many of the structures, patterns, and assertions of the past cannot be shored up or maintained any longer nor can the past be retrieved in some idealistic way. Rather we must renew or realign ourselves into new patterns in which respect for one another is nourished."

The "Call To Openness And Trust" continues, "We see alternative attitudes, when freely chosen, as a conflict in life-styles rather than a denial of Jesus Christ...Common consent or the will of the majority, charitably exercised, decides which patterns shall be maintained in a given group...Denominational identification should not be used to bind consciences...We believe that faith in God is expressed by the quality of our relationships to people even more than by formulating precise doctrines about God and man...Those who exercise authority in the church must honor the Christian's freedom to speak, write or act according to his convictions concerning Christ, the Scriptures, his fellowship with his community or any other aspect of Christian faith and life. When these conditions do not exist, people are manipulated..." The document ends with this statement, "The Gospel (that is, Christ) is not a doctrine which equates the Gospel with the Bible...We specifically hold that differences concerning: (1) the manner of the creation of the universe by God, (2) the authorship and literary form of the books of the Bible, (3) the definition of the presence of Christ in the Lord's Supper, (4) the moral obligation of Christians in individual or corporate action, (5) the question of factual error in the Bible, and (6) the role and authority of clergy in the church, are not to be the basis for inclusion or exclusion of people among the true disciples of Jesus Christ or for membership in the LCMS."

Before the Frey-Lueking group and ELIM were organized, there was no necessity for such organization, because the party of the left had captured the key leadership positions of the entire Synod as the majority party, including elected officials and staff. They controlled the publications, the St. Louis Seminary, the Lutheran Laymen's League, the Mission Board, and many other entities. They were controlling the Synod by procedural tactics, but when those loyal to Synod and its Biblical confessions felt constrained to organize, the party of the left started challenging procedural matters, demanded openness and trust, named anyone who opposed them loveless, but never answered the theological questions. Those who shamelessly captured the Synod also were bold in their use of Synodical structures to attain their purposes. They pushed the new Sunday School course, *Mission: Life*, onto the Synod; this series turned out to be a fiasco and a financial disaster to Concordia Publishing House.

The *1973 Concordia Pulpit* carried such ELIM leaders and participants as authors, "Dean Lueking, John Tietjen, Dale Hansen, George W. Hoyer, William Goerss, Walter Rast, Kenneth Frerking, Samuel Roth, and Justus P. Kretzmann."

A number of District Presidents became a political force and used their positions to influence their Districts and the Synod. Those District Presidents who were in full scale rebellion against the church which ordained them and later elected them to office felt free to reject the Biblical faith of their Synod and to organize against the Synod. There were the Seven, the Eight, then the Dallas Nine, the Expanded Dallas Nine, all involved in political maneuvers to support the St. Louis faculty and its theology which was a full assault on the Biblical faith held by the LCMS for its entire history.

We who were loyal to the historic faith of the Missouri Synod were charged with being divisive, as can be seen by a paragraph printed in the Oct. 31, 1976, New England District Supplement of *The Lutheran Witness* (quoting the District President): "My prayer is that those who have brought about our present circumstances may yet repent of the divisions and offenses they have caused - of the pain and hurt they have brought to so many - of the legalism which destroys God-given rights and eventually hope itself - of the besmirching of the Christian reputations of its own pastors and people - and above all of the diminution of the Gospel of our Lord Jesus Christ."

Some of these District Presidents were clearly playing politics rather than being churchmen who followed their theological beliefs. Several were working with us and actually signed the *Faith Forward - First Concerns* document and were part of the movement. The October 19, 1976 *Forum Letter* tells about the great difference between the private and public behavior of some of these and states that one "is reported to be living with a painful dichotomy between private convictions and public posture."

Some of these I found particularly sad. One example will illustrate the problem: Dr. Paul E. Jacobs, President of the California-Nevada District and I met in a St. Louis hotel for a long visit, and he strongly and unambiguously confessed and stood where the Missouri Synod had always been. He also showed deep concern about the theology of the St. Louis faculty. He said that he needed to think about this. After he returned home, we had a telephone conversation in which he stated that he was preparing an essay to present to various circuits and areas of his District to try to bring a peaceful solution to the entire matter. History records that this essay was an attempted compromise of affirming both the historic Biblical position of the Synod and the new theology, and asking for peaceful co-existence. He felt that he could lovingly straddle the fence and keep his District in mission.

At the June 26-29, 1972, Colorado District Convention, he presented the essence of his new religious philosophy in an essay, *Freedom and Authority in the Church*. He used the universal reconciliation of God to himself as the argument to proclaim, "A reconciling community would not want to use separation or expulsion as the means by which he carries out the purposes of God." He placed Christian freedom in opposition to Christian order and obedience. He said with agreement, "The only authority the church has is love." He said, "The history of the church records the procrustean attempts to process people through a certain doctrinal mode expressed in formulations which, if you do not quite fit, you are either cut to size or stretched."

Jacobs quoted Gustav Wingren, "No Lutheran Confession contains any doctrinal statement concerning the origin of the Bible...The Word is not primarily thought of as a written Word or as words in a book, but as the spoken Word, as words on the lips." Jacobs, like the St. Louis Seminary faculty, equates the Scriptures as the Gospel itself and places any other questions of authority and content in opposition to the Gospel. He correctly identifies "Gospel Reductionism" which is "a rather strange word that has crept into the vocabulary of the Synod lately. 'Gospel Reductionism' is the charge that Holy Scripture is minimized or placed in a less important position so long as the Gospel is kept central, naming justification by grace through faith, which is confessional shorthand for the whole Christian truth." However Jacobs claims, "Yet this is what the Confessions constantly keep advocating, for without the Gospel there is no Christ and no church."

Strange talk which echoes the St. Louis faculty is heard in answer to Jacob's question, "In every discussion of inerrancy we need to ask: inerrant for what?" About the Synodical Presidents' "A Statement" he said that it "tends to be a kind of neo-papism of which the Synod has been wary throughout its history." He does not like the "we reject" of the statement, "The danger of the 'Reject Section' is that we can get so caught up in its specifics on facticity and literalism that we miss out on what Scripture is really after, and thus become so concerned about the carton that we fail to drink the milk that the carton packaged." This was a real straw man: I have been around the Synod in many places for 47 years and possibly the kind of people that he describes are hiding and have no vocal cords, but I have not found any yet.

The January 17, 1977 *Missouri In Perspective*, carries the resignation statement of Jacobs from his District Presidency. He offered six principle reasons for resigning: "a growing administrative legalism in the Synod, which is 'frustrating and hindering the Gospel'; the exclusion of members who disagree with prevailing Synodical policies and beliefs; the interference of Synodical administration in 'the life and decision-making of member congregations', contrary to Article VII of Synod's Constitution; the 'endless' arbitrary rulings of the Synod's Constitutional Commission which are produced 'to get rid of those who disagree' without giving them an opportunity even to appear before the Commission; the manipulation of people at Synodical conventions through slogans like 'Tietjen must go!'; the destruction of 'the unity of faith' by elevating human opinions above sound Scriptural doctrine and by never-proved allegations against fellow members of the Synod." He said, "Synods are not sacred; people are." I was under the impression that people organized the Synod for the people's sake, rather than the Synod organizing people for the Synod's sake. In other words, the Synod was being responsive to the majority of people who were loyal to the Synod's Biblical and Confessional position. There were a number of District Presidents who did not want to abide by that fact.

I was very saddened by the major change from the former unsullied beliefs which Jacobs showed when we visited in a hotel room years before when compared to the complicated "new hermeneutic" faith which he showed when he resigned the District Presidency. The same is true of some other District Presidents, professors, and pastors with whom I attended the seminary, and others who were friends or acquaintances after I entered the ministry.

I believed at that time, as I believe now, that what is required in the Synod is not the organization of political parties of any kind, but of a consistent show of integrity in leaders and members alike, in pastors and laymen, from Synod to Districts to Circuits to congregations. Our efforts to get the Synod back on its Biblical track with integrity was particularly bothersome to the party of the left. That is why the Lutheran Congress of 1970 in Chicago was conducted.

1970 CHICAGO LUTHERAN CONGRESS

After the election of J. A. O. Preus as President of the Synod in 1969, the party of the left intensified their battle as Preus tried to take some corrective measures. By 1970 there was a great need to get the synodical loyalists to understand the nature of Biblical Lutheranism and how to struggle ethically in the battle for the Bible and for the church. This resulted in organizing the Lutheran Congress, held at Chicago from Aug. 31 to Sept. 2, 1970. I was Chairman of the Program Committee and so was responsible to contact and work with the various presenters who were invited. The book, *Evangelical Directions For The Lutheran Church*, prints the essays presented at this Congress. In the Foreword the co-editors, Dr. Erich H. Kiehl(now a professor at Concordia Seminary in St. Louis) and I, wrote the following:

"We must remember that most Lutherans have never walked this way before. Most of us have never experienced a situation where God's Word is openly questioned, where eternal truths are relativized, traditional theological terms are emptied of their Biblical meanings, and the process of normal communication between brothers in faith is made difficult with endless ambiguity.

"What shall we do as we face a new humanism, a new theology, and a new hermeneutic parading as permissible options for the Lutheran Church in the Twentieth Century? Speakers at the Lutheran Congress were conscious that many are deeply perplexed and pained by these challenges to the firm Biblical moorings of the historic Christian faith. The program was planned to give Scriptural and evangelical guidance and direction regarding the nature of Scriptural truth, faithful confessional life in the church, and evangelical communication of the Word."

The Essayists and Presentors were the following:

Congress Call to Order - Dr. Edwin Weber

THE NATURE OF SCRIPTURAL TRUTH
1. God's Word - Dr. Paul Zimmerman
2. Theologies - Dr. Martim Warth
3. Truth Versus New Humanism and New Theology - Dr. Francis Schaeffer
4. Shaping Society-Social Action - Dr. Richard Klann

FAITHFUL CONFESSIONAL LIFE IN THE CHURCH
5. The Confessions and Confessing Today - Dr. Manfred Roensch
6. Confessional Subscription - Dr. Robert Preus
7. Confessional Declaration - Rev. Alvin Wagner
8. Confessional Polity - Dr. George Wollenburg
9. Confessional Practice - Dr. Waldo Werning
10. Confessional Ecumenism I - Dr. Ralph Bohlmann
11. Confessional Ecumenism II - A Case Study in Communion Practice
    - Dr. Lowell Green

EVANGELICAL COMMUNICATION OF THE WORD
12. Christian Education - Dr. Erich Kiehl
13. Professional Education - Dr. Edwin C. Weber
14. Evangelism - Rev. Wm. Gast
15. World Missions I - God's Harmony and Man's Discordant Notes
    - Rev. Elmer Reimnitz
16. World Missions II - The Gospel Imperative - A Call For World Missions
    - Dr. Eugene Bertermann

GENERAL
17. Lutheran World Federation - Dr. Martim Warth
18. A Protestant Evangelical Speaks to his Lutheran Friends in a Day of Theological Crises - Dr. Francis Schaeffer
19. Greetings - Dr. Herman A. Sasse
20. Ordination Vow - Mr. Alfred Tessman
21. Confirmation Vow - Mr. George Mohr
22. Go Home Confessing - Dr. Wilbert Sohns

This book, *Evangelical Directions For The Lutheran Church* [31], is available from *Biblical Renewal Publications*, 1914 Wendmere Lane, Fort Wayne IN 46825 for $9.95 each.

ELIM and its "Missouri Out of Perspective" found the Congress and the publication of the book, *Evangelical Directions for The Lutheran Church*, very threatening, so in the Nov. 24, 1975 *MIP (Missouri In Perspective)* carried a special editorial and an editor's note which asked, "How did the Missouri Synod ever get into the mess it's in?" The answer, "A key factor unquestionably has been the elaborate political organization of so-called 'conservatives.' " They were unwilling to recognize that they had taken over the Synodical administration and system for purposes alien to God's Word, the Lutheran Confessions, and the Synodical Constitution. They were also unwilling to answer theological questions, so they distorted the whole issue by complaining about the big political machine of the party of the right. They found particularly menacing the suggestion that loyal members of the Synod become extremely active in the synodical structure in a legitimate way to confess their Biblical faith and to participate in the process of bringing the Synod back to purity in doctrine and practice.

The editor of MIP wrote, "Perhaps the most important paper of the 'Congress of Evangelical Lutherans' as the participants called it, was by Waldo J. Werning, who has through the years been recognized as one of the most powerful of the 'conservative' organizers." They found particularly threatening the 14-point "Blueprint for Winning the Confessional Battle." In this essay on "Confessional Practice" I suggested in earlier paragraphs, "We need creative scholarship in theology which produces materials and books that will lead pastors to an aggressive ministry. Let books be written to direct all churchmen toward evangelistic endeavors which confront modern man with God's truth and the power to straighten out the mess in the world, rather than accommodating our ministry to what the world wants to hear...Required is parish renewal in congregations and renewed commitment on the part of individual Christians in order to win the world for Christ. Theology should lead the way by a holy reverence to God's Word, teaching faithfully to break down human barriers and to build fires for mission outreach. There is a great urgency for retooling for our mission, and faithful theologians can direct us by challenging us to prepare for a lively ministry to reach the world in our lifetime."

This was followed by this encouragement, "There are many forms in which vigorous Confessional activities take place. The Confessional Lutheran should be a person whose authority is found in God's Word alone. He must be a man of faith - trusting Christ for his salvation and the Holy Spirit for his power. He must be a man of prayer and mean business for God."

The proposals for action were written and presented at a time when there were many in the Synod who were disheartened because the administration even under a new President seemed to be impotent in situations where people should expect their Synod to pursue Biblical and Synodical policies and practices. Undoubtedly, those who had taken the Synod hostage were the opposition, but today I regret the use of that term because it seems too confrontational. I did not intend these blueprints to be a call to war, but to confess

107

boldly in Christian love (Eph. 4:15). The proposals were:

"1. Take and keep the initiative at all times on the basis of the Scriptures and Lutheran Confessions, which are our only standard and norm."

"2. Name the questions and issues that are at stake. Never let the opposition divert attention to secondary matters or confuse the points under discussion."

"3. Don't get into arguments about words and definitions - use traditional terms and traditional meanings only."

"4. Keep the opposition on the defensive and show them to be disloyal. Thus stress not only the theses of every issue, but also the antitheses. When the opposition indicates disagreement, then insist on an explanation and definition; when shown erroneous, ask whether this is what they want. This insistence on antitheses and where they lead will make clear that the opposition is disloyal."

"5. Keep repeating that we are polarized and split theologically in most Lutheran Churches, and that it is those who are teaching contrary that are divisive. Our goal is not organizational unity, but unity in God's Word and in the Christian faith. We seek unity of Christ's believers through the Word which the Father has given, and then organizational unity and loyalty will follow."

"6. Be salesmen for the faithful Scriptural and Confessional Lutheran position. Be well prepared. Do your homework. One great fault of Lutherans: they read too little! Read such books as Francis A. Schaeffer's "Escape From Reason," and "The God Who Is There." Read Norman L. Geissler's "Christ: The Theme Of The Bible."

"7. Encourage vocal support and witness to the faithful Lutheran position and practice by leaders and all members, and speak against all unfaithfulness to the Scriptural and Confessional standard."

"8. Urge responsible leaders at every level to continue exploring the unresolved doctrinal problems within your own church and between churches and efforts to promote the true unity of the Lutheran Church. Seek discipline of errorists, even to their exclusion. Make them face their errors instead of the faithful running. Don't give up the church to errorists but ask them to withdraw. That will be the result of our 'State of Protest...'

"9. Encourage and participate in serious Bible study in our homes, schools, churches, and conferences to the end that we continue to learn the truth of God's word and will for our lives and apply it in practice."

"10. Alert others through regular channels in our parishes, areas, and districts to the crucial needs of the church in this hour, and invite them to be active Confessors of the truth, and admonish any who err so that they might repent and experience forgiveness in Christ."

"11. Show exemplary and dedicated stewardship, missions and evangelism efforts locally and throughout the world."

"12. Support officials on the local and district levels who provide positive Confessional leadership for the constituency. Support the leaders of your church in their efforts to supervise doctrine and life, remembering them in our private and corporate prayers."

"13. Outline and formulate a strategy that includes reading of essays and presenting of lectures on Scriptural and Confessional loyalty in the search to be an authentic Lutheran Church at all conferences, meetings, and at all occasions on all local, area, district, and national levels."

"14. Plan rallies and influence the various boards and committees to which we belong to utilize prominent speakers who will speak on Scriptural and Confessional loyalty in seeking to be an authentic missionary Lutheran Church." [32]

Reviewing that the "Blueprint For Winning the Confessional Battle" is confessional in tone, the *DC Trumpet* reprinted in the May 20, 1974, *Christian News* (page 2) the 14 points together with the appropriate quotations from the Lutheran Confessions: While the article talked about opponents, the Confessions called them adversaries. It was seen that the Lutheran Confessions do not allow indifference, lack of diligence in exposing the false opinions of the "erring party," and that their teachings are not to be tolerated. The Confessions show that these controversies are not, as some may think, mere misunderstandings or contentions about words, with one party talking past the other, and they do not reflect a mere semantic problem (FC, SD, Page 502). The Confessions speak about rejecting anything that is opposed to the confession of our faith, and to forewarn everyone of the errors contained here and there in the teachings of certain theologians. (507:19) Once again, the ELIM party avoided the issue of their unfaithfulness to God's Word, and tried to divert attention to procedures and semantics.

1971 Christian Herald Article

The January 1971 *Christian Herald* presented a classic example of what the party of the left (so-called liberal but misnamed moderate) and the party of the right (Biblical and misnamed conservative) struggle was all about. Obviously, party politics was on front stage, but it should be obvious that the presentations by author Kenneth L. Woodward, Elim member Omar Stuenkel, and I were authors of articles about the LCMS struggle: "The Missouri Synod Lutheran Civil War" by Woodward, "Here Moderates Stand" by Stuenkel, and "Here Conservatives Stand" by myself.

Woodward's article named the ALC-LCMS fellowship matter "unduly parochial in light of the 'global village' modern technology." In other words, since culture and technology had already decided that we are one world, so we should be one church, and Biblical doctrine is not germane. He told of the August 1970 meetings of the left and right parties in Chicago in which he states that I outlined a 14 point "blueprint" for winning the "confessional battle": "Don't give up the church to errorists, but ask them to withdraw. That should be the result of our state of protest." While 500 of us were meeting at a downtown Chicago hotel, the party of the left had 50 at Grace Lutheran Church in River Forest at which F. Dean Lueking stated, "Our intention is to be fully supportive of the resolutions of our Synod and to devote our efforts to working within the Synod as responsible Lutheran churchmen." These were no more than assuring words for the media, for the next five years would provide evidence of what great disagreements these self-claimed "moderates" had with Biblical theology.

Woodward did share that one of the stated goals of the LC-MS has always been "the conservation and promotion of the unity of the true faith and a united defense against schism and sectarianism." Woodward claimed that Jaroslav Pelikan, Martin Marty, and Arthur Piepkorn were "authentic Lutherans" and that we who hold faithfully to the synodical doctrinal positions are "fundamentalistic Lutherans."

Omar Stuenkel's article listed "What does it mean to be human?" as the first question to face, and then mentioned that the struggle relates to "questions of authority. Some take a rigid and static view of the Bible which easily becomes literalistic, dogmatic and judgmental. I believe they endanger the church at a crucial point." He is right in stating that the Bible is not a legalistic club and that if questions are to be considered honestly, openness must be possible in church to state convictions, but then he proposes tentative conclusions. His was a very short article which actually dealt with religious philosophy, not with confession of the true faith.

Because my article deals very directly with the issues involved, clarifying the theological and political questions, my entire article will be reprinted here.

HERE CONSERVATIVES STAND

The President of The Lutheran Church-Missouri Synod is under attack for maintaining the position imposed upon him by the Lutheran Confessions and for trying to do what his church's constitution requires of him. He is complying with the solemn charge to which these attackers are also committed by their ordination vow and their voluntary signature to the constitution. At stake here is not a "conservative-liberal" battle, but the very Gospel itself.

The only reason for the existence of a Lutheran church is that a group of people treasured the Gospel so highly that they made a covenant with each other to give their lives to hold and share it faithfully with each other and the world. The LC-MS has from its beginning had scriptural distinctives which include the centrality of the saving Gospel of Jesus Christ, the unique authority of God's Word with a determined confessional position as seen in its reformation symbols, the priesthood of all believers and the evangelization of the world. This puts us in a spiritual fellowship with all other true believers in Christ which we seek to express in such a way to encourage all fellow Christians, while holding to Lutheran distinctives in our particular group, to contribute to the entire body of Christ. This Gospel heritage has been held sacred in mutual trust through voluntary pastoral vows without reservation to the Holy Scriptures and the Lutheran Confessions and the signing of the Synod's constitution. The Confessions show the Gospel in the narrow sense to be the consoling proclamation of God's grace in Christ, true God and true man, who through his death gives believers forgiveness of sins; and in the general sense the Gospel embraces all scriptural doctrine because Christ wraps himself in the eternal word which claims total accuracy for all its parts, historical and miraculous.

As the Confessions do battle for true doctrine for the Gospel's sake, so the LC-MS without becoming Biblicist or fundamentalist holds solemnly to an infallible, written Word. If we violate any part of that Word, we violate the Gospel. Our Confessions say that the "immutable Word of God" does not err nor lie. (The church which will not hold to Scripture **alone** will not long retain Grace **alone**.) Therefore, we hold to a miraculous inspiration and inerrancy of the Bible rather than an historically conditioned book with only temporary validity. With the Confessors we believe that divinely revealed truth can be articulated in correct formulations. This is not an academic preoccupation, but a pastoral concern for justification by faith aimed at life for the welfare of people and for mission. We are convinced people will die from thirst if we do not have a trustworthy container that holds water, whether physical or spiritual.

When something foreign to the Gospel and the Confessions seeks to enter the LC-MS, all the members are bound to act firmly and evangelically. One foreign body we resist is the higher critical method with presuppositions which reduce the Bible to inspired literature, some true and some undependable. With Scripture, we reject a diversity which allows such independent and individual treatment of the sacred writings, where everyone does what is good in his own mind. Holding with the Confessions that the "church needs a consistent doctrine" and that we must "state true against false doctrine," the LC-MS and its Commission on Theology has upheld pure doctrine as it condemned a false diversity claimed by a few members of this body. Freedom in Christ does not allow irresponsible, academic opinions to conflict with the pure doctrine of the Gospel. Nor does it give license to use freedom for reason to exert its independence, only to be entangled in another bondage.

Scripture asks that Christ be worshiped with one mind and one voice, and our Confessions demand a unanimous agreement. The recurring theme of "unanimous consent" allows no loopholes so that believers and nonbelievers alike should not be offended. Where unanimity is lacking, the Confessions ascribe this to Satan, who sirs up discord to pride and arrogance and to ignorance and stupidity. This is why there is a strong objection against those who in doctrine and practice go beyond or reject the mutually agreed standard. The constituted body entrusted with giving continued direction is the Synod in convention. When the convention speaks on doctrinal matters, it does so to apply the Scriptures and Confessions to a particular issue to reinforce its Gospel and Confessional position. The last three LC-MS conventions passed doctrinal resolutions which revealed substantial problems of a small vocal minority seeking to ignore the church's position.

The 1965 Detroit Convention faced a request that professors abide by adopted statements as officials of one district "verified by personal confrontation that certain members of Concordia Theological Seminary in St. Louis do not consider Cleveland Resolution 3-17 [The Synod beseeches all its members by the mercies of God to honor and uphold the doctrinal content of the Synodically adopted statements] binding upon them, but feel free to carry on the differing conclusions of their theological explorations into their classroom..." Another district in early 1970 stated in a resolution that evidence testifies that "certain professors at our Synodically supported schools teach contrary to part of Christian doctrine," on such issues as authorship of Scripture, Virgin Birth, historical nature of Genesis, etc.

Recurring topics of the last four conventions that spoke of existing problems and sought to correct critics, were raised in the 1969 Denver actions in ten resolutions affirming the authorship of the Pentateuch and Isaiah, the Scriptures as the infallible, written Word of God, preservation of doctrinal unity through proper supervision, historicity of the New Testament and the Synod's historic position of the Word. Last February the Council of Presidents reaffirmed those resolutions as they prayed that "unity may be restored."

It is obvious that this is no "conservative-moderate-liberal" struggle, but a simple question of integrity and of keeping a sacred trust between brothers in Christ. To preserve our Gospel mission we have accepted supervision mutually which we did not consider servitude: we took our vows voluntarily. Taken with full knowledge of their demands, these solemn agreements are not a repression or restriction of anyone's rightful freedom. So when Biblical doctrines are disregarded and discipline is called for, such phrases as "heresy trial" and "head-rolling" becomes cruel secular judgments of the church's spiritual process of edification, which includes discipline.

If the Confessions remind an earthly emperor that it is his duty to watch that pure doctrine not be suppressed (Apology, AT. XVI), we should not be surprised that the LC-MS at its Denver Convention resolved "that the President of the Synod and others responsible for doctrinal supervision be earnestly and prayerfully encouraged to continue such supervision...and that all members of the Synod be encouraged to support and cooperate..." (2-06). When the president answers this request, he is not on a private vendetta, but obeying Synod's will. The Synod does not desire schism, but it will not avoid disciplining, maintain a false peace or permit room for unscriptural activities.

This persistent record of LC-MS action is sufficient proof that the great majority (not a clique) is anxious to get off the sidetrack which perverts scriptural truths, and be busy sharing the Gospel while there is still time. The LC-MS has the choice of holding pastors and professors faithful to the mutual covenant under God or to be honest and change its Confessional and constitutional standards. It cannot allow an unwillingness to keep this trust or a cowardice that does not stand openly. If the Synod fails in this, it will deserve the contempt of outsiders as well as the condemnation of our Savior whose Gospel we share.

Only the sure Word of promise will keep us effective in the Gospel mission, and only obedience to the truth of the incorruptible Word will assure a fruitful witness to a world whose only hope is the eternal Christ of the Bible. Such a witness must be given at all costs.

- -

It must be told that my article was printed only because of the contact which I had with the secretary of Grace Lutheran Church of River Forest (revealed also in James Adam's book, "Preus of Missouri"), who informed me that Rev. Lueking and his party of the left were boasting that there would be a bombshell before the Milwaukee Convention in the publication of an article by Kenneth Woodward on the Missouri Synod. Upon hearing this, I contacted the Editor of the *Christian Herald* and told him that we had learned that such an article was being published, and was it true? He said it was. So I said that I knew that he wanted fair treatment of the entire subject and that it would be advisable to have an orthodox member of the LCMS to state the historic position of the church in this day of conflict. Obviously, he agreed and so asked Omar Stuenkel to write for the party of the left and me for the party of the right. Lueking's group made copies of the article to use as propaganda before and at the convention. [33]

The party of the left was well-befriended by the public media, which regularly was used to paint the loyal Missourians as the bad guys and the rebels as the good guys. *Newsweek*, July 12, 1971, published an article, "Lutherans to the Right." It was claimed, "On the right, the LCMS has spawned a dozen factions that are conducting a spirited fight to purge their church of liberal scholars and socially active clergy. On the left, a handful of comparatively disorganized liberals are fighting - mainly through mimeographed newsletters - to keep their seminaries free of outside conservative pressure and their pulpits open to ecumenical exchange." That was pure leftist propaganda that came out of their headquarters at Grace Church in River Forest. I had access to all of the materials, activities and program of the Frey-Lueking group, and it was clear that this was not a one-horse outfit.

The *Newsweek* article correctly assessed the situation in this statement, "The issues dividing the LCMS involve doctrine, discipline and ecumenism." *Newsweek* also correctly quoted me from a long telephone visit with an editor in which I said, "There's a lot of dishonesty going on among liberals." Indeed, there will always be people who will misunderstand God's Word or move away from it in any church body, and they can be dealt with as long as there is honest communication instead of double-talk and semantics that result in theological confusion. The article states that church liberals labeled the inquiry into the St. Louis Faculty a "witch hunt." Looking at it now 20 years later and seeing the results of the theology of the AELC and ELCA, where former liberals are now "conservatives," no historian would dare call it a witch hunt. There is gross denial of God's precious Word. This article was written in preparation for the 1971 Milwaukee Convention.

After a quick glance at a sheet which I found in my files on which I had written some of the memorials on doctrine at the Conventions from 1962 to 1969, an observation on the use of convention resolutions about true doctrine and practice should be shared. A summary of the main memorials to these conventions included the following:

1. *Cleveland, 1962*: –3-17 - uphold Synodically adopted statements; –3-10 - preserve and promote pure and correct teaching in our institutions; –3-09 - supervise doctrine and practice; –3-18 - emphasizes sure truth.

2. *Detroit, 1965*: –2-01 - reaffirm unwavering loyalty to Scripture as the inspired and inerrant Word of God; –2-06 - supervise doctrine and practice; –2-08 - uphold and honor doctrinal content of Synodically adopted statements; –2-14 - respect Scripture; –2-17 - reaffirm "Quia" subscription to the Lutheran Confessions; –2-20 - confess Christ as the only way to heaven; –2-26 - reaffirm our belief that Old Testament prophecies of savior are fulfilled in Jesus Christ; –2-27 - reaffirm the historicity of the Jonah account; –2-35 - author-

ship of Pentateuch and book of Isaiah.

3. *New York, 1967*: –2-16 – reaffirm our position on Scripture; –2-30 – reaffirm our position on certain doctrines; –2-31 – affirm our position on Creation, the Fall and related subjects; –2-37 – deal decisively in cases of alleged false doctrine.

4. *Denver, 1969*: –2-01 – authorship of Pentateuch and Isaiah; –2-02 – continued exercise of doctrinal discipline; –2-03 – reaffirm our position on the Word; –2-06 – preserve doctrinal unity through proper supervision; –2-16 – reaffirm the historicity of the New Testament; –2-27 – honor and uphold the doctrinal statements; –2-20 – assure Synod's intent to abide by its Scriptural basis; –2-23 – affirm the desire to follow orthodoxy; –2-35 – abide by the historic position on the Word; –2-38 – affirm inerrancy and request the CTCR to give further clarification; three memorials raised the issue of church discipline.

The 1971 Milwaukee and the 1973 New Orleans Conventions were just more of the same. As you look at this line-up of affirmations and reaffirmations, what impression do you get, and what is your reaction? This is what hit me like a ton of bricks as I looked at these: here is a confessional Lutheran church body in which rebels had perverted the doctrine and the system and in which Synodical and District officials were either incapable or unwilling to act according to their Biblical and constitutional requirements; church discipline had broken down, and the adjudication system was not available or not used. Instead, every two years or so, the ecclesiastical trumpets were sounded at a convention with clarity by a majority (while a minority were voting against fidelity to the Word in doctrine and practice). Here we see the church fractured by the rebels into two warring parties - one which was shouting procedures and love, while the other was passing resolutions on remaining faithful to Biblical doctrine and practice.

Neither party were using the church system properly. That's no way to run a church. We should deal evangelically with the disobedient and never again allow a shouting match, name-calling and labeling. Unfortunately, all kinds of public forums such as the Great Theological Convocation in St. Louis from April 14-18, 1975 (where theologians on both sides were lined up at the microphone, and nothing was settled except much steam was released), were conducted in which the public denunciations continued, rather than facing each errorist with his own words and actions through Matthew 18 and then the adjudication process of the Synod.

In the midst of this the Synod's Board of Directors in response to the "Declaration of Determination" by Frey and Lueking to the Board meeting on January 28, 1971, called upon the "vocal few on the right and on the left to lower their voices" and get on with the work of the Church. Unfortunately, the Board had no more to offer than pious platitudes about a hope that somehow Christ's reconciliation might govern our relations with our brothers without offering any concrete suggestions or action or assistance to pursue Matthew 18 and the system which had been unused by either the party of the left or of the right. The only hope for success, the Biblical way, was completely ignored. In the meanwhile, some of the loyalists became impatient and organized the Federation of Authentic Lutherans, some of whom entered the Wisconsin Evangelical Lutheran Church and the Evangelical Lutheran Synod sometime later.

Those were very frustrating days for those of us who wanted to pursue Biblical procedures in settling the grave Synodical problem. As the leader of the conservative group until the election of Dr. J. A. Preus as President in 1969, I did not feel comfortable with dependence upon a political party of the right and to use *Christian News* as the mouthpiece. However, no other alternatives or options appeared since the Synodical system was closed to us, and none of us had any other insights as to what the right course might be under the circumstances. Under God, we did the best we could. As I look at it even today, I can think of no other way that the turnaround could have been accomplished, even though

I am very uneasy about using a political organization to do what Biblical procedures should have done, but they were not available to us because the party of the left held us hostage.

I am sure that President J. A. O. Preus felt about the same as I described in the previous paragraph. Before too long, *Missouri in Perspective, Christian News, The Badger Lutheran*, and *Affirm* were expressing unhappiness about the way the Synodical administration was handling things. Quite consistently, explanations and defenses had to be made by the Synodical President about what he had said or done by political tactics which he felt had to be carried on in order to win the battle. Whether it was a "deal," or "talking out of both sides of the mouth at the same time," or "moving toward the middle," or condemning "both extremes," or hoping that ELIM can find "its proper place" within the Synod, the Biblically-oriented members of the Synod were driven to desperation by some of the pronouncements of the Administration.

Soon after the election of Dr. Jacob Preus in 1969, the Council of Presidents on October 3, 1969, passed and sent a resolution condemning *Christian News* to the Missouri Synod, and printed it in the *Lutheran Witness*. It should be noted that some of the District Presidents soon withdrew their signatures, while others at least privately, if not publicly, regretted their action. The COP statement asserted, "We are of the conviction that the publication now known as *Christian News* disseminated with or without the prior consent of those who receive it is an obstacle to the furtherance of the objectives of the Synod, breeds mistrust, creates unnecessary tensions, and disturbs God's servants in the performance of their tasks. We, therefore, unanimously repudiate this publication and caution against lending credence and support to it. We pledge to help the pastors, teachers, and congregations of the Synod attain a greater measure of mutual confidence and joy in their service."

This was a very unchurchmanlike action on the part of the COP for a number of reasons: 1. None of them had the courage to go to Rev. Herman Otten to point out his alleged misrepresentations of the situation in the Synod; 2. Instead of using the church system to correct an alleged wrong, they used the media to try to condemn and intimidate; 3. Some of the District Presidents were covering up their own delinquencies and not facing the reality of their own sins, and in essence were like "the pot calling the kettle black"; 4. The fact is that some of those on the conservative side, including Preus, had been in an alliance with Rev. Herman Otten, as I was. In a way, that could be justified under the circumstances. Otten requested a thorough investigation of *Christian News* formally of the COP, but they ignored it, which made their public criticism very hollow. Preus said that between January and July of 1977 that Otten told 57 lies, but he never identified one, as he said that they cannot even be counted.

When the President in 1978 to 1981 got into a fight with *Affirm* magazine, the *Affirm* editors responded that the President was guilty of a low blow and a cheap shot. Various letters and telephone conversations were exchanged between the *Affirm* Editor and the President. *Christian News* finally found its editor compelled to write in a March 16, 1981 (page 4), article: "The Chief Backroom Politician in the LCMS, the Pot calls the Kettle Black": "Resolved, that Balance Inc. express its appreciation to the professors and the past President of Concordia Theological Seminary, Springfield, Illinois, for their contributions and their personal encouragement..", Otten wrote.

"Some of the 'back room politics' Preus now condemns took place around his ping pong table. The conservatives who worked with Preus were at times referred to in the inner circle as the 'ping pong' club. Prior to Preus' election in 1969 he approved of various open letters which appeared in *Christian News* exposing the fact that the administration of LCMS President Harms was defending liberals at Concordia Theological Seminary, St. Louis, and elsewhere in the LCMS. We were in close contact with Preus. But immediately after his election in Denver in 1969 he acted in public as if he hardly knew us. When the press reported that he disavowed us, he called from Denver to tell us that Dr. Walter Wolbrecht was actually responsible for the story and he pleaded with us not to reveal our association."

Let it be said emphatically that if there would not have been a Rev. Herman Otten and *Christian News* before 1969 and even up to 1973, someone else would have moved into that vacuum. The Synod administration, most Boards, the church press, and most of the system were not available to orthodox Missourians. The problem with fighting the left's political tactics with constitutional procedures by the President was that it made it appear that he was a politician like them, which was not really true. Utilizing administrative strategies instead of a simple Biblical approach to confront theological aberrations with theological questions and appropriate theological charges allowed the left to get into a cat-and-dog fight which served their purpose and which they used to regularly shout, "Foul!" Their's was a tactic of "show of right," but it worked, for it even gathered some conservative loving people who saw the strife as a procedural one rather than theological. Unfortunately, they discovered the truth too late, after they had been part of the AELC or even the ELCA.

President Jack Preus' theological positions and goals were absolutely correct. The Elimites dare take no comfort that there was a difference of opinion between J. Preus and these loyal Missourians. The Elimites were clearly wrong!

On a number of occasions both in personal and telephone visits and in letters, I tried from early on to encourage the President, my good friend and ally, to avoid administrative and political tactics as much as possible, but to follow Biblical procedures, to major in theology and to avoid depending too much on procedures. I believe that a series of private letters to the President during 1970 and 1971 will be quite revealing when they are read by men who are trying to gain an historical perspective of the administrative strengths and weaknesses in the years following 1969.

A February 25, 1970, letter indicates concern about an appeal to the "so-called middle," while criticizing the two extremes was no way to lead a church. Disillusionment was expressed on the part of my colleagues also about the use of political tactics in the place of consistent Biblical and Handbook strategy.

I wrote a March 24, 1970 Memo to the President which asserted, "The Synod loyalists seem to be saying:

1. Everything must be done that everyone understand the confessional, Scriptural, and Handbook basis. Anything less than this is not only confusing and self-defeating, but further degrades the Synod by continuing the path of the previous administration. This requires consistency and avoidance of contradictory statements or action.

2. The work cannot be done by an underground which gets private assurances and quotations that things are happening at one place and another, but leaders cannot be quoted. The only thing that will cause faithful members to work is what they hear publicly from their President and leaders. Pipelines will no longer carry reliable information which will be believed.

3. Private and public assurances that 'things are being taken care of' have lost their credibility with the previous administration. When people hear this today, they think something is being hidden or is being allowed to happen.

4. There can be no more talk against polarization. Tietjen and the liberals are warning against polarization because it is their only hope to make it a political issue. Everyone knows that this is a dead issue, for the Synod is totally polarized!

5. Definite and consistent **action** is required. This action means regular reporting to the

Synod of actual problems that have been learned through the press and other channels(if they don't get reliable information - though only partial - they will get unreliable information from other sources and conclude the President is not interested). Next, action means doing something about cases that have been properly brought step by step to the President and now demand action. Right now most of the Synod is convinced that it does no good to take the proper steps because from past experience nothing will be done anyway. Now every time anyone is asked to write a letter or bring a complaint or take some other action against someone, the first point raised is what assurance do we have that our leaders will do something about it (they say that it is a waste of time). Only action on the part of leadership will convince members that it is worth doing what is requested and required...

6. Proper decisions must be made when requested on individual cases. Delay and no answer are the wrong actions. When the Constitution and by-Laws clearly state the facts and the situation calls for action, then the Synod cannot tolerate the argument, 'We are afraid we can't win this one.' Who decides that required action be denied because allegedly it can't be won? What Scriptural or constitutional reason is there for such an attitude? Can the Synod long survive that course? This is completely self-defeating.

7. The Synod's Constitution and By-Laws are sufficient to get the job done. The provision of the Constitution and By-Laws give stated officials the power to take definite and firm action in cases where men teach contrary to the Scriptures and Confessions. The same is true of men who are involved in unionistic worship services. The troublemakers do not have a constitutional leg to stand on."

That was written 22 years ago, and is still valid today.

A letter of December 14, 1970, to the President requests that the matter of polarization be clarified because the party of the left is using it to their advantage: the one who is confessional in speech and action is painted as divisive and guilty of polarizing; its true meaning relates to those who are disobeying Synod's doctrine and practice. The letter also encourages Synod's Praesidium, loyal District Presidents and other Synodical officials to take a public stand on basic issues and continually ask, "How can this be right? How can we tolerate this?," and challenge what is wrong. We must stop private assurances of Synod and District leaders while maintaining public silence. Why must we depend upon a political organization instead of active leaders to bring the Synod back to its historic Biblical position? This is no time for second-guessing and saying, "I am afraid we cannot win this one, so we will do nothing."

I wrote, "The basic issues before the Synod involve **obedience to God and His Word,** and if we really expect a victory **for God,** then we had better fight with spiritual weapons and not with political guesses which are essentially forms of unbelief or doubting God's Word. There certainly are legitimate concerns for timing, but such questions as doctrinal affirmations, discipline, correctness of the St. Louis Seminary inquiry, ALC fellowship, adoption of doctrinal resolutions are not to be decided by political measurements as to whether we can win or lose..." The letter continues, "We dare not worry about how the secular and church press handles Missouri when it ultimately is turned about to be a true servant of the Scriptures and the Lutheran Confessions. Missouri will be shown to be the worst Biblicist, fundamentalist, legalistic, 16th Century archaic, negative, church body by them!"

On November 23, 1971, I wrote to the President with carbons to four Synodical leaders and two laymen concerning inconsistencies which were harmful. It was written in response to word heard from many members of the Synod, "The President will not do a thing." This letter contained a lengthy discourse on the total frustration I had as Chairman of the Board For Missions in response to the President imposing his political tactics, second-guessing, requests that are regularly changed or countermanded to the confusion of all, and regular change of signals.

A December 14, 1971, letter raised more concerns about confusion created in the Board for Missions because of presidential interference.

Much later, on May 5, 1975, I find a letter in which I made a strong plea against political tactics and fuller Biblical procedures, consistent and dependable leadership rather than vacillating. I provided five reasons why the political approach was unacceptable:

"1. The current approach depends upon political means to the extent that it violates the Scriptural approach.

2. Its strength comes from human organization, ingenuity, at the expense of the power of the Holy Spirit.

3. It is predictably self-defeating because it alienates all who are listening for a Word from God, who only hear a word from a man and his men who give political direction and assurance.

4. It is a Vietnamese 'no-win' war fought in the spiritual bushes on the spiritual Viet Cong terms and on their ground and will as surely as the U. S. involvement in Vietnam find The Lutheran Church-Missouri Synod in the situation where the loyal troops are running and bailing out while the Cong is on the attack...We must unite the church on the Word while the ELIMites stand mute and humbled before that Word. This is the only thing that is going to shut them up so that they no longer shout back every time you or we say something!

5. It is **wrong**! Anything that is wrong is not right. Anything that is wrong will not have the blessing of God...What we want to do is what is right, what regains our integrity, what the Lord says, and consequently what will win at Anaheim and forever!'' A copy of this was sent to Vice-President Ed Weber.

Political Tactics of the Left

Administering a church on the basis of a political party or political tactics soon degenerates into a question as to who can outwit the other, who can gain the most power, who can play poker the best, and who can outlast the other. Analysis of the tactics used by the party of the left, and now by the party of the right, reveals some of the following characteristics:

1. There is an attack on persons, not discussion of issues. Unwarranted and untrue accusations are used to intimidate. They are divisive and polarize, but maintain that the others are divisive.

2. Public trials are conducted through the press and media, avoiding Biblical procedures. There is incessant repetition of accusations against the victims of their campaigns.

3. The Eighth Commandment is broken consistently and false charges are brought against the faithful by begging the question, half-truths, rationalizations, semantics, guilt by association, straw men, arguments, generalizations on the basis of one example, judgments on the basis of no evidence, evidence which does not allow the illogical conclusion, false reasoning, and failure to distinguish between the antecedent and causality. There is dishonesty and deception.

4. A theological ''elite'' is established who introduce new presuppositions, new terminology, new definitions, and then utilize either the old or the new depending upon the

situation and the opportunity to deceive. To correct this, two lists need to be established by churchmen - the historic and the pragmatic terminologies - and at any point of confusion to request identification of which list is being used. Require accurate labeling.

5. They claim to hold the high ground, and claim it is a battle between the good guys against the bad guys.

6. Political parties are organized as pressure groups.

7. The ecclesiastical system is perverted, and procedural tactics are utilized.

8. There is gang tackling or group pressure by the academic mafia and their supporters.

9. There is an insistence to be "pastoral" which means to procrastinate and fail to deal with the situations deliberately and Biblically.

10. They are reactionary, and do not pursue the basic issues, follow personal whims instead Biblical instincts.

11. The church is held hostage by people who have another agenda. There is vicious individualism with no concern for the brotherhood.

12. Everything is to be tentative, and they retreat when confronted, while giving meaningless assurances.

13. Undergirding the activities and tactics of church political parties is the giving of continued words of assurance, which later turn out to be false hopes. These assurances are given via speeches, letters and general rumor. There is much untruthfulness.

14. Another important aspect of church conflicts between warring parties is the writing of letters and trying to out-distance the other's party in getting support from individuals and churches through letter writing campaigns. I was a recipient of such letters myself when I was chairman of the Board for Missions during the years when the mission staff was in rebellion against the Synod. Very few letters had anything of substance and had no supporting evidence, only opinions and judgments on one side or the other. Letter campaigns are futile, because our Lord did not give the injunction to write letters to church administrators to complain about the actions of the other person to request correction of doctrinal errors. It is disconcerting to find many who would condemn a brother simply on the basis of the propaganda and half-truths which were found in some documents by the liberal mission staff or printed in MIP. The public trial was organized and kept alive by the party press.

15. False dichotomies are presented, as choices are offered between two complementary ideas that are made to be contradictory (for example, pitting the Gospel against the Bible).

There was no text book available which defined the nature of the church conflict and how to fight such a battle, what to do when the odds are completely against you or if you face impossible odds. Knowledge of the history of previous theological perversions introduced into the Lutheran Church in Europe and the confessionals battles of the Missouri Synod before 1950 offered no hint as to the street-fighting and meanness which can be experienced at the hands of the rebels who have captured a church body.

The Missouri Synod has never recovered from the trauma of all these years of internal conflict, and I am convinced that this is the basic reason for our dysfunctions today. Too many are still in denial, and who dares talk about it? We have and continue to hold our feelings inside and are unwilling to talk about it, and so we still do not trust one another. I believe that the reason for this is that we remain strongly on the political track, and have not yet even entertained the thought how we could seriously get back on the Biblical course in order to become spiritually functional again.

Walking into uncharted territory related to the liberal take-over of a church provided the scene in which the Missouri Synod already weakened, administratively disordered and disoriented, with many perplexed about the substance and the nature of the issues, and everyone wanting to be evangelical in action, made the Missouri Synod ripe for being bullied by the Synodical Administration and the party of the left to enter fellowship with the American Lutheran Church which was a catastrophe, spiritual adultery. This tragic matter is discussed in the next chapter. Until we purge our memories and our consciences from the guilt incurred from this corporate deception of ourselves, I see little hope for being the healthy and functional church that God wants us to be.

CHAPTER 6

THE SYNOD BUREAUCRACY AND PARTY OF THE LEFT PRESSURE THE SYNOD INTO ALC FELLOWSHIP.

By a thin majority vote Denver Resolution 3-23 on ALC Fellowship plunged the Missouri Synod into twelve more years of spiritual trauma. There is no way that this action could keep from adding pain, strain, and continued upheaval to the Synod, for it was the result of a bureaucratic and political campaign which honest historians must find nothing short of self-deception.

The carefully worded, ambiguous resolution contained the following half-truths and some truths, "WHEREAS...reveals consensus in the preaching of the Gospel...diversities of practice which do not constitute a denial or contradiction of the Gospel can be understood better, and agreement can be developed more easily toward a consistent evangelical practice for mutual edification, when Christians are united in the work of the Lord...Resolved, that the Synod recognize that the Scriptural and confessional basis for altar and pulpit fellowship between The Lutheran Church-Missouri Synod and The American Lutheran Church exists...that the Synod proceed to take the necessary steps toward full realization of altar and pulpit fellowship... that the Synod urge all its representatives and officials to work earnestly and sincerely toward a unified evangelical position and practice in areas of church life where disturbing diversities still exist...that the Synod direct its officials to make arrangements for promoting the widest possible mutual recognition of the doctrinal consensus and its implications for church fellowship among the entire membership of the Synod..."

THE FELLOWSHIP, THE CURRENT QUEST OF THE LUTHERAN CHURCH-MISSOURI SYNOD AND THE AMERICAN LUTHERAN CHURCH FOR ALTAR AND PULPIT FELLOWSHIP booklet was produced by the Lutheran Church-Missouri Synod and based on a preliminary presentation of this material on November 30, 1967, to the Council of Presidents, the Board of Directors and the Council of Administrators, and sent out by President Oliver R. Harms. The above booklet tells about the 1967 New York resolution 3-23 which stipulated the promotion of "the widest possible mutual recognition of the doctrinal consensus and its implications for church fellowship among the entire membership of the Synod." (page 8) It should be noted that the document also states that in preparation for the 1967 convention resolution that "in a final session held in January 1967 the commissioners addressed themselves to the unresolved issues before them. More precisely, they did not attempt to find a final settlement to the differences between the Synods. These differences related to the diversities that appear in the application of doctrine to practice." (page 7)

The bureaucracy was at work between 1967 and 1969. In an apparent attempt to try to make it appear that all of us who were presenting evidences and facts of various doctrinal aberrations in the ALC (as admitted in the above 1967 document), President Oliver R. Harms stated in an address to the Council of Presidents on September 11, 1968, "I realize too that we are now hearing echoes of past controversies and past indoctrination and rumor. There are instances in which reasons for our separation have been repeated so long that they have gained credence and prominence...I am mystified that we who have so wisely and wonderfully made the important distinctions between the heterodox and the Lutherans, now seem to have forgotten what it is that makes Lutherans distinctive from others and binds them together in a confessional embrace...again and again we have found doctrinal agreement among us as Lutherans who are loyal to the Scriptures and the historic Lutheran Confessions. And now, just as we were to promote the widest possible recognition of that consensus are we tempted to use our offices to thwart the will of Synod and promote disunity among us and between us?''

In response to the reports by District Presidents about serious doctrinal aberrations among ALC pastors and congregations in their areas, Harms stated, "These reports show there are many more who see the purpose of conversations with members of the American Lutheran Church to be an opportunity to discuss our differences - rather than an opportunity to explore the consensus which exists in the Gospel...It becomes evident that the proposed discussions will hardly be very evangelical, Biblical, or Lutheran. I fear they will be marked by a kind of sectarianism or separatism and by legalism." Can any one be blamed for coming to the conclusion that the gun was placed at the heads of the district presidents and of the Synod itself. In other words, "Don't disturb us with the facts."

As we will see later in this chapter, this speech as well as the entire campaign for ALC fellowship was based on the minimum and narrow consideration of a John 3:16 Gospel, not the entire Bible which brings us the Gospel. Revealing how shallow and desperate the situation was, the speech continues, "There is no hard and fast list of areas in which differences and diversities exist, simply because there is no hard and fast list of ways in which the Gospel may be denied or compromised." Many of the ALC discussions and transactions of those days were as embarrassing as this statement because of their denial of reality. But the speech assured, "because we respect one another's intentions, we are hopeful." Here was an agreement based on intentions, not action.

One of the examples of contradictions in this speech attempted to gain assent to ALC fellowship because their "United Testimony" had an orthodox paragraph on the Inerrancy of Scripture, "There have been hints that the United Testimony no longer has binding force in the American Lutheran Church. I have been assured again that this confessional statement stands. I have been assured that there is no desire or intention to get rid of the term inerrancy. I have been assured again that ALC pastors who deny the inspiration or authority of Holy Scriptures or the resurrection of Jesus Christ would be disciplined. Further, it has been explained that Dr. Schiotz's paper regarding the Scriptures was written for a very specific and limited purpose. It should be examined and criticized in this restricted context."

Read this assurance in the light of a report in the ALC *Lutheran Standard* (June 28, 1966) more than two years before the Harm's statement in which the ALC President Dr. Schoitz told the North Pacific district of his church that "inerrancy of the Bible applies to truth, not to the text." The official ALC magazine reports Dr. Schoitz declaring, "This Lutheran position saves us from deifying the book and frees us from a fear of historical criticism. Historical criticism has been a help to faith. In interpreting the ALC Constitution, which speaks of the Bible as 'inerrant' Dr. Schoitz said that inerrancy does not apply to the text but to the truth revealed for our faith and life." Later years revealed that the main theologians and leaders of the ALC totally affirmed the same unscriptural belief.

St. Louis Seminary President Alfred O. Fuerbringer in the *Concordia Theological Monthly* (November 1968, pp. 643-652) in an article, "What's Your Prediction?" continued the misrepresentations of the entire issue. Some of it was pure propaganda, "There are, as is well known, those who are firmly convinced that the time is not ripe and the proper conditions are not present for the full implementation of that fellowship. Although comparatively not really large in number and with relatively very few laymen involved, this group is quite vocal and very energetic, and evidently speaks out of genuine conviction. It is interesting, however, to note that some of the leaders of this movement favor and actually practice selective fellowship with ALC people...There is another group of people

- and it is fairly large, although not in any way organized - who are in favor of and hope for a declaration of fellowship, but in view of the spirited opposition, do not think 'it's worth the battle' at this time." Note how the author rewrites history and makes ours a small group, and vocal and energetic, but ELIM is fairly large and not in any organized. However, the most striking fairy tale here is that some of the leaders of our conservative movement "favor and actually practice selective altar fellowship with ALC people" - I knew them all and never heard of even one who fits this description. One wonders why the author felt constrained to fabricate this story.

Fuerbringer uses a hard hand and even speaks for God when he condemns those who found evidence to reject ALC fellowship, "It will amount to an evident rejection of the guidance of God the Holy Spirit to hold back the hand of fellowship..." He tried to sell the reader on the claim that if there were a plebiscite by secret ballot in the Missouri Synod that a majority would vote in favor of the declaration and its implementation.

It took twelve long years of anguish and dysfunctional life before the ALC fellowship was rescinded in the 1981 convention. *Christianity Today* [34] tells about these years of hypocrisy and spiritual adultery, "Although theological discussions between the two denominations held regularly over the twelve-year period, differences were not narrowed; in fact, they increased. Those differences included the inerrancy of the Bible, what subscribing to the creeds entails, ordination of women, abortion, and membership in ecumenical organizations. Lack of progress prompted the LCMS to move four years ago to a status 'fellowship in protest' implying that no significant progress was made or that if no significant progress were made, the altar and fellowship link should be broken." In those twelve years the hindrances to the fellowship of the ALC were not removed, but were actually clarified and proven to be there all the time.

There are several reasons why the ALC fellowship was so harmful to the LCMS and continued us on the dysfunctional path: It introduced a new notion of Biblical authority which undermines the historic Lutheran doctrine of the divine origin, absolute truthfulness and normative authority of Scripture and made this heterodox view equal with the historic position of the Missouri Synod. It introduced a new kind of ecumenism which ignores the Biblical doctrine of the spiritual unity of Christ's church through Biblical agreement and makes the unity of the church depend upon outward structures and on what the church says it believes rather than what it preaches, teaches and practices. It pressured a fellowship by political campaigns rather than allowing the Word of God through the Holy Spirit to produce true unity of faith.

Loyal Missourians produced various materials and provided presentations for various occasions to present the facts and the truth about the ALC issue. Besides the ones that I wrote and delivered which will be reported in the rest of this chapter, Dr. Robert D. Preus offered two: "To Join Or Not To Join" presented at the February 13-16, 1968, convention at Grand Forks in the North Dakota LCMS district, and distributed by that district; "Fellowship Reconsidered," delivered at the April 13-15, 1971, Wyoming District Pastors conference and distributed by Mt. Hope Lutheran Church of Casper (which showed why ALC fellowship should be rescinded). Then ALC pastor James Brooks of the ALC from North Dakota distributed a pamphlet, "Some of the Things That Concern Us Within Our Church." In the Fall of 1969 he published, "A Voice From the Parish," which listed his grave concerns about the doctrinal delinquencies of the ALC. As late as 1987 Dr. Rudy Skogerboe wrote of his objections to ALC apostasy in a book "dedicated to the faithful ALC pastors who have kept the light of truth alive in an increasing hostile culture." His book was titled, "Who Has Stolen My Church?"

In an attempt to give a short background of the issues which we faced in the years previous to 1969 when fellowship was declared with the ALC, I will summarize a major essay which

I have presented in various parts of the Synod and sent out to all pastors under a letter by Rev. David Wallschlaeger of Benediction Lutheran Church of Milwaukee on April 29, 1969. This document was titled, "Issues in Deciding The Lutheran Church-Missouri Synod and American Lutheran Church Fellowship Matter." This is the document:

Introduction to the ISSUES Presentation

"These pages are written because others requested that they might read what they had heard in a lecture on the American Lutheran Church fellowship issue to be decided at the Denver Convention of The Lutheran Church-Missouri Synod in July 1969. Far too many members of the Missouri Synod are confused because they hear well-known speakers on both the pro and con sides of this matter. Some feel they have full information only to learn that since 8 years ago there is a new American Lutheran Church, both organizationally and theologically. A recounting of the history of negotiations between The Lutheran Church-Missouri Synod and the American Lutheran Church is really beside the point, and such discussion does not provide valid insights for the decision to be made at Denver.

If the Missouri Synod knowingly takes this course of complete change, that is one thing. If she votes for fellowship with the American Lutheran Church with the thought that no changed commitments are made in Scripture and in fellowship principles, then she is deceiving herself!

This booklet is mainly one of quotations and witnesses (by design), so that firsthand facts can be gained as to what is really involved. It was designed to provide information required to make a proper and honest decision regarding fellowship with the American Lutheran Church at Denver. We cannot wish away such information, but it must be dealt with. All the recorded writings stand before us and will be a witness against us after Denver if they are not allowed to be a witness to us before Denver.

Our contacts with the ALC have been regular, and these have enforced the material presented in these pages. This is unfortunate because there are many ALC members who either are not fully aware of the problems or do not know what to do about it. We know of ALC members who even hope that the LCMS will not vote fellowship with the ALC so that their church will have reason to reconsider its teachings."

ISSUES IN DECIDING
THE LCMS-ALC FELLOWSHIP MATTER

(Invitational Presentation Given Originally in shorter form by Waldo J. Werning at St. Paul's Lutheran Church, Austin, Texas, at Croydon, Pennsylvania, and at meetings and rallies in Wisconsin - edited and printed at the request of various participants.)

The ALC Fellowship issue must be faced by all of us at two levels: first, there must be a discussion of the consensus and divergences with ALC pastors and people according to New York Res. 3-23; secondly, there must be a presentation of facts to members of the LCMS who are dependent upon factual material so that the full situation might be known. Unfortunately, the second phase presents some difficulties: If the full truth is not told, then the Synod is not prepared for the decision to be made at Denver and great harm can come to the Synod; if the full facts are revealed, it may make it more difficult to communicate later with our ALC counterparts in conferences where these matters might be resolved. Only honest and frank discussion on both levels will under God bring the blessings we seek, or we will face greater disunity within the LCMS and a great divisiveness between the two bodies if fellowship should be wrongly declared.

New York Resolution 3-23 speaks not only about recognizing a confessional basis and promoting recognition of an alleged doctrinal consensus and its implications, but also that there be work toward an unified position and practice in areas of church life where "disturbing diversities" still exist. Thus a responsibility is laid upon us to seek rectification with the ALC, and also to discuss and face such problems that still exist so that an intelligent vote may be made on whether there are still disturbing divergences that have not been corrected or dealt with. Is there any other alternative for God-pleasing fellowship or true unity?

True Fellowship to be Sought

Fellowship in the New Testament is seen as a union which individual Christians have with their God and Savior Jesus Christ established by the Holy Spirit through the means of grace, and the unity that exists between Christians through their common faith in Christ. Christians must ever look upon the fellowship with one another through Jesus as a precious gift, and this is to be cultivated. Eph. 4:3-6. There is also a fellowship in which Christians unite in an outward organization in order to carry on jointly acts of worship and the religious works with which Christ has commissioned His people. It certainly is the will of God that the inner unity which the Spirit has worked be given outward expression in common acts of worship (pulpit and altar fellowship), mission work, and other phases of activities designed to extend the Kingdom of God through the Gospel. Christians are earnestly to work for the external expression of the unity worked by the Spirit, not only by preaching the whole counsel of God and the Truth and by edifying the brethren through all means of communication, but also by rebuking error and admonishing erring brethren, and by separating from persistent errorists. We are seeking zealously the external expression of fellowship with all who have a common confession and loyalty to God's Word. Even while seeking fellowship, Scripture forbids us to tolerate error.

The "Theses On Fellowship" document produced by resolution of Synod (1947) and sent out by Dr. John W. Behnken on February 15, 1949, states that "the history of the Lutheran Church bears record to the fact that many errors arose within that church also (e.g., the controversies which led to the composition of the Formula of Concord). The warnings against false teachers are not restricted to teachers outside the fold, and there is no reason in Scripture to believe that the Lutheran Church has been exempted from the danger that Paul said threatened the church at Ephesus: 'Also of your own selves shall men arise speaking perverse things to draw away disciples after them. Therefore watch' (Acts 20:30 ff). Hence it behooves also the Lutheran Church to remember the injunction: 'Try the spirits whether they are of God' (1 John 4:1) and: 'Prove all things, hold fast that which is good' (1 Thes. 5:21). Consequently, when we consider the question of Lutheran unity or of fellowship between different Synods, two things must be taken into account: 1. Whether the church body has officially subscribed to the Lutheran Confessions. 2. Whether doctrine regularly proclaimed in that body deviates in any way from the Scriptures and the Lutheran Confessions as a true exhibition of doctrine taught in Scripture...The subscription to the Lutheran Confessions must always be implemented by the actual teaching and preaching of only sound doctrine, for the orthodox character of the church body is determined equally by its official confession and by the doctrine actually taught in its midst." (page 16)

GOSPEL

"Toward Fellowship" records some facts concerning agreement in the Gospel between

Lutherans: "For Lutherans the basis for unity or for declaring and practicing fellowship is to be found in the Augsburg Confession. Article VII of the Confession says this: 'The church is the congregations of saints in which the Gospel is rightly taught and the sacraments are rightly administered. And to the true unity of the church it is enough to agree concerning the Gospel and the administration of the sacraments.' "

To show the breadth of the Gospel, "Toward Fellowship" properly makes the following point: "The Lutheran Church-Missouri Synod has explained this article of the Augsburg Confession in its own document entitled 'Theology of Fellowship.' It says: 'The doctrine of the Gospel is not here to be understood as one doctrine among many, or as a bare recital of John 3:16, but rather as a doctrine composed of a number of Articles of Faith. For the doctrine of the Gospel cannot be understood or preached without the Article of God, which the Lutheran confessors say they teach **magno consensu**, (AC 1), the Article of Original Sin which shows man's need for the Gospel, the Article of the Son of God, who became incarnate and redeemed man.' The true understanding of Article VII of the Augsburg Confession is truly set forth by Herbert J. A. Bouman as follows: 'This does not mean that the specific locus **De Justificatione** considered by itself is all the Lutherans consider indispensable. Rather they regard the entire **corpus doctrinae** as bound up inextricably with justification. All doctrines have their place in this doctrine. All doctrines stand or fall with the doctrine of justification.' "(page 14)

"Toward Fellowship" quotes the ALC in its official statement at the founding of the new combined church: "The American Lutheran Church addresses itself to this point in its 'United Testimony on Faith and Life' as follows: . . . The Holy Scriptures bid us to continue in Christ's words (John 8:31) to beware of the leaven of the Pharisees (Matt. 16:6), to be on guard against false prophets (Matt. 7:15), to discern those who make a pretense of piety (Matt. 7:21), to mark them which cause divisions and offenses contrary to the doctrine (Rom. 16:17), to avoid being unequally yoked with unbelievers (2 Cor. 6:14), to regard as accursed to preacher of 'another gospel' (Gal. 1:8). It is our solemn duty to try the spirits whether they are of God (1 John 4:1), to continue steadfastly in the apostles' doctrine (Acts 2:42), to do nothing against the truth, but be faithful and admonitions can be ignored by the church only at great peril to its own spiritual life.'"(p. 14)

The LCMS document "Theology of Fellowship" is quoted by "Toward Fellowship" as continuing concern that the Gospel not be perverted in church fellowship: "By resolutely confronting, exposing, and excluding all that threatens to vitiate and destroy the fellowship, whether it be a satanic intrusion from outside the church or a satanic perversion from within." (p. 15)

It is very unfortunate that the impression has been given too often that in fellowship the word Gospel is the narrow understanding of justification, and that everyone who insists on more than that is legalistic and loveless.

Consensus and Diversities

New York Res. 3-23 ("Toward Fellowship," p. 9) not only speaks about an alleged confessional basis existing and about promoting recognition of this doctrinal consensus (its ambiguity will be discussed later), but it also requires that we "work earnestly and sincerely toward a unified evangelical position and practice in areas of church life where disturbing diversities still exist, particularly in reference to unchristian and anti-Christian societies.." That "disturbing diversities" must be settled before Denver's vote is also evident from "Toward Fellowship", p. 7: "In a final session held in January 1967 the commissioners addressed themselves to the unresolved issues before them. More precisely, they did not attempt to find a final settlement to the differences between the synods. These differences related to the diversities that appear in the application of doctrine to practice."

"Toward Fellowship," page 11, tells how the preamble of the Commissioner's "Joint Statement and Declaration" records: "The preamble recognizes that it is necessary to work toward the adoption and development of practices that conform to the Gospel we confess." The third essay states, 'Churches endeavoring to establish or preserve unity in the church need earnestly to raise these questions in the course of their mutual endeavors. They need to apply themselves in love to a correction of errors that conflict with a pure proclamation of the Gospel. They need also to concern themselves with the cleansing of practices that endanger the purity of the Gospel message." (*Essays*, p. 14)

That official statements, confessions and professions are not the true test of a church alone, but must be taught in classrooms and preached in pulpits, is also recorded in "Toward Fellowship," page 16: "By the way in which they employ the Word of God and the sacraments such church bodies proclaim their faith in the operation of the Holy Spirit to achieve God's desired results by means of the Word of God." This is also recorded in the Commissioner's Essay on the Church: "It is not sufficient that the Gospel is correctly stated in the church's confession. It must actually be proclaimed in the pulpits and taught in the church." (p.12)

The Word

The LCMS has a strong statement on the Holy Scriptures. The LCMS "Brief Statement" records: "We teach that the Holy Scriptures differ from all other books in the world in that they are the Word of God. They are the Word of God because the holy men of God who wrote the Scriptures wrote only that which the Holy Ghost communicated to them by inspiration, 2 Tim. 3:16; 2 Pet. 1:21. We teach also that the verbal inspiration of the Scriptures is not a so-called 'theological deduction,' but that is it taught by direct statements of the Scriptures, 2 Tim. 3:16; John 10:35; Rom. 3:2; 1 Cor. 2:13. Since the Holy Scriptures are the Word of God, it goes without saying that they contain no errors or contradictions, but that they are in all their parts and words the infallible truth, also in those parts which treat of historical, geographical, and other secular matters, John 10:35." (p.3)

We have already read from the Commissioner's Joint Statement and Essays and the Brief Statement that we are not to judge a church only by its confessions, but also by its public teachings and its practice in church life. The record of the ALC unfortunately shows some serious problems in this regard. We will study this issue chronologically.

1. One of the significant problems on the Word appeared first in a publication "THEOLOGICAL PERSPECTIVES" (A Discussion of Contemporary Issues in Lutheran Theology) written by members of the Department of Religion, Luther College, Decorah, Iowa, and produced by the Luther College Press. Luther College President E. D. Farwell wrote in the Foreword that they were originally "delivered as public lectures in the Fall of 1962", and they "represent an attempt by faculty members of Luther College to stimulate a serious consideration of the theological position of the Lutheran Church." Wilfred F. Bunge writes, page 42: "Luke is definitely wrong in saying that Paul agreed to these requirements." Page 46: "These are the words of the risen Lord speaking through the confession of the church and not the words of the Jesus of history." Gerhard Forde writes, page 56: "In the final analysis the verbal inspiration method is based on a theory - a human theory." None of these essays have been retracted.

2. In 1964 the ALC Board of Parish Education sponsored "The Bible: Book of Faith," written by theological professors of the ALC. Pages 71-76 are especially filled with the theory of multiple authorship of the Pentateuch (J, E, D, P), denying the Mosaic authorship. "The infallibility of the Scriptures is the infallibility of Jesus Christ and not the infallibility of the written text...Inspiration of the Scriptures is primarily a statement of faith

about the effective working of the Holy Spirit" (p. 148)

4. From that time enough controversy apparently resulted so that in 1966 ALC President Schoitz delivered an essay, "The Church's Confessional Stand Relative to the Scriptures," at two ALC District conventions and it was printed by vote of the ALC Church Council. The essay spends considerable time trying to establish the human side of the Bible and contains the very controversial statement: "The ALC holds that the inerrancy referred to here does not apply to the text but to the truths revealed for our faith, doctrine, and life."

5. The ALC Church Council officially adopted a generally good document at its sessions in Winnipeg, Manitoba, Canada, June 22-29, 1966, but which because of a very controversial statement opened wider the breach between the outstanding statement on inerrancy in the ALC's United Testimony and its public teachings. The LCMS "Toward Fellowship" makes absolutely no reference to this statement entitled, "Doctrinal Concerns," for it ignores the fact that the ALC "Doctrinal Concerns" paragraph C records: "To assume that the church can arrive at human concepts or expressions that are in every respect correct is as much a symptom of pride as to assume that the church or its members can achieve sinlessness in their daily lives. Both in living the faith and in knowing or expressing the faith, we all need daily forgiveness and amendment which the Holy Spirit alone can give." (p. 3)

Rev. Alvin Wagner, member of the LCMS' CTCR, quite accurately criticizes this official ALC statement by writing: "a. It virtually challenges the possibility of attaining correct doctrine. b. It calls the assumption of having correct doctrine 'a symptom of pride'. c. It makes a radically false and unbiblical analogy between the attainment of correct doctrine and achievement of a sinless life. d. It fails to make the vitally important and necessary distinction between objective propositional truth (assertions - doctrines) and subjective obedience to that truth. e. It misrepresents the Confessions on this point. f. It betrays a view of Scripture and the Confessions that can result in nothing but continued theological and Confessional erosion." (p. 4) Dr. Herman Sasse wrote to Pastor Wagner: "You are quite right in taking issue with the incredible statements in 'Doctrinal Concerns' about theological formulations...What a nonsense!...True Lutheranism has never and can never accede to that. The moment it does it has lost its sound confessional character and its certainty of the Gospel."

6. Charles S. Anderson (a professor at Luther Seminary, St. Paul, and an ALC Commissioner who helped form the essay on the Scriptures) writes in an otherwise generally good book, "The Reformation, Then and Now" (Augsburg 1966), the following statements that are confusing and cast doubt on the accuracy of God's Word: "The biblical writers, inspired by God to present his Word, his answer, wrote against the background of their view of the world. Their ideas of science, e.g. of geography, are not essential to the Christian answer; they are not relevant; in some instances they are not even correct..."

7. Paul Jersild, professor in the religion department of Luther College, Decorah, Iowa, wrote "What Are Those Theologians Saying?" in *Luther*, Vol. 4, Spring 1967, No. 2: "Our American Lutheran Church is rather obviously divided today on certain theological issues. Perhaps the one most basic and obvious difference among our churchmen has to do with their understanding of the doctrine of the Word....We who teach at Luther College cannot subscribe to scriptural inerrancy because our knowledge of Scripture prevents us from making such a claim." This statement has never been retracted. He places personal love and concern in the place of the authority and absolute Truth of God's Word when he writes, "As long as we are doing our work with a love and concern for the church and her mission in the world, you have nothing to fear!"

8. Philip A. Quanbeck, ALC Professor at Augsburg College in Minneapolis, wrote in

"When God Speaks," (1968) an Augsburg "Tower Book" to teach laymen: "Just as it is true with the Old Testament, so it is the case with the New, that the authors or editors wrote or edited the books without an awareness of writing Scripture." (p. 29) "In a similar way we would say that we cannot expect the Biblical writers to know more than their age allows them to know." (p. 31) "This is not to say that the Bible is not revelation. But it is to suggest that it is not a revelation which is somehow perfect, if by perfect is meant either without error or unambiguous or unequivocal." (p. 39) All these sentences are so foreign to the testimony of Scripture itself and to the Lutheran Confessions that it almost seems impossible that there is a defense of the ALC's position on Scripture.

10. After the experience of many gatherings of the ALC-LCMS pastors in the midwest it became a common experience to hear of a different commitment to the Word in the ALC than that which is found in the constitution of the ALC. There was no disagreement from the floor and very little after the meeting when an ALC pastor said at a joint meeting of pastors of the ALC-LCA-LCMS in Milwaukee on September 10, 1968: "The Bible makes God known that it is identified with THE WORD, but it is not identical with the revelation or THE WORD - for the revelation took place in history and God cannot be reduced to a book...I believe that one of our greatest idolatries can be our insistence on putting the Bible in the place of God for an authority, or source of authority..." This essay was discussed at a later date and all ALC pastors in a group affirmed that they tend to agree with the essayist. At a later conference this was discussed with yet another group of ALC pastors, where several stated that they disagreed - and one related that he was so upset about the content of the essay that he wrote to ALC Synodical and District officials, but received replies to "cool it!"

11. On January 12, 1969, the same attitude toward the Word continued as ALC Professor William Weiblen (Wartburg Seminary, Dubuque, Iowa, and author of one of the challenged statements in "Bible: Book of Faith") met in dialogue with Dr. John W. Montgomery at Concordia Teacher's College, River Forest, Illinois. He said, "We are not being called today to see whether our fathers wrote correctly or not...I cannot see how anything we say here can be correct....I do not deny diversity within the ALC, but God is beneficent enough to forgive....Our theological books are bound to be filled with incompleteness and excessive statements...Let room for diversity....It is impossible and meaningless to separate between human and divine, between error and non-error in Scripture."

12. The new Tower Book of Augsburg Publishing House entitled, "Creation, Fall, and Flood," (Feb. 1969) by Professor Terence E. Fretheim of Luther Seminary, St. Paul proposes Biblical errors, evolution, and a denial of the Flood: "Genesis 1-11 cannot be properly understood unless it is seen in relation to the entire historical work of J and P. We will now take a look at the cathedrals that J and P built to see what place Genesis 1-11 has in their respective structures." (p. 13) "One of the implications of this is that we today (as historians) cannot consider as factual some of the things which they thought had actually happened. This is the case with much of the material which we find in Genesis 1-11." (p. 31)

"It is quite reasonable to suppose, for example, that God's method of creating the human race was by means of development from one of the higher animals...The validity of one's faith in God as Creator does not depend upon whether the theory of evolution is wrong or right." (p. 39) "There is no doubt that the authors of the flood story in Genesis believed that the flood had actually occurred at some time in the past. Such a point of view is impossible for us today, however, at least as far as the details of the flood story are concerned." (p. 107)

If the LCMS closes its eyes and accepts the ALC with its present record on the Word, it will have repudiated Dr. C. F. W. Walther, its founder, who rightly said in his "Theses on the Modern Theory of Open Questions" (*Lehre & Wehre* XIV, p. 318 ff.): "7. No one has the liberty, and to no one may liberty be granted, to believe and to teach otherwise than God has revealed in His Word, whether that pertain to primary or secondary fundamental articles of faith, to conduct, matters historical or pertaining to the realm of science, matters of weight or seemingly unimportant."

LCMS Fellowship Matters

This part of our essay reveals the type and extent of confusion and ambiguities that have been experienced by the Synod since the New York Convention's Res. 3-23. Added to the already existing evidence of a lack of unity in the doctrine of Scripture, fellowship principles, and the lodge, it is difficult to comprehend how it is possible to unravel all the confusions that have existed and are growing, in order that an intelligent and God-pleasing vote may be taken at Denver.

Some have felt that there is a withholding of or even a rewriting of history in some instances in telling the fellowship story. Certainly, there has been an attempt editorially to create position and policy in regard to fellowship. With it there has been a tendency to propagandize. Added to this are the current unionistic abuses and fellowship violations where unionistic services including pastors and congregations have been conducted without any evidence of effective disciplinary action, and a casual and relaxed approach to the difference between the Synods in regard to membership in unChristian secret societies. A survey of District Conventions will reveal wide degrees of disagreement and consequent confusion about constitutional rights and validity of procedures. Does a District have a right to memorialize Synod not to vote for ALC fellowship or to ask for a referendum? Synodical leaders supported the opinion that Districts may not petition the Synod through Memorials concerning the pending fellowship with the ALC, and this influenced the District Conventions that were held early in 1968. This writer was among those who challenged this "Opinion" in a document entitled, "The Right of Districts to Petition the Synod." The result of contacts by many of us was an agreement on the part of Synodical officials that a District may memorialize Synod in this regard, but some Districts had already been influenced by the contrary opinion stated at their Convention.

Decide on the Doctrinal Basis, not Emotional Appeals

The *Lutheran Witness Reporter* of March 16, 1969, in its article "Reason For Fellowship" starts with two emotional appeals for fellowship - one by a LCMS mother with a son and daughter in the ALC, and another by a layman from a congregation where the majority came out of other Synods. These certainly are not happy situations and pull at heartstrings, but they still must be decided by honest and fair discussion of doctrinal facts and Synodical commitments. All such appeals are pure emotion, and no more. Some "pro fellowship" pastors will tell about years of wonderful association with certain ALC men with whom they say that are in full agreement. We certainly rejoice if such agreement has been discovered and experienced. Such pastors see no reason why they should deny themselves fellowship centering at the communion table. Let us ask some questions, however: Did such LCMS pastors discuss with them the disturbing resolution of the 1964 ALC Convention of "Bible: Book Of Faith" and the "Symptom Of Pride" statement of the ALC Church Council in 1966? Did they discuss the many books and articles subsequently written that prove that the ALC now has a completely new stance on Scripture? What are these ALC men (with whom some of our men feel they found complete agreement) doing about all of these contradictions and offenses? Did they solve the lodge problem and offense? Certainly, they are responsible to help correct the situation.

Selective Fellowship

The *Australian Theological Review*, September, 1957 [35] presents a major article on "Selective Fellowship" by Dr. Herman Sasse. Dr. Sasse writes as a theologian, not as a church politician. He states that "it is necessary to emphasize this at a time when theology is in danger of becoming the tool of church politics...And not what is opportune, what is useful, but what is true, what is the truth taught by God's Word."

In this article Dr. Sasse writes: "According to the Lutheran Standard, April 6, 1957, Page 12, the American Lutheran Church has adopted a resolution which reads: 'Wherever congregations and pastors of the ALC find they are mutually agreed in confession and practice with congregations and pastors of other Lutheran church bodies they may in good conscience practice fellowship of both worship and work.' " "The questions which arise out of this plan are: (a) Is it true that there are no doctrinal differences between the churches concerned, but only differences of practice, as the authorities of the ALC think? (b) Is selective fellowship, as suggested by the resolution, a means of overcoming existing disunity?...What has happened during the past 30 years to justify the statement that the various Lutheran churches concerned are no longer separated by doctrinal differences, but by practical issues?...But a confession cannot remain a real confession, if it is only inherited. It must be confessed..."

"In such an age we must teach our congregations and pastors to be very careful in exercising their rights and powers and to make no decision which may be fateful also for themselves. By no means can we give them the right to make a decision on church fellowship for themselves without taking regard to their Synod and church body, as long as they belong to that body. Synod or church body fulfills duties which the individual congregation or the individual pastor could not fulfill, if the decision on church fellowship were left to them. Suppose two pastors of their congregations would establish the fellowship envisioned by the resolution of the ALC. Either side would find that no difference in doctrine and practice exist between them. That may be true for the present. Would it also be true some years later, the congregations change rapidly, old members die or move to other places, new members come in? Also the pastors may change.

"The consensus which existed some years before might no longer exist. Suppose as a congregation of the ALC and a congregation of Missouri in one town, they would establish fellowship on the conditions prevailing at the moment. Would not the desire to maintain at all costs the fellowship established lead to indifference and finally the loss of that sense of the confessional obligation which always has been one of the outstanding characteristics of the Lutheran Church?...Our confession establishes not only the bond between those who now live, but also with those who have confessed true faith throughout the centuries. An agreement between two congregations would express only the consensus fratrum, not the consensus with the fathers and the future generations which will confess the truth of the Gospel to the end of the world. The catholicity of the confession in space and time would be destroyed if the church body which confesses 'magno consensu' were atomized and pulverized into a mere aggregation of individuals or small groups. In other words, selective fellowship would not further, but rather destroy the unity of the church bodies, and this means that measure of unity which had been attained."

Dr. Sasse continues, "Thus 'selective fellowship' is not the answer to the problem of Lutheran unity...It is misleading and cannot even be justified by the fact that within one and the same church a person may be compelled by his conscience to avoid the sacrament of a minister whose doctrine is doubtful or even false, as Luther has made it clear in his letter to the Christians at Frankfurt in 1532. How can we lay the grave burden of deciding whether or not **communio in sacris** can be practiced with members of congregations of another church body, on our pastors and laymen as long as even our bishops, church presidents and theological scholars cannot tell them what the unity of the Lutheran Church is which we are seeking?..."

It is not the personal conviction of the individual minister or congregation that can decide the question whether or not inter-communion is possible, but solely the entire membership of an entire church body acting together as a Synod. It is a wrong pietistic understanding of the great article on the true unity of the church to assume that if a minority or even half of the Christians and congregations of a church body at a given moment feel that they are in agreement, they are entitled and even obliged to have church fellowship. Will the LCMS fall prey to this pietistic thinking on the church and its unity?

A Summary Of The Issues

1. Recitation of the history of discussions with the ALC is irrelevant because we are dealing with a completely new ALC, both organizationally and theologically.

2. The public statements of the ALC on the Word are not only found in its Constitution and the United Testimony, but also in its 1964 Convention on "Bible: Book Of Faith" and the 1966 Church Council statement on Doctrinal Concerns. Furthermore, our Brief Statement and the Commissioners "Joint Statement and Declaration" ask us to test public teachings, not just look at an official statement of a church body.

3. John 17 and the High Priestly Prayer of Jesus dare not be evoked as Christ's will for a "Yes" vote on ALC fellowship at Denver. Christ's will for a specific situation cannot be known by anyone over others in regard to organizational fellowship at any given point.

4. To argue that "both churches have doctrinal problems" is to ignore responsibilities to our own church and to close eyes to a specific responsibility of correcting errorists in either church. It is not only a weak argument for fellowship, but a wrong one.

5. When the ALC declared fellowship with the LCA, another destructive barrier was placed between ALC-LCMS fellowship. We cannot expect the ALC to deny its declared fellowship with the LCA, because we have no agreement with the LCA.

6. The lodge issue is also a crucial question, for if we are in fellowship with the ALC which can no longer handle its lodge problem, we have approved something which our constitution and our doctrinal stand does not allow us to compromise.

7. When it is argued that we must trust both ALC and LCMS leaders when known facts in the ALC show otherwise, and when we are told that a majority of the Synod are for fellowship now, this can be considered only a pious opinion, but not a fact. It is not a majority in any case that dictates right, because only Biblical truths and the facts can dictate the right procedure.

8. The kind of selective fellowship proposed is worse than no fellowship. It goes against all Confessionalism, will be destructive, and leads to full fellowship and complete unionistic practices.

9. When an "Inter-Synodical Commission" is promised to help counsel and work out problems, the point seems to be that we can endure differences in position and practice because these matters "will be worked out." How can we expect the ALC to take problems seriously after fellowship is declared if we do not seriously discuss the same matters before it is declared. If they show no serious recognition or seriousness in facing doctrinal problems now, where will the motivation come to change or even listen later?

10. How can there be consensus with a group which has two positions - public statements on one hand, and public teachings and writings on the other hand? Is the consensus with

the official statements or with the public teachings?

11. Any church that faces the ambiguities and confusion that the LCMS has experienced in the past two years must first stop all ecumenical plans and get its facts straight and clarify issues before it decides a major issue. 18. The facts in such essays as "To Join Or Not To Join" by Dr. Robert Preus have not been answered or disproven. They stand as a witness that a consensus does not exist. It is painful for some to admit the reality of roadblocks.

12. ALC fellowship is not the most important issue, but a commitment to God's Word, missions, and Kingdom advance. We are for fellowship, but for ALC fellowship only when principles are kept. What the LCMS owes to the world in faithful adherence to the Word for the sake of Gospel outreach is as great a concern as what we owe the ALC.

13. We have fellowship agreements to honor with brethren in Europe (such as Germany, France, and Finland) and a desire for fellowship with Australia. Some leaders of the churches of Europe and of the Lutheran Church in Australia have indicated strongly that the LCMS cannot have fellowship both with the ALC and with them. If ALC fellowship is voted, then we have cut ourselves off with many of our brethren overseas.

14. If ALC-LCMS fellowship is voted, then the LCMS has put privilege over principle. This essay has provided numerous examples of the breaking of the Biblical and Confessional principles on various questions, including unionism and the lodge. If we put privilege over principle, we will lose both principle and privilege.

15. Let us keep all discussion on the issues. Too often we have heard emotional responses that have been improper and unfair conclusions that would lead to chaos and destruction. One such emotional reaction comes when ALC doctrinal problems are listed, and the retort comes, "Don't you even consider them Christians?" Such conclusions are a hindrance and greatly detrimental to communication in our Synod.

*   *   *   *   *   *   *   *   *   *   *   *   *   *   *

OBSERVATIONS FROM DR. HERMAN SASSE OF AUSTRALIA

THIS DOCUMENT WAS PRINTED AT THE REQUEST OF PARTICIPANTS WHO RECEIVED COPIES AT THE LLL MILWAUKEE ZONE SEMINAR ON MARCH 2, 1969.

Dr. Sasse wrote the following before the Denver convention regarding the article that follows:

"Dear Brother Werning: Yesterday I mailed to you a manuscript. You are free to publish it in any way you think fit. I wrote it as an historian, and mindful of the grave concerns which we all have. When I wrote this I was thinking of Dr. Behnken. Before each of the great synods and the crucial decisions he asked for my opinion, not to follow my advice, but to know what other conservative Lutherans were thinking. This is what I would have written to him in this case. Yours in Christ, Herman Sasse."

THE DECISION OF DENVER
by Herman Sasse

As The Lutheran Church-Missouri Synod at its Denver convention of 1969 decides whether or not it will establish church fellowship with the ALC, an irrevocable decision will be made which will not only determine the entire future of Missouri, but will also be of vital importance to the whole of Lutheranism in the world. In the beginning of the

19th century, under the influence of the Pietistic and Rationalistic movements, the end of the Lutheran Church as a confessional church seemed to have come. Entire Lutheran churches, among them the largest (the Lutheran Church in the older provinces of Prussia), had accepted the union which wiped out the historic border-line between Lutheran and Reformed churches...

The Lutheran synods in the Middle West of the U.S.A., consisting of German and Scandinavian immigrants, became a new stronghold of Lutheranism in the world and the center of Lutheran confessionalism. Through the influence of Walther's "Lutheraner," the older type of American Lutheranism became again conscious of its confessional heritage...

The great tragedy of confessional American Lutheranism was the split on matters of doctrine which occurred time and again and paralyzed its power. It began with the great dissent between Walther and Loehe on the question of church and ministry. This led to the schism between Missouri and Iowa which extended later to other synods, especially when the "Gnadenwahlstreit," the controversy on predestination and election, broke out. It is pathetic to see in this last of the real theological controversies within the Lutheran Church Walther and Missouri fighting alone for Luther's *De servo arbitrio* against their fellow Lutherans who were too deeply influenced by those remnants of synergism of which Pietism could never get rid. That all endeavors to solve these problems came to nothing may be regretted, but it should not be forgotten, that even the European scholars were not able to help their American brethren.

The decision of Missouri at Denver will be the final end of these endeavors which in the negotiations of the past decades have been going on. But the various documents published reveal the fact that the real issues between Missouri and what has become in 1960 the American Lutheran Church are no longer the issues of former generations. **New questions** have arisen, the most important being the doctrine of Holy Scripture, its inspiration and inerrancy, and the problem of the confession of the Church, the nature of the dogma of the Church, its binding force and its application in the problems of modern church life. Both churches continue in their doctrinal **statements** the old doctrines of Scripture and confession, **statements** on which there was never a disagreement between the fathers of either church. One often observed in the past that a pastor of the ALC preached as orthodox a sermon as his colleague from Missouri. It was on the whole a sound orthodox theology which was taught at Wartburg and at Capital some years ago. The students of that time did not differ very much from their fellow students of old St. Louis. And yet something has happened which has created a totally different situation. It is a profound change in the attitude of the ALC towards Lutheran Confessionalism. While Missouri has maintained, at least in its official statements and its conventions, its confessional status, the ALC does no longer want to belong to the outspoken confessional churches in contrast to a mere nominal Lutheranism...

Hence the answer to the question with which Missouri finds itself confronted, only an unqualified No to the offer of the ALC and a definite end of all negotiations with the ALC in doctrinal matters. The question is whether Missouri is strong enough to give such a reply. It would presuppose that Missouri itself is aware of its own weaknesses. Too long has Missouri seen itself as the stronghold and guardian of Lutheran orthodoxy. We do not intend to discuss the false doctrines proclaimed by the theologians of the ALC. Such a discussion would immediately lead to the question whether not the same doctrines have been proclaimed in Missouri by men in St. Louis whose orthodoxy is being taken for granted (by some)...

The **first thing** we have to **regain** is a clear understanding of the Word of God which was for Luther always simultaneously the written word of the Bible and the faithful proclamation of this Word in the preaching of the Church. They cannot be divided just as either is inseparable from the Word Incarnate. When we accept the Bible, we accept it as God's own Word, given by the inspiration of the Holy Spirit and, consequently as truth, as the inerrant Word.

The **second thing** we have to learn again is the great dogmatic heritage of the Ancient Church in the great Creeds which we confess with the church of all ages. Since the content of these creeds is thoroughly Biblical, as the Nicene Creed expressly claims, we do not allow a rejection of their contents, e.g., the Virgin Birth of our Lord and His bodily resurrection for alleged historical reasons. We reject expressly the error spread in our days that human language cannot express the truth of God sufficiently. The ALC has officially stated: "To assume that the church can arrive at human concepts or expressions that are in every respect correct is as much a symptom of pride as to assume that the church or its members can achieve sinlessness in their daily lives. Both in living the faith and in knowing or expressing the faith, we all need daily forgiveness and amendment which the Holy Spirit alone can give" (Statement on Doctrinal Concerns, Exhibit G. Approved by the Church Council of the ALC in 1966.)...

The **third thing** we have to learn again is the meaning of the confessions of the Lutheran Church. It is a most remarkable fact that the Church which in the 19th century became in many ways the confessional conscience of Lutheranism has not been able to develop the full Biblical and Lutheran understanding of the confession of the Church. This may partly be due to the error of churches like Iowa which regarded as binding on the church only such statements which were introduced in the confessions with a solemn formula such as "we believe, teach and confess," regarding all other questions as "open questions."...

The **danger** is that the administrative problems are solved by adopting the methods of the world. So the churches in Europe are governed after the methods of the states, while in America they follow the example of the big business concerns. The central administration makes the decision. The task of the church papers is to "sell" this decision to the people and to prepare the governing convention. All this is not ill will, it is the necessary consequence of a system whose primary victims are the church administrators themselves. They are or have been Christian gentlemen, perhaps very good pastors themselves. But the system makes them "administrators" whose main task is to see to it that the policy is faithfully carried out as it has been determined by the governing body. Human traditions and decisions, then constitute the unity of the church. We have practically adopted the African and the Roman system. He is considered a good pastor who renders unquestioned canonical obedience to his superiors. Whether he preaches the pure gospel and administers the sacraments as Christ has instituted them, this is a subordinate question. "We take that for granted," as the late Dr. Fry (LCA) used to say. But can it be taken for granted in our churches today?

How things have changed in our churches, even in those which seriously want to remain orthodox, is shown by the great example of "Marburg Revisited." The Convention of The Lutheran Church-Missouri Synod of New York 1967 did not find any fault with the Lutheran-Reformed Discussions reported in "Marburg Revisited," although in these discussions the Lutheran doctrine of the true Body and Blood of Christ was negotiated away and replaced by a mere personal presence. The same happened in India, where under the leadership of Dr. Martin Kretzmann in a document which rightly has been incorporated into a collection of union documents of our time the doctrine of Luther's Catechism ("It is the true body and blood of Christ") was abandoned. This happened in the year of the 450th anniversary of the Reformation. No one would have any serious objection against a Lutheran-Reformed dialog, as we all have to be prepared to give account of our faith and to learn whatever we have to learn from Christians of other denominations. But every serious dialog must be based on certain presuppositions. The participants must know what they are talking about. They must know what either part believes. At the time of the Reformation the colloquists had certain common beliefs. The resurrection and ascension of Christ were to them unquestioned facts of the divine revelation. This they are no longer today.

If we in conclusion may express a wish for the delegates at the Denver Convention, then it is that they all come well prepared to make a conscientious decision. This requires not only the thorough study of the convention papers, not only a critical perusal of the church papers, but a clear concept of what they want Denver to be. Should it be the end of Missouri as a confessional Lutheran Church and the transformation of the old Missouri into one branch of a unified Lutheran Church which allows everybody individually to understand the Lutheran confessions as he likes? Or should it be the new beginning of a confessional Church, bound to the Scriptures and the Book of Concord, and therefore **not in fellowship with the liberal and ecumenical Lutheranism of our time**. By fellowship we mean what the theologians call "comunicatio in sacris," altar-fellowship. This would not mean that we refuse such cooperation as is possible with Christians of other convictions and especially those with whom we are connected through a great historic heritage. The old slogan, "Lutheran pulpits for Lutheran pastors, Lutheran altars for Lutheran communicants," may be a bad formulation, for neither a pulpit nor an altar can be Lutheran. But this old Galesbury Rule of our fathers expresses a rule which has been valid in the church at all times since 1 Cor. 10:16f has made it clear that the communion of the sacramental body of Christ belongs together with the **communio** of the mystical body. None of us wants a repetition of the old strifes between Lutheran and Christians which so often have made the witness of the Church incredible. But we are deeply convinced that Christendom as a whole needs more than ever the unadulterated witness of the Gospel. The more we see around us the decay of the substance of the Christian faith, the less we are ashamed of giving a witness which no one else could give today. It would be the utmost lack of Christian love and true ecumenicity to refuse this witness.

This witness will be given at Denver, we are sure of that. May God give to those who have to speak that humility which helps to convince the erring brother more than anything else. Let your witness first of all be the confession of our own guilt, of our lack of courage perhaps to speak when clear speech was required. There is a time to be silent, and there is a time to speak. Sometimes there is a last opportunity to speak. It happened in a decisive hour in the church history of Germany that a churchman of great authority was asked to speak a certain word. He promised to do it. But he remained silent. Later he said: "I wanted to speak. I tried to open my mouth. But I could not open it. It was as if a mighty power kept it shut." In such cases we need Him who looses our tongue with His mighty: "Ephphatha."

May God bless the confessors of Denver and make this synod an "Ephphatha" Convention.

Herman Sasse

*   *   *   *   *   *   *   *   *   *   *

To Inform the Synod Why We Could Not Support The Fellowship Declaration

Despite pressure from the Synod administration not to break rank with the Counsel of Presidents in favor of the ALC fellowship, thirteen district presidents offered their own resolution to the Synod. This resolution which was suppressed and criticized told this story:

WHEREAS, we have been working and praying that the Holy Spirit would direct The

Lutheran Church-Missouri Synod to a God-pleasing fellowship with The American Lutheran Church; and

WHEREAS, extensive contacts and discussions have shown a wide divergence between American Lutheran Church constitutional statements and the teaching and preaching practices in the areas of Scripture, ecumenical principles and lodgery; and

WHEREAS, no official statement of agreement has been published as a result of the joint meeting of the theological faculties of The American Lutheran Church and The Lutheran Church-Missouri Synod; and

WHEREAS, we deplore the lack of basic theological discussions toward Scriptural agreement between The American Lutheran Church and The Lutheran Church in America which The American Lutheran Church agreed was necessary in dealing with The Lutheran Church-Missouri Synod. The Lutheran Church-Missouri Synod recognized both proper principles and improper involvements, in 1940, when it stated, "We do not see how the Missouri Synod could enter into church fellowship with The American Lutheran Church if the latter establishes fellowship with a church body which does not share our joint doctrinal basis." (DOCUMENTS OF LUTHERAN UNITY IN AMERICA, R. C. Wolf, Document 164, page 405); and

WHEREAS, the declaration of a type of selective fellowship reveals the impatience of men in the place of Spirit wrought unity sought by a church through discussion of all divergences in doctrine and practice; and

WHEREAS, the Constitution of Synod, Article VI, point 2, and the BRIEF STATEMENT of our Synod have made it obligatory that there be full agreement in doctrine and practice before declaring pulpit and altar fellowship, and

WHEREAS, fellowship with The American Lutheran Church would involve us with all the fellowship commitments of The American Lutheran Church, such as Lutheran World Federation, World Council of Churches, and other associations as well as fellowship with the Lutheran Church in America;

THEREFORE, we, the undersigned, take this means to inform the Synod that we could not support, for the above reasons, a declaration of fellowship with The American Lutheran Church at this time; and

We recommend a course of continued theological discussions with the prayer that the Holy Spirit may, in His time, bring a God-pleasing unity.

Signed:

E. C. Weber
Herbert W. Baxmann
Ellis Nieting
Alwin Reimnitz
Elmer Reimnitz
H. W. Niermann
Edmund H. Happel
Lewis C. Niemoeller
Victor L. Behnken
G. F. Wollenburg
Herman C. Scherer
Carl H. Bensene
Leonard Eberhard

More From Dr. J. W. Behnken

It has been often repeated if we do not learn from history, we are doomed to repeat it. Dr. John W. Behnken provided wise leadership for our Synod on the basis of Biblical procedures, and there was not a political bone in him. This chapter is concluded with several paragraphs from an address delivered by Dr. Behnken to the American Lutheran Conference at Rockford, Illinois on Nov. 14, 1946, and sent to all Lutheran pastors in American.

Dr. Behnken said, "I realize that we have been accused of over-emphasizing the need of doctrinal unity, but you cannot get away from the fact that the Word of God throughout emphasizes doctrinal unity. The history of the early Christian church clearly shows what emphasis was placed upon doctrinal unity. God-appointed leaders in the Apostolic Church issued earnest warnings against false doctrine... Or think of the Lutheran Confessions. Much time and effort were spent to express things so definitely and precisely that there should be no misunderstanding. Think especially of the Formula of Concord. Years were spent in its formulation before it was adopted. Then, however, it settled the controversial issues, removed the dissension and safe-guarded sound Biblical doctrine... Such agreement must be reached, not only between official committees, but also out in the field between members of our congregations.

"There are those who have grown tired of doctrinal discussions. Some have claimed that we have unity, since Lutherans in America by resolutions have subscribed to the Lutheran Confessions. It is true that doctrinal discussions in some places have revealed that much has been accomplished. However, it is also true that some doctrinal discussions have revealed a decided lack of doctrinal unity...

"It grieves a person whose heart is interested in genuine unity that there are those who would brush aside doctrinal discussion and boldly claim that agreement has been reached, since we subscribe to the Lutheran Confessions. It grieves a person very much to hear that men are not willing to consider further doctrinal theses. It grieves a person to be told that this way to doctrinal unity is closed.

"Today efforts are being put forth toward fellowship via cooperation. Cooperative efforts have been proclaimed and heralded as harbingers of Lutheran fellowship and Lutheran union. Let me speak very frankly. If such cooperation involves joint work in missions, in Christian education, in student welfare work, in joint services celebrating great events, then cooperation is just another name for pulpit and altar fellowship. Without doctrinal agreement this spells compromise. It means yielding in doctrinal positions. Such fellowship will not stand in the light of Scripture."

May God always give us Synodical leaders at all levels who speak with such doctrinal clarity and Biblical integrity!

CHAPTER 7

THE PARTY OF THE LEFT HI-JACKS LCMS MISSIONS

When I became Chairman of the LCMS Board for Missions, I was interviewed by the editor of one of our church newspapers who asked what my Mission goals were. The following goals were printed: "To set infinite value on the soul of every person in the world; To encourage a fresh vision of the evangelistic nature of the mission and the sharing of the saving Gospel by every Christian in every field; To exhibit daring willingness to use every legitimate means and method to disciple the nations where we have accepted responsibility and to share jointly with indigenous daughter churches this responsibility under the infallible Word of God; To have a vivid awareness that time is short because many souls are daily meeting their maker without a saving knowledge of the Lord Jesus Christ."

Unfortunately, my Biblical vision was hampered and destroyed by men who had their own private agenda in concert with the former St. Louis faculty. By 1974 the majority of the missionary staff walked out, just as the seminary faculty did. My greatest hope for Synod's missions when I became secretary of the Mission Board in 1966 and chairman in 1971 were shattered, as my co-workers and I attempted valiantly to pursue the Great Commission with fidelity. This chapter will record the struggle that was necessary in order to stop the rebels from destroying the mission entirely. However, we and the mission were held hostage until the departure of the staff in April 1974.

Many hours and days were spent in conflict in order to accept a mission policy statement. The "Board for Missions Resolution on Policy" was renounced by the ELIM staff even after the New Orleans convention resolved to accept it officially. As you read it, try to imagine at least twenty men (mission staff, ELIM board members, and ELIM advisory members) making objections to paragraph after paragraph. This statement addressed the urgent mission issues of that day.

BOARD FOR MISSIONS RESOLUTION ON POLICY

WHEREAS, The Board for Missions is charged with the responsibility to formulate, recommend, review and supervise the mission policy of Synod, guide Synod's mission outreach in keeping with such mission policy, and to do all else necessary to provide for an aggressive and united mission effort for the Synod; and

WHEREAS, There is no greater imperative than to disciple the nations and no more urgent need than for Christians individually and collectively to proclaim and share the saving Gospel of Jesus Christ and to demonstrate Christian love in every facet of their lives; and

WHEREAS, There needs to be a clear understanding of our Synod's theological principles in the Board's policies and practices, implementing through the Holy Spirit the New Testament process of repentance and renewal to hold the purity of the Word, and the unity and peace of the church; therefore be it

RESOLVED, That in consonance with the Scriptures, the Lutheran Confessions, the policies of Synod and the Board for Missions, we affirm at this time the following principles to serve as the major guidelines for our mission activities:

1) The indispensable heart and core of God's mission is the ministry of the Word (Acts 6) in which the proclamation of the Gospel takes precedence. This proclamation may be

chronologically preceded by or accompanied by efforts at education work, medical missions, social work, etc., but if these become ends in themselves and do not provide occasion for a verbal witness to Christ as the only Savior, the mission is not accomplished. The Gospel is a message, and, as such, it is communicated by words. Actions, however Christ-like, do not in themselves convey the Good News that God forgives those sinners who trust in Christ. The deeds of love that flow from the Gospel at work in the lives of God's people are necessary in the life of the Christian but they cannot by the nature of Christian faith replace the indispensable heart and core of salvation which is offered only through special revelation in the Holy Scriptures. Our deeds of love do not take precedence in God's plan of salvation, but rather that position of primacy is occupied by God's acts of love in Christ, revealed in the Gospel, as the chief doctrine of Scripture and the heart of our theology. "All who would be saved must hear this preaching, for the preaching and hearing of God's Word are the Holy Spirit's instrument, with, and through which He wills to act efficaciously, to convert men to God, and to work in them both to will and to achieve." (Solid Declaration, Article II, 531:52) Therefore, our mission in our culture and also across cultural boundaries is structured so that everywhere in planning, policy making and programming, the church will carry out its task without neglecting, subordinating, or eliminating the verbal communication of the Gospel.

2. Our work of missions is to reflect strongly the means (Word and Sacraments) by which sinful man comes into right relationship to God, even while properly emphasizing the Christian's relation to his fellow men in love and service. The New Testament gives us the Apostolic norm for proper balance between proclamation (kerygma) and service (diaconia), and primarily emphasis is to be given to verbalizing the Gospel and discipling the nations rather than to physical ministries or social action. We hope to respond to the challenge and opportunity of bringing the Gospel of Jesus Christ to unevangelized peoples everywhere through evangelistic ministries supported by Christian service.

3. The Christian's life of love and service is the consequence of his having been justified by grace through faith in Jesus Christ. Faith is a living, active thing, always seeking the welfare of the neighbor. God's people should participate personally in prayer, witness, service, and sacrificial stewardship directed toward the release of troubled souls and toward the prevention of those conditions that cause trouble. (Social Ministry Affirmations, 9-07 Milwaukee Convention).

4. Theological awareness demands that we recognize that there are spiritual forces inimical to the Christian faith which are growing stronger and more aggressive. (1) We are aware of a "new universalism" which falsely believes that because Christ died for all, He will sovereignly and out of love bring all men to salvation(even though some never have faith in Christ as their personal Savior) or holds falsely that all men are "reconciled" in the sense that those who have met Christ through the means of grace have advantage above those who have not, but the difference is in degree, not in principle, for some simply are not conscious of the riches they possess. In our Synodical Mission we emphasize the Biblical truth that there is no salvation outside of the means of grace without faith in Christ. (2) We are also conscious of a syncretism which attempts to unite and absorb diverse non-Christian thoughts, philosophies, and practices to use them as if they are saving truth, but the writers of the uniquely inspired Holy Scriptures combated the syncretistic tendencies of their age. We affirm our intention to do likewise. (Article VI, 2, LCMS Constitution) (3) A new humanism has manifested itself in several ways in mission practice, such as mission without proclamation. The Bread of Life alone gives fulfillment to life, and we provide bread where needed as a witness of our Christian love to give sustenance of life.

5. Concerning church unity and fellowship as we learn it from the Scriptures and have experienced it in The Lutheran Church-Missouri Synod, we recognize that it is a unity given

by God to be preserved within our church by speaking the Word to each other. It is a unity of belief in submission to the entire Scriptures, centering in the person and work of Jesus Christ, and it is a unity for the fulfillment of our mission responsibility throughout the world. We affirm that the Scriptural and Confessional principles of fellowship to which The Lutheran Church-Missouri Synod has bound itself are no less binding in all our efforts elsewhere. Thus we wish to exercise a prophetic voice toward the sister churches overseas to exhort them to remain faithful to the Apostolic faith and we wish to exercise our God-given right as fellow Christians to take measures to help them move in the right direction when we believe they are gong in the wrong direction. God commands such love and concern (Gal. 6:1; 2 Thes. 3:14, 15; Mt. 18). At the same time, the Apostolic Word is to be spoken by sister churches to us. We discourage unScriptural differences of faith and doctrine between us and our sister churches for it fosters splits and schisms. In Acts 2:42, Rom. 15:4-13, 1 Cor. 1:10; Gal. 5:10, Phil. 1:27 and 4:2 God reveals only one Savior (who unites and removes all differences), one Scripture-Word (one admonition and hope derived from one doctrine or instruction), one mind (one conviction which God produces), one confession (the mouth which speaks Scripture confesses but one truth), one fellowship (in Christ we receive one another, and Christ is not divided), one goal (one faith, one joy and one peace). Oneness in **doctrine** and **practice** is vital in world missions because unScriptural compromises within the church confuse the outside world, cause consternation among believers, cause conflict in the churches, cause evangelistic activity to wane and cease, and deny the practice of true Christian unity. Therefore, the mission program of the sister churches throughout the world should be consistent with the Apostolic Word and the Lutheran Confessions both as to theological and ecumenical standards in doctrine and practice; and be it further

RESOLVED, That we also affirm that the following be guides for our mission efforts:

1. The adherents of non-Christian religions can receive salvation only through faith in Christ. We reject the idea that "Christian presence" among such religions is a substitute for the proclamation of the Gospel. Conversion is the aim of the Gospel and is thus our aim. Men of all religions are invited to believe and be baptized in the name of the Father, Son, and Holy Ghost, for Christ is not anonymously present in non-Christian religions.

2. God's gift of eternal salvation comes through the means of proclamation of the Gospel and by faith in Christ. EVen though the act of salvation is complete for all men (objective reconciliation), individuals are not born again and have no peace with God until they are brought to faith in Christ (subjective justification).

3. Gospel proclamation should everywhere lead to the establishment of the church with the means of grace, through which God accomplishes His saving work in the world.

4. Our mission purpose and goals are (1) rooted in Christ, (2) anchored in the Word, (3) directed by the Holy Spirit, (4) related to the culture, and (5) geared to the times; and be it further

RESOLVED, That as we seek unity of purpose and mind and spirit within our board, the mission staff, and all expatriate and national workers in our world-wide fields, all members of the Synod be herewith assured that the Synod's Board for Missions wholeheartedly adheres to the Synod's official position in doctrine and practice, and that we join our hearts in prayer that God would cause us to administer the mission thrust of our church faithfully according to the Scriptures and the Confessions, and that He would prompt all workers and members of our Synod to proclaim His Word faithfully, in all its truth and purity; and be it finally

RESOLVED, That copies of this resolution be sent to the President and Board of Directors of Synod, and to all of the personnel of the Board for Missions overseas.

You can get a good idea about the unethical tactics used by these men as you read the following comments made by William Danker in a December 6, 1972 release entitled, "Retreat From Mission" (My comments are interspersed: 1. "...Needless and outdated controversy rages on methods of Biblical interpretation." Comment: Loyal Board members were insistent that the St. Louis Seminary "new theology" should not be imported to our seminaries in our churches over seas. 2. "...Unprecedented calling back of overseas missionaries during the past triennium..." Comment: We were not only stopped from sending more missionaries, but the staff without board knowledge recalled missionaries from Japan, even though the Synod by-laws says that this is the sole responsibility of the Board itself. The staff wanted to jettison the entire mission staff from Nigeria, but were stopped. 3. "The same forces that are embroiling the church at home in needless controversy are now seeking to tear up what has been achieved overseas." From the documentation in this chapter, you will see that it was the mission staff and some of their ELIM missionaries who were transporting the St. Louis faculty theology and tearing up the fields. We have a sufficient number of letters from orthodox missionaries who strenuously objected to what the staff was doing. 4. "Some board members, like a few other synodical functionaries, are resisting the Synod's official mission policies as expressed in numerous resolutions at one convention after the other...The staff refuses to be coerced into defying the official mission policies of The Lutheran Church-Missouri Synod." Take one look at the "Board for Missions Resolution on Policy" printed in the previous paragraphs, and you will see official mission policy that was passed over the strenuous objections and rejection by the ELIM staff. Who was defying the official mission policies of the Synod? 5. "Other backwards steps may be attempted." I can assure you that the only backward steps were back to the Bible and the by-laws.

Considering the false claims quoted in the above paragraph, listen to a national Vice President of one of our overseas sister churches, who is now the president of his church as he writes about his experience in the Hong Kong consultation: "The Hong Kong meeting was not organized by overseas churches. The resolutions would not have been written that way. This was organized by people in the United States, and was not a meeting of overseas fellows." What he meant was that the overseas nationals were manipulated by the St. Louis ELIM Staff. He also complained about some of the ELIM missionaries: "Already in 1968 we knew you had theological problems and I told a professor that if I were president of the LCMS I would have repatriated some of your missionaries then. We had a pastor being trained by the St. Louis faculty and when he returned with the St. Louis theology we excommunicated him. When I was at the St. Louis Seminary, I didn't believe I was in a Lutheran church. Some of the pastors don't even believe there is a hell and don't know what the ministry is."

The *Mission Affirmations* were ambiguous and could be interpreted in many places in two ways, but they were the Bible for the ELIM staff. Dr. Wilbert J. Sohns, when a member of the Board for Missions, wrote in *AFFIRM* on June 13, 1973 an article, "Mission Affirmations: Inadequate, Inappropriate." He wrote: "The Minority Report for the Board for Missions in the New Orleans *Convention Workbook* speaks in glowing terms about the Mission Affirmations, and one gets the impression that they supersede the Constitution and Bylaws of Synod."

On the other hand, the Board Report on Issues first commends the Affirmations for "various important Biblical emphases" which "rightly and eloquently show a deep compassion for men in their spiritual and physical condition," but also says, "it appears that at times they have been regarded as sanctioning many types of mission and ecumenical policies which are beyond the Scriptures, the Confessions, and Synodical Resolutions which clarify such matters" (Page 11, 1973 *Convention Workbook*).

The Board Report states: "We believe that the Affirmations lack clarity and are ambiguous at certain points and have allowed for some confusion in Mission doctrine and practice. They seem to lack a proper emphasis on the Word of God as the source and norm of the Mission, on the necessity of faith through which salvation is obtained (subjective justification), on the recognition of the Visible and Invisible Church (and the reality of differences between denominations), on the political involvement by the church as an institution (no clear distinction between the two kingdoms), the use of Law and Gospel in missions, the hostility of the sinful world against the faithful Church, the proper balance between Gospel proclamation and social involvement, the eschatological aspect of missions (Matthew 24:14), and on the ultimate goal of eternal life. The Mission Affirmations are somewhat inappropriate because they do not address themselves to some of the major issues of mission concerns in any age: problems of humanism, universalism, synergism, ecumenism, the so-called 'anonymous Christian', and revolution liberation theology."

The Board majority suggested a need for sensitivity toward "the doctrine of the two kingdoms, recognizing that our mission is unique and different from any secular group or government. It is directed toward putting man's existence under Christ's Saviorship and Lordship through faith by the Holy Spirit. We seek to avoid secularization of the Church. To present missions only as a form of Christian compassion for the underprivileged is a distortion. Nor is the Church an agent of social revolution. Yet the Church stands against sin, injustice, bigotry, prejudice, and it seeks to correct the human nature which produces human problems. The Church, as an institution, should not take a political stand, but do its work through its individual members who witness and influence, working individually and corporately through all levels of government."

What is the inadequacy of the Mission Affirmations? Although the Board minority speaks in glowing terms about them, there certainly is a need to correct their deficiencies at a number of basic points.

Detroit 1965 Synod Convention Resolution *1-01A** refers to "redeeming the world" and "reconciling all things," but it does not effectively treat the fact of subjective justification, as the Board majority points out. While it refers to the Holy Spirit, not one word is said about the Word of God through which the Spirit alone works. It tells of the missionary dimensions of worship, service, fellowship and nurture, but not one word is stated about the fact that all men are sinners, that sin has produced death and damnation and enslavement to the Devil, and that only those who repent and believe will be reconciled to God and be saved from sin now and for eternity.

1-01B* though quoting John 3:16, refers to a "universal redemption," and approaching men of other faiths, which is subject to misunderstanding for it would certainly allow universalism. Rightfully, we are told that sister mission churches in other lands are not subservient to us, but to the Lord, but it does not tell us what this partnership with these churches really means.

1-01C* confesses the matter of confessionality as it emphasizes the matter of institutional barriers or separation. Certainly, the Lutheran Confessions do both - they confess and they also protest, and in their protest they make us a separate and distinctive denomination. One of the great weaknesses of this Affirmation is that it does not address itself or define "the Visible and the Invisible Church," and the reality of differences between denominations. A theologically liberal person can affirm this Affirmation. This section ought to define the true marks of the church in its mission to itself and to other churches.

1-01D* is confusing when it says that there is no area of life which may be termed "secular" in the sense that it is removed from the Lordship of Jesus Christ. The fact is that there are secular aspects of life, which are under the the control of the Devil, and need to be given over to the Lordship of Christ. The statement that we recognize the difficulty of understanding in every instance whether God desires Christians to act corporately or individually or both in His mission to the whole society is a totally inadequate way to get at the point itself. Scriptural and Lutheran principles should be spelled out at this point in order to get ourselves out of the confusion and misunderstanding in which we find ourselves today in the matter of individual or corporate action in the world. This section confuses the question of the relationship of the Church to society, seeming to maintain that the Church is to redeem society. There's no question that the Church should influence society as its individual members participate in everyday life. But this does not suggest that the institutional church should be involved in the politics of government. The Affirmations do not even imply that it is a hostile world and that the world will practice hostility against the faithful church. This section should also concern itself with the reality of the "social Gospel," while it stresses the importance of ministering to the physical and social needs of man.

*1-01E** is unsatisfactory because of the lack of clarity of three words: church, missions, and whole man. Christ conferred on His Church the mission to seek and save the lost by proclaiming the saving Gospel and infallible Word. The Affirmations should make clear that no man is whole until he has faith in Jesus, as Jesus said, "Thy faith hath made thee whole." This Affirmation is also erroneous when it states that the demonstration of our faith in Christ "adds power to its proclamation' for the power comes alone from God's Word and the Holy Spirit, not from us.

1-01F is as weak as the other points, as it deplores anything that seeks to divide what God has joined together, such as racism, multiplication of sects, wars, etc., but it does not intimate anything about false doctrine, i.e., the Board's majority exposed the danger of universalism, syncretism, and a new humanism of our day.

The Mission Affirmations are inadequate because they do not center the Mission of the Church around the means of Grace. The orientation appears to be one of the betterment of humanity. A *Statement of Scriptural and Confessional Principles* affirms the Biblical orientation: **We believe, teach, and confess that the primary mission of the church is to make disciples of every nation by bearing witness to Jesus Christ through the preaching of the Gospel and the administration of the Sacraments. Other necessary activities of the church, such as ministering to men's physical needs, are to serve the church's primary mission and its goal that men will believe and confess Jesus Christ as their Lord and Savior. We therefore reject any views of the mission of the church which imply: That an adequate or complete witness to Jesus Christ can be made without proclaiming or verbalizing the Gospel.**

In the Church, we dare not talk missions if we omit the mission assigned by Christ to the Church. We dare not stress a "loving approach and understanding" and omit the message of the Law and the Gospel, of Repentance and Remission of Sins. Note what the Lutheran Confessions say: **In the last chapter of Luke (24:47) Christ commands that penitence and forgiveness of sins should be preached in His name. The Gospel declares that all men are under sin and are worthy of eternal wrath and death. For Christ's sake it offers forgiveness of sins and justification, which are received by faith. By its accusations, the preaching of penitence terrifies our consciences with real and serious fears. For these, our hearts must again receive consolation. This happens if they believe Christ's promise that for His sake we have the forgiveness of sins. (Apology IV, 62) and In these matters, which concern the external, spoken Word, we must hold firmly to the conviction that God gives no one His Spirit or grace except through or with the external Word which comes before. (Smalcald Articles III, vii 3)**

The Mission Affirmations are inappropriate because they do not address themselves to the primary need of man in any age, much less the 1970's. Nor do they address themselves to the real issues facing the Church in Mission.

The church should reiterate its certainty about the validity of **Biblical Affirmations** in this age of change. The church must lift its voice and show discernment when the institutional church is afflicted with doctrinal uncertainty, theological novelty, and outright apostasy. The church needs to "discern the spirits whether they be of God." Non-Christian religious systems pose an oppressive threat to the growth of the Church and demand careful assessment and response. Many Biblical and Lutheran distinctives are being blurred today.

AFFIRMATIONS are needed to declare a clearer understanding of evangelistic mission in which every member must be involved. it must show a deeper compassion for the spiritual lostness of men and women for eternity with the realization that there can be no substitute for speaking the Gospel so that all men will hear of Christ before they die. **"All who would be saved must hear this preaching, for the preaching and the hearing of God's Word are the Holy Spirit's instruments in, with, and through which He wills to act efficaciously to convert men to God, and to work in them, both to will and to achieve" (Formula of Concord, Solid Declaration** II, 52). They should speak about the necessity of all believers receiving Scriptural indoctrination, meeting together constantly under the impact and teaching of the Apostolic Word, mobilizing and equipping believers for the great task of evangelizing our generation.

The Gospel requires of those who preside over the churches that they preach the Gospel, remit sins, administer the Sacraments, and, in addition, exercise jurisdiction, that is, excommunicate those who are guilty of notorious crimes and absolve those who repent." (Power and Primacy of the Pope 60)

If a person will not hear preaching or read the Word of God, but despises the Word and the community of God, dies in this condition, and perishes in his sins, he can neither comfort himself with God's eternal election nor obtain His mercy. For Christ, in whom we are elected, offers His grace to all men in the Word and the Holy Sacraments, earnestly wills that we hear it, and has promised that, where two or three are gathered together in His name and occupy themselves with His Holy Word, He is in the midst of them." (FC, SD, 57) [35]

Dr. Wilbert J. Sohns

Certainly, there were many good things in the Mission Affirmations, but they were obviously being abused by the ELIM staff and board members to the advantage of bring the new theology into the Synod's mission enterprise. Dr. Martin L. Kretzmann, architect of the Affirmations, created severe theological problems within the mission endeavors, as can be seen in the following critique of his essays and documents, which I wrote after some years of working with him and also special meetings which I or several of us had with him.

CRITIQUE OF MARTIN L. KRETZMANN'S ESSAYS AND DOCUMENTS — AND HIS REACTIONS TO THEM

I. On October 28, 1971, at Geneva, Switzerland, before a witness I asked this question: "What are the standards that would allow Kretzmann to say in a LCMS Board meeting in October 1970 that the LCMS is less Lutheran than those members of the LWF?" No recognition of a problem was shown because of this statement, despite the Missouri Synod's refusal to join the LWF.

II. Question: What standards would allow such statements as these presented by Kretzmann for the LWF "Committee on the Church and the Jews" to the Commission of World Affairs in Asmara, Ethiopia, in an essay, "On The Theology of the Church's Relation To Judaism," Page 8? He said, "We as Lutherans affirm our solidarity with the Jewish people...This our solidarity with the Jewish people is to be affirmed not only despite the crucifixion of Jesus, but also because of it..." This our solidarity with the Jewish people is grounded in God's unmerited grace, His forgiveness of sin and His justification of the disobedient. Whenever we Christians, therefore, speak about 'rejection' and 'faith', 'disobedience' and 'obedience' in such a way that 'rejection' and 'disobedience' are made to be attributes of Jews while 'faith' and 'obedience' are made to be attributes of Christians, we are not only guilty of the most despicable spiritual pride, but we foster a pernicious slander, denying the very ground of our own existence; grace, forgiveness and justification." I pointed out that our solidarity with the Jewish people is not, as Kretzmann suggests, grounded in God's justification of the disobedient in the subjective sense, for that requires faith as we are justified by faith alone. Thus the opposite is true of what Kretzmann says about **rejection**, faith, and obedience, because rejection is an attribute (damning of the Jews while **faith** and **obedience** are made (saving) attributes of Christians - this is neither despicable spiritual pride, a pernicious slander or a denial of our own existence by grace, forgiveness and justification. This is a terrible confusion of objective and subjective justification...

III. Question: What are the standards that will allow our Lutherans to confess with the Reformed or other Protestant churches, as suggested in the Ghana documents? Here M. Kretzmann quoted from Page 7 of the Ghana document, offering a third alternative, which is commended to the church in Ghana as a valid expression of its self-understanding. The statements questioned are the following: "b. It should be possible for members of other churches to attach themselves to the 'Lutheran' ministry in Ghana without severing their institutional relationship to their own church. c. Since the Lutheran fellowship can only continue to grow in strength through a constant feeding on the Word and Sacrament, it is important that this be a large element in the life of the fellowship, including the participation in the Sacrament by people who have other institutional relationships...It would seem important that we would develop 'conversation centers' where people could gather for fellowship, study, and training in the witness of service. They should not be known as Lutheran Churches, since no nomenclature would automatically serve to exclude a great many people. But I would see no reason why the Christian fellowship in such centers could also not have a full worship life."

Kretzmann later states that if he personally was physically involved in the ministry in Ghana he would probably resent very much the type of program proposed, perhaps not for **theological reasons**, but for **practical** reasons. This shows a misunderstanding of the Scriptural and Confessional theology involved as held by the LCMS in its Constitution, By-Laws, and resolutions. We pointed out that other Protestants and Catholics cannot attach themselves to our Lutheran ministry **without severing their own church relationship**, and that they could not be included, as he suggests, in the Sacraments and thus included in the Lutheran fellowship, and that the **full** worship life cannot involve members of the other Lutheran bodies since he already stated this included the Sacraments. Kretzmann could not understand why there was any suggestion of wrongness here.

IV. "The Call To Openness And Trust" document.

1. The entire document requests a freedom which is contrary to Confessional and LCMS Commitments, as seen in Chapter 5; This ELIM statement was rejected by the Synod. As the CTCR and 1971 Milwaukee Convention resolution indicate, there

are grave offenses in this document against the Scriptures and the Lutheran Confessions, and the position which the LCMS holds in doctrine and practice. Kretzmann kept on referring to the question of the types of literature in Genesis and the Old Testament while Werning affirmed the historicity of these matters and also the verbal inerrancy of the Scriptures in the traditional sense of the Missouri Synod. Kretzmann questioned how Lutheran Werning's position was, but said he was entitled to hold to that position. Kretzmann indicated that Werning had no understanding of the theological problem.

In defense of this "Openness and Trust" document, Kretzmann wrote on **March 10, 1970** "On what grounds do you base the statement that there are 'great errors in this document which contradict both the Scriptures and the Lutheran Confessions'? I can only conclude that you did not make an effort to understand the document but tried to find phrases which could be distorted for your own ends. **I must categorically state what I believe that the statement is in harmony with the Scriptures and the Lutheran Confessions."**

President J. A. O. Preus and Dr. William H. Kohn received copies of this correspondence, and even though the CTCR indicated that this document is unfaithful to God's Holy Word and our Synod's position in doctrine and practice, and though Kretzmann had been reminded of this several times, he did not care to discuss this matter further or change his views. On December 10, 1970, he wrote: "You must know that my acceptance of the Scriptures as the Word of God and my subscription to the Lutheran Confessions will not permit me to withdraw what I believe is in harmony with both the Scriptures and the Confessions." This was stated primarily in relation to the three controverted essays, but also covered the commitment to "A Call To Openness And Trust." On January 7, 1971 in a visit between Kretzmann and Waldo J. Werning in the presence oft the Board's Executive Secretary, this matter was again defended by Kretzmann.

V. *Three essays* concern us. A full critique of these essays was provided Kretzmann with a letter of October 30, 1970, and were covered in a discussion on January 7, 1971, with Kretzmann and the Executive Secretary of the Board. In summary many of these quotations and criticisms were repeated briefly at the meeting with Kretzmann at Geneva on October 28 in the presence of Dr. Arnold Sovik. Following are some of these quotations, together with a brief summary of the criticisms of the theological inadequacy of the statements:

1. What are the Scriptural, theological, and LCMS standards that would allow the following statements in "What On Earth Does The Gospel Change?" (Lutheran World, Vol. XVI, No. 4, 1969)

A. "A great many doctrines in the church's library are a witness to the earnestness with which men have tried to reduce the mysteries of God, of the world, and of human life, to concepts which we can understand. Unfortunately, they are also often witness to the extent to which theologians have forgotten the Gospel and forced systems of doctrine which prevent men from hearing the Gospel. We are thus offered a great many propositions, ranging from a specific doctrine of creation to the condition of man's soul after death which we are asked to believe, as if we were saved by doctrine instead of by grace." (Page 315). The Lutheran Confessions and the LCMS Constitution or public doctrine never were understood in the sense that we were saved by doctrine instead of grace, but the most disturbing part of this statement is that a great many doctrines in the church's library are said to be a witness only to the **earnestness** with which men have tried to reduce the mysteries of God, etc., to concepts which we can understand; also, that they are often witness to the extent to which theologians have **forgotten the Gospel** and forge systems of doctrine to prevent men from hearing the Gospel. He stated that our stand on the lodge would be an example of forgetting the Gospel and forging systems of doctrine which prevent men from hearing the Gospel.

Kretzmann stated that it is neither Scriptural or Lutheran to insist that a staff or Board member of Synod needs to administer his work according to Synod's doctrinal resolutions, for all matters must be decided by the Word of God. He said that he stands on the Constitution that he does not have to abide by Synodical doctrinal resolutions.

B. "One must ask oneself, for example, what would happen to a 'doctrine' of the place of women in the church, or a literalistic doctrine of creation, or some particular doctrines of the inspiration of Scripture, or explicit explanations of the mystery of Christ's presence in the Eucharist, or a doctrine of church orders, or of church government, or a host of others, if we would put them to the test of the question, 'What has this to do with the Gospel?' Would we not quickly see that they have no essential connection with the Gospel and therefore find ourselves able to live with many divergent formulations of doctrine in our common understanding of, and commitment to, the centrality of the Gospel?" (Page 315) For the **Gospel's sake** and to show its understanding of the Lutheran Confessions and Scriptures, the LCMS has a position on the place of women in the church, of the literal understanding of creation as seen in Genesis, position of Christ's presence in the Lord's Supper, doctrine of inspiration of Scripture, etc.

The last four conventions have asked that the members, including Synodical staff, honor the Synodically adopted doctrinal statements. Regarding Genesis and the historical account of creation versus evolution, he stated that it depends upon the type of literature we have there. We pointed out that there is an essential connection with the Gospel when we are discussing any number of historical and miraculous portions of the Old Testament, such as Jonah and the Flood (II Pet. 2:4-5, and 3:4-7, 10). How can he make this flood anything but historical and not connect it with the Gospel when in Mt. 12:39-40 the flood is tied up with the Last Judgment? Take away the historicity of Jonah and his three days in the big fish, and you take away the historicity of the claim of Jesus and His own resurrection. The Gospel is involved.

2. What are the Scriptural, theological and LCMS standards that would allow the following statements in the essay "Where Is The Church Going In World Missions?" (Papers & Proceedings, Workshop on Church-Ministry, Concordia Seminary, St. Louis, MO., July 29-31, 1961, Concordia Seminary Print Shop, 1970)

A. "All of us, as men, are not only related to the One God, but are also related to each other in the incarnate God who has taken upon Himself our common humanity, has united all men in Himself, and by His death on the cross and His resurrection has initiated the new creation, in which all men are involved just as much as they are involved in the natural creation. When a church in mission to the world begins its theology at this point, we see how unfortunate such expressions are as 'the God of the Bible' or 'the God of the Christians.' " (Page 36) We as **men** are **not** related to each other in the **incarnate God** (Christ) because there is no fellowship between believers and non-believers. All men are not united

147

in Christ and all men are not involved in the **new** creation as much as they are involved in the **natural** creation — where non-believers have nothing but condemnation and are outside of Christ....

B. "...We realize then how close we are to them (non-Christians), because God's mercy nourishes and preserves them as much as it does us, that they are also created by God as we are, that Christ Jesus has also died to free them, that their freedom is at hand, that they too are reconciled to God." (pages 36-37)...God's mercy is experienced through baptism, regeneration, forgiveness, none of which the non-believer has accepted — and that's a world of difference. Further, the statement that "they too are reconciled to God," continues this mistaken idea, for God has reconciled them to Himself, but in Christ we are to beseech them: "Be reconciled to God' (2 Cor. 5:17) through baptism and faith in Christ.

C. "We are saying that our relationship to our fellow Christians is to be determined by the concern for the fulfillment of Christ's mission, and not by whether we happen to agree or disagree on the way in which certain doctrines are formulated." (Page 42) The Scriptures, Confessions and our LCMS Constitution and doctrinal position do not allow us to say that. "The second aspect of our understanding of the relationships which must exist in the church in mission to the world is that of our recognition of the Oneness of Christ's mission as it is expressed by His one body throughout all of the churches." (Page 41) He says that we are to understand our denominationalism and then to determine our relationship **by the concern** for the fulfillment of Christ's mission, rather than **by doctrinal agreement and Confessional formulation**. As Missouri Synod staff and Board members, we are committed to the Confessional and Constitutional requirements in doctrine and practice, which affects our organizational relationship to other Christian groups or denominations.

3. What are the Scriptural, theological, and LCMS standards that would allow the following statements in an essay "Theological Education" (Presentation to the Board of World Missions, LCA, November 11, 1968)?

A. "Much of the material that now forms the body of what we call systematic theology, worship patterns...are not uniquely and distinctively Christian but are part of the general experience of mankind." (Page 4) We particularly pointed out that the **material** which forms the **body** in what we Lutherans call systematic theology is unique and distinctively Christian, and not a part of the general experience of mankind. Luther's **Catechism**, Pieper's **Dogmatics**, Walther's **Law and Gospel**, and other important books, are not part of the general experience of mankind, but uniquely and distinctively Christian!...

B. "This would serve to free us from many of the hang-ups which plague us in so many parts of the church, the hang-up of creation or evolution..." (Page 5). Creation versus evolution is not a hang-up, but a plain Scriptural topic of utmost importance. Genesis 1 and 2 provide historical fact, and evolution is unbelief. Kretzmann said that this is not decided by convention, that the Synod can't resolve how the world was created, but only God's Word does that.

* *

After the majority of the mission staff resigned in April 1974, I worked with the Executive Committee to list the many acts of disobedience and rebellion on the part of the former staff, and this became dramatic evidence of the insubordination of the ELIM staff against the Synod which we of the board were forced to deal with. It was not an easy task, nor a happy one. My colleagues joined me wanting to lead the Synod in mission outreach, but we had to fight for the very survival of the Synod's mission operation.

The evidence of the adversarial position and activities on the part of the staff majority fill a box of file folders. The Executive Committee and I condensed these into about 20 pages which was then shared with synodical and district leaders and anyone who had questions about the board's activity. If you find the following summary tedious to read because so many incidences are enumerated, then imagine how it felt to experience this for a period of ten years, especially the last five. These 20 pages of individual items have been substantially reduced by excluding 50% of the document:

SUMMARY OF MISSION ISSUES

The program and approach which the Board of Missions employed in the past four years is totally consistent with the constitution, by-laws and resolutions of The Lutheran Church-Missouri Synod. In the elections of the past two conventions it was obvious that the Synod wanted members on the Board (and other boards) who will fulfill their Board membership, as the by-laws of Synod state, within "the intent and resolutions of the Synod." The Board majority faithfully adhered in an evangelical manner to the purpose and reason for their elections, and never deviated from the path assigned by Synod itself.

What the **Board (majority)** really **affirms:**
While we individually would state it in different ways, basically the Synodical loyalists on the Board for Missions affirm:

1. We are on **Christ's mission**, and we are to speak the words which he has given and which He has decided in the written Scriptures. It is His mission, and He has left us His clear Word and Gospel to proclaim.

2. The Doctrine of Justification by faith alone is essential to Christ's Commission: One must hear the Gospel and accept it by faith in order to gain eternal life, and the alternative is eternal damnation.

3. The nature, meaning and role of the Gospel must be kept clear and central, but not separated from Scripture (the written Word) or from the use of the Law (avoid Antinomianism).

4. We get directions for the mission from the Scriptures, not from the world, culture or individuals, avoiding a kind of "culture-Christianity," for the church in mission must speak with "**one word**, voice, faith..." (Rom. 15:4. 5; 1 Cor. 1:10, Confessions).

5. The **Lutheran mission is Confessional** - and requires a correct understanding of the Biblical nature of Christian doctrine as opposed to non-Biblical nature of other religions.

6. The Mission Affirmations are an acceptable statement and are to be used freely (within the understanding of the recent CTCR document), and they are **not** a license for variant theologies, unionism or separatism, and they assume proper undergirding with Scriptural principles.

7. There must be a Biblical balance between Gospel proclamation and the deeds of love. The Gospel and Word are primary (marks in the church) while deeds of love flow out of the Christian faith, and so also are necessary.

8. Missions must reflect the Synodical position in doctrine and practice. The LCMS By-Laws are a common agreement and are to be honored with integrity. They are set by people for people to work at common tasks and goals. When there is disagreement, we are

to follow the agreed-on process for correction. When we face problems, admit their existence, define the issues, communicate evangelically as brethren, and then make a decision (even the hard ones) and live with them in forgiveness in Christ. Use the Scriptural channels in identify and correct problems.

9. We are to follow ecumenical principles that are Scriptural and Lutheran. We expect sister churches as partners in mission to be true co-workers and partners and to be aggressive in mission. There is to be mutual encouragement and correction. We are to have an aggressive outreach as Lutherans with Lutheran structures and Lutheran workers.

10. We uphold the sovereignty of the sister churches and the need for their self government and for exercising a growing dependence on their own resources.

We should plan more aggressive mission outreach, using proper church growth principles and strategies, accepted procedures for church sowing and reaping and building, and constantly reaching into new areas and to all areas in the world until they have been covered.

The faithful Board majority followed the Synod's Agenda as it was given by the Synod itself through its By-Laws and resolutions. These efforts were frustrated by contrary objectives, goals and personal agendas of those who disagree with the Synod itself, not only with the Board majority. The Board held carefully to setting and directing policy, but the ELIM staff either disobeyed or misinformed the public via MTP to make the Board look bad. One frustrated lay-Board member told the staff that if they wanted to set policy, to resign their staff position and get elected to the Board by a Synod convention. As there are two theologies in Synod (1974), so there were two theologies in the Board and former staff. As there was a Seminex, there was a Missionex.

Evidences of questionable theological commitments or actions by the former staff and some Board members who opposed Synod's doctrinal position:

1. The March-April 1975 South Wisconsin ELIM Prospective, Dr. Kretzmann showed his continued bias against the historical LCMS doctrinal commitment (which he equates as that of the "Preus party"): "...the Preus party has departed from the Scriptural and Confessional basis of the Synod..."

2. Several staff actively involved and supported the 1970 and 1971 "Call to Openness and Trust" and the "Declaration of Determination," both of which were disapproved by Synod's Board of Directors, and the "Call to Openness and Trust" was rejected in Milwaukee Convention Resolution 2-50.

3. Rev. James Mayer at the 1971 Moorhead, Minnesota, meeting of the Board after a Synodical loyalist stated that "for doctrine and conscience sake" the Board could not accept but must revise the "Evangelizing Is" document, former staff James Mayer said, "bull shit!" Dr. G. Nitz, a representative of President Preus, observed the bad treatment given the five Synodical loyalists by former staff and their Board supporters.

4. At the November 1972 Minneapolis Board meeting former staff James Mayer charged the Board with spiritual adultery, which could not be stated unless the Board was charged with theological deviation.

5. The staff meeting minutes of October 18, 1971 state: "William Kohn then reported on the special meeting with Dr. Preus and Dr. Werning on the evening of October 15. The meeting was initiated by the Chairman of the Board, and its purpose was to share individually what the Chairman and the Executive Secretary believed to be the objectives, goals and tasks in mission and what the problems are that need to be solved in order to unify the work of the Board and the staff...Acknowledge some differences in the understanding of the objectives and goals of the Board." Several such meetings were held at which time, President Preus and Werning found themselves on one side of the theological and ecumenical spectrum in opposition to former staff Kohn. Then in 1972 Preus requested Vice-President

Weber to meet with Kohn and Werning in order to try to achieve such unity, which was originally requested by Werning so that the Board could be unified in theological doctrine and ecumenical practice. Both President Preus and Vice-President Weber confirm that in all instances there was real disagreement as to what constituted Missouri Synod theology and practice and that former staff Kohn refused to affirm verbally or identify in writing the areas of theological concern, but discussed only in vague terms. It could be said that Werning, Preus and Weber were holding to Synod's Agenda, while former staff Kohn held to his private agenda in this positive and creative attempt to take a churchmanlike step to lead the Board in the right direction.

6. On December 2, 1971, Missionaries Brehmer and Bunkowske were dismayed that former staff Reinking would not affirm the Scriptural fact that a Yala man who did not hear of Christ or believe in Him would go to hell, and they asked Kohn and Reinking why they sent the missionaries to Africa if they held such a belief (witnessed by the Executive Committee).

7. In the June 11, 1971, *Lutheran Witness* seven missionaries stated that they read with concern the statements of the Synodical President and the St. Louis faculty and that they expressed their "complete support of the seminary faculty in this matter. We have full confidence in its **theological** integrity and in its unyielding loyalty to the inspired Scriptures and the Lutheran Confessions."

8. When the officers and members of the Board periodically suggested taking controverted theological documents on issues to the CTCR or CCM, Kohn would object.

9. *Christianity Today*, August 31, 1972 told about 1200 "moderate-liberals" meeting in St. Louis and that "Missions Executive William Kohn said he thinks that some key **doctrinal** resolutions adopted at New Orleans are **unconstitutional**."

10. The Chairman (Werning) re-elected in September 1973 gave a presentation attached to the minutes that the Board "declare war on spiritual poverty" and indicated the theological nature of battle, calling the Board and the Synod to marshal all of its resources in this responsibility. This was met by a response of a minority Board member to ask for equal time to dissent.

11. September 20-22, 1973, Minutes No. 38, shows a motion carried: "In view of the position he (Kohn) took at the New Orleans Convention over against the **'Statement'** of Synod's President and of Synod's **doctrinal** position, and in view of Dr. Kohn's joining the St. Louis Seminary demonstration against the action of the New Orleans Convention...we pray that it may be resolved successfully according to the Word and will of God."

12. The Mission on Six Continents meeting at Zion, Illinois, in October, 1973, (where Board and staff were present) did not center on evangelism or evangelistic outreach, but on cultural and societal matters. In a plenary session the necessity of faith for salvation was openly challenged, and not at all affirmed (Kohn and other staff were present). We had met for two days when the question was raised by Werning about when the group would get to evangelism and Gospel sharing, Werning gave as gracious a testimony as possible on salvation by grace through faith in Jesus Christ, and the necessity of evangelism that grows out of that. Emilio Castro, who was invited by the Mission staff to be present as an observer, now in 1992 head of the World Council of Churches, rejected the necessity of belief in Christ for salvation. At that time, Werning recited some Scripturally confessional statements, especially from the Athanasian Creed, about the absolute necessity of faith for salvation, and that he who dies not believing will be damned. Castro stated that he did not believe this. When I stated that this truth was affirmed in the Athanasian Creed to which all Christians are bound, he stated that he did not care where it came from, he did not accept it. Among all of the LCA, ALC, and LCMS mission representatives, not even one LCMS staff man would stand to affirm the truth of the Athanasian Creed. At

that time, Werning stated that at least he would like to confess it before the group for what it was worth.

13. Former Executive Secretary Kohn said in the October 13, 1973, Personnel Committee: "No matter how we explain 3-01 of New Orleans, it was wrong to pass it. I don't believe that the Preus' *Statement* in all its parts is *Scriptural*...Synod can pass **doctrinal** resolutions for discussion, but they cannot be binding."

14. The January 20, 1974, letter of mission staff to President J. Preus criticized the *Statement* and the CTCR guidelines (Dr. Ralph Bohlmann objected to that letter in a letter of February 20, 1974).

15. A February 22, 1974, letter of former staff Bill Seeber to BFM: "Recent attempts by some Board members to bind the consciences of missionaries and staff members by requiring subscription to **extra-Scriptural doctrinal** statements and by insisting that missionaries and staff disassociate themselves from mission movements within the Synod which seems to be **contrary to the Gospel** as well as the Constitution of our church body."

16. At the February 28, 1974, Board meeting, a former staff stated: "Gordon, I know you and I have **differences in theology.**" Board of Directors representatives were present.

17. In the May 2, 1974 Board meeting ELIM member Paul Harms openly questioned the necessity of faith for salvation in all cases, which gave many Board members a concern about his universalistic view.

18. Observers of the Mission Board meetings on reconciliation discussions gave testimony to the theological and ecumenical questions and problems which arose during the course of the past several years. Such men were Dr. Ralph Bohlmann, Dr. Sam Nafzger, Dr. Edwin Weber. Problems which were isolated in the reconciliation discussions with these men present were stated thus: "Tensions come from **theologies** which come out of two roots in the Mission Board: 1. Unionism versus separatism; 2. Relation between a Confessional Church and the Holy Christian Church."

19. August 22-24, 1974, minutes –497c in the resolution to ask Rev. Heerboth to be director of a policy study and development project, show that the 1973 Board statement on policy centered on **theology**: "Because of a desire to remain united in mind and thought (1 Cor. 1:10), the Board for Missions adopted a Statement on Policy (April 5-7, 1974) which, it had hoped, would restate a Christ-centered and Scripturally sound Confessional base for our work, alert us all to certain **theological errors of our day**, and thereby assist us all in carrying out the Savior's directive (Mt. 28:18-20)." The 1973 New Orleans Convention "**commended** the Board" for the **theological** principles in this Policy Statement.

20. Dr. Ralph Bohlmann was quoted on October 17-19, 1974 mission minutes –525c: "A good clear affirmation of what we mean by church, authority, missions; a digging into the Scriptures and learning that this voice of God is to be practiced, not argued." Dr. Bohlmann at the same meeting told a minority Board member: "I heard four or five cases of unmitigated Schwaermerei in what you said." Dr. Bohlmann was in dialog and disagreement with Seminex Professor Herbert Mayer.

21. Professor Nelson Unwene, Vice-President of the Evangelical Lutheran Church of Nigeria, spoke publicly about his tragic experience at the St. Louis Seminary, which the former staff defended, and how their theology was unLutheran. He also complained about former staff Bill Reinking. At the same time, Professor James C. Gamaliel of the India Seminary complained about the theology of the St. Louis Seminary and what he heard former Executive Kohn say at a presentation at the Seminary.

22. The January 4, 1974, LCMS press release reported that the Rev. Wilbert Sohns, Chairman of the BFM Personnel Committee said, "The Board problem is not basically one of tension between Board and staff, but one of disagreement between the Board and staff

on expression on the Synod's position on **doctrine and ecumenical practices** and the philosophy of missions."

23. The March 25-27, 1974, meeting of the CTCR passed a resolution regarding tri-Lutheran activities, stating that all Synod's members are to refrain from practicing altar and pulpit fellowship with church bodies with whom the Synod has not declared fellowship and to refrain from selective fellowship. The subsequent CTCR document on the Lutheran Stance Toward Ecumenicism was discussed in the Board for Missions and attacked by the minority as **unLutheran.**

The Board majority also sought to follow Synod's By-Laws and resolutions in regard to policies and general administration. Examples of problems inflicted on the Board by the former staff which touch on policies and general administration that hampered the Board from doing its work effectively according to Synod's requirements:

1. Synod's Executive Director on December 19, 1968, wrote to former Executive Kohn on the Board of Directors resolution that all future appropriations for special ministries must have "specific approval of the Board for Missions and not of its staff alone." Denver Resolution 1-11 then stated that "all expenditures of funds for projects in the area of special ministries be approved by the Board for Missions." The former staff did not obey this resolution so that on July 22, 1970, a letter to the Board of Directors stated that the minutes do not show **approval** of any expenditure for special ministries, former staff to those who want to hold the Synodical policy.

2. Early in 1973 former staff James Mayer worked with leaders of the New Guinea Church to develop the "New Guinea Church-Mission Relationships Document" which merged the mission into the church without the knowledge of or approval of the Board. Also he did not in any way refer to the Board's new "Church/Mission" policy statement. Despite Board policy that the Board have an opportunity to act on any such actions overseas, Mayer did not inform the Board but allowed the New Guinea Church to accept this document at its June Convention without the knowledge of the Board. When faced with this sad delinquency in performance at the September 20-22, 1973, meeting, Mayer indicated that he would restudy and rework the document with the New Guinea Church according to Board suggestions, but nothing has ever been heard about it since that time. Thus Mayer cut out the Board in its direct responsibility.

3. The Board on February 12, 1972, resolved to ask an Ad Hoc Committee to develop a policy document on "Church/Mission," which was fought against by former Executive Kohn and to which he had various objections. A good statement with excellent assistance by staff man Heerboth and Board member Hintze was developed and accepted. This document was requested after discovering that Africa Executive Reinking had imposed a non-existent policy on Nigeria in which he stated that the mission had to merge with the church (without the Board's knowledge). The former Executive Kohn would not inform the African Church that there is no policy as proposed by Reinking, so there ensued another difficult struggle between Board and the former staff, which was brought to a head on December 2, 1971 at which time it was learned that Reinking had sent a message to Missionaries Brehmer and Bunkowske that this was the policy, **which was not true.**

4. At the September 20-22, 1973 Board meeting former staff James Mayer stated that the India President had written a letter to state that he wanted a team (Pero and Goetting) to visit India. In October when a Board member was sitting with Mayer on the airplane between New Guinea and India, Mayer stated that he needed to apologize because he did not have such a letter and admitted an untruth, and that he wanted to win that so bad that he "overstated the case a bit."

5. Following proper procedure Mr. Ralph Marten on September 20-22, 1973, presented a letter and a motion about his concerns about Executive Kohn who participated in anti-

Synod activities during and since the New Orleans Convention.

6. On October 30, 1973, the Executive Committee interviewed a pastor recommended by Executive Kohn for the position of "Expatriate Project" director, and Kohn objected to theological questions being asked of this man.

7. Advisory members favorable to ELIM in the 1971-1972 biennium became a political power group with the Board minority and former staff to the extent that the Board, to protect itself, adopted suggested guidelines on attendance of advisory members at Board meetings.

8. Former Executive Kohn failed to take seriously strong letters of complaints to the Board from Missionaries of Japan and New Guinea and refused to allow the Board to discuss them. Statements from various faithful missionaries and sister church leaders indicated that the former staff was misrepresenting the Board's position to the field and the field to the Board, and that the Board's reputation was being blackened. Nothing was done about the pan-Christian communion practices, to which some campus pastors refused to go because they disagreed with the content and program so strongly.

9. The joint Board of Directors and Board for Missions Overseas Visitation Team Report was given to the January 10-12, 1974 BFM meeting, and the minutes state: "It was the consensus of the Board that staff should study the report and recommendation and bring their actions to the next meeting, and that further opportunity will be given for discussion." Instead, former staff sent it all over the world to missionaries and sister churches, which then became the cause for a battle cry from ELIMite and liberal elements against "the Board interference overseas, wrong procedure," etc. It should be noted that three members of that team were from the Board of **Directors** and **two** members were from the Board for **Missions.**

10. Former Executive Kohn and his staff complained bitterly and made a major issue of the non-reappointment of former staff James Mayer in the January 10-12, 1974, meeting. It must be noted that the BFM followed a carefully outlined and evangelical re-appointment policy and procedure, which went far beyond what the Synod required.

11. A January 24, 1974, statement by Kohn lectured Synod's administration on what is wrong in the Synod and the "demand that the seminary Board of Control reconsider its recent decisions. We raise our voices on behalf of the faculty and the student body...The tragic factor of the Mission staff is that we see something similar developing in our own Board..."

12. The January 28, 1974, letter of staff to President Preus with copies to District Executives and Presidents, and overseas churches and personnel: "We ask for the elimination of the first objective of the study of missions as proposed by you and resolved upon by the Board for Missions. We further ask that the **Ad Hoc Committee** appointed by the Board for Missions be dissolved..." Subsequently, Kohn and former staff refused to work with or cooperate with the Board in the review of these objectives, goals, and organization, and actually boycotted the committee meeting. These are the same people who attended the ELIM organization meeting and went out under ELIM's sponsorship throughout the country.

13. On February 1, 1974, Executive Kohn and some staff walked out of the Executive Committee when the plea was made to have dialog and hear their complaints.

14. On February 1, 1974, the Executive Committee, Executive Kohn and some of his staff met with the Board of Directors, at which time the Board of Directors was able to see which parties followed Synodical policies and which ones had personal agendas. Reuben Schmidt stated that we are to work only under the Gospel, and was uncomplimentary about the Handbook. Secretary Dr. Herbert Mueller took exception to the comments. On February 4, 1974, Secretary Mueller reported the Board of Directors resolution encouraging the BFM

to have meetings "to define precisely areas of agreement and disagreement," which the Board attempted to do while the former staff was in rebellion against the Board and produced "Mission Updates" without the knowledge of the Board which were sent to unspecified people in Synod, and a telephone brigade and contact system was set up by former staff under the leadership of Walter H. Meyer to some District Mission Executives who were to call other District Mission Executives to keep them informed as to staff views and complaints against the Board. (A protest was lodged about this by at least one District President.)

15. The April 8, 1974, letter by Kohn for the staff states that they intend to carry on their work "without reference to the Board for Missions for the present. Unless you show more willingness to respond to the **mission staff stance, commitment and proposal,** including the suggested forms of reconciliation, than was evidenced at the meeting on April 5-6, we see no purpose to be served by staff by participation in Board meetings or in conversations with spokesmen..." (This came simply because the Board would not accede to preconditions and untenable demands at the outset.)

16. A March 29, 1974, letter by Kohn, Mayer and Seeber for the staff to District Mission Executives and Presidents, and overseas sister church presidents criticized the Board of Directors for proposing the mediation program with a 5-man commission to study the entire mission operation.

17. The entire Hong Kong consultation in July 1974 indicates private agendas of former staff in partnership with ELIM through contacts, phone calls, distribution of materials, etc. Taiwan leaders disapproved of the Hong Kong actions, and the India Church Council disassociated themselves from all actions except one. The Board was a victim of a propaganda war in which former staff and ELIM were involved.

18. Except for materials sent out by the officers of the Board in February and May 1974, the Board has kept silent as far as the church and field have been concerned. On July 15, 1974, the Chairman (Werning) wrote to the Board for Missions: "While our Board is carrying on its discussion and work, and most of us believe that we are making good progress, our resigned staff members are creating difficulties by visits to many places throughout the country, and two resigned staff even went overseas to follow the footsteps of President Preus and our co-worker, Rev. Paul Heerboth. During the past several months we have received many letters of criticism and of encouragement, while District conventions and pastoral conferences have acted upon information given by the resigned staff with no information from the Board itself...Ignoring the negative and critical activities by our resigned staff has not helped the situation and both the liberals and conservatives of the Synod are requesting answers to these criticisms..." However, the Board continued its silence and continued to receive improper criticism on the basis of slanderous statements and the breaking of the 8th Commandment.

19. While the Board is to supervise missionaries and missions, Dr. Thomas Coates was transferred from Korea to Hong Kong without the knowledge or approval of the Board, and the Board has still not been informed as to what process was used, although recently the Board extended his stay for one year (everyone realizing that if the Board did what it should have done, it would cause another blow-up). Dr. Coates has given ELIM support consistently.

The former staff was active in ELIM while serving as Synodical staff and befriended its theology and practice. Considerable evidence is available to show **former staff involvement in ELIM:**

1. At the 1973 New Orleans convention there were activities and participation on the part of some staff and ELIM leader Ewald and ELIM Board member Mahler in the Frey-Lueking-Roth group ("moderate") meetings, presentations before the Mission Floor Com-

mittee on behalf of the Board minority and staff views, on the floor against the "Statement" and on behalf of the faculty majority named in Resolution 3-09.

2. Executive Secretary Kohn participated in a protest meeting with the St. Louis Seminary faculty and others in July after the 1973 convention.

3. Involved at the formal organization of ELIM at Chicago in August 1973 were the following:

- LCMS mission staff member James Mayer who spoke at the meeting and gave suggestions for changes in the group's "Protest Document." He allowed himself to be consultant to organize a sixth region of ELIM which subsequently was organized. At least three other staff attended this meeting (Reinking, Bulle, Kreyzschmar).

- Missionary Elwyn Ewald of New Guinea who spoke and stated: "New Guinea where I come from and many of the mission fields are doing many of the things today that **this group** wants to. We have moved in our ecumenical understanding in relation to other Lutheran Churches and other Protestant churches and the Roman Catholic church far beyond what I believe the majority of you have moved, and far, far beyond what any Lutheran Church in the United States has moved. I think it is imperative that someone who knows and is informed about overseas missions must be on the Board of Directors of this organization...I would therefore like to suggest and make a motion that a sixth region for this organization be formed and that in the next few weeks or months with **Jim Mayer and staff** in dialog for ways and means of organizing the allowing or **offering of overseas missionaries an opportunity to organize and select** someone to serve on the Board of Directors be made available to them." Dr. John Tietjen called the motion which was adopted without objection from Mayer or any other Missions' staff present. Ewald subsequently became Executive Secretary for ELIM.

- Paul Harms, member of the LCMS Board for Missions, who stated at the meeting: "We need broad representation... (this organization) needs to pick up missions which might possibly be dropped by the Synod...It needs to provide fund raising committees and a fund raising program..."

4. Elected to the Board of Directors of ELIM is the Rev. Kenneth Mahler, missionary in Panama.

5. We have not been informed of most overseas ELIM organizations, but a missionary in New Guinea objected to the ELIM activities of Missionary Spruth and to the letter which Spruth sent to the LCMS missionaries of the Wabag Lutheran Church in New Guinea on December 28, 1973. Spruth wrote: "...I have become a part of the confessing group within the LCMS known as the ELIM and have agreed to serve as their contact man in New Guinea..." Then he quoted from almost two pages of ELIM material and criticized the Board for Missions' Policy Statement, which was commended by the New Orleans convention.)

6. Staff member Walter H. Meyer on February 5, 1974, went especially to speak about the mission problem (without Board knowledge) to the South Dakota District Convention. When the convention refused to allow Meyer to speak to the convention, Meyer accepted an invitation to speak at an ELIM meeting despite advice against his speaking from a Synodical Vice-President and a Board of Directors' member.

7. The New Guinea President and Missionary Spruth (New Guinea ELIM leader) arrived in St. Louis from New Guinea on February 19, 1974, with a series of demands. They stayed at the home of ELIM Director Elwyn Ewald. Dr. Kohn used the presence of the New Guinea President as evidence of the crisis. Apparently. ELIM offered to pay the expenses for travel to the U.S. for New Guinea and India representatives, for the two India representatives stated that they "were offered financial help from ELIM but turned it down although it was accepted by New Guinea."

Subsequently, ELIM and Partners in Mission sent two Seminex candidates to New Guinea, to which Vice-President Weber responded in the *Lutheran Witness* official notice that this does not have the approval of The Lutheran Church-Missouri Synod.

8. ELIM sponsored the February 15, 1974, Synod-wide letter to pastors and teachers from Dr. Kohn and his Staff against the Board and Seminary Board of Control. The letter was sent to all people getting "Missouri in Perspective."

9. At the national ELIM meeting on February 15-16, 1974, in St. Louis, Kohn, Mayer, and the New Guinea President gave speeches. Mayer alleged foul play in both the Seminary and in the Board for Missions: 1) Unethical practices against people; 2) Deliberate subverting and overlaying of Synodical positions by interpretations; 3) Abuse of power.

10. Walter H. Meyer spoke at Houston, Texas, February 24, 1974, criticizing both President Preus and the Board for Missions. He used various half-truths and untruths, such as claiming that Appendix 6 of President Preus' mailing proved later to be frankly fraudulent. (Note: It was not.)

11. John Tietjen and Kohn were featured speakers at an ELIM Service in Minneapolis, March 10, 1974. Kohn said that the reason for Jim Mayer's termination was not credible. An ELIM membership application was given out to which there was a specific objective stated: "To get support for an alternative channel for people and groups to fund **any and all mission programs** of the LCMS."

12. Walter H. Meyer spoke at Lincoln, Omaha, and Seward, Neb., on March 21-23 at ELIM rallies, and said the Board was guilty of mishandling people, unChristian dealing with people, breaking the 8th Commandment and Matthew 18, and re-judgment, having double standards, defamation of character, corrupt use of institutional power, stacked decks, the end justifies the means, and of having "conscienceless power." He criticized the "fraternal discussions," and he stated, "We maintain that when you are dealing with the Gospel of Jesus Christ that there is nothing to negotiate."

13. The Synod's Board of Directors took action against ELIM. The Board for Missions facing rebellious action on the part of some missionaries, and former staff, presented a resolution at the January 10-12, 1974, meeting about ELIM (suggesting responsible steps for the Board to take) and referred this to the staff and Executive Committee, but nothing ever became of it.

14. The ELIM Coffee Kits contain several brochures written by former staff members which not only condemn the BFM but also tell various untruths. One eight-page brochure written by former Staff Walter H. Meyer **contained 36 errors**, and strong objections were shared repeatedly with ELIM leaders and Meyer (evidence given to the MSC), but none of these were ever corrected and this slander continued to be passed out throughout the country.

As I reviewed the Mission files again during the past weeks, several situations reveal the intensity of dishonesty, misrepresentation, and insubordination which we faced. These were the activities of the Asia Mission Executive, the Africa Mission Executive, and the Executive Secretary himself. When present and future historians search these documents, they will find considerable evidence which reveals the tactics which the ELIM staff utilized, and the grave problems which we confronted as a result. Kohn's tactics were relentless and time-consuming.

You may recall in the "Summary of Mission Issues" that the first thing that I did when I was elected Chairman of the Board was to write a letter on September 30, 1971, to Synod's President telling him "to take the initiative to try to bring agreement and concord in the Board for Missions...This would start with the Executive Secretary and the Chairman working for similar goals and methods which grow out of our theology and objectives. Therefore, I would like to solemnly request that you take under advisement a meeting with Dr. Kohn and myself in order to have such a sharing and discussion time..'' The result was that a number of meetings were held where either President Jack Preus or Vice President Ed Weber were involved. A large file folder tells of our honest attempts to try to unify under the Biblical commitment which the Synod imposed upon the Board of Missions, revealing two theologies of mission. Reviewing the files of Mayer and Reinking also gives one a great sadness.

Even a greater tragedy was the number of overseas national leaders who were harmed, some irreparably, by the training they received from the St. Louis faculty and from the influence of the ELIM mission staff. Some great talents and wonderfully loving people became warped and some were corrupted. They were led away from the Biblical theology and practice enunciated in our "Mission Policy Statement" which you have read earlier. In one case, serious allegations were made against the leader of one of our national churches both in his own church and from first-hand experience in The Missouri Synod, but this leader refused to even communicate in any form.

The Hong Kong Theatrics

What about the Hong Kong situation in 1974 and 1975 in which I was featured in MIP? It would be easy to recount factually the historic record of my forced apologies to the Hong Kong church for a legitimate answer to a letter from concerned pastors and congregations of the Hong Kong Lutheran Synod to me as Chairman of the Board. But I will not take time and space here to recount the evidence of what really happened, only summarize it.

Obviously, politics influenced by ELIM with its theology divided the Hong Kong church into two warring camps. Our Missions staff was encouraging their own clones in Hong Kong to proceed with the ELIM agenda, while those loyal to The Missouri Synod were bruised and battered. Our ELIM Mission staff did not want the loyal Board to discuss the matter since they had it all going their way, and all I did as Chairman was to assure the victims of the ELIMite campaign in Hong Kong that the Board would consider their pleas. If such a fair Christian response was wrong, then no one has proven it. Records show that that letter was condemned by the ELIM faction in Hong Kong, who then used *Missouri in Perspective* as their mouthpiece to hold public court, and there was no way that I could have any reasonable communication with them to deal with the real issues.

When I tried to communicate via correspondence with a key missionary, I received no answer from him; instead, the basics of my concern in that letter were published in *MIP* with front page headlines. I wrote to the missionary and told him of his wrong, but all that happened was more printing of headline articles and editorials in *MIP*. It is significant that about eight years ago I received a letter from this former missionary, now a pastor in the U.S., who said he was sorry for what he had done; he wrote that he had prepared a sermon, which he could not preach the next Sunday until he had asked me for forgiveness for the way he had treated me, and I gave him full and free forgiveness. In view of this later clearing of the decks, the events that follow proved to be even a greater tragedy than what they appeared at that time: in order to try to get the Mission Board and his Synodical administration extracted from the public trial conducted in *Missouri in Perspective*, the Synodical President planned a settlement behind the scenes in which he extracted an apology from me, which I told him would not be sufficient to stop the ELIMite campaign in Hong Kong. The Hong Kong ELIMite majority toyed with that one and accepted the apology partially and said that it was "a step in the right direction," but more was needed. At that time, the Synodical President and the Executive for the Missions Study Commission and also several members of the Board of Directors urged a strengthening of the apology. The

President wanted this apology because he said that this would stop the attacks on me and get the focus back on the issues in Hong Kong; I said that I did not believe that it would stop them, but I was assured that if they did not accept the apology and kept on attacking, he would then be in a strong position to defend me fully and to criticize the Hong Kong leaders. There was more planning behind the scenes while more public court was held in MIP.

At that time, I engaged a Synodical layman, a lawyer, as my personal counsel because I was becoming weary of the political handling of this situation. I even received a letter written by an agent of the President to sign with the assurance that, if I did sign, the Board of Directors might pass a resolution complimenting me for this gracious act, and this would be put into the public relations releases. When I asked how the Board of Directors got involved and what they had to do with it, this agent told me that they are in no way involved. After this telephone visit, while the Board of Directors was still in session I received a phone call from a member of the Board of Directors with the same basic message that the previous agent had conveyed and put on the same kind of pressure. I simply stated over and over that I was going to write nothing more, and that no clarification would be acceptable by the Hong Kong ELIMites but be used for further attacks on me through the Hong Kong General Conference and MIP.

The next day I received another phone call from the agent, and the following day from the President himself, who used the same kind of arguments and pressure as did his two emissaries in three long-distance phone calls to get me to sign the letter. Several days later, a letter from the President to the members of the Board for Missions carried an exhibit entitled, "Proposed Letter by Werning to Chiu," which was the same letter which his agent read to me over the phone the previous Thursday night. It did not state that this was a letter proposed by the President, his emissaries, and the Board of Directors, but was submitted as though I had written it. Not only were the Hong Kong ELIMites trying me in **absentia**, but also the Synodical leaders were engineering something that had little semblance to Biblical procedure.

MIP in its Feb. 24, 1975, letter gloated, "The Chairman of the LCMS Board for Missions has issued a second, more comprehensive, apology for his participation in actions and correspondence that led to a schism in the Synodical Hong Kong mission." (Note: See how I was blamed for a conflict which was created by the ELIMites in Hong Kong when all I did was to respond to the victims that the Board would consider their pleas.) MIP: "The Rev. Dr. Waldo Werning made the apology at the Board's February meeting at the persistent urging of the Synod's President, The Rev. Dr. J. A. O. Preus. The initial draft of the apology was prepared by the Synod's Board of Directors and was designed to cover all the areas of 'assurance' requested by the Hong Kong Mission." Please recall that I was assured by the President's emissary that the Board of Directors was in no way involved. This MIP article continues, "In a press release, Dr. Preus noted that the Board Chairman's action indicated that the Synod is 'willing to ask for forgiveness even when in doing so it feels that it has been wronged.'" I rest my case on that last statement!

Please do not feel that I am unnecessarily revealing information which should be kept confidential, for this is all a part of public record and much of it was spread all over the pages of *Missouri in Perspective* for several years. Even at that, it is very painful for me to review the public record in this book. But if we do not learn from our past mistakes of political maneuvers instead of following Biblical and by-law procedures, we will not have learned to avoid political ways that sidetrack us. Not only I, but the entire Mission Board loyal majority was being interfered with. Can you imagine how we felt and reacted when we learned of speeches or read stories in MIP about statements which made the faithful members of the Board for Missions look inept instead of the capable servants of the Lord which they were?

The April 28, 1975 MIP reported part of a speech given by the President in Kansas, in which he painted himself as a referee in an unnecessary feud between the Board for Missions and the ELIMite staff: "I do not think that the feud which arose should have arisen...I think they (Board) were very distrustful...In the case of the resignations, I asked everyone of them to reconsider...I did not feel that the conflict was of such a nature between the Mission staff over the old traditional position of the Synod. I didn't feel that it was such a problem that it could not be adjudicated or settled...It was sort of a comedy of errors...I'll go so far as to say now I advised and made contact with Jim Mayer to talk about the possibility of doing something to recognize, legitimatize, regularize, or whatever you call it, the **Partners in Mission**. (**Note:** this was the ELIMite rebel mission group trying to destroy the Synod's missions.)...I, for one, very much support the contentions of the former staff. I think they were more right than wrong. I think they were wrong in some of their procedures by taking some of the things to the church, but philosophically, I think that some of the things were right."

The July 15, 1974, MIP reported, "Missouri Synod President Jacob Preus has expressed public support for positions maintained by Mission staff workers in their long-standing dispute with the so-called 'conservative' leadership of the Board for Missions. Dr. Preus has placed himself at odds with positions espoused by Mission Board leaders and in line with the thinking of Mission staff leaders, several of whom resigned recently to protest Board policy."

Another move was to get the Board of Directors officially involved through a committee which created many months of maneuvering through procedural questions and tactics which avoided the issues and allowed the ELIMite staff an opportunity to do more propagandizing. The final result was that the Board of Directors then in their March 28-29, 1974 meeting resolved to appoint a five man study commission "to make a thorough study of the entire Mission operation for the purpose of assessing the efficacy of its present operation and further to propose to the Board of Directors and the Board for Missions recommendations as to objectives, purposes, goals, structure, operation and any other aspect necessary to determine how the church's mission can best be served."

Quoting from a summary of the information which I supplied to this Mission study commission on March 24, 1975, you will learn that "Dr. Werning shared with the commission his concern over the extent of involvement of President Preus and others in the affairs of the Board for Missions. With respect to President Preus, there are various aspects to this: Various strategies discussed by President Preus in advance with mission staff at the headquarters...Dr. Werning is bothered by all the 'third party' involvement by both friend and foe. Interferences made it difficult to be his own man - there are people in St. Louis who are deciding courses of action for him. He has conscience problems with this."

The following is the analysis and report which I gave to the Mission Study Committee, the Board of Directors, and Synodical leaders regarding the work of the Mission Study Commission when it was completed:

SOME COMMENTS AND OBSERVATIONS
ON THE MISSION STUDY COMMISSION REPORT (1975)

It is good to recall that Executive Secretary, Dr. Eugene W. Linse, stated to the Board for Missions on April 11 that the Commission reserves the right to withdraw any or all parts of the report between now and the convention and during the convention.

BASIC EVALUATION OF THE REPORT

There is much obvious good, to which we will not point for brevity sake. Some areas are inadequate, and these observations focus on the inadequacies. Our immediate problem arises in that the M.S.C. report makes rather harsh judgments of past actions of the Board on the basis of surface symptoms and the noise of strife. This requires an analysis. The criticism by the M.S.C. which will be reproduced under "Quotations" require of us an open and honest approach in stating our actions, not taken for personal gain or selfish standards, but solely for the good of the Synod on the basis of Synodical requirements.

How unfortunate that the M.S.C. report attempts to refight a battle that has ended, for our new Executive Secretary is on the job with the daily call, "Go Forward!" New objectives and structures cannot be planned effectively by replaying only the symptoms of the war, ignoring the total mosaic of which the mission problem is only one part.

Summary Observation: THE M.S.C. FAILED TO DETERMINE THE REAL MOTIVATIONS AND REASONS FOR THE BOARD'S ACTIONS, DID NOT ACCURATELY ASSESS THE SITUATION, AND DID NOT UNDERSTAND EITHER THE SHORT-RANGE OR LONG-RANGE IMPLICATIONS OF THE CONTROVERSIES.

Specific Observations: We find

(1) SWEEPING GENERALIZATIONS ON INDIVIDUAL OR MINOR ITEMS, OR PARTIAL AND SELECTIVE INFORMATION, WHICH GIVES THE WRONG IMPRESSION OF WHAT THE REAL SITUATION WAS.

(2) OPINIONS NOT SUFFICIENTLY SUPPORTED BY FACTS AND EVIDENCES - OR A SUPERFICIAL READING OF THE SITUATION.

(3) INDISCRIMINATE CONCLUSIONS - DOES NOT DISCRIMINATE BETWEEN THOSE WHO ARE GUILTY OR NON-GUILTY IN BOARD, STAFF, OR FIELD, NOR DISCRIMINATE BETWEEN CAUSES AND SYMPTOMS, BETWEEN ISSUES AND PERSONALITIES; FAILS TO PERCEIVE THE REAL ISSUES AND CAUSES.

(4) OUT OF HISTORICAL CONTEXT.

(5) INSINUATIONS OR INNUENDOES.

(6) UNNECESSARY RHETORIC OR INTEMPERATE WORDS AND PHRASES.

(7) SEEMS TO CENTER ON PERSONALITIES AT TIMES AND ATTACKS PEOPLE IN A WAY THAT GETS AWAY FROM ISSUES.

Throughout this critique **the above numbers with brackets** will be used to indicate where it is felt that the above Evaluation Instrument applies in the text and the report.

This report has several major omissions: It completely ignores the documented fact that the Mission Board and St. Louis Seminary issues are tied together and that the mission problem is one with the total Synodical problem. It ignores the commitment and activities on the part of the former staff in the Synod's liberal movement (Frey-Lueking group, followed by ELIM). There is no indication of the excesses or errors in the life of certain missionaries and sister churches overseas. It does not commend specific faithful missionaries and fields such as Nigeria. It gives the impression that exhibits and evidences are on hand for all opinions and judgments, and that there is a volume of evidence on various judgments made, which is **not true**. It fails to recognize a major factor that former staff regularly proposed: Trust us, the Board has no business in getting involved in this. Then the former staff either would not perform or would come in with their biased recommendations; when biased recommendations were brought into the meeting, they controlled the meeting with their friends on the Board itself, advisory members, and a large staff; thus loyal members were intimidated or effectively controlled by such strategy. The report does not recognize the strong commitment of the Board majority, who as volunteers were faced with insurmountable tasks of giving days and weeks for being properly prepared with factual and historical resources against the constant attack and campaign by the former staff, staff's friends on the Board, and advisory members; it does not recognize the patience exercised for six years by some.

The program and approach which the Board for Missions majority employed in the past four years is totally consistent with the constitution, by-laws and resolutions of The LC-MS. The Board majority faithfully adhered in an evangelical manner to the purpose and reason for their elections, as well as that of the entire administration, and never deviated from the path assigned by Synod itself.

QUOTATIONS OF PROBLEMATIC OPINIONS AND JUDGMENTS

All **underlined** are **ours,** not in the text of the Mission Study Commission, and are done in order to point to specific instances in paragraphs which are quoted.

Pages 28-29: "...Comes as no surprise that Board and staff became **embroiled** in conflicts over questions of theology, missiology, and support for **personal proposals** for missions, questions of **internal strategy,** questions of **semantics** and other matters. The result was a **constant flow** in recent years of majority and minority reports to the church-at-large and in convention...Its largely **ineffective response** to problems was unique..." (1) (2) (3)

Page 32: "...**Private agendas** were the **order of the day,** strategies for winning achieved new priorities, and the membership of the church-at-large was **solicited to take sides.** Majority and minority reports to the New Orleans convention in 1973 **failed to reveal** the **intensity of the struggle** that was going on." (1) (2) (3)

Page 32: "Through **precipitous action** by members of the Board and the former staff in the **internal affairs of sister churches,** sister churches became involved in the conflict..." (1) (2)

Page 60: "...**preoccupation** over **organizational powers,** over **personal preferences** and **private agendas,** the area of world missions has also been affected...**Representatives** of the Board for Missions have **acted hastily** and drawn conclusions **without having all of the facts** or **without a proper understanding** of all the historical and contextual circumstances of churches in other lands..." (1) (2) (3) (5) (6)

Page 61: "...Confounded by the **indiscriminate actions** of some of its own members...Comedy of errors..." (1) (2) (3) (6)

Page 62: "...**Claims of interference** in the domestic affairs of churches in other lands have been made against TLC-MS, **perhaps with some justification**..." (2) (3)

EXAMPLES OF INADEQUACIES OF THE MSC REPORT

I. The Theology Of Synod

Given the entire context of the report, we question the adequacy of the statement, "While the Commission acknowledges an **awareness** of a growing theological debate over the past decennium...There are few who will dispute the fact that the basic theology of the LCMS has remained remarkable constant since its inception in 1847." (Page 11) It seems to ignore the fact that the Missouri Synod is **in a civil war** (1974) and that our Synodical President who said at New Orleans (quoted in the *St. Louis Globe Democrat* editorial of July 12, 1973), "Someone in this church ought to have authority to determine how we today interpret, confess our Lutheran faith and maintain it in our pulpits and classrooms", has been criticized for demagoguery, lying, and that his theology is unLutheran and unScriptural. It ignores the fact that the majority in the Synod agree with seminary acting President Ralph Bohlmann who said as late as the recent St. Louis Convocation, 'It is better to be divided for the sake of the truth than to be united in error.'

II. The Problems In Mission Theology

The report states on Page 11 that "the fundamental mission theology of the LCMS has undergone little change during the century-and-a-quarter plus years of her existence." Oversimplified and confusing again is the previous statement on the theology of the LCMS. The body and recommendations of the M.S.C. Report do not follow a statement about "two theologies" clouding mission expressions.

III. General Concerns about the Opinions by the Mission Study Commission Report

A. General

Page 30: "For a time the Board for Missions and the former staff developed policies independently of each other...A notable example is the independent development of a policy statement for campus ministry." (3) The fact is that the Executive Committee and certain resigned staff were to develop a campus ministry statement, but staff stubbornly insisted on inclusion of a statement for tri-Lutheran agencies despite the fact that it had been shown that the Synod's By-Laws, resolutions, and CCM took a position against them. It is indiscriminate criticism to hold the Board officers guilty in this regard, while they were holding to Synod's agenda.

Page 30: "To date, no policy statement of criteria has been adopted against which an assessment can be made as to whether or not a mission field has reached maturity necessary for sister church status." (3) The fact is that in late 1970 the Synodical loyalists finally got a resolution through the Board that the staff in January 1971 should present such criteria to the Board in preparation for the Milwaukee 1971 convention. The staff never did present these to the Board.

Page 33: "These position descriptions, drawn up in 1967, have been reviewed. Moreover, the Board for Missions seems to **see no need in updating** these job descriptions...The Board of Directors of the LCMS instructed the Board for Missions to update the position description for the Executive Secretary prior to issuing the call...The Board for Missions called the new Executive Secretary on the basis of the old job description. The Board for Missions failed to comply with the Board of Director's request." (1) (2) The fact is that 1) the Personnel Chairman was working completely in harmony with the Executive Secretary of the Board of Directors in this matter; 2) The Board of Directors had ordered the Board for Missions not to call any more staff until the M.C.S. report had been finished (which immediately nullified any attempt to update positions which might no longer be proposed after the M.S.C. report). A June 5, 1974, memo from Herman H. Koppelmann to Staff Members and Will Sohns stated that the Board of Directors resolved that "none of the vacant positions on the Mission Staff" be filled "until the M.S.C. completes its work on or about November 1." Koppelmann wrote "This rather invalidates any proposals we might now make." The Mission Board was not taking an independent action, but was stymied by the interference of the Board of Directors through its contradicting statements and resolutions.

Page 50: "**Some say** the church should get out of service programs - such as schools, hospitals, and the like - and concentrate on the proclamation of the Gospel..." (1) (2) (3)

(5) Who says this? Not one of the BFM Board members say it, yet this purports to be a report about the Board's activities.

Page 61: Referring to the overseas visitation report: "Representatives of the BFM have acted hastily and drawn conclusions without having all the facts or without a proper understanding of all the historical and contextual circumstances of churches in other lands.." (3) The fact is that the Overseas Visit Committee involved **three** members of the **Board of Directors** while there were **two** members of the BFM who jointly proposed this report. Without a recognition of the previous facts stated that this had been bootlegged to the fields by former staff, this matter will be totally misrepresented. The MSC report confuses and compounds the problem more.

B. Board of Directors

Page 24: "**Resentment** of and **resistance** to direction or suggestions from the Board of Directors or the President of Synod all too frequently concerned time on agendas. Surely **this does not speak well of men** committed to the mission of Christ. Is it any wonder that in many areas the **mission has run aground**?" (1) (2) (3) This is a cruel judgment and does not square with the facts. The BFM consistently faced political tactics and "end-around-runs" by the President directly or through the Board of Directors, which had no relation to Synodical policies and procedures.

Page 59: "Neither the President of the Synod nor the Board of Directors have exercised the kind of power for which they have been criticized." (1) (2) (3) NOTE: Without judging motives or seeking reasons, it must be candidly stated that on a number of occasions without consultation with or the knowledge of the Board for Missions or its officers, the Board of Directors or President made decisions arbitrarily which affected Mission work for which the BFM is responsible to supervise and counsel in various countries. The Board of Directors or President, although informed by representatives G. Nitz, V. Behnken, E. Weber of difficulties caused by former staff and anti-Synod Mission Board members, at no time gave support to the BFM in its proper stand on Synod's doctrine, by-laws, and policies (except in the case of Denver 1-11). If such support would have been evident, it would have put an end to the rebellion. Instead, the Board of Directors and President became third parties who heard complaints or gave advice in such a manner that BFM authority and power to act was effectively diffused.

C. Mission Study Commission And Its Executive Secretary

The March 28, 1974 Board of Directors resolution stated that the MCS was to "propose to the Board of Directors and the Board for Missions recommendations as to objectives, purposes, goals, structure, operation, and any other aspect necessary to determine how the church's mission can best be served," and "to promptly present their findings conclusions, and recommendations to the Board for Missions, the Board of Directors, and the President for implementation."

1. Instead of presenting findings, conclusions, and recommendations to the three parties mentioned above promptly, the MCS consistently went to the Board of Directors **while the BFM was kept in ignorance.** The MCS also presented its final report to the Board of Directors and to the Synod for its convention workbook without the BFM having heard anything or seen anything about it. This is totally in opposition to the Board of Directors resolution and the agreement which the BFM accepted with the Board of Directors. With all the difficulties that Synodical loyalists in the BFM have had, this only compounds the problems considerably more.

2. The November 2, 1974, resolution to the MSC recommended that the Board of Directors take such action (ignoring the BFM) as is necessary to assure the appointment of the Executive Secretary to the BFM, to be effective only after consultation with sister churches. The BFM was not informed by the Board of Directors until over two weeks later. The BFM had asked Board of Director's representatives to telephone the chairman, whose shock and the ensuing problems were reported to the BFM in a letter of November 25, 1974, to the BFM. This action of the MSC also did not follow the March 1974 Board of Directors resolution and policy.

FROM THE "BATTLE NOISE" REACTION OF THE MSC TO BASIC STRATEGY AND ISSUES

Past Synodical Conventions themselves have acted positively in areas where the MSC made condemnations against the Synodical loyalists on the BFM. The Synodical Board majority was often forced to stand alone to loyally confess the Synodical position for over six years. The Mission faithful were shown as men who enjoy doing battle and who consequently are thrown the blame for Synod's mission problems.

Is it not more accurate to portray them as men who have faithfully held to the Scriptural, Confessional and Synodical positions in doctrine and practice amidst most difficult situations and with great cost personally and to their families in one arena of the Synod's overall "civil war"?

The Board should be commended for attempting to deal with the various problems on the basis of Scriptural and Synodical policies instead of on the political level as did the Synodical administration. Hopefully, the Executive Secretary of the MSC will follow his own advice - that the MSC reserves the right to withdraw any and all parts of the report from now and until the convention or during the convention. We believe the facts indicate such a **withdrawal** and a complete **revision** for the sake of truth, fairness and justice.

* *

This chapter will end with the statement which I gave to the Synod on April 10, 1974 at the occasion of the resignation of Dr. William H. Kohn as Executive Secretary of the Board. This reveals again the Board's endeavors to be faithful servants of the Word and of the Synod:

"The Board for Missions is sorry that a way could not be found to work with Dr. William H. Kohn that would unify the LCMS mission on the basis of its Gospel commitment as required by the Synod's constitution and resolutions. We are not happy that the disagreements ended by such a drastic step as resignation, but we commend Dr. Kohn for acting in such an honorable way.

"Our board is responsible to the Synod to reflect the church's position, intention and resolutions in mission policies and practices. We have no authority to promote another position or variety of positions, but only that of the church for which we serve as the mission arm.

"This matter has a relationship to the entire doctrinal controversy in our church regarding the basic question of the interpretation of the Bible. This has resulted in differing proposals for mission theology and practice from those we have known from the Scriptures and those our church has practiced in the past.

"Acting as best and faithfully as we know, we tried in the face of difficult circumstances to act evangelically to reach our common mission objectives and goals. We were frustrated to find conflicting goals between the Board and Dr. Kohn. We were greatly surprised to learn on January 18 of a letter sent out by Dr. Kohn and his helpers criticizing the Synod's Board for Missions for legalism, arbitrary use of power, separatism and other matters. We were grieved to learn of three other letters sent worldwide also without our knowledge attacking the Board without our having an opportunity to give witness to our own dedication to truly Gospel and Scriptural goals for mission.

"An attempt by the officers of the Board on February 1 to ask questions and listen to Dr. Kohn ended in an immediate walkout without his speaking to us. The Synod's Board of Directors' attempt to assist our Board in conducting fraternal discussions between February 28 and April 5 ended in frustration as the Board's three representatives twice went to St. Louis (and were told a third time that there was no need to come) for discussion with Dr. Kohn and two staff members, only to be informed by the Board of Directors that Dr. Kohn still had not agreed to the format of the discussions. During this time, Dr. Kohn and others spoke publicly throughout the country against the Board.

"This has become an administrative problem because of an unwillingness to state clearly the issues side by side. The Board has been very intent on discussing the real issues as they see them, believing that this would lead to a successful resolution of the differences. The Board has been waiting for three months to face these issues in fraternal discussion. Thus, on April 6 we passed an enabling motion to go into serious discussions while we pursued our mission responsibilities as the Synod required of its elected officials.

"The Board had been presented with ultimatums which made impossible the Board's attempts to resolve the issues. Some of these demands involved synodical resolutions to which the Board is held. This hindered our attempts to resolve these issues which were presented to us as ultimatums...

"Despite Dr. Kohn's action, we hope the staff will gladly join with the Board to resolve any issues that may confront us. The Board's primary concern has been, is, and will be to carry out the mission of the church as desired by the members of the Missouri Synod. We thank Dr. Kohn for his service and wish him well."

* *

These last two chapters provided facts about the activities of the party of the left - the St. Louis faculty and the ELIMite mission staff, and all their supporters throughout Synod. They do not begin to reveal the carnage of wonderful students, pastors, teachers, laymen, missionaries and anyone else, all of whom believed the "party line" and did not take the time to learn the truth. They simply did not know what the real issues were. They were led to believe that the cause of the St. Louis faculty and the mission staff problems were legalism, procedural dictators and heartless tyrants. The ELIM followers allowed themselves to be manipulated through the rumor mill and the public press, not realizing the half-truths and propaganda they were being fed.

Today, some of those who left the Missouri Synod have returned, while many others are unhappy as members of the ELCA. To quote Richard Neuhaus, they have complained in the ELCA about quotas, social action, political initiatives, and completely false doctrine in the place of Gospel witness. Some theologians and pastors of the ALC and LCA who were prominent liberals in theology twenty years ago are today complaining about unBiblical theology in the ELCA. Nine hundred of them, including many former LCMS members (AELC) who are unhappy in their new church home, gathered together at St. Olaf college, Minnesota in June 1990 for an independent theological conference, "Called to Faithfulness".

The July 11, 1990 *The Lutheran* reported, "In major lectures at a three-day 'Called to Faithfulness' Conference, prominent Lutheran theologians chastised the ELCA for its ecumenical policies, its approach to social involvement, its mission philosophy, the content of its periodicals, its encouragement of illusive god language and its alleged lack of theological direction." Significantly, one thing missing was the ordination of women as pastors.

The Lutheran article continues, "Speakers suggested that the two-and-a-half-year-old ELCA's troubles are largely the outcome of failures to be faithful to Biblical theology and Lutheran confessions. 'Heresy'(unorthodox belief), 'Apostasy'(abandoning of the faith) and 'Gnosticism' (the claim of salvation through knowledge rather than faith) were frequently heard." Dr. James Kittleson of Ohio State University said, "...we have abdicated our responsibility to teach the faith. We happily whore after every cause that appears - Ecumenism, Episcopacy, quotas, the environment, inclusiveness - everything is more important than the Gospel."

Professor Robert W. Jenson of St. Olaf's college wrote in an editorial in the Autumn, 1991 *Dialogue* explaining why Dr. Carl Braaten left ELCA's Lutheran School of Theology in Chicago, "In the seminaries of the ELCA there is now a theological censorship of a stringency previously unknown in Lutheranism outside the Missouri Synod...His chief axioms are perhaps: (1) Biblical and historical study is for the purpose of liberating from the language and opinions of the Bible and the traditions; (2) 'God' is a complex of metaphors, protected from our religious needs and social evaluations; (3) The church is a volunteer society of the religiously like-minded, which we continuously re-institute as our religious minds change...what made Carl Braaten overturn his licensing judgment; (4) seminaries of the ELCA are now institutions emphatically inhospitable to theological work and instruction, and are likely to remain so for the foreseeable future."

The Sept. 14, 1991 *FORUM LETTER* discussing the organization of ELCA, reports, "As somebody has surely said, it was **sola structura** (structure) all the way. The ELCA as a result has no coherent doctrine on ordained ministry. We do have a real cracker-jack quota system. Someone has said that the quota system and pressure for social action substitutes with law what it lacks in virtue. It establishes legalism to replace the Holy Spirit."

A word needs to be spoken to those who are members of the Missouri Synod and those who have left who made President J. A. O. Preus their whipping boy. We can in no way criticize President Preus for his theological commitment to doctrine and practice, and for his gracious attempts to try to do what his office demanded of him. We may have disagreed with some of his political procedures, but that does not negate in any way the validity of his cause or that he was right. Nor did it justify ELIM's organization and actions. This became an occasion for the St. Louis faculty and the ELIMites to change the focus from themselves and their own rebellion to tactics which they claimed did them in.

I agree with the axiom that "you do not fight fire with fire." In this case, we should not have fought wrongful political tactics and theological aberrations with political tactics, no matter how righteous the cause. However, President Jack Preus inherited a Synod in disarray and that was committed to institutional answers to practical matters. His political moves should not have become an issue for claiming that the Missouri Synod was treating the rebels badly. I believe there was a better way for him to handle it, but he was the President and he had to make the decisions — it was not our task. The important thing is that we learn our lesson and make a change of church paradigms when we face a church conflict.

CHAPTER 8

THE PARTY OF THE RIGHT BECOMES A POLITICAL MACHINE AND HOLDS A SEMINARY HOSTAGE — GOD'S MEN DOING BAD THINGS

Minutes before I was ready to begin writing this chapter, the U.S. mail delivered a copy of "A Theological Statement of Mission" (CTCR, November 1991). The entire document consists of eight parts and proves to be an excellent one. However, there is one vital addition I would make: God's mission can be hampered or destroyed by political parties and institutional Lutherans.

That booklet which effectively summarizes the mission of TLCMS stands in stark contrast to the wayward, contentious and destructive mission of the March 30, 1992 *Christian News* which arrived yesterday. Already the Feb. 24 headline read, "ORTHODOXY WINS," claiming some dubious political "victory" for Dr. Robert Preus. If this is all "Confessional Lutherans" or "Orthodoxy" have to offer the church and the world, Lutheranism is terribly sick.

Apparently, the *CN* Editor received a copy of the Indiana District Adjudication decision which tells of the sins of Dr. Preus in the charges made by the Synod's Praesidium. The *CN* Editor erratically wrote on March 30, 1992, 'Now we can assure our readers that Preus is guilty of no great crime which should lead to the termination of his membership within The LCMS...trifling matters... Much of the document reminds us of a silly, stupid, and waste-of-time family squabble...Preus did make some unguarded statements. We do not defend all of his statements or actions...The entire historical context must be taken into consideration. We also find it difficult to defend all of Luther's preposterous statements. None of us are perfect." Beyond that, there are less than complementary inferences made regarding the acumen and theological perception of the Indiana Commission members who are given a "compliment" of being "sincere Christians who tried their best." This chapter will share the facts of this Indiana decision.

CN blames President Bohlmann for all the evil in the LCMS in much of the rest of the article. There is a slanderous attempt at satire: "The final audience or Missouri at 2010," is shameless ridicule of President Bohlmann, Dr. Sam Nafzger, and others; a review of eight imaginary books uses sarcasm to ridicule Synodical personalities and church growth.

Whatever the cause, God's mission never gives license for such bad treatment of brother Christians. Such spiritual barbarianism of *CN* is used to blunt the guilt of Dr. Robert Preus. This chapter will deal with the necessity for honesty, integrity and Christian ethics in contending for the faith. It calls for the politics of responsibility, not of sarcasm and liquidation. It exposes the old tactic, "Attack the personality and confuse the issues."

Because this chapter provides various negative experiences which I had at the Seminary in order to provide necessary documentation, I must assure the reader that none of this is shared out of any feeling of deep hurt, bitterness, or any personal reasons, but only so that the carnage inflicted upon many excellent servants of God might stop. If there had been any motive of anguish, I would not subject myself to additional emotional trauma in writing for any reason. To put it bluntly, I have been urged very strongly by some Seminary professors and other Synodical leaders to tell the truth kindly, and to provide evidence in the hope that the political campaign can be stopped. I had been told by some Seminary professors already three years ago that I had much less to lose in taking the steps required than any others who were not of retirement age. Already then, I was willing to pay any price to make my contribution to stop the destruction of outstanding workers in our Seminary and to help bring back healing. It would be unfair and wrong for any partisan to assume anything else regarding my motives than what I have written here.

Robert Preus Party Tactics

There are close similarities between the Tietjen-SL Faculty-ELIM-MIP tactics of twenty years ago and the Robert Preus-CN-FW Academic Clique-"Confessional Lutheran" maneuvers against the true mission of the Missouri Synod today. Both ELIM and "Confessional Lutherans" developed powerful political campaigns for waging their unwarranted war, as the historical records provide considerable documentation. Both used argument and accusation while ignoring and denying evidence and truth. Neither recognized that contentious shouting and allegations or complaints are not evidence or documentation to make a legitimate case — yet that is precisely what they did.

Both the ELIMites and the Preus party were in denial and could not accept reality. Each had functionaries who were in bondage to the party, and didn't know it. I was one of the last loyal party members to bail out of the Robert Preus boat — in fact, I was kicked out. I apologize to The LCMS that I did not go out in protest earlier, but I was dealing patiently in the hope that matters would get better. I was a hero to these people twenty years ago, but now a bum. I have not changed, but they have.

As soon as the evidence of the Ft. Wayne situation grabbed me by the throat to see what was happening, I privately brought the aberrations to the attention of Dr. R. Preus regularly. After he became convinced that I was serious and wanted Christian communication and believable answers, he terminated me. Very soon, the word went out, which Rev. Herman Otten can affirm, that I was "losing it," and had turned liberal. Others before me experienced the same. None of these party-line critics ever faced me to discover the truth, but passed on the party line slander instead. What I have seen first-hand during the past four years are the same tactics and politics of irresponsibility utilized by the ELIMites twenty years ago.

Like the ELIMites, the Preus "Confessional Lutherans" used various political tactics in the name of Christ. Both became entangled in human manipulation through political power plays. Both believed and stated loudly that they were serving our Holy God in a "righteous cause." Both were holding the Synod hostage through use of party-line professors, students, and clones in the Synod. Neither one could tolerate true scholarship and evidence, so they changed the focus to bashing those who have the evidence, using ridicule to discredit and repeating half-truths.

This lengthly chapter provides documentation and commentary on the tragic Robert Preus episode at the Ft. Wayne Seminary for almost ten years, but there is much more. The Preus pipeline was served well by his professor friends, which was easily identifiable by listening to the Faculty gossip channel that was very active. There were always those in the Faculty who were basically uncommitted but remained good friends with the Preus people, so we personally heard the "news" within a day on campus.

Once the managed news was leaked by the pipeline to the public, then the public trial began in *CN*. As will be seen in this account, when support was not strong enough, then ordination of women and other doctrinal concerns were thrown in to raise fears. The "faithful" would read the latest party line neatly packaged in *CN*. The Eighth Commandment was evoked to lecture critics about "putting the best construction on everything," while those saying this had been tearing down the reputation of some pious people, including the Vice Presidents of Synod.

The game plan has been to utilize over-statements, begging the questions, rationalizations, failure to distinguish between antecedent and casualty, semantics, guilt by associa-

169

tion, half-truths, strawman arguments, generalizations on the basis of one example, conclusions on the basis of no evidence or evidence which does not allow the illogical conclusion, etc. Often, the arguments raised fears and gave a slant on the subject directly or implied through a jungle of fallacies. The worst tactic is the conducting of a public trial through the press and media, thus avoiding Biblical procedures, As such, the attack is on persons with broad strokes or generalizations which involve half-truths that avoid the issues. Unwarranted accusations are made.

Theological elite "Confessional Lutherans" have existed to introduce new presuppositions or red flags, such as church growth, decision theology, evangelicals, charismatics, theology of glory, which do not describe the real situation. They never confront any individual who might be guilty of something, but intimidate everyone who would dare to use an idea or a methodology which the party will not allow. Recently, several seminary students told me that when they came to Fort Wayne, they should have been given two lists of definitions as they pertain to "Confessional Lutherans" or to regular Lutherans, as they perceive the "Preus-faculty loyalists" by their statements to be enemies of santification, evangelism and missions.

False dichotomies are presented, as choices are sometimes offered between two complementary ideas that are made to appear to be theologically contradictory. There is the merging of santification with justification, and subjective justification with objective justification. This will be shown in this chapter.

The political party of the "right" claims to hold the high ground, and maintains that this is a battle between the good and the bad. There is much rumor and untruthfulness. There is gang-tackling of group pressure by the Seminary academic elite and their supporters.

A major aspect is the letter writing campaigns. Recalling the letters I received during the mission conflic 20 years ago from both sides, some letters had little substance and had no supporting evidence, only opinions and judgments. Such letters are useless, and sometimes sinful. Some of the condemnations in those letters were retracted later because an individual who thought he had reliable information.

Why this Book?

Under normal circumstances, I would not share information on individuals and their public performance. These abnormal times call for uncommon actions, publicly "speaking the truth in love." At a time when evangelical church discipline and the Synod's Adjudication system have been corrupted to the extent that our Commission on Appeals overturned proper decisions based on evidence and then proceeded to conclude my case with an absolute untruth, there is no other recourse that to tell the church. I apologize for any pain that may be caused, but I see no other alternative. Anyone who complains about this disclosure should go to the Synod's Commission on Appeals to complain because they closed the door to any Biblical procedures and adjudication. I tried to face the individual Commission members with correction through their District Presidents, but the Presidents did not believe it was their responsibility.

Our Handbook 8.07,b states that there are situations where a person "shall be free to enforce or defend his rights in the civil courts," despite the warning in 1 Cor. 6:1-7. Even though the Seminary Board of Regents and Synodical Officials have failed to protect my rights in the Robert Preus case, costing me tens of thousands of dollars, and despite the fact that the Commission on Appeals has corrupted the system, I simply do not believe in going to court against my Synod. I believe firmly that all fair-minded and clear-thinking members of the Synod, including those of the Robert Preus party, will honestly look at the documentation of this book, and then come to the proper conclusion and learn a lesson that will help the Synod find a better way to handle conflict.

A pastor who recently ordered this book on the basis of the publicity folder clearly caught my purpose and motive for writing it when he wrote, "You seem to have taken the position that the time for politics and partisanship is over. We must get on with the Kingdom work and the mission God has placed before us. Although you have long had a reputation as being an arch-conservative, I get the impression that you are still a faithful, confessional Lutheran but you have an even greater concern, namely, that we rise above our separatism, and search for and propose various steps to bring our church body together once again." Indeed!

This book is a plea for all of us to be obedient to God's Word and our Lutheran Confessions, and to utilize only Biblical and Synodical procedures to deal with any one whom we believe is not keeping on the Biblical course. The only Scripturally allowed path for correcting perceived or real wrongs is to follow Matthew 18 and the Eighth Commandment, which imposes upon us the necessity of dealing directly and use private channels with anyone we believe has offended in doctrine and practice. The Scriptures do not allow any complaintant to try his case against another by holding his own public court through the media. This Biblical pattern has been destroyed in our Synod, which leaves me only the civil courts or writing a book for telling the public in as a loving a way as possible.

Introduction to the Robert Preus Problem

Now to study the documentation in the tragic Robert D. Preus dispute. I kept accurate records and files as a normal procedure, as others do. The Preus party and *CN* have made statements that imply that I was looking for "trouble," which is a tactic to obscure the truth and to make my motives suspect. A person is not to be criticized as suspicious when he discovers mud has been thrown in his face, and then recognizes that the same happened to his colleagues. Now I became aware of how important it is to keep files current and accurate. I was offered volumes of materials from others' files, too. This documentation is so voluminous that, despite much summarizing, this chapter became far too long, so that it is necessary to choose only basic materials. The reader should keep this in mind when summaries of documents are provided instead of direct quotations. The files remain evidence of the accuracy of this account.

If Dr. Robert Preus had been open to Biblical procedures, if all his allies had pursued the Scriptural system, if *CN* had not broadcast false allegations, and if the Board of Regents (BOR) would have used Christian tough love, then we would all have been spared the anguish and distress of the past two years; Dr. Preus would have been lovingly confronted by faculty members and the BOR with his mistakes which were destructive to the brotherhood; then the Preus party would not have been organized and gotten into their public trial which God does not allow; then *CN* would not have exclaimed week after week, month after month, "What is Dr. Preus' lie?" Church leaders do not owe Rev. Herman Otten an answer to that question because God has not given him any authority to become the public judge in the Missouri Synod.

It is now time to look at the issues, to evaluate the methods used, and what can be done to find a God-pleasing solution to it. I write as one who was a very close friend and associate of Dr. Robert Preus, one who appreciated his gifts so deeply that I encouraged his continuation as President even amidst growing difficulties. I was supplied his "pipeline" information about the dismissals and forced separations of various professors since 1976 when I came on the scene. I believed much of it until facts did not coincide with pipeline fiction. Even at that, I did not bail out, but was terminated (not "honorable retirement" at the age of 67) in May 1988. Despite that, I struggled to keep the bond between Dr. Preus and me until the BOR meeting on May 20, 1989.

However, already on Nov. 12, 1988, when I was offered an unscriptural contract by Dr. Preus, I found the price too high and discovered that I had to sell my integrity in order to keep working for him even by contract. Even though I had by that time seen and experienced sufficient events which caused my conscience to cry out, "No more!," I had little comprehension of how much information had been misintrepreted or withheld by Dr. Preus and his pipeline.

That presents a terrible dilemma: one wants to go both ways at the same time, but Christian values do not allow that. I had deep friendships not only with Dr. Robert Preus, but also with Dr. David Scaer and Professor Kurt Marquart. Yes, I do have a sense of humor and enjoyed jesting and wise-cracking with my friend David, and theologizing and philsophizing with my friend Kurt, and missionizing with my friend Robert.

But then why write a book now? Friends from the Preus party may ask, "Why do you turn your back on your friends?" I am not turning my back on any friends, including the three named, but I am *facing* them as I always have — but more honestly that I have in the past two years because Dr. Preus and Dr. Scaer were not interested in communication, only in manipulation or annihilation.

As representative of the many victims of the Fort Wayne saga, how can I write these words so that many sincere brothers in the Preus party may work through their denial and experience reality? Will they accept evidence and documentation for what it is — the truth about some very dear friends of ours? My task has been made much more difficult because of so many of the allies of Dr. Preus have been programmed to believe propaganda passed through consistent hype and brain-washing page after page, week after week of *CN* from our erring brother, Rev. Herman Otten.

I want to believe that my good friends who have been supporters and spokesman for Dr. Preus and his party will with aroused consciences accept the truth and look toward healing rather than promoting and reinforcing what is gross sin that is dividing a church. Good brothers, Dr. John Klotz, Mr. Henry Hilst, Mr. Armin Ottemoeller, Dr. Edwin Suelflow, Dr. Al Barry, Dr. George Wollenburg, and Dr. Ed Weber, will you be the influence and be the conscience for leaders of *Balance*, *Affirm*, *RALI* and the "Free Conferences," and help the "Confessional Lutherans," to get off the band wagon immediately? Will you minister to Rev. Herman Otten who appears god-like in the sight of the Preus party members? If you really want to have Biblical solutions, then please move out of the denial state and begin to deal with the evidence which now is available to tear away all binders, and see the scandalous breaking of the Eighth Commandment, and indeed a scandal to the Gospel itself.

The account that follows is not fabricated. It is documented history. There are many victims, but most of them will be found in the Preus party itself because they were deceived. Hopefully, many will discover how Dr. Preus and his party crossed the line between contending for the faith to being contentious and blindly following the party line.

First Media Incident

The June 7, 1978, S.L. Globe-Democrat reported that Dr. Robert D. Preus "has turned down a proposal apparently designed to move him out of the Presidency of the Synod Seminary in Fort Wayne, Ind." The offer to revise the works of Dr. Franz Pieper came from "The Synod's Board For Higher Education, which would have required Dr. Preus to leave the presidency of Concordia Seminary in Fort Wayne," and was "an effort to give him a gracious way out of his post," Synodical officials said. The article tells, "Dissatisfaction with Dr. Preus' administrative skills has grown steadily among the faculty and the Higher Education Board..'' The writer claims to have interviewed some faculty members who expressed dissatisfaction with the impulsiveness and vindictiveness of Dr. Preus. It was no secret that the Synodical President, Dr. J. A. O. Preus, wanted to move his brother out of this position.

In response, the faculty passed a resolution in support of Dr. Preus. That situation calls for an analysis. Most of us in administrative positions, including mine as staff in the Development Office, were well aware of weaknesses in Dr. Preus' administrative ability and/or performance. This was not a big deal because there were so many other strengths which we believed actually helped overcome any weakness in administration. It is significant, however, that a former Academic Dean, the Heads of the departments, and various administrative officers by 1982-1985 saw manipulations and personnel treatment which were very bothersome.

Most of those who experienced forced departures were ones who quietly and properly shared concerns with the President or privately disagreed with his conduct in one matter or another. These were not met with a sympathetic ear, but with a hard hand of pressure. Most of them were administrators, who felt the wrath of the CEO who painted them in a corner as an organized gang who were trying to depose him. Dr. Preus even said that some were allegedly holding secret meetings organized to dump him. Not once did they get together as a group; they were not organized to depose him. Comments made to me in 1992 by some of them was that if that had been their goal, it would have been easy to do because there was sufficient evidence for it.

The five were followed by a middle-of-the-road group of nine faculty members, who were offended that they were being asked to sign statements of support, that they were being asked to participate in political campaigns. They wanted to remain neutral and faithfully work at their jobs without being forced to take one side or another. The historical record shows a letter they produced to express serious concerns. However, these nine also soon were considered the "enemy," who were to be destroyed. In other words, any kind of Biblical approach with Dr. Preus was unwelcome, no matter how much he stated that he was open and cooperative. He was able to convince the BOR and others who were in positions of influence to counteract legitimate concerns about real injustices and manipulative actions on his part.

I was somewhat confused upon hearing that various ones who were dismissed or voluntarily left in disgust had uncomplimentary things said about them through the "pipeline." It was very difficult to separate fact from Preus' pipeline rumor. I lived in the comfort of the big middle group of the faculty and staff who did not get involved, and wanted to live and let live. It is significant that such a strong supporter of Dr. Preus as Dr. Norbert Mueller was targeted by the Preus party and attacked immediately when he did not give the kind of public support that Dr. Preus demanded. In other words, a person was not allowed to be his own man or be independent; he had to get on the political team or be treated as an enemy.

When some of the District Presidents, Synodical administrators, members of visiting teams, and faculty members whose good reputation and service cannot be disputed attempt to "speak the truth in love" to this valued churchman whose actions had become destructive, it is not right to call them liberal, but listen to their findings.

Visiting teams who interviewed faculty indicated that there was always a hard core group of faculty "true believers," who still remain in total denial and who would not admit evidence regardless of how it is presented. Until the last few years, this group may have represented 30% of the faculty. Then there was the middle 30% who recognized the great problems, but felt that they were called to teach, so they would in no way become involved. Then there were those who left because their consciences would not allow them to tolerate the deception and destruction of the mission.

Problems Begin to Become Identified

Typical of the departed Faculty members was this letter sent to the Chairman of the LCMS Board for Professional Educational Services (BPES), "Effective...I will no longer be on the faculty of CTS which places me in an unique position over my colleagues to be able to speak out and voice my concern for the welfare of one of Synod's Seminaries and my Alma Mater without fear of reprisal. I am **NOT** writing out of vindictiveness or hatred; I am not that kind of person. Rather, I am writing to you out of deep concern with the hope that as Chairman of the BPES you might be able to work to bring about positive change at CTS for the good of the whole church. One of the most frustrating obstacles in serving at Concordia Seminary is the authoritarian style leadership which is practiced by the President. Some of my colleagues have regrettably coped with this situation by ignoring it, others chafe under the situation and just live with it. These were not options for me because the situation prevented me from doing my job as well as I knew it could be done which became increasingly frustrating. Thus I have, as others before me, chosen to leave. I cannot have a clear conscience about leaving, however, without voicing my concerns according to the appropriate procedures. I have spoken with Dr. Preus as well as members of the BOR about these matters. I have a great respect for Dr. Preus as a theologian, scholar, and as a person. The issue does not revolve around any of these points. The bottom line is that Dr. Robert Preus is unable to function effectively as an administrator, namely, President of CTS. His style in leadership is blatantly authoritarian, and he demonstrates no ability to significantly modify this style."

This professor continues, "Enclosed is a list of items exemplifying what I am talking about...Recent actions of the BOR of CTS have convinced me that they are either unwilling or incapable of dealing with the heart of the problem. I am therefore requesting that you appoint a neutral third party to investigate the situation for the good of all the individuals involved. If I may, I would suggest that this third party might, with the strictness of confidence, interview faculty members and staff. This may be somewhat difficult because the level of trust is very low around here, some faculty being fearful of reprisal should they speak their true feelings..."

Another administrator who had many years of proven faithful, balanced administration, also wrote to the Board for Professional Educational Services complaining that there was "no due process" in the Preus administration and that the most recent dismissal was a "precipitous and highly unjust" act. He added, "There is something perversely disturbing if such a situation goes unheeded...The climate is not conducive to equipping pastors to be servants of God to administer to his chosen ones. My concern is that wrong will be made right, that the spirit of Matthew 18 have an opportunity to prove its truth, that things be done in decency and order for the good of all concerned."

Sadly, Dr. Preus always had the opportunity to present his views of every person and every situation in the privacy of board meetings, and I learned as others did that the legitimate concerns about the Seminary were seldom if ever allowed to be heard by the board, but they were offered misrepresentations. What the individual or sometimes the faculty heard was entirely different than what the BOR apparently heard. What the facts were and what the Preus pipeline of faculty supporters told were two different stories.

Take the situation of Dr. Alvin Schmidt, for example. The Synod has heard so much through *CN* about his alleged views on ordination of women and the $40,000 settlement that the facts of the situation have been lost. The fact is that the "ordination of women" issue did not enter in until the final steps when public pressure needed to be applied by Dr. Preus. Dr. Schmidt got in trouble with Dr. Preus when Schmidt refused to change data in an ATS report back in 1978. Already then, Dr. Howard Tepker as Academic Dean reported that Dr. Preus said, "Schmidt must go." Can you imagine the attitude Dr. Preus had toward Dr. Schmidt when he as the spokesman of the Faculty Concerns Committee reported the very unsettling findings in the January 27-28, 1984 meeting of the Board of Regents. Schmidt became an innocent victim when he together with others on that Faculty Committee were given a task by the BOR as a result of a Jan. 1983 team of visitors sent by the BPES, who reported, "...there is no question to anyone visiting the campus for several days that a morale problem exists in a significant number of faculty members. This appears to be due in part of the recent dismissal of the Academic Dean, the combination of a series of administrative turnovers in recent years. An atmosphere of fear prevails in parts of the campus." On May 3, 1983, the BPES wrote a letter to the BOR asking it to respond in writing with respect to a number of concerns that the BPES found as a result of the team's visit. The letter asked how the problems listed in the report would be eliminated. One of these problems was the "atmosphere of fear" on campus.

At the BOR's November 1983 meeting, a resolution was passed asking the Faculty Concerns Committee to examine this alleged problem and to report to the BOR in its January 1984 meeting. The Faculty Committee asked questions based on the complaints which were heard by the BPES team, in order to ascertain how accurate and widespread these complaints were. Twenty nine out of thirty faculty members responded to the survey. Two of these responded by written comments without returning the questionnaire. What was the action of the BOR? Dr. Preus convinced them that he could handle the situation and that the written statistical report should be destroyed; then the Board asked representatives to go with Dr. Schmidt to burn that report in a nearby fireplace. Fortunately, for historical accuracy and judgment, copies of the report were not destroyed. An actual copy reveals the following facts:

PREUS FACULTY QUESTIONNAIRE OF JANUARY, 1984

Questions 1-20 are items seeking your opinion or perception. Mark only **one choice** (agree, undecided, or disagree) for each question.

	Agree		Undecided		Disagree	
	#	%	#	%	#	%
1. A morale problem exists in a significant number of faculty members.	18	67	02	07	07	26
2. The present administration of the seminary is insufficiently open and communicative.	12	44	04	15	11	41
3. The president conveys a posture of being pastoral in dealing with problems of faculty members.	13	48	04	15	10	37
4. The administration conducts the affairs of the seminary in a way that is often demoralizing to the faculty.	15	57	02	08	09	35

5. The president fosters an atmosphere of openness and freedom of expression so that the faculty need not think about fear or reprisal. 07 27 08 31 11 42

6. An atmosphere of fear prevails among a significant number of faculty members. 17 63 02 07 08 30

7. The president at times demonstrates a posture of vindictiveness. 13 48 05 19 09 33

8. The seminary's administration is at times arbitrary. 17 63 02 07 08 30

9. The president has on occasion used inappropriate methods in order to gather information on some faculty members. 13 48 08 30 06 22

10. Traditional administration patterns are often confused. 12 46 08 30 06 22

11. Faculty meetings are commonly conducted without much regard to Robert's Rules of Order. 08 30 05 19 14 52

12. The way the president conducts faculty meetings makes it easy to disagree publicly with his viewpoint. 11 41 05 19 11 41

13. The president at times polarizes the faculty on matters that could be mediated. 13 50 03 12 10 38

14. A morale problem on the part of a significant number of faculty members exists in part as the result of the high turnover (more than twice the rate of synod's other terminal schools) of administrative appointments. 15 56 05 19 07 26

15. The president at times manipulates the faculty in order to obtain support on controversial issues. 13 50 04 15 09 35

16. There is inconsistency and inequity of administrative decisions. 14 54 04 15 08 31

17. The president is generally more democratic than authoritarian in his administrative posture. 06 22 08 31 12 46

18. Lines of authority in the administration are not always followed. 16 64 06 24 03 12

19. The president sometimes acts on the basis of rumor or gossip from either students or faculty without telling these "reporters" to first talk to the person(s) who is the object of the rumor or gossip. 13 50 08 31 05 19

20. I sometimes fear the president not because he occupies a position of authority, but because of the way in which he uses power. 13 50 01 04 12 46

21. Do you know where the president has made significant promises, either in writing or orally, to faculty members which were not acted upon? 11 41 07 26 09 33

22. If you had a significant problem, personal or otherwise, would you go to the president in confidence? 11 44 02 08 11 44

23. In recent years a number of administrative appointees have been relieved of their administrative positions. Do such terminations in your opinion add to an "atmosphere of fear"? 15 56 06 22 06 22

24. The week before Christmas of 1983 the faculty learned that one of its colleagues was notified in writing that his faculty contract would not be renewed. Does this particular action, in your opinion, add to an "atmosphere of fear"? 14 52 06 22 07 26

25. Do you at times feel as though someone is "looking over your shoulder" as you teach your seminary classes? 06 23 01 04 19 73

26. Do you mimic the students' saying of "cooperate and graduate" by behaving in a manner that could be described as "cooperate and survive"?	09	36	00	00	16	64
27. Do you know of given faculty members who have been called into the president's office on the basis of some gossip or rumor that was without basis in fact?	12	44	05	19	10	37
28. Have you ever been one of those faculty members who has been called into the president's office on the basis of rumor or gossip?	18	67	00	00	09	33
29. Do you feel comfortable discussing issues with your colleagues?	14	56	04	16	07	28

30. Additional comments, if you wish. Please write on the back.

*　　　　*　　　　*　　　　*　　　　*

What is so tragic about this 1984 Faculty Questionnaire is the anguish experienced as a result of this situation: many who are victims, others who cannot tolerate conflict of any kind, and others in denial who simply rubberstamp anything that their leader says and does. All of those who were exterminated are real people, many of them highly gifted and are a great asset to the Synod. One by one their ministry to which God called them was systematically destroyed by one who was honorably retired by the BOR instead of legitimately terminating him for cause. None of the faculty had proper evaluation or due process, but faced an arbitrary administration.

Yet one of the "Confessional Lutheran" spokesman, Rev. John Pless, had the audacity and spiritual recklessness to write in the Dec. 25, 1990 *Forum Letter* (p. 2), "I am still bewildered why he brought in some faculty members. I would venture to suggest that Preus should have fired more, not less, faculty and staff..." Yet the Preus machine at the Seminary helped organize the Student Association's "Integrity Series" to invite Pless in March 1992 to speak on the campus where faculty members reside, about whom he had made slanderous and heartless comments. Pless spoke without giving an apology, which shows the level of ethics practiced here in 1992 by Preus supporters.

Typical of the pain felt and alienation undergone by victims was the experience of a professor who served faithfully and ably in another Synodical institution and is doing so at yet another one today, who recorded his observations especially from 1984 and 1985. He sent a five page letter to the BOR to tell of his experiences. At a private farewell with five professors present, he wept and said, "David Scaer eviscerated me physiologically and emotionally." The mistake that this professor with a Ph.D. and known as a kind Christian gentleman made was that he called to Dr. Preus' attention administrative perversions which caused him conscience problems. In 1984 this administrator learned that the file of a former CTS student who had transferred to the St. Louis Seminary (who today is a pastor) was missing; he learned that the file had been destroyed by orders of President Preus. He also confronted Dr. Preus concerning another situation with telling an untruth to the ATS after checking the records and the actual accounts; the ATS Executive Secretary's account revealed that the statement of Dr. Preus was totally incorrect. When Dr. Preus was confronted with what this administrator revealed as an example of dishonesty, Preus denied that he had ever said that about ATS rules having been violated. Significantly, the professor at a later date was verbally rebuked by David Scaer for contacting the ATS and for not taking Preus at his word.

This administrator also challenged the fulfillment of Dr. Preus' approval of the colloquy achievements of one colloquy student who withdrew from Greek, and had all of his academic courses by audit except two. The administrator wrote, "I think the transcript qualifies as a farce and not as a colloquy program."

The irony of this professor's situation was that the day before the BOR took action to terminate his service (May 17, 1986) that he received a letter from Dr. Preus dated May 16, 1986 which stated, "I know that you will be struggling and praying over the divine call that you have received...I want to assure you that I will be praying for you that you might find the will of God as you give your response, remembering that you also have a divine call here. Our Board of Regents which has given you the call here, inasmuch as they are meeting tomorrow, know that you would want to consult with them before you make a final decision. They too want only to follow the will of God and is leading as they counsel you in this important decision you have to make." There was **no consultation, no discussion, just a dismissal the next day!**

Little wonder that this professor on October 4, 1989, wrote a letter in which he said, "The brevity of this response is disproportionate to the magnitude of my feelings regarding several confrontational experiences involving both Preus and Scaer. Matters pertaining to the 8th Commandment and what I considered to be a blatant disregard for the Christian ethic were very much a part of these experiences. I became one small victim of the storm. I did indicate my concerns about conflict to Dr. Preus but he neither acknowledged nor accepted responsibility for those conflicts.

"I have some twelve pages of type-written, single-spaced notes, summarizing a series of unpleasant sessions with Preus and Scaer that took place in the spring of 1985. Intimidation, heavy-handedness and managerial conflicts weave their way through these 'seminary soap-operas.' While I do not relish a reliving of the events, I relish even less the prospect of their repetition."

A letter by Academic Dean Howard Tepker to the faculty on May 29, 1984, stated, "...Many of our colleagues have in the recent past left our faculty...what troubles me is that in so many cases they have left us with deep feelings of bitterness and frustration...some feel they have been treated unfairly...(Names deleted)." On June 12, 1990, Dr. Tepker wrote a Memorandum to me, "In 1984 I personally confronted Preus with the fact that some faculty members felt that he should deal with his colleagues in a more brotherly and pastoral manner. They suggested that he should become reconciled with men whom he had offended such as (Names deleted). I am sure that Robert Preus will remember the conversations that six of us had with him on three different occasions in 1985."

On July 5, 1985, Dr. Tepker wrote to Dr. Preus, "...Enclosed is a letter in which nine members of our faculty are expressing their concerns...You will see that among them are some of your closest friends, who have supported you." Included with that was a July 2, 1984, letter to Dr. Preus from nine faculty members, in which they said, "...We were heartened by the last sentence in your report in which you stated: 'I pledge to do everything in my power to remove any obstacle I can to reconciliation.'...In view of the intentions of the faculty, we would like to urge you very strongly to try another approach to reconciliation and accept President Ralph Bohlmann's offer to provide a Committee whose purpose will be to assist the Seminary's difficult task of bringing about reconciliation between you and these men...Among the rest of the faculty also there are feelings — not animosity — but feelings which range from anger, frustration, and disappointment on one hand to fear, apprehension, and uncertainty on the other. Some feel that the above cases should have been handled in a more pastoral manner...''

The Board of Regents passed a resolution on May 26, 1984, which stated, "...7. that a procedure be established for dealing with faculty grievances; 8. that a systematic process be established for evaluating faculty and staff performances expanding on P.4.38 of the Faculty Handbook." (Note: This was never pursued by Dr. Preus or managed by the Board.)

Another faculty member with the consensus of others made this assessment in 1984-1985: "Uneasy surface calm but deceptive, nothing changed. Not dealing with but covering up the root problem of confession of sin and dealing spiritually with the complicated matter of raw politics. Explosive situation with regard to personnel turnover. Continuing friction; ill-advised actions and outright disdain for some of the standard procedures of academics. The 'Preus Men' are in place and moving on. Astonished and bewildered at some of what the Board of Regents permits. There is question whether the Board desires to solve the problem. Faculty are being forced to sign statements of support. Preus not only had not made an attempt to reconcile to faculty members, but says he had done no wrong. Each has his own tensions and fears because of the President's authoritarian and unethical attitude...Preus is vindictive, accepts no restrictions and circumvents regulations at will. Steamroller tactics will continue as Board will not stop it."

When Dr. Preus complained to the Board of Regents about an administrator without telling him what the criticisms were, this administrator in self defense drew up a list of things that Preus had been doing that were wrong and unethical. This was shared with the Chairman of the Board, who asked for a copy of the list of 41 points. The professor replied that this matter was not to be a subject for the Board agenda for the Board ought to be aware of them already. It was given to the Chairman after much pressure with the stipulation that it was not to be shared. When the administrator was called in to the Board, the Chairman brought out the list, but the professor said that this was not to be a matter for Board discussion. That apparently was used for cause as insubordination, and the Board approved the firing of this man. The professor never had an opportunity to talk to the Board about the issues. So ended another saga and another professor's call to the Seminary.

Dr. Preus' Handling of Two Divorce Cases

Particularly bothersome to some professors yet today was the involvement of Dr. Preus in approving several instances of divorce: in one case, Dr. Preus gathered together a number of professors to hear a relative of a lady give an account of an impending divorce in one of Synod's congregations, wanting to gain approval from the faculty members. The Pastor of the congregation was present to defend himself, and his District President and several other pastors served as witnesses. There was strong objection on the part of one professor that there were no Biblical grounds for divorce; the question was never answered as to why a seminary faculty should be drawn into such a congregational conflict, which was a real irritation to the pastor who basically was boxed in by Dr. Preus intruding himself and the Seminary in the spiritual business of a congregation. Dr. Preus said that separation was not the solution, for the woman would get a divorce anyway. He asked this relative not to cause the pastor any trouble while Dr. Preus committed the Seminary representatives to a divorce that had no Scriptural basis.

Another case involved a pastor who insisted on a divorce from his wife, claiming "irreconcilable differences." The wife contested it. Written documentation shows the following: the wife wrote to the pastor-husband, "I don't believe that we need to listen to lawyers on how to dissolve our marriage, but to godly counselors who can lead us to see how we need to change according to God's Word to build up our marriage...Since I am committed under God to make our marriage work, I cannot and will not be a party to its dissolution by acquiescing or by responding in agreement to your demand for dissolution...You left without me, and despite the fact that I said I would and wanted to go with me, you told me that you did not want me to come along. Despite this fact, various people around have said that they heard you tell them that I refused to go with you. You know that this simply is not true, but that you refused to let me go along. Your attorney's letter stated that I should stop trying to seek reconciliation and that you want to get out of our marriage..."

Ignoring this evidence, Dr. Preus approved and the District President transferred this pastor to another District where he was received and soon became married to another woman. This former wife still holds grave offense against Dr. Preus, the Seminary and the Synod which concurred in this unBiblical divorce. Unfortunately, Dr. Preus and his pipeline told another story to make it look as though the wife was guilty, and various people, including some faculty, never learned the truth.

Visiting Teams and Reports

A special 7-person LCMS task force for the BHES reported on a visit to the Seminary on January 23-25, 1983: "A morale problem exists in a significant number of faculty members...The situation requires attention...During the 1978 visit, there were suggestions of a somewhat high-handed arbitrary administration, especially in the Presidency. Some of these accusations were still heard during this visit...Lines of authority may not always be followed and thus traditional administrative patterns become confused...The administration of the Seminary is insufficiently open and communicative...The criticism then would settle on the alleged inconsistency and inequity of administrative actions...The administration is presently perceived as arbitrary by a significant portion of the campus family."

A report of six District Presidents Visit Team on March 19, 1985 tells, "There are serious problems...it was expressed that the Board of Regents does not understand the complexity of the situation...many of those who have concerns are fearful of approaching the President of the Seminary...It is clear that the President is seen by most as the focal point of the tension...Faculty is severely divided as to whether his decisions are always fair, wise, and evangelical...There are those who, while they signed the letter of support for the President, at the same time willingly shared their frustrations, hurts and misgivings about the leadership of the President."

District Presidents Ellis Nieting, Al Barry and Arnold Kromphardt visited the campus on Sept. 6-8, 1985. This being a consultation, it basically had some loving suggestions for reconciliation. It recognized grave problems without stating them because apparently it was not in the nature of the visit and report to put that in the written report. One of the prominent faculty members of that time this week told about some of the faculty who related their deep griefs about Dr. Preus, and it is significant that he mentioned that District President Al Barry was one of them that was present. Obviously, Dr. Barry knew firsthand of the grave problems caused by Dr. Preus at that time.

Consultation Report to CTS by ATS (Marvin Taylor and Jean Marc Laporte on Sept. 15-17, 1985): "The passage of time has probably enhanced the problem rather than diminished it. Hence those who had hoped 'Time will heal' are surely exacerbating rather than alleviating the situation. We could not find evidence to confirm the BOR's judgment in Nov., 1984 that progress had been made...One of the earlier Visitor's reports indicated the presence of an 'in group' (who are consulted) and an 'out group' (seldom if ever consulted)...A decision to circulate and obtain Faculty signatures on a letter of support for the President following one of the external visits we believe has been a tragic error in strategy. The clear purpose was to demonstrate that the report was inaccurate in its perceptions. Since a significant number of Faculty declined to sign — a substantially greater number than the small group of former administrators identified above, the letter actually served the opposite purpose, illustrating the fact that the visitors had not been inaccurate. Thus, a well-meaning, but ill-advised letter added to the polarization without aiding the President...Continuing existence for over three years of turmoil on campus, conflict which does not appear to be diminishing in intensity...Near universal agreement that a major problem of morale does exist on the campus..."

Vice President Will Hyatt on April 22, 1985, wrote to Dr. Preus with copies to the Board of Regents and President Bohlmann: "Robert, I cannot understand why you took that kind of insubordinate action...Just when I believe you are beginning to hear, we get another manipulation of the Faculty and, I might say, of the Board of Regents...to get (the Faculty) to pass a resolution at variance with the Board's resolution before you even tell them about the Board's resolution is manipulation beyond anything I have ever experienced. I believe you should call a meeting of the Faculty, apologize for the sequence of events, give them a copy of the Board's resolution and ask them to start all over again...Robert, I feel terribly betrayed."

Wesley Reimnitz Selective Propaganda

How sad that Rev. Wesley Reimnitz, and the Decatur Circuit of which he was Counselor, claimed to have objective evidence that there was no documentation to show that there was no turmoil at any time, implying that all the visits by outside teams at the Seminary showed nothing but positive comments. Reimnitz produced a "Chronology of Recent Events at CTS, FW, and Other Related Events" which he claims was "gathered from court proceedings, depositions, letters, taped presentations, and other documents." Anyone who carefully checks these will find that Reimnitz selectively chose the good that he could find, and completely ignored the criticisms which are produced in this book.

I wrote to Reimnitz several times to tell him that his was basically a document of misinformation. He obviously did not realize that court depositions are very selective in that each side carefully tells only what they want to divulge at that time and that they are not necessarily accurate. Furthermore, one of the depositions for Dr. Preus had a complete untruth about me, which that professor after considerable contact apologized to me for making it; however, Dr. Preus until today has in no way encouraged or allowed any change in that false testimony in the Allen County Circuit Court Deposition, to which I refer.

There are other statements in those depositions which I would also question regarding their reliability, which are pure propaganda. Such was the source of documentation of W. Reimnitz, besides whatever Dr. Preus or his agents gave him. The tragic thing is that Reimnitz was asked to give this presentation at a "Confessional Lutheran Forum" at Pilgrim, Decatur, Ill., and other places. This and other biased documents were produced by Reimnitz and given wide distribution through the various Confessional Lutheran reporters and *CN*.

The Decatur Circuit with Reimnitz as Circuit Counselor sent an overture to the Indiana District Convention in 1991, "to set the record straight." Page 3, number seven of that document carried a complete distortion of 1 Cor. 6 and the Synodical Handbook By-law 8.07b which is quoted, "In such cases each party to the disagreement, accusation, or controversy shall be free to enforce or defend his rights in the Civil Courts." The Synodical By-law allows a member to go to court only as a last resort, only if he has failed to gain the restitution he desires and no further adjudication channels are open. Dr. Preus went to Allen County Circuit Court on August 8, 1989 and finally sent a brief to Synod's Commission on Adjudication on Sept. 23, 1989 — six weeks after he had gone to court. Yet he allowed his spokesmen and CN regularly to say that adjudication was closed to him, when he never tried it until six weeks later. Ultimately, the judge ordered that the church adjudication process be utilized. The Reimnitz propaganda was used to base much of the campaign and war against the Synod, the BOR and the Praesidium.

My 1987 Memo and Essay to Preus

While reviewing this entire matter, I found in my files a document about which I had forgotten. It reveals personal concerns which I had from my own experience which were shared with Dr. Preus. This is the Memo of 1987 to Dr. Preus:

"Some time ago you sent a Memo to a number of us asking what can be done to help give the Seminary a positive image in the Synod in view of some of the criticism related to Church Growth. I think you know that I took offense at the 'sloganism' criticism by one of our professors at the May 1986 Missions Congress. I feel that you are not being made aware of the various negative statements being made by a number of the faculty to students individually and in smaller groups on campus, even in classrooms and out in the field (like Scaer's in Texas). I have noted some of them, not all of them...The enclosed 'Confidential Documentation' has been shared with Kurt Marquart and Eugene Bunkowske. I had a chance to visit with Kurt about the Scheiderer essay, and he agreed that at least half the criticisms I made were valid...The problem in all cases is that the speakers are not even aware that what they are saying is subject to question, misunderstanding and in most cases rejection. I am sharing this because I believe that first of all we need to know what the problem is before we can find a solution..." The following is the "**CONFIDENTIAL DOCUMENTATION**" which I shared with Preus, Marquart, and Bunkowske:

CONFIDENTIAL DOCUMENTATION, 1987

This documentation for private channels to several Seminary Administrators is produced in order to provide evidence of a very unhealthy confrontation in matters of doctrine and practice in the LCMS, which requires more clear and loving communication by Seminary personnel than accorded to date. The private documentation is kept out of the main essay in order to keep the study and discussion issue-oriented, not person-oriented.

If it makes the reader nervous to read this documentation of difficulties related to our Seminary, it should be kept in mind that District Presidents, executives and parish pastors have heard them, and that some faculty members are grieved by them. The issue is not one of recounting unresolved problems, but the fact that these matters were spoken to the public in one forum or another by faculty members without recognition of the problem they created.

Writing with the greatest fear and trepidation, this author does not write as a Visiting Professor, but as a concerned and experienced LCMS pastor who sees a divisive issue in which the truth needs to be spoken in love. The goal is to heal and bring peace. It is a divisive issue full-blown, not merely about to become an issue. The confrontational approach of some of the critics of church growth and evangelism programs, who have been aggressively on the offensive, have ignored those who have a valid contribution to make. It seems as though catch-all criticism of being Reformed and Armenian settles the matter.

As a Christian and as a pastor in the LCMS, my conscience is bound to live with integrity. As a stewardship consultant and author, this writer is facing the public constantly in Districts, areas and congregations. When he is faced with these criticisms, he cannot lie or deceive. "No comment" on our part is totally unacceptable and inadvisable to those who bring their concerns. These matters call for mature, humble and common-sense biblical response. It is assumed that the main Essay and the special *Appendix* to the CTS faculty have been read.

Indiana President E.H. Zimmermann's outline and presentation to the faculty, "How Some in the Synod Look at the Ft. Wayne Seminary (Faculty)" is a very shocking statement. What Dr. Zimmermann reports has been heard by some out in the field from alumni, pastors and laymen — also by recent graduates. They love the Seminary, and the faculty who have great abilities and expertise in certain areas, but they are bothered by the traits to which Dr. Zimmermann refers.

Dr. Zimmermann stated that "perceptions are not always correct, but they need to be regarded seriously, because some of the church at least think they are true...As a group, the faculty is sometimes seen as:

"A. **An Armed camp** — the center of controversy, anger and fear - a struggle to be right...a poor role model for students for Ministry - people who do not practice the basic Golden Rule, 'treat each other as Christ treats you.'

"B. **A political force** — often single-issue oriented, feeding on fear, mouthing shibboleths and lining up sides... -- the goal at times seems to be to prepare people who can recite right answers to theological questions. Not enough attention is given to help students to relate orthodoxy to common tasks in the parish and to care for people as redeemed beloved of God.

"C. **A self-seeking body** — no longer viewed by the church in the servant role. A direct contrast to the 60's and early 70's. It is as though something needs to be proved (like 'we are the **true** voice of Lutheran orthodoxy.').

"D. **A group that has changed through the years** — once warm and loving, now cold, uncaring, legalistic and rigid; a group that doesn't know much at all about pastoral care and pastoral needs..."

Various statements by some faculty members and some student involvement provide evidence of the concerns voiced by Dr. Zimmermann. Have we paused to consider these serious criticisms? Are we dealing with them? For this essay, documentation is in the author's files with names and source material. If anyone feels that these matters should not be stated but ignored, they need to be reminded that there is no immunity from Biblical principles in our conduct in academic circles. There is no reason for us to acquiesce in a matter which has been destructive to effective communication in the church. It should be recognized that these matters have caused offense which needs to be faced gently and kindly until the offense is removed.

Student Condemnation

A copy of my pamphlet, "New Steps to Security and Happiness," was placed under my office door with the following note: "This is neither Lutheran nor helpful. You have essentially made Christianity a religion of morality. Your steps 6 and 7 basically deny the work of Christ in His life, death, and resurrection and of the Spirit in Baptism. Hopefully, none will be lead astray by this stuff." Fortunately, the student signed his name, and so he was called in for a visit. I expressed gratitude to the student for his candid expression, which is always appreciated, and that it is important to communicate and discuss misunderstandings and differences. He was asked to take another copy of the booklet and select statements which he challenged Biblically on the basis of his criticisms. First, he was a bit adamant and stated that he did not have time, nor was it necessary because he thought not much would be accomplished. When he discovered that I insisted that a critic who has so blatantly charged someone with false doctrine has the Christian responsibility to answer, he said he would try to find time to mark the booklet with criticisms. After a few days, he return-ed and shared about a dozen statements which he said should be challenged. We looked at each of them, asking, "What Biblical truths have been violated or obscured?" He ultimately agreed that not one of them was Biblically in error. I reminded the student that he was very wrong according to Biblical principles and in human relations to make such severe condemnation without first sitting down and trying to understand what was writ-ten and learn whether he might possibly also have misunderstood. One can only surmise that the student had some faculty role models which he may unfortunately have been following.

All one has to do is to listen to student discussion to learn that some of this is also being done by some elitist-minded students who appear to be mouthing criticisms heard by professors they admire. The way I heard about the seminary debate with Dr. Kent Hunter in 1986 was from some students whispering in the halls. Later more bold proclamations were heard, "Did you hear about the debate with Hunter? We will get the enemy in our camp and beat him." Soon the whispers grew into loud voices of triumphalism. There was no hint of careful communication, but rather of clobbering the enemy. The outcome was predicable: various students said, "No one changed their mind." Who changes minds in a battle or war?

The Feb., 1987 DQ Party again provided good fun and humor, but the fixation on Church Growth was so prolonged and repetitious that it finally became obnoxious and offensive. It ended being very counter-productive.

April 1986, Mission Congress

Two faculty members made statements which raise questions and which provide similar concerns raised by President Zimmermann. Six panelists were to respond to the following theses for discussion entitled, "Panel on Church Growth: A Missions Perspective." The theses were the following:

"1. God brings the growth of His Church, externally and internally, through the means of grace (the Gospel, Baptism and the Lord's Supper) administered through the agency of culture-bound people in a culture-bound world.

"2. The divinely-appointed means of grace are a receptor-oriented communication by which God creates, nurtures and preserves His relationship with His children, the Church.

"3. Effective communication of the Gospel is entirely man's work; accurate communica-tion of the Gospel is the responsibility of God's people.

"4. Accurate communication of the Gospel cannot be assumed because cultural, psychological and physical factors may distort the Gospel message at both the source and receptor ends, and in the communication process.

"5. Accurate communication of the Gospel requires both receptor orientation and fidelity to God's intended content of, and intended response to, the Gospel."

Both professors (Marquart and Weinrich) on the panel, who were in different disciplines than Pastoral Ministry, totally ignored the carefully stated and defined theses which were intended to help understanding and agreement, but they made various negative comments, mostly unrelated to the clear definition of the theses. The tape recording shows that both became severe critics of church growth according to their own limited perception, and avoid-ed speaking to the theses.

One of the professors (Weinrich) said we should not flagellate ourselves as though we haven't been doing a good job and that we are really Germanic all the time. He complain-ed that a Synodical study showed that many in the field feel that the seminaries are not training students for the real life ministry, and stated that he lives in the real world as he has had to change diapers.

Weinrich selected one word, "God," and parsed that word on the basis of his negative feelings about church growth. He made several severe criticisms, "We need to express con-cerns about what we have right here on the campus...we have sloganeering, such as *Supply-side Stewardship*, (Werning's book), as though it is found in the Bible...we have lost discern-ment...we need a theology of money management...we're hankering after growth..." There is a serious professional and academic problem here, besides one of Christian behavior: the professor criticized what he has not read or at least not "properly read." Such an ap-proach is intellectually indefensible. This instance basically shows the problem of others in disciplines other than Pastoral Ministry or Church Growth or Missions who have done little or no study or research in the area, but who make strong public criticisms about a matter in which there are experts on the campus who may have read 50 or 60 books on the matter and have taken training in the area of their discipline. Only when a person who is outside of his discipline has studied a number of texts and dialogued with those who are proficient in that discipline will their misconceptions, misunderstandings and ignorance be erased.

The result of this particular provocation: a number of students, including those from my class, indicated offense at the remarks. President's Advisory members were present: one wrote a note to say to ignore it completely; another told another professor that "it is sad that there were signs of no humility at this institution, it was arrogant to criticize publicly another servant who has a valid contribution to make." A pastor wrote, "I want to share with you my deep hurt concerning the 'pot shot' taken at your new book by one of your colleagues at the Mission Conference panel discussion a few days ago. I was em-barrassed for you, but especially for our seminary. Our seminary is doing so much good for so many, but why does this method of what I consider unprofessional behavior con-tinue to be so prevalent among some of our professors?"

Another professor on the panel (Marquart) began by saying that he wholeheartedly subscribes **quia** to the theses, but that he selected only one word among them, "culture." One must question whether anything positive was contributed by his statements, for the professor stated such things as, "We glibly throw around the word 'culture'...I regard the theses as a statement of the problem. They are not a statement of the solution (Author's comment: this is incredible in view of the carefully written theses that are a valuable con-tribution toward clarity in communication.)...we need to realize that the Bible does not use the word or the concept 'culture.' Nor is it a confessional term. What do we mean theologically when we say, 'culture?' I suggest this is something we need to work - serious, theoretical work for which touching anecdotes are no substitute. I'm reminded that the prophet Isaiah in his vision did not respond, 'Woe is me, I'm a man of culture-bound lips and have dwelt amidst a people of culture-bound lips.' That sort of mentality is the pro-blem that arises from some other source...when we talk culture, we cannot distinguish as glibly as we think we can - well, this is theological, this culture...I've noticed a tendency, as it appears to me, to place too high an evaluation of culture at the receptor and cor-respondingly too low an evaluation of culture at the source end...it seems that the whole business of conversion and the so-called decision for Jesus finally rests on cultural fac-tors...we have to say that when all is said and done about culture that the basic obstacles are always spiritual."

As one reads carefully the transcript of that speech, the ignoring of the five theses becomes catastrophic as continued misunderstandings and confusion related to **communication**, are

186

displayed. The efficacy of the means of grace was never in question by the Church growth thesis. The professor missed the whole point of communication and culture, for we certainly believe neither in **opera ex operata**, nor of helping the Holy Spirit in conversion.

District Wide Conference By One Of Our Seminary Professors

After a presentation at a conference in a District by a Seminary professor (Scaer), a District executive who had met our professor for the first time at this conference wrote to him that he 'condemned the Church Growth movement, certain favorite hymns, variations in liturgy, the use of statistics, the use of directional signs at the church, evangelism methods such as Kennedy, and other practical ministry undertakings. On what basis do you speak as if you are an authority on these varied subjects? In making so many strong pronouncements and judgments, were you speaking as a representative of the Seminary, or were these personal opinions? You owe this clarification to any audience especially when you make such strong statements as you did without any printed hand-out reference material.'

The letter continued, "I asked you following the meeting...why, in your condemnation of the Church Growth movement and in your quoting of Lutheran sources related to Church Growth, you avoided quoting from Dr. Werning's books since he is a well-known LCMS author who happens to be a Ft. Wayne seminary professor. You responded by saying that you were not familiar with Dr. Werning's material on the subject, and quickly reminded me that he was not a member of the faculty...'The Radical Nature of Christianity'...should be safe to read since Dr. Robert Preus wrote the Foreword...to identify what's wrong with some aspects of the Church Growth movement in the context of what's right with the movement is not only acceptable but necessary; however, to condemn the entire Church Growth movement as you did is deplorable, especially from one who has limited knowledge concerning the movement, much less an authority on the subject. The...District has a number of congregations that are successfully combining Church Growth principles with solid Lutheran theology. I would love to have you spend some time in the congregation of one of your former students...your presentation impacted on three areas for which I am directly responsible: evangelism, recruitment and stewardship. When faculty and staff from the same seminary present conflicting opinions relative to ministry methodology, it has a negative impact on the church's mission." Obviously, this is strong evidence of the problem raised by President Zimmermann.

Other Concerns

A faculty member told me at a faculty coffee, "Kent Hunter is the enemy." When I stated, "No person is the enemy," he responded, "Yes, you're right." The first statement shows a confrontational attitude which needs to be changed from person-oriented to issue-oriented.

Members of the Seminary Alumni Board appear to be very uptight about the reputation of the Seminary because of some statements by some faculty members. Some statements that have been shared are, "Some faculty are living in the past...some Doctor of Ministry students are ready to rebel, some are saying, 'these men don't know what's going on in the parish...some have a warrior complex...some are presenting 17th century theology without application.' " They also object to labeling tactics from professors who have no expertise or clear understanding of the area which they are criticizing. They appreciate these professors in their own disciplines and are eager to learn from them in those disciplines, but object to them as brittle, inflexible and intolerant in their use of pejoratives as elitists determined to make judgments that have basically been conjured up in their own minds."

187

When discussing sanctification in my Stewardship Class early in the third quarter, 1987, six students felt constrained to volunteer their concern that several professors in their classes have warned them against preaching sanctification, or left negative attitudes toward it in one way or another. They affirmed each other's account. Another of our professors in his homiletics course was asked by a student, "Do you mean that I can preach sanctification?" The student stated that his concern came after hearing another professor warning against preaching sanctification. Local pastors told about students and field workers who verified this.

Panel on "What About the Future of Church Growth in the LCMS?" at CTS in February, 1986

I was out of the city at the time and so was unable to attend. At the Feb., 1987, Central Illinois District Pastoral Conference, five pastors including a District Executive, approached me with the question whether I had seen the video tape of this CTS panel discussion. When they learned that I had not seen it, they suggested strongly that I view it because the Seminary representatives on the video tape were representing the Seminary badly related to Church Growth. Upon return, I viewed the tape, took careful notes with this report. We will not summarize the good points made by any of the speakers, but merely point out the problem areas:

First presentation by Marquart: "Church Growth was a reaction to the social gospel." This originated with the Scheiderer essay, which is untrue, for McGavran became interested in it because of insufficient mission procedures and non-growth. "The policy grows out of philosophy, out of Armenian theology...that idea of conversion is now being received into the Lutheran Church." Methodology and theology must be separated. Church Growth methodology did not grow out of Armenian theology. This is also part of Scheiderer's faulty thesis.

Wenthe's first presentation: taking examples from the Old Testament and New Testament, he indicated that we have a kingdom which is hidden compared to Church Growth goals with society's values. Unfortunately, he totally misunderstands and misrepresents the Lutheran Church Growth approach. Wenthe confuses the issue by putting theology and science as a mixture, rather than doctrine and methology. Wenthe showed a misunderstanding of the whole growth question, as though Lutherans believe that the using of a formula, a program or a method guarantees results. He implied that by using the example of Jeremiah and others that non-growth is the norm, contrary to the Book of Acts. Hunter later made an issue of this, to which Wenthe did not answer but rather spoke in generalities about "rejoicing over God's whole company," and that the "prediction of the future is not full of glowing terms."

Prof. Houser felt compelled to make a statement that he was quite disappointed that an invitation was given to his colleagues not acquainted with Church Growth, for he teaches the Church Growth course here. He said, "We can debate anybody, and we will all have our little following, but come and see what we are teaching. I teach in the Lutheran form, not Armenian. I want the scarecrows of fear removed from this campus, dialogue with me and together we can fight the errors of the Church Growth Movement, but we teach those things in Church Growth which are a great blessing in reaching lost souls." Houser later did criticize Hunter for seeming to open the door to Charismatics.

Marquart improperly called Church Growth dangerous because it allegedly substitutes technique for truth. No true Lutheran will allow that.

The inadequacy of this forum was also evidenced when one of the questioners quoted from my book, "Vision and Strategy for Church Growth," and made an inaccurate point about the book which no one corrected. We do not need that kind of misrepresentation.

Generally, the panel discussion left much to be desired. It is easy to see why the C. Ill. District pastors and other pastors in the Synod have been highly critical of this effort on the part of the Seminary. They suggest that the video not be distributed. This writer must reluctantly concur.

Church Growth Thesis and Criticisms by Graduates

On October 1, 1986, a pastor provided a printed essay which he presented at the Ontario District Pastoral Conference, "A Comparison of 'Church Growth' and Confessional Principles." He wrote, "In searching for someone to quote from a presentation for this conference, I found that Steve Scheiderer has written an STM thesis on this. I also learned that Prof. Marquart and Wenthe debated Church Growth supporters Wagner and Hunter over the merits of the Movement... I've drawn up this list with the help of Scheiderer's work referring back as much as possible to the original works cited." His essay then proceeds to **misinterpret** Church Growth on the basis of the **misrepresentation** in the Graduate Thesis sold in our bookstore.

The Scheiderer thesis is also the source of an injustice against me. When the Circuit Counselors of that District met in Feb., 1987, one of the Counselors (a graduate of Fort Wayne seminary) reported that a Seminary Student Study analyzing my stewardship process used in that District was criticized and found faulty. Knowing this to be a total untruth, I called that pastor, and he said that it was reported to him that this thesis was the source of this criticism against my stewardship materials. The direct opposite was true, for the thesis writer (Scheiderer) even refused to deal with my book on Church Growth. This provides further proof as to the serious problems created by this thesis approved by this seminary. It is a very unhealthy matter.

Here are 20 of the many errors of Scheiderer's Master's Thesis:

Thesis, page 17, footnotes 5 and 7, no such statement or reference could be found in Wagner's book pages 23-25. There was something similar in Hunter's book, pages 23-25, but Hunter is not talking about conversion, but about the mind understanding and the matter of communication, which is a valid concern. This is dishonest scholarship which criticizes alleged statements which are not found in the text!

Thesis, page 22, footnotes 24 and 25: by taking a part of a sentence from Hunter's page 38 and a phrase from page 82, the writer makes one sentence, which is not what Hunter said. Dishonest scholarship!

Thesis, page 23, footnotes 31 and 32: by taking a phrase from a quotation by Wagner and another from Hunter on page 97, the writer makes Hunter make a statement which **he did not make.** Dishonest scholarship!

Thesis, page 27, footnote 26: From Hunter's page 102, two different phrases are used and put together in such a way to make an interpretation, not a quotation, but makes it seem like a quotation. Dishonest scholarship!

Thesis, page 34, footnotes 86, 87, 88, 89: footnotes 86 and 87 are selective phrases quoted from two authors (Glasser and **George** Hunter) while footnotes 88 and 89 put two of Kent Hunter's phrases together and make them apply to the previous statement of the two other authors, in which the thesis writer makes a completely unwarranted criticism. Dishonest scholarship!

Thesis, page 44, footnotes 133 and 134: The thesis writer: "The Church Growth view could reduce the Holy Spirit to a mere presence (133) which works as the Christian 'sets the state' and 'context.' " (134). Looking at footnote 133 (Hunter, page 182), one can find nothing of the sort on the page, and then the writer uses two different phrases from Hunter's page 76 to make Hunter say something which he did not at all say. Dishonest scholarship! The thesis writer consistently makes statements such as "this **could** or that **could**" happen. Any book or thesis that so consistently talks about what **could** happen is of no value to readers because one could state that a thousand things **could happen** - anything **can** be abused. The question is: does it or does it not? A thesis filled with so many "coulds" must be challenged as being bad scholarship.

Thesis, page 47, footnotes 147 and 148: by taking a phrase from Hunter's page 76 and another from page 82, the thesis writer takes two different points (conversion and Church Growth principles) and puts them together into his own statement, not the author's. Dishonest scholarship!

Thesis page 62, footnote 206: one word (homogeneous unit) which is not in quotes is found in Hunter's page 102, but the word "winnable" which is in the quotation is not found on that page. The purported quotation does not exist. Dishonest scholarship!

Thesis page 79, footnote 1: The writer, "the Church Growth 'renewal' is seen by some as God's eternal plan for the Church..." which supposedly is a quote from Hunter page 20. Hunter states that "Church Growth is **a renewal of**," not God's eternal plan to renew the Church. There is a big difference between the quotation and the misquotation. Dishonest scholarship!

Thesis page 79, footnotes 3, 4 and 5: **In one sentence** the writer uses quotations from Hunter pages 181, 17, and 14, and the writer makes his own interpretation of what he thinks the author stated and makes it appear that this is what Hunter stated. Dishonest scholarship!

Thesis page 80, footnotes 13 and 14: In two sentences from Hunter pages 181 and 151, the thesis writer misrepresents Hunter's reference to Church Growth, whereas the entire section is about what the **Church** is doing — a misleading paraphrase. The second quotation does not say that Church Growth is bringing renewal, as the writer misquotes, but Hunter says that, "these biblical, New Testament principles are bringing a renewal..." Dishonest scholarship! Church involves methodology as well as biblical principles.

Thesis page 87, footnote 62: The writer misquotes Hunter, "Therefore God has raised up, even for Lutherans, the 'Church Growth consultant.' "(62). All that Hunter says is that "professional consultants are now available for the Church." Compare that with what the thesis writer stated. The terrible thing about this is that on a number of occasions in the rest of the thesis the writer uses this as a quotation that Church Growth states that God has made a calling of Church Growth consultants. Incredible invention by the writer repeated regularly by him. Incredibly dishonest scholarship!

Thesis 89, footnotes 73 and 72: The writer sates, "Whatever a person's gift, he can have a part in the 'priesthood of all believers' (73) by seeking and using his 'spiritual gifts.' " (74) By simply taking two words or two phrases, one from Hunter's page 61 and another from page 85, the essayist makes Hunter say something which he did not say. Dishonest scholarship!

Thesis page 90, footnote 79: Using numerous misquotations, the author makes another misrepresentation, by combining phrases from various places and to make Hunter say what the writer wants him to say. Dishonest scholarship!

Thesis page 104, footnote 144: The writer states, "It is incorrect to say that 'growth is an essential characteristic of the Church.' " What does the writer's statement do to Ephesians 2:20-22 and 4:15, Col. 1:6, 1 Pet. 2:2,5, 2 Pet. 3:18, Titus 1:5, Acts 4:4, 5:15, 9:35, 16:5, 17:6, 19:10, which show that growth is an essential characteristic of the Gospel?

Thesis page 123, footnote 218: Quoting several phrases from Hunter's page 9, the writer now adds to the phrase, "consultant, in a sense as having an immediate call," which is his own invention and interpretation. This is a misinterpretation that is later picked up by the writer as his alleged "direct quotation" from a nonexistent source. Dishonest scholarship!

Thesis page 125, footnote 230: On page 60 Hunter states that the pastor's "training does not establish him as the one to do the ministry for the people, rather it enables him to be a resource person. He is not a replacement for the people's ministry." The writer changes this Hunter statement on page 60 saying, "...the pastor is reduced to a mere 'resource person'..." Hunter is not denigrating the pastoral office one bit, but shows the pastor as the chief equipper in the congregation. If the pastor does not have that task rather than a layman, who does? This is a total misrepresentation of what Hunter stated. This "mere resource person" misquotation is repeated later also. Dishonest scholarship!

Thesis page 126: A model manufactured by the writer, not by any church growth author at any time or any place, is then compared to the biblical model-total misrepresentation, which the writer uses to pontificate on what all is wrong with that fabricated model, which goes on for pages. Frankly, this critic finds it hard to comprehend what the writer has concocted, which seems to be from another world. In the succeeding pages the writer again picks up the "mere resource person" misquotation again. He also states that Church Growth proponents incorrectly assume that Eph. 4 speaks of God giving the "gift of consultants" shown previously to be a reprehensible misrepresentation. Dishonest scholarship!

Thesis page 163, footnote 28: Misquoting, the writer claims McGavran said that "Christians can do anything 'to give tremendous power to Christ's will.' " McGavran was speaking about evangelical (Gospel) awakening, but the writer changes McGavran's original statement. McGavran did not write such a statement fabricated by the essayist. Dishonest scholarship!

Thesis page 179, first paragraph, first two sentences: When the writer says that Church Growth certainly is not a reincarnation of the 19th century Reformation, etc., it is incredible fantasy, while there is no direct quotation. Hunter plainly talked about reformation of **practice**, not of theology. Dishonest scholarship!

*   *   *   *   *   *

Summary: Succeeding chapters of Scheiderer's Essay re-assert what previous misrepresentations had stated. Then these chapters build misrepresentation on misrepresentation, quoting misrepresentations as facts. There are possibly up to 100 more major concerns about quotations and misrepresentations which allow the conclusion that somehow Church Growth can only be Reformed or Armenian, and all that Lutherans can do is build Church Growth under "a waterfall," that it is hopeless. Using only a small number of actual misquotations of the thesis, this critic has shown that the writer has built strawmen by selective quoting from various phrases and various pages to place them in one sentence. Because of its relation to CTS and because it is sold through the Concordia Bookstore, this thesis is giving cause to many Synodical officials, District officials and pastors in many places to associate it totally with us and condemn us thereby.

Unethical Tactics

The 20 preceding quotations from "The Church Growth Movement: A Lutheran Analysis," by Steve O. Scheiderer with Professor Kurt Marquart as advisor presents a classical example of several things: 1) This was the source of the unBiblical campaign against church growth which has been waged in the Missouri Synod for the past five years; 2) The manipulative and dictatorial tactics which Dr. Robert Preus employed to accomplish his purposes.

I am providing an analysis of how this entire matter was engineered to where Synod is experiencing its anti-church growth fiasco today. The war began in the Systematics Department of the FW Seminary with Prof. Marquart's approval of an unethical essay. No legitimate and well-reasoned response could stop these men at any point from distorting this issue.

You will note in the previous document that Dr. Preus requested response from the faculty, including me, about "What can be done to give the Seminary a positive image in the Synod in view of some of the criticism related to Church Growth." Dr. Preus, Prof. Marquart and Dr. Bunkowske received the preceding lengthy document. Dr. Preus and Prof. Marquart never acknowledged it. The Scheiderer essay received close scrutiny by me only after I was facing fires about it through my work in several Districts, and so I decided to study it carefully. I had read it previously in a superficial manner, and while I was disturbed by it, I did nothing. When I took two weeks to study carefully also the footnotes and the original book sources, I was astounded to find about 200 errors or very questionable statements. Of the 40 total misquotations, 20 are listed in the preceding section.

As a result of my research, I made a 19-page "Critique and Review" of this Master of Divinity church growth thesis and sent it to Scheiderer and shared it in a visit with Prof. Kurt Marquart. After naming specific problems, I wrote some conclusions to Marquart and Preus, "The Essay is intellectually and academically indefensible. Often the author uses a quotation from one man and pins it on the entire movement, then continues to generalize throughout the Essay about the errors of the movement which he assumes he found by his circuitous reasoning and sophistry. He transfers the sins of other denominations' doctrinal errors to church growth recklessly without clear evidence. He imposes his interpretation upon writers by misquoting or misrepresenting, and then pontificates against them on the basis of his misrepresentations. Extremely repetitious! A very loose use of words, 'they, some, the movement, many, could, might, seems to' — totally unacceptable for a Master's thesis. He writes like a blind man feeling an elephant's legs, trunk, etc., and then trying to explain what an elephant is. Many times I do not know why he is covering a point since it is not related to church growth. Sometimes I do not know what he is talking about at all. I do not recognize the church growth movement which the essayist fabricates. It appears that almost everything he learned in Dogmatics and Historical Theology is pulled in by the ears."

Typically, there was no response from Dr. Preus. As advisor, Prof. Marquart in a visit admitted that half of the examples which I presented were misquotations. He would do nothing about it except to say that if I would get Kent Hunter's books out of the Bookstore, then he might encourage the same for Scheiderer's essay. Please recall that this Master's thesis was used as the "gospel" against Church Growth by many sources, and since that time all the other criticisms were built upon this thesis as its foundation, which was pure sand. Recall also that this was advertised in the Seminary Newsletter and regularly in *CN*.

I carried on fruitless correspondence with Rev. Steve Scheiderer (who today does not serve in congregation). He did not make it possible for me to visit with him personally when opportunities presented themselves. All of this started in 1986 and came to a head when I received a May 27, 1987, letter from Dr. Preus to Scheiderer which stated, "The following action was taken by the Board of Regents on May 16 in regard to the altercation between you two: **E. Scheiderer/Werning Affair. RESOLVED** that the Board, having taken note of the correspondence, request both parties to cease all correspondence in this matter. The Board has asked me to make myself informed whether you are both complying with the Board's request." This was typical Preus manipulation of by-passing Biblical procedure and interfering with personal Christian rights. The Board received only the selected information which Preus chose to give them without my knowledge, and the Board without the facts took action which was totally an unBiblical procedure. Here Preus' tactic protected this destructive essay with its proven distortions.

In response, I sent a June 16, 1987, Memo to Dr. Preus and the Chairman of the Board of Regents, which stated, "Even though it could be said that I am made to appear to be a troublemaker who needs to be curbed, the situation seems to be one which could be settled very easily and quickly...There is more than sufficient evidence to warrant the Seminary to determine that the thesis by Scheiderer is too controversial and questionable to be sold through the Bookstore. Secondly, the entire subject should be removed from the Regent's Agenda and Minutes without prejudice. The Seminary needs to clear itself of the damaging criticism growing out of the Scheiderer thesis that will continue as long as it it sold through the Bookstore..."

Typically, there was no Preus' answer to this Memo, so I sent the following letter to the BOR, which provides all of the necessary background to understand how the Church Growth controversy in the Missouri Synod had its birth and grew with approval of Dr. Preus: "I was surprised and mystified by the information that the Board of Regents on May 16 resolved 'E. Scheiderer/Werning Affair. RESOLVED that the Board, having taken note of the correspondence, request both parties to cease all correspondence in this matter.

"Mine were private communications which adhere to Biblical injunctions and also involved personal Christian rights. This correspondence did not properly belong to anyone else. Why and how is the Board of Regents involved in a matter which 1) is rooted in a Biblical procedure that has entered the first phase of Matt. 18; 2) does not involve policy matters? The correspondence in the hands of the Board must have been partial, and the information must have been very fragmented and incomplete.

"How and why did I become involved? I am not a novice in the area of Church Growth and all of its aspects, having written the first book on the subject by a Lutheran. I wrote this book because I saw that church growth was the same as the old Spiritual Life Missions, which the Missouri Synod conducted 25 years ago. Some Missouri Synod pastors immediately called Church Growth 'Reformed' because of its non-Lutheran source. When Dr. Bunkowske, Dr. Houser and I conducted a Church Growth seminar class at the Seminary, Scheiderer attended and became so obnoxious that Dr. Houser told him to keep quiet. Because Scheiderer informed us that he was writing a Master's thesis on the subject, both Dr. Houser and I asked him to share his thesis with us while it was being written so that we could reflect on it. He told Dr. Houser that he would show the thesis to him before adoption. Although Scheiderer states that he does not recall this, both Dr. Houser and I in each other's presence verified that these discussions with Scheiderer took place. Neither of us was informed about the completion of the thesis. On hearing that his thesis was being sold in the Bookstore, I purchased one and read it and felt it to be academically irresponsible and logically indefensible. Being very busy, I left the matter stand without doing anything.

"Having had about 300 seminars and meetings in various parts of Synod during the past 6 years, I started hearing a few complaints about the thesis by ones who bought it from the Seminary Bookstore. The climax came several years ago at the Ontario District Pastoral Conference where I had a presentation. One of our graduates gave a paper on Church Growth based mainly on the Scheiderer thesis This caused some dissension in the Pastoral Conference and some of the pastors offered criticisms of the Seminary.

"At that time, I determined to read the thesis more carefully, and spent at least two full weeks checking out most of the footnotes, which not even the thesis advisor had done. I was horrified to learn that footnotes showed that some sentences were put together from two and three different pages to make up statements which the authors did not say at all, but were imposed upon them. In several instances there was only word or no word from the several pages which were cited in the footnote that could be found as the basis of Scheiderer's claim of a quotation.

"My critiques are available, providing my detailed research. I made 200 negative criticisms, finding some of his fabricated quotations to be so bad that one would not believe it unless he personally searched the original texts. There are spiritual judgments and ecclesiastical ramifications of the irresponsible judgments made in this thesis. Then I concluded that I have not seen anything so irresponsible and unethical in any religious writings outside of the Jehovah's Witnesses and other such sects. If anyone disagrees, let him spend several weeks of studying the texts and footnotes compared with original sources.

"During the past year, beginning at the Indianapolis Synodical Convention, I have been repeatedly contacted by irate pastors, even alumni who are terribly upset by the fact that this thesis is being sold through the Seminary Bookstore. They are also angry because some of the clones of Scheiderer and his friends are propagandizing in their areas, aggravating fellow pastors and even District officials. These men are holding the Seminary responsible for causing disagreements and fights in their regions because of this misinformation.

"After I wrote my critique of the Scheiderer thesis, I sent it to him together with a letter, which had no condemnation in it but rather showed empathy toward how he might feel and react to such serious criticism against his thesis which he held dearly. His response was a critical letter which went to various professors at the Seminary. Even though this was a review of a public document, which calls for public review, I chose to do it privately because I would have been satisfied merely to get the thesis off the market and forget about it, not to condemn it publicly. I properly have written to Scheiderer to say that I have taken offense to his drawing various people into the matter which is now even a bigger offense because the Board of Regents has chosen to enter into it even though I am following Matthew 18 in a private manner...

"When I was at the Pastoral Conference as an essayist for the Central Illinois District in February, he did not care to visit. Indeed, the Board should know that he went to the District President and to the District Pastoral Conference Program committee insisting that my invitation as essayist be canceled. He calls me an unrepentant sinner and refuses to commune with me.

"I am assuming that since the Board of Regents has now learned the facts of the matter, the Board will insist that the Scheiderer thesis not be sold through the Seminary Bookstore. I have always been cooperative with fellow Christians, colleagues, and the boards, and I am willing to do anything as long as it does not violate Biblical principles and injunctions. Let us build our opinions and actions on Biblical requirements, and you will always find me totally submissive and cooperative. Waldo J. Werning"

The Board did not reply. Dr. Preus sent me a July 13, 1987, letter with a copy of Scheiderer's letter to Preus which stated, "In the spirit of Christian love and freedom, I will abide by the wishes of said Board." Preus wrote a word of thanks to Scheiderer, hoping that the matter would now be put to rest, and then added a P.S. which referred to Dr. William Houser and me, "...I, therefore, am simply sending a copy of the Board action and your letter and mine to these two brethren to not pursue the debate between you and Dr. Werning any longer. In other words, when the Board wants the matter dropped, it certainly means dropped by everyone concerned."

I gave copies of the Master's thesis with 225 marked numbers and my 19-page critique and review to several professors, and they were as horrified about its content as I was.

I dropped the matter and left it at that. I wanted to keep my job. However, had I known that this thesis would be the false basis of the full-blown church growth controversy in the Synod today, I would have been ready to pay whatever price had to be paid to stop this in order to stop this political campaign when it was still young.

194

I did make one more try: I shared an essay, Church Growth Principles and Practices,'' and an Appendix with Dr. Preus to share with the entire faculty. The following is the Appendix written for the faculty:

Appendix to "Church Growth Principles and Practices" for CTS Faculty

The LC-MS experiences a great divide between **doctrine** and **practice.** Professional theologians dedicated to doctrinal orthodoxy do not always fully comprehend how the ecclesiastical machinery in practice nullifies what they teach. Many pastors generally feel overwhelmingly frustrated over the demands of a maintenance ministry which seems to collide full force with the biblical ideals and purpose for which they are called to a ministry of Word and Sacrament.

The over-riding message of congregational meetings and church body conferences and conventions is "more, **more, MORE!**" More money and workers to do the job. More planning meetings. More discussion of challenges and programs. More minutes to inquire, clarify and inform. More letters and bulletins to read before we know what to do.

The Missouri Synod needs "bridge people" who will help bridge the chasm between doctrine and practice with thoughtful minds, gentle hearts, and helpful hands, confronting all the issues biblically in love. Professors and pastors need to understand the inadequacy of fighting for the authority and inerrancy of the Bible while dealing softly with or ignoring the practical implications of its doctrines in the daily life and practice of the church, especially in the area of sanctification.

We must avoid a brittle, inflexible, intolerant spirit, one of pride, theological or spiritual elitism, judgmental attitudes, and negative or hyper-criticisms. Where and when these exist, there is a need for repentance, finding us committed to witnessing and healing instead of being confrontational. Pejoratives and ridicule by theological elitists have no place in this bridgebuilding process, for they must demonstrate to the church the practicality and spiritual dimension of their theological discussions.

Piety is no substitute for effort. Today's theological frontier is not more equations about doctrine, to which we solemnly hold and agree, but to clean up and unify our church practices to be compatible with our doctrine.

In understanding this task, we will avoid dividing people into **we** and **they.** We will avoid pinning offensive labels or making criticism in imprecise and misleading ways. We assume that we ourselves need to practice consistently simple courtesy, fairness and respect for those with whom we disagree, and to avoid divisive actions.

Church Growth Perceptions

Various District leaders, sharing concerns of criticism against church Growth, made specific criticisms against the seminary in these phrases: "...Don't get caught up in all the stuff people sling at Church Growth especially...Ft. Wayne Seminary...get seminaries to stop their embarrassingly ill-informed attacks on Church Growth...include strategic class time at our seminaries...too many young pastors are graduating from our Sems with a negative concept of Church Growth...sick and tired of hearing all the negatives our Seminaries are foisting on our future pastors...help the Ft. Wayne seminary to understand Church Growth and to cease and desist their uninformed criticisms...go on the offensive against anti-Church Growth philosophy in Sems..." These criticisms were sent by a Synodical leader to all District Presidents, as well as read by the participants at the Orlando Church Growth Conference.

Fighting perceived wrongs from across theological disciplines is not the correct route to find what is right. Some 20 Districts of the LCMS have been or are engaged in an organized Church growth process. The process is in place, affecting the activities of parish life and also structures.

Current debates and arguments are apparently serving only to produce increasingly firm polarization of positions brought about by two sets of divergent understandings. One comes from proper training, reading and experience and the other comes from superficial contact and looking through "systematic glasses." Harmony can be brought if those who are Biblical and expert in the area are given an opportunity to be heard.

Because of the furor created on campus about the process, the qualified professors have shied away from continuing to conduct church growth seminars in the summer session, which were conducted for about four years. Meanwhile, the St. Louis Seminary in its June, 1987 offering, has scheduled "Church Growth I" and "Church Growth Through Small Groups and Life-style Evangelism." Offerings for 1988 are "Church Growth II," and "Congregational Self-Evaluation." St. Louis is holding a Church Growth Symposium in May, at which Kent Hunter is one of the main presentors. St. Louis has one trained church growth teacher, while Fort Wayne has four. We are losing by default.

Meanwhile, criticisms about church growth have been voiced by some professors in other disciplines in classrooms, out in the field, and to individuals, without valid proof that our Lutheran Church Growth process is infected with Reformed and Armenian theology.

The Role of the Seminary

Proper questions must be asked when considering the role of the Seminary in Christ's plans and purposes for His Church. Is the Seminary concerned mainly with correct views of the Bible and the inculcation of true doctrine or is it also concerned about spiritual formation and function? What does the theological Seminary have to offer for effective stewardship and evangelism? What is the place for Church Growth? How is the Seminary to concern itself with the Great Commission? Does the Seminary curriculum reflect God's priorities? How much does the "maintenance mentality" dominate the thinking? How is stewardship, which constantly demands the leadership of every pastor and the attention of every member, taught to reach every student so that each one is capable of providing effective teaching and leadership to change the maintenance model to one of grace?

Some have voiced the opinion that the students can learn church practice and stewardship in the parish. Some have expressed the view that there is not a great need for this at this Seminary, and so let it be a subject of a workshop — thereby unnaturally dividing theology and practice. With congregations being the scene for activistic Christianity separated from grace theology, there is a great need for deepened theological considerations of church practice. The curriculum which has its roots in the 16th century is not the best for a tremendously changed and constantly changing world. The curriculum must prepare ministers for the parish as it exists today. In a nation quickly becoming humanistic, secularistic and materialistic, the curriculum must deal with preparing pastors not only to cope with problems but to provide positive leadership for all related issues, including how the Gospel is presented to non-Christians and how to multiply new congregations.

The pastor's task is not to impress his people with his ability to present true statements and to refute errorists, but to be able to present a positive theology of grace in order to make disciples, teaching them the whole counsel of God. To the extent that we fail in this task, pastors will not have sufficient practical theology and will easily fall for pragmatic time-serving, leading people mostly by means of methods and techniques. To denigrate practical theology to the "tricks of the trade" and how to "plan programs," is to misunderstand sanctification and its relation to the parish. To the degree that we have misunderstood and failed to train people effectively, there are crises in parishes today. There is no place for the kind of armchair theology which does not relate the context of a working ecclesiology — combining and balancing soteriology with pneumonology.

Let us avoid at all costs the kind of abstract theologizing that fails to tackle the hard issue of interpreting the Bible in the areas of practical concerns of the ministry of Christ's Church in all of its complexities. Theological education must be functional within the context of the issues of our own culture and time.

Providing bits and pieces of Christian teaching have often been contradictory and almost always incomplete. Needed are pastorally wise presentations that speak to Biblical sanctification — Christian virtues, conduct and relationships. We need to understand our responsibility to guide students and congregations into biblical **practice**, not presenting doctrine in the cognitive without reference to practice.

Seminaries will want to avoid the kind of abstract theologizing that does not face the hard issues of sanctification, renewal, and practical concerns of ministry in today's world. Academia and systematics should not be suspicious of the contribution and worthwhileness of pastoral theology and New Testament studies in the area of the priesthood of all believers. We need to learn from other disciplines beyond the comfortable boundaries of the traditional range of our own disciplines.

We sometimes find ourselves attacking symptoms instead of the cause, fighting the Reformed, Armenians, Church Growth, Fuller Seminary, charismatics, the electronic church, etc. These are not our enemies. The enemies are not those who hold other beliefs. The enemy is also in our church, the lack of proper indoctrination on our part — educationally weak members who are susceptible because they are so spiritually weak and undernourished. A diseased tree does not bear good fruit. A tree, not watered and fertilized through a theology of grace, will not bear good fruit.

*   *   *   *   *   *

The response to this essay: Dr. Preus did not answer, while Church Growth Convocations were organized in which Prof. Kurt Marquart, the thesis advisor for Scheiderer's irresponsible essay, was the leading voice. The Systematics Department took the lead in the attack while the Church Growth professor (Houser) at the seminary was silenced. The only way that he got on the program was to speak from the floor.

After the second Church Growth Convocation was announced and before it was held, I talked to Prof. Marquart and gave him my book, *Vision and Strategy For Church Growth*, and also *Renewal For The 21st Century Church* (emphasizing Chapter 9 on church growth). I requested him at least to be academically honest since this is a production by an LCMS author and experienced consultant, that he should either acknowledge that a Lutheran has done a Biblically responsible job or that he criticize what is wrong. Prof. Marquart **ignored it totally** in his presentation, preferring to follow the same old line. This is not a matter of talking past each other, but of Systematics Department representatives with Dr. Preus' approval and encouragement taking the initiative by criticizing church growth on the basis of reformed denominational theology, rather than dealing with Missouri Synod Lutherans in what was actually happening in Districts and congregations.

Certainly, there are several statements in Dr. Kent Hunter's book, *Foundations For Church Growth*, which are faulty, but that does not destroy his thesis or prevent a Lutheran approach to church growth. Significantly, these critics have not said one word about Hunter's recent church growth book, *Moving the Church Into Action*, published by CPH. Marquart and his Systematics friends have also studiously avoided any mention or reference to the CTCR report, "EVANGELISM AND CHURCH GROWTH," with special reference to the Church Growth Movement, Sept. 1987. It is no overstatement that everything proper and positive about Lutheran church growth is simply ignored as though it does not exist, and as though there is not a proper Lutheran understanding. This shows how unfair this political campaign has been. When a man does a responsible job, they simply ignore it. When some author makes several faulty statements, the critics shred the entire book and throw out the entire program.

Significantly, Dr. David Scaer with Dr. Howard Tepker, attended a special meeting with the Fuller School For World Missions Faculty to discuss church growth. Scaer came back to inform the faculty that these men were doing some responsible thinking and knew the difference between theology and sociology. Obviously, soon he joined Prof. Marquart to build the anti-church growth campaign.

Ignored also by the systematicians is the document, "Toward A Theological Basis, Understanding and Use of Church Growth Principles in The Lutheran Church-Missouri Synod," prepared by the Church Growth Strategy Task Force and distributed to the faculty in June of 1991. Several members of the Fort Wayne Seminary faculty were part of that Task Force, which produced an excellent document to cut through the verbiage and confusion created by those who act as though the 1987 CTCR document does not exist.

The campaign to discredit Missouri Synod Lutherans who use church growth can easily be shown to be unfair, unkind, and untrue because of generalizations, guilt by association, half-truths and numerous other inexcusable tactics. Basically, none of the critics have done their homework. Some of them raise valid criticisms which are true in isolated cases, but they use these to discredit all Missouri Synod Lutherans who use church growth principles under the authority of God's Word. Under the editorship of David P. Scaer, only negative articles have been printed in the CTQ about church growth, none of them really helpful or fair. The same is true of the presentations which his Systematics Department have had at the annual Symposiums related to church growth.

The Spring 1989-1990 *REFLECTIONS*, a student publication of the Fort Wayne Seminary, has a lengthy dissertation on the church growth movement and quotes Glen Huebel from the July-Oct. 1986 CTQ as the only church growth source. He makes a very unkind statement that is not true of most Missouri Synod Lutherans who utilize church growth principles: "Doctrine is not a vital ingredient...rather what makes a church tick, like a fine Swiss watch, are pragmatic, organizational principles, many of which are patterned after the business model." Possibly, he **could** find ten Missouri Synod pastors and congregations who might take that position (although proof is required, not careless accusation), but if there are, let him go directly to them and criticize them, rather than using his "strawman" to try to discredit loyal Missourians who use church growth faithfully according to Biblical standards.

In January, 1988, the Fort Wayne Systematics Symposium featured Carter Linberg with his assignment, "Pietism and the Church Growth Movement in a Confessional Lutheran Perspective." During a social hour I asked Prof. Linberg what church growth books he had read or what he knew about it before he received this assignment from David Scaer. He said he knew nothing about it, had read no books on the topic, and wondered why Scaer had asked him. He did read several books in preparation for his essay, especially McGavran's *Understanding Church Growth*. Of his 47 Endnotes, only 14 apply to church growth.

I wondered before and after the essay what pietism and its history with Spener and others had to do with today's Church Growth. The next day there was a panel of speakers with Marquart as moderator who read a written question handed to him, "In view of the Fort Wayne Seminary being against Church Growth and other methodologies for mission outreach, what does CTS have to offer to the church to take its place?" Marquart said that this question should be directed to the Academic Dean and the Vice-Academic Dean (Scaer and Wenthe). Scaer started with few generalities and then said something like this, "Since the Board of Regents meets in about an hour or two, I'll be careful what I say. (laughter) I will ask Carl Linberg to answer that question." When Wenthe was asked to answer the question, he said, "I would recommend that we send Norman Negel to conferences throughout the church to provide help." Men from the Pastoral Ministry Department sat mute while a systematician and an exegete had no answer for the good of the Seminary. Dr. Preus then took the floor and tried to defend the Seminary.

Once again, in the April-July 1990 CTQ David Scaer invited Carter Linberg to write an article, "Church Growth and Confessional Integrity." He begins his article by saying that if he had not been invited to the 1988 CTS Symposium, he would "still be blissfully unaware of the Church Growth Movement." He states, "In preparation for this study, I have been able to use some writings of which I was unaware when I made my first effort to evaluate the Church Growth Movement." He admits then that at the first time he did not even know about Kent Hunter, yet that essay was to speak about a **Lutheran** view! He did not know about my book. He also lists the irresponsible Master's thesis, "The Church Growth Movement: A Lutheran Analysis" by Steve Scheiderer which helped him evaluate Church Growth. Linberg's footnotes even refer to a quotation of Scheiderer's, which contained at least 40 thesis quotations which were fabricated. Significantly, of the 64 endnotes of Linberg, only 10 come from Church Growth sources.

Even Richard John Neuhaus got in the act in the Reformation, 1990 *Lutheran Forum* (pp. 18-24). This is basically a critique of David Luecke's book. If that was his goal, then it should have been titled as such, not as the title he selected, "What's Wrong With The Church Growth Movement: THE LUTHERAN DIFFERENCE." Space in this book does not allow quoting the seven points that he raises in his conclusion. When he writes, "We have considered, then, seven problems with the Church Growth Movement," those statements were his own assumptions, which provided absolutely no evidence. In fact, the 14 Endnotes list no church growth book. Then he lists seven false and interrelated propositions, none of which is held by any Missouri Synod Lutheran Church Growth leader whom I know. The least the author could have done was to quote directly from some reliable authority among Missouri Synod Lutherans who allegedly holds such a false view.

Then there is the shameful ridicule and tirades which go beyond all reason, all Christian behavior CN and its columnists, especially Dr. Gregory L. Jackson. See what the scandalous 1985 Fort Wayne Master's thesis on Church Growth approved by Prof. Marquart has contributed to:

1) *CN*, March 18, 1991(p. 18): *"Lutherans in the Church Growth Hall of Shame"*. "Although the Church Growth Movement began among liberals, Pentecostals, and phrenologists, conservative Lutherans were quick to join the apostates of Fuller, exchanging inerrancy for errancy, the Sacraments for ordinances, the historical liturgy for revivals and cell groups." Every statement here is a false and vicious judgment, and the most bizarre is "phrenologist," which Webster defines as "a system, now rejected, of analyzing character from the shape of the skull." Immediately following this are the men who are apparently guilty of some terrible sin to put them in the "Hall of Shame," beginning with me. The article states that I was a student at Fuller Seminary, which is a total lie.

2) Dr. Gregory L. Jackson's, "Pure Baloney: The Church Growth Movement," covers almost two pages of *CN* July 10, 1989 (pp. 16-17). Despite the fact that there is no documentation, Jackson writes, "The Church Growth Movement has advertised itself as the essence of the Gospel, when in fact it is nothing more than pure baloney." The Gospel reference is untrue, for methodology is not Gospel. Through guilt by association, my book, *Vision*

and Strategy For Church Growth is listed in that article. This article again is filled with judgments, pejoratives, insults, and smart aleck comments.

3). *CN*, April 8, 1991, prints the article, "Werning and the Church Growth Movement, Biblical Errantists, the Reformed, and Unionism." It is followed by the question, "Was Wagner flaky when he wrote the Preface for Werning's *Vision and Strategy For Church Growth?*" All of this is pitifully sub-Christian, and slanderous.

4) *CN* on Dec. 23, 1991 (p. 18) finds Jackson sharing the "Church Growth Commandments," sent to him by Mr. X. A sensitive Christian would call this unreasonable and irresponsible ridicule.

5) Jackson in *CN*, Oct. 14, 1991 pontificates, "Church Growth Movement is Now a Hearse."

6) *CN*, April 29, 1991, published outrageous ridicule, half-truths and a breaking of the 8th Commandment under the title, "Reasons to Oppose the Church Growth Movement." This article gives 33 "reasons for avoiding the Church Growth Movement like the plague, unless one is a liberal (Reformed, Pentecostal or Mainline)." The May 20, 1991, *CN* carried a good parody of that article, which criticized the silly accusations, labeling, guilt by association, and other tactics of *CN* and its writers; Rev. Steve Howe wrote, "Ten Reasons to Oppose the Lutheran Reformation Movement." I will select only some of these, the first being the reasons to oppose Church Growth, and the second the Lutheran Reformation movement:

a. The CGM was founded by a non-Lutheran, Donald McGavran.
The Lutheran Reformation (L.R.) was founded by a non-Lutheran.

b. The CGM was promoted by C. P. Wagner....
The L.R. was endorsed and promoted by Martin Stephan, a well-known womanizer...

c. The CGM is not supported by any serious Lutheran theologian.
None of the serious Catholic theologians of the day supported the teachings of Luther.

7) There have been various attempts at satire, which stoop to such unChristian ridicule that one has to question the author's and the publisher's ethics: *CN*, June 5, 1989 (p. 15), "The Church Growth Movement" by Gregory L. Jackson; *CN*, Oct. 28, 1991 (p. 21): "Just Released From the Purple Palace - the Home of 'Church Growth Eyes', 'An Order of Worship Guaranteed to Excite, please and keep those dollars and people rolling in.' " The anonymous author slanders our Christian brothers and tries to get off the hook in his last paragraph by saying, "Herman, Luther said that humor is good for the soul. A lot of this is humor." Herman, it is sick, and *CN* is a garbage can. More sick attempts at satire have been printed in recent issues of *CN*.

CN's low level of handling facts is seen in other of Otten's writers, for example, "A good book but.." by Don Matzat (*CN*, June 27, 1988, p. 8). Even though he states that he does recommend my book, *Renewal For The 21st Century Church*, "primarily as a means of discussing the issues of church renewal," he raises arguments and accusations as others have in *CN* without documentation or evidence. Among those are:

1) "A regurgitation of other existing programs.." Which? I am very eager to know.

2) "...heavily mixed with Calvinist superstitions...lest you give the Calvinist impression.." No proof, only accusation.

3) "...It seemed to me that Werning ignored much of our rich heritage and chose to offer us C. Peter Wagner, Lyle Schaller, Win Arn, smatterings of Cho and Schuller mixed together with some Calvinist and fundamentalist presuppositions." All fabricated and undocumented fantasy! What can you say when a person is that completely dishonest? Just another day at *CN*!

4) *CN*, Sept. 5, 1988 (p. 4) quotes from my letter printed in the July 18, 1988, CN, "The book ("Renewal") proposes and looks only into the Bible...This is not a study on Lutheran approaches but on authentic and classical Biblical approaches...Unfortunately, the reviewer has only one theme — Lutheran overshadowing the Bible completely...The book sticks only to the Bible, not to any tradition! In fact, it criticizes the fact that churches, including Lutheran, depend more upon tradition than the Bible." Matzat writes, "...His contention that the failure to follow such 'Biblical principles' is disobedience to God (e.g., pg. 78) confuses Law and Gospel, mixes obedience with faith as being the essential marks of the church...THAT'S CALVINISM." Where in all the world have I ever said or written that "obedience with faith" is one of the "essential marks of the church"? Another fabrication. Apparently, the word that I have heard these many years that we are not to use the words "obey or obedience, for that is Calvinism," is still going strong. My answer to it is that Jesus said, "If you love Me, obey My Commandments." (Jn. 14:15) I did not know that Jesus was a Calvinist!

Matzat writes, "I strongly question Dr. Werning's recommendation of C. Peter Wagner's 'Spiritual Gift Identification Program.' " Pure fabrication: I do not recommend that program and even caution against a Lutheran approach in my book, which Matzat ignores but proposes his own myth instead. I wrote in *Renewal*, "Great care should be taken to avoid overemphasizing self-discovery of spiritual gifts...Warnings need to be heeded that leaders properly and fully train their members through sound Biblical teaching...can easily sidetrack people to become overly occupied with discovery instruments and other tools such as tests and questionnaires which may be more an American phenomenon than an educational need...There is a danger of 'gifts inventory' instruments becoming mechanical and leading to negative effects because of careless use..." (pp. 83-84). Now check Matzat's CN statement again, and cry.

All of these unkind and untrue condemnations were built basically on the foundation of the Seminary Master's thesis, which was academically bankrupt, but approved by Prof. Marquart and stonewalled by Dr. Preus.

An analogy can be made between Church Growth and preaching, both of which involve communication. We don't Lutheranize preaching any more than we Lutheranize Church Growth. As Lutherans and Reformed utilize preaching, so Lutherans and Reformed utilize Church Growth. It is faulty to dissect Reformed or Armenian theology, and then use that as proof that the Church Growth process is Reformed or Armenian. On that basis, one could take sermons by Reformed or Armenians, and indicate that since false doctrine has been discovered, false doctrine is inherent in preaching. The same point relates to Church Growth. If a Lutheran brings faulty theology to his practice of Church Growth, it is **his** theology that needs criticizing, not Church Growth.

Church Growth does not mean a set of sociological principles added to biblical faith. Biblical faith is the base for Church Growth. The LCMS already owns the basic Church Growth documents: the New Testament written by missionaries to missionaries — the Gospels, the book of Acts, the Epistles. Church Growth is as old as the first century, but we must learn those presuppositions and principles. That is what Church Growth is all about theologically for Lutherans under a Word and Sacrament ministry.

The church consists of countable men and women, and there is nothing particularly spiritual or meritorious in not counting them. To be sure, no one was ever saved by accurate membership counting and no one was ever cured by a thermometer. Yet the physician uses a thermometer. Statistics do not cure, but they tell a great deal about the condition of the patient. So does the evaluation and diagnosis in Church Growth, which helps dispel the fog of good intentions, pious thoughts unrelated to reality, promotional inaccuracies, hoped-for outcomes, generalizations, and general ignorance which hides the real situation from leaders and workers.

In order to understand the background in which people live, sociological, psychological and cultural emphases are important, but they are not a substitute for or an aid to the Means of Grace. Strategies do not build the church and are not a Means of Grace. Strategies are not used to motivate people to work, but are plans to organize the work of motivated members.

In evaluations, leaders first look at the negative side for roadblocks, such as poor communication, lack of training or skills, failure to be committed to the task, closed minds and slavery to traditional methods, procrastination, lack of planning and organizing.

On the positive side, Church Growth looks at the functions of leaders: communicating, directing, planning, organizing, coordinating, controlling, staffing and team building.

Biblical forms and functions suggest even more questions: how do we improve effectiveness as Christian leaders, change or replace ineffective leaders, improve administrative procedures in the church, get more members involved and committed, utilize youth more effectively, get the right members in the right jobs, get more done in less time, develop job descriptions for church positions, and delegate successfully? Why should we get upset if Church Growth raises these questions?

It is really curious why I could give three presentations on stewardship at the First U.S. Convocation on Church Growth at Robert Schuller's Garden Grove Church in California in 1976 with Dr. Robert Preus present and approving, while today "Confessional Lutherans" and Herman Otten put me in the "Church Growth Hall of Shame." Most of the prominent Church Growth leaders of that time were on the program. Dr. Preus and I did not approve of every word spoken, but we were hearing responsible churchmen, not a bunch of idiots as Greg Jackson and Herman Otten treat them.

Don't Confuse Style With Substance

At the end of Chapter Three I presented a short study of substance and style. Critics using *CN* as their soapbox give evidence of fusing the style with substance, and the method of communication with essence of the message. Starting with Scheiderer's unfortunate essay and continuing throughout the Church Growth convocations and the Church Growth topics at the CTS Systematics Symposiums, and *CN*, there has been unethical treatment and illogical criticism about the Lutheran Church Growth message related to the legitimate use of sociology and methodology. Some of the writers in *CN* have gone so far overboard that one cannot escape the conclusion that they despise the arts unless they are used with the traditional Lutheran German form. Such critics refuse to recognize the pure Lutheran substance which is present because a different mode of communication is utilized.

Let it be declared loudly again that the substance of a Lutheran Church Growth approach is the pure Word of God and Sacraments, the Law and Gospel, and a Biblical Doctrine of the church. Missouri Synod Lutherans who are using Church Growth methods with proper sociological and methodological approaches should stop the mouths and pens of the irresponsible critics. Let the instigators of the Missouri Synod anti-Church Growth campaign confess their wrongs and admit the deception that began and was managed by a few at the Ft. Wayne Seminary. These "doctrinal experts" are practicing religious quackery. The evidence presented in these pages suggests no less than that kind of statement.

THE ROBERT PREUS-DAVID SCAER TEAM

As you read this account, please remember that Dr. Scaer had been a good friend for a number of years, and Dr. Preus a very close friend and ally in Christ's mission. In studying my files with all the Memos and documentation, I noted that my contacts, when it became necessary to disagree with either one of them were always private and only when there were wrongs to be righted. The messages were always to edify and to encourage faithfulness to our Biblical and confessional faith. The evidence over the next several years show that consistently both men shared private matters politically with selected people and always moved the matters toward the public arena in a political manner. At the same time they would not give me appointments to meet with them personally so that usually I had to communicate by Memos.

As matters unraveled and deeper problems were experienced, it became evident that Dr. Scaer had come to the aid of Dr. Preus on a number of occasions in getting faculty members into line and to get signatures for Dr. Preus, and now Dr. Preus was returning the favor.

I tried to help Dr. Preus to recognize that Dr. Scaer needed correction, or he would bring Dr. Preus down. Another professor asked Dr. Preus several times, "What does David Scaer have on you that you are protecting him?" Until this time, I recall on several occasions some pastors in the field complaining about some very offbeat statement in presentations by Dr. Scaer, but I refused to believe them and thought that these men misunderstood. By personal experience during the last three years, I saw that there was a real problem.

Soon after my 67th birthday, on May 26, 1988, Dr. Preus asked me to come to his office and handed me a resolution passed by the Board of Regents on May 21, which thanked me for my years of service to the Seminary, and "RESOLVED, that the President notify Dr. Werning that his present contract is terminated as of June 30, 1988...and RESOLVED, that Dr. Werning vacate his office on campus and space currently utilized no later than June 30, 1988." After 12 years of faithful and able service, no "honorable retirement," only termination and one month to vacate the office, even though I was requested to continue to serve the Seminary Development on a contract basis. Dr. Preus, who went to civil court over his honorable retirement, officiated at another termination at the Seminary. Let no one think that this caused any regrets on my part for myself, but only for the Seminary. Indeed, soon after the Chairman contacted me to say that the service would continue until the end of August, I pleaded to keep it at the end of June because I was much better off. I was finally free, no longer under bondage of a sometimes tyrannical administration.

Problems Created By Dr. Scaer

If Dr. Scaer had kept true to the agreement we made in December of 1989 when I forgave him, his story would be out of place in this book. But as you will read, Dr. Scaer not only created more offenses but refused to meet and talk with me about them. It will become clear also that he was an integral part and an enabler in the entire Preus procedures.

After Dr. Scaer failed to answer several Memos, I wrote the following to him on Dec. 9, 1987: "I have valued our friendship very much over the years and hope that it can be retained amidst a very distasteful spiritual responsibility on my part explained in this letter...You went to the Board of Regents knowing that you had not discussed this matter with me to learn the facts and that taking it to the Board of Regents would be embarrassing to me as though I was some kind of ignorant stubborn individual who is trying to use the Seminary for his advantage. I must charge you with sub-Christian and poor administrative procedures. You may try these tactics on other people, but I have too high regard for the Seminary and its ethical procedures to allow you to get by with this one. This is not done for my sake. If it were only a personal matter, I would forget it, but when this is a procedure that can be used on other people too, someone has to call a halt to it...I ask for mutual agreement on a way to correct this injustice that was created...In conclusion, you will note that this is a personal Memo to you, and I trust that all these matters can be dealt with evangelically and lovingly between us as brother to brother and that no further steps need to be taken in order to correct these offenses...You may contact me at my office or if I am away, make an appointment through my secretary...''

On Dec. 28, 1987, I sent the following Memo: "My Dec. 9 Memo, together with two other Memos on the "Sanctification" essay have received **no response** from you. This is cause for great concern. Let us first put the entire matter in proper perspective. There is a necessary functioning within the body of Christ which we cannot ignore. Our interrelatedness under Christ, our Head, is reason enough to pursue this matter. Indeed, my commitment is that 'everything be done for edifying.'...Please keep in mind that my action is actually a reaction and not something that I initiated...I am sure that you fully realize that there are consequences to what you say and do which relate to others around you and the entire church. **Loose tongues** are dangerous, and no amount of jesting will take away personal responsibility of the effects on others in the Body...If you are holding the rest of us accountable for our actions, **so we hold you** accountable for yours. Since you choose to ignore my first spiritual steps to get you to correct what needs to be changed, I am now prepared to take the second step, to bring two or three with me as witnesses. I don't understand why this is necessary because you are a sincere and committed Christian who understands the Biblical pattern for relations within the body of Christ. Christian practice is not a theory to be ignored, but something to be lived. We have a pastoral role that needs to be exercised in our daily life, and that includes being role models. Role models are especially needed at the Seminary...'' I found out later that Dr. Scaer gave this to Dr. Preus.

Another Memo of mine which Dr. Scaer gave to Dr. Preus was a follow-up on Jan. 4, 1988: "I want to make certain that you know how much I hesitate taking another step in matters presented in the previous Memo and that I do it as a Christian friend, not as an adversary. It should be obvious, too, that my actions are taken from a totally spiritual perspective, while I must candidly share with you that your actions have appeared to be political and adversarial...we are here to build each other up, not to embarrass each other or tear each other down.''

The following Memo (Adjudication Exhibit M) refers to a meeting which I had with Dr. David Scaer on Feb. 17, 1988: "My visit was requested because of the concerns raised in previous correspondence which was unanswered...(Note: Then the problems are summarized. The reader needs to know that I was gone for several weeks in Nigeria and when I returned, my pastor approached me about the problem, which will be explained next.)

The Memo continues, "Scaer mentioned his hurt about getting a Memo that indicated that he needed to repent. I told him that a Fort Wayne pastor recently told me that a Seminary student had told him that Werning had brought charges against Scaer, and that this pastor then asked one of our Seminary professors whether he knew anything about it, 'and the Seminary professor said yes it might be true. When I asked Dr. Scaer on what basis did he take a confidential, private Memo, which dealt on a spiritual level between two people and tell the public about it, he defended himself by stating that when he gets attacked this way, he needs to go to other people to see what their opinion is. He showed no understanding about Biblical procedures and no sensitivity toward wrongfully going public with this. After more questioning, he had refused to acknowledge that his going to students and faculty, and whoever else he may have gone to, was irregular from a Biblical viewpoint...'' (Note: At this time I reminded Scaer about his Faculty office building being a gossip center for the faculty.)

The Memo continues, "I did mention to him that this faculty is notorious as a gossip and slander mill, to which there was no response...Our meeting ended by mutual assurances of friendship, and my impression is that we just drop the entire matter, and we hugged each other and we wished each other God's blessings and went our way. I must note that there was a deep feeling of regret on my part that this discussion was not on a spiritual or Biblical plane, but purely on the managerial and political level of trying to work together amicably. It left a deep concern in my heart, but as I told Scaer, 'It's your problem, not mine.' "

The day after the above notes were dictated, I recorded some additional reflections about the Feb. 17, 1988, visit with Dr. David Scaer (Adjudication Exhibit N): "Some meditation and prayerful consideration left a dull thud in my heart about the action and reaction of my brother in Christ and friend David Scaer related to the issues in my visit of Feb. 17 in his office at the Seminary. Specifically, my concerns focus on the following matters: He always concentrated on the procedural issues, and his only discussion involved statements which appeared to rationalize and justify his actions. He never dealt with the spiritual issues involved, and my claim of offense given and sins against me, together with my request that he repent, was treated by him in a political fashion to Seminary students and faculty members. He showed no understanding or sensitivity towards spiritual relations which Jesus established for individuals facing each other and dealing with the issues without first involving other people. He totally refused the spiritual route which I wanted to pursue, but used a political approach of coming back repeatedly to procedures. He showed no sensitivity toward the Eighth Commandment and Matthew 18, and seems to use information and disclosure to others as a weapon against those he wishes to criticize..."

Adjudication Exhibit O tells of a meeting with Scaer on Feb. 25, 1988: "I told him I was waiting for a copy of his essay that he gave to the Systematics Department. He stated that he had not planned to give it to me, and why did I want it? I told him that this was one bit of unfinished discussion that we had and that he had agreed in our previous discussion that I could get a copy so that I could review it in the light of one contested sentence which we need to discuss yet. He said something like this, 'I am done discussing, I can't take it, it takes everything out of me...' "

During 1987-1988 Dr. Scaer got into a conflict with some in a conservative group in the Northwest District because of what he said in a speech. In a July 12, 1988 letter a layman wrote to President Preus with a copy to the BOR Chairman that the issues were not faced. He wrote, "Although Dr. Scaer states in his 1-20-88 letter that on his part his general and vague statements bring the matter to a peaceful solution and conclusion, he should realize that he did not deal with the issues. When he states that, 'Any of my statements that may have raised concerns should be understood in the light of those rather extensive statements in the presentation,' he states a contradiction. If his statements which caused concern are understood properly, they are in direct conflict with certain confessional statements as we understand them, which seem to contradict his controversial statements. He did not deal with his general demeanor, conduct, and attitude which were an offense to a number of the attendees. We also are concerned that his students might adopt this same kind of conduct in the Seminary classroom. Dr. Preus, will Dr. Scaer admit that his demeanor may well have been flippant and condescending as some attendees believe? Will he admit that the Bible does not say that Peter has the primary authority for the Office of the Keys?" I was given the opportunity to see a video tape of Scaer's presentation at that meeting, and his performance was as bad or worse than what this layman states, who was speaking for other people, too. Dr. Preus supported Dr. Scaer and refused to do anything about this offense.

On Apr. 19, 1988, I sent a Memo to Dr. Preus and Scaer and other administrators, asking about the cancellation of my stewardship class in 1988-1989 for all three quarters in view of the fact that it had been taught every quarter since I had come to the Seminary and that the Synod had passed a number of resolutions requesting the Seminaries even to make this a required course, not just an elective. There was no answer from Preus or Scaer. At least twenty five students came to me all voluntarily to ask why the class was not scheduled and I told them to talk to the Academic Dean.

One of the pastors who was ordained the summer of 1988 had regularly complained to me about the speech and actions of Dr. Scaer in class; when he graduated, I told him that since he felt so strongly about it, he ought to put it into writing, which he did. This is it (also part of the exhibits):

"Dear Dr. Werning:

As you have asked me to do, I would like to relate the following with regard to the character of Dr. Scaer.

1. During my second year at the Seminary in Fort Wayne I witnessed a birthday party for Dr. Scaer in the south classroom building on the second floor where a group of seminarians created a mock worship for Dr. Scaer's birthday. They used lecterns and torches from the Chapel, one of the hymns they sang was "Jeremiah Was a Bull Frog" and toward the end of the service they brought a live pig into the hallway which was subsequently kissed by Dr. Scaer.

2. I was a student in Dr. Scaer's Christology class and felt that his personal style seemed to be one of entertaining students in Christology much like a stand-up comedian. At one point I can remember him saying about the Virgin Mary that "she got knocked up" and said that he could use stronger language but would refrain. Of course, this got a lot of laughs.

Another point in question during this class was the issue of praying to the saints. Dr. Scaer left questions in the minds of the students as to whether it was advantageous or not to pray to saints. According to the Confessions, we claim that praying to the saints is idolatry. In my opinion, his character is less than pious, and he is a poor example of the pastoral office.

I personally feel that Dr. Scaer is not qualified to maintain his position as professor and academic dean at Concordia Theological Seminary for the above-mentioned observations and that disciplinary measures should be taken.

Respectfully," (Name deleted), Aug. 1, 1988

*   *   *   *   *   *   *

After such behavior as noted above, one was not surprised to learn that a veteran Japanese pastor who was studying at the Seminary for a short time, was heard by a professor and others to walk out of Dr. Scaer's class one morning very irate and saying, "That man does not belong in this Seminary. He does not belong in any church institution anywhere!"

I heard various concerns from time to time, especially at the beginning of 1987. In the fall of 1988 some students volunteered to show notes they wrote. Here are some Scaer' quotes, which are not one hundred percent verbatim, but accurate: "There will be no prayer in this class; pray in the chapel. Don't pray for me, if you do, may you choke on your prayers...The LCMS is a Marcionite Sect...'I am a higher critic.' Prophets sometimes misunderstood their prophecies and improved on God's instructions. Prophets are as much unbelievers as anyone else. God adjusted to the situation, He is a Lutheran, not a Calvinist in this respect...Isaiah did not believe the prophesy in Is. 7:14 about virginity, nor did Isaac...'The Virgin Birth substantiates the New Adam, not the mythical Adam of the Genesis myth?...Satan appears in the Genesis myth...'I gave up an inerrancy long ago.' Now we are fighting the evangelical-prayer crowd. I preferred fighting the liberals, there you could use your mind."

Although various students questioned the content and style of Dr. Scaer's classroom lectures, they said that they did not take him seriously. There are others who thought it was hilarious. Some students, as do most Seminary professors and pastors in the field, have severe problems with this kind of lecturing and decorum related to the role model expected of a Seminary professor on the basis of God's Word. Humor and satire have their place, but this kind of classroom action does not fit the qualifications which Paul states that God requires. The sad thing is that this is only a part of the story in which Dr. Scaer is involved.

An Interlude To Gain Perspective of the Documentation That Follows

Before continuing, I am stopping to ask you, "Is this what 'Confessional Lutheranism' is all about?"

Our answer will depend upon our mental screen or paradigm we bring, also on our capacity to identify, accept and endure truth. This is where denial enters and becomes a factor which may cause one to take the following documentation and discard it for a number of reasons: this deals with people whose reputations are at stake (the victims are also real people and the facts must be studied to discover what the issue is and who is at fault); some cannot handle it emotionally because of close friendship or relations (but problems which strangle us do not get up and walk away); there are others who are doing worse things (one sin does not give license for another, besides then we should deal with both); Synod will survive this crisis like others in the past (the war must end, or we will be permanently dysfunctional); the documentation may be unreliable (on several occasions I asked Dr. Preus to charge me with false accusation, for I am prepared to present volumes of documentation and many witnesses.)

If anyone feels that I should have hidden the truth because it might hurt the several leaders of the Preus camp and also the members of Synod's Commission on Appeals, then I will show you 100 people for every one of the Preus party who have been injured by Dr. Preus or one of his agents. If I knew another way in which I could contribute to stopping the terrible battle which is causing great havoc, I would stop the presses immediately.

Dr. Preus, Dr. Scaer, Prof. Marquart, Mr. Ed Hinnefeld, Rev. Herman Otten, the LCMS Commission on Appeals, and many "Confessional Lutherans" have refused to open their ears to the truth. Now they will have to painfully review the entire account publicly. If the Synod fails to deal with these brothers Biblically now, I believe that the Synod basically has no hope to be functional again.

The account now continues from August-September 1988 to April 1992.

Dr. Scaer-Dr. Preus Beginning with August-September 1988

Adj. Ex. P (an Aug. 11, 1988 Memo from me to Dr. Scaer) recorded, "...For the sake of peace, I was willing to hope for the best after our Feb. 25 meeting. I have sufficient evidence in hand to be satisfied that you must be brought to an awareness of the seriousness of your sins, none of which you recognized in the least in our Feb. 25 meeting. Having prayerfully and carefully considered the entire matter, I must inform you that I am compelled to take the second step of Matthew 18 in order to bring you to an understanding and consciousness of your wrongs. I am asking for a meeting with you as soon as you come back to Fort Wayne, and I shall bring two or three witnesses with me. At that time,

At that time, I shall state clearly the charges, some of which were previously shared with you but which you did not comprehend..."

A Memo to myself, which became Exhibit 15 in my personal dealing with Dr. Preus, recorded a visit with Dr. Scaer on Sept. 6, 1988 as a follow-up to my Aug. 11, 1988 letter. I wrote, "Wanting to know how the matter could be settled, I recounted some of the grievances. Dr. Scaer wanted to hear what all the specifics were, so I gave him my Sept. 1 14-page letter and dropped off the exhibits in the afternoon. Early during our visit, he said that if he had offended me in any way he was sorry, and that if I would say the same, we could settle the matter. I told him that it was considerably deeper than this kind of assurance, that we were now reaping what he had sowed, which needed to be dealt with. I wondered also what kind of apology says that 'if I have offended you in **any way**'...Definite things were pointed out to him last Friday and previously in Memos...My Sept. 1, 1988, letter provides considerable evidence. When Dr. Scaer asked me both in our February meeting and in today's meeting what is meant by 'fruits of repentance,' it appears to me that he revealed one of his basic problems...His actions and reactions intuitively indicate political, administrative, and social understandings and response rather than the deep Biblical and spiritual imperatives of the Gospel which involve the central issue of repentance and forgiveness. Not once so far in our visits has he shown that he has done anything wrong whatsoever or that he is hurting people by his actions, but all he keeps repeating is that he is being hurt badly...I told him that I had selected three pastors as witnesses, who were to serve strictly as witnesses of what was said by the accuser and the accused, and not to take sides. This matter also irritated him...When Dr. Scaer learned that I was firm in my spiritual approach of repentance and forgiveness, not just shaking hands with some general expression of regrets that there may have been some offense given, Dr. Scaer jumped up and said, 'Let's go.' He was visibly angry and distressed, and that was the end."

On Saturday morning, Sept. 10, 1988, I was requested to meet with BOR Chairman Ray Joeckel and Rev. Bud Fehl as representatives of the BOR. My notes show that the Board Chairman said that Preus had told him that Preus had told me not to do anything in the Scaer matter and to drop everything because Scaer has the power to take me out of my class. This coincides with what I actually recall the President telling me on several occasions. In that meeting, these Board representatives told me that Dr. Scaer and Dr. Preus had duplicated some of my Memos to Dr. Scaer and given them to the BOR. Rather than meeting with me with several witnesses, Dr. Scaer cut off my Matthew 18 dealing with him, and now he and Dr. Preus threw it into an administrative level without my knowledge. The Board Chairman apologized three or four times for this getting into their hands, but now that they had it, they wanted to discuss the matter with me.

They asked me about my views on the matter. I suggested to the Board Chairman that the Board employ a "conflict management organization," and learn objectively what the real problems are at the Seminary. These men agreed to take this suggestion to Dr. Preus, who was leading a Faculty Forum at that time nearby. After visiting with Dr. Preus, the Chairman informed me that Dr. Preus refused this, but said that he would conduct his own investigation, to which the Chairman agreed. I was assured that the Board of Regents would take responsibility for the supervision by Dr. Preus, and so I agreed with these two Board representatives to **suspend** my Matthew 18 action against Dr. Scaer to allow the Board of Regents and the President to handle this matter. I sent a Memo to President Robert Preus on Sept. 12, 1988, to inform him of this, and added, "My personal concern is that Dr. Scaer at this time needs a lot of love and personal counsel not only to see what wrong he has done to others, but also that God loves him and that he can be rehabilitated as a professor."

The next day, Sunday, Sept. 11, the Seminary Opening Service was held. On Sept. 14,

1988, I wrote this Memo, "On Monday and Tuesday, Sept. 12 and 13, a number of professors told me that Arthur Just had canvassed some professors on Sunday, Sept. 11 before and after the Seminary Opening Service with the general approach that since Werning wanted Dr. Scaer out as Academic Dean, he should be defended and would they please write a letter to President Preus saying something good about Dr. Scaer. When he was asked by one professor how that could be said, he said that everybody knows that. When told by another professor that it was wrong for Just to do this and that conflict management principles do not allow this kind of political approach, he again asked that a letter be sent to the President with favorable comments about Scaer."

It was untrue that I ever said or asked that Dr. Scaer be removed as Academic Dean! In another paragraph of the Memo, I mentioned that these actions were contrary to the agreement I made with the Board of Regents and that this was politicizing the situation in a matter in which Matthew 18 was to be used, and that it was the BOR's business to handle this, not a young professor politicizing the faculty into two camps.

Another Memo reveals that on Sept. 23, Prof. Dean Wenthe was taking around a short statement(several lines) with support for Dr. Scaer and asking faculty members to sign it.

At the Sept. 26, Faculty meeting, the essay of Dr. David Scaer on sanctification with the Christology statement was presented by Dr. Preus. My Memo quoted several professors telling that the President made the recommendation that the faculty accept it as a perfectly orthodox statement. After various questions, Dr. Preus demanded several times that a resolution be passed to accept the essay. Finally, someone proposed a resolution even though a number of faculty members indicated that they had not had adequate discussion regarding the controverted statement, the Faculty Minutes report, "B. Scaer Article entitled, *"Sanctification in Lutheran Theology"* — A charge of false doctrine has been lodged against Dr. Scaer. Copies of the article in question have been circulated to the Faculty prior to the meeting. After discussion, 'It was moved and seconded that from our (faculty) point of view this article neither contains nor promotes any false doctrine.' Adopted."

A personal Memo based on professors' reports about this Sept. 26 Faculty meeting stated, "The President also requested everyone to sign the statement of support which Dean Wenthe was passing around to Faculty in support of Dr. David Scaer. Some faculty members reported disgust over this pressure tactic, and even some who signed expressed disgust over themselves that they did it even though under pressure." It was inconceivable that any serious theologian would railroad a resolution like that through a faculty without an objective study. If an opportunity had been provided for me or someone else to present a valid study of this unBiblical statement, I would have given what I prepared to expose the error of the Christology statement, such as:

Scaer's Christology Statement

The controversial statement in the Sanctification Essay in the April-June 1985 *CTQ*, FW, was the **very last sentence** of the Essay. "ANY ATTEMPT TO MAKE CHRISTOLOGY PRELIMINARY TO THEOLOGY, OR ONLY ITS MOST IMPORTANT PART, BUT NOT ITS ONLY PART, IS A DENIAL OF LUTHER'S DOCTRINE AND EFFECTIVELY DESTROYS THE GOSPEL AS THE MESSAGE OF COMPLETED ATONEMENT."

It appears that what the author is trying to say is what Lutherans and the Confessions have always said: Christology is **central** to all theology. This statement, however, confuses that truth and goes beyond it especially because it not only says that Christology is the only part of theology, but it makes an **exclusive** statement that any attempt to make Christology not its only part (that Christology is the only part of theology) is a denial of Luther's doctrine and **effectively destroys the Gospel as the message of completed**

atonement.

The Bible and the Lutheran Confessions show that the Father and creation are a part of theology. If one believes that the Bible teaches that the Holy Spirit and sanctification are a part of theology, does this mean that he has denied Luther's doctrine and effectively destroyed the Gospel by stating that the Father and Holy Spirit are a part of theology? That Christology statement is an **exclusive** statement, disallowing the Father and the Holy Spirit to be part of theology.

The exclusive claim creates a conflict with the Athanasian Creed. The unclarity and confusion of the Christology statement which excludes everyone except Christ as a part of theology, lies not only in its failure to establish proper distinctions (Father, Son and Holy Spirit), but that it actually erases **necessary** distinctions which the Athanasian Creed makes clear: "...One God in three Persons and three Persons in one God, neither confusing the Persons nor dividing the substance...glory equal...co-equal...in this Trinity, none is before or after another; none is greater or less than another..." The unity of God and the "Christ alone" truth does not allow Lutherans to say arbitrarily that Christology is the only part of theology, thus excluding the Father and the Holy Spirit, placing Christ before, making Christ more equal than the Father and the Holy Spirit.

It is side-stepping the real issue if it is said that the statement in question must be taken in the context of the entire article. Of course, every sentence in an article must be taken in context. But the context cannot be expected to "rescue" an incorrect, inaccurate or weak statement. If it is claimed that the controverted statement can be acceptable within the whole article, which quotations of the context correct the statement that excludes the Father and Holy Spirit from theology?

Neither the Scriptures nor the Lutheran Confessions ever make the claim that the work of one person in the Trinity is all of theology. They never pit the work of one person in the Trinity against that of the other two. The Lutheran Church always refused to subordinate any person of the Trinity to the other two.

The statement is also in conflict with the Scriptures. Jesus Himself did not exclude the Holy Spirit as part of theology as he stated: "Unless I go away, the Counselor will not come to you; but if I go, I will send Him to you" (Jn. 16:7); Jesus did not exclude the Holy Spirit from Christian theology; indeed, He told later that people would not understand who Jesus was unless the Holy Spirit gave light to them; how can it be said that the Holy Spirit is not part of Christian theology? John 14:15-25 concerns the same thing. If the Father and the Holy Spirit are not part of theology, why is Jesus asking the Father that He should send the Holy Spirit? John 15:26 says the same. John 7:38-39 is also a strong testimony to the Holy Spirit and His work as Jesus includes the Holy Spirit as an integral part of theology.

Jesus said that when you pray, say, "**Our Father**, Who art in heaven..." He did not teach, pray, "O Jesus..." If the Father is not part of theology, but only Jesus is, then why did Jesus ask us to pray to the Father?

The argument about the hymn, "Jesus, Jesus Only..." is bad semantics because that hymn does not state that Jesus is the only part of **theology**! If the Christology statement is true, then those people who baptize only in the name of Jesus should not be condemned because somehow Christ represents the Father and the Holy Spirit in a mystical way, as they are not part of theology.

This is not a tempest in a teapot, nor some theologians quarreling over phrases or terminology, but it is a tragic overstatement which leads to heresies. We cannot improve on the Lutheran assertion that Christology is central to theology nor the formulation of the Athanasian Creed. The statement that Christology is the only part of theology is disastrous. We must avoid semantic theological assertions which will confuse laity and pastors alike.

The statement on Christology which appeared in the CTQ is inadequate, confusing, and wrong. We believe that the article under discussion does not take into account sufficiently the fact that in today's religious world, various Christian bodies and theologians tend to emphasize one person of the Trinity more than the others.

In contrast, we in the LCMS, in accord with the Ecumenical Creeds, have always confessed the three persons of the Trinity to be equal in all respects. Can we really expect readers to see the name of "Christ" as synonymous with the Trinity? Can we accept a change of the orthodox Lutheran position of Christ's centrality in theology to an unwarranted claim that the doctrine of Christ is the "only part" of theology? To maintain a clear confession of our faith in the present religious climate, it is essential that we avoid statements that can be misunderstood or misapplied, such as the unBiblical Christology assertion.

It is not "Christology alone" that has been described as the doctrine on which the church stands or falls; instead, that distinction goes to the doctrine of justification, namely, that we are justified by grace, for Christ's sake, through faith.

*　　　　*　　　　*　　　　*　　　　*　　　　*

Dr. W. E. Griesse gave the Synod's Commission on Adjudication this criticism dated Nov. 2, 1991: "...The Trinitarian formula of baptism in the Great Commission gives equal emphasis to each Person of the Trinity. The doctrine of the Trinity does not flow from Christology. Christology flows from the doctrine of the Trinity. The use of the term 'only part of theology' is grammatically and syntactically incorrect...The Scaer statement has the effect of elevating Christ above the other members of the Trinity as in the ancient Modalistic heresy. There are other persons in Scripture, viz.: the Father, the Holy Spirit, angels, Satan, etc., and there are theologies about each of them. This statement, coming at the end of a treatise on sanctification, becomes an improper mixing of justification and sanctification."

On Sept. 29, 1988, at 2 p.m. I visited with Dr. Preus, who told me that the Christology statement in the Sanctification essay of Dr. Scaer had been settled, as the Faculty adopted the essay. He asked me, "Will you now drop it?" When I indicated that there are basic problems with the essay which have not been faced, Dr. Preus stated that he will ask the Board of Regents to accept the faculty adoption of the essay and the case will be finished. He said that the Board of Regents will pass it. He said that the Faculty is upset when one of their men is attacked, and they resent it. I reminded him that I did not attack Scaer, and that I was using a private approach according to Matthew 18 with Dr. Scaer and that this matter went to the BOR only because Scaer personally duplicated the material and both of them gave it to the BOR. I said that this was breaking the Eighth Commandment and that the Faculty had been fed a lie which has not been corrected. Preus was adamant.

On Sept. 30, 1988, I wrote a Memo to Dr. Preus giving the basic criticisms which are contained in my critique reproduced above. Dr. William J. Houser wrote a letter based on his notes at the Faculty meeting: "Dr. Preus then spent the next 35 minutes subjecting the Faculty to his rhetorical skills and intimidations, false statements, and manipulations. I copied the following statements while Dr. Preus spoke showing that most of the time he claimed that Dr. Werning was trying to remove Dr. Scaer as Academic Dean: 'I am not asking you to stand up in front of the Council of Trent. I am just asking for a vote of faculty harmony...We want to avoid giving the Board of Regents a feeling of faculty polarization or of the faculty having a morale problem...We are voting for collegiality and being bound together...The one word that the Board wants to hear is harmony...The Board wants us to 'o.k.' David...Get a faculty member off the hook and 'o.k.' David...Step up and support one another...No one can get rid of a faculty member like Scaer but me." "

Some of the tactics of Dr. Preus caused me real anxiety, but I trusted that he under the supervision of the Board of Regents would handle the problems fairly as should be expected. As I had done regularly in the past, I believed that a thoughtful study of the Biblical approach versus the political approach in personnel matters would be helpful. Thus I wrote the following Memo together with "A Biblical Model or Paradigm or Prototype for Christian Relationships," which I hoped that Dr. Preus would share with the Faculty and Board of Regents. There was no acknowledgment, no recognition that it was received.

Memo from the desk of Waldo J. Werning (EXHIBIT 22)
To Dr. Robert Preus
Date: Oct. 25, 1988

I have been prayerfully agonizing to try to make a positive contribution from a Biblical perspective related to the current situation, which is impartial and watches out for the good of everyone. I have shared "A Biblical Model or Paradigm or Prototype For Christian Relationships" with some veterans who are trusted confidants, and they believe that this is a very positive, honest, earnest, and fair document which, if we can agree on the model, could lead to total healing. Even though it is being sent only to you, it is not a private document and may be used within the Faculty and Board of Regents. May the Holy Spirit make it a great blessing.

A BIBLICAL MODEL OR PARADIGM OR PROTOTYPE FOR CHRISTIAN RELATIONSHIPS (EX 22A)

Since my Matthew 18 approach and spiritual approach to overcome certain difficulties have been misunderstood and somewhat distorted, I am writing this little document to explain fully what I mean by a proper spiritual approach to spiritual problems and life conflicts. I look to God's Word for directions for building and living our relationships. This is the structure or Biblical framework from which I live and relate to others.

I approach my work and my life relationships with the knowledge that I am prone to mistakes, having a depraved nature and unholy self (Old Adam) constantly in battle with the new nature. Recognizing this, I am alert to assess thoughts before they are translated into speech and actions, and then also continue to evaluate words and actions so that they conform to the Christian principles of truth and love. Being introspective and also dependent upon trusted confidants in true openness and honesty has given me a security and strength which should not be mistaken as arrogance or feeling that I do not make mistakes. I am daily prepared to apologize or repent of any statement or action that is indeed in error when the facts indicate it. By God's grace, I live by the spirit of repentance and forgiveness.

I earnestly invite study together and reaction for building these principles into what I term, "A Biblical Model or Paradigm or Prototype For Christian Relationships." Being committed to reconciliation in every situation, I have tried to develop principles for an "edifying life style," and in unity amidst diversity of personalities, talents, and positions.

The assumption is that all of us are completely committed to God, His Word, fellow Christians, and that we are sincerely motivated. The problem often lies in ability for self-understanding, openness, and willingness to be edified by others.

The model with its counterpart is presented as Level #1 - "Biblical Objective Model" and Level #2 - "Human Subjective Model."

Level #1 Biblical and Objective	Level #2 Human and Subjective
1. Biblical - spiritual strength	Political - power tactics

The contrast here is between Biblical-spiritual means or quick results through political means which are more easily gained by simply doing it our way and using the power of human authority. However, our only God-given and God-authorized strength is spiritual power.

2. Tell facts - take spiritual steps	Tell opinions - judge, attack

The question here is whether discussion and contacts consider the **facts** and then take spiritual steps such as Matthew 18 when disagreements are to be resolved or whether **opinions** and judgments will confuse matters and legitimate concerns. The first approach will help solve difficulties, while the second one will not.

3. Attitude of servant (servant to others under Christ)	Institutional or corporate attitude (control, dictate)

The contrast here is between a servant mind or an institutional-corporate mind. Phil. 2:5 directs Level One so that we have a servant mentality under Christ, whereas Level Two attitudes seek to control and dictate human actions and affairs. Level One centers us in Christ's way, "Be one in thought and in love, live in harmony, keep one purpose in mind. Do not act out of selfish ambition or with conceit, but in humility think of others as being better than yourselves, while at the same time not being concerned about your own things, but rather about the things of others. Have the same attitude that Christ Jesus had" (Phil. 2:2-5). Level Two consists of maneuvers to help keep people in line.

4. Priority on spiritual transformation of self and others - speak the truth with love (Eph. 4:15)	Conform to world's principles and relationships in treating others - fail to speak the truth and/or do not always with love

A transformed mind lives under Level One according to Rom. 12:2-3: "Do not follow the pattern of this world, but let yourselves be transformed by a renewing of your minds so that you can test and be sure of what God wants, namely, what is good and pleasing and perfect...keep your thoughts in bounds. Consider how God has given a measure of faith to each of you." Level One living will be accompanied with humility and introspection that is open to course correction when necessary. Level Two centers on behavioral standards, rules and regulations to make people shape up; games are played, as the truth is not spoken with love.

5. Live and act by faith	Reason intervenes or over-arches at times

"Our faith is the victorious conqueror over the world" (1 Jn. 5:4). "Take faith as the shield with which you can put out all the flaming arrows of the Evil One" (Eph. 6:16). Faith on Level One is accompanied with loving one another as Christ commanded us (1 Jn. 3:23). "Trust in the Lord with all your heart and lean not on your own understanding" (Prov. 3:5). Any dependence on human reason and ability on Level Two is destructive of relationships because it is carnal and dependent on the flesh.

6. Doctrine leads to consistent practice of love for others at all times	Doctrine as head knowledge sometimes becomes a security for ignoring consistent practice of love and sensitivity

"Therefore, everyone who hears these words of mine and continues to follow them is like a man who had sense enough to build his house on the rock" (Mt. 7:24). "For whoever does the will of My Father in heaven is in reality My brother and sister and other" (Mt.12:50). "If anyone loves Me, he will obey My word, and My Father will love him, and We will come to him and make Our home with him" (Jn. 14:23). Level One involves doctrine and practice of love, being pastoral in mood and tone. Level Two concerns itself with saying the right thing (head knowledge), but not being concerned whether actions are political and carnal in relating to others or how they are treated.

7. "Public and community" faith (expressed in practice)	"Generic church" faith that remains private (sometimes not translated into action)

A faith which is expressed only generally or generically is not confessed specifically in private or in daily life. In making judgments about people, Level Two spirituality uses arguments to claim that the other person is to be openly criticized, because he is not being loyal to our **team**. Level One refuses to make judgments about people, but rather sticks to the issues without referring to the personalities involved and uses private Biblical channels.

A major issue here is the problem of remaining very general but not specific in repentance and confession, publicly making general confession but nothing specific even in private. Involved here is the true form and content of Office of the Keys as evidenced in the Law and Gospel, and repentance and forgiveness.

Without realizing it, we can have a form of the grace which contains only absolution and forgiveness without repentance and confession, leading to Gospel without Law. Grace involves both Law and Gospel, resulting in repentance and confession which is followed by forgiveness and absolution.

8. Concerned and open discussions (hold to issues)	Gossiping and quarreling, even sometimes slandering (attack personalities)

Level One always looks at other Christians as fellow members of the body of Christ, connecting faith with the community of believers. Level Two finds a faith, which is not translated into action or real love. Here matters are settled by gossiping and quarreling, trying to pressure others into silence or submission by intimidation or harassment.

"Get rid of all bitterness and temper and anger and shouting and slander, along with every way of hurting one another" (Eph. 4:31). "Stop talking against one another, my fellow Christians. Anyone who talks against his fellow Christian or judges him, talks against the Law and judges it" (James 4:11). "I am afraid that there may be quarreling, jealousy, angry feelings, selfish ambitions, slander, gossip, and disorderly conduct" (2 Cor. 12:20b). Our tongues must be restrained in talking about others (Prov. 13:3; James 1:26). Our discussion about others should be sensitive to people. Gossip and backbiting shows insensitivity to other people. The rule should be, "Don't talk **about** people, but talk **to** people."

9. Repentance (change)   Regrets, but little change

Level One repentance is not just some doctrine or something that others need to do. "Daily repentance" is not just a religious cliche. A Level Two life of expressing shallow and impersonal regrets allows the person to keep on doing what has been done, where there are neither repentance or fruits of repentance. Level One is followed by change and fruits of repentance. Level Two finds a person vague and willing only to say, "**If** I have offended you in any way, I am sorry" (such statements have been used since the beginning of time to displace Level One spiritual conduct). This Level Two statement and attitude is a formalistic approach, which does not meet the deep spiritual needs of life or relations between people.

10. Life lived by grace in practice   Legalistic, manipulative

Level One is a life filled with the possibilities of grace, while Level Two, with its legalism, is filled with manipulation and self-centered protection of personal turf claimed at the expense of others.

11. Impartial   Partiality, favoritism,
                                          prejudicial

"Do not pervert justice; do not show partiality to the poor or favoritism to the great, but judge your neighbor fairly" (Lev. 19:15). "He would surely rebuke you if you secretly showed partiality" (Job 13:10). "...To keep these things without prejudice and without preference for anyone in anything you do" (1 Tim. 5:21). "Have you not shown favoritism and become judges who give corrupt opinions?" (James 2:4). The typical Level Two life is exemplified in 1 Cor. 1:11-12: "...You are quarreling...I mean that each of you says: 'I belong to Paul,' or 'I belong to Apollos,' or 'I belong to Peter,' or 'I belong to Christ' " (1 Cor. 1:11-12). Failure to take seriously the faults of a person or charges against him shows a Level Two partiality and favoritism.

12. **Rehabilitate** (edify, love,   Annihilate (destroy,
    gentleness), all win   dismiss, separate, fight,
                                          win arguments), win-lose

This factor can be subtle. Level One of rehabilitating is performed by one who is on solid ground to deal with a brother who needs correction and encouragement. Level Two finds the use of annihilation, destruction and dismissal as a simpler settlement of a situation. Level One requires edifying or building up the other (Rom. 14:19; 15:2; Eph. 4:29) in order to keep the bond of peace and unify brothers and sisters in Christ, all built upon proper love (Mt. 22:2; Eph. 4:15; Jn. 13:35; 15:2; 1 Thes. 3:12). Level Two is destructive as it causes separation and puts the other person in a negative position and makes him a loser. Level One with its unifying approach through love and gentleness (2 Tim. 2:24; James 3:17) aims to have all win because each one through repentance and forgiveness is being built up in love. Level Two in its fighting, winning of arguments and separation, is a win-lose proposition, as the one who wants to win uses Level Two tactics so that the other will lose.

13. Patiently take time to follow   Do not take time to be
    spiritual principles, channels,   informed or apply Biblical
    and methods (No judgments)   principles, thus shortcutting
                                          Level One (Judgmental-
                                          impatient)

Level One is patient, recognizing that all of the Biblical steps take time, as judgment is delayed even though the facts and issues may show need for correction. Level Two shows impatience and immediate private and public judgments, and not taking time to be properly informed. Level Two conducts public court, trying to win a victory by intimidation and by show of right through political means.

Use The Model To Build Relationships

This model, paradigm or prototype will be useful to all if there is agreement that it is usable to prevent eroding relations or to bring healing and unification when there is conflict. Even though this model has been created only at this time, Level One has been consciously in mind to follow in my relationships, and Level Two is one which I have studiously sought to avoid. If all of us can agree to a specific model with the two levels, we will have an instrument which will be objectively helpful to avoid unnecessary strife and to be mutually edifying.

In my work and relationships, I have sought to follow Level One of this model because I recognize the inherent weakness within me. Level One presents various characteristics for avoiding conflict and for building good relationships. Because I, together with all others, am inclined toward human frailty, I have taken steps to keep this within my private life and not to allow it to make inroads in my public life. This is done not only by daily personal repentance and forgiveness with full awareness of the need for analysis and introspection, but also to tap the resources of the body of Christ. For that reason, I have at least five regular confidants, all of whom understand Level One Christianity and who are not ''yes men,'' but are capable of speaking the truth in love to me at all times under all conditions. They know that I expect such honesty and openness, otherwise they will no longer be my confidants, only friends. This insures as much as is humanly possible that human weaknesses and sins are displayed on the private level, where they are corrected before they can be expressed publicly in word and deed.

I am committed to the same lifestyle today, as a pastor, and as a representative of the Seminary and of Synod. My aim by God's grace is to bring no discredit upon the Seminary or upon the Synod, and not upon myself either, because I do not want to discredit Christ in any way. The Scriptures show that we are to avoid coarse sins, which are also part of Level Two, and that we are not to be slaves to sins of the tongue, but rather to be edifiers in the body of Christ. If and when I ever am guilty of a sin in word or deed against others, I am prepared to repent genuinely and to make the appropriate change; if I do not see it myself, my confidants will see it and tell me. This approach certainly helps a person from having to backtrack because potential mistakes are caught when they are in the mind or before they are expressed in any public arena. This gives me a feeling of peace and serenity, knowing that my imperfections are prevented from being put on public display or hurting others to the dishonor of my Savior. I will not lock myself into a course of action without giving serious consideration to alternatives or possible consequences, being concerned especially to keep on the Level One track.

It is a healthy thing to scrutinize our own actions by the **Model or Prototype For Relationships,** ascertaining whether we are acting on Level One or Level Two. Let each make their own analysis on the basis of the available evidence. Sorting our the current situation on the basis of this Model has the potential of getting us all on track. Presenting the facts as I know them, I am suggesting that we individually evaluate actions which are on Level One or Level Two related to Werning, Academic Dean, President, Faculty, Board of Regents, and the LCMS.

(NOTE: Nine pages are now deleted which deal with individual problems created by the former President and former Academic Dean until October 1988, naming 13 separate issues for Dr. Scaer and six for Dr. Preus. Then the question was raised related to each of the three: Which one of Werning's statements or actions needs to be changed to conform with Level 1? Which of the statements and actions of the Academic Dean need to be changed to conform to Level 1? Which one of the statements or actions of the President need to be changed to conform to Level 1? Then the document continues.)

Living on Level One

We will all agree that God not only has much to say about this entire matter, but that He wants us living and acting on the Biblical level — Level One. Can we close ranks and defend each other and protect each other on the basis of Level One? Will we? This is is necessary if we are to survive.

If we are to become unified, it must be on a Biblical basis, not on personal loyalties to one or the other, or continue to follow Level Two. We will find protection only in committing ourselves to Level One, and that is without exception.

What is required?

1. We all need to affirm each other and everyone with our strengths and weaknesses, but each committed to continual growth and change by God's standards (repentance-forgiveness). We need to be committed that no one be dismissed or that no one's privileges and services to the Seminary be diminished in any way, no exceptions.

2. We need to close ranks with and for each other on the basis of Level One, and then live by mutual edification, looking not only to our own interests, but also to the interests of others.

3. We must consciously and determinedly live on Level One of the Biblical Model or Paradigm or Prototype in Christian Relationships(#1-#13). This means that each one of us needs to **be free** to speak the truth in love (Eph. 4:15), and each needs to listen to the truth in love, no matter how difficult it may be to hear it. This means that we will be speaking to each other without fear of retribution, and not speak about each other to others. This is Christ's prescription. Then each of us will be free to do the work for which God has given us the ability and to which we were called.

Failure to commit ourselves totally to the Biblical model of Level One will cause us to self-destruct. When one or several of us are harmed or destroyed, then all of us are affected and harmed. When each one of us is committed to Level One, then all of us are protected. May the Holy Spirit give us this mind and this attitude to give us a needed victory in Jesus Christ.

(NOTE: Significantly, Dr. Preus did not answer this Memo, but convened a secret Faculty Committee which reported to the Board of Regents with complete distortions, including a statement that was totally untrue which he later admitted, on the basis of which the Board passed a resolution which they later declared non-operative. This is all reported in this account.)

*   *   *   *   *   *

I was not prepared for the shock of a visit with Dr. Preus on Nov. 16, 1988 when evidence became clear that Dr. Preus cleverly managed this whole matter from Sept. 10 to the Board meeting of November 12, 1988 which stacked the deck. Dr. Preus handed me some documents, which included a Faculty Committee Report on the "Scaer-Werning Matter." Without informing me, Dr. Preus appointed a five-man committee who stated that they studied the "evidence" submitted to them, for example, the allegation that Scaer had transgressed the procedures of Matthew 18 and sinned against the 8th Commandment. With the documentation which Dr. Preus secretly selected for the Committee, they declared that "the exhibits in our possession does not in our opinion substantiate these claims."

You have read the documentation that several times Dr. Scaer jumped the Matthew 18 track in order to play to the galleries. The worst problem with this secret document was the statement, "The remaining charge which we are invited to consider was the President's understanding the assertion of Dr. Waldo Werning that Dr. Scaer does not possess Christian faith." Dr. Preus admitted that he had told the Committee this. I exclaimed that I have never said this about anyone in my life, because only a church can take steps of excommunication, and that I do not think or talk like that. Dr. Preus told me that he knew that I did not say that. Yet he took this lie to the BOR and let them believe it, and never corrected it!

Please notice the Resolution passed by the BOR on Nov. 12, 1988, and note the first RESOLVE that the Board fully concurs in both the "Members of the Board of Regents" Memo from President Robert Preus (which I never saw even to this day, so I am not aware of whatever untruths he may have told), and also that they concur with the Report of the Faculty Committee, in which Dr. Preus later admitted that there was a lie, which he passed on and did not correct. Theologically, it was a bad document. On May 20, 1989, Rev. Ray Mueller admitted that he wrote this Resolution. On Dec. 20, 1988, I wrote eight pages of a Memo to the Board of Regents to show that this was absolute stone-walling my Matthew 18 action, and that their action and Resolution contained a number of errors.

On Dec. 20 I wrote, "The question must be faced whether the Board action was on a Biblical Matthew 18 basis or on a managerial and political basis.." I referred to previous documentation that the Board had accepted false witness against me without even trying to check with me about the actual facts, and in this case, of a slanted, prejudicial opinion of a Faculty Committee Report in which I did not even know that there was a Committee judging me and never saw the report until after the Board's action. It was not true that I was treating Dr. Scaer as if Christ had not fully covered his sins and shortcomings in objective justification, but rather that I was true to the Office of the Keys and Confession in requiring repentance (Lk. 17:3). In a peculiar twist of logic, I am said to be guilty of a potentially damning sin if I believed I had "no flaws or shortcomings of the flesh" (when did I ever imply that?) or "to treat Dr. Scaer as if Christ had not fully covered his sins and shortcomings."

Added to this unBiblical theology of giving absolution without confession was the "Contract and Agreement" offered by the Board which Dr. Preus delivered to me on Nov. 16 and signed by him that day which requested me to violate Matthew 18 and the 8th Commandment when it requested that "all charges, formal or informal, against CTS and any administrator, faculty, or staff employed at CTS currently pending will be dropped with the assurance that these will not be revived thereafter." Under no condition could I work for a church institution which violates Matthew 18 and the 8th Commandment to the extent that the Board of Regents and Dr. Preus did, and then insist that I drop it all.

It must be noted that on Dec. 14, 1989, the Board of Regents Chairman Reuben L. Garber and Secretary Stuart Tietz presented a Resolution which was passed by the Board in its January 26, 1990, letter that "The Board of Regents apparently did not have all the pertinent information required for making an appropriate decision...said Resolution could be subject to misunderstanding...the Faculty Committee, though acting in good faith, apparently did not have at its disposal all pertinent information...subsequent events indicate that this Resolution did not lead to closure...RESOLVED, that the issues...pertaining to the Werning/Scaer matter now be considered an open matter to be decided through appropriate Synodical channels.." Dr. Preus was responsible for all this disinformation to the Board! Because I wanted to narrow my focus, I dropped the charges against the Board at that time despite the fact that this agreement in no way rescinded the previous motion. I was told that legal considerations might prevent that.

On January 4, 1989 I wrote an eight-page letter to Dr. Preus, "Prayerfully, I am coming to you one more time to plead with you to correct the great injustice that is happening to me and others at the Seminary because of the actions of Dr. David Scaer and your support of him. I have valued our association as close friends for many years, and I intend to keep that fellowship, even though it would not be reciprocated...This does not mean that I will bind my conscience to what you say or want others to do in every situation. Unfortunately some of your methods leave much to be desired, and at times are destructive...I have every right to go to the Synod's Board on Adjudication, but I felt that both you and the BOR members are men of good will who allowed yourselves to be misguided for a time. Even though I and others have been annihilated, by God's grace I am totally committed to repentance and forgiveness, which is designed to correct and rehabilitate. I will not treat others as they treat me when I am treated wrongly...If this is painful for you to read, then realize that not only I, but a good number of others in the past, have found it very painful to experience the autocratic treatment from Scaer and you...There is a blind spot or other side which is autocratic and dictatorial by which you harm or destroy the other person if he does not bow to your wishes or is not obedient to your strategy, no matter how flawed it may be.

My letter continued, "It is not necessary to bloody or destroy others in order to get this marvelous mission work done. By allowing David Scaer to harm and destroy others, you have harmed yourself severely. I mentioned this to you several times that if you continue to support Scaer and his sinful ways, he will bring you down. At one time, your answer was, 'He has been loyal to me'...Bloodied and dead bodies are all over: gifted men with sensitive spirits and hearts, who were completely committed to God and the Seminary. Simply because they would not sign a letter of support for you or for David Scaer, they became marked men. The judgment was made, 'That man must go.' How often that has been said! That man's only crime was that he did not want to sign for or against anyone, but he wanted to do the work of the Lord faithfully."

The letter to Dr. Preus continues, "I heard (name deleted) say to a number of people that when he was interviewed by the President for professor at the Seminary, that the President told him about the good guys and the bad guys at the Seminary and about the ones that had to go. (Name deleted) stated that he told you that this was none of his business and why was he being told this even before he had a call...If you do not believe that Tepker, Rosin, and I and many others are telling the truth when we say that there are many faculty members who are gravely concerned even though they may acquiesce because of intimidation, then let it proved by having a 'conflict management group' come in to test the true convictions and opinions of individuals who may wish to remain anonymous. Every faculty member is in bondage to human control and rule...They are intimidated...because they will be annihilated...This tears me apart, too, because I love you very much, and it has pained me to see you destroy yourself. However, I am totally committed to stand with you if you, together with David Scaer, will repent of these wrongs, make restitution, be reconciled to **all** those whom you have made your enemies, and let all this be known to the total Faculty, the appropriate staff, and the Board of Regents.

I wrote, "You are the key to the solution to this entire problem for healing or if there will be more destruction...You may be angry and you may be hurt as you read these lines, but realize that there are many wonderful men who are gifts of God who lie bloodied and dead as far as the Seminary is concerned, and who are more hurt and pained than you, because of the treatment they received from the Seminary administration under your leadership...More plotting and strategy to isolate 'critics' compounds the sins of the perpetrator and multiplies the hurt of the victim." I wrote, "I am open to honest discussion with you, not debates, rationalizations, excuses, recriminations or arguments. All this documentation shows that I remain on the spiritual level. If you respond with proper repentance, fruits of repentance, restitution and reconciliation with those who have been harmed without any 'ifs' and 'buts', then you will have been the key person to solve this entire problem...I ask only that this scandal be resolved by you in a Biblical, God-pleasing way. If it is not, I will ask the BOR to do that task. If the Board of Regents does not do it, I will ask the Synod's Commission on Adjudication to do it..."

On January 24, 1989, I received a letter from Dr. Preus that Dr. Scaer is guilty of nothing and that he does not need to perform the fruits of repentance, nor that he himself had been remiss in his duties toward the Seminary by defending and supporting Dr. Scaer. I suggested that my next step would be to go to the Board of Regents.

On January 17, 1989, I wrote to the BOR [This is my letter which Preus copied and gave to some members of the Faculty. There is no Biblical authority to ask the Faculty to act as Synod's Commission on Adjudication.]:

Board of Regents, Concordia Theological Seminary, Jan. 17, 1989

Dear Co-Workers in Christ:

The action of the Board of Regents on Nov. 12, 1988, finds me in a state of disbelief regarding the untenable position and the indefensible action which the Board has taken. EX-HIBIT 27 provides my commentary and analysis of this Resolution, which explains my dismay and consternation. EXHIBIT 28 tells the basic reasons why I must reject for conscience' sake the contract and agreement offered by the Board. I will not repeat the substance of EXHIBITS 27 and 28, but rather let the message of these exhibits provide the information I have prepared for you.

Since the BOR through its Chairman accepted the responsibility of continuing the process of Matthew 18 with Dr. David P. Scaer, I withdrew totally from any participation during that time. Since the Board now has declared Scaer innocent of all charges by closing the case, that action now stands in judgment in the court of God and of the church. Please remember that I was prepared to take two or three witnesses with me, but I deferred to the Board for this next step. Since I am convinced by conscience and by trusted confidants that the Board's action is in total error, I have prepared to take this case to the Synod's Commission of Adjudication.

It seems to me that the BOR in a weak moment felt that it would be an easier route to clear Scaer and leave me standing with charges which would now appear to be frivolous, trite and unreasonable. Another possibility is that I allegedly brought false charges against him. In both cases, the Board owes it to me not to offer a contract to me, but to offer counsel and correction because I then am responsible for all kinds of divisive and disruptive actions.

Reading carefully the proposed letter to the Synod's Commission on Adjudication, you will find all the evidences and exhibits for the charges which are being brought. It might be added that not only was the Nov. 14, 1989, Essay of Dr. Scaer one more evidence of the road that he is traveling, but all one has to do is to talk to students in his classes this fall to learn that he continues to make all kinds of confusing statements and remarks that are untenable in the context of a seminary classroom. Indeed, some observers say that his comical way of lecturing is a way in which he introduces his aberrations on the priesthood of all believers, clergy, etc., for one really never knows if he is joking or not about these sacred matters. Professors did not take him seriously when he was solely serving the professor ranks, but when he became Academic Dean his actions took on a totally different perspective. It is a significant factor that the heads of the four departments all objected to him being named Academic Dean when that event happened, some of them rather strongly. Yet this was not heeded by Dr. Preus and now we are living with the scandal at the Seminary and in Synod.

In previous communications, I stated that problems don't go away or dissolve by themselves, but they grow bigger if they are not faced. By merely closing the case in a situation where letter writing campaigns and political actions were substituted for the spiritual responsibilities of Matthew 18, the Board actually swept everything under the rug. The problem is now bigger than ever. It really is grievous when such a cover-up or whitewash is the response of a Board that has the responsibility to face the realities of harmful actions on the part of personnel for which they are responsible. The political move of choosing to side with the Academic Dean and the President against lesser personnel like myself has created an ethical and theological problem for the Board.

It seems to me that the Board together with the President felt that I could be isolated in such a manner as to look like an oddball or troublemaker who is unnecessarily stirring the waters. It also appears that the Board and the President felt that I did not have the resolve or Christian fortitude to take the next step, which meant that I would have to take on "city hall." Might does not make right, but right makes might.

The proposed letter to the Board on Adjudication has been sent to you because I want to give my brothers in Christ on the Board another opportunity to correct this situation and to stop the pretense, and even dereliction of responsibility. This will mean that many hours will be required to read carefully the documentation and all the exhibits. I have given the same opportunity to the President, who has been a close friend, for I have wanted nothing but good for him, as for you. The fact that you have gotten this letter means that the President has chosen not to change and not to face the reality of sin involved in this entire matter, as well as others in the past. Even though the Board has stated that it considers "the case to be closed," which frees me to take it the next step to the Commission on Adjudication, I want the Holy Spirit to have another opportunity to work among us to produce repentance and forgiveness.

Pastors and professors are first of all Christians. Augustine, preaching about pastors, observed that "we are Christians for our own sake; we are leaders for your sake. The fact that we are Christians should serve our own advantage; the fact that we are leaders should serve only yours." We are to see ourselves as servants, and act that way. It is easy to let our personal spiritual life get swallowed up and to let pride detract us from our servant relation with others. At this time, we must strongly affirm the true expression of our faith in our leadership roles as servants.

Churches have a right to expect their leaders to be "above reproach," which is the first Biblical requirement of a church overseer (1 Tim. 3:2). We are to be examples to the flock, whether it is members of a congregation or students of a Seminary. Christian leaders who show pride and do and say offensive things should be treated like any believer who needs correcting. Not to do so may ultimately end in the destruction of the brother of himself by default, because the members of the Body have failed to help him and correct him.

God's Word shows that crucial qualities of pastors and professors are to be temperate in the exercise of emotions, possess spiritual wisdom and common sense, be gentle, humble, not self-willed or prone to unilateral actions, but one who enjoys what is good (1 Tim. 3). Godly character is a substantive issue. It is not merely academic, theoretical or an ideal.

221

The qualities of godly character are the behavioral realities of the Christian faith. It is a painful thing to see an able professor like Dr. Scaer to continue with his serious flaws and aberrations, but it is even more painful to see his leaders fail to correct him. The quality of leaders is usually reproduced in students and in church members. The flaws which Dr. Scaer has shown would not be acceptable in a local congregation, so why are we tolerating them here? A person has to be blind or in a state of denial not to admit that Dr. Scaer needs counsel, correction and rehabilitation. This is a scandal on the campus and somewhat throughout the Synod, so why can the President and Board not recognize this scandal?

Unfortunately, this entire matter has placed us all in bondage. I was in bondage while serving the Seminary, even half time, because I knew that if I spoke to the President or the Board what many professors and students are saying, and many alumni are thinking, that I would put my job in jeopardy. I want to apologize profusely to the Board for being such a coward and for failing to be obedient to my Lord. I am sorry and repent for this. However, I am now free of that bondage, while many others are still in bondage and do not have an alternative like I do in the freedom of retirement. Consciences have been burdened and continue to be burdened. Consciences of those who support Dr. Scaer and who campaign for him have been deadened and seared so that they are not capable of sound reason in applying Biblical truths to the practical areas of their seminary life and in the life of sanctification.

The victims include the nine professors who tried to be healers but were inflicted with more wounds. The victims include sensitive Christian pastors and professors, who still today bear the scars of being torn apart emotionally and psychologically by Dr. Scaer and others. I speak no allusions or fabrications or misrepresentations. Others have tried to share this truth, but have felt the big shoe of authority pressed upon them brutally. We get inklings of treatment of those in the past. All I know is that I have been judged in a number of instances by the Board of Regents without representation and without my knowledge, and judged in absentia in matters which Dr. Preus should never have taken to the Board without first being brought to me so that I could either correct them if guilty or I could present the truth if the President or Academic Dean was in error. Under the administration of the Academic Dean and the President, the gossip and rumor mill runs rampant (and I told them this to no avail). The fact is that the Board did not abide by the Eighth Commandment in various instances. That is the reason why Bob Rahn said that the Board "acts without facts."

There are a good number of men with a loving and evangelical spirit who have volunteered to go with me or to provide written evidence to the Synod's Commission on Adjudication of serious harm done one way or another by Scaer, the President and the Board's concurrence. The fact that either Scaer and/or the President are completely unreconciled to pious men who have been harmed and offended by these two men should be a serious concern to the Board. The Scriptures insist that there should be reconciliation, but the Board does not even seem concerned about such a Biblical requirement. Instead, the Board simple closes one case after another, or terminates the service of one or another.

Though most of us hate confrontation, Scripture demands it. We must discover the real story firsthand, not get half-truths or fabrications. It tells us to "show him his fault" or to "reprove him." It does not judge in absentia and conduct kangaroo courts. It speaks the truth in love to a brother. It seeks recognition of those faults and a seeking of repentance and change. It also clarifies the alternatives. There are appropriate and inappropriate ways to handle these matters, but it is never easy to correct a brother.

Why has not a "conflict management group" been employed to come in to test the true convictions and opinions of Faculty, staff, and students in view of the autocratic and dictatorial atmosphere which is maintained by the Administration? The time for PR tactics and management of information is far past. There are few who will speak openly or allow their names to be attached because of fear of recrimination, and that fear is real on the basis of the experience of a good number of people who are long gone. After the District Presidents Committee was on campus in 1984, over 50% of the Faculty said that they had told the District Presidents that they were distressed over the administration of the President and the quality of training pastors at the Seminary. However, once again nothing was done about it.

I have in a determined manner kept this entire matter from the public so that it can be handled in a Biblical manner. I seek no embarrassment of anyone, and no "pound of flesh." In fact, I pray fervently that the President may be corrected and restored because he has much to offer the Seminary under a Biblical style of management. I urge you to read carefully EXHIBIT 22, "A Biblical Model or Paradigm or Prototype for Christian Relationships," and then focus on the conclusion. Let there be an end to political power plays. Let us be committed to spiritual procedures that edify, even while correcting — and to reconciliation on a Biblical basis...

Please keep in mind that I am only reacting to my experiences at the hands of Seminary personnel and the Board which had stood with it. If you feel that this is confrontational, try being an employee of the Seminary as many of us have experienced it. If I can force the moment of truth that will direct toward complete reconciliation on the part of everyone, I am even willing to be misunderstood and misrepresented. I can only conclude that the Seminary administration wants separation, not reconciliation, by their words and actions. What I have written in the Memo to President Preus is important for the BOR to consider at this time.

This Memo is my formal request of the Board of Regents to look at this entire issue with open minds and eyes, and to deal Biblically and openly with the matter. This is one more attempt evangelically and pastorally to get a solution to this matter at this level, rather than going to the Synod's Commission on Adjudication. I ask that this matter not be delayed, but that it be treated in a Biblical and responsible way at the January Board meeting. This matter has continued to fester far too long.

May God in His grace give us a Biblical and responsible solution now.

A wounded healer, Waldo J. Werning

*   *   *   *   *   *   *

I attempted through above letter and phone calls to get the officers of the BOR to allow me to speak to them at the January meeting, then again at the March meeting, but this was denied. This letter was simply ignored.

On Feb. 20, 1989, I wrote to Indiana District President Reuben Garber with a copy to Dr. Preus, "On January 19, a message on my answering machine service at my office requested a phone call to a pastor in the city. In my subsequent call to him, he told me that he was disturbed that certain professors at the Seminary are criticizing my new book, as some seminary students told him. Later he stopped in my office and began with the startling statement that somebody ought to put a sign up in front of the Seminary that states, 'The Spirit of God is not welcome here'...He said that some seminary students who come with an evangelistic spirit have it squelched...A member of the Seminary Alumni Board who attended one of my recent seminars told me that he had been lied to...This is a matter of sinful acts against various people, which have not been admitted or recognized, that are an offense to the Seminary community and general church...

The letter continues, "It is as though our dear friend Robert Preus is two people: one a wonderful person with unusual and exceptional talents and interests in Biblical theology and in missions with many followers who have been rightfully gained because of wonderful deeds; the other person is brutally political, shows partiality and favoritism, is mean-spirited, annihilates workers simply because they do not play his political games and bow down to him. Thus we have a terrible enigma, which is difficult to face emotionally and psychologically...(Note: The following charges had documentation, which is deleted because it is printed later in this Chapter.):...1. DR. ROBERT PREUS HAS DEFENDED AND STOOD WITH DR. DAVID SCAER IN HIS SINFUL ACTIONS WHICH ARE NAMED IN ALL OF THE ENCLOSED DOCUMENTATION....2. DR. ROBERT PREUS SUPPORTS CONFUSION AND PERVERSION OF BIBLICAL DOCTRINE, AND THUS IS GUILTY OF FALSE DOCTRINE IN THE AREAS OF THE CONTROVERTED CHRISTOLOGY STATEMENT AND ALSO THE MATTER OF OBJECTIVE AND SUBJECTIVE JUSTIFICATION RELATED TO THE OFFICE OF THE KEYS AND CONFESSIONS IN THE AREA OF CONFESSION-ABSOLUTION AND REPENTANCE-FORGIVENESS, AND THEIR PLACE IN THE LIFE OF SANCTIFICATION AND A LACK OF BALANCE BETWEEN LAW AND GOSPEL...3. DR. ROBERT PREUS DOES NOT OBEY THE INJUNCTIONS OF MATTHEW 18 BUT RATHER UTILIZES POLITICAL CAMPAIGNS TO ACHIEVE HIS AIMS...4. DR. ROBERT PREUS SUPPORTED THE BREAKING OF THE 8TH COMMANDMENT AND BROKE THE 8TH COMMANDMENT HIMSELF...5. DR. ROBERT PREUS IS NOT RECONCILED TO A NUMBER OF MEN, WHOM HE HAS TREATED BADLY, SHABBILY, AND TOGETHER WITH THEIR RELATIVES AND FRIENDS SAY THAT THEY WERE TREATED IN AN UNGODLY AND UNCHRISTIAN MANNER (KNOWN ALSO BY MANY FACULTY MEMBERS). 6. MANY OF THE PREVIOUSLY MENTIONED POINTS INDICATE A VINDICTIVENESS, JUST LIKE DR. SCAER, WHICH HAS REAPED HAVOC ON THE SHIELDS, GARCIAS, WILBERTS, SCHMIDTS, TEPKERS, ROSINS, AND NOW WERNINGS...I am not willing that this matter be delayed any longer. As far as I am concerned, it must be handled in terms of days and weeks, not months or years. I have delayed going to the Synod's Commission on Adjudication only to allow one more chance to settle it immediately...(All the points included documentation)." There was no action by the BOR.

On Feb. 28, 1989, I wrote a letter to District President Garber with copies to Dr. Preus and Dr. Scaer, sharing again the concerns of the continued and mounting assault that they were conducting. On March 10, 1989, I wrote to President Garber with copies to Preus and Scaer, telling him that "in a long distance telephone visit with a host pastor for one of my seminars that he said that at a Pastoral Conference that morning that one of the pastors said, 'that Werning had brought charges against Dr. David Scaer for false doctrine, etc...The pastor was wondering what it's all about..' There's no need to try to track down how John Pless learned about it, but I do know that he had written for the Seminary CTQ and has other connections with Dr. Scaer and others at the Seminary. Once again, we see that the public has been brought in, and I am not sure what role they are expected to play - advocates, arbitrars, gossipers, supporters? This breaks every principle which Christ has set for us and it presents a grave problem: Do I now answer in the Stewardship Seminar in Minneapolis in two weeks? Do I give this pastor the truth about the entire matter and let him announce it to the Pastoral Conference? By what Biblical right does anyone in public have the right to be involved by Scaer, Preus or anyone? Who knows how many all over Synod know about this because of the grapevine and networking that comes out of Dorm A and the Administration of the Seminary?"

Faculty Disobedience Led by Dr. Preus

During the middle of March, I was told by some faculty members that the Preus faculty pipeline was saying that there may be a resolution of censure against me at a faculty meeting. At that time, I contacted District President Garber and Board Chairman Ray Joeckel to tell them that if they allowed that, I would personally hold them and the Synod responsible for any slander that happened. I asked for protection which my Synod membership guarantees according to the LCMS Constitution.

On March 28, 1989, Garber hand-delivered a letter to me, as he did to Dr. Preus and Dr. Scaer, officially requesting the faculty not to discuss the Scaer-Werning matter in any way. The BOR held a telephone conference meeting on March 27. They asked Dr. Preus to immediately place the following in the the the hands of the Faculty: "The Board of Regents is deeply disturbed to learn that information regarding the disagreement between CTS administration and Dr. Waldo Werning has been rather widely disseminated. This is a serious breach of ethics even by secular standards, and is certainly contrary to the manner in which our Lord Jesus asked us to deal with a Christian brother. We, therefore, respectfully urge and request that you refrain from further discussion regarding this matter..."

On March 30, 1989, I wrote to Chairman Joeckel and Garber, "Thank you very much for the hand-delivered March 28, 1989, letter delivered by President Garber early Wednesday morning, March 29. I am glad to have in hand a statement which is also to go to the Faculty that the Board 'intends to deal with this matter fully, appropriately, and in a timely manner'....I feel completely assured from my visits with President Garber that the Board sees the network of all these basic considerations in their entirety in order to make CTS function in a healthy manner once again..."

On Apr. 18, I was informed that the Faculty in a meeting of April 17, 1989, passed the following resolution, "We reject as unfounded and untrue the description of the actions and character of the BOR, the President, the Academic Dean, the faculty of Concordia Theological Seminary, which Rev. Waldo Werning has disseminated..." The secret ballot tabulated: 13 affirmative; 1 negative; 8 abstentions. On April 25, 1989, I wrote to the Board of Regents telling about this rebellious incident, saying, "...Dr. Preus' failure to obey the 8th Commandment, and the requirements of Matthew 18 presents open rebellion against the BOR. District President Garber told me on Sunday, April 23 that Dr. Preus had sent a copy of the Resolution to the BOR, but he did not send me anything. Now this is a formal request that the BOR assure me that this Faculty Resolution will be forever deleted from the Minutes and proper substitution of Minutes be made so that all who have the Minutes will have this slanderous Resolution deleted..."

An April 18, 1989, Memo to the CTS Board of Regents exposes the lies which Dr. Preus entertained in that motion and the problems that it created: 1. There was no evidence that Werning made any unfounded and untrue descriptions of the actions and character of the BOR, the President, the Academic Dean, and the Faculty, and that nothing of the sort ever included the BOR and the Faculty (Note: the transcript of the Synodical Adjudication meeting shows that I questioned five faculty members, including Prof. Marquart, and that not one of them could identify any documentation that they had received, nor any descriptions that were untrue; these faculty members were also asked where they got their materials, and they said from Dr. Preus and the Seminary administration, not from Werning.); 2. The resolution contained another lie that I had disseminated it, whereas it was

Preus and Scaer who did this; 3. It was open rebellion against the BOR, who had ordered the Faculty not to discuss this matter, because the Board was dealing with it. Indeed, the Faculty heard Dr. Preus saying at the meeting, "The Board cannot tell this Faculty what to do. It is lame duck Board."

Eight different faculty members wrote letters which are in the Adjudication exhibits, of which short excerpts are reproduced here: "...I immediately began to feel very uncomfortable since just days before I had received the CTS BOR letter which was addressed not only to me, but to all faculty members...Not the business of the Faculty, and that we as individuals and as Faculty should refrain from carrying on further discussion on the matter...I found myself in a most uncomfortable position...Before the discussion could go any further I immediately asked for the floor and strongly suggested that it was out of order...My point of view was overruled by the Chairman(Preus)...It was a moral dilemma for me to be asked to make a judgment about Dr. Werning on the basis of undesignated documents which to the best of my knowledge I had never seen...It was unethical to discuss matters which concerned Dr. Werning without him being given the opportunity to be present to explain his side of the situation and to defend himself..."

Other professors wrote, "I was very uncomfortable as the CTS Faculty was being backed into what I felt was an unethical corner...In the end, a vote was forced...The discussion and subsequent vote on the resolution required that I compromise given loyalties...A violation of conscience and would harmfully divide the Faculty...The Faculty was asked to pass a resolution rejecting information that I was not in possession of...The question constantly running through my mind during the April 17 meeting was, 'How many of us have spoken directly to Dr. Werning about these concerns?' I believe that the April 17 meeting created a tragic and unnecessary breach within the Faculty and as a Faculty toward Dr. Werning...A number of faculty members objected because the Board of Regents' letter prohibited such an action...Dr. Preus was very adamant concerning the Board letter and instructed the Faculty to ignore it..."

The Professors continued, "Dr. Preus spoke of Rev. Werning in a derogatory fashion...I felt ashamed...I felt I was treated with a lack of respect by Preus who was visibly at odds with the vote. Dr. Preus indicated we lacked the courage/backbone to support the resolution. He chastised those who disagreed with his position...I was saddened to learn he had so much animosity toward Rev. Werning and those faculty members who disagreed with his (Preus') stance...I felt very uncomfortable...The Faculty had been instructed by the Board of Regents to refrain...Clearly in violation of the order of the Board of Regents...Also in violation of the most essential mandates of Christian love, in that a brother (Dr. Werning) was condemned without personal attempts at understanding and reconciliation. My signature to this open letter indicates my own displeasure in the method in which the Faculty addressed this matter...I had not received the statements, nor had I read them. The methods used to coerce votes against Dr. Werning from those of us who had not been informed caused me to abstain."

On Sept. 20, 1989, I addressed the following letter to the Faculty:

"Dear Brothers and Co-Workers in Christ:

On April 17, 1989, the Faculty passed a Resolution with some negatives, many abstentions, and several absences, which criticized me in a Biblically unjust manner. I was not given the courtesy of getting a copy of this unfortunate Resolution, but some faculty members with burdened consciences inquired whether I knew that I had been judged **in absentia** and without my knowledge. Since the Scriptures require that accusers must face the accused personally and with facts, this April 17 action cannot stand before Biblical scrutiny, and must certainly be an unrighteous act before the throne of God. Furthermore, the President and the Faculty had been informed specifically by the ecclesiastical authorities (the BOR) that they were not to enter into this matter which was properly before the BOR. This is a Matthew 18 action, which requires careful direction from the Word of God.

This matter is now before the Synod's Commission on Adjudication, and it would seem that the Faculty would not want to continue to be involved in a matter in which an action was in direct disobedience to the authorized authority of the church, the Biblical procedure, and the facts which are known by the Board of Regents and the Commission on Adjudication in over 300 pages of documents with about 50 exhibits.

I would be pleased to learn that the Faculty has rescinded the April 17 motion and forever deleted it from the Minutes, and that even that motion to rescind would not be entered into the Minutes. Where there is confession of sin and repentance, there is forgiveness and absolution in Christ.

I ask all of you as dear co-workers and brothers in Christ to join me to 'speak the truth in love' (Eph. 4:15) and to 'give an answer...with gentleness and respect' (1 Pet. 3:15). 'Let all things be done to edify' (1 Cor. 14:26) and let us do only 'that which is good to the use of edifying' (Eph. 4:29).

Yours in Christ, our Savior and Lord, Waldo J. Werning"

*   *   *   *   *   *

There was no answer at any time from Dr. Preus or the Faculty as a body. **UNRESOLVED ERRORS - UNFINISHED BUSINESS:** Once again, I announce publicly - this time in a published book - that I will not allow this slander and breaking of the 8th Commandment to stand as a public record, and request the Faculty and the Board of Regents formally to rescind this motion and to forever delete it from the Minutes! If they fail to do so, then I request the appropriate Synodical officials to perform their responsible duty toward this Faculty.

May 20, 1989 Board Of Regents Meeting

What was the reaction of the BOR against whom Dr. Preus was disobedient and rebelled in saying that the Board could not tell the Faculty what to do? Obviously, the most ardent Preus supporter would have to admit that this was cause for immediate dismissal. Instead, the Board took a step to try to get Dr. Preus to retire honorably. The former Chairman of the Board spoke with Dr. Preus a number of times over a long period of time to encourage him to do so. This is what the Board did: At its May 20, 1989, meeting, the Board invited me to make a presentation to them in the presence of Dr. Preus, Dr. Scaer, and Secretary Trudy Behning. In the middle of my presentation, Dr. Preus snickered and was making motions of ridicule(which was not just a nervous reaction), and I called this to the attention of the Chairman, who did nothing. I gave the Board a nine-page document entitled, "Issues Presented to the BOR, CTS, FW, May 20, 1989 from Waldo J. Werning." An introduction states, "This accompanies previous enclosures sent to the BOR with several letters and over 40 exhibits related to offenses related to Dr. David P. Scaer and Dr. Robert D. Preus. This document summarizes the issues under consideration. Instead of going to the Synod's Commission on Adjudication after the Nov. 12, 1988 Board meeting, I chose to give all parties one more chance, which now awaits the action of the Board of Regents...This is presented humbly by the grace of God with the compelling conviction that I have no other choice to pursue in this matter..." I asked for action before the July Wichita Convention, hopefully at this meeting.

Former Academic Dean Howard Tepker asked me to share a statement from him with the Board, which follows:

[Howard Tepker: "I want this shared with the BOR, because I have a stake in this, too." 5/20/89]:

"A Look at the Situation at CTS, Fort Wayne Ind..

My concern in the case of Dr. Waldo Werning has to do for the most part with the spiritual and doctrinal implications that are involved. Every pastor must become concerned when Christians give offense to other Christians and when a pastor brings charges against another pastor, especially when such charges are as serious as those which Dr. Werning has brought against the present administration at Concordia Theological Seminary in Fort Wayne. My concerns focus especially on the following facts:

(1) The faculty at the Fort Wayne Seminary has experienced frustrations, uncertainty concerning its future, fear of reprisal, on the part of the administration, and even a measure of resentment for more than five years. Numerous members of the faculty and their families have been hurt by the arbitrary action of certain administrators. Dr. Waldo Werning is only the latest to be go through this painful experience. As the Board knows there have been a number of attempts made to ease the tension and restore peace. These include pastoral visitations by the President of Synod and on two separate occasions by District Presidents. The Association of Theological Schools and the North Central Association — our accrediting agencies — conducted an investigation and reported a serious morale problem on campus. Still nothing seems to have changed over the years. The Board has letters and documents to verify these facts.

(2) I am not sure that the seminary administration fully understands and appreciates the hurt which it has inflicted on some faculty members and their families. It is so easy to reduce these problems to the administrative level and conclude that the president and the academic dean are within their rights as administrators when they seek to reduce tensions and frustrations by dismissing members of the faculty instead of listening to their concerns. It is so easy to regard threats and aggressive acts on the part of an administrator as innocent personality traits or see them as evidence of strong leadership. It is easy to see such tactics as necessary if there is to be unity on a faculty. But in the opinion of some respected members of the faculty such aggressive actions often have spiritual and doctrinal implications.

(3) The members of the faculty are divided on the question whether or not certain administrators have committed offenses that require repentance and reconciliation. This raises the important question: "When is an offense against a brother so serious that the offender should feel constrained to confess his sin and ask the brother's forgiveness?" All of us know that we Christians ordinarily overlook many of the offenses that are committed against us. But Scripture and the Lutheran Confessions clearly teach that there are sins which endanger one's faith. When is an offense so serious that repentance is called for? Apparently members of the faculty have different answers to that question. That is one of the issues facing the faculty at the seminary.

(4) In such cases where the members of the faculty disagree, the Board of Regents has a special responsibility to assist the faculty in arriving at a God-pleasing answer. The Board must ask itself whether it has faced up to that responsibility. Fortunately, Luther provided help in his Small Catechism when he states: 'Before God we should plead guilty of all sins, even of those which we do not know, as we do in the Lord's Prayer, but before the pastor (or before our brother whom we have offended) we should confess those sins which

we know and feel in our hearts? Now what kind of sins should trouble us and lead us to go to a brother and repent? Luther again answers: 'Here consider your station according to the Ten Commandments.' This implies among other things that especially those who are in positions of authority such as father, mother, master, mistress and (we could add Seminary President, Academic Dean, Board of Regents, pastor, etc.) have certain responsibilities toward those over whom they exercise authority. Among them is the relevant point that they should be ready and willing to confess their faults if 'they have grieved any person by word or deed.''

Dr. Werning has brought charges against two members of the administration accusing them of sinning against the eighth commandment, deliberately and willfully attempting to destroy his reputation. That charge cannot be passed over lightly. If true, it requires that the offender confess his sins and ask God's forgiveness, but does he feel in his heart the necessity to confess his faults also to the brother whom he has offended, and will he also try to change his way of dealing with his Christian brethren?

Since the faculty is divided on this question, may I respectfully suggest:

(1) That a careful study be made of Matthew 18 to determine proper procedure when offense has been given. Decisions in a case such as Dr. Werning's must not be based solely on the Synodical Handbook.

(2) That the results of this study be used to bring about reconciliation between the members of the faculty and the administration.

(3) That a study be made of Synod's doctrine of the divine call, and that the seminary's practice be brought into conformity with our doctrine.

It is my sincere hope that the Board can at this time take such appropriate action as will bring about true reconciliation between all members of the faculty and the administration. We should be willing to settle for nothing less.'' Howard W. Tepker

*   *   *   *   *   *   *   *

What was the Board's action on May 20, 1989? Though I came to present the issues of the document which I gave to everyone present, I was told by the Board Chairman that they were wondering whether I would consider going back to Preus and Scaer one more time to see whether this matter could be settled. Why should I go back to them, when the Board absolved Scaer in the Nov. 12 Resolution, closed their eyes to his clever political maneuvers between Sept. 10 and Nov. 12, 1988, and allowed Dr. Preus to sit there before them without having reprimanded him for his rebellion against the Board in the April 17, 1989, Faculty meeting? It was so incomprehensible to me that I came to the obvious conclusion that either this Board was unwilling or incapable of facing documentation or the reality related to its responsibility. Several times, the former Board Chairman continued to ask whether I would go back and deal with Preus and Scaer again, so finally I stated, "I was not elected to do the work of this Board. It is your responsibility, not mine."

I wrote several letters to the BOR to verify what did and did not happen at my May 20 appearance with them. On July 3, 1989, I sent a 19-page document to the BOR entitled, "Crisis of Leadership Created By Seminary President Robert D. Preus and Academic Dean David P. Scaer at CTS, FW." Several quotations, "This document is basically a summary of the May 20, 1989, issues presented to the BOR, CTS, FW. Several critical items which were excluded from that document are added, and this is updated for the crisis faced by the BOR and the Synod itself by continued actions by Preus and his allies. This report is based upon previous enclosures sent to the BOR with various letters and over forty exhibits related to the offenses by Dr. Scaer and Dr. Preus. It should be noted that if anyone complains about the amount of materials (one-hundred-fifty to two-hundred pages), the reason for this is the inaction of the BOR between November 12, 1988 to May 20, 1989...My May 24, 1989, letter, to the BOR together with my report said to the Board about the May 20 meeting, 'Crisis created by the Board of Regents on May 20, 1989, CTS, FW,' was very prophetic in view of the current political action on the part of President Preus and his army in organizing the Synod to fight the BOR. The current war by the Preus faction was predictable in view of the Board's decision to face Dr. Preus on May 19 and 20 with another political approach of retirement rather than spiritual of repenting of ethical errors and sins of rebellion. The motivation of the Board undoubtedly was right, but the action invited a continued high intensity political war which was engineered by Dr. Preus (and Dr. Scaer) within the faculty and the Seminary within the past five years, and now within the Synod itself.'

The July 3 letter added more: "**The current crisis situation**: Two weeks ago President Preus sent a two-page letter to the faculty presenting his version of the Executive Session and actions of the BOR on May 20, together with the resolution which was defeated according to his report, 3-4. As in the past, this was a signal for writing another statement of support for Dr. Preus, and circulating it throughout the faculty — this time by Professors Kurt Marquart and Arthur Just...As reported previously, it is no secret that Dr. Preus has shared the fact that he has friends and allies named by the Commission on Nominations as nominees for the BOR who are willing do his bidding....Obviously, he is counting on the new Board to ignore evidence and facts, and to rule politically as he has in the past.

"Apparently the new Faculty statement for Preus was signed by only one-third of the men, while many felt totally pressured and coerced, so this was withdrawn. Of course, the Board Members know through the phone calls and letters which they have been receiving from the field that the Preus faculty members and Preus army have been very active on the phone in the Synod to get pastors to write and phone Board Members to try to influence their views. This Preus' publicity has also been fanned by a letter to the Alumni and the convention delegates. This is totally predictable on the basis of the method of operation of the past by Dr. Preus. Can you begin to imagine the pressure and intimidation of the faculty by this political engineer?...We simply dare not put out fires with fire, or stop political campaigns by another political move of getting a retirement or dismissing a man without gaining corrections of wrongs.

The spiritual, Biblical level is the only solution to this tragedy and dilemma which faces us today. Indeed, I prophesy that if the Board does not deal with this on a spiritual level soon, there will be such a fire that the Board will find it almost impossible to deal with on the offensive in a Biblical manner.'"

NOTE: LOOK AT WHAT HAD HAPPENED BETWEEN JULY, 1989 AND APRIL, 1992, AND WE SEE THAT MY PREDICTION WAS ABSOLUTELY ON TARGET. THERE IS AS GREAT A POLITICAL AND PAPER WAR CONDUCTED BY THE "CONFESSIONAL LUTHERANS" NOW AS THE ELIMITES DID 18 YEARS AGO — BOTH USING THE SAME TACTICS AND BOTH GETTING AWAY FROM THE REAL ISSUES AND TRUTH AND BOTH GETTING INTO A PROCEDURAL WAR. PLEASE RECOGNIZE THAT IT WAS BIBLICALLY CORRECT FOR THE BOR TO TERMINATE OR RETIRE DR. PREUS. THEY HAD VOLUMES OF EVIDENCE WHICH THEY KEPT TO THEMSELVES. BUT THE TACTIC OF "HONORABLE RETIREMENT" INSTEAD OF TERMINATING HIM FOR CAUSE HAS BEEN USED AS A PLOY OR SUBTERFUGE FIRST BY DR. PREUS AND THEN BY HIS PARTY TO ACT AS IF THEY HAD SOME KIND OF VALID ISSUE.

My July 3, 1989 document to the BOR continued, "Dr. Tepker's references and experiences are affirmed by others that Dr. Preus **rules the Seminary by the 'Kingdom of the Left' " - by law and not by grace.** Not only has an **autocratic managerial style** been his method of operation, but it has been administered in a god-like fashion without any semblance of a proper use of the Eighth Commandment and Matthew 18. His 'Kingdom of the Left' theology of the church and its practices must be challenged as being un-Biblical...Now the July 3, 1989, issue of *CN*, pages 7-8, conveys the 'Preus Story', together with copies of three letters from Indiana pastors to President Garber — all a gross breaking of the Eighth Commandment and Matthew 18. It is noteworthy that Dr. Preus has the use of *Accord* (sister publication of *Affirm*) which published a highly selective and slanted story that is a classical political campaign which is daring and carnal, bizarre and scandalous. Frankly, it is an expected response from Dr. Preus to any Board request for him to retire, as he can survive only on a political field. It is noteworthy that the *Accord article uses nothing but* **ad hominem** arguments...

"A diseased body with diseased members require a surgeon who knows when to prescribe the right thing and when to operate when necessary. Intervention is required in a drastic way because the Seminary faculty as a body has been infected by a severe virus which requires that the two principals (Preus and Scaer) together with such "legmen" as Professor Arthur Just and Professor Dean Wenthe and now Professor Kurt Marquart who have been out selling professors on the need to sign statements and to provide support must realize that they have been part of a carnal political machine totally outside of Biblical procedures.

"The faculty and its members, have been so severely hurt emotionally, psychologically, and spiritually during these years of political bondage and battering, that it would be wise to offer **intervention counseling** where Biblical procedures are followed and total Biblical reconciliation is experienced with all of us included, and no one excluded. Those who have been victimized need love, comfort and encouragement. The faculty has experienced trauma as a body which has undergone a raging virus unattended for too long a time, and which needs radical treatment...

Since I could have and should have gone to higher courts of Synod after the November 12th Board meeting, but patiently gave all parties another opportunity if any actions which are appropriately expected are not taken, I will begin with the Synod's Commission on Adjudication the day after the next Board meeting. Please do not construe this as a threat, for it is not, nor is it an attempt to put on pressure. The Board needs to know simply that my patience at that time will have been tested beyond endurance. If it becomes necessary also to involve the Board, it should be known that since adjudication would undoubtedly go beyond the time of membership on the part of some Board members, the case would be brought against every individual member of the Board, not against the Board itself...May God give everyone the Christian faith, strength, wisdom, and grace to act in a manner that will bring correction and reconciliation through repentance and forgiveness by our precious Savior, Jesus Christ!"

On July 11, 1989 I wrote to the BOR, "Having spent two days at the Wichita Convention...at breakfast the first morning I was accosted by Dr. Carl and Dr. Anne Driessneck criticizing me bitterly for daring to complain about Dr. Preus, that I was all wrong and should stop now. They reminded me that they had all the facts, that I was doing harmful things to Dr. Preus and a disservice to the Synod and the Seminary. I reminded them that I had many pages of evidence. They said that they had not talked to Dr. Preus, but they had talked to people who had the facts and that the Board of Regents was doing a terrible thing.." (Note: This insistence by Preus allies that they have had the facts and that the Board of Regents does not has been carried on for 33 months now; it should be noted that in 1990 when Mrs. Driessneck saw me after chapel on the campus, before various witnesses who were shocked by her statements, she lectured me and asked what I was doing on the campus, and what right I had on the campus, because this is Dr. Preus' Seminary!)...My July 11, 1989 letter to the BOR continued, "Dr. Preus' letter to the delegates and to the Alumni was likewise disturbing...People all over the church were talking about this because Preus' friends on the faculty who were phoning and contacting especially pastors all the Synod to urge them to contact the Board of Regents."

Rev. Raymond Mueller

A very important part of this July 11, 1989, letter to the Board of Regents said, "Normally, I would withhold this information about contacts which my friend, Pastor Ray Mueller, BOR member, made with me, but the request was plainly a public one, and I will share it with you because it was very bothersome. On Friday morning at Wichita, Pastor Mueller came to me to ask me to pass the word around that if Dr. Robert Sauer was elected President that Robert Preus would retire and that there would be no blood-letting. Apparently, Pastor Mueller, a member of the Board, was involved with some kind of a deal with Dr. Preus. What was disconcerting was that on Saturday afternoon after President Bohlmann was re-elected, when I passed Pastor Mueller going to lunch, he said, 'Now Dr. Preus will be President for three more years.' After this sunk in a little and I found it shocking, I quickly ran after Pastor Mueller and asked him what he meant, and he simply walked off without saying a word." I did not realize until that moment that Pastor Mueller involved himself politically for Dr. Preus in this matter as he had.

It should be stated that in 1988 when the Synod's Standing Committee on Pastoral Ministry visited both Seminaries as a result of a 1986 Convention Resolution in order to learn how the congregations and the Synod can better support the Seminaries and how the Seminaries can better serve the congregations, that there was a very negative reaction from Dr. Preus and his allies. An article in the student publication, *Cornerstone*, caused some furor. The members of that Committee, including Dr. J. A. O. Preus, Dr. Wil Sohns representing the District Presidents, former District President Edwin Happel, and others visited the Seminary, while Dr. Preus brought to Fort Wayne Pastor Ray Mueller to be with them wherever they went. At the end of the faculty meeting where this visit was discussed, Dr. Preus said to five of his allies within the hearing of other faculty members that his contact man on the Board of Regents, Rev. Ray Mueller, will take care of this.

In January, 1989, I visited with Rev. Mueller for about 1 1/4 hours in the Seminary dining hall to encourage him to save Dr. Preus, and to get the Board to deal firmly but lovingly, and shared with him various things which he as a Board member should know. The only observation which he made about doing something was that if this gets out, Dr. Bohlmann will be re-elected in Wichita. I was shocked at his political attitude.

There was no answer to the July 11, 1989 letter to the BOR. About Sept. 1, 1990, over a year later, I learned that Pastor Mueller had allegedly written a letter to me and the BOR taking issue with what I had written in my July 11, 1989 letter. Had I not accidentally gotten it, I would not have known about this complete distortion. Mueller's July 25, 1989, letter to Werning and the Board of CTS recorded: "...Here are several statements which need to be clarified and/or corrected. First, Dr. Werning stated that my 'request was plainly a public one.' The facts are, that Dr. Werning told me - I took it to be in confidence - that some of the faculty at Fort Wayne were expressing the hope that Dr. Bohlmann would be re-elected as Synodical President since the election of Dr. Robert Sauer would guarantee that Dr. Robert Preus would remain President of our Seminary, a situation which Dr. Werning and these unnamed faculty members viewed as disastrous. Taking this concept as his basis for action, Dr. Werning was talking to delegates as they arrived in an attempt to persuade them to vote for Dr. Bohlmann. I happened to overhear Dr. Werning as he was speaking to two or three delegates along this line. Second, Dr. Werning's letter states that I asked him to 'pass the word around that if Dr. Robert Sauer was elected President, that Robert Preus would retire and that there would be no blood-letting.' That is an inaccurate report of my words. I did not use the word, 'would,' but the word, 'could'..."

On Sept. 5, 1990, I wrote to Pastor Ray Mueller with a copy to the BOR, "Last week I was shown a copy of a July 25, 1989, letter which you addressed to me and the BOR at the FW Seminary. I never received that letter and did not know it existed until last week, and I wonder why it would be in the hands of the BOR, and I did not get one when it is addressed also to me and it makes some very serious charges against me. You know very well that I respond to such issues in the church when I am involved, and I wonder why you did not contact me when you did not receive a response from me...It is obvious that the Board did not take it seriously. Thus my concern is with you and for making the record straight...It is true that you encouraged me to pass the word around that if Sauer was elected President, that Dr. Preus (would)(could) retire, etc. I heard 'would,' but if you say you said 'could,' I will not argue. I shared your thoughts with only a limited number of people and quoted you. I did not give it as my own idea."

I wrote, "It is a total fabrication when you wrote, 'the facts are that Dr. Werning told me - I took it to be in confidence - that some of the faculty in Fort Wayne were expressing the hope that Dr. Bohlmann would be re-elected as Synodical President, since the election of Dr. Robert Sauer would, etc..' Fact: I was not and am not for Bohlmann as President under any condition. I never heard from others or thought myself that Dr. Sauer's election would guarantee that Preus would remain as President (your letter that I didn't receive until now was the first that I heard or thought of something like that.)....I was for the election of Sauer...Provide me with the names of these delegates and if they will confirm what you said, I will face them with their lies."

I added, "In January of 1989, we sat for about an hour and a quarter in the dining hall of the Seminary when I related to you a number of things which Dr. Preus had done. Your only response at the conclusion was that this dare not get out and nothing be done because it will get Ralph Bohlmann elected at the July Convention."

Pastor Ray Mueller was at the Opening Service of the Seminary in Sept., 1990, and I asked him about and showed him a copy of his July 25, 1989 letter addressed to me and the BOR, and he said that he did not recall writing such a letter. I showed him what he wrote and he still could not recall. I gave him a copy of a new letter from me dated Sept. 5, 1990. I asked him when we could visit about it, and he said that he would phone me when he had time while in Fort Wayne, but he never did.

On Oct. 15, 1990, I wrote to Rev. Mueller, "Since you did not phone me while at the BOR meeting in early September, I was awaiting a letter or phone call from you soon after about the letter which I hand delivered to you about the problem raised by your letter of 1989: I believed that I would have heard from you weeks ago because this is not a small matter and not something to ignore. I cannot imagine that it would take that long to figure out how to respond. I await an early response from you regarding this issue..."

On Oct. 31, 1990, I wrote to Rev. Mueller, "I talked to you after the opening service at the Seminary in Fort Wayne on Sept. 9, at which time I gave you a copy of your July 25, 1989, letter to me and the Board...for five weeks you ignored this formal request for correction of your mistakes, so it became necessary for me to write you a letter dated October 15...I have not received an answer to that letter, which was sent over two weeks ago. Because of your failure not only to correct your mistakes, but not even to have the courtesy to answer two attempts to get a response from you, I have no other choice than making this the first step of Matthew 18 to confront you with your sins against me and others. For starters, I am requesting the following information: 1. Who are the delegates to whom

I was allegedly speaking as they arrived in an attempt to allegedly persuade them to vote for Dr. Bohlmann? 2. Who were the two or three delegates to whom I was allegedly speaking when you allegedly overheard such an alleged conversation? Find them and I will show you some liars. 3. Give me evidence that I was allegedly for Bohlmann as President, and not Sauer. 4. In view of the fact that the Synod's Commission on Adjudication found Dr. Preus guilty of breaking the 8th Commandment and Matthew 18 in two major areas (and this is not discussing the case but merely **reporting a decision**), and in view of the fact that my July 11, 1989, letter to the Board of Regents was part of my Matthew 18 process of trying to correct Dr. Preus, show me where your false allegation that I broke the 8th Commandment against Dr. Preus is true and accurate. Since when does following Matthew 18 in private channels in pursuing proper complaints constitute a breaking of the 8th Commandment?...'' (Note: Another longer paragraph in that letter exposes his denial of the Office of the Keys and Confession, as he did in his writing of the Nov. 12, 1988, Board resolution.)

On Dec. 3, 1990, I wrote Rev. Mueller another letter recounting all of my attempts made to get a personal visit or a telephone call or a letter from him, and added, "On Nov. 5, 1990, after the services in the Chapel, I sought you out to ask why I have not received any communication, and you told me, 'I will write you a letter soon.' It is now Dec. 3, 1990, and since you have not communicated personally by letter or by telephone, this letter is my announcement that I am starting Matthew 18 with you...I will be willing to come to Cleveland if that is necessary...I do not want this to drag out, for you have already delayed it for three months...''

On Jan. 7, 1991, I wrote to Ohio District President David Buegler, with a copy to Rev. Mueller, "Enclosed is correspondence initiated by the Rev. Raymond Mueller, pastoral member of the Ohio District, by a letter of false allegations dated July 25, 1989, to which he has not given response after repeated attempts by me to settle the matter in the Biblical manner...As distasteful as it is for me, I have no choice but to ask you as District President what steps I should take to get Rev. Raymond Mueller to make corrections in a Biblical manner...''

On Jan. 21, 1991, District President Buegler wrote to Rev. Mueller and me, "...I therefore stand ready to serve as a loving witness or arbitrator for truth's sake, should you both agree to a meeting with me. I much prefer, and believe, that you have it within your own mature Christian commitment to settle these matters without delay...''

On Feb. 11, 1991, I wrote to Rev. Mueller, "I assumed that I would hear from you after the letter from District President Buegler. I have a meeting in Hamilton, Ontario, and would be willing to take the much longer route via Cleveland, but I would be passing through Cleveland on Thursday morning, Feb. 21, any time between 9 a.m. and 12 noon. Since I have made all the contacts and have received no responses, I would be very happy to hear from you by telephone or a letter by return mail...''

On May 22, 1991, I wrote to Rev. Mueller, "Several times I talked with you personally and I wrote a number of letters to attempt to get the problem settled which was created by your breaking the 8th Commandment and slandering me in your July, 1989, letter...Last weekend several hours before the BOR met here in FW, I learned that the Board was meeting. I am wondering why you failed to contact me so that we could have a visit. It appears to me that you have no interest in erasing the sin you committed against me in breaking the 8th Commandment.' On May 30, 1991, I wrote to Rev. Mueller, "You were in Fort Wayne again several times during the past month and did not inform me beforehand or contact me in order to have a visit to discuss your sins against me...I thought that was the agreement also when you had a visit with Pres. Buegler...''

Since by this time the original guilty verdict against Dr. Preus in my case with the Synod's

Commission on Adjudication against Dr. Preus based on documentation had been overturned by the Synodical Commission on Appeals, and they had done it on the basis of a total untruth and deception, I had to make the decision that I would not subject myself to Rev. Mueller to an adjudication and appeals system that had been corrupted by men through dishonesty. Whatever else can be said, Rev. Mueller's refusal to communicate was a sinful neglect of obedience to Matthew 18 in a case where he was guilty of breaking the 8th Commandment. There are various other ones who should face their sins, but the Synod's adjudication process has been corrupted, so this scream of agony comes by the published page. This is the same Rev. Mueller who cannot recognize the documentation presented to him before the Board of Regents, but discounts it in favor of Dr. Preus and his allies. He is the same Rev. Mueller, who together with the new pastoral member of the Board of Regents, Rev. David Anderson, offered in July 1989 to the Board of Regents to make an investigation of the Preus matter by themselves and report to the Board.

Charges Sent to Commission on Adjudication

Getting back to 1989, on Aug. 7, 1989, I wrote to the LCMS Commission on Adjudication and brought charges against Dr. Preus, Dr. Scaer, and also the Board of Regents for failing to act and failing to protect the rights of this pastor. In December, 1989, I had a meeting with two Board representatives and and decided to treat the matter delicately, and because it was a newly constituted Board, to forgive them and accept an ambiguous statement as a settlement.

The July Convention issue of *Accord* (companion to *Affirm*) carried an article which was reproduced twice in *CN* to tell about the May 20, 1989, meeting of the BOR: "The Fort Wayne Story - a story of attempts to remove Dr. Robert Preus from the Presidency of Concordia Theological Seminary - is one of intrigue, and insinuation, rumor-mongering, secret meetings, selected 'leaks' of Board of Regents actions...it is no exaggeration that the report spread like wildfire through the Synod...on the basis of the resolution **and facts provided by Dr. Preus**, we have pieced together the following account..." The insinuation was that BOR members made selective "leaks," which is not true at all. After several hours faculty members knew about this May 20 meeting action and it spread throughout the Synod and some of the pastors who called stated that they had been phoned by faculty members to tell them about it. Dr. Preus himself was quoted in some places, even stating which Board members voted for and against him. Dr. Preus branded as a "fabrication" the Board statement that the Board "has become convinced that the Faculty of CTS is divided and that there is turmoil within the faculty and staff to such an extent that Dr. Preus is no longer able to serve effectively as President of said institution." Read the extensive documentation of this book and try to convince any court or jury in our country that Dr. Preus and *CN* were not guilty of doing the fabricating.

Degner's Letter

Dr. Preus also stated that no faculty member had ever spoken to him or contacted him to tell about their disagreements. There were definitely some, such as Dr. Waldemar Degner, who wrote Dr. Preus on July 1, 1989, "Please permit me to reply to your letter of June 19, in which you request help from your colleagues 'during this time.' Though we have already talked about these issues privately, the need for making this more formal response to your request arises from the fact that another letter is being circulated amongst the faculty which, while seeking to support you in your office, yet involves methods and draws conclusions which I cannot support...Word has just reached me that the designated letter may not be sent to the BOR for lack of support among the faculty...as I stated to you orally, I would urge you to accept the resolution of the BOR without demur. I reminded you in our chat in your office that your Biblical and confessional theology will probably be enhanced by your willing submission to the Board's wishes..."

Degner continues, "Should you choose to refuse to submit to the Board's will and strive to retain your present office, only your own personal desires can be satisfied, but much harm accrue to the Seminary, the Synod and the cause of confessional Lutheran theology...I can think of any number of charges which may be directed against you in this Seminary should you choose to follow your own path. People will not only charge you with violating the 4th Commandment of the Decalogue by not heeding the will of the Board, but they will also bring up many other matters: They may charge you with excessive absentee-ism from campus; with permitting doctrinal and practical deviations at the Seminary; with engaging in excessive politicking in Synod; with failure to provide leadership in curricular construction at the Seminary to meet the changing conditions in theological education; with tolerating and abetting a kind of sacerdotalism at the Seminary which ill-equips our students to work well in parish settings...The pervasive hatred which seems to motivate and direct so many administrative actions at the Seminary and throughout the Synod may be compared to children playing with matches beside an open gas can...My fervent prayer is that you will do the God-pleasing thing, and that your true legacy to the church - your confessional theology - may not be lost through fleshly pursuits."

Post-July 1989

The summer of 1989 was a very intense one for the Synod, as the Preus party began to claim the high ground of "Confessional Lutherans," who organized with greater precision to fight the "demon," Ralph Bohlmann, alleged false doctrine against anyone who disagreed with them, and that there is a grand design to close the Fort Wayne Seminary. This has been orchestrated to a high pitch in the past year. By the end of 1989, not only I, but such orthodox conservative stalwarts as Dr. Degner and Dr. Eugene Klug were approached by recent graduates of the Seminary to tell them that they heard in the field that they had turned liberal (obviously, because they did not join the Preus party).

By late summer, 1989, my May 20, 1989, document given to the Board of Regents, Dr. Preus and Dr. Scaer, was summarized in *CN*. Such propaganda without objections from Dr. Preus was so blatant that I wrote the following, which was published in the Sept. 11, 1989 *CN*.

Statement of Conscience

When Biblical procedures are not followed, all kinds of problems are created. When the 8th Commandment and Matthew 18 are violated, all kinds of false assumptions, guestimates, and slander are presented by uninformed persons to an unsuspecting public as legitimate views via written word, telephone or personal visits in matters in which God has not called them to speak. Having been named on several pages of the August 7, 1989, *CN* (pages 4 and 10) in the Dr. R. Preus matter, I must ask the reader to withhold judgment against me and the FW Seminary Board of Regents and about the generalizations in support of Dr. Preus. There is evidence of uninformed or misinformed judgments and half-truths that are untenable. I refuse to enter the cesspool of the untamed tongue and refuse to prove or disprove anything in the public area even though there is slander involved. I will not attempt to defend my name by entering the same unbiblical arena as the uninformed critics, but continue to follow the spiritual procedures of Matthew 18 which

Christ has imposed upon faithful Christians. I am not answerable to ecclesiastical guerrilla fighters, but to the authority of Christ's church. God has not authorized me or any other complainant to hold public court. May I plead with my brothers to obey Christ, "Do not judge, or you will be judged. For in the same way you judge others, you will be judged, and with the same measure you use, it will be measured to you" (Matt. 7:1-2).

There will be an appropriate time when the facts as they pertain to me will be revealed on the basis of Biblical principles. Until that time I am exercising patience. I practice privately what I have written publicly in *Renewal For the 21st Century Church*, pages 35-36 and 111-116. As for the reader and editor, I ask for the Gospel's sake, before you speak or write or publish, please be sure God has ordained you to be His spokesman and that you have exhausted all Scriptural channels and procedures.

I pray for a halt to Biblically unauthorized wagging of tongues and also of wiggling of pens in printed pages. I also pray for confession that leads to absolution and repentance that leads to forgiveness in Christ.

Waldo J. Werning, Fort Wayne IN, Aug. 9, 1989

*   *   *   *   *

Rev. Robert Schaibley Imposes Himself

On Sept. 15, 1989, I received a letter from Dr. Scaer's pastor, Rev. Robert Schaibley, in which he complained that portions of my May 20, 1989, document to the BOR were printed in *CN* with reference to objectionable and unChristian ways of one of his members in good standing. It is a lengthy letter, so I will just summarize a few points. He recognizes that I did not desire that these documents be made public, but "the case that those statements have been made public, to the hurt, damage, and detriment of Dr. Scaer." Schaibley wrote that he held me responsible for this damage, and he would not stand idly by and have one of his members in good standing be vilified. He now claimed that I had made **public charges** that were unfounded, incorrect and harmful because he had conducted pastoral consultation with Scaer during the past three days, and he asserted with a clear conscience that my charges were unfounded and incorrect. That is no surprise, because he did not sit down with me and look at the full documentation.

In response to Schaibley's letter, I wrote on Sept. 19, 1989, "...1. The matter of Dr. David P. Scaer is now before the LCMS Commission on Adjudication based on proper procedures of the church established according to Biblical confessional standards. 2. This has been an 8th Commandment and Matthew 18 issue from the very beginning, as can easily be determined by those who are involved according to Biblical procedures. 3. I am not responsible for any of the rumors or the publication of a Matthew 18 and 8th Commandment procedure which have been divulged in varying public forums. My documentation provides evidence as to which people are the source of these 'selective leaks.' ...I telephoned the (C.N.) Editor several times to plead with him not to print anything about this seminary situation, and that Matthew 18 and the 8th Commandment had been broken to make it appear that this is a public matter...You did not first seek to discuss the matter with me, but made a false judgment on selected information which you had. I had no knowledge that you were holding court against me in an unBiblical fashion which resulted in your judgment against me..."

On Sept. 26, 1989, Rev. Schaibley continued his insistence that he had a right to intrude into the adjudication process at the congregational level, writing, "I am dealing with the public airing of complaints which you happened to raise before the Board or Regents last

May and which came to public notice this month...I am addressing the damage which results from the publication of charges, purporting to come from you, which relate to David Scaer as a member of Zion...I am fully aware of the fact that these things came to public light through unauthorized channels. Indeed, others are involved as the source of this damage...you are in fact responsible for the consequences of 'rumors,' as you call them, whether you valiantly sought to squelch them or not!...Meanwhile, we now have another little problem between us, namely your false and injurious accusation against me (which you sent on to the Board of Adjudication, thus violating the 8th Commandment and Matthew 18 over against me!)...I did not come to judgment over against you in my last letter...P. S. I also ask you to keep your copies of both of our letters in a file, privately, with the exception of the now necessary apology concerning your false charges against me which you raised appropriately to me, but then sent(inappropriately) to the Commission on Adjudication...I'm sure that your files provide safe storage for these documents should you feel the need to bring them to light in the future.' The time has come to bring them to light because Rev. Schaibley kept on the attack as you will see in the information that continues.

On October 5, 1989, I wrote to Rev. Schaibley, "...I am not responsible, nor will I be held responsible for anything that appears in *CN* or is shared by anyone through any channels because I have been holding carefully to Biblical procedures of the 8th Commandment and will continue to do so. Your concerns about public airing of complaints and of damage which results from the publication of charges must obviously be dealt with the publisher of those matters...You should be assured that the answers to the questions you raise are the issues before the LCMS Commission on Adjudication..."

On Oct. 6, 1989, Rev. Schaibley wrote, "The time has come for me to move on with this difficult but necessary responsibility concerning the damage that has been done to the reputation to David Scaer, and therefore indirectly to the congregation in which he communes, by public allegations for which you are substantially, albeit certainly not solely, responsible...Unless you publicly express your regret to Dr. Scaer for suffering caused to him due to this manner in which a dispute between the two of you has surfaced publicly...you have since also ignored my second letter(Note: you just read part of my Oct. 5 letter to him)...I now insist on the necessity to deal with this matter face-to-face in the company of at least one other member of my congregation...I will wait in public silence for ten more days to give you time to agree to this meeting and for it to occur. If you choose to ignore the growing damage that you have done, chiefly to Dr. Scaer, but now also to me and his congregation, I will have no other alternative but to tell the matter to the church, which I will do publicly in the appropriate context..."

My response was to write to Ind. Dist. Pres. Garber, with a copy to Rev. Schaibley and Synod's President on Oct. 10, 1989, "This letter is sent to inform you of the problem which the Rev. Robert Schaibley is creating by three letters which he wrote in which he is intruding himself in the charges related to the Rev. Dr. David P. Scaer as Academic Dean of CTS of FW. The enclosed correspondence will inform you that he is using the occasion of the decision of the editor of *CN* to publish parts of a private document related to the Preus-Scaer-Board concerns which I raised through totally private channels. The facts show that I am not responsible for, nor can be held responsible for the publication of this matter, and so it is obvious Rev. Schaibley's target should be the editor of *CN* and those who submitted the document to him...I am asking you as District President to use your office to cause the Rev. Schaibley to cease and desist in his wrongful judgment of me as being guilty of making public charges against Dr. Scaer, thus bringing false charges against me and bearing false witness against me, because his allegations are a total untruth. The Synod's constitution assures me protection of my rights as a member of the Synod, and I am ask-

238

ing you formally as District President to make certain that my rights are not violated related to the 8th Commandment related to this matter. Inasmuch as Rev. Schaibley is a pastor under the jurisdiction of the Indiana District, I am making this request of you."

On Oct. 11, 1989, Garber wrote to Schaibley, "...I will get in touch with you when I return to Fort Wayne and look forward to the opportunity of sitting down with you and with others as may seem necessary in order to deal with this matter in a proper manner.." On Oct. 20, 1989, Rev. Schaibley wrote to Garber with a copy to me, saying, "...This note is to confirm our meeting at your office on Friday, Oct. 27 (sic) at 1:30 p.m. Meanwhile, I will suspend any actions with regard to Rev. Waldo Werning until after we have met." That was the end of this episode.

This is reported because Rev. Schaibley has been a very important cog in the entire Preus machine. He was the theological consultant to Dr. Preus during the Adjudication meetings which were held in my case against Dr. Preus. It was obvious that Schaibley embraces the same theology as Dr. Scaer and Dr. Preus related to Christology, false views on the Office of the Keys and Confession, and other related matters. Rev. Schaibley reveals a complaint against those in the Synod who understand the Great Commission to mean that all Christians are to be actively witnessing of their faith by God's grace, as he questions the vital role that every Christian has in evangelism and missions to accomplish Christ's mission. Three examples follow.

On July 22, 1990, Rev. Schaibley preached a sermon in Zion Church, Fort Wayne on the Great Commission text, Matt. 28:18-20: his pretext was the first part of Luther's Explanation to the Third Petition, "Thy will be on earth as it is in heaven." A cassette recording reveals that Schaibley stated, "Luther said that the good and gracious will of God is done indeed without our prayer. It is done without our action. We think and do as though it cannot be done if we don't pray or do (mission work). We are just like the disciples. We have applied the Great Commission in a way that reveals our doubts. Church leaders often use these famous words, 'Go ye' without meaning to and significantly mistranslate them. It becomes the "Great Obligation" of the church or the overarching reason you are in the church. We talk and act as though the will of God is stuck and can't be done without our action. We put things into the text as though they are there. We interpret it as though Christ is wearing handcuffs and is on the sidelines as our coach...as if when the church is not preaching the Gospel to the ends of the world that the job is not being done. We come to the conclusion that He is an absent God and act as if He only prays for us as though He has gone away and let us do His job...as though if we don't do them, they won't get done. We handcuff God. The way the Great Commission is preached today, it depends upon our resources, our conduct and the way we package the Gospel as to whether His work will get done...This is the 'new-found' enthusiasm for the Great Commission that has been talked about in the past half century."

Schaibley continued his sermon, "What did we get for the application of the Great Commission that has been missing for 1900 years? We Christians comprise the smallest percentage of population since the Fourth Century. In our own LCMS in the past three decades, the Great Commission has been used in describing everything. What do we have to show for it? Fewer missionaries than 30 years ago. No wonder we shudder to hear another sermon on the Great Commission. The bottom line is doubt...His kingdom will come without our prayer...our doubt gets us into trouble and to misuse the Great Commission...Gathering around preaching and Sacraments you will gather disciples from every nation and sustain them. We cannot hinder His mission."

Schaibley's evangelism consists of getting people into church services, not going out and sharing the Gospel with them as Jesus said. My basic criticisms of this sermon are: misinterpreting the Matt. 28:18-20 text on the basis of a misinterpretation of Luther's Explanation of the Third Petition, and using his misinterpretation to criticize the historic correct exegesis of the Great Commission; he failed to delineate between command and promise, between the third use of the Law and of Gospel; he perverted the Third Petition as well as the Second and Fourth Petitions by butchering Luther's Explanations to them and tearing them out of the context of what Luther was really saying. On the basis of Schaibley's sermon, we need never pray, "Thy Kingdom come, Thy will be done on earth as it is in heaven," because God is going to do it anyway. So we just walk around and trust that He will do it without instruments and agents! He also fails to emphasize properly the Christian's function in the Kingdom of Grace, which is the focus of this Petition, and not Christ's kingdom of power which Christ exerts daily through nature without our help. He fails to deal with Bible truths such as: "Ask the Lord of the Harvest, therefore, to send workers.." (Matt. 9:38); "I urge, then, first of all, that requests, prayers, intercessions and thanksgiving be made for everyone.."; "(God) who wants all men to be saved and come to the knowledge of the truth" (1 Tim. 2:1,4). God does command us to pray and witness. This sermon denies the instrumentality of the redeemed, as though God does His work directly while our activity is incidental or inconsequential.

This is a denial of God's plan of involving believers to perform His work on earth (Eph. 2:10; Jn. 15; 1 Cor. 3:6-15; 2 Cor. 9:8). The sermon fails to show that God's grace involves both Law and Gospel. It denies the truth of the Parable of the Talents (Mt. 25:14-30) and presents an ugly picture which distorts the body of Christ as functioning according to Christ's and Paul's revelation: Eph. 4; and 1 Cor. 12.

On Oct. 6, 1991 on the Festival of Missions, Rev. Schaibley preached a sermon, "God's Plan for Missions" on Is. 2:1-5. In it he said, " 'God's Plan For Missions Is Quite Different From Man's Plan For Missions As Usually Heard In The Church.' That's quite a title for a sermon...Today in our congregation when we remember mission work in general and the work of the LWML in particular...Well, what is heard in the church? Isn't God's plan that we hear? 'Go therefore, etc..' Well, no! That is **God's** assignment (**Note:** Apparently Jesus is giving **Himself, not His disciples,** the instructions to **go.**)...But how will the church accomplish this goal?...What we hear all too often is man's plan for the church's mission (Note: Then Schaibley uses several paragraphs of caricatures of what the great faithful LCMS majority are doing in the way of mission work, which is a judgment by generalization)...Man's plan for God's mission is a variation on the theme: What do I want? So that's how we plan to complete God's mission, by playing off what we think people want, which is always filtered through the filter of what we think we want. And that's the plan for God's mission which we usually hear in the church. (Note: Is this true?)...On this day when we especially think about God's mission, wouldn't it be a good idea to take a little peek at God's plan for His mission?' (Note: this appears to be an arrogant condemnation of our LCMS brothers.)

Then comes a portion of the Isaiah text which deals with Law, and Schaibley says, "Here it is, here's the plan! Here's how God's work gets done...So the key to God's plan for missions, according to Isaiah, is the temple and the Ark of the Covenant, the appointed place of the presence of God among His people. Today, Isaiah's answer still remains true." So he opts for missions to get people to come and sit in worship; he excuses people from following the Great Commission, "Go!" The rest of the sermon tells the hearers that the key to God's mission is right here in the church building where believers are "gathered around the sacramental system of God's grace in washing and proclaiming and absolving and communing power of the Gospel of Christ."

He says, "For many years now, we've been taught by well-meaning people that we have to get God's people out of the church and into the world if God's mission is to be accomplished. Sadly, that's just another one of man's plans for God's mission. The truth is that we have to get the people of God to realize what it is that we have here in the church!...That's God's plan for His mission." This theology ties in closely to the anti-sanctification "cathedral" theology which has lifted its head at the Seminary, which will be shown later.

Besides the problems created in these sermons in sanctification, Rev. Schaibley's sermons, writings and activities are listed here because he has been a strong enabler for Dr. Preus and his party by concurring with Dr. Preus during the Adjudication hearings in un-Biblical views on Christology and the Office of the Keys and Confession. He also defended Preus in his breaking of the 8th Commandment, and also because he hosted a national meeting of the Preus' "Confessional Lutherans" in one of their strategy meetings during the time of the Seminary Symposium in January, 1991. Some professors, including Dr. Scaer, are members of his congregation.

"Lutheran Preaching" Article

Even though there are excellent points in Schaibley's article, "Lutheran Preaching: Proclamation, Not Communication," in the January 1992 *Concordia Journal* (pages 6-27), Schaibley has an overly sacerdotal emphasis (emphasizing the role of the priests as mediators between God and man, while effectively cutting out some aspects of the priesthood of all believers). He begins with an uncomplimentary statement that "our Synod is in deep trouble in the area of preaching, that conviction heightened as it is by the notion that sooner or later, I must turn over all my parishioners and all of my loved ones to one of these preachers..." I get worried when a pastor speaks about "my" parishioners when referring to the people of God, and when he trusts only himself for this care. Schaibley builds some strawmen and weights them with his own meaning, and then burns his own creations with his own theories. He does recognize his sacerdotalist commitment, as he says that he will "gladly settle for 'sacerdotalist.'" To place proclamation in contradiction to communication as he does in this essay is a grievous thing.

When Schaibley says that, "the Lutheran sermon is not Bible study," one wonders whether he believes that there should be expository sermons or a concern about knowing and recognizing the needs of the hearers. Yet that is exactly what flavored Paul's letter and preaching to the Corinthian congregation, where there were real needs which needed to be addressed. Schaibley says, "We are encouraged to 'be uplifting' in our presentations, but these demands often conflict with the text, with the theology of the cross under which we live." It is my impression of Scripture that we do not keep people in the Law, but give them the uplifting Gospel. Is there to be no resurrection after "Good Friday misery" which our people experience? Is preaching of the Resurrection after Law and repentance emphases really "the theology of glory"? He does not deal with the legitimate aspect of identifying the real needs of a specific congregation or people, which is what Paul did in his preaching and writing. Yet Schaibley calls this concern "pernicious."

Schaibley restricts "communication" to what he calls a "micro-meaning," which restricts it to skills as enunciation, pronunciation, voice usage, etc. It can be assumed from Schaibley's warnings against recognizing the felt needs of the audience that it would be best to blindfold the pastor in his preaching so that he will remain immaculately abstract, and will avoid any semblance of acknowledging the problems and situation of his audience. He crudely and cruelly condemns any attempt to understand culture through one's proclamation when he says, "The hearers need not hear the sound of culture, but the sound of Christ," as though these are opposites, whereas our Gospel proclamation is always in a cultural setting. Or does he believe that Lutheran pastors today should preach only in the cultural context of Luther's day and thus prove to be **true** Lutherans? It is not surprising when he summarizes, "In short, what Lutheran preaching needs to deliver is not 'communication,' but rather, 'proclamation.'"

Schaibley unfairly condemns communication because he says it "works within what might be called a 'synergistic' framework. That cuts out Romans 10 with all that it means, without any concern as to whether the hearer is understanding the words or not. If there is to be no cooperation of the hearer because it is 'synergistic,' then how does the proclaimer avoid the criticism of being 'synergistic' when he dares to become the instrument of God in proclaiming the Word? If synergism can be applied to the hearer, it can just as well be applied to the proclaimer. This is an example of Schaibley making an opposite out of something that is not. The hearer is not empowered by his own strength any more than the proclaimer is empowered to proclaim by his own strength. So he concludes, "Proclamation works within what might be called a 'monergistic' framework, in which the proclaimer proclaims, but the hearer must obviously be present, but this does not necessitate the cooperation or hearing of the hearer." False antitheses! Try that one for logic.

On page 14 of his article he makes the peculiar statement that "the proclamation model **bestows being.**" The Word of God bestows being. If proclamation can bestow being, then communication can also do the same by the same Word and Holy Spirit.

After studying *Webster*, I became even more confused: to **communicate** means to make known, and communication means information given, a message. **Proclaim** means publish abroad, pronounce, declare officially, while **proclamation** means act of proclaiming, official notice to the public. Does Schaibley mean that the Lutheran proclaimer is giving official notice, take it or leave it, without any reference to the context or whether he is communicating at all?

It was very distressing to read, "The communication model is now offered as a better way to deliver information and to move hearers to action, especially in light of this new age in the life of the pastoral office within our Synod, the age in which the pastor is forced to say, along with the now defunct Frank Borman, 'we have to earn our wings every day.' The communication model is in fact a concession to this minimalistic point of view concerning the pastoral office, as it legitimizes this synergistic process of 'sharing' truth." Whatever this may mean in the context of the entire essay, it is a judgment without any example or documentation in fact. Indeed, the entire essay has only one Bible reference, even though Lutheran preaching is first of all thoroughly Biblical.

Schaibley does have some good things to offer, of course, but he often proclaims very sloppily: "By means of proclamation, Lutheran preaching justifies!" We know what he means, but he says something else. That's the reason why there must be communication, so that the proclaimer does not merely pontificate and assume that he is even saying it right. But Schaibley cuts out the hearer altogether by implying, "Shut up and sit and listen!" His paragraph on "sanctification" carries some strong condemnations, but he does not explain it in any way from a Biblical viewpoint.

It is difficult to understand how anyone can place effective communication in contradiction to proclamation when adequate communication involves such essentials as recognizing people's mental screens and paradigms or barriers to communication, recognition of the communication code, choice of code and channel, and feedback to ascertain whether the message is even understood. There are all kinds of communication noises which need to be recognized or proclamation can be as effective as speaking to a stone wall. There would simply not be anything for the Holy Spirit to work on. This essay overemphasizes the preacher-speaker, while ignoring the hearer and the thinking process which deals only with getting the facts right, not with faith or belief.

The account of Schaibley's sermons and essay are very pertinent to this entire case because of him being an enabler for Dr. Preus and Dr. Scaer.

Dr. Scaer's Unsettled Settlement

On Dec. 19, 1989, I signed a statement with Dr. Scaer, co-signed by Dr. Eugene Klug, to accept Scaer's sincere regrets for any real or perceived wrong against me, and agreed to relieve him of any accountability regarding my documentation. This is the statement to which we agreed:

> "Dr. Werning had charged that the last sentence of Dr. Scaer's essay ('Sanctification in Lutheran Theology,' CTQ April/July, 1985, p. 194) was inadequate because 'it is an exclusive statement which excludes the Father and the Holy Spirit as part of theology.'
>
> At the suggestion of the committee Dr. Scaer offered to provide an emended interpretation or change in wording, to read:
>
> 'Any attempt to make Christology preliminary to theology, or even its most important part, but not **its primary, central core in the light of which all articles of faith are interpreted,** is a denial of Luther's doctrine and effectively destroys the Gospel as the message of a completed atonement,'
>
> (the underlined words replace:...its only part...')
>
> "Dr. Werning approved of this change in wording, satisfied that no exclusion of the Trinity was intended or suggested in the original wording. In a spirit of collegiality, Dr. Scaer agreed that notice of this change would appear in an upcoming issue of the *CTQ.*"

In April, 1991, I received the January 1991 *CTQ*. There was not a statement from Dr. Scaer, but one from "The Editors," with a heading, "An Interpretation." I had stated to Dr. Scaer in the presence of Dr. Klug that we should avoid any interpretations and correct them if we hear anyone making them. The Editors, not Dr. Scaer, in the *CTQ* give the impression that it was merely an interpretation, and the February 12, 1990 *Reporter Alive* said that my charge against this statement resulted from a "misunderstanding of a disputed sentence." On Dec. 19, 1989, I said to Scaer and Klug that I understood it very well, and that the "change in wording" was because this was false doctrine, not a misunderstanding on my part.

Several recent Fort Wayne graduates who were Scaer supporters after reading this in the CTQ and *CN* criticized me for making an issue of this since I signed the statement that said that "I was satisfied that no exclusion of the Trinity was intended or suggested in the original wording." The statement I signed was far from satisfactory, but since it took Dr. Scaer a long time to come this far, I felt that he would have the good will to change his ways if I forgave him. Only a person can intend something, not a statement, so in my mind I included, "...was intended or suggested 'by Dr. Scaer' in the original wording." Writers for the *CN* made an issue out of this, at which time I contacted Dr. Scaer to ask him to make a statement that would stop this paper war about this matter.

Matters were made worse when Dr. Preus in the Adjudication Hearing stated that I had bullied Dr. Scaer into making this change (this was said in the presence of Rev. Robert Schaibley, the pastor of Dr. Scaer). Dr. Eugene Klug wrote on June 7, 1990, "The Reconciliation Agreement...was arrived at without any sort of pressure, bullying or cajoling on my part or that of other Reconciliation members...Through what might be described as shuttle diplomacy by phone over a period of three days, a mutually accepted statement and resolution was arrived at..." Because of other problems, I wrote to Dr. Scaer on Sept. 14, 1990, and asked, "Do you condone or agree with the words and actions of Dr. Preus and your Pastor Schaibley in claiming that I bullied you into a correction?" He did not answer that question or address other concerns.

David Scaer-Charles M. Brooks Encounter

In early Sept., 1990, Charles M. Brooks, a new student at the Seminary, was staying in a visitor's dormitory with his family. During the time of the Seminary Opening Service, he met and became acquainted with Rev. Raymond Mueller of the Seminary BOR while shaving in the morning. Rev. Mueller asked him whether he had heard about the Preus problem. Brooks said that he had not. Mueller suggested that Brooks visit Preus and learn about it. Brooks then contacted Dr. Preus, and they had a meeting in the Preus home. Dr. Preus said that he could not say much about his case, but that he had deposited depositions and other materials in the Seminary library, and he suggested to Brooks that he read them.

As you read the following account, it should be noted that this started with BOR member Raymond Mueller, then Preus, then the library, then Scaer. I did not know Charles Brooks until he phoned me for an appointment and visited with me on Oct. 28, 1990, to say that he was disturbed about what Scaer had said about me. I visited Dr. Scaer to ask about the allegations against me which were attributed to him. Before I could go any further, he stated that Brooks is no longer a student here. I told him that the status of Charles Brooks at the Seminary had nothing to do with my questions because here is a fellow Christian who asked me questions about a visit with Scaer that needed to be verified. In an Oct. 31 Memo to Scaer I recounted what Brooks had told me, and that Scaer denied everything. After a number of attempts to make an appointment with him, I wrote a Memo on Nov. 6, 1990 to Scaer telling him that I was concerned about his refusal to meet in the presence of Charles Brooks in order to correct his allegations. At the same time, I wrote to Brooks, asking him for a written account of his encounter with Dr. Scaer. Brooks wrote:

Dear Brother Werning:

My warmest and most sincere personal thanks for your letter of Nov. 6th pertaining to the David Scaer matter I brought to your attention on Oct. 28, 1990. At that time I inquired of you what problem existed between you and Dr. Scaer after a long and most distressing meeting with him over the Preus' Papers in Walther Library. I thank you for being so honest and forthright in answering my questions for, Seminary student aside, I am a concerned and informed layman of TLC-MS and care deeply for its peace and welfare. I am most disappointed that Dr. Scaer will not meet with us; I had considered him an outspoken and forthright individual! Please also be advised that Dr. Scaer is also my Advisor so these matters are quite unsettling for me. I am happy to answer the questions posed in your letter in order.

1. While meeting in Walther Library, examining the Preus' Papers, I became quite concerned with certain documents authored by Werning and Tepker — this matter explained gross injustices, abuses and other matters which affected me deeply. Naturally, I inquired of Dr. Scaer who these individuals were and if, in fact, the data presented was true. He was most agitated and annoyed and called Tepker a "brainless fool" and Werning a dangerous "trouble-maker" who has plagued the place until he got kicked out. I asked Scaer why he should feel this way regarding Werning, and he mentioned a "Christological Controversy" that had arisen and that Werning accused him of false doctrine. He informed me that "he" (i.e. Werning) misunderstood the whole Christological matter. Being familiar with Schaller's treatise on "Christology" (as well as Pieper, Hoeneke and Luther on the subject), I found his answers to my question regarding the nature of the contro-

versy made no sense whatsoever and confused me more. My only impression, strictly as a neophyte, was that he sincerely believed in the supreme divinity of Jesus Christ - but gave me the impression that the Holy Spirit and God the Father were of little significance. From this discussion I sincerely hope that you understand fully that I did not hear about this "Controversy" from anyone else!

2. When I inquired as to what form of settlement to this issue was raised, Dr. Scaer became most defensive and produced a paper from his vest-pocket known as the "Agreement" between Werning and himself. To my recollection it was a single piece of paper, rather 'legal' in its aesthetics, with two signatures at the base. He stated that he "carried it everywhere." I returned this document to him and made little more about it. I can unequivocally state that I am not, and never have been "psychic."

3. After leaving Walther Library, in front of Kramer Chapel, I commented on the interesting nature of the new "Confessional Lutheran Dogmatics" edited by Dr. Preus, and my recent reading of his (Scaer's) "Christology" volume. I asked him why such a pedantic series was necessary since we have Pieper's "Gold Standard" and that I understood that Dr. Bohlmann was producing a new "Dogmatics" to help address key issues in the Contemporary Church. He responded that the "Synodical" Dogmatics were really the ramblings of Howard Tepker - a "brainless ass" who "did not have an original thought in his head" and that Dr. Bohlmann (sic., "the other side") was using this as just another avenue to destroy "the Lutheran identity of the Church." When I reminded Dr. Scaer that, not knowing Bohlmann personally but having read his "Principles of Biblical Interpretation...;" I strongly felt he was a truly Confessional Lutheran who didn't impress me as being some liberal lunatic! It is interesting to note that I did not know that the "Other Dogmatics" was being edited by Dr. Tepker or know Tepker. How else could I have known these facts? Dr. Scaer also compared this project with the two-volume "Dogmatics" of Braaten!

During the bizarre and disjointed blustering about the "Christological" issue Dr. Scaer referred to Werning as a "Jackass...Pain In The Ass..Etc." I'm sure that the witnesses to our document ramblings in the Library will remember these statements as they were not ethereal in tone!

5. Outside of the Administration Building, entering the Radio Station (The Manager Will Testify We Were There That Day) I asked Dr. Scaer, "What Is Going To Happen To The Church?" His reply, bordering on allegorical vitriol was "They" (i.e., Synod and Bohlmann) will "Kill It" and Church Growth will just bring us to the same position as the Southern Baptists are now...

6. The following day, after Chapel Service, Dr. Scaer called to me across the Piazza and when I approached him, he came directly to my face and threatened me with, "If you utter a single word of what we talked about in the Library yesterday, you will be ridden out on a rail — that's a Promise!" I asked him what prompted such angry words and he replied, "Its not time yet, we have fought this battle five times before." I did not know what he was alluding to. He also gave me a short Eulogy on Robert E. Lee - a complete nonsequitor - and I chased him into the classroom building demanding a **clear** explanation, but to no avail.

In summary, I do agree with you that this is a very serious matter and cannot understand why Dr. Scaer will not state the truth in these dialogues? (Name deleted) overheard most of the library conversations; (Name deleted), I believe, served at the Library Desk; and (Name deleted) oversaw Dr. Scaer summons me on the Piazza. Dr. Preus also told me that

I would find suitable answers to his "unfair" treatment by consulting these documents. Dr. Scaer's main concerns, as he told me, was that "he could care less about the Preus matter - he only wanted to save his own neck from any more attacks." After prayerful consideration, and after calling upon our Lord to guide me, I must conclude that Dr. Scaer has sinned against me and accused me of lying.

I sincerely hope this deposition will amply settle the obvious discrepancies that have occurred in this unfortunate matter, and I will gladly have this document notarized if it will assist in any way.

May Our Lord Jesus Christ Continue To Guide And Direct You As You Answer His Call For Service And Evangelism!

YOURS IN OUR RISEN SAVIOR, CHARLES MARTIN BROOKS Sem. I, Concordia Theological Seminary

cc: Dr. David Scaer

*   *   *   *   *

On Nov. 15, 1990, I wrote a letter to Dr. Scaer, "...Please let me discuss the testimony of Charles Brooks and try to establish where it would be difficult to prove that he is not telling the truth. First, I am sure that you will agree that you met with him at length at the Library while looking at the Preus files. It is obvious, too, that there was considerable conversation between you and Brooks. Also, I never knew or heard about Brooks until he contacted me in late October. Likewise, he knew nothing about me. Obviously, he is not psychic, and so could not know or manufacture such reports as Werning being a dangerous 'trouble-maker' who had plagued the place until he got kicked out. Or that he should know about the 'Christological controversy,' and that 'Werning accused you of false doctrine.' Also, he was accurate about an 'agreement between the two of us.' It is also significant whether he could manufacture a report on the 'Synodical Dogmatics,' when he knew nothing about it or that Howard Tepker whom he did not know was the chief editor, unless you told him during that discussion. There are other issues in this, but I will let this suffice at this time..." This letter was not acknowledged.

On Dec. 4, 1990, I wrote him another letter to ask him for a meeting, which was not answered. When Brooks was notified that he was suspended as a student, he was told that he could appeal the decision through due process. Brooks appealed, and even though he went to four levels of Synodical Administration, he received no answer and was **not given due process**. One can assume that he was "driven out on a rail," as Scaer warned him.

Other Concerns about Dr. David Scaer

Two years earlier, at the Nov. 14, 1988 Faculty meeting, Dr. Scaer presented an essay to the Faculty entitled, "A New Look at the Matter of Ordination of Women into the Pastoral Ministry of Word and Sacrament." Apparently, he shared some of his favorite theological views which are quite confusing in light of Lutheran and Missouri Synod doctrine, for Dr. Waldemar Degner criticized the essay very strongly at eight points where he felt the essay was disturbing: a denial of the priesthood of all believers, some kind of affirmation of the sacramental nature and essence of ordination, that ordination gives full authority without a call from a congregation, the pastoral office is only an office and not a function (Walther said it was a **both-and,** not an **either-or**), the Pastoral Office is derived from the Second Article and not the Third Article, showed a Donatist view of pastoral acts that are said to be invalid because they are done by women, etc.

Scaer's article, "Sanctification in the Lutheran Confessions" (CTQ, July 1989, pp. 165-181) presents questionable statements on sanctification, "Good works naturally flow from the preaching of Christ...The preaching of the Gospel in the moment that it is preached justifies the sinner and makes him abound in good works...Good works which flow naturally from his faith in Christ...In these positive affirmations, the old man is no longer in view. Theoretically in the moment of the Gospel the old man becomes nonexistent, though as a threat to faith he is always active...Negative prohibitions in the moment of the Gospel and of faith are no longer necessary, since the Christian is alive to Christ and dead to sin and the law..." All of this is a confusion of the old man, new man tension and struggle, of Law and Gospel, and a denial of the 3rd use of the law.

On March 23, 1992, Dr. Scaer preached for the chapel worship at CTS on John 1:29-34. Speaking topically on Christ taking away the **sin** (singular) of the world, Scaer stated, "Lengthy Lenten celebrations can result in an unhealthy preoccupation with sins, which can degenerate into self-absorption of the worse kind. Jesus Christ and not counting sins is what Lent is all about. Self-absorption is only the reverse side of calculating spiritual endowments. In each case each one of us is living...in our cubicle...without God."

He continued, "Self-recognized sanctification is its own deception, a denial of the Truth. Socrates may have said, 'know yourself,' but that does not work, at least for Christians. A Christian who really believes he can search his heart for sins which are at first evident will become proud of the success with which he finds them. Spiritual self-centeredness puts ourselves and not God at the center of our existence, and in the words of Luther's explanation of the First Commandment, we begin to reverence ourselves as idols...Stay with the confessions that no one can know his sins, 'Cleanse me from secret faults.' Absorption with sin nullifies our justification by grace for the sake of God. If we can perfectly examine ourselves, and then the lives of others, the law has conquered our hearts, and the saving and free grace of Christ has been defeated. Without the Gospel, individual sins take on a life of their own. Their enormity overshadows God's grace or we become impressed with our abilities to overcome them. Sin which can be overcome is too trivial to be called sin, and the enormity of sin is lost."

After a very beautiful Gospel interlude, he continued, "Lent is not a season of sins in the plural but sin in the singular, the one sin - the sin of the world." After talking about baptismal sanctification and that eucharistic worship heals, Scaer continued, "One Lord, one sacrament, one Holy Church, and only one sin to be forgiven, not many, and there is one sinful humanity and not many to be restored...there are no individual separate burdens, only one burden...The burden belongs equally to all, but is completely carried by each one...Never look at another person and say, 'There but by the Grace of God go I,' for that other person is you...That cannot mean that God catalogs sins. If we are to computerize sins according to the Commandments, God does not. If we catalog sins, we will by comparison be too generous to ourselves and too severe with others. Sin is a totality, a seamless garment and not the sum of its parts...Behold the Lamb of God that takes away the **sin** of the world, **not many sins**, but one sin." He ended with rich Gospel which did not change the apparent denial of actual sin and for the need of repentance of individual sins.

In contrast, Augsburg XII (pp. 4-35) affirms actual sins, of which we need to repent daily. Luther's Small Catechism under "Confession and Absolution," asks, "What sins should we confess?" He answers that "before God we should acknowledge that we are guilty of all manner of sins, even those of which we are unaware..." Examination of specific sins, which Scaer denies, is found in Tappert 350:20-29. Luther believed in confessing particular sins, not just sin in general (Original Sin).

Scaer's philosophical arguments are contradicted by 1 Cor. 15:3; 15:17; Gal. 1:4; Col. 1:14;

1 Tim. 5:22; Heb. 1:3; 2:17; 10:17; Jas. 5:17; 1 Jn. 1:9. Important also are Ps. 23:7; 79:9; 69:5; 51:9. Scaer's view of the purpose of Lent is quite different from what we Lutherans have always thought and practiced. There is no passage in Scripture that will support what Scaer is saying: That Lent is not the time to search our hearts and repent of individual sins. Scaer is going way beyond the notion of an obsession with our sins that loses sight of Christ's cross. The Bible makes us aware of our sinfulness by pointing to individual sins that we commit. The Seminary community has become so accustomed to this kind of theology from Dr. Scaer that this did not cause a ripple, except some students said that this was one of the best sermons that they had ever heard. Dr. Scaer has introduced "No Fault" religion into the LCMS.

ADJUDICATION WITH DR. PREUS

It should be emphasized at this point that not only I, but also Indiana Dist. Pres. Reuben Garber and his secretary, tried a number of times to find a solution and affect a reconciliation with Preus and Scaer. This is recorded here because Dr. Preus on several occasions in the adjudication process stated that I never followed Matthew 18 in my approach with him. The many letters written to him, the reconciliation meeting with two pastors in Dec. 1988, and this evidence shows that Dr. Preus was not telling the truth. Garber's secretary wrote, "As requested I am confirming with you that from Jan., 1989, through Aug., 1989, at the request of Dist. Pres. Garber, we (Pres. Garber and myself) have tried unsuccessfully either through correspondence or telephone calls to set dates and times for meetings between Dr. Scaer, Dr. Preus, and yourself with Pres. Garber, individually or collectively. There are at least two letters on file requesting such meetings, giving many dates and times when Pres. Garber was available. However, when phoning to confirm a date and time neither Dr. Scaer nor Dr. Preus were available for any of the dates or times suggested."

Yours in Christ,

Mrs. Janet Koenig, Secretary to Pres. Garber, June 7, 1990

In the adjudication process, I wrote several major letters and documents outlining carefully all the charges and the issues presented in over thirty exhibits. On June 11, 1990 I sent a "Final Brief" to the LCMS Commission on Adjudication which included analysis of the 238 page transcript of the hearing. This is the outline of the issues from that Brief which I summarized and presented in 1991 (edited for this publication):

A STATEMENT OF CONSCIENCE TO THE LUTHERAN CHURCH-MISSOURI SYNOD

The decision of the LCMS Commission on APPEALS (APPEALS) dated March 26, 1991, denied a motion for a rehearing in the case of Dr. Waldo Werning against Dr. Robert Preus, which followed a Jan. 17, 1991, decision of APPEALS that failed to deal with the evidence at hand but declared forgiveness for all, and closed the matter. On Aug. 23, 1990, I personally received an undated "Decision of the Commission on Adjudication" (ADJ) which declared Dr. Preus guilty of breaking the 8th Commandment, but failed to act in two major statements involving false doctrine (one member, Dr. Wilbert Griesse, opposed the ADJ decision in order to add the rejection of the Christology statement as incorrect).

Letters to APPEALS on Aug. 27, 1990, Sept. 20, 1990, Feb. 5, 1991, Feb. 27, 1991, March 22, 1991, and March 25, 1991 presented my argumentation based on **evidence** from the transcripts and documentation that Dr. Preus is guilty of false doctrine in two theological statements, and of breaking the 4th and 8th Commandments in areas beyond the two issues in which ADJ found him guilty. In my Feb. 5, 1991, letter and subsequent letters to AP-PEALS (as response to their erroneous decision) with copies to ADJ, on the basis of evidence which was ignored, I charged the individual members of both Commissions with allowing and participating in the sins of breaking the 8th Commandment and of being guilty of false doctrine in two areas where Dr. Preus is theologically wrong, and requested a rehearing from them. They denied a rehearing.

Bylaw 8.69 states that all decisions of APPEALS shall be binding upon all parties to the case and not subject for review, reversal, amendment or modification. The APPEALS Commission refused a rehearing. I announced to both Commissions in requesting a rehearing which was denied that my next step will be to tell it to the church, giving it to the delegates at the Pittsburgh Convention and writing a book for LCMS members to decide whether the evidence is conclusive related to the guilt of Dr. Preus in breaking the 8th Commandment and in defending two theological statements which I believe constitute false doctrine.

THE ISSUES SUMMARIZED

Issue 1: The ADJ declared Dr. Preus guilty of breaking the Eighth Commandment in leading and supporting the Fort Wayne Seminary Faculty to pass a resolution of condemnation against Werning on April 17, 1989, without the knowledge of or an opportunity for Werning to present the truth. That Faculty resolution contained these falsehoods: that Werning made unfounded and untrue descriptions of others, against the Faculty, and that Werning had disseminated materials with unfounded and untrue allegations. Through interrogation, no Faculty member could define what these alleged false allegations might be and which materials which they may have received, and showed that they had no evidence that Dr. Werning disseminated anything; but on the other hand, they recognized that some materials were disseminated by the Administration through Faculty mail and at the Faculty meeting. Indeed, almost all of the Faculty interviewed believed that the resolution was a sin against Werning. Nine faculty members gave oral or written evidence, and I was actually stopped from interviewing more because the ADJ would not allow more time.

APPEALS overturned the ruling of ADJ, despite the written evidence and oral testimony of the events that showed that Werning was not guilty of any of these false allegations. Indeed, the APPEALS added that the Faculty did nothing wrong and had the right to pass the resolution with false witness and allegations in Werning's absence.

Issue 2: A BOR Mar. 28, 1989, letter requested Dr. Preus to share the Board's message with the Faculty: "The BOR is deeply distressed to learn that information regarding the disagreement between the CTS administration and Dr. Waldo Werning has been rather widely disseminated. This is a serious breach of ethics even by secular standards, and is certainly contrary to the manner in which our Lord asks us to deal with a Christian brother. We, therefore, respectfully urge and request that you refrain from further discussion regarding this matter."

Werning brought charges to ADJ and APPEALS on this basis that Preus broke the 4th Commandment when the faculty discussed and passed a resolution on April 17, 1989, with false allegations against Werning, but ADJ refused to consider the matter because they claimed that Werning had no standing to bring the complaint about the 4th Commandment to them (even though Werning was the victim). APPEALS maintains that Preus did not violate the 4th Commandment and that he had the right to go to the Faculty (despite orders to the contrary from the BOR) with false allegations against Werning without his

249

knowledge or presence.

APPEALS wrote, "The BOR's asking the Faculty not to discuss the matter was understood not to bar the Faculty from discussing Werning's charges among themselves...any such gag order, if made, would raise serious questions of interference of the Faculty's right to discuss theological issues." Fact: The BOR hand delivered a letter to Dr. Preus which contained a direct message to the Faculty **not** to discuss this matter in any way.

APPEALS erroneously wrote, "The Faculty was doing what they understood the BOR wanted...." But there were a number of faculty members who publicly stated that they understood the opposite from what APPEALS writes. One faculty member in the meeting even stated that it was untenable that the Faculty should discuss this or try to act on it because the BOR had ordered it not to (Dr. Houser is very plain on this in the Transcript). This was not a gag order but a request to obey the 4th Commandment. It was not a theological issue, but a matter of obeying the 8th Commandment with unproven allegations placed before the Faculty about unfounded and untrue charges without the presence of the one criticized. Dr. Preus even went so far as to say that the BOR could not tell the Faculty what to do. Can one come to any other conclusion than that this is blatant defiance and a breaking of the 4th Commandment?

Issue 3: The ADJ found Dr. Preus guilty of breaking the 8th Commandment in writing a letter to the Board of Directors of God's Word To The Nations Bible Society, which was filled with false allegations and also with gossip which Preus admitted that he wrongfully shared. The APPEALS dismissed the ADJ ruling with the statement that "Dr. Preus confessed his sin in regard to these letters," but did not note that Preus never corrected this statement to those who received them, nor note that Preus appealed the ADJ ruling against him because he did no wrong. Yet APPEALS absolved Preus where ADJ found evidence of his guilt.

Issue 4: Dr. Preus requested a retired Faculty member to give a deposition to the Allen County Circuit Court on Aug. 31, 1989, which contained falsehoods, slander and defamation of character. This deposition is available to the public also in the Seminary Library. Many attempts to gain corrections failed because the professor stated that Dr. Preus asked him not to respond. After many months when Werning took it to the District ADJ, the professor began discussion. The professor provided a signed statement to correct the wrongs, which was stapled to the deposition in the library. Both ADJ and APPEALS refused to act on this despite the fact that Preus consistently has refused to acknowledge the falsehoods in the deposition for him and used by him, which still stands before the Allen County Circuit Court for him with its untruth.

Issue 5: A Lutheran couple in Florida (donors to the Seminary) complained that when they talked to Dr. Preus about a commendation for Werning's service to the Seminary, that Dr. Preus and a pastor with him stated that Werning had taken advantage of the Seminary while working at the Seminary. Not only has no evidence ever been provided for such defamation of character, but a signed statement from Werning's supervisor at that time has been given to show that **Werning gave advantage** to the Seminary, rather than the reverse. Dr. Preus in the transcript stated: "If I knew that the statement was false, I would defend him." Both the ADJ and APPEALS ruled that Preus did not break the 8th Commandment. Never once has Dr. Preus made this false allegation to Werning directly either while at the Seminary or since, but it was shared with the Florida couple and also with a Seminary staff person eight months later, who informed Werning. Preus has never corrected it. Dr. Preus is guilty of breaking the 8th Commandment both with the Florida couple and with a staff person in the false allegation against Werning.

This couple said that the two people who were with Dr. Preus were Mr. Ed Hinnefeld and Pastor Mark Bergmann. On Dec. 28, 1989, I wrote to Hinnefeld, "Because of what Dr. Preus said at a meeting with me on Dec. 13, 1989, I need to give you this information and ask you a question. Related to the incident in early February in Ft. Lauderdale in which (names deleted) said that they spoke to Dr. Preus about giving me an honor because of faithful work with the Seminary, Dr. Preus told them that I had taken advantage of the Seminary in favor of my own work while in the employ of the Seminary. They said that Dr. Bergmann even made it a bit stronger. At the Wichita Convention, you indicated that you were there and you heard it. At my Dec. 13 meeting with Dr. Preus, he said that he did not say it and that his wife Donna would say the same. He said that you told him that you had said it. This changes the story from what (names deleted) told me in February and again confirmed in a telephone call a week ago, and what you told me in Wichita. I wonder on what basis you would have made such a statement which only a Seminary administrator or CEO could make. If you said it, why were you told by Preus, but not I? Dr. Preus' new claim complicates the matter and raises even more questions than I ask here."

As usual Ed Hinnefeld never answered the letter. Without my knowledge, Pastor Bergmann on April 19, 1989 wrote to Dr. Preus, "...The actual conversation was of my origin, secondly founded on the fact of direct information that I received in conversation with Mr. Ed Hinnefeld..." For the record, I don't care which one of the three said it; they can keep on arguing about it amongst themselves, for the fact is that Dr. Preus as President was party of slander of which he had knowledge, and which he actually shared also with the new development director of the Seminary in Oct. 1988, which was confirmed by a letter to me from him. The fact was that because the Seminary did not provide adequate secretarial assistance, that I utilized over $1000 per year of secretary work at my cost, and I paid for all my flights all over the country. The Seminary paid only for car rentals to make visits in those areas. I was giving the Seminary the advantage. This is typical of the rumors that Dr. Preus started at the Seminary about people he wanted to under-cut.

Who was taking advantage of the Seminary? Dr. Preus and I participated in the ordination service of Pastor Doris Jean-Louis in Haiti on Jan. 15, 1989. In Dec., 1988, I received a short Memo from Dr. Preus' secretary, Miss Trudy Behning, stating that Dr. Preus was offering me payment from the Seminary for the round trip flight to Haiti. I immediately turned this down, saying that I would not use Seminary money for such a trip under any condition. Who was taking advantage of the Seminary? This came at a time when Dr. Preus was trying to win my favor.

Dr. Preus revealed a double standard in fund-raising. On May 11, 1988, Dr. Preus wrote a letter asking me to help raise funds for *Affirm*, even from members of the Seminary President's Advisory Council: "As *Affirm* begins to crank up for the next convention, they are...trying to get names of people who might give to the cause...If you have any names of people, would you please contact (name deleted). I wouldn't mind if you mentioned even some names on our P.A.C...." — I did not submit any PAC names.

Another issue which I consider an ethical question is the decision by Dr. Preus to produce a *Dogmatics* in competition with the one which Synod resolved to publish. The CTCR was made responsible for this, and a letter of Dec. 9, 1986, was sent to 57 LCMS professors and pastors to invite them to participate in writing. Out of these, four declined, and only Dr. Preus and Prof. Marquart did not respond at all to the letter. After another contact later, Prof. Marquart declined. The Board of Regents did not give approval to Cr. Preus to publish a competitive *Dogmatics*. The records show that Dr. Preus personally contacted members of the Seminary Presidents' Advisory Council and raised $22,925 from 22 people **for his own project**. This is the same Dr. Preus who started rumors that I was taking advantage of the Seminary. Furthermore, Dr. Preus approved of a graduate student to work for Dr. Scaer and the Systematics Department for the Dogmatics research at Seminary expense until the BOR learned about it, stopped it, and transferred him to the library. Who was taking advantage of the Seminary?

Issue 6: Dr. Preus characterized a controversial statement on Christology as a profound statement, which appeared in the April-June 1985 CTQ, which was previously treated in this book. Preus said that Scaer was wrong in changing the statement, which disallows the Father and the Holy Spirit to be part of theology. Werning informed the ADJ and APPEALS that he rejected this statement as false doctrine, and that he refuses to accept the statement's indictment that thereby he is denying Luther's doctrine and effectively destroys the Gospel as the message of completed atonement. I sent them the critique which was reproduced earlier in this chapter. Both ADJ (with the objection of Dr. Griesse) and APPEALS said that this is not false doctrine or theologically wrong. The ADJ Hearing Tr. 71, lines 2-5 quotes Dr. Preus making this astounding statement about Christology, "They (Father and the Holy Spirit) don't have to be named. When you say Jesus Christ...The (Christian) knows that you are including the Father and the Holy Spirit." This direct quote raises the question of fusing the three Persons of the Trinity into one without distinctions between the Persons.

Issue 7: Dr. Preus stated in the transcript before the ADJ, "That is what Jesus is talking about when He says, forgive, forgive, forgive. He never said that they have to repent first. He never said that they have to ask for forgiveness," and later he stated, "God has already forgiven them" without repentance. Another instance was the Nov. 22, 1988 BOR resolution which gave forgiveness without repentance, in which Dr. Preus led. Neither the ADJ or APPEALS found these denials of the Office of the Keys and Confession, even though he offers forgiveness without repentance, and absolution without confession contrary to Lk. 17:3, 1 Jn. 1:9, Acts 8:22-23, Rev. 2:5, 2 Cor. 7:9 and Large Catechism (Tappert 458:10, 15; 460:28, 30). As Werning charged Dr. Preus with false doctrine in this denial of the doctrine of repentance-confession and forgiveness-absolution, so he also charged the members of both Commissions, which had no effect on them, as they seem to believe that the Preus' statement is perfectly orthodox.

Issue 8: Despite my urging to ADJ and APPEALS to take both false theological statements to the CTCR, both ADJ and APPEALS failed to do so. Synod Bylaw 8.51f states that at the request of either party, the ADJ or APPEALS **shall** seek interpretation of theological issues. Werning has reminded both Commissions that they disobeyed Synod Bylaws and violated their trust with the Synod which elected them to conduct the church's work, and that they are disobedient in their Christian and ecclesiastical obligations.

On April 18, 1991, I received a letter from Chairman Walter Dissen of APPEALS in which it is said, "The simple truth is that you never made a proper and timely request for an advisory opinion from the CTCR." My March 25, 1991, letter to the Commission on Adjudication and Appeals recorded a partial list of times when mention was made of presenting the two theological matters to the CTCR: 1) Sept. 14, 1989, letter to ADJ, page 2, para. 4, lines 6-8: "Let us be open and honest about this and let the CTCR make a decision." 2) Sept. 12, 1990, letter to ADJ for rehearing, page 1, para. 2, line 7-9: "It seems incredible that the ADJ has not requested a theological ruling on two doctrinal issues from the CTCR." 3) Aug. 27, 1990, letter to APPEALS with copy to ADJ, page 7, lines 31-38, "I recall in our March 15, 1990 hearing in St. Louis that a member of the Commission stated that theological matters would have to be studied by the CTCR. If the ADJ persists in its erroneous decision in this regard, a way will be found to get a theological ruling from the CTCR..."; page 9, lines 3-5: "This is another case where the CTCR needs to react, and overrule the Commission, if necessary." 4) Aug. 27, 1990 letter to APPEALS, page 2, lines 9-10 to page 3, line 1: "I requested the ADJ to take this to the Synod's CTCR, but they failed to do it. And ignoring or denial of this point cannot be done without a CTCR decision." 5) Sept. 20, 1990 letter to APPEALS with copy to ADJ, page 3, para. 4, lines 1-3. 6) Feb. 5, 1991 letter to APPEALS with copy to ADJ, page 10, para. 2, line 8ff, "Neither the APPEALS nor the ADJ did what was urgent and proper in this regard: Take the statement to the CTCR."; para. 3, lines 9-12, "One wonders why the APPEALS did not go to the CTCR for a decision. That's why the CTCR exists."; page 14, para. 2, lines 6-9, "Since I am charging that both theological issues are unscriptural, I will persist until the CTCR reacts to these two unBiblical statements." 7) Feb. 7, 1991 letter to President Bohlmann with a copy to APPEALS and ADJ, requesting him "to do what APPEALS and ADJ did not do - take the two theological statements to the CTCR." The APPEALS denial for a rehearing is dated March 21, 1991, which is six weeks after these early February letters and eight months after the first cited statements.

Then came the **April 16, 1991**, letter from APPEALS that I never made a "proper and timely request for an advisory opinion from the CTCR." I ask: When the APPEALS read all of the above statements in the letters and documents, what did they make of it? Did they think or say that Werning obviously is making an issue of APPEALS taking this to the CTCR, but technically he has not stated it in a formal and proper manner, so we will ignore it? If that is the case, one would expect that APPEALS would remind me that I may have thought that I made a request but I did not put it in the right terms. **The Bylaws do not mandate the exact form in which the request should be made, so how can my way of saying it repeatedly be termed "improper"?** Ethically and morally, I was urging AP-PEALS to take it to the CTCR. The Synod dare not accept APPEAL's attempt at a "show of right" or "appearance-management" tactic to avoid what I clearly was asking to be done. APPEALS was disobedient to the Synod By-laws in this matter!

Issue 9: Preus' attorney, David Keller with the approval of Dr. Preus in the hearings (see transcripts) and in their documents was guilty of "name-calling," making the following judgments and false allegations against Werning without any presentation of evidence: "Werning brought a frivolous case...guilty of a perversion of the system...an injustice seeker...guilty of bullying...abusive, paranoid-like, manipulative, unethical." Werning was not on trial and charges were not to be piggybacked in this case, but both ADJ and AP-PEALS allowed this false witness against a Christian brother despite the fact that no evidence was presented for the allegations and that it was called to their attention immediately and in letters. The members of both Commissions have been charged by Werning to be guilty of breaking the 8th Commandment in allowing this to happen without objection. Their decisions simply ignored the fact that Preus is guilty here of false allegations, judgments and name-calling.

Issue 10: A number of issues of the Visit Teams were brought to the attention of the Commissions that impact negatively upon the administration of Dr. Preus. These were summarized previously.

Issue 11: Another issue brought to the attention of the Commission on Appeals is the fact that Preus' allies, *CN* and *Affirm* have perpetuated a falsehood in behalf of Dr. Preus related to his violating 1 Cor. 6 and going to civil court. *CN* had regularly printed misinformation from various allies of Dr. Preus. I personally heard one of the spokesmen say at Emmaus Lutheran in Fort Wayne on the night of March 10 **in the presence of Dr. Preus** that Dr. Preus had to go to civil court in order to have the adjudication process open for him in The Lutheran Church-Missouri Synod. Fact: On Aug. 8, 1989, Dr. Preus went to the Allen County Circuit Court and on Sept. 23, 1989, he filed a complaint with the LCMS Commission on ADJ against the CTS BOR, against Pres. Ralph Bohlmann and 1st VP August Mennicke. **Six weeks after** he went to civil court, Dr. Preus went to the Synod, yet he has allowed the persistent untruth that he had to go to court to make the adjudication process in the LCMS open for him.

Issue 12: The Erroneous APPEALS Decision:

Despite all the evidence in the transcripts and the documentation which have been summarized, and despite the fact the Dr. Preus continues to say that he has done no wrong, the LCMS Commission on Appeals on Jan. 17, 1991 declared: "Dr. Werning acknowledged his own sin and declared that he forgave Dr. Preus (TP4/26/90, TP165,178-9). Preus apologized for any wrong he had done Dr. Werning and forgave Werning in the same way. (ID., P.212, 22-3). Forgiveness of sins given and accepted is final...When forgiveness is sought and absolution is given, the matter is closed. In that spirit, the Commission on Appeals declares this case closed."

This above statement and conclusion violates the facts of the Transcript and is an **untruth and a deception:** The transcript shows that I testified that I made a mistake in signing a support letter for Preus in 1985 against my better judgment, so I told the BOR on May 20, 1989 that I asked Preus for forgiveness for being "chicken" and signing because I wanted to keep my job. The cited pages do not show that Preus forgave me for signing that statement in his behalf, nor that I repented for bringing any charges against him. (Please note that the BOR meeting was three months before I **started** the Adjudication process.) The transcript shows that I "forgave him in the spirit of Christ" (which means that I forgive him in my heart), but I stated that **"I cannot absolve or forgive him according to the Office of the Keys."** Obviously, APPEALS took the first phrase totally out of the context of T165 and 178-9, for the next phrase, and the entire Transcript, and all the documents reveal with great clarity that no forgiveness was given **because there was no repentance.** The Transcript and documentation show the **opposite** of the APPEALS' conclusion: Dr. Preus consistently stated that he did no wrong!

Having received a copy of Dr. Preus' Feb. 20, 1991 letter to APPEALS which rejected all my charges and which added charges against me, and looking at the Transcript and documentation in which Dr. Preus said he had done no wrong, and remembering that APPEALS erroneously stated that "Preus apologized for any wrong he had done Dr. Werning," I asked Dr. Preus for a visit on April 12, 1991, to ascertain the accuracy of APPEALS' conclusion that Dr. Preus had admitted his wrongs. Since this statement was not consistent with the evidence of the past two years, I sought clarification on April 12 in the hope that there was a genuine change of heart.

The meeting was amiable, but sadly I must report that nothing changed. In answer to a number of questions, Dr. Preus said several times that every bit of the case and every charge was frivolous on my part, and that there was no substance to my charges, that he had no idea how he wronged me, and that he did not sin against me in any way. This experience revealed again that he does not understand what edification, correction and mutual consolation of believers is all about. My heart grieves at my experience of the past two years with Dr. Preus in my facing his confrontational, win-lose approach so consistently that one must conclude that he does not know how to live in an edifying atmosphere and situation which alone can lead to true and lasting repentance-forgiveness.

A REVIEW OF THE ADJ AND APPEALS DECISIONS

On August 23, 1990, I received an undated "Decision of the Commission on Adjudication" (ADJ) which declared Dr. Preus guilty of breaking the 8th Commandment in two major areas, but failed to deal with two statements involving false doctrine. Jan. 17, 1991, was the dated decision of APPEALS that failed to deal with the evidence at hand but declared forgiveness for all, and closed the matter. The decision of the Commission on APPEALS dated March 26, 1991, denied a motion for a rehearing in the case of Dr. Waldo Werning against Dr. Robert Preus.

Letters to APPEALS on Aug. 27, 1990, Sept. 20, 1990, Feb. 5, 1991, Feb. 27, 1991, March 22, 1991, and March 25, 1991 presented my argumentation based on **evidence** from the transcripts and documentation that Dr. Preus is guilty of breaking the 4th and 8th Commandments in areas beyond the two issues in which ADJ found him guilty and of false doctrine in two theological statements. In my Feb. 5, 1991, letter and subsequent letters to APPEALS with copies to ADJ, on the basis of evidence which was ignored, I charged the individual members of both Commissions with allowing and participating in the sins of breaking the 8th Commandment and of being guilty of false doctrine in two areas where Dr. Preus is theologically wrong, and requested a rehearing from them. They denied a rehearing.

Bylaw 8.69 states that all decisions of APPEALS shall be binding upon all parties to the case and not subject for review, reversal, amendment or modification, which makes the APPEALS' refusal for a rehearing the final step to victims of wrongs. I announced to both Commissions in requesting a rehearing which was denied that my next step will be to tell it to the church, giving it to the delegates at the Pittsburgh Convention and writing a book for them and LCMS members to decide whether the evidence is conclusive related to the guilt of Dr. Preus in breaking the 8th Commandment and in defending two theological statements which I charge constitutes false doctrine.

The sins of Dr. Preus now also belong to ADJ and APPEALS. This is a public offense. They are Synod's official representatives properly to administer Law and Gospel and to reflect evidence exactly rather than their misinterpreting, re-interpreting or taking things totally out of context.

Objections Sent To APPEALS From Participants

Dr. Howard W. Tepker, my theological advisor, who observed the entire proceedings and has read all the documentation wrote to the APPEALS: "Recently I had the opportunity to read the decision of the Commission on Appeals in the matter of Waldo Werning and Robert Preus. I regret to say that I am perplexed and saddened that the LCMS APPEALS has apparently discounted much of the testimony of witnesses, and reached the conclusion that the matter has been resolved. Brethren, the last paragraph on page 9 of the Commission's report, to the effect that both Dr. Werning and Dr. Preus confessed their sins and received forgiveness, is **not an accurate assessment** of what transpired in the meeting of the Commission.

"As Dr. Werning's theological adviser, I attended both meetings of ADJ and heard the testimony. I have reread numerous times the charges brought by Dr. Werning. What is more, I know the heartache, anguish, and in some cases bitterness that past and present members of our Faculty have felt because of action taken by various administrators, including Dr. Preus. In my opinion it is simply unthinkable that some of the more important oral and written testimony could so easily be discredited and disallowed by both Commissions.

"It appears that APPEALS simply concurred with ADJ when the latter found Dr. Preus innocent of the charges. And in cases where the ADJ found that Dr. Preus had sinned, APPEALS reversed the opinion of ADJ and exonerated Dr. Preus, despite oral and written testimony.

"Even more serious is the fact that APPEALS in its report did not deal more resolutely with the charge of false doctrine brought by Dr. Werning against Dr. Preus when Dr. Preus defended an incorrect statement on Christology written by Dr. Scaer and published in the CTQ — even after Dr. Scaer agreed to an important change in language. When there is disagreement on doctrinal issues such as this, the matter should be referred to the CTCR for an opinion. But this was not done.

"One has a right to expect more of a Commission which is entrusted with The responsibility of serving as the final court of appeals in The LC-MS. Yours in the interest of Christ and His church, Howard W. Tepker, Th. D."

Dr. Erich H. Kiehl, professor at the St. Louis Seminary another theological advisor, wrote the following:

"On April 10th, 1991, I received a letter from Dr. Robert Preus. In this letter he states that the Werning-Preus case had come to an end with the recent decision of the Commission on Appeals...Since I serve as one of several spiritual advisors of Dr. Waldo Werning and hence have in my confidential files the facts in the matter, I find the action of the ADJ and on Appeals very perplexing. I was asked to attend one of the meetings with the ADJ.

"The 1989 Synodical Handbook under VIII Reconciliation, Adjudication, and Appeal, A. General Principles, –8.01 Purposes and Objectives, states: 'The provisions of this article are established in order to provide a means consistent with the Holy Scriptures to find the truth, provide for justice, and safeguard the welfare of the Synod, the members of the Synod, and those (whether or not members of the Synod) holding positions with the Synod, or with an organization owned and controlled by the Synod.' "

"D. Rules of Procedure, 8.51 Establishing and Amending Rules of Procedure, a. states as a basic principle: 'A Commission shall be governed in its acts, procedures, and judgments by the Holy Scriptures and Christian principles.' "

"A careful review of all the documents in my confidential files clearly indicates that both the ADJ and APPEALS need prayerfully in the presence of God to study all the data to see whether the proper Scriptural and Christian principles were followed in this case. To follow these in every instance, regardless of who is involved, is part of the solemn oath of office. It is important to remember that all involved in this case stand before the just and righteous God and must answer for whatever was done and whatever decisions were made in the light of the extensive evidence available. It is important also to remember as the Apostle Peter stated in Acts 10:34: 'In truth I perceive that God shows no partiality' (New KJV).

"I must conclude that both commissions and especially the Appeals Commission have failed to recognize **on the basis of the evidence** that the actions of the defendant were wholly inconsistent with Biblical principles and that the two controverted theological statements are totally in conflict with the Scriptures and Confessions. I am deeply grieved by the injustice of the decision. Yours, in Christ, Erich H. Kiehl"

On April 13, 1991, Dr. Waldemar Degner wrote to APPEALS:

"Dr. Robert Preus placed into my mailbox at the Seminary under a cover letter dated April 6, 1991, the findings of APPEALS 'In the Matter of Waldo Werning, and Robert Preus.'

"Included in this report, page 5, is my own testimony given on 4/26, 90 p. 25 of the Transcript. Please be informed that my testimony in the APPEALS version is completely inaccurate, that it is in contradiction to the intention, and that it is unrecognizable to me.

"If such distortion of witness is accepted as evidence by the Commission on Appeals, I fear for the future of TLC-MS. Our dear Lord was sentenced to the cross on the value of false testimony. Certainly, brothers in Christ will not permit such practices in the Church.

"For the sake of the Church's integrity and mission I trust that you will do what is necessary to correct the records. Sincerely, Waldemar Degner"

On April 23, 1991, Dr. William G. Houser wrote to APPEALS:

"On April 26, 1990, I appeared as a witness to give testimony in a hearing in the matter of Dr. Waldo Werning and Dr. Robert Preus. The decision of APPEALS is simply untrue which maintains that the faculty had the right in its April 17, 1989 meeting to discuss false allegations against Werning and to pass a resolution with false witness despite the Eight and Fourth Commandments and the warning by the BOR.

"I gave testimony (Transcript 28-36) to ADJ, which is confirmed by other faculty members that some members of the faculty were guilty of insubordination in view of the BOR's request that the faculty not discuss this matter. The faculty resolution broke the Eight Commandment by presenting falsehoods against a brother who was not present. Dr. Werning did not disseminate unfounded and untrue descriptions of the faculty or anyone, and so was falsely accused.

"You have done a great injustice to a Christian brother and against the Church in your decision which helps establish an untruth. Speaking the truth in love, Dr. William G. Houser"

On April 15, 1991, I wrote to APPEALS to inform them that Professor Robert Newton made strong objections against the severe distortions and misrepresentations which Appeals made of his testimony in the Adjudication Transcript. Prof. Newton expressed his grave concerns directly with the Commission on Appeals, and so chose to keep his letter private.

"Appearance Management" Decision

The APPEALS decision is obviously an "appearance-management" document, which is a classical example of "making a show of right" by presenting many matters totally out of context to such an extent that those who read the scurrilous document can only conclude that Werning was such a zealot in bringing false allegations against Dr. Preus and that the Faculty had to come to the aid of themselves and others. This "appearance-management" document is the worst kind of breaking the 8th Commandment. I counted seven untruths, 12 misrepresentations, and a number of conclusions in the APPEALS Decision which are not supported in any way by the evidence.

As difficult as it is, and as fearful as this act is in presenting charges against my brothers, I have no other choice for the sake of the purity of the Gospel and God's Word in a church that has been crippled by a lack of Biblical consistency and practice. I come to the church as a sinner humbled by the fact that I do sin daily, and one who is always prepared to repent of any specific sin against a brother where evidence is shown, and to be forgiven by fellow Christians.

This has been a painful experience, as I refused to recognize the severity of the spiritual problem of a good and true friend, a respected world renowned Lutheran theologian. The one thing that must permeate friendship is the reality of Law and Gospel in personal behavior that centers on actual repentance and forgiveness daily. I and others have accepted a false peace for too long. It is time to go beyond friendships and symbols of orthodoxy, and get back to God's way in godly practice in the church.

CHARGES VS. COMMISSION ON APPEALS

On Feb. 5, 1991, I wrote a 17-page letter to the individual members of APPEALS with copies to the members of ADJ, stating among other things, "I will show that the conclusions of APPEALS are political, wrong, and unBiblical because they ignore those people whom Dr. Preus has offended by his sinful actions and allows those sins to stand without repentance; the APPEALS ignored the documentation that showed Dr. Preus standing firmly with his contention that he had done no wrong..." Please note that on May 14, 1991 (after APPEALS claimed Dr. Preus admitted no wrongs), Dr. Preus sent a letter to the Faculty, together with his evaluation of the presentation by Dr. Ralph Bohlmann to the Faculty on May 1, 1991, in which he said, "...I refuse to be bullied legalistically into repenting of things I have not done or things I have done which are good works, pleasing to God for Christ's sake." Consistently, Dr. Preus has said that he has done no wrong, yet APPEALS lied and deceived the Synod when it said, "Dr. Preus admitted his wrongs," and then closed the case.

I wrote more than three letters to members of Appeals, and will quote directly from my letter of May 29, 1991:

LCMS Commission on Appeals

Mr. Walter Dissen	Rev. Alan Barber
Rev. Harlan Harnapp	Rev. Victor T. Hellman
Rev. Edward Saresky	Rev. Marcus Strohschein
Mr. Robert Doggett	Mr. Walter Tesch
Mr. William Killion	

LCMS Commission on Adjudication

Rev. David Caspersen	Rev. David Bode
Rev. Wilbert Griesse	Mr. David Jarratt
Rev. Carl E. Mehl	Mr. Robert Moeller
Mr. David Piehler	

Dear Brothers in Christ:

On April 25, 1991, I sent a letter to the LCMS APPEALS with a copy to the Chairman of ADJ, for the members of that Commission, which raised the same issue related to both Commissions in my appeal for a rehearing, which was denied. In a February letter, I reminded the members of both Commissions that if a rehearing was not granted, that I would charge all with supporting the breaking of the Eighth Commandment and with false doctrine in two areas. I have not heard whether my April 25 communication has even been received.

My April 25 letter pleaded with individual members of APPEALS, and now also with all the individual members of ADJ, to face the issues individually. You are being charged individually, and it is time for you to face your conscience and your Lord that you may recognize that your decision (except for two matters by ADJ) is a misrepresentation of the facts and that in essence you are deceiving the church. As indicated, I am not asking for an apology for myself, but a statement of repentance to the whole church, and specifically the witnesses and advisors who participated. If I were you pastors, I could not preach another sermon until this was cleared before the Throne of Grace. If I were you laymen, I could not partake of Communion one more time until repentance and forgiveness had taken place.

I have great sorrow over what you have done to yourselves, and I am especially concerned about the **author** of the APPEALS decision, for that is totally corrupt. You have my information related to my statement in my 16-page "Statement of Conscience," page 14, that when I met with Dr. Preus on April 12 to ask him what wrong he had done (since the Commission's conclusion stated that he admitted his wrong), he said he had no idea what you were talking about or what wrong he had done, and that he had not sinned against me. Brothers, you have published a blatant lie. I did **not** forgive him for all his wrongs because he admitted not wrongs. I did **not** repent of various sins against him, and your words are a lie...

For those of you who do not indicate repentance for your faulty actions and false doctrine, if I do not hear from you soon, I shall attempt to encourage your District Presidents to admonish you. I am sharing this only so that it will not come as a surprise if you do not individually take steps to disassociate with and to repent over the wrongs you have supported.

I hold no animosity toward you, but only have grief in my heart. It is very painful to see men hurt themselves and the church to the degree that you have.

May God graciously favor you with new understanding of this situation and to heed His Word and His will. Grace and peace in our Lord Jesus Christ!

Yours in Him, Waldo J. Werning"

*   *   *   *   *

No Disqualifications of Appeals Commission Members Who Had Conflicts of Interest

Another complaint against APPEALS is that they did not disqualify one of its members, Dr. Harlan Harnapp, who took an active part for Dr. Preus against the BOR in writing a letter to the Board as an advocate for Dr. Preus; nor did they disqualify him for being named on the *Affirm* masthead, which provided advocacy for Dr. Preus, which would disqualify him in civil court. Pastor Harnapp failed to recognize that he might later become part of the Appeals process, which was the time for him to make a judgment instead of expressing himself earlier even without evidence. Any member of the Synod's APPEALS should have the ethical standard not to get involved in any conflict at any level because each issue potentially could end up in that Commission. Yet the APPEALS refused to disqualify Pastor Harlan Harnapp. His July 19, 1989, letter stated, "Before God who reads and judges the hearts of each of us, it is appropriate that each member of the BOR look ing into the eyes of Christ asks himself, 'What God-pleasing service do I render my beloved Savior if I should vote for the removal of Dr. Preus...What will I have done to promote or hinder the spreading of the whole and pure Word of God.'"

Both Dr. Harnapp and Walter Dissen should have been disqualified to serve on the Preus' panel. Fact: *Balance, Inc.,* parent body of *Affirm* and of the "Legal Defense Fund," which has supported Dr. Preus, made reports in 1987, 1988, and 1989 as truthful under penalty of law that Harlan Harnapp was Secretary and a member of the BALANCE trustees, and received annual funds of $1765.49, $733.49, and $408.86 as expenses reimbursed; the same IRS reports showed Walter Dissen to be a trustee of BALANCE, and as such received $1068.77, $333.09, and $1050.70 for annual expenses reimbursed. Read the articles supporting Dr. Robert Preus in *Affirm* and the pleas for financial support for his legal defense, and you must agree with the letter of protest which the BOR sent to the APPEALS on March 4, 1992, reminding them that the BOR has approached APPEALS many times, seeking the disqualifications of Harnapp and Dissen, and on all occasions, Appeals refused.

The BOR letter records that Harnapp was on the editorial staff of *Affirm* until Feb. 1992, and by virtue of his editorial position with the magazine which had articles soliciting contributions to the "Legal Defense Fund" for Dr. Preus, would prove a conflict of interest. The current BALANCE secretary on Nov. 21, 1991, wrote a letter to certify that Harnapp was not involved with the establishment nor the administration of the "Legal Defense Funds," **but that was not the issue.** The issue was that he was on the the BALANCE Board and the editorial committee which was responsible for appealing for funds. On Nov. 12, 1991, BALANCE secretary Bergmann, in a notarized statement, stated that he had examined the records of BALANCE INC. and nowhere at any time in the past or present has Mr. Walter C. Dissen been on the Board or in any way officially connected with BALANCE INC. Significantly, Bergmann **does not deny** that Harnapp was secretary of the **Balance** Trustees! The BOR letter states that Dr. Bergmann's letter lacks any credibility in saying this, for "the IRS requires that all payments to officers, directors, and trustees by tax-exempt entities be reported on form 990's. For all three years the returns show payment of expenses to you (Dissen) as a trustee, and to Rev. Harnapp as Secretary," and this was reported by two different treasurers. Were the payments fantasy figures? Notice that Bergmann's letter does not assert that Harnapp was not on the Board of Trustees, which leaves him still hanging.

Who lied? The treasurers Suelflow and C. M. Davis, or the new secretary, Pastor Mark Bergmann? The IRS is involved and should be interested in these two contradictory statements made by supporters of Dr. Preus.

"Where Did Preus Lie?"

Issue after issue of *CN* made repeated references to the case which the Praesidium brought against Dr. Robert Preus, and repeatedly campaigned against the Vice-Presidents as villains who must be deposed at the Pittsburgh Convention because they are allegedly "pawns" of President Bohlmann. Otten's approach is what can be termed "accusation journalism." There are many important and valid matters against Dr. Robert Preus that are documented, but the limitations of space in this book allow only selected summaries of the decision of the Indiana Commission on ADJ in the case of the Praesidium against Dr. Preus. The vote always was on termination of clergy status for Dr. Preus. The Indiana Commission's decision does not repeat the documentation, but only provides the conclusions:

Count 2, "Refusal to cooperate with reconciliation efforts as disobedience to God's Word and as violation of Synodical By-laws": Findings of fact: 1. Dr. Preus did refuse to cooperate with reconciliation efforts, as were properly recommended on Oct. 10, 1989, by the Synodical ADJ...2. This refusal to cooperate with reconciliation efforts was manifested by Dr. Preus throughout the five-month period...Nov.-Dec. 1989-first quarter 1990. 3. The decision to refuse to attempt such reconciliation was knowingly made by Dr. Preus... The decision was that Dr. Preus was "disobedient to God's Word,...violated the By-laws of our Synod..." All voted for termination.

Count 5, "The complaint for declaratory judgment is a false complaint before the Allen Superior Court": Fact: "1. Dr. Preus did misrepresent the truth in his allegation that 'all of the defendants are working in concert as agents of the Synod' to keep him from access to the ajudicatory bodies of the church. No factual basis was presented by Dr. Preus to support this allegation...2. Dr. Preus did further misrepresent the truth in his allegations that Dr. Bohlmann had been acting as his 'enemy'...No factual basis was presented by Dr. Preus to support these allegations...3. Dr. Preus did further misrepresent the truth in his allegation that Dr. Bohlmann had acted as 'Chief Justice' and Attorney General of the church. No factual basis was presented by Dr. Preus to support it...4. Dr. Preus did further misrepresent the truth in his allegation that the Commission on Constitutional Matters dealt in judicial matters. No factual basis was presented...6. Dr. Preus is responsible for anguish and injuries because of these misrepresentations of the truth...8. The Church, at large, has been spiritually hurt by these misrepresentations contained within the litigious acts of Dr. Preus before the Allen Superior Court. 9. Dr. Preus withholds confession, and, hence contrition, with respect to any sin on his part...Conclusions:" (Note: five points are given at that point which indicated that Dr. Preus erred in five misrepresentations, and has been disobedient to the Word of God.) All voted for termination.

Count 6, "**The letter to** *ALIVE*, published on May 14, 1990, as an untruthful publication": "Facts: 1. Dr. Preus did misrepresent the truth in his April 14, 1990 letter...(in respect to four statements)...5. Said misrepresentations have resulted in spiritual anguish and injury to Dr. Bohlmann and Dr. Sohns...7. Dr. Preus withholds confession, and hence contrition with respect to any sin on his part...Conclusions: Dr. Preus has erred by making the aforesaid misrepresentations and by offering the same for publication, and thus has been disobedient to the Word of God.." All voted for termination.

Count 7, "THE NOV. 29, 1990, LETTER FROM DR. PREUS TO THE SYNODICAL COMMISSION ON ADJUDICATION AS (A) A FALSE ACCOUNT OF HIS DEALINGS WITH DR. BOHLMANN AND OTHERS, AND (B) A VIOLATION OF HIS NOV. 14, 1990 PROMISE TO MEET IN JANUARY, 1991, FOR RECONCILIATION PURPOSES": The facts of the documents here show that Dr. Preus misrepresented the truth in five matters, and that Dr. Preus erred and was disobedient to the Word of God. All voted for termination.

Count 8, "THE DECEMBER 8, 1990, LETTERS FROM DR. PREUS REGARDING DISTRICT PRESIDENTS GARBER AND SOHNS AS BEING CONTRARY TO CHRISTIAN PRINCIPLES FOR DISPUTE RESOLUTION": The facts of the document show that the Praesidium was right in their accusations against Dr. Preus, and the conclusions confirm that Dr. Preus has erred and been disobedient to the Word of God in various ways, and that he as in the other counts is unrepentant. All voted for termination. This case contains so many facts in the Transcript and even the summary in the decision that there is no space to reproduce the documentation.

These issues of the Praesidium's case against Dr. Preus with their documentation and the Commission finding him guilty in five counts are separate and different from all of the ones with documentation that I have presented in this book. My documentation happened before July 1989, while the Praesidium's documentation began with July 1989. What a volume of evidence of the guilt of Dr. Preus!

AN ORGANIZED CAMPAIGN WITH ENABLERS AND ENFORCERS

Enablers and enforcers are basic influences in waging political warfare in the church in order to advance personal agendas. Enablers are ones who supply the means, give influence, power and authority to fulfill one's objectives, and help, equip or give sanction to one's cause. Enforcers compel action, urge, constrain, and see that people stay in line.

As with the ELIMites twenty years ago, the Preus party-"Confessional Lutherans" have a well-organized system of enablers and enforcers to keep their crusade alive and healthy. This part of my report will reveal some of the enablers and enforcers, who may be church functionaries, family, seminary faculty, students, *CN, Balance* and *Affirm,* "Confessional Lutheran" organizations and periodicals, and Free Conferences. These enablers are organized and kept active to conduct the holy war against the "enemy" who allegedly is trying to take away our church, its doctrines, all of which allegedly is part of a secret operation. The Preus party-"Confessional Lutherans" are the good guys, and everyone who does not join them or disagrees with them are the bad guys. The enablers use all the tactics of fear, changing labels, holding public court, always keeping on talking and writing regardless of their mistakes, ignoring all the legitimate documentation, and complaining about wrong procedures.

Breaking The Eighth Commandment And Holding Public Court

The biggest offense and sin of which Preus' enablers are guilty is the sin against the Eighth Commandment. First, they abuse this Commandment by stressing the second part of Luther's Explanation (that we should defend and speak well of others) in order to try to stop the legitimate pursuit of Matthew 18 by their victims; then they proceed to break the Eighth Commandment through slander against anyone who dares to use Matthew 18 against their leader, Dr. Preus.

Already in 1984, I received a letter from a former student, now a pastor, who wrote, "I would ask one favor of you as a professor and a friend. And that is to teach against gossip. The amount of gossip at the Sem bothered me when I was there...I believe this is a major problem. Perhaps you are in a position to help." The September, 1991, Seminary Administration and Board letter to the Fort Wayne Student Body to discourage students from getting involved in the Preus matter or insisting on sharing Preus' allegations was met with condemnation by the students. Secretary Stuart Tietz, Secretary of the BOR, wrote, "Contrary to well-established Synodical guidelines, there have been rather widespread discussion on various actions pending before the ADJ and APPEALS. Such discussions frequently result in rumors and misstatements of facts that have been damaging to individuals, the Seminary, the Synod and the church-at-large. The BOR fervently requests that the students and faculty at CTS adheres strictly to the By-laws of the LCMS which are set forth in the 1989 *Handbook* concerning these matters."

Various students have complained bitterly about the constant breaking of the 8th Commandment by some faculty and a number of students. One student in 1991 prepared a "Manifesto Against Tale-Bearing," in which he wrote:

"We find that there is a good deal of tale-bearing happening on this campus. Some have found out the hard way, others through warnings that confidences will not be respected, and damaging rumors, whether true or false, will be reported to the authorities. We find that this practice is very destructive of community, as people are reluctant to trust others with their feelings or needs. All of us are sinners, and what we need is mercy, forgiveness, and healing, and not condemnation or harassment.

"We are supposed to be training men for the holy ministry. Pastors are expected to respect confidences, but tale-bearing erodes trust. As pastors we are committed to caring for people in their needs, but expressing weakness makes one a target for harassment. We find that this institution has the mentality of a police state. This is a deplorable state of affairs.

"We will not assign blame or judge anyone. We are going to take moral responsibility for this state of affairs and repent. Irrespective of when this practice started, or who is responsible for continuing it, we are going to take collective responsibility for stopping it. And the first stage is repentance. Following the prayer of Daniel 9, we repent for ourselves, for anything we have done in the past, and for the whole seminary. We pray for God's mercy, that He will forgive us and supply us with grace that this evil practice be stopped.

"As Christians and Seminarians, we pledge ourselves:

— To love one another, and so fulfill the Great Commandment.

— To respect confidences and not bear tales, true or false, that will harm anyone at CTS, and to carry out the 8th Commandment.

— To contribute what we can to improve the spiritual atmosphere of this seminary, that friendliness should replace suspicion, and pastoral care be given to those who express needs. We also pledge to work out these resolutions both in our personal devotions and lives, and in our dealings with other students in this seminary.

— To pray against this evil practice, until the Seminary be delivered from it." (Student name deleted)

I submitted to ADJ an Exhibit from the May 27, 1991, CN, simply signed by an "LCMS professor," which asks questions numbered A through Z, most of which blatantly breaks the 8th Commandment. One question asks, "Does the LCMS know about the connection between Waldo Werning and the Bohlmann Administration?" The only connection I have had with his administration were several insignificant formal telephone inquiries, which Dr. Bohlmann never answered. Thus the Preus camp and *Christian News* - tremendous enablers for holding public court.

Almost a classical example of the breaking of the Eighth Commandment which is happening in many places was the experience which I had in a conference in March with about twenty retired pastors in which the enabler, a pastor friend of Dr. Preus, gave a good presentation, but then ended with criticism of a an unnamed Seminary professor who gave a presentation at his church together with several students. This pastor said that there was Reformed and Decision Theology, and Church Growth, you know how bad that is. When as graciously as possible I said that I could not believe that one of our Seminary professors would be guilty of this, and I wanted to know who it was, this enabler refused to tell but repeated the accusation. A little later, he agreed to tell the name of the person. I refused to believe that this professor was quoted accurately. Then the enabler stated that the professor did not say it, but that it was in a film. All kinds of undocumented accusations were made, so I asked why we were being told this and what Biblical role were we to play? I asked why he was broadcasting this to people who were not involved and have no Biblical responsibility for it. The enabler became very agitated, and some of the pastors present also were very unhappy about me raising the questions. I have learned that it is very unpopular to try to raise questions about obeying the Eighth Commandment when supporters of the Preus party are present.

Enabler Hinnefeld

Many of the members of the Seminary President's Advisory Council (PAC) became very good friends of mine. Among them, I counted Edwin Hinnefeld as a very dear and close friend. Not only was he seen as a very able Christian, but also one who consistently practiced the Christian faith. I was very aware of his very fine credentials, which have been advertised repeatedly in *CN* by the "Confessional Lutherans." How did my friend Ed Hinnefeld enter into denial and be brought into the "big lie" which would ignore all the documentation and evidence which showed that Dr. Preus needed correction and rehabilitation.

It was first in Sept. 1988 during the time of a Seminary PAC meeting when he, Dr. Eugene Bunkowske and I were speaking about what we could do to help Dr. Preus in some of his administrative difficulties. When I expressed concern about actions of Dr. Preus and Dr. Scaer which Dr. Preus was to handle and take to the BOR at the Nov. 12, 1988 meeting, both Dr. Bunkowske and Mr. Hinnefeld encouraged me strongly to let the BOR handle it, which I said I had already agreed to. But Hinnefeld showed an intensity in encouraging me to drop the entire matter. "Drop it!" is the word that I've heard from my friend Ed several times since that time, no matter how severe the problem was.

On Apr. 11, 1989, I wrote to Hinnefeld to tell him that I knew he was experiencing emotional turmoil about the Preus matter. I wrote, "...Dr. Scaer and Dr. Preus will have to hold themselves responsible for sharing this news in many areas of Synod, and providing partial and slanderous information...The evidence also shows that there has never been a serious effort on their part to deal with this on a Biblical and spiritual level, but always by political approaches. I must say that I was somewhat shocked to hear you say during our visit at the Sept. 1988 PAC meeting that you would go to the BOR and bring some PAC members to defend Dr. Preus. By this statement, you involved yourself totally and had the appearance of mounting a political campaign to back a person in order to discount the facts of this situation, no matter how true and valid. The perception is that you would without facts counter it with a numbers game. Your encouragement to me to drop everything and walk off was also shocking in view of my being victimized in an unChristian manner, as have others before me, and a largely unhappy and divided faculty and student body. I have never so openly been encouraged to disobey God and been intimidated by a man to go against conscience and instruction by God's Word, as your suggestion to me. Bruised and bloody bodies are all over, and I'm asked to close my eyes and walk off..."

The letter continued, "It is note-worthy that you say you get many calls from laymen and PAC members about this matter. This is somewhat surprising since laymen are not that active in the pipeline, so obviously someone is feeding it. I have no assurance that you are not a willing agent of that pipeline. There were various signals in our visit you had accepted the political interpretations which had been fed to you by others, and I've heard some of the same statements shared by faculty members who have heard it from the mouths of the Scaer-Preus group at the Seminary...I was simply amazed that I am intimidated, criticized and dealt with as if I am the trouble maker, rather than a victim...How will the untruth be corrected? I have written this only because of your raising the issues in our telephone visit, when I perceived that you were rather aggressive in being a part of the administration political efforts..." This letter indicates that I already perceived Ed Hinnefeld as a strategic enabler from the beginning. He never answered that letter.

On July 10, 1989, I wrote to Mr. Hinnefeld, in which I reviewed our visit at the Wichita Convention, "...you allow Dr. Preus and Dr. Scaer to violate Biblical truths in a Christology statement, and break the Eighth Commandment and Matthew 18 flagrantly. You want me to disobey Christ's commands ...'Drop it and forget it' is your consistent urging upon me, even though this is only one of a series of situations over the past years, which now has become a scandal in the Church...'Ignore it!' Ed, I still can't believe what I am hearing from your lips, and I can't believe the intensity with which you are urging me to become a participant of another man's sins, which Christ in no way will overlook; He calls rather

264

for repentance. I am completely shocked that a Christian business man who does so tremendously well in practicing the Christian faith in business and is so successful, but, when it comes to Church affairs and Christian relations, he becomes sure of himself by listening to a man who has thoroughly discredited himself because of his breaking of the Eight Commandment, Matthew 18, and giving misinformation...We who have the facts are belittled, and you who have heard only from a breaker of the Eighth Commandment, know it all..."

Instead of an answer to my letter, Mr. Hinnefeld proceeded to hold public court in an article in the Aug. 7, 1989, *CN* to which I responded to him, "Your 'Letter to All Laymen - URGENT' written by you causes great heartache because it is basically fraudulent and dishonest...You pose as an expert with all evidence and facts in hand. With service to well-known corporations, the implication is that this is a man with an impeccable reputation and absolute integrity who is telling the truth in the same way that he has serviced these corporations...The Robert Preus issue finds you stating that 'what may happen next is the removal of other devoted and confessional professors, then the consolidation of the two Seminaries, and then the initiation of liberal teachings to our young Seminarians so eventually true doctrine will not be taught or required...We must protect true doctrine, we must defend that the Bible is inerrant, we must stop this enormous demonstration of **Power without Love**..."

The letter continued, "Your first paragraph (in *C.N.*) came directly from Dr. Preus, heard by various faculty and staff members, recited by the wife of the PR man to a number of seminary wives, and heard by you obviously when you were on campus shortly before the Wichita Convention to visit Dr. Preus. Ed, there are so many witnesses that Dr. Preus was saying this before they heard it from others and from you, that the witnesses are sticking out of our ears...Just this week some faculty members were together and claimed that they could count up the twenty five people who have been axed in one way or another by Dr. Preus since he began in Springfield. What about Alan Nauss, Randy Shields, Wilbert Rosin, Albert Garcia, Warren Wilbert, etc., etc., etc." Note: here I informed him about the faculty questionnaire of 1984 which has been previously printed in this book.) The "Confessional Lutherans," and *CN* have repeatedly stated what Hinnefeld published in the Aug. 7, 1989 *CN* about closing the Seminary, liberal teachings, and removing Confessional professors. This came right out of the mouth of Dr. Preus and faculty and staff supporters.

On Sept. 26, 1989, Mr. Hinnefeld abused his recent appointment to be Chairman of the President's Advisory Council (PAC), by inviting the members of the PAC to meet with him in a rump meeting at the Holiday Inn in Ft. Wayne on Oct. 13. He stated, "We must discuss the firing of Dr. Preus, the removal of Dr. Scaer as Academic Dean, the removal of Prof. Dean Wenthe as the Dean of Graduate Students and the removal of Prof. Kurt Marquart as Chairman of the Systematics Department. In addition, Rev. Robert Roberts was removed from his relationship with the PAC."

Since that time some PAC members have reported that they have received letters from Mr. Hinnefeld to inform them about "what is going on at the Seminary," acting as the self-appointed source of "information," which has been filled with allegations. Through Free Conferences and meetings throughout the country, he has been one of the chief enablers of the entire Preus campaign, seeming to legitimatize the allegations so that they appear to be truths.

I wrote him three more letters after that without getting any answer, and also wrote a letter in early April 1992 to tell him that I would be mentioning his enabling work in this book, and that I honestly seek communication from him. He was a dear Christian friend who can speak all over the Synod to provide false accusations, but he does not answer a person who wants him to face the documentation.

Regarding the rumor about closing the Seminary which Hinnefeld started in Aug., 1989, enabler Rev. John Fehrmann editor of the **Confessional Lutheran Reporter,** is quoted in the Minneapolis Star Tribune several weeks ago, "Bohlmann wants to close the Seminary. Just watch." This is groundless rumor that Hinnefeld started in August 1989 in *CN.* Only a Synodical Convention can close a Seminary.

We can wholeheartedly agree with many of the mission and Synodical goals which Hinnefeld has enunciated in his Free Conference speeches. However, some of his financial information about Synod is misleading, which has been clarified by the Board of Directors. It never pays to overstate one's case, but that is what Hinnefeld is doing, besides encouraging withholding of funds.

Family Enablers

It is sad to know how much pain a family experiences through publicity of one's father's problems. Especially one of the Preus sons, Rolf, participated aggressively as an enabler in his father's campaign. Rev. Rolf Preus wrote an article entitled, "Werning's Rubic Cube Theology," in *CN* on May 20, 1991 (pages 14-15).

Among the undocumented accusations and false witness of the *CN* article was the following, "...more than malicious vendetta...Waldo Werning does not think like a Lutheran...Werning's theology works like the rubic cube...Werning could not tolerate David Scaer...in the light of the undisguised animosity which he had against him...Werning knew that when he charged Scaer that Scaer's position of the doctrine of the Holy Trinity was sound...Werning's charge of false doctrine against Scaer cannot be disassociated from his own personal dislike of Dr. Scaer...It is simply intolerable that a man should use doctrinal charges as a personal weapon to punish those who displease him...Ridiculous charges...His dogged persistence in obtaining either surrender to his will or his pound of flesh, portrays the same self-vindicating spirit with which his so-called 'Statement of Conscience' is filled...Some of what Werning accuses Preus are allegations of years ago which have been thoroughly discredited. For example, issue 10 (Note: these were the Visitation Team reports from the Seminary between 1983-1985, and the faculty questionnaire of 1984, etc.)...

Rolf Preus' *CN* article continued, "Werning's accusation had no merit...Werning's persistence finally induced Scaer to agree to revise the statement...Werning never was interested in safeguarding the doctrine of the Trinity, but in bullying those who refused to submit to his will...Such a charge should not be entertained merely to satisfy the craving of a bully...Waldo Werning has done much to promote the false stereotype of conservatives which is often used to discredit solid, confessional theology...which parades itself as orthodox...in condemning this statement (forgiveness without repentance), Werning clearly rejects the doctrine of objective justification...If Werning really believes that you cannot forgive those who sin against you unless and until they repent, he is objecting to the Gospel itself...The Christian does not insist on identifying certain acts committed against him as being sinful acts before he forgives...To forgive — without insisting on repentance first — is not cheap grace, nor is it a denial of the Office of the Keys...By this exercise, Werning condemned the true and evangelical statements of both Scaer and Preus..."

I wrote to *CN* on May 21, 1991, that this article has "17 instances of false witness and a number of instances of false teaching." On May 21, 1991, I wrote to Rolf Preus, "Your breaking of the Eighth Commandment, your ignoring and discrediting of evidence, and your promotion of false doctrine in two areas make it necessary to call to your attention that these sinful acts must be corrected...This letter is my first step of Matthew 18 to point out your sins for which I call for repentance and correction...I simply will not be a party to charges and countercharges in an unBiblical way to conduct a public trial through *CN*... There are over 700 pages of documentation to disprove your 17 false allegations."

After I received no answer from him. I contacted him by telephone, but he said that he did not want to talk to me. The next day, June 18, 1991, his secretary phoned to say that he did want to talk. In our lengthy telephone visit later, Rolf Preus merely repeated many of his allegations, while I asked again, what documentation he had to make such accusations. He continued to repeat the accusations, but gave no evidence. He said, "I could have been much stronger than what I wrote in *CN*." He suggested that we should carry on our communication through the pages of *Christian News*. He said, "You are so filled with malice and you have filled your malice with Matthew 18...After talking to you, I will not allow you to pursue this with me."

In a letter of June 20, 1991, I reminded Rolf Preus that I had followed Matthew 18 and the Synodical adjudication provisions. This letter told that in our telephone visit for one hour that he did not answer one of the questions of my May 21 letter. I wrote, "He revealed failure to understand the difference between personal opinions and evidence according to universal standards...According to the Synodical Handbook, I am sending a copy of this letter and my previous letter and all pertinent documentation through the South Wisconsin District President, Dr. Edwin Suelflow, who, according to the By-Laws, is to try to affect reconciliation. I trust that he will be able to assist you in providing evidence for your false witness."

On June 20, 1991, I sent a letter to S. W. District President Suelflow, telling him that I was following By-Law 8.05 which gives an opportunity to him to settle the matter. I reminded Suelflow that Rolf Preus wants to hold public court with claims and counter-claims, judgments and counter-judgments, and condemnations and counter-condemnations. I believe such an approach is destructive of Christian fellowship and is condemned in God's Word. Therefore, I have made it plain that I will not counter in *CN*, as Rolf requested. All I request is that Pastor Preus make a public statement that he retracts all of the condemnations and judgments which are false witness which he published in *CN*."

After several months, I received a Sept. 3, 1991, letter from Rolf Preus. His five-page letter admitted no wrongs, and in many cases simply restated the accusations. At the end, he wrote, "You and I both have had our say in the public forum, that is, in *CN*. Let us leave it at that. Please accept my apologies for any hurt I have caused you...I wish I had not replied to your 'Statement of Conscience.' Please understand that I will not under any circumstances, either publicly or privately, admit that I have lied about you or promoted false doctrine..."

In a Sept. 10, 1991, letter I took time to respond to Rolf's argumentation in his Sept. 3 letter, but reminded him that one of his big problems was the fact that he was a third party, acting as an advocate in making charges against me for David Scaer and Robert Preus. I wrote, "The question always arises as to why you think you have the evidence when all you have is third-party allegations and impressions...Therefore, I charge you as a third party intruding yourself as a public judge. Your ill-advised judgments confuse the issue, and clarifies nothing, nor does it edify...Please note that I am not trying the Robert Preus case with you, because that is not your business, but my charge deals with your error of intruding yourself as a third party..."

On Oct. 2, 1991, Rolf wrote that he would not send a statement of regrets or correction to be printed in *CN*. He maintained that he was not a "third party" in involving himself. Again, he wrote that he believed that I had sinned in publishing my "Statement of Conscience" document after APPEALS had whitewashed the Robert Preus case. He wrote, "...your case against Robert Preus was and remains thoroughly without merit or substance..." He stated that he would not make a public statement of retraction because that would lend credibility to my charges. He ended by stating that if I signed a withdrawal statement of my "Statement of Conscience" that he would make a statement to withdraw his *CN* article, "Werning's Rubic Cube Theology."

On Oct. 11, 1991, I wrote to Rolf, "In response to your Oct. 2, 1991, letter unfortunately it is a repetition of allegations of the past in holding to untenable judgment. It is impossible to communicate when a person insists that evidence disappears simply because he says so." I reminded him that I was again asking S. W. Dist. Pres. Suelflow to deal with him.

On Oct. 11, 1991, I wrote to Suelflow, "I assume that you have been discussing the problem of Rev. Rolf Preus with him, but I do not find any change of attitude or understanding in his letter concerning his sins of breaking the Eighth Commandment. I am making a solemn request of you, on the basis of the Synodical Handbook procedure by which you have been working the past several months that you as District President try to settle this matter between us and get brother Rolf to recognize that he simply cannot publish judgments against a brother as he did in *CN*...It would be good news to hear from you that Rolf has listened to you, changed his mind, and cleared his sin against the Eighth Commandment.."

On Oct. 25, 1991, Suelflow wrote, "I am convinced that Pastor Preus holds no malice or ill will against you. I do not see him in violation of the Eighth Commandment. Criticism in and of itself is not a sin...I, therefore, suggest that you and Pastor Preus sit down together in the presence of a third person, if you desire, and talk out your differences as brothers in Christ. I will not bring this matter to the Adjudication Committee of the South Wisconsin District."

On Oct. 30, 1991, I wrote to Dist. Pres. Suelflow in response to his Oct. 25 letter in which he said that he did not see Rev. Rolf Preus in violation of the Eighth Commandment: "Rolf did not follow Biblical procedures when he made charges against me as he presented them publicly in *CN*. He publicized them instead of speaking to me. He acted as a third party...made public judgments...I pray that you will change your statement that you 'do not see him in violation of the Eighth Commandment.' Any ecclesiastical or civil court would find him guilty on the basis of these untenable judgments...I repeat my solemn request of you of Oct. 11, 1991 on the basis of Synodical Handbook procedure that you as District President try to settle this matter.."

On Nov. 11, 1991, I wrote another letter to Suelflow reminding him that there were two articles of false doctrine in my charges, too. I wrote, "...I pray God's grace and mercy that you will be successful in counseling him and in gaining a Biblical correction." That is the last that I've heard from Rev. Rolf Preus or from District President Edwin Suelflow. I assume that Suelflow was able to get a promise that Rolf would no longer use *CN* as an advocate for his father and as a critic of people like me, because I have not read anything in *CN* from him for a long time. However, Rolf has spoken at a few Free Conferences and other meetings. Since the Adjudication system has broken down in the Missouri Synod, I have not pursued this matter further, but am revealing it in this book.

Faculty Enablers

Evidence of faculty involvement as enablers and enforcers has been provided throughout this chapter. The main enablers are Dr. David Scaer and Prof. Kurt Marquart, who is now the theological advisor of Dr. Preus, and who has been a strong advocate all the time. Faculty enablers and enforcers have been active since the time the loyalty statements were taken around almost 10 years. Some faculty members complained about David Scaer putting pressure on them to be loyal to the "boss" and sign a statement. Other lieutenants were very active in getting signatures, and all were active in getting the word and rumors out throughout the faculty, student body, recent seminary graduates and to other friends.

1991 graduates Craig Stanford and Karl Weber naively provided evidence of these faculty members' involvement as enablers and enforcers when they wrote **a word of thanks** in their recent publication, "A HOUSE DIVIDED (CONCORDIA THEOLOGICAL SEMINARY)": "I would like to express a word of thanks and deep appreciation to those faculty members who offered encouragement, wise counsel, good humor, and protection to the graduates and students whose only desire was to speak the truth, confess the faith, and defend others against wrong-doing." Stanford and Weber merely acknowledged what everyone knew was the truth: there are faculty enablers who have taken an active part for Dr. Preus against the Seminary BOR and the Synod, helping also **to maintain the pipeline to "Confessional Lutherans" and** *CN*, either directly or indirectly. The students were led to believe that what they were saying was speaking the truth and confessing the faith, whereas they received their misinformation and allegations directly from the Preus pipeline. There was no other place from which to get it.

In June, 1989, Prof. Kurt Marquart, in one of his acts as an enabler, took a statement, "AN URGENT PUBLIC PLEA TO THE PRESIDENT OF SYNOD" with the help of Prof. Arthur Just and others to faculty to get signatures of support. Because it did not receive general support, it was withdrawn. In May 20, 1991, Enabler Marquart wrote to *CN* to object to me naming Marquart as a chief advisor of Dr. Preus. He defended Preus' defense of Scaer's false Christology statement. Marquart was the chief enabler for the war fought against church growth by approving the dishonest Master's thesis (mentioned earlier), and later refusing to stop its circulation. Keep in mind that this is a Seminary committed to the Gospel of Jesus Christ, and such scholarship should not be condoned by Prof. Marquart.

Marquart showed the theological elitism of the Preus party when at the Wichita Convention he stated that the ordinary pastors and delegates could not understand the ministry issue because there were only a few theologians present there. The next day he apologized for that statement.

Student Enablers

This is the most tragic part of all. A good number of students during the past several years have been perverted through propaganda from the Preus party, mainly through faculty members who are enablers for Preus. In a way it is understandable: the majority of the faculty have determinedly kept out of the campaign and rumor mill because it was not their business, and it was wrong to get involved. Therefore, they went quietly about their business. The Preus faculty enablers were very active, speaking as though they were knowledgeable in this entire matter, and they showed great interest in the students. Because of the loyal faculty members' non-involvement, they appeared to be unconcerned about the students' concerns and dilemma. If you are a student, then who do you speak to and spend time with? Obviously, the one who shows interest and who has tidbits to share.

Besides, Dr. Preus was always there at the Dining Hall and other places, and gave invitations to his home, to play the role of a victim and to keep on saying that he has not been told what wrong he had done. Recently, several students told me that they were very uncomfortable sitting in the Dining Hall with other students in visits with Dr. Preus, as some of the students were sitting there "drooling on their shoes" while listening to this dear abused man, who is one of the greatest Lutheran theologians in the world, and also whom the BOR is denying them an opportunity for them to have him in class.

The student enabling system was working perfectly. Craig Stanford and Karl Weber, fourth year students in 1990-1991, appeared to have been the chief enablers among the students that year. There were others who are named in their book, "A House Divided, mentioned in the previous paragraph. Their book is filled with rumors, including one about me in March, 1991. I attended the Free Conference in Chicago in early March, driving by myself, and I recall passing two seminary students whom I did not know — later I learned that it was Stanford and Weber. A week or so after the Conference, I heard a rumor going around the Seminary that I was writing names of students attending the Chicago Conference to give them to Interim President Norbert Mueller. When I saw this rumor in *CN* about someone giving Mueller names of students who had attended, I contacted Herman Otten by telephone on March 20, 1991. He said that he phoned Norbert Mueller to ask whether Werning gave Mueller names of students of CTS who were at the Free Conference. Obviously, I neither made a list of students, nor told Mueller or anyone, because I didn't know who Stanford and Weber were or that they were there. On March 26, another student told me that Stanford and Weber told him about the name list and that Werning was doing "terrible things." This student asked, "What is he doing?" Stanford said, "I really don't know. Ask Werning." That is the integrity of the Preus rumor mill.

What role were the students to play in the Preus affair? Where should their information come from, and how authentic was it? Who authorized them to be involved? The involvement of the activist enabler students was about the same as the St. Louis seminary students in 1973-74 in backing Dr. John Tietjen. As in the case of Tietjen, these students received their information from the pipeline. They could not receive accurate information from the BOR, so the only source was either directly or indirectly from Dr. Preus, which invariably appeared in *CN*. What proof did they have that Dr. Preus was abused other than his allegations? When the students were warned by the administration not to be involved, they attacked the administration as being dictatorial and guilty of mistreating Dr. Preus.

Stanford had written a previous book, *The Death of The Lutheran Reformation*, which told about his unfortunate experience with liberalism in the former LCA. That book appears to be well-reasoned and fairly documented as good as can be in a personal account. He used that book to claim credibility in his writing a book on the Fort Wayne situation. He wrote that he found himself, with the help of Karl Weber, "again fulfilling the role of chronicler from inside the classroom of a theological institution whose integrity is being threatened by forces that wish to take away from the church, sound confessional Lutheran theology." That is an untruth without any documentation, which came first from Edwin Hinnefeld in August 1989, who was mimicking what he heard from Dr. Preus and friends.

It is not surprising that Stanford continues, "The LCMS is involved in a theological battle of the first order. These battles are just as serious as those in the 60's and 70's." No documentation is given as to what the false doctrine might be. But still he states that through faithful Lutheran laity, that "God would use this report in some way once again to cause our people to come to the defense of God's Word..." There you see the "holy war" of the "Confessional Lutherans" against all of us "liberals."

On page 3, he states, "The seminary was moved to the campus of Fort Wayne in 1976 as a result of the doctrinal struggles and upheavals." There is no evidence or documentation for making such an untrue statement.

When Stanford states, "From time to time a faculty member did depart from God's Word," his footnote indicates that one of these was Dr. Alvin Schmidt, of whom he says that he "was found guilty of false doctrine, then sued the Synod and received a $40,000 out of court settlement." What Stanford does not say is that the Synod's APPEALS made this judgment while the Synod's Commission on ADJ and the BOR did not declare him guilty of false doctrine, nor that APPEALS had no authority to do so, and did not even face Dr. Schmidt personally or have a hearing with such a charge, and did not get a ruling from the CTCR. Neither did Stanford or *CN*, report that the apparent reason why Schmidt won an out-of-court settlement for $40,000 was that this was only reimbursement for lost salary in a case in which the BOR itself recognized that Schmidt was done an injustice by Preus' violation of procedure; the BOR went to the Commission on Constitutional Matters which recognized that Preus had used wrong procedures and that **Schmidt was not given due process**. APPEALS also acted in theological matters without a ruling from the CTCR. So what Stanford and *CN* is trumpeting is unproven allegations. Only after APPEALS took their wrong action did Dr. Schmidt take the Synod, the Seminary and Dr. Preus to court, as the Synodical By-Laws allow after all procedures have been exhausted by an individual. Yet *CN* tries to make a virtue of Dr. Preus taking the Synod to court because Dr. Schmidt did the same thing.

Stanford writes, "Claims and charges of turmoil among faculty, staff, and students under Dr. Preus, either in 1984-1985 or 1988-1989, are simply false and cannot be sustained through a study of the facts." The documentation from those reports in this book destroys that untruth.

Next, Stanford provides the chronology of recent events of CTS in the "Reimnitz Report." My book also has provided documentation to show that Reimnitz only covered selected events which Preus and his allies fed him. The unreliability of the Wesley Reimnitz fabrication can be known by his mostly secondary sources and third parties!

On page 13, Stanford complains about the letter of the BOR, which he titles, "Students Warned not to Discuss or Comment on the Matter." By what authority can students be involved in a Board matter? He also stated, "Historians in the LCMS have noticed an increasing phenomenon, which factors heavily in the Preus case..." Who are these historians who have already pontificated on a current matter? Are they some faculty enablers?

There are references to the 8th Commandment related to "protecting the name and reputation of our neighbor." That apparently is the justification for student involvement and the letter which the majority of the student association sent to the BOR on Sept. 29, 1989, which appeared in *CN*.

Stanford gives the student account for their invitation to Dr. Preus to be the speaker at their closing banquet. The AAL banquet was canceled and the Preus' supporters conducted a special appreciation dinner sponsored by "Stanford Publishing," with the help of private contributors. Stanford provides the introduction which Joseph Brennan gave. Brennan is another enabler, now a pastor who has written some rather vitriolic letters to various people and places.

Stanford totally distorts the message of Rev. Norman Groteleuschen, speaker at the 1991 Call Service. Stanford wrote, "Instead of encouraging candidates to remain faithful to the Word of God in doctrine and practice, he spoke critically of those who emerged from the Seminary too confident of their theological training. Rather than sending them into their first call with the Gospel of forgiveness of sin ringing in their ears, he used Law to weaken their proclamation. Instead of speaking highly of the theological training the students received under the fine theologians of CTS, he spoke negatively of its ability to prepare men for real life in the parish..." I heard that sermon, and heard something entirely different from what Stanford's mental screen allowed him to hear. The one big point which Groteleuschen made, which Stanford transposed into his allegation, was that graduates need to remember that they are at "entry level proficiency." Even after 47 years of pastoral ministry, I will speak for myself to say that I had only "entry level proficiency" when I was ordained. However, the "Confessional Lutheran" students at the seminary consider themselves to be the "theological elite."

Without any documentation, Stanford, now a pastor, makes the public **false allegation** that the BOR (with the two notable exceptions of Pastor David Anderson and Raymond Mueller, who he claims have shown themselves to be fair-minded men) are "either intentionally or unintentionally destroying the financial, academic, theological, and spiritual integrity that have come to be associated with the Fort Wayne Seminary campus."

Student Association "Integrity Series"

On Nov. 6, 1991, the self-claimed "Integrity Series" featured Dr. Scaer, Prof. Marquart and Dr. Wenthe. The third program featured Ft. Wayne Grads John T. Pless, and Harold Senkbeil, both of whom are featured in other parts of this chapter. The Student Association and the Systematics Department were very transparent in the planning of the program. I was invited by one of the student Student Association "Integrity Series" leaders while in the Library to attend the third program but I declined because I stated that this situation was simply not objective.

The Seminary Student Association became part of the enabler system through the "Integrity Series," which the Dec. 1991 *Cornerstone* reported "debutes at CTS." It is very clear from the content and the speakers that students who were influenced by these men, and that the Preus party initiated it.

Dr. Scaer's presentation on Nov. 6, 1991, was titled, "The Integrity of a Christological Character of the Office of the Ministry." Alluding to Loehe's more sacerdotal view of ministry rather than Walther's, he said, "We may never be able to toss the word 'ministry' back into Pandora's Box, but for the sake of integrity we cannot simply read these multiple uses of the term back into the New Testament." It should be said that the LCMS has done a credible job in holding to the New Testament meaning of ministry (diakonia), but Dr. Scaer and his high-church collaborators simply cannot tolerate anything beyond the **pastoral ministry**. Furthermore, there is a tendency to transfer to the pastor upon ordination rights which belong to congregations, taking away some of the responsibilities of the priesthood of all believers and congregational polity. They hold only to proclamation and preaching, and forget about mutual exhortation and edifying. They simply wipe out any Biblical doctrine of other ministries as shown in Eph. 4.

Dr. Scaer has been known to make all kinds of unsettling statements that appear to be sacerdotal. When he says, "Since our ministry is only Christ's, the words 'effective' and 'successful' ministries can have no place in our vocabulary," he places the pastoral ministry totally outside of any evaluation or any recall for cause. That is the position which Dr. Preus has held. Apparently, it is arrogant for a Christian congregation under the Word to believe their own eyes and ears when they first perceive the actions and words of a pastor who has been totally ineffective and even unfaithful to his call. Scaer states, "The Lutheran Confessional writings of the 16th Century are all we need for the direction of the church today." Thus he puts the Confessions in contradiction to proper supervision of pastors.

There is a legitimate side to measuring effectiveness by the pastor himself or by those who are responsible for his spiritual health in the Synod and in the congregation — a District President, a circuit counselor or elders. Aspects that will benefit from evaluation are theological (Is committed to, understands and applies Biblical and confessional truths), personal (strong in the faith, faithful in family relationships, communicating Christian love, serving as a role model), professional (equipped to disciple, nurture, proclaim, and administer faithful in all his work). The pastor should be a true shepherd, and not a dictator in any sense of the word. Seminaries should be expected to certify only those men who have proven themselves to be committed to such theological, personal, and professional effectiveness in their attitude and commitment. Consistently, there have been several graduates who have not lasted more than one year in their congregation because of their dictatorial behavior, while others have been passed around from congregation to congregation until the breaking point is experienced.

Dr. Scaer and his associates need to recognize that the LCMS in its official documents and the work of the CTCR have faithfully enunciated the New Testament teachings of the public ministry and of other ministries which grow out of that. When he asks, "Is the church so insignificant and is Baptism so meaningless that we will not be content until everyone is a minister?" The question should be asked, "When will Dr. Scaer and his friends recognize the fact that the Christian priesthood of all believers has already given a general or even specific role to all members as servants or ministers outside that of the public or pastoral ministry? There is no sense in trying to retain the title "minister" to apply only to pastors. It is as simple as making the distinction between ministers in general and the pastoral ministry. but Dr. Scaer wants to keep the "fight" going by confusing the issue.

Ministry is a generic word in the New Testament and even used with Mary serving Jesus. Culturally today there is no way that the word "minister" by itself can be equated with the pastoral or public ministry because there are so many different kinds of ministers in the world that each one must be defined individually. This in no way weakens the unique call and position of the Lutheran pastor.

In the meantime, debates about documents like, "The Divine Disposal/Dismissal of Ministers of the Word and Sacraments," should be debated in the Council of Presidents and before the CTCR through responsible representatives rather than doing it irresponsibly through labeling and unjust criticism through *CN* or forums for propaganda purposes.

Not only have the Seminary students been influenced to exert pressures through the Student Association, but also propagandized through social affairs such as the Seminary DQ parties each year. This year the party was held in one of the dorms on March 15, 1992.

The student DQ or now IQ party, under the influence and direction of a proper mentor could be wholesome with its humor and satire, but not under the coach or guru, Dr. David Scaer. I attended one DQ party about seven or eight years ago and enjoyed the proper humor and satire, but eventually found myself very uncomfortable with the excessive ridicule and drinking when my conscience started being aroused. I enjoy a good laugh, and have had some enjoyable jesting with Dr. Scaer for some years until it ended in 1988. Then I saw a man who would use humor to belittle students and faculty in their presence while seeming to joke about it, but in reality deeply offending and hurting them. Scaer has a thin skin and is easily hurt himself, but he expects others to see his ridicule as innocent fun. That's the way the DQ and IQ parties are set up. If you do not enjoy it or if you feel offended, you simply do not have a sense of humor. The perpetrators of this satire-ridicule use their unspoken interpretations and understanding, and criticize those who disagree as too sensitive.

The reader needs to be asked some questions: What do you make of a situation where Dr. Preus, Dr. Scaer, Professor Marquart, Professor Judisch with BOR members Ray Mueller and David Anderson present at the March IQ Party have encouraged the students together with Scaer and Preus in their "humor" at the expense of some professors who were not present, and the Pastoral Ministry and the Mission Departments to the extent that a number of students were very offended? How do you interpret the finishing of two kegs of beer by 10:30 P.M., with a few students later vomiting in the sink downstairs? How do you handle the news that some Student Association leaders said that this IQ party was not as bad as some of those in years past (recalling that Dr. Scaer is the guru of them all)? How do you answer an offended student who notes that Scaer's Systematic Department and Pless' presentations at the "Integrity Series" were not lampooned, but that of Professor Newton of the Mission Department was?

My questions of the students, faculty, and two Board members who were present are these: "Would you feel free to tell your congregation where you hold membership all that happened at the IQ party ? If 'no', what would you not tell them and why? Was the Eighth Commandment in its real Biblical sense honored or broken at this party? Do you believe that it is fair or proper to lampoon, spoof or caricature pastors or professors who are not present, when these men are conducting their ministry for the Lord with dignity, faithfulness and success? Is it edifying to ridicule fellow Christians simply because they raise their hands to God sometimes when they say, 'Praise the Lord'? Do you believe that the presence of two BOR members at the party was appropriate without them either halting the proceedings or making a public statement of rebuke about the things that were offensive to others?''

I visited with Professor Marquart on March 16th, 1992 in his office and asked him why he thought some students would be offended at what was said and done at this IQ party. He answered, "I put the line on taking the name of the Lord in vain." I asked him, "so the Eighth Commandment and other questions of ethics do not concern you." He had no answer. At the next faculty meeting, the question of offense at the IQ party was raised, and both Dr. Scaer and Professor Marquart indicated that there may have been some things that happened which were not right, and they would talk to some people. That is all that was said and done.

Preus-Scaer-Marquart Group As "Confessional Lutheran Gnostics"

Throughout this book I have avoided labeling and name-calling, but have attempted to properly criticize only the wrong **actions** of various people. However, in the case of the theology and practice of the self-claimed "Confessional Lutherans" some are convinced that they are guilty of gnosticism so severely that it is proper to name them "Confessional Lutheran Gnostics." This is my definition and explanation of the term:

Confessional Lutheran Gnosticism

There is no substitute for correct doctrine. The authority, integrity and accuracy of the Bible must be held and confessed, and taken seriously in the daily life of the church. However, there is a gnosticism that makes Christian faith primarily a matter of the mind. That is, correct teaching is viewed as having right doctrinal positions without insisting that there be balance in application. Focusing mostly on the correct way of saying doctrine in traditional formulations as the only test of orthodoxy finds the Gospel message of salvation and transformation reduced to correct information about Jesus and God's plan of redemption. Thus the heart, though regenerate, remains stagnant and coldly formal, while there is no application of God's grace as the power of transformation of life. This gnosticism, which centers on head knowledge, right formulations, and keeping of church traditions at the expense of practice, then manifests itself in the bickering and backbiting which has characterized church politics.

When faith in Christ has been reduced to correct doctrine, then Law and Gospel have been confused and abused, and a great part of grace has been lost. Then, correct doctrine is Law. This does not have the power to change people. This results in displacing God's grace which affects the entire life, not just the mind undertaking doctrinal studies for their own sake so that everyone gets it right. This will be followed by high church ritualism and even sacerdotalism, leaving the people basically unfed spiritually for the battles they face in their daily lives. It even results in criticism of people's felt spiritual needs, which are real and on target, and contending that all that people have to do is come to hear the preaching of the pure Word.

The basic problem is that an overemphasis on justification diminishes the Gospel message to correct information about Jesus. Thus the main appeal of this kind of preaching is to people's minds to gain assent to truths. Their hearts and spirits are not served with Biblical truths that guide them in living their faith. The term that the early Church came up with to describe a religion which was entirely centered in the mind was gnosticism. Hence when doctrine is separated from life in Christ and reduced to correct information only, the result is confessional Lutheran gnosticism. This is a confessional position that appeals to the mind only, and does not cultivate the whole man, body, soul, and spirit.

The "in Christ" formula used by St. Paul in his epistles describes the true life of the Christian. St. Paul supports sound doctrine (1 Tim. 1:10), but he makes other things very essential, particularly love (1 Cor. 13). To separate doctrine from everything else that characterizes the life "in Christ," loses that life. However, Paul does not present doctrine in competition to love.

Confessional Lutheran Gnosticism allows a lack of vibrant Christian faith on the grounds that the person has been justified and confesses true doctrine. The solution to this situation is to recognize it, repent of dead works (Heb. 6:1), and feed people spiritually through the Means of Grace. As the body is fed three times a day to sustain it and give it life, so also it is necessary to feed the New Man, the regenerate spirit, daily so that it might bear fruit in good works acceptable to God by the Spirit. This historic Lutheran teaching is the answer to Confessional Lutheran Gnosticism.

What is the essence or substance of Confessional Gnosticism in its Missouri Synod Lutheran manifestation? Its basic theological ingredients involve the theological aberrations which I have quoted in the writings and sayings of Dr. Preus, Dr. Scaer and some of their followers. Various ingredients of their "new doctrine" are mimicked by the "Confessional Lutheran" student followers of Dr. Preus at the Seminary. These ingredients are: A Christology formulation which fuses the Father and the Holy Spirit into Christ, and so if you say "Jesus," as Dr. Preus said, everyone knows that you also mean the Father and the Holy Spirit. This has resulted in assimilating sanctification totally into justification, so that any preaching of sanctification is seen as legalism. Various students have been disturbed, telling trusted faculty members at Ft. Wayne about being warned about preaching sanctification.

This isolation of practice from doctrine has allowed them to minimize stewardship and missions, as is seen in Rev. Schaibley's sermons. It reaches to a denial of the Office of the Keys and Confession in Dr. Preus' proposal of forgiveness without repentance, and absolution without confession. Dr. Scaer took it to its final conclusion in his sermon of several weeks ago in the denial of actual sins, holding that it is dangerous in Lent to evaluate one's self on the basis of sins, but there is a need for forgiveness only for sin in the singular, original sin. Therefore, there is an emphasis on objective justification to the exclusion of subjective justification. There is an emphasis on Scripture Alone and Grace Alone, but a neglect of Faith Alone. In other words, the perception is that man is saved by grace in Christ, but we are saved and forgiven whether we have active faith by the Holy Spirit or not. This is a dangerous Christian universalism which appeared in the Nov. 12, 1988 BOR resolution which Rev. Raymond Mueller wrote, and in the teachings of Dr. Preus and Dr. Scaer.

It is natural, then, that there should be an overemphasis on the part of the pastor and of worship services at the expense of priesthood activities, for it is now the main duty of the members to show up for worship and go through their liturgical exercises. It is amazing that many fine laymen in the Synod have bought into this crude doctrine of Sacerdotalism (overemphasizing the position of pastors at the expense of the priesthood of believers). I certainly cannot understand how this anti-laity theory could be acceptable in Phoenix with Mr. Marion Winkler.

What the "Confessional Lutherans" with Dr. Preus, Dr. Scaer and Prof. Marquart have ended up with is doctrine isolated from practice at the points which they choose. Since they need to hold public court and utilize *CN* as their voice, the 8th Commandment is no longer essential. Now it is easy for Prof. Marquart to place the ethical line at taking the name of the Lord in vain, but forgetting about the 8th Commandment. Misrepresentation and cheating in Master's Theses then are not of great concern.

What results in Confessional Lutheran Gnosticism is pure doctrine in the head, ears and mouth, spinning and spinning without any real contact with the heart, hands, feet and life. This separation of doctrine from practice in daily life related to the 8th Commandment and truthfulness is very similar to the cultural spirit of situational ethics. However, this is a distinctive version with conservative confession but habits which destroy the Christian community that is to be built by consistent practice of the confession. This is another "Higher Critical Method," which allows changing of the Biblical text that in the case of the Preus-Scaer theology excises sanctification in the areas of gossip, slander and lies.

Just like the ELIMites who forged their own "doctrines," so the "Confessional Lutheran Gnostics" have as one of their main principles, "the end justifies the means." After all, the "others" are trying to take pure doctrine away from us, close our Fort Wayne Seminary, and soon they will be ordaining women. Just watch! Fear which is constantly aroused by *CN* and the "Confessional Lutheran" reporters keeps the troops writing letters, meeting in Free Conferences and in District caucuses, and labeling anyone who disagrees with them.

I have not changed theologically or in church practice since my day of ordination, but I am miles away from the tactics of the "Confessional Lutheran Gnostics." It is not difficult to see who moved. Yet, in order to keep the fires burning high, I am now said to be a "flaming liberal, and off my rocker." Keep in mind that I am just one individual who experienced this. Think of what would happen if another dozen victims would open their files on the Preus administration and the "Confessional Lutherans." The editor of the "Confessional Lutheran Reporter," Rev. John Fehrmann, began his Nov. 1991 issue with, "REMEMBER! SHARE THE FACTS AND THE TRUTH!" Rev. Fehrmann sent letters in 1990 to various pastors, whose names he received from other "Confessional Lutherans," to encourage them to be a voice for them in their region/area and to try to constitute themselves and officially organize as a Confessional Lutheran study group in their District.

In a September, 1990, Confessional Lutheran Reporter, Fehrmann tells about his propaganda, "DISSEMINATE THIS STUFF! It is your responsibility to reproduce these materials and disseminate them to all of the clergy and laity of the district who are of like mind." I requested him to put me on his mailing list, for which I would pay, but he refused. Fehrmann's Reporter said this of me, "It should be noted that Rev. Werning is still on the clergy roster of the LCMS and is even considered to be in good standing." I talked to Fehrmann on the telephone to object to this insinuation and other untruths in his writing, and he expressed regrets but never made a correction. These men are in such great denial that they have not recognized truth for several years.

On March 7, 1992, the co-editor of the New Jersey Confessional Lutheran wrote me with much pretension and condescension, "As one of President Bohlmann's apparent fellow travelers, we are aware of the fact that you instituted some ecclesiastical charges of your own against Dr. Preus...It would seem that the adjective 'litigious' would be a fair characterization of Waldo Werning." He stated that they intended to use the word to describe me in the next issue, and if "either I or my lawyer feel that such an adjective is misplaced in the intended context, please advise us." I wrote to tell him that my dictionary said that the word meant, "to tend to engage in lawsuits." I have never in my life engaged in a lawsuit against anyone and certainly do not believe in going against a Christian unless the circumstances demand it. I reminded him that this idea originated from Dr. Preus himself in the Adjudication meeting. I did not advise him whether or not to print it, but wrote,

"If you do print it, you have just one more sin against the 8th Commandment to repent about to your Lord." His March 19, 1992 letter contained more judgments, labeling and stated about my allegations against Dr. Preus that these are "uncorroborated assertions, which, in their best light, may only be termed as hearsay and idle gossip." This has been the normal response from "Confessional Lutherans." One must face them with this question: What documentation do you have and where did you get it to make such an outrageous judgment?

A letter to Rev. Philip Meyer of Terre Haute, IN, on June 25, 1991, tells about his condemnation of me at the Indiana District Convention in Indianapolis when he scolded me mercilessly without any reference to any specific wrongdoing on my part. I wrote to Rev. Meyer, "Your irrational and unBiblical treatment of me last Saturday at the Convention was very grievous and inexcusable. It wasn't even civil. What made it even more dismaying is the fact that a layman stood there to witness the entire debacle, and I assume that he was your lay delegate. I am sorry that I did not ask him whether he approves of this type of treatment and unprovoked action by a pastor. I had not seen you for a year or two and was coming happily to greet you. You immediately gave me a complete dressing down with judgments and condemnations that I wanted to wipe out of my mind and not want to consider as reality. **Without any evidence** you made wild charges against me, which ended in telling me that I had a bad spiritual problem. If you are a responsible Christian and insist on holding the pastoral office and being a Circuit Counselor, you are accountable for your actions on the basis of Biblical principles. You have violated several of the most basic Biblical standards for which you must be held accountable for your own sake. I did not provoke it, and if you are complaining about my Biblical actions against Dr. Preus, then you are entering as a third party. I have asked Dr. Preus to bring charges against me if I have sinned against him in any way, but he refuses to do so.."

When I did not receive an answer for two and one half months, I wrote to Rev. Meyer on Sept. 16, 1991, "It has been over 10 weeks since I wrote you the June 25 letter related to your unBiblical judgment and breaking of the 8th Commandment against me at the District Convention. Your intemperate action is not fitting of the office of the Holy Ministry, and it is not to be tolerated...I pray that the Holy Spirit will give you the courage to be a faithful Christian and pastor by making confession of your sin to that witness and me. How can you preach another sermon without absolving yourself? I await an early answer from you.." There was no answer from this "Confessional Lutheran" until this day. Since the Adjudication process of the Synod has broken down entirely, I am not allowing criticism for publication of this matter. I want to document another instance of aberrant behavior by a "Confessional Lutheran."

Theology of Glory

The "Confessional Lutherans" use various labels and "red flag" words. One of their favorite is "theology of glory." This is a very useful pejorative to use in order to put the other fellow in place. The ELIMites, the party of the left, originated that against the conservatives 20 years ago. They exclaimed in the July 7, 1975, *MISSOURI IN PERSPECTIVE*, "The theology at the helm of the Synod today is its arch enemy — 'a theology of glory'...Biblical faith — the 'theology of the cross' — calls on people to stop lusting after the supernatural, because that can become a form of self-justification, and instead to start trusting humbly on the mercy of God who revealed His real power on the cross. The conservatives' 'theology of glory' manifests itself most clearly in their unyielding insistence that everyone accept their definition of the word 'inerrancy' as applied to the Scriptures...What is troubling the Synod today is its understanding of God, of faith, and of the

Scriptures is an un-Lutheran 'theology of glory'...." The ELIMites defined 'theology of glory' as centering on God's glory, power, wisdom, otherness, majesty, superiority, and miraculous ability. Properly, it is an emphasis on the resurrection of Jesus Christ and the power that God gives us by the Holy Spirit.

The "Confessional Lutherans," like the ELIMites, have confused the entire issue and use "theology of glory" for labeling purposes without any careful definition regarding the target. Luther's Explanation to the 21st Thesis of the Heidelberg Dissertation properly emphasizes both the theology of the cross and the theology of glory, the suffering and the resurrection, the weakness and the strength of Christians. Actually, Luther's criticism was toward those who were guilty of works righteousness as having a "theology of glory." The "Confessional Lutherans" have used it loosely to include anyone who believes in resurrection power. They want us to stay on Good Friday and forget about Easter. The real "theology of glory" is in what man does, while the "theology of the cross" glories in what Christ does. That's how Luther used it, not how the "Confessional Lutherans" are tossing it around carelessly today. The next time you hear someone criticizing someone who is not present as having a "theology of glory," ask that person what he means, and how it applies. Ask him also whether he has directed his criticism to the Lutheran brother or group whom he is publicly criticizing.

Many of us have some days which seem like Good Friday and others which appear to be Easter. Actually, no matter what kind of day it is, we have a "theology of **hope**" given us both by the cross and the resurrection! Abraham did not have a theology of glory, "Against all hope Abraham in hope believed..." (Rom. 4:18). Both the cross and the resurrection assure us, "For in this hope we were saved" (Rom. 8:24). The Scriptures are the source of the cross and of glory which give us hope, "for everything that was written in the past was written to teach us, so that through endurance and the encouragement of the Scriptures we might have hope" (Rom. 15:4).

We are not to stand only at the cross, but live in hope because of the glory of resurrection. The next time a "Confessional Lutheran" criticizes you for having a "theology of glory," about your anticipation about Christ's coming, you may wish to tell him, "While we wait for the blessed hope — the glorious appearing of our great God and Savior, Jesus Christ" (Tit.. 2:13), our hope comes not only from the cross, but also from the resurrection.

BALANCE — RALI

An Umbrella Publication of "Confessional Lutherans" published RALI, with a BALANCE INC address in St. Louis. The March 15, 1991, issue named the list of Confessional Publications/Groups throughout the Synod, 21 at the time besides *CN*. That issue, as other "Confessional" papers, carried considerable misinformation about the Preus matter and a lot of preaching. On Feb. 1, 1991, RALI with a covering letter by Dr. Edwin C. Weber, sent out a document, "Reclaiming Lutheran Identity." With a proper interpretation, I could very joyfully sign that statement, but I would not want it administered by these "Confessional Lutheran Gnostics." Unfortunately, *Affirm* magazine, which I strongly supported and to which I contributed editorially and financially, and which played a very important role in the past in its reasoned discussion of various issues, has also become a pawn of "Confessional Lutherans." During the past two years, issue after issue has distorted facts related to the Preus matter.

One fine orthodox Missourian, who was held in high esteem by the current "Confessional Lutheran Gnostics" in the past but now has been ostracized because he does not agree with the sins of Dr. Preus, wrote, "They have restricted thinking which sees no evil in the church other than liberalism, decision theology, church growth; the 'we-against-them' mentality obstructs fraternal discussion; there is no fault, wrong-doing or stupidity in any who espouses our cause; they dismiss anyone with whom they disagree with labels and pejoratives such as Reformed, fundies, etc." They want only those elected or appointed to official positions whose only qualifications are that they are members of the "Confessional Conservative" party.

Some wonderful things have been done in the conservative movement and still are. Men and women have risen to serve their church in self-sacrificing ways to the glory of God. However, the "Confessional Lutherans" have become a self-serving group filled with haughty attitudes, self-justification, face-saving, contempt for critics, vendettas, ulterior motives, pretended innocence, twisting the facts, etc. All such misbehavior in the church is of the evil one and must be so treated in ourselves and in those whom we love and admire. The "Confessional Lutherans" respect only their own agenda.

Like other "Confessional Lutheran" magazines, the *LUTHERAN VANGUARD* has been part of the propaganda machine. It grieves me that my good friends Armin Ottemoeller and Marion Winkler have sometimes been very careless with facts and the truth. The April 1992 *Vanguard* makes such wild assertions about Synod as, "staff have signed 'loyalty oaths', all Vice-Presidents have been conquered... Called servants render obeisance or starve...Some have sold their souls. Opposition everywhere is swept away...Thought control is working...The Synodical treasury has been plundered...Religion is a front...Theology is being changed...Missouri is being secularized. Our Confessions are being forgotten. Lutheranism is being diluted. The Bible is being changed. We are no longer a church...The Third, Fourth, and Fifth Vice-Presidents have utterly disgraced themselves and are not electable.." This irresponsible journalism is a blatant breaking of the 8th Commandment in sentence after sentence, accusations without any possible documentation or evidence. This is another example of "accusation journalism."

Harold L. Senkbeil's Book and Articles

Suddenly, a very fine Missouri Synod pastor, Harold L. Senkbeil became an overnight sensation when his book, *SANCTIFICATION: Christ In Action* (Harold L. Senkbeil: *SANCTIFICATION: Christ In Action,* (Milwaukee: Northwestern Publishing House, 1989) was published, and "Confessional Lutherans" encouraged its distribution, and reviews were presented in various magazines. This was followed by an article in the *Lutheran Witness*, and invitations to various conferences, together with several appearances at his alma mater, CTS in Fort Wayne.

That book began as a thesis, *Sanctification: The Evangelical Challenge* (May 8, 1986), written for the Master of Sacred Theology degree with Dr. David Scaer as Advisor, who recommended that it be published as a book. In his introduction for one of Pastor Senkbeil's presentations at the Seminary, Dr. Scaer indicated real pride in this work of his student. The problem is that these works go far beyond mere apologetics or polemics.

The question is: Must orthodox Lutherans abuse Biblical ethics? Do we teach our people to be orthodox, avoiding false doctrine, but tear apart other church leaders and representatives in doing so? There is a legitimate and important use of apologetics in which members at appropriate times are informed where other church bodies veer from true doctrine. We have always done that and need to continue to do so. However, the books under consideration and the behavior of "Confessional Lutherans" today goes beyond all reason and Biblical behavior, and is very counter-productive.

Senkbeil's article, "A Lutheran Look at the 'Evangelicals,' " published in the Feb. 1991 *Lutheran Witness* does not recognize that there is a great variety of evangelicals, and it makes criticisms of evangelicals in general that do not describe many evangelicals. Senkbeil does not follow his own advice in his article, "I submit that Lutherans, rather than simply criticizing evangelicals, can help define a truly evangelical Gospel for our troubled world..." After that, he makes unwarranted judgments against evangelicals without once quoting any examples or evidence of his criticisms.

As a response to Senkbeil's article, I received a letter from Dr. Billy A. Melvin, Executive Director of the National Association of Evangelicals on April 1, 1991, in which he asked, "Would he represent the majority view within the LCMS regarding evangelicals?" Dr. Melvin was aghast that Senkbeil's description would be the general view of the LCMS. I wrote Dr. Melvin that this article "is a completely distorted view by a representative of a small and strong theological clique in the Synod. Many of us are embarrassed, and I personally apologize to you and many other evangelicals for such breaking of the 8th Commandment. I was so sad about this article that I contacted the L.W. Editor by telephone. I learned that there was more response than they had had in a long time and that 95% of the people were against the article..."

I enclosed a questionnaire with the letter to Dr. Melvin, which I gave to evangelical leaders in a national meeting and also at the Fort Wayne Evangelical Pastor's Conference. There were possibly about 20 denominations represented in the answers which I received. The statements were posed **directly** from the criticisms and statements which Pastor Senkbeil made in his *Lutheran Witness* article. In most cases, the answers of these evangelicals were 100% opposite of what Pastor Senkbeil erroneously wrote, and in many cases, about 80% against the views he imposed upon them. Here are some of the statements and how the great majority answered (sometimes unanimously):

1. No one comes to faith except by the Holy Spirit, who prompts the decision to receive Christ — True.

2. Salvation is God's work from beginning to end — True.

3. Salvation remains beyond the reach of the human mind — True.

4. The Christian Gospel is God reaching down to man, not man reaching up to God — True.

5. The Gospel is merely historical information about Jesus and the cross — False.

6. God is always in the driver's seat. He always does things His way, not ours — True.

7. We can make God work according to human expectations — False.

8. The Gospel is primarily historical data rather than "the power of God unto salvation" (Romans 1:16) — False.

9. Saving faith is essentially the decision of the human will rather than a free gift of God — False.

10. Christians can be motivated to live holy lives by instruction in God's law presented primarily as "how-to" lists rather than out of forgiveness, life and salvation He gives us in His Gospel — False.

11. Christian worship is essentially a human tool to recruit and motivate people for Jesus rather than the primary setting where God meets His people in the Word and Sacraments — False.

12. We need more teachings of rules and regulations for the sanctified life — False.

13. We should not "market" the Gospel to perspective customers like we would so many

potato chips — True.

14. Obedience to sets of "Christian principles" saves us — False.

15. We need human ingenuity and techniques to get God's work done — False.

16. The Christian's renewed life is the basis for certainty of salvation — False.

The least that Pastor Senkbeil could have done was to make a scientific study of how valid his caricature of evangelicals is. I do not claim that my questionnaire was scientific at all, but it was just given out at random to Evangelicals in two meetings which I attended. With Senkbeil's misrepresentation of at least a large segment of Evangelicals, it is not surprising that apparently 95% of the letters which came to the Lutheran Witness were critical of his article. That did not impress Dr. David Scaer in his remarks when he introduced Pastor Senkbeil at the Seminary, or Professor Kurt Marquart in his *AFFIRM* November 1991 article, "In our Synod people have become touchy about truth which is distinctive and awkward. Here, too, the culture is running wild. Several random examples will do: When Pastor H. Senkbeil published a splendid article in the *Lutheran Witness* explaining important differences between Lutheran and pop-'Evangelical' beliefs and approaches, he was greeted with a torrent of hostile mail.." Possibly, the mail was very negative because the article was filled with distortions, as I discovered with the Evangelicals which I tested! Statements which I put in my questionnaire appeared in one way or another in Senkbeil's article, and I could not believe that that's what most Evangelicals believe. That article suffered from lack of evidence in making conclusions on the basis of untested assumptions, and made unwarranted judgments against believers in other denominations with whom we have some obvious differences in doctrine, but not the ones which Senkbeil focused on. We should have dialogues with these other Christians, not close the door by distorting their beliefs.

Senkbeil's book, *SANCTIFICATION: Christ in Action* attempts to analyze sanctification as understood by Evangelicals by using selected writings of Charles Swindoll. Senkbeil makes some of the undocumented criticisms of Evangelicals that he made in his *Lutheran Witness* article. These will not be repeated here.

Senkbeil is correct when he criticizes Calvinist, Armenian, and Pietist beliefs, but we can read that in other books which present polemics without breaking the Eighth Commandment. Unfortunately, he does not meet his stated objective for his book, "This book is not directed **against** 'Evangelical Christians.' Rather, it is directed **toward** the recovery of a New Testament understanding of the life in Christ which is both thoroughly Biblical and absolutely practical." Tragically, chapter 5 on "A Lutheran View of Sanctification," begins with great promise, including steps away from Pietism, as he suggests that a Lutheran view of sanctification will be provided. The promise is **totally unfulfilled** in the chapter as it **reveals only justification!**

"The Power for Sanctification" (p. 119) provides no grace or strength from the Holy Spirit, such as 2 Corinthians 9:8. Instead, the author wrongly presents the Lutheran view of sanctification primarily as salvation and eternal life. The quotation from David P. Scaer on page 21 is not only confusing, but wrong, "Justification and sanctification are not two separate realities, but the same reality viewed from the different perspectives of God and man." They are not one reality but two realities where sanctification follows justification, where justification is completed, but sanctification is not. The author's discussion on pages 122 and 126 is not a Lutheran view of sanctification, but of justification. It is an error to promise a large chapter in a book on sanctification, but offer justification in its place. The subject appears to be strongly legalistic, as it mentions only Christ's cross (being saved) as a motivation and specifically as a reason for serving God, but does not direct the reader toward grace and Gospel power that is the strength for sanctification.

The question of man's activity and responsibility in sanctification, and what the true nature of sanctification is, is never answered in a book that promises to do so. The stated goal of the book was sanctification, not justification, sacraments, absolution, and worship. This book does not offer a Lutheran view of sanctification, but only promises to do so. Senkbeil makes some surprising claims without any documentation and which will surprise most Evangelicals, for example on page 38, "...many wings of Evangelicalism are happy to use Higher Critical approaches to Scriptural interpretation..." Who are they? How many? What is the evidence?

His short critique of Swindoll's theology and books is quite confusing. There are short headings and then quotations from Swindoll's books, but often Senkbeil does not state whether he agrees with him or not. He simply has pages of titles and paragraphs of quotations. Sometimes he makes an opening statement in a paragraph, but the quotations do not always coincide with Senkbeil's commentary.

Generous commendations of this book are made by Herman Otten, John T. Pless, and others. Otten wrote in the Dec. 9, 1991, *CN*, "The book classically and distinctly portrays the confessional mind of a Lutheran." He requests readers to study Senkbeil's book. Otten writes, "You will know at least in part why conservatives within the LCMS are promoting Senkbeil as one of the Vice-Presidential positions within the LCMS..." Pless reviewed the book in the Summer 1990 *Lutheran Quarterly*, emphasizing justification issues, while ignoring the fact that there is no Lutheran treatment of sanctification in that book. A review in the *Concordia Journal* of April 1990, very succinctly focuses on the problem of this book, "In the end, this book is more about Christ and His cross and about justification than about sanctification..." Unfortunately, the reviewer states, "This is not a criticism, but an affirmation for that is the way it should be." Are we Lutherans really incapable of writing a book on sanctification which is truly Biblical sanctification? *CN* and others have promoted this book, saying, "Every concerned Lutheran should read this book." Unfortunately, it is being used with its distortions as a textbook at some of our colleges and at the Fort Wayne Seminary.

Senkbeil has been featured at several District Pastoral Conferences, and one of his presentations, *"LITURGY AS MISSION: A Response To The Challenge Facing Lutherans From 'Evangelicals' in America Today"* was reproduced in *CN*, on July 22, 1991. This article has some of the untenable statements which were published in the *Lutheran Witness* article, and also in his book.

What is wrong with this book and approach, and these articles and materials? 1. It gives the impression that somehow doctrinal errors of other denominations cannot be adequately known by our people through basic apologetics, but they must be attacked publicly in order to warn our people of how dangerous these people are; 2. It does not recognize that if we strengthen the Biblical knowledge of our people so that they gain a deepened faith by the Holy Spirit that they will not fall into the trap of other denominations' errors. If we have done a poor job of keeping our people spiritually strong, public distorted criticisms must not be substituted in the attempt to protect members by continually warning them about the spiritual devils out there who will devour them if they cannot name all of their theological aberrations; 3. It is a total law and legalistic approach, not one of grace (it is lecturing, not educating); 4. It goes beyond all reason and common sense and is counterproductive, i.e., a number of our members are offended by this type of crass attacks on others. A diet of "spiritual vinegar" will not make our members spiritually strong to recognize or fight the real enemies.

Christian News — Enabler Rev. Herman Otten

During the past three years, Rev. Herman Otten has been a very destructive force within TLC-MS because of positioning himself and being positioned by "Confessional Lutherans" as judge and jury of anyone and any activity he decides does not fit his "Confessional Lutheran gnosticism." There have been sufficient examples already in this book which demonstrate this point. I am sitting here and looking at a file of 200-300 examples of distortions, untruths, half-truths, and misrepresentations from *CN* during the past three years. Many of these are violent treatment against brothers in Christ. There are no Biblical grounds for such behavior.

I have written various letters and made a number of phone calls over the past three years to try to appeal to Otten's conscience, but to no avail. Anyone who does not agree with him is a dangerous person, a liberal or divisive. No one dare have the effrontery to refuse or fail to answer Otten's questions. On Nov. 5, 1990, I visited with him for about 30 minutes on the telephone and told him that he had betrayed and violated my confidence, friendship and trust, and that I would not communicate with him again until he proves that he is a trustworthy Christian, When you disagree, with him, you are a dangerous person.

Otten printed, "The Logic of Rumor," in the April 1, 1985 *CN*, as he "piously" analyzed the rumors about Robert Preus, while he himself as the master rumor-monger with his "Missouri Insider," "Missouri Outsider," "The Wonderer," the "Quaester," etc., etc. He slanders pious Synodical Vice-Presidents and charges then with "caving in to the pope." (Feb. 11, 1991 *CN*) He ranges all the way to the bizarre, "Peglau Making Phone Calls from Heaven to Defeat Bunkowske" (*CN*, April 1, 1991). He published an irresponsible attack on Dr. James Dobson. Without any real evidence, he keeps on repeating that the Missouri Synod is getting close to ordaining women.

The Sept. 16, 1991, *CN* printed this article, "Scaer And Marquart May Be Next 'Tied To The Dunking Chair' — LCMS Officials Continue Vendetta Vs. Conservatives," contained nothing but hype and no substance.

The May 7, 1990, *CN* contained 32 pages on the Holocaust, attempting to prove it never happened. For a long a time we were treated to news about "The Debate of the Century," until it was announced that "The great debate fizzled." Some correspondents like Catherine L. Mueller of Albuquerque tried to reason with him by facts but to no avail. Mrs. Mueller ultimately published two booklets to expose Otten's fallacies. On Feb. 5, 1991, she wrote that Otten "has a double standard. . .there are more apologies in *CN* for Hitler and the Third Reich than there are positive articles about our LC-MS." She also criticized his slanted coverage of the Gulf War. I believe that she correctly evaluates the situation of *CN*, "An independent Lutheran newspaper which at one time was the voice for conservative Lutherans became the voice for a radical viewpoint, and in the process lost its credibility among the Lutheran community. . .We find that we have no common ground. . .Further verbiage would be an effort in futility. . ." She complains about being constantly misrepresented as Otten regularly gets the last word to distort the views of the other person. She writes, "I trusted Herman implicitly and expected above everything else. . .HONESTY."

We leave it to the reader whether Otten was honest or not in this situation: Around 1978 Dr. Robert Sauer, Dr. Herbert Mueller, and then Cent. Ill. Dist. Pres. Arthur Kuehnert met with elders/officers of Otten's New Haven church, together with Dr. John Baur representing Otten. These men showed these officers and Baur evidence of some untruths which were published in *CN*. The only response which the officers made was that they did not read *CN* and were not aware of this. In a following issue, Otten claimed that these men tried to intimidate his officers, but no comment was made about the fact that the officers had no answers for the untruths published in *CN*. The unBiblical activity of our erring brother, Rev. Herman Otten, can be known by a study of his advocacy for Dr. Robert Preus and against anyone who dares to disagree, and also his constant battering of anyone who would dare to use the word Church Growth, as is documented in this book. His committing of *CN* for the full use of the political campaign of the party of the right — the "Confessional Lutheran Gnostics" — has acted as a battering ram to intimidate anyone who has an important and valid viewpoint.

The result has been a dysfunctional Synod in which leaders and many members alike fear to speak out even against Dr. Preus' false doctrine and practice violating the 8th Commandment and Matthew 18. Leaders and members have been intimidated to allow these untruths and distortions to be unchallenged because "we can't correct everything." Readers of *CN* imbibe this religious philosophy and proudly take up the fight for "pure" doctrine, while creating fear in the hearts of those who have a Biblical contribution to make. One of these areas is the matter of substance abuse. *CN* has given considerable space to books which destroy any opportunity for communication in the church to gain Biblical solutions in the area of substance abuse.

Otten's Publicity of Bobgan's "Twelve Steps To Destruction"

CN has given prominent reviews to "TWELVE STEPS TO DESTRUCTION, Co-dependency Recovery Heresies" by Martin and Diedre Bobgan (Eastgate Publishers, 1991). My review of this book is made necessary because apparently some Lutheran Church-Missouri Synod pastors have believed that this book accurately portrays all Christian 12-Step programs and recovery groups and that the book is a result of fair and faithful research among all Christian 12-Step books, recovery and co-dependency groups. It misrepresents the facts related to various Christian authors and counselors in this field.

With a broad brush of condemnation that all Christians who in any way use the 12-Steps, recovery programs, and co-dependency ideas, *CN* reviews give 100% agreement to the Bobgan's book in its total censure and reproach against any endeavor, including those who use proper truths in psychology. It is distressing to hear some of our pastors commend the book and give credence to it. This review reveals the dangers of this book.

First, this book does properly portray the evils of theories by non-Christian psychologists. It gives instances of several Christians who have apparently made confusing statements in the controverted areas, but the authors used these several instances as the platform for launching a broadside on any Christian who makes a proper use of the arts, such as psychology and sociology, those who have effective and orthodix Christian recovery programs, and who have an effective Biblically sound Christian version of the 12-Steps, and especially those who deal with healing emotions. The authors believe they are right because they said so.

The book also properly portrays the true Christian message of sin and grace which alone gives true salvation, and which is the base of full recovery. If only they had stuck with that and not used guilt by association and generalizations simply when they saw the word psychology or saw a Christian recovery program.

The book uses such denunciations of many faithful Christians by generalizations that it becomes extremely harmful from a Biblical viewpoint. One reviewer mimics the authors' quote, "It would be laughable if it (12-Step Programs and Groups, and co-dependency counseling) were not so pitiful — so destructive to thousands of sincere, misguided people. Pastors, Christian therapists and Christian medical doctors have swallowed the tenets of Freud, Skinner, Adler, Maslow, Rogers and others of that humanistic ilk. Rephrase them in theologically-sounding language, then dispense their malarkey to sincere disciples of

Christ who think such medicine will 'make them whole." " Faithful Christian counselors and recovery groups are called "God's enemies." The authors assert that "without a scintilla of evidence, it (co-dependency) does not even the slightest good for the patient."

Another intemperate criticism, "Authors of books on co-dependency/recovery base their ideas on unproven psychological theories and subjective observations which are based on neither the rigors of scientific investigation nor the rigors of of exegetical Bible study." The authors give the impression that they have fairly researched all the books in all these areas to the extent that a reviewer writes, "The one thing we like about the Bobgans: **they do their homework!** They totally research everything they write about and you know you are receiving a fair and equitable evaluation of the subject. . .We offer it our unconditional endorsement!" As will be shown in my Review, this is untrue. It is said that the new wave of co-dependency groups which have joined the hundreds of dependency ones, including ones promoted by Christians, are all based upon unscientific myths.

Have the authors done their homework and fairly represented the various Christian groups and counselors who are as orthodox in their Christian faith and practice, as the Bobgans claim to be? There are 15 to 20 books and programs which would indicate that the authors' claim is false. Let us look at **just a few:**

1. **Alcoholics for Christ** centered in Detroit now has 43 groups in that area, 81 all over the United States and 6 in other countries. Read their "Statement of Faith":

"A/C is a non-denominational, non-profit Christian fellowship for the alcoholic and his family and is dedicated to the propagation of the Gospel of Jesus Christ, as well as sharing His burden for the lost and hurting individuals.

We believe that 'God as we understand him' is the Triune God, 'God the Father,' 'God the Son,' and 'God the Holy Spirit,' and that acceptance of Jesus Christ as the Personal Savior is the doorway to fullness of life in the Spirit as well as the means by which we can turn our lives and our wills completely over.

This fellowship uses the Word of God as its primary source of direction and those leading the meetings are all 'born-again' compassionate Christians, dedicated to the service of Jesus Christ.

Our chief goal is to direct or restore the alcoholic, his family, and/or concerned persons to a sincere and dedicated relationship with Jesus Christ and, through the written Word of God, make the alcoholic aware of the mighty tools available to him as a 'born-again' believer. Jesus begins by healing the inner man and working outward, and we believe that as the alcoholic dies to self and is reborn to Christ (2 Cor. 5:17) he can be totally released from the oppression and fear that find their roots in alcoholism (John 8:36).

The alcoholic is encouraged to remain active in his local A/C, AA, NA, etc. group and, where possible, to continue to worship within his own body of believers. We suggest that there are no strong church ties existing that the alcoholic become active in a Bible-believing church of his own choice."

I have met leaders of this group and know that they practice the Gospel they preach. Will you accept the unjust condemnation of the authors that the thousands of Christians involved in A/C are dishonoring Christ?

2. David A. Seamands, a conservative evangelical counselor and professor, centers on the theology of grace (Law and Gospel), and uses only proven truths of psychology. His books, including "Healing Grace-Freedom From the Performance Trap," are so centered on justification and God's unconditional love in Christ that no quotations are needed.

3. The "RAPHA'S" 12-Step Program for OVERCOMING CHEMICAL DEPEN-

DENCY by Robert S. McGee, Pat Springel, and Susan Joiner (which the Bobgans severely criticizes) is a truly Biblical study course which exposes false beliefs and Satan's lies. Page 40 presents, "God's Truth: Your worth - what God says about you - Justification (Rom. 3:19-25; 2 Cor. 5:21): I am completely forgiven; Reconciliation (Col. 1:19-22); I am totally accepted by God, Propitiation (1 Jn. 4:9-11); I am deeply loved by God, Regeneration (2 Cor. 5:17); absolutely complete in Christ." This is the consistent basic Gospel theology of this book, which the Bobgans erroneously claim is missing, and criticize that is unChristian.

4. J. Keith Miller in his book, "A Hunger For Healing, The 12 Steps as a Classic Model For Christian Spiritual Growth" begins his Chapter 16, *"THE BOTTOM LINE,"* with Gen. 3:9-10 to show that this Christian program takes sin seriously, and also states, "What we have received from the Gospel: 'There is therefore now no condemnation for those who are in Christ Jesus. For the Law of the Spirit of life in Christ Jesus has set me free from the Law of sin and death' (Rom. 8:1- 2);' and also quotes 2 Cor. 5:17. On page 174, he writes, "The Christian message is that God's love and God's power, revealed in the life and death and resurrection of Jesus Christ, can reconcile us to God, make us 'new creations', free us from sin and the disease that it spawns, and sends us out as ambassadors to spread God's truth about life. (See 2 Cor. 5:17-20.) Step Ten gives us practical ways to keep accessing that love and that power, 'one day at a time.' " While Miller's book is not filled with the message of sin and grace, and while we do not concur with everything that he says, sin and grace are strategically placed to show that these are the foundation of the entire recovery program which he proposes, and the counseling in which he is involved.

5. The ELEEO Ministries of St. Charles, IL (headed by a Baptist pastor who is a recovering alcoholic through the use of the 12 Steps), is a ministry of recovery through justification and salvation. They have about 30 units in their area now based on the 12 Steps which center on being justified by grace through faith in Jesus Christ. Other Christian groups throughout the United States unashamedly declare the Biblical message of sin and grace, all of which the Bobgans ignore and act as though they do not exist. The Bobgans' lack of scientific research of all such sound Christian groups betrays the fallacy of their demand for scientific research where facts speak for themselves.

6. Sandra Dee Wilson in her book, "Released From Shame, Recovery for Adult Children of Dysfunctional Families," provides a totally Christian orientation to give evidence of her counseling (she is a member of the Evangelical Free Church). In her Appendix 1, she writes, "Renunciation of Occultic and Satanic Influences. These practices may open our lives to the Enemy by providing a foothold for him (See Eph. 4:27.)" She lists 26 items under "Some Occultic Practices To Renounce" and 12 items under "Occultic and Satanic Religions to Renounce" and 3 under such "Influences to Renounce," including dungeons and dragons, drug use, heavy metal music. She also includes some "Sinful Attitudes and Practices to Renounce." She offers a prayer of renunciation through the cleansing power of the blood of Jesus. Pages 183-194 are headed, "Your Identity in Christ," which provides Bible passages to help the individual start to see himself as God sees him in Christ, and lists 18 different New Testament Bible verses which provide full information on justification and reconciliation with God through Jesus Christ, the only Savior. Pages 195-196 list 12 attributes of God which show Him to be the God of justice and God of love. Sandra Wilson was terribly abused as a child, but the authors with an uncaring and unloving magic wand call that kind of witness as anecdotal. Wilson is joined by hundreds of thousands of others who have not conjured up their brutal experience by psychology or hypnosis. There are many Missouri Synod Lutherans among them.

7. I attended the first two meetings of about 500 Christian professionals and non-professionals from churches and Christian recovery groups who met in Colorado and

organized "Free Indeed." It is not anecdotal that I and others actually heard with our own ears with a spirit of discernment based upon God's Word from speakers and participants who centered all their work on the doctrine of justification by grace through faith in Jesus Christ. They would tolerate nothing else even in their Christian interpretation of the 12 Steps. The National Association for Christian Recovery of La Habra, CA is a new organization which provides a collective voice for professionals and non-professionals alike who are as strong Christians as the Bobgans claim to be, and who provide a Christian solution in counseling, recovery programs, and the 12-Step approach.

One of the big errors which the authors make is that they demand something of the original 12-Step leaders and program which the originators and current leaders of the secular 12-Step program do not intend. The secular 12-Step program is designed to overcome addiction to alcohol, not to give eternal life. Other secular programs to overcome other addictions are similarly based. THEY NEVER HAVE CLAIMED, NOR DO THEY CLAIM TODAY TO OFFER SALVATION OR JUSTIFICATION FOR SOULS. The Bobgans' judgment that the 12-Step Program is satanic because it does not bring salvation but brings damnation is illogical, unfair, and untrue. The original 12-Step program is to be judged on the basis of what it claims to be — a recovery from alcoholic or other substance addiction, not a way of salvation. PREACHING THE GOSPEL IS THE CHURCH'S RESPONSIBILITY!, not that of a secular 12-Step program.

The other issue related to the strained logic is that the same kind of tactics of begging the question, building straw men, generalizing on the basis of one error by one counselor or book, semantics, and guilt by association is found throughout the book, samples of which we will share. One must conclude that the authors' logic is somewhat the same as that used by the Jehovah's Witnesses in their refusal to have blood transfusions and for Christian Scientists and faith healers in not using doctors and medicine. The Bobgans use very carefully selected and isolated examples of real problems, and generalize to the extent that they impose the non-Christian theories of psychology upon Christians who accept truthful observations of human nature that grow out of sin and grace while using certain sociological and psychological truths. Thus an inaccurate assessment is made of Christians who conduct a thorough and orthodox Christian ministry through recovery programs, including co-dependency, and find a Christian basis for the 12 Steps which the originators used purely on a secular basis.

The authors consistently begin with the Law when sinners acknowledge wrong and are looking for a solution while needing the Gospel. The book offers no solution except splashing more of the doctrine of justification by faith on saved people with deep problems. These have not been helped to work through their emotional hurts and have found no assistance in their church for their addiction, but had to go to a secular agency to find it.

It is not anecdotal that I have a brother who is a recovering alcoholic, and there are also Lutherans with real names and real alcoholic experiences right here in Fort Wayne, who found recovery from their addiction through the original 12-Step Program, not a church. There are over 180 12-Step Recovery meetings held in Fort Wayne each week, and another 60 related to co-dependencies. I have personally talked with confessing Christians who are members of these groups, but the Bobgans call them anecdotal. Many are sharing the steps of recovery from addiction while emphasizing even stronger the necessity of being rescued from the slavery of their sins by the grace of God through the blood sacrifice of Jesus Christ. How judgmental and unloving to say that these people imagined their alcohol and chemical dependencies and that they are destined to hell because they found their recovery from addiction in the 12-Steps in an area where churches failed. Regularly, there are statements which name some author and a book as the source, but the statements have no quotation marks so that it is impossible to know whether the quotation is accurate or not, unless one reads the original book. Often they criticize someone for not having any research evidence, but the Bobgans criticism provides little valid research evidence.

Among the hundreds of concerns marked in the Bobgans' book, I will name a few examples:

1. Page 39 tries to make the point that most people's experiences are fairy tales and stories which were conjured up through manipulation by psychologists. This ignores the fact of abused wives, children, or even husbands. It is pathetic that all of the experiences of deeply scarred and hurt people are summarily dismissed by the generalization, "Such stories and case histories should be regarded as biased and contrived...Such stories and testimonials give a reality to the psychological theories promoted by the authors of the various books." Let the authors face the tens of thousands in recovery through the Gospel ministry of Alcoholics for Christ, Eleeo Ministries and others, to tell them such unloving and uncaring condemnation. The authors' solution in this book is apparently to quote John 3:16, and if that won't do it, nothing will.

2. The Bobgans state that most books written by Christians "rehash the same psychological definitions, diagnoses, explanations, and treatments that the pop psychology books offer. However, those written by professing Christians have enough Christian sounding language and references to God and the Bible that unsuspecting readers assume they are getting sound Christian, Biblical understanding advice. Such books, while appearing to be helpful to Christians, are often more dangerous than the purely secular books." Who are "they?" I have quoted some books and counselors who do not fit this description in any way and who are slandered by such descriptions as the Bobgans make.

3. AA Step One says, "We admitted we were powerless over alcohol — that our lives had become unmanageable." Despite that clear and simple statement, most of this chapter deals with "disease" and makes the statement, "Step One of AA is the admission that the problem is **not** sin, but rather disease - that one is not under the dominion of sin, as clearly stated in the Bible, but under the domination of a destructive disease." No matter how one dissects and exegetes that Step One for overcoming addiction, he can find no evidence of the misinterpretation which the authors impose upon it.

Page 91 makes the astounding statement that Step One is a dangerous counterfeit for both Christians and non-Christians and that "it serves as a substitute for acknowledging one's own depravity, sinful acts, and utter lostness apart from Jesus Christ...", etc. They also say that many Christians "generally substitute powerlessness for sinfulness and admit a life that is unmanageable without confessing disobedience." What a vicious judgment against orthodox Christians and Lutherans who use Step One who are totally Christ-centered. These statements impose upon the original 12 steps a mission which they do not intend (not an evangelistic tool for salvation), whereas they plainly state that they are only for overcoming a specific addiction, and that salvation is the business of the church. Once again, we read a judgment on page 93, "How grievous it is when hopeless and despairing people are sent to something or someone other than the One who is our only Hope!" Obviously, they see no purpose in doctors, orthodox Christian counselors, even psychologists who use that God-given art in a true and proper manner without obscuring or denying Christianity.

4. Page 89 criticized the *Serenity: A Companion for 12 Step Recovery,* which is the New Testament with 12 Step commentaries together with directions to read various Bible verses which deal with sin, salvation, sanctification — all authentic New Testament texts. Step Three in this Bible, for example, refers to Eph. 2:8-9 in one of its readings as God as the Christian understands Him. Note that Rom 5:1; 7:18-19; 8:1, 26-28; 10:9-15: and 12:2-3

(among many other Law and Gospel verses) are used for references to various Steps! Yet the authors write, **"Serenity"** includes the New Testament laced with unbiblical co-dependency/recovery psychology and religion. They write, "This insidious implantation of psychological notions and Twelve Step religious ideas into the Bible severely undermines the Scriptures." They also erroneously maintain another interpretation of Step One which is untenable, "Step One relieves the Twelve Step believer from both responsibility and guilty feelings." The Bible references in the Serenity Bible under Step One do not allow such a misleading statement. They continue on page 90, "Step One may actually give license to excuse oneself from certain genuine responsibilities and valid commitments...may also serve to exonerate self from responsibility to others." This deduction is irrational as one reads the actual Step One.

5. Page 95 lists AA Step Two, as much of the chapter does not deal with the statement as it stands, but rather talks with the Oxford group, Charles Jung and other psychologists, the occult and the New Age. How can all that be read into the text of Step Two. There is no logic to support that type of deduction.

6. Page 117 provides Step Three, while the rest of the chapter is a dissertation on the "self" philosophy which misinterprets this step. The authors say that AA denies being a religion, but they insist that AA groups are a religion because they should be saving souls instead of holding themselves to helping people overcome addictions. So it is not surprising to find on page 122, "For a professing Christian to be a member of AA yolks him with unbelievers..." The authors will not allow AA to refuse to be a church or to do the work of the church, but simply deal with addictions on that level. It is not surprising to read on page 125, "AA religion is Christless and offers a counterfeit salvation without the sacrificial death of Jesus Christ." Read all of the 12 Steps word by word and you will **not** find in them or in the AA current purposes that they are offering any salvation, so how can they offer a counterfeit salvation?

7. Page 137 presents Step Four, "Made a searching fearless moral inventory of ourselves," which is followed by a chapter filled with condemnations of self-serving, power of sugges-tion, Freudian psychology, etc. Much of this chapter again has nothing to do with the ac-tual statement of AA Step Four, but is simply a space shot into the far yonder with various unrelated criticisms.

8. Page 163 presents Step Five, "Admitted to God, to ourselves, and to another human being the exact nature of our wrongs," which becomes the springboard for dissertations on toxic faith, subjectivity, self-deception, being tied to secular psychology, none of which are related to the simple statement of Step Five. The authors begin by saying, "Step Five looks good on the surface," but they go subterranean and start mining another field 1000 miles away from Step Five and throw all of that dirt onto Step Five. They even throw in mystical experiences and transpersonal psychology, and psychoanalytic and humanistic theories and mystically force them into the simple statement of Step Five.

9. Page 212 gives the amazing prescription, "Christians do not need the help of Steps Eight or Nine or any of the others for that matter. All that is needed is in the Bible." It is no more irrational to say that churches and Christians need not provide Bible study courses for any topic, because it's all in the Bible. When people have deep personal pro-blems which they cannot solve themselves, hand them a Bible and tell them the solution is in it. It is not surprising that the authors continue, "When churches adopt and adapt 12-Step programs, they are telling the world that the Bible is not sufficient to deal with problems of sin." So throw a Bible at the hurting and suffering, and no more.

These are only a **sample** of over-statements, non-sequitors, begging the question, men-tal handsprings, over-simplification, personal attack, rationalizations, false generalizations, conclusions on the basis of no evidence, etc. I found the book to be an illogical jungle of fallacies, even though there were two basic truths that were expounded - that there is non-Christian psychology to be avoided like the plague and that people need the true Christian Gospel. It is almost impossible for readers to know that there is indeed evidence in various Christian discovery groups and books of the **opposite** of what the authors state.

Reading this book is a misuse of time which should be used in learning the Biblical foundation and Biblical methodology to reach the myriads of hurting people who are as sheep without a shepherd, and who even are told that the sectarian help from the AA from addictions is evil. Apparently, the hurting people are to stay in their evil until they are mystically excised from their addiction and rescued through some disciples of the Bobgans. This reviewer has found some Missouri Synod pastors who received a totally distorted view of the entire subject by reading this book, thus closing their mind to any possible realistic and authentic Christian solution through Christian recovery groups. Let the Bobgans print their book, for this is a free country. However, *CN* becomes grossly guilty of slandering strong Christian witnesses by promoting this book.

I believe that the July 22, 1991, *Christianity Today* had a balanced assessment of the strengths and weaknesses of the 12-Step Program and also of the Christian recovery groups, unlike the legalistic attack with illogical connections and conclusions by the Bobgans.

The *Lutheran Witness* is beginning to provide assistance with understanding substance abuse and other kinds of abuse. The Oct. 1991 *L. W.* published three excellent articles, and the "Fellowship of Recovering Lutheran Clergy" was publicized. *The Reporter* in its June 10, 1991, issue carried an article by the founder of that group, Rev. Richard Hill.

Unfortunately, the Synod's Task Force on Alcohol and Substance Abuse through some of its professional chaplains has discouraged production of books and materials by Missouri Synod Lutherans in this area, contending that the materials from the Hazelden Foundation of Minnesota are sufficient for use in our church. I have read at least 15 of the Hazeldon books or booklets and found them very philosophical with very little, if any, sin and grace, and Law and Gospel. Meeting with several of these chaplains was a very troubling experience because of their legalistic condemnation against Lutherans who would dare encourage and support Lutheran groups in the 12-Step program. I have written such a manuscript, *New Steps To Security and Happiness, Twelve Steps To Freedom and Peace*, which provides also for 15 weeks of Bible study. I have been asked by the editors of Concordia Publishing House to re-work the manuscript considerably and will do so, but not on the basis of the demands of those who refuse to accept a Christian version of the 12 Steps.

*   *   *   *   *   *

WORSHIP, LITURGICS — GRACE OR LEGALISM?

There are dissonant sounds in our Synod about liturgical and worship practices so that effective communication is difficult in this area. The "Confessional Lutherans" are utilizing *CN*, the *LUTHERAN FORUM*, and other opportunities to claim the "Biblical" ground of true worship and liturgy. Can we as a Synod adopt a variety of liturgical forms which enhance the worship of us all, which are not in conflict with true Lutheran doctrine and practice?

I cherish very highly my musical and liturgical heritage received from William B. Heyne and Gustav Polack during my Seminary training in St. Louis from 1941 to 1945. Dr. Polack helped direct Lutheran historical insights of worship in the writing of The Lutheran Hymnal, while Dr. Heyne took us to spiritual heights through participation in J. S. Bach's, *St. Matthew's Passion, Mass in B Minor, St. John's Passion* and other classical Lutheran originals.

These deeply spiritual worship experiences continued for me at the Fort Wayne Seminary in listening to the same and other historic European selections of Bach, and also Handel, Haydn, and others. Dr. Dan Reuning and Prof. Richard Resch have done a great service in helping preserve and in encouraging use of these classical musical formulations and the historic liturgy which bring us God's Word in musical form. These are a priority in my life and will remain so, but there are other orthodox Lutherans to whom this does not communicate because they are not of European extraction or culture. Does this mean that their worship is less Lutheran than mine? Does this mean that I am right, and they are wrong?

Impose European Culture on the Lutheran Church in Africa?

I have just come back from my ninth visit to Nigeria, and once again endured a tedious and plodding "participation" of Page 5 in The Lutheran Hymnal where its German cultural music style was imposed upon African culture. As we labored through the liturgy, I read the words Introit, Gradual, Collect, and Nunc Dimitis, but no one present, including the preacher, knew what these words meant. Surprisingly, there was no collection when it was time to Collect. These African pastors assume, because of their Seminary training, that they must follow early German musical settings or William Loehe's 19th Century "Common" service in order to be truly Lutheran. The strong impression came to me that they have been cheated by a mindset or mental screen that there is only one cultural mode of music and worship that is Biblical. This legalistic or austere practice is lost when these Lutherans sing their own African Christian songs with a beat when they take their offering, when the choir sings, and especially when in other worship settings.

As I recall other worship experiences in different parts of the world and also with other ethnic groups in the United States, including our black congregations, I ask whether all of them must be taught to appreciate European music settings such as I enjoy in order to be true worshipping Lutherans. Such liturgy purists in music and style need to recognize that even the selection of the Scriptures in the liturgy is a pattern made by church leaders in a dated past.

Liturgical Time-line

If we look at the liturgical time-line, we see that only in the Fourth Century did Chrysostom enlarge and define the liturgy. The framework of the Roman Mass was determined in the Fifth Century. All components of the liturgy were written by the Seventh Century. Luther wrote a new form with German hymns and congregational participation in the 16th Century which was radical - apparently so that there could be effective communication between God and man in worship. In 1888, several Lutheran bodies issued the "Church Book." 1912 saw the production of the first LCMS English Hymnal. *The Lutheran Hymnal* was produced in 1941, followed by *Lutheran Worship* in 1983. Were the Christians ten or fifteen centuries ago less Biblical in their worship than the liturgical purists today?

If men of the past could construct a Biblical liturgy with specific European cultural expressions that we use today, then 15-20 LCMS worship leaders in our day can design a truly Biblical liturgy with contemporary music that is as correct as the one we have. Let the Germans have their "German" liturgies, and the Americans have their contemporary liturgy. But we should attempt to introduce all members to our historic liturgy. Also, either extreme form will not work in most parishes. This is not an "either...or" matter.

The church is not limited today to the extent that only our forefathers could formulate a form of worship and liturgy true to Scriptures, but we somehow cannot. By the Holy Spirit under grace, we can organize new and uplifting styles of worship based wholly on God's Word. It is arrogant and legalistic to claim that only one cultural group — Germans or Europeans or any other — is capable to provide and absolutize a church musical style for all cultures, all nations, and all time. It is a deception to state that a different cultural musical style corrupts the Biblical text or that God's Word can only be sung in European cultural formulations. We will be a dying church if we insist that the Lutheran Church be a separated ethnic church with **only** a German style or a 16th Century cultural expression in church music.

"Worship Toward 2000"

"Worship Toward 2000," produced by the LCMS Commission on Worship correctly states, "Our vision portrays people filled with such a sense of God's presence in Word and Sacrament that they rejoice in the surprising varieties of music which can serve as vessels of both the Word and our response." This is the way of grace.

The Lutheran Confessions say the same: "We believe, teach...that the community of God in every locality and every age has authority to **change** such ceremonies according to circumstances as it may be most profitable and edifying to the community of God...that no church should condemn another because it has fewer or more external ceremonies not commanded by God as long as there is mutual agreement in doctrine and in all its articles as well as in the right use of the Sacraments" (Tappert 493:4-5). This is also grace.

We are told that change may be expected in localities and in different ages, but we have brothers who insist that we are locked into 16th Century German or European or it is not Lutheran nor Scriptural. This is pure legalism. Grace does not allow us to prescribe a specific liturgical form of worship as a command. Yet the Liturgical Symposium at CTS in FW in January, 1991, heard that "congregations should follow the order of worship exactly as it is printed in TLH or LW" (*Called To Serve*, Spring, 1991, p. 3). This is law.

The **true test** of worship is whether it is built upon the Word of God and focuses everything on Christ and Him crucified, having the Triune God as the object of worship, but also communicates in the language/culture of the worshipers and is relevant to the people's spiritual needs. Culture must be translated in time and place every bit as much as language.

The current situation in the LCMS finds Synodical leaders on worship intimidated by voices that sometimes are not based on logic and reason, and sometimes legalistic. The result is a vacuum which the more vocal "Confessional Lutherans" are filling.

Biblical Variety

Variety in worship and liturgy is both Biblical and confessional, and it does not mean that "anything goes." Luther's emphasis on worship in his own culture was an **example of change**. He showed that clarity of **communication** is important for worship. The argument of traditionalists normally emphasize that form must remain constant, but why should every century be locked into any specific century or culture? Is not good communication **incarnational communication** — the Word becomes **flesh** in the **people's own culture**? Jesus did not come only for the Jews or for the Gentiles. Jesus spoke the language of the people, observed their customs, and celebrated their festivals. He knew what the learners knew and then formulated His message and communicated knowledge to meet that need. Jesus met people at their point of need; does that make Him consumeristic or a marketer?

Bible translation is itself an example of an incarnational approach to communication. The missionary does not begin by teaching the natives English and the new Christians the

16th Century liturgy or the forms of **Lutheran Worship**. They begin where people are in their own culture and teach God's Word to change their spiritual condition, not the parts of their language or customs which are neutral. Many critics are throwing reckless barbs at effective Lutheran pastors who try to understand people's needs in order to communicate God's Word clearly. The Gospel penetrates best when it is in the heart language of the hearer. That heart language is different than it was 500 years ago. We have a challenge in every age: We have a changeless message to proclaim in a changing challenging era. Are our worship practices supporting or distorting the transmittal of our Christian faith?

"Liturgicate" is not in opposition to communicate. Liturgy must communicate the Word in musical forms that are understood, and we must communicate through liturgy. When Dr. Herman Gockel raised this issue in the Dec. 1990 *Lutheran Witness*, some LCMS pastors reacted with such nonsense as, "To intersperse the readings of the sacred Word of God with one's own thoughts is to mix the holy and the profane in a most unsalutory manner. Or do we wish your own words to be seen as having greater significance than the word of the Holy Ghost?" Taking that at face value, our sermons would constitute only the literal reading of the Word of God, and we would not dare try any exegesis or homiletics! Unfortunately, that quotation shows the difficulty of communicating with some of the critics today. Another stated that to explain the liturgy or to summarize a Scripture reading for better comprehension of the Word is to "undermine the liturgical heritage of the church," calling this a "man-centered approach." That writer wrote that voices such as Dr. Goeckel's "despise the precious jewel of liturgical worship." The Scriptures do not allow such locking into a particular time and place for its liturgy or worship.

German Culture Bound John T. Pless

The Fort Wayne CTS *Cornerstone* (April 1992) has an article by Rev. John T. Pless who spoke on liturgy and worship for the so-called "Integrity Series," promoting more of the theological politics of the "Confessional Lutherans." He reveals, as do his mentors, that they have made a drastic change from Walther's theology in the doctrine of the Ministry and the Church to Wilhelm Loehe's priest-centered theology, from the body of Christ to the cathedral. Pless said that nowhere is integrity "so obvious as in the congregation gathered around the pastoral office at the font, pulpit and altar." This apparently disqualifies the priesthood of all believers-the body of Christ to gather around the Word in their homes or when God's people are busy edifying one another, as God shows in Ephesians 4.

Pless makes the untenable statement, "The substance/style distinction made popular in LCMS circles by David Luecke and endorsed by the recent report 'Worship Toward 2000,' is an example of theological and ecclesiastical schizophrenia." He continues with the astounding statement that where the "substance of the Word and Sacraments does not shape the style of their delivery, the integrity is lost and the Means of Grace are in jeopardy." The style of the Word was Hebrew and Greek, so we ask whether we have lost the substance because we are now communicating in English? This is again an irrational fusing of substance and style, of the Word and its communication. The article uses caricature and ridicule against unnamed "marketers."

In a *LUTHERAN FORUM* article reviewing the LCMS "Worship Towards 2000," Pless becomes contentious as he distorts that brief 13-page document. He badly misrepresents what this document says about worship, and puts the worst construction on the "Findings From The Worship Survey of LCMS People," which he ridicules as a consumer's survey. Reading carefully and prayerfully this LCMS document, there is no warrant to call our worshipers "shoppers," or that the shape of the survey instrument is anthropocentric, or that the "consumers" answers are offered as "guides for marketing Lutheran worship."

Pless distorts when he says that there is little evidence that those responsible for the report heeded their own advice that worship is not to be driven primarily by market forces; or that their assumption is that the needs and the desires of the "audience" will decide the service; or that instead of beginning with Scripture, the point of departure of this document is sociology. Despite such statements in the document as, "God comes to us and, through Word and Sacrament, offers us life and salvation," Pless says that "the New Testament reality that Christians have access to God only through the 'external Word' of Gospel and Sacraments is lost in *Worship Toward 2000.*" Pless opts for Loehe's "cathedral" Lutheranism (which he misrepresents as austere worship) against Walther-Body of Christ Biblical Lutheranism. The problem is that the "cathedral" liturgists denigrate and squeeze out the "Body of Christ" liturgies altogether, instead of "both-and."

Typical is this statement, "One wonders how long it will be before the CTCR promulgates a doctrine on the inerrancy of ecclesiastical surveys." One can seriously criticize Pless and his friends for claiming inerrancy of earlier century music and liturgies — pure legalism! He adds, "Style controls the substance." Pless missed the basic point that *Worship Toward 2000* is descriptive in its report of the survey, not prescriptive.

In a succeeding *LUTHERAN FORUM*, Victor Gebauer for the Commission on Worship correctly shows some of the errors of the review by Pless and says that Pless' reporting was "not honest." After pointing to the Word-Sacrament commitment of the document, Gebauer points out two major inaccuracies in the Pless' assessment. Gebauer pleads that discussion be directed to the report as issued, not by misrepresentations by Pless and his allies. Pless in the *Lutheran Forum* and *CN* again had the last word in a later issue, confusing the matter more.

More of the Same

The Rev. Harold L. Senkbeil, wrote an article, "The Liturgy is the Life of the Church," in the February, 1992 *LUTHERAN FORUM*. The **Word** is the life of the church, while liturgy is just **one** form of communicating that Word.

That article fuses substance and style, message and modes of communication. When Senkbeil says that "The liturgy is the source and shape of the church's life in Jesus Christ," then we ask, "If this is so, then the Catholic Church should be a vibrant church and there would be no need for a Reformation." The Word is the source and center of everything in the church, proclaimed in the church building and studied in the Christian's home. The Book of Acts and Ephesians 4 reveal varied forms of the Christian life. Senkbeil does say that liturgical forms are adiaphora, but that is inconsistent with his central theme that "the liturgy is both the **source** of the church's life and the **shape** of the church's life." The source and shape is the Word, which is not adiaphora. He is critical of any Lutheran who would shape Scriptural liturgy in contemporary form and music. He makes the legalistic statement, "You can't tinker around with the style of a church without changing its doctrinal substance." I ask, "Really?" Our liturgy has evolved even in *Lutheran Worship* using new tunes or creations by Professors Paul Bunjes, Richard Hiller, Carl Schalk, Thomas Gieschen and Ronald Nelson without tinkering with the substance, but enhancing it.

In a Seminary Chapel service this academic year, we were told by a student preacher that criticism of the liturgy as being German for us Americans cannot be accepted, for if that criticism is valid, then God is German, because that German liturgy is God's word. I repeat, "Really?"

The *Lutheran Forum* book review editor, Leonard Klein, spoke at the FW CTS "Confessional Symposium" and "noted that Lutherans having emancipated themselves from the traditional liturgy by introducing new forms, sometimes changing each Sunday...had already forfeited their right to oppose the 'non-sexist' formula..." (CALLED TO SERVE-Spring 1992, p. 5). Again I say, "Really?"

Frederick W. Baue also places the discussion out of focus in a guest editorial, "MISSOURI'S VIETNAM," in the Reformation, 1990, *Lutheran Forum*. Baue utilizes his visit to The Lord's Community Church (Lutheran) where he said the pastor had taken a plateaued Missouri Synod congregation and turned it into a growing church. Baue uses what he maintains he saw in that worship service as a springboard to clobber the entire Missouri Synod and even judges us as having our own "Vietnam." He says that the LCMS is hysterically looking to church growth techniques like an alcoholic and his family look to a revival-tent conversion. He then puts the LCMS on a "couch" and without giving any specifics except the isolated case of that one congregation to tell that we are in denial and dysfunctional. The article has little more than judgment and condemnation, not any real positive contribution from a Biblical viewpoint.

Proposing liturgy as pastoral care, and liturgy as evangelism, Arthur A. Just, Jr., in the CTS *Cornerstone*, January, 1991, keeps the "good word" rolling with his assault, "Even an informed layman recognizes that most contemporary Lutheran liturgies and hymns foster subjective worship and crass emotionalism...the grass-roots liturgical movement threatens and will destroy everything that it means to be Lutheran." Let him and Pastor Baue go to the offending pastors and congregations to correct them or bring charges against them. It is much easier for them to blast away in *CN*, the *LUTHERAN FORUM*, and the *Cornerstone*. Professor Just also states, "Liturgy serves to transform the culture...the church exists to convert the culture." The church exists to bring the Word for the conversion of **people, not of culture.**

Professor Just, in an essay, "Liturgy and Pastoral Care," makes a number of untenable statements. He writes, "The prophecy that the liturgy has adapted to the culture has been fulfilled, and the people of God at worship are being treated to all manner of liturgies in the name of education or therapy...There are but a few voices in the wilderness crying out that liturgy and pastoral care are to be considered together." Our concern is that he is really serious in his broad generalizations. Prof. Just quotes Kenneth Korby, who is a great admirer of Wilhelm Loehe, "The ordinary means for pastoral care are the sermon, catechesis, the liturgy..." Professor Just says that counseling, visitations and any personal discourse come from the social sciences. What? Does he mean pastors are capable of sharing the Word only through liturgy? I believe they misrepresent Loehe as a cathedral-chaplain, whereas it might be more accurate to see him as a missionary interested in the liturgy of his "day."

One wonders where the documentation is for Just's statement, "More pagans became Christians through the liturgy in the earliest centuries of the church than any other means." I have ransacked the epistles of Paul and the Book of Acts, and I find many conversions through the proclamation of the Word in large audience settings and with individuals or in groups, but there is no mention of liturgy. Just's essay cuts out Bible study groups and study in homes when he places liturgy and worship as **the** means by which the Word of God is brought to the congregation and its members. He states, "In the final section of this essay, we return to a part of the tradition where liturgy and pastoral care were one and the same thing, to a time when Christianity was kept alive through the liturgy..." Survival? That kind of talk does not make a positive contribution to the necessary discussion that needs to take place today related to defining Scriptural liturgies in contemporary form as an option to the historic Lutheran liturgy, where both forms are offered to the congregation.

Indicating an unwholesome attitude, one student wrote in the January 1991 CTS *Cornerstone* a very reactionary point of view, "If our Reformed brethren condemn the breaking of the Host, then let us not only break it, but elevate it as well. If they prefer 'non-liturgical' services, then should we not prefer Gospel processions, incense, and Easter Vigils? If their worship facilitators prefer polyester leisure suits, then let our ministers proudly support their clerical collars, but also cassocks and copes as well." The March 1992 *Cornerstone* also takes some cheap shots against responsible Lutherans related to worship.

Another *Cornerstone* article has an interview with Dr. David Scaer, who regards liturgy as evangelism. Scaer says, "Lutherans should not be embarrassed, as if we are still in the 15th Century," for the "liturgy is an effective evangelism tool." I believe that there should be a healthy debate in our Synod and in the Christian church in general concerning the use of the worship service, especially the liturgy, as the primary means of evangelism. Worship and liturgy are for people who know God, who are responding to the Word and the grace that they have experienced. How can an unchurched person worship and praise a God whom he does not know? The specific Scripture or topic of any particular worship service may be totally unfitting for various persons, and they cannot comprehend it or get anything out of it. The same is true of inactive and delinquent members. The primary purpose for worship services is for Christians to worship by Christians, not to do evangelism.

Instead of going to the homes of delinquents or members making evangelism calls on the unchurched to invite them to church, elders and church members should go to the prospect's homes to share God's Word with them. The elders and members have often become tongue-tied, and so the pastor becomes the only spokesman for the church. This is not the New Testament pattern. In worship we need to communicate Biblically with people in language and terms they can understand. The understanding and needs of mature members is totally different than the inactive members or the unchurched. When we begin to train our elders and members sufficiently so that they can go into homes to share God's Word in a series of relevant Bible studies, then basic evangelism will take place outside of the walls of the church, where Christ commanded Christians to go, rather than invite people inside the church where many of these inactives and unchurched find the language and liturgy incomprehensible. When people truly know this great and living God and the Savior Jesus Christ, they will rush to worship Him.

Luther and Music — Varieties of Liturgy

In "Luther and Music" by Daniel Reuning (CTQ Jan., 1984) we are told that Martin Luther edited seven liturgical pieces, and provided a vernacular alternative with hymn paraphrases of the ordinaries, and authored six occasional services, plus six occasional services and others. Luther certainly gave the example of Lutherans being free to create liturgies and hymns which pursue a variety of structures that contain a great amount of God's Word. The question is not one of creating various liturgies or hymns, but of whether they are Biblically oriented or not. Many years ago, Rev. Elmer Kettner produced a variety of contemporary liturgical forms for which he was strongly criticized by those who hold that Lutherans dare only use the several forms that are oriented to past centuries.

Bo Giertz in "Liturgy and Spiritual Awakening" (CTS Press, p. 4) correctly states that a variety of liturgies and forms of worship are permitted, but he comes to the wrong conclusion that "they will be inferior." Giertz writes, "It is possible to live for a short time on improvisations and on forms that are constantly changing and being made over. One may use only free prayers and yet create a new ritual for every worship situation. But the possibilities are soon exhausted. One will have to repeat, and with that the making of rituals is in full swing...but it would not be wrong to say that the new forms that grow up in this way are usually less attractive and more profane than the ancient liturgy. They contain less of God's Word. They pray and speak without Scriptural direction. They are not so much concerned about expressing the whole content of Scripture, but are satisfied with one thing or another that seems to be especially attractive or popular. The new liturgy that grows in this manner is poorer, less Biblical, and less nourishing to the soul than the discarded ancient order." Why? To whom? German Lutherans, Swedish Lutherans, who? Who says so? We must not force a legalistic "either...or."

The solution to this situation is that TLC-MS as a body should work together for a variety of worship services and liturgies which do meet all the necessary criteria. Instead of allowing a vacuum to be created in which individual congregations or small groups enter with limited resources and meet Scriptural standards, but without high quality, the LCMS ought to plan a high-level liturgy writing workshop. Contemporary liturgies will allow true worship for people who find the ancient liturgy to be a foreign language which simply does not communicate to them. It is not a foregone conclusion that these contemporary liturgies are profane, or contain less of God's Word, or pray and speak without Scriptural direction, as Giertz erroneously concludes. Surely, the Holy Spirit is available to Missouri Synod worship leaders today to write new and fresh contemporary liturgies to complement the ancient liturgy.

Worship and Emotions

Unfortunately, Reuning's article on "Luther and Music" makes a major point about emotions on the basis of Manford Clynes research on Sentics (printed in *CN* July 19, 1982) without providing convincing documentation. One can rightly assume that the **"sentics"** theory is a pious idea of just one man. Reuning writes, " 'Sentics' major premise is that music is a communicator of independent forces, namely, "two kinds of emotions, that elicit from us two different reactions, Dionysian and Apollonian." Reuning maintains that sentics is a new academic discipline which proves that Luther was correct in his assessment of the effects of music as he used the old words "Dionysian" and "Apollonian" to help us understand the phenomenon. Certainly, there is truth in Reuning's claim if we are comparing Rock music with Classical music, or even those in the general ball park of each. Reuning uses the phrase "man-directed" with Dionysian music, which is an untenable generalization. How can one prove that Apollonian music is directed by God, while Dionysian music is directed by man? This is simple labeling without foundation, which the research of one man has little validity to prove. Dionysian music does not have to dote upon human experience and feelings, as Reuning argues, for it can be applied totally also to Scripture verses even without human paraphrases. As Reuning places emotions in contradiction to life itself, he unconvincingly tries to claim that the limited research on sentics proves this pious notion to disqualify any kind of Gospel music or Negro Spirituals. How can anyone really research the depth of spirituality that anyone else feels and know how genuine and valid those emotions are?

When Reuning states, "The church must take Luther to heart and believe that music's dynamic can either poison or support the church's theology," we ask where did Luther say that? If he did, where is that found in the Scriptures? Can a specific melody change a Scriptural statement into heresy? Apparently, Reuning means that the poison is becoming engrossed in personal feelings and emotions, and may even involve moving a part of one's body such as raising the hands. Is folding hands also "Dionysian," since the body and emotions are also involved? What about kneeling and emotions?

We should also question the statement, "We know that Luther used not bar-songs, but the Apollonian resources of Gregorian Chant and ancient Latin hymnology." Luther certainly not only went beyond the ancient tunes but also utilized pop tunes and folk tunes of the day, and even faster rhythm at times.

Unfortunately, this entire "sentics" matter places emotions against truth, as some today pit psychology against Scripture. When one worships and participates in liturgy, he should not be expected to leave his emotions at the door and deny his own psychological make-up. God's Word shows that there should be a reasonable degree of self-evaluation (I Cor. 11:31), adequate spontaneity (Jas. 1:22; Prov. 19), and adequate response (Prov. 17:22). Paul believed that there were three elements to human personality - body, soul, and spirit (I Thes. 5:23), which completes man's "psyche." Paul uses "I" and "me" at least 42 times in Romans 7, and he talks about the will. He speaks of sorrow in his heart (Rom. 9:2). Paul recognized his deep emotional experiences, as he went through sorrow (2 Cor. 2:1), joy (2 Cor. 2:3), anguish (2:4), sincerity (2:17), and in 2 Cor. 4, he lists more emotions, as he is in distress, perplexed, depressed but he found relief from these (verse 11). What is Biblically wrong for Paul or us to express these emotions at appropriate times in our worship through prayer, praise or hymns?

Jesus calmed the hostile (Matt. 5:28), helped the fearful and anxious (Mk. 4:40), aided the discouraged (Mk. 5:11-24), and encouraged the frustrated (Mk. 12:15). Does the Bible show that the expression of these emotions and seeking help must come only in counseling outside the church walls or dare we deal with them also in the liturgy and worship?

Proper emotional response to worship is provided by a form used by Guido Merkens of San Antonio, Texas, which is worthy of serious consideration. It is not an "altar call," but at the end of worship services an announcement is made by the pastor that worshipers are invited to respond to the Gospel message by sharing their problems, sorrows, joys, and successes individually with the pastor or the elders at a selected place after the service near the altar, where someone will be prepared to pray with them. The pastor joins the elders after he completes the greeting of the worshipers as they leave the church. Various people readily respond, because they are helped individually by such action on the part of the body of Christ, rather than being ushered out of the service without having anyone with whom to talk meaningfully.

Encourage Synod Worship Leaders to Lead Creatively

The Synod's Commission has provided the American Version of Divine Service III, and provided ethnic resources for the Hispanic and African-American culture. We should expect the Synod's Commission on Worship and the Seminary worship classes to provide a number of basic patterns which give a variety of expressions in worship, both ancient and contemporary.

The strident voices of "Confessional Lutherans" have caused intimidation and left a vacuum in some measure. Offended leaders and members should give support to the Commission on Worship to proceed aggressively and courageously to provide various worship forms for a variety of cultures, including the Boomers.

Dave and Barb Anderson (The Fellowship Ministries, 6202 S. Maple, Suite 121, Tempe, AZ 85283) have something constructive to offer, too. In a March 15, 1992 Newsletter they write, "A couple of months ago, at a meeting with some of the top music and worship people in the Lutheran Church, there seemed to be a craving to fill a void in reaching out to help churches in their worship and music ministry. There were so many needs identified, and no one to carry them out. They implored the The Fellowship Ministries to take on the challenge and burden of helping churches and their leadership be more effective in sharing the Gospel with both their members and the unchurched in their communities. Collectively, they said that if The Fellowship Ministries did not respond to this challenge, there was no one else out there to pick up the ball, **leaving ministry opportunities unfulfilled**. Our board met just after this leadership meeting and agreed to take on the burden and the challenge. They include training, developing resources, modeling churches that are making a significant impact, and networking those involved on a day-to-day basis in worship and music."

What should be done to provide the full choices required in this day of cultural diversity? Work with our Synod's Commission and Seminary leaders to lead and bring us together in traditional and contemporary worship music. Let the Synod Commission on Worship with the aid of experts at the Seminaries and in the parishes produce a variety of liturgy and worship forms for contemporary use, besides emphasizing again the beauty of traditional liturgies.

Encourage congregations to provide two kinds of liturgies each Sunday, if they can; there are normally two groups in most congregations with cultural differences with whom to communicate. We dare not take away the rich old liturgy best enjoyed by those of us who were raised on it; we dare not deny Lutheran contemporary worship to those who do not understand or appreciate a liturgy which does not communicate to them.

Why not do what is done at CTS at Fort Wayne: use both hymnals, where a large percentage insist on holding on to the old. The Synod should publish a contemporary hymnal with contemporary liturgies and hymns, which are not found in *Lutheran Worship*, giving us creative new forms without sacrificing our theology. Then we can be finished with other liturgies and songs of lesser quality, even though they may be Biblical.

There should be more variety than the traditional "mass" forms of *LW* that are not reaching or sustaining the real spiritual needs of a growing number of Missouri Synod Lutherans who want to honor and worship the Lord in truth and purity. Liturgy and worship should not be a hindrance toward effective communication of the saving and everlasting Gospel.

We need to reconsider the "packaging" of the liturgy. Are some of our liturgical formulations causing a dead formalism of worship? We certainly can be guided by the Holy Spirit to have contemporary liturgy and worship forms that are distinctly Lutheran, centering on Word and Sacraments and emphasizing justification by grace, and the Law-Gospel dialectic. We dare not disenfranchise either the members who worship best with the historic liturgy and hymnody or those who require communication in contemporary forms. Messages should not be overshadowed by the medium (such as heavy metal and other dissonant sounds), or sacrifice the sacramental and sacrificial elements of worship. Distinctive Lutheran worship will not allow the medium to dominate the message.

Most congregations should be able to provide a two-level approach - one the traditional, and the other the contemporary. In many cases it may be discovered that chanting often gets in the way of modern people because of the tedious task of trying to get the tune right and then losing the message. I personally am distracted from really praying the Lord's Prayer when I am required to chant it in a 16th Century form. Even the traditional Divine Service may have to see modification or even the burial of the Introit, Gradual, and Prefaces or seek more meaningful worship expressions to replace these liturgical formulations which are increasingly experienced as archaic. This will require leadership from the Synodical Commission on Worship and our Seminaries, our musicians, worship leaders and pastors in our churches. Both Seminaries should be expected to have training and exposure to the best in contemporary liturgy and worship. What we need is the faith of our fathers in the language and culture in which we live.

Fort Wayne Seminary Vicar Patrick Boomhower voiced the conviction of many Biblical oriented Lutherans as they look at the need to communicate the pure Word of God today in worship in an article, "Simplicity, Sincerity, Truth," which was published in the *Cornerstone*, December 1991. Significantly, he received some unsigned hate mail from Fort Wayne, but also many commendations. Boomhower tells of his change in a congregation where he needed to learn how to communicate God's word, as he writes, "...The pipe organ has been replaced with a synthesizer and a guitar, and the standards of Bach and Mozart have bowed to the music of Sandi Patti and 'Shouts of Joy'...Well, what's happened? Have I changed everything? No. I have merely adapted my life style to fit the conditions of my vicar parish in order to be effective in my work with the people here. The outward symbols of my life I gladly give up...to worship as they worship. In fact, both my faith and health have become substantially stronger...and I am discovering that outward forms and practices mean less and less to me because I have seen the true essence of Christianity which exists in the life of these people. It is not tied to dress, life style, or worship forms. It is rather, a profound inward faith which is indelibly imprinted on the hearts of these wonderful souls as they daily confess their Christian convictions in simplicity, sincerity, and truth - oftentimes in the face of overwhelming suffering...It is this faith that shows itself in growing and loving and learning in the Lord...I have broken free from the bonds of self-imposed ecclesiastical restrictions (Tappert P.49) and have embraced the true meaning of the word, 'Christian.' " I obviously disagree with Boomhower that the organ is to be replaced with a synthesizer and a guitar, for it is definitely a "both...and."

All seminary students need to learn the richness of our traditional heritage and also the spiritual wealth that can be gained through Biblical contemporary worship at the Seminary. Aids for a variety of forms should be provided to the congregations by the Synod. We should utilize various Biblical, Lutheran worship and liturgical forms which provide integrity as they communicate truth. Let us worship under grace, and avoid making legalistic judgments, but rather enjoy creative variety which the Gospel allows.

USE SYNODICAL CHANNELS ONLY

CN, April 27, 1992, presents the Central Illinois District officials as the saviors of the Synod, while those who are victims are pictured as the ones who have created "anarchy," related to the Synod's APPEALS. *CN* presents their presidential candidate making a public pronouncement against the Fort Wayne BOR and he says, "If this action by the Board is allowed to stand, no pastor in the Synod will be safe from the same type of personal and professional treatment." My book provides evidence of the lies and deception of which APPEALS is guilty, which provides documentation that no pastor of the Synod will be safe if the APPEALS members are not removed or faced with their sins.

Who will help Rev. Otten to recognize the truth of the facts behind the Indiana District Commission on Adjudication decision so that he no longer translates it into a "friendly family squabble"? The April 1992 *Affirm* violently attacks the Fort Wayne BOR for daring to refuse to bow before the ungodly decision of a Commission that has corrupted itself. Using both Old and New Testament Bible verses, and quoting their enabler, Presidential candidate Al Barry, *Affirm* charges the victims as the criminals. Individual items: 1) "Personalities in Missouri" (p. 3) by Ken Schurb about personality over substance requires other conclusions; when Schurb refers to personality over substance, innuendoes and rumors, this is a precise description of how the "Confessional Lutherans," *CN*, and even *Affirm* in a lesser degree treated President Bohlmann; their entire campaign was one of personalities, rumors, innuendoes; 2) "Accepting Judicial Verdicts" uses Deut. 17:8-12 and Heb. 10:26-27, 31 to try to prove that the Fort Wayne BOR stood "in contempt of God Himself," when they rejected the untenable action of APPEALS; 3) "Who's Next?" states, "Appeals is a bulwark that members of the Synod have against arbitrary and capricious actions"; *Affirm* does not consider the Synod's plight when Appeals takes more than arbitrary and capricious action, but sinful action in the Preus-Werning case, in which they made a conclusion which is in direct contradiction to the very words of Dr. Preus.

Rev. John T. Pless went into his *Forum Letter* pulpit again (Apr. 19, 1992) to extol the unproven and unwarranted condemnation of all evangelicals by Rev. Harold Senkbeil in the Feb. 1991 *Lutheran Witness*, which was reviewed in this chapter. Pless cleverly changes the theses of that article, ignoring its generalizations, false logic and half-truths which I exposed in my review, and he writes that "Senkbeil triggered an avalanche of letters hostile to his suggestion that Confessional Lutherans and evangelicals do not share in a common confession of the Gospel." That is not the proposition which the great number of letter writers and I objected to, but you will not know it from Pless' distortion of the issue.

Pless again uses this platform to launch another broadside against Church Growth by extolling *The Ultimate Church* (Zondervan, by Tom Raabe, 1991), a satire on mega-churches, liturgies, spiritual gifts surveys, homogeneous principles, etc. The book is humorous, but in reading it when I saw senseless ridicule which readers will use to make indiscriminate condemnations against faithful LCMS pastors and congregations, I alternated between praying for God to deliver us from such unbrotherliness or wanting to cry. In fact, a thought which came to me several years ago came again in sharp focus that someone should write a book of satire on the LCMS institutional Lutheran congregation and pastor to show the humor of the inflexible cathedral mentality which shuts out considerable Biblical sanctification and New Testament Christian community living because such proposals do not fit the Systematic's paradigm, mindset and the terminology of the cathedral chaplain. After a few moments of reflection, I concluded that this would be cruel and merciless treatment of my brothers who are institutional Lutherans, as identified in Chapter 1. That is no way to try to communicate or to gain them to join me on a Great Adventure. Institutional Lutheranism and maintenance mentalities are no joke, because those who pursue these paths are deadly serious, and they love their Lord as much as I do. I will not hold them in ridicule, even though a satire might be hilarious.

BIBLICAL-PASTORAL VS. MANAGERIAL-LEGAL-POLITICAL PROCEDURES IN THE CHURCH

I was shocked in the Adjudication meetings with Dr. Preus that ordinary Biblical routines were unacceptable, and that not only legalistic but also legal tactics were substituted for the Biblical in a way that effectively destroyed the possibility for communication between two brothers. I became so disturbed that on April 26, 1990, I presented the following document to the Synod's ADJ as a matter of public record regarding my concerns.

What are the procedures and dynamics of the churches' Matthew 18 use and approach, and how are they consistent and primary on the personal, congregational, District and Synodical levels? Legal aspects are proper within limitations of Biblical principles, as God's Word is the authority and directive for Christian relations and actions when there are disagreements or conflicts to be settled between Christians (1 Cor. 6). No procedure is to be guided by any legal tactics when such tactics pervert or mix improperly God's will and way with legal and civil court procedures, resulting in a situation where the Word does not remain the primary rule of conduct.

1 Cor. 6 indicates that Christians are not to resort to civil courts to settle their disputes, but to do so within the polity of the church itself. Matthew 18 together with all Biblical counsel on conflict management do not allow legal or civil court tactics to be used as a dominant factor in settling problems in the church.

See how Paul handles the Corinth congregation members with all their spiritual problems, confronting them with various sins which needed Biblical correction. He presented his case without advice from an attorney, and without facing the legal advisors of the Corinthian Christians who would maintain that his individual admonitions were inadmissible. Paul complained about the intrusion of politics in the form of a party spirit in Corinth, but apparently they did not line up letter writers to counteract Paul's criticisms, nor did they use legal tactics to accomplish Biblical aims. We will also avoid the confusion of the two kingdoms or bring the Kingdom of the Left into the Kingdom of the Right. Our conflicts are to be handled within the polity of the church, using only means that are consistent with Scripture.

The Synod has clearly shown that the adjudication process must be directed only by God's Word unimpeded by human tactics. Handbook 8.01 records that the provisions of Section VIII on Adjudication and Reconciliation are established to "provide a means consistent with the Holy Scriptures to find the truth, provide for justice..." 8.51a states that "a Commission shall be governed in its acts, procedures, and judgments by the Holy Scriptures and Christian principles." God's Word reveals that Christians should operate in God's court under Law-Gospel, not legalistic law. Use of legal or civil court schemes then dare not interfere with communication between the accuser and the accused so that the issues and substance of the case become lost in the midst of challenges oriented toward the court room more than God's Word. No legalistic tactics dare be used to dominate or control a brother.

What does this mean for the meetings in the Adjudication process in the Synod?

First, the Word of God should rule without legal or civil court procedures intervening or coloring the Biblical authority related to contact between principals or witnesses.

Second, objections of admissibility of evidence should be made only for Biblical reasons, not for legal or civil court considerations, which allow any persons to avoid their Biblical responsibilities or that denies the offended ones their Biblical rights.

Third, whenever legal or civil court tactics dominate or derail the Biblical Matthew 18 procedure, the goals change to "win-lose," to a political campaign of "beat the opposition" by getting bodies lined up for and against. This approach closes the possibility for Biblical repentance and forgiveness, thus diminishing the chance for reconciliation or actual recognition of faults on the part of the accused one because he must stoically play the legal game of admitting no guilt whatsoever. It invites spiritual disaster, as both accuser and accused must get their attorneys primed and all four face each other daringly eyeball to eyeball, hoping that the other party blinks first. This offers little hope for a Biblical solution and reconciliation.

If improper legal intrusion is not Biblically proper between Christians in the congregation or between a pastor and an erring member, then it is not proper on the Synodical level. As Lutheran Christians, we must insist on a consistent Biblical approach.

March 15, 1990 Meeting

Objections must be raised to some of the legal tactics used by Dr. Robert D. Preus and his attorney David Keller in the March 15 Adjudication meeting when Keller requested that the April 17, 1989, Seminary Faculty Minutes not be admitted as "evidence" because they were not signed, as well as calling Professor Houser's letter "hearsay." Thereupon, Werning asked Dr. Preus as Presiding Officer of that meeting whether he recognized the motion from the Minutes to be authentic, but Preus and Keller refused to answer the question as Keller demanded that the Faculty Minutes were inadmissible without a signature. Christian procedure would require Dr. Preus, as the presiding officer present, to answer the question of authenticity of that faculty resolution. As of today, April 26, the current Faculty Secretary has affixed his signature, and a number of faculty have expressed their written opinions. All of us as Christians knew they were authentic on March 15, but we were forced to pay the legal game in what should have been a Biblical Matthew 18 setting.

Conclusion

Why have we as Christians complicated the simple procedure for acknowledging and correcting offenses? Legal procedures are acceptable only as servants of the Word and the church. Whatever the subject or issue, the Bible provides adequate parameters for relationships and conduct of meetings, while employing "Robert's Rules of Order" or Rules of procedure which Biblically and practically define relevance and admissibility as the tools of orderliness insofar as they do not disrupt the Biblical principles for settling disagreements or for establishing or maintaining proper relationships. The predominance of legal tactics over Biblical procedure — which can only be explained as sinful personal pride that refuses to bow before God or serve one's neighbor in love — will prevent the use of spiritual solutions to spiritual problems, which is contrary to God's Word!

My conclusion to all of this is that any legal predominance or **legal**-Biblical perversion blocking Biblical freedom is no way to conduct Christ's work or to run His church. We will want to avoid anything which does not contribute to facing each other freely by free expression of substance and the issues by Biblical standards.

*   *   *   *   *   *

CN, May 4, 1992, is a classic example of what we have experienced during the past two years from *CN* and the "Confessional Lutherans" by way of half-truths, generalizations, untruths, accusations without evidence, guilt by association, etc. "A Breach of Trust!" gives misinformation regarding the 50% of the Fort Wayne candidates who did not receive calls: They were not **denied** calls, for there were not enough calls, and half of those that were received were from congregations which stated that they would not accept a Fort Wayne graduate for reasons obvious to many in Synod; it did not indicate that it is the congregations, not District Presidents, who extend calls; neither did it show that District Presidents every year have urged congregations to call candidates, yet there has been a shortage of calls during the past few years, which have been filled by summertime.

"Stop the Rebellion" is filled with accusations and some misinformation by BOR minority members Raymond Mueller and David Anderson, and criticizing the BOR for its stand of conscience against a corrupt APPEALS. "Bohlmann's Abuse of Presidential Authority," ignores the validity of the Indiana District Commission on Adjudication's decision in finding Dr. Preus guilty of untruths. "What Does The LCMS Have To Offer Today?" claims to have both secular and religious media headlines, to show how frequently the public has heard about the LCMS and Seminary problems: Otten does not tell that almost all of these headlines are from his own *CN*!

"Lutheran Leaders Asked to Renounce Defiance of 'Supreme Court' " by Robert Noland, together with his "A Review of the Structure of 'The New Missouri' " is almost totally personal opinion and accusation — accusation journalism. "When Will President Bohlmann Come Clean and Tell the Truth?" is filled with half-truths by Ed Weise, for he deals only with Dissen and avoids the issue of Harnapp altogether: instead of trying to whitewash the question of Dissen's membership on the *Balance* Trustees, he should take this to the IRS and let them decide whether the original signers or the new one is telling the truth; also, significantly, he does not face the issue that for the three reporting years Walter Dissen accepted large amounts of expense money from *Balance, Inc,* but for what services? The silence about Harnapp's membership on the *Balance, Inc.* Trustees is deafening!

Otten's cartoon on President Bohlmann, stretching, twisting, and distorting truth (p. 21) fits Herman Otten 100%, so next week Otten should run the cartoon again with his face in it. Joseph Brennan's invitation to the Praesidium to face Robert Preus and Ed Hinnefeld on June 6 at Pittsburgh is nothing but a shallow media event in which Brennan wants to make his forum plausible and acceptable in the place of regular Synodical channels. Brennan was one named in the Craig Stanford book. There is nothing in the Bible that should allow the orthodox members of The Lutheran Church-Missouri Synod to tolerate this kind of ungodly political haranguing any longer without the Synod voting and authorizing Otten to be the judge and jury for the Missouri Synod.

Criteria for Synodical Elections

Before the party of the Right was formed in 1965, there is no question that the party of the Left had "king makers," who were moving people they had selected as candidates into leadership positions. This includes positions for Synodical elections. Many of the leaders were not members of a party, but most of them were tools whether they knew it or not. The party of the Left represented basically the supporters of the St. Louis Seminary.

We who helped form the party of the Right in 1965 were aware of the necessity to at least inform all the orthodox delegates of the 1965 Detroit convention that they had a choice related to some of the "liberal" issues before the convention, also regarding elections. Many faithful delegates became quite depressed and thought that there was little they could do. As in our "Faith Forward-First Concerns," the leaders of the newly formed party of the Right gave encouragement to concerned delegates to learn of the real issues, voice their concerns at the convention in an effective manner, and try to learn who the candidates for office were who were loyal to the Synod's doctrine and practice. Even though the Detroit convention passed the controversial Mission Affirmations, which were later shown to be defective and are now long past gone, loyal Synod members began to exert a proper influence on the Synod.

The 1967 New York convention found the Synodical loyalists, which is a more accurate name than the party of the Right, working together to the extent that many concerned delegates would request an evaluation of the candidates for elections because they did not know whom they were voting for. An evaluation had been made by a number of orthodox leaders from various Districts to ascertain the theology and practice of the various candidates as best as possible. We followed carefully the principles enunciated in the recent COP document, "Ministry of Influence," in answering the queries of delegates who simply had no knowledge where the candidates stood. It is ethical and proper to ask trustworthy ones regarding their evaluations. We never told delegates how to vote, as the delegates made their own choice. We made certain that this was fair and kind to all concerned.

The same approach was used for the 1969 Denver convention, at which time Dr. J. A. O. Preus was elected President. Only those who were blind to how the Synod was moving quickly away from its historic position in doctrine and practice would be bold enough to criticize this legitimate "Ministry of Influence." The fact is that we learned that over half of the delegates in various Districts were eager to get a fair evaluation of the stance of the candidates for election. Even though this was voluntary and private, history shows that the party of the Left and their friends became quite furious at this helping of orthodox delegates who wanted leaders who would abide by the Synod's Biblical path.

As indicated in Chapter 5, I stepped out of the leadership position of the party of the Right but kept involved and informed as much as possible for some time. In 1973, I learned that the Balance group was preparing to publish an election list. Through *Balance* channels I registered a strong complaint against such a tactic, indicating that it was unwise, unnecessary, divisive, and wrong. I believe then, as I do now, that the **publication** of a list to be broadcast goes way beyond the **private influence** of individuals of a private group, but will cause difficult problems: First, orthodox candidates who are not on the preferred list may find themselves embarrassed by such publicity. If the orthodox leaders in the Synod and in Districts are not willing to work to make information available to delegates who desire such information in a private manner, this is no excuse for the over-kill of a public list. It had allowed the party of the Left and anyone else who objects to a public list to look at the preferred candidates and vote against them. This is unnecessarily divisive.

For at least four more conventions I wrote memos to the *Balance* and *Affirm* leaders about my strong objections to the publishing of such lists. They were fearful that the private ministry of influence would not accomplish their goals, so they insisted on publishing lists. At some of the past conventions, the Nominations Committee selected candidates for election who almost unanimously were people loyal to the Synod's position on doctrine and practice, yet the *Balance* and *Affirm* leaders insisted on a published list.

The party of the Left also had a written list, which usually did not get such broad distribution, but it was a reality. Furthermore, since 1981 some District Presidents became active especially for nominees who appeared to be inconsistent related to Synod's doctrine and practice. While some of these District Presidents complained about the political activity of *Balance* and *Affirm*, they were just as busy for their own cause to influence the elections. Today, we have a total politicized situation where *Balance* and *Affirm* insist on publishing their lists despite proper arguments against it, while on the other hand, inconsistent District Presidents and their followers have actively campaigned for their candidates.

At this late date, can this political campaigning be stopped so that rational debate can go on by using proper "Ministry of Influence" guidelines regarding the qualifications of nominees at the Pittsburgh convention? I believe so, and will suggest here what can be done for each of us to extend our ministry of influence in a proper manner.

Criteria and Questions which I would pose in the selection of the next President of The Lutheran Church-Missouri Synod, assuming that all candidates have the ability to administer the affairs of Synod: 1. Is the nominee being supported by a political party such as *Affirm, Confessional Lutheran Reporters, Christian News,* or any party on the other side? 2. Is the nominee supported by political partisans such as a group of District Presidents with their own agenda, who have given a margin of support in the Presidential elections in the past two conventions? 3. In his daily work, has the nominee enunciated and given evidence of a mission vision and plan for the Synod which will take us beyond marketing, planning procedures, and public relations endeavors to assure the Synod that we are faithful in God's mission? 4. Is the candidate sufficiently non-aligned and capable of bringing healing and direction to the Synod and of helping us have peaceful relations between each other? 5. Is the nominee able to provide firm but evangelical leadership to bring a Synod with diverse patterns, ideas, and hopes to adopt a truly Biblical course and faithfully adhere to it?

As a concerned Missouri Synod Lutheran, I would urge delegates to ask these and other questions in evaluating the candidates, and then prayerfully cast their vote to provide us with a leader whom God would use to bring the Missouri Synod out of our "30 years spiritual war." We do not want peace at any price. We want the peace which God alone can give through faithfulness to His Word and to His ways.

A Treacherous Time: Changing From Party Politics to Biblical Channels

Chapter 4, "BIBLICAL LUTHERANS ARE EVANGELICAL AND CONFESSIONAL IN DOCTRINE AND PRACTICE" presents the Biblical and confessional expectations in the administration of the church both by leaders and members. Building on those Biblical principles, we have the immediate challenge to decide how our behavior will be ordered both at the Pittsburgh Convention and in the months following. The next year presents a critical challenge to make the change from private agendas and party politics to deal with each other in such an honest and open manner that there will be no dealing under the table. Only Biblical channels are to be utilized in clarifying issues and problems so that we might become unified once again. These are treacherous times when human instincts and fears tempt us to use human tactics and control, living under the law rather adopting grace ways, and instead of dealing evangelically with each other and using tough love when necessary.

The very first issue facing us is whether we will try to reconcile people while ignoring contradictions in doctrine and practice which require a solution before there can be unity. This is not a superficial matter of shaking hands and making up, and merely acting peacefully. As indicated in Chapter 4, our divisions will be healed only as we follow the example of Paul, "I appeal to you, brothers, in the name of our Lord Jesus Christ, that all of you agree with one another so that there may be no divisions among you and that you may be perfectly united in mind and thought" (1 Cor. 1:10).

More than organizational peace and unity is required. We have a divine mandate for spiritual unity in doctrine and practice: "May the God who gives endurance and encouragement give you a spirit of unity among yourselves as you follow Christ Jesus, so that with one heart and mouth you may glorify the God and Father of our Lord Jesus Christ" (Romans 15:5-6). This issue needs to be faced squarely in relation to differences in ecumenical practices, lodge policy, ordination of women, the doctrine of the call and ministry, communion practice, the charismatic issue, and changing our church practice from being institutional Lutherans to Biblical Lutherans.

We all must use the Biblical structures and systems that are available in the church. This does not mean that we cannot meet as interest groups or have Free Conferences. It does mean that such meetings do not become a place where anyone makes judgments against any other without first having spoken to the individual and having used proper church channels. It means that *CN* will no longer be a vehicle where the editor or disgruntled members of the Synod may vent their anger irresponsibly by slandering people with whom they have not dealt Biblically. This requires that *CN* should change immediately from its unChristian slander to become a respected magazine for apologetics in the best sense. Such a magazine of polemics or arguing issues in order to reveal what true and false doctrine are, rather than trying to determine who is a heretic, can serve our Synod. Even though this is a free country, we will no longer tolerate a *CN* which attacks people rather than arguing doctrine in a positive manner.

It would be well for *Affirm* to amalgamate with *CN* and become one respected magazine which stays out of party politics, not being an advocate for people who have a complaint, and stop trying to be the conscience of the church or spokesman for orthodox Lutherans. It is imperative that all "Confessional Lutheran Reporters" of various Districts, and such publications as "Vanguard," disband immediately.

It is unrealistic to think that *CN* will be closed, but it must be expected that it will be transformed into a viable and helpful publication to help unify thinking on basic doctrinal issues. Rev. Herman Otten claims to be very Biblical and wants to be very ethical, so it should not be too big a problem for him to recognize that his approach has been completely unBiblical, and that he has indeed slandered many people and has been a divisive force in the Synod. He must make the commitment to make the necessary change to understand loving apologetics. If Otten does not make this change, then members of the Synod and leaders of the Missouri District should initiate discussions with Otten's congregation in New Haven and get him to see the Biblical light.

What about the "Confessional Lutheran" organizations all over the Synod, and the national network and also *Balance Inc.*? Our Synodical Commitment makes it mandatory that Synod's channels and forums be used to exert our influence. There should be no dissident groups meeting privately. Meetings should always be open so that such people are not just talking to themselves and that, above all, they do not allow anyone to talk about or criticize another person publicly if they have not pursued the proper spiritual approach. This will require considerable self-discipline. If there are real problems or even perceived problems, it is legitimate to discuss what procedures should be used in the church to achieve our Biblical goals and to make the necessary changes if there are identifiable problems in doctrine and practice.

A few years ago, I attended several private District caucuses and found the programs to be so unedifying and some of the talks so destructive and contrary to the 8th Commandment, that I simply could not subject myself to attending that kind of meeting. Just a week ago, one of my truly orthodox friends, who a few years ago was active in one of those District groups, told me that he will not attend any more of such meetings because they made him bitter against five or six of the brothers because of their irresponsible denunciation of Synodical leaders and others with whom they disagreed. There are a large number of truly orthodox Missourians throughout the Synod who simply will not associate with that kind of perverted sense of "church work." It is safe to say that today "Confessional Lutherans" do not represent confessional Lutheranism at all. It will be difficult for many of us to identify ourselves as **confessional Lutherans** simply because of the corruption of the term by the extreme party of the Right with its unBiblical conduct, which has been documented in this chapter.

Some of these "Confessional Lutheran" leaders in Synod and Districts, together with their mentors at the Fort Wayne Seminary, need to be deprogrammed. While *CN* and the "Confessional Lutheran Reporters" have been trying to annihilate people, just as Dr. Robert Preus and Dr. David Scaer have done, we do not want them treated as they treated others. They need to be rehabilitated. I urge love and compassion to Rev. Herman Otten, Dr. Robert Preus, Dr. David Scaer, Prof. Kurt Marquart, and other "Confessional Lutheran" leaders in the Synod and in Districts. These are our brothers whom God has endowed with gifts which can bless the church. I believe that they have been sincere in what they do, but they must be helped to get out of denial and see the reality of their sinful actions in the light of Scripture. This may require intervention counseling, tough love, and loving care to give some of them sabbaticals in order to have time to be rehabilitated. If any needs evangelical discipline, let us do it tenderly under grace to regain them for an effective and constructive Gospel ministry once again.

Consistent with Chapter 4 on our Synod being evangelical and confessional in doctrine and practice is the matter of positive leadership by the District Presidents in their own District work, and also in their mutual encouragement through the Council of Presidents. District pastors and members should work through their District President and encourage him and pray for him in his very important assignment. District Presidents, like the Synodical President, should not worry about being re-elected, but always make Biblical decisions in the fear of God, not worrying about the consequences politically. There have been far too many instances in the past years where even District Presidents known for their orthodoxy have shown partiality to certain pastors or congregations, which has been disturbing the unity of the church. Some have dealt with members behind the back of the pastor without helping the people follow proper procedures. There have been times when it is perceived that District Presidents have sided with the pastors against the congregation and made it almost impossible for the congregation to experience relief from a bad situation. There is often far too much procrastination.

It is time for the District Presidents through the Council of Presidents to agree that the Synod's position on doctrine and practice in controverted areas is to be honored at all times in their Districts, and that they are responsible for any aberrations on the part of pastors or congregations in their Districts. If a District President disagrees with our traditional or historic practice, he has only one choice: make certain that his pastors and congregations are obedient to that doctrine and practice; if a pastor or congregation and even if the District President disagrees with the Synodical practice, he must present his views to the Council of Presidents and to the CTCR. Let us be done with subverting, undermining, and making end-runs for any reason. Once again, Chapter 4 of this book provides Biblical guidelines, and we invite anyone who disagrees to come up with ones more Biblically oriented.

What will be necessary so that all of us will speak with one mind and voice, and to practice this faith, as the Scriptures require? It begins with the election of a Synodical President, who evangelically and winsomely can enunciate our Biblical position in doctrine and practice, with consistent encouragement through Law and Gospel. It will require a Praesidium (President and Vice-Presidents) who are above reproach and fit the qualifications of bishops in the true sense to be able to be a catalyst in the Council of President and with individual District Presidents to lead us toward one doctrine, one faith, and one practice in areas where God requires it. Required is a Council of Presidents, which meets to confront, not evade, the issues presented by other brothers in the Council, listen to one another, speak Biblical truth to one another, bow before the Word from God, and be obedient in faith. No District President should be allowed to play games that would continue our disunity and further trouble our Synod.

Circuit Counselors should never reflect their own personal views or private agendas which conflict with our historic doctrine and practice. A number of Circuit Counselors from various Districts complained about the Pheasant Run Circuit Counselor's meeting in 1991 that in the sectional meetings that there were statements made by some Circuit Counselors that were indefensible from a Biblical viewpoint, and that this was not corrected. When the Synod conducts another "Circuit Counselor Conference," the basic program need is to present areas of disagreement and contention regarding our Synod's position in doctrine and practice in controverted areas. The obvious rule must be that God's Word is to be directed to the issue and problem, and that God's Word will settle it, not a majority view, not a minority view, nor a synthesis between the two. If we through God's Word cannot arrive at agreement in Biblical truths, then we are no longer a viable Synod unless that matter is settled.

Great care must be taken that gross misinterpretations are not allowed such as introduced by the St. Louis faculty in the 1960's and 1970's, and the ELIM party, nor the legalistic interpretations in the controverted areas which have been introduced by "Confessional Lutherans" in this decade. But the Missouri Synod has always known what is exegesis and what is not, and we need not get into semantic arguments about that. Utilizing the same approach used in developing the Lutheran Confessions, we can and must achieve unity in doctrine and practice if we are to get back to our proper mission. There should be no party politics, no *Christian News*, no "Confessional Lutheran Reporters," only "speaking the truth in love" (Eph. 4:15) by using Synodical procedures to face one another and share what is in our hearts and minds. If the Holy Spirit cannot unify us that way, it will never happen.

Controverted Areas That Need Immediate Attention

The unfortunate thing is that when the Synod was being attacked by the party of the left 20 years ago, the problem was handled more by procedural methods than by obligating dissidents to sit down and discuss the Biblical truths to which the Missouri Synod holds faithfully, and how they impact upon what we teach and practice. In the past few years, the Robert Preus party has distorted the entire matter by raising false issues and claiming that any critic of Dr. Preus was a liberal or wanted to change Synodical doctrine, wanted ordination of women, and wanted to close the Fort Wayne Seminary. As a result of their ill-conceived tactics, these "Confessional Lutherans" have actually weakened the Synod and made it more difficult for orthodox Lutherans to deal with the problems and made it easier for those with liberal agendas to keep working under cover. In other words, the Preus party has helped speed the Synod into a kind of chaos in which ones who disagree with and want to change the Synod's historic position in doctrine and practice can flourish and actually make headway.

What are the basic issues to be discussed and settled?

1. Fellowship and Ecumenical Questions.

We must go much deeper than the current "Inter-Christian Relationships" document prepared by the CTCR. It will be well for the CTCR together with a larger group of participants from all over the Synod in a special meeting to study once again such documents as: **a.** "Thesis on Fellowship" produced by resolution of Synod in the 1947 Chicago Convention, and sent out by Dr. Behnken with a Feb. 15, 1949 letter; **b.** "Selective Fellowship" by Dr. Herman Sasse, reproduced in "The Australian Theological Review," Sept. 1957; **c.** "Theology of Fellowship," which grew out of studies initiated by a resolution of the 1956 St. Paul Convention, revised and adopted by the joint faculties in October, 1960, and revised again as a result of the 1962 Cleveland Convention action.

Regarding the "Inter-Christian Relationships" document (Feb. 1991), I have time and space only for several major observations. The 13 point analysis of the Fort Wayne CTS faculty to the CTCR dated Oct. 7, 1991, presents many valid items which the CTCR should consider in revising their document. The CTCR basic presentation itself appears to be good, but the case studies will definitely give the wrong impressions to those who believe that some of these aberrations discussed are viable options. I believe it would have been much better to present a case study, and then to ask the participants to provide Biblical reasons why they believe that these statements or situations are right or wrong, rather than debating between those who go with one position and those who go with the other. The discussion tactic appears to be divisive, rather than unifying.

Here again, objections should be presented to the CTCR and raised during study of the document at pastoral conferences rather than printing the judgmental article by Robert E. Noland of San Jose, CA in *CN* Nov. 4, 1991 and "Lutheran Vanguard," Jan. 1992. It is more than counter-productive but wrong for him to write, "...You purposely equivocate the meaning of many terms. This is referred to as subterfuge in the business world...You now would recommend that it is OK to rub elbows with heresy or error, but you give no theological, God-pleasing reason for the opinion...You don't agree with our constitution, nor with the Book of Concord for that matter...You attack the doctrine of faith itself. Therefore your document is heresy...Your teaching is not only heresy, it is a lie!...Maybe you just don't have any real experience in explaining the Lutheran faith to others...using your influence to mask your malice against our constitution and Confessions...Your document would have me no longer think about Lutheran doctrine which is well-founded in God's Word...I am sure that I will not be the only person unleashing unkind words in your direction...May God have mercy on you!" We are not helped by such a tirade.

The editing of this "Inter-Christian Relationships" document will be helpful if it enlarges the document to incorporate some of the previous carefully enunciated Biblical principles of fellowship and ecumenism of our Synod. There should be clarity in expressing our practice regarding open communion without allowing the policy to become meaningless through lack of clarity. It should reject individualism and selective fellowship. The word "unionism" which is in our constitution should be used in its proper sense. There needs to be a sharpening of the distinction between cooperation in externals, and altar and pulpit fellowship. I see an ambivalence that needs to be made clear about joint participation with others in regular and official public services in contradiction to occasional services, which some critics rightfully may criticize as being vague and evasive in order to allow wrongful individual exceptions or selective fellowship. I see selective fellowship as an attempt to hold the Missouri Synod together as a political body without proper confessional boundaries or restrictions.

Practices such as those in which Southeastern District President Richard T. Hinz has been involved should be questioned and discussed with proper Synodical officials, not through editorials in CN. Possibly my concerns are similar to many others in our Synod. I do not believe that it is edifying for Dr. Hinz to enter into "A COVENANT" between Dr. Michael C. D. McDaniel, Bishop of the ELCA North Carolina Synod himself as publicized in the June 1991 in the *S.E.D. News*. The document is masterfully written with carefully selected words and phrases to make it sound very pious to the extent that it really ends up to be useless and misleading. Anyone who reads the *Lutheran Forum*, learning what is being said at the Conferences held at Northfield, MN by ELCA pastors, would have to ask if Bishop McDaniel recognizes grave problems in the ELCA which need attention. When one scrutinizes this "COVENANT" between Hinz and McDaniel, they would find the activities which they intend to undertake constitute selective fellowship. Dr. Hinz is a very astute pastor, and it is inconceivable that he could be so blind as to fail to ask the right questions and to deal with the real issues which divide us from the ELCA. That's what makes this document appear to be deceptive. It is a well-known fact that many in the Synod, including orthodox District Presidents, disagree greatly with some of the doctrine and practice of fellowship of Dr. Hinz. His document "A COVENANT" exudes love for our Lutheran brothers and sisters, and I ask Dr. Hinz to utilize that love to sit down in discussion with the Synod's Praesidium and Council of Presidents not only to discuss "A COVENANT," but also the ecumenical practices which he allows in his District. Unlike his dialog with the ELCA bishop, all the cards would be laid on the table and all questions should be answered Biblically. There should be no evasion of any question or problem that any member of the Praesidium and Counsel of Presidents would raise. Let it be done lovingly and brotherly, but also honestly.

2. Ordination of Women

Some may use interpretation arguments in a way to make the Scriptures appear to be ambiguous related to God's command that women are not to be pastors. But the Scriptures are not that unclear, nor has the LCMS been wrong in this matter. The LCMS has possibly allowed confusion about the woman's place in the church otherwise, and this certainly needs to be clarified in order that women are not disqualified for church service as they have been by some pastors and congregations.

Regarding women's eligibility for ordination into the Pastoral ministry, there is absolutely no reason to believe that Paul's prohibition is only cultural, when he states in 1 Cor. 14:33 that this is the "Lord's command." Neither is it cultural nor subject to another interpretation when 1 Tim. 3:2 states that the bishop-pastor should be the husband of one wife.

It is redundant to say that a woman pastor cannot have a wife. Three corrective passages in Scriptures insist that sexual distinctions be made for the **pastoral ministry**: 1 Cor. 11:2-16; 14:34-36; 1 Tim. 2:11-15.

I believe that those who disagree with the LCMS position on ordination of women should immediately get involved in formal Bible study with others in their circuit and District and discuss it until they come to a common understanding and position in this regard on the basis of the CTCR document "WOMEN IN THE CHURCH" (Sept. 1985). This document states, "The main application of these passages (1 Cor. 14:33b-35; 1 Tim. 2:11-15) in the contemporary church is that women are not to exercise those functions in the local congregation that would involve them in the exercise of authority inherent in the authoritative public teaching office (i.e., the office of Pastor)." This discussion must also involve the many ways in which women can be properly and actively involved as teachers, deaconesses, and the exercise of women's abilities as members of congregations in the fullest sense except those of pastor, elders, or taking authority over men in spiritual matters. In this situation, it appears to me that many "Confessional Lutherans" must sit down with their peers and their brothers and learn that some of their restrictions are blatantly legalistic, and not allowed under grace. Orthodox Lutheran men must encourage consistent practice throughout the LCMS in women's service in congregations, which is Biblically legitimate.

Those LCMS members who disagree with our position on ordination of women should write and state their concerns to the CTCR on the basis of Scripture and to any other official group in the Synod which has the authority and ability to deal with such issues. Every legitimate view should be heard lovingly and evangelically without condescension. This is the only way that we can come to the agreement which God wants us to have. Accordingly, the views expressed in the recent book, *Different Voices/Shared Vision, Male and Female in the Trinitarian Community* (by Marie Meyer, Marva Dawn, Dot Nuechterlein, Elizabeth A. Yates, Richard T. Hinz, with an Afterword by Paul R. Hinlicky; ALPB Books, Delhi: New York, 1992), should be studied carefully by the CTCR since this is offered publicly to the LCMS, and give these people a response in areas where their ideas have been helpful and where they are incorrect.

A number of provocative thoughts would be helpful in dialog on this issue, but there are also untenable statements and proposals which not only confuse the issue further, but contribute nothing to the discussion that is Biblically correct. Obviously, it is not helpful or productive to be lectured by the ELCA on "Why Women May Be Ordained," and "An Appeal To Missouri For The Ordination of Women," which appear as the last two articles of the book. I wrote to District President Hinz to ask how he could be involved in a book on women's place in the church which concludes with such advocacy for women's ordination. Hinz sent me a letter from Mrs. Marie Meyer to Dr. Paul Hinlicky, who was Editor of the book and publisher of the last last two articles on ordination, and Hinlicky's answer to Mrs. Meyer. Mrs. Meyer said that the group of authors agreed not to raise the question of ordination so that they would not raise any "red flags." Even though the other authors did not know beforehand that the ordination articles would be printed at the end, Meyer writes, "After consultation with the above and prayerful consideration, it was my decision to continue distribution (of the book) without retraction, defense or apology...The greater danger is to avoid re-examining how the Synod arrived at existing practices." Dr. Hinz did not answer my basic questions, "Were you aware of the fact that the Afterword and the Appendix articles would be included? If not, do you at this date disavow them completely and will you make a public statement to that effect?" Hinz did not disavow the publication of those two chapters, and so did not offer a public apology.

I am sure that a great number of loyal Missouri Synod pastors and laymen will join me in asking the CTCR, the Praesidium, and the Council of Presidents to deal with this issue forthrightly with Dr. Hinz to get it resolved. Our Synod will not become united in this matter when individuals make public pronouncements as trial balloons or as attempts to influence others to join them. The only Biblical approach is to sit together, open our Bibles, and start talking frankly and patiently. This should be a primary concern of the Council of Presidents, who should discuss not only this and the ecumenical procedures of Dr. Hinz and friends on the COP, but also any other troublesome issues.

When the issue of ordination of women is studied further, I suggest that participants obtain and read a copy of "RECLAIMING THE WOMAN'S RIGHT TO BE A WOMAN" by Deaconess Irene Campbell, Zion Lutheran Church, Terra Bella, CA. This is a very careful and thoughtful Bible study with additional quotations from Luther to show that women's position will be elevated and not degraded by obedience to God's Word.

3. Charismatic Movement

Productive dialog on the basis of the CTCR document on the charismatic question should be continued with the Renewal In Missouri representatives. Legitimate thoughts and concerns should be heard and acted upon. Those in the Synod who have legalistically gone beyond what the CTCR document states should listen more than they speak so that they comprehend what the real issues are. Renewal is available through much Bible study, not charismatic practices.

Chapter 9

STEWARDSHIP DYSFUNCTIONS AND GIVING SHORTAGES CURTAIL MISSION OUTREACH AND BECOME PERMANENT PROBLEMS

With the exception of the New Testament church itself, everything that is available on stewardship in books and articles indicates to me that stewardship has basically been a step-child of the church, seldom having an integral connection or relation to grace. Whether it was subtle or gross legalism, stewardship has generally been law-centered, many times being merely a fund-raising program for maintenance or survival, with hardly any attempt to tie it to its New Testament reality of sanctification.

I really wasn't prepared for what I faced in the parish when I became a pastor, for I immediately discovered that grace theology had little to do with financial matters in the church. When the church needed money, they would set a budget, ask people to give, and keep on asking until there were enough pledges to make the budget. Need as determined by the leaders was the measure by which people were to give. Usually, the church got what the leaders asked, but people were not giving what God asks according to Biblical standards.

The method of stewardship utilized institutional goals, rather than grace theology through education to reach Biblical goals. People were told what to give, rather than told how to give. As stated in the Introduction, Dr. John Herrmann, the first Stewardship Executive in the Synod, taught me grace stewardship theology, which changed my paradigm from needs to Biblical principles.

I will never forget the first day of the Synodical Fiscal Conference where the Synod budget was set, when I became Assistant Stewardship Counselor of the Synod in 1952. I heard District leaders debating that the Synodical budget must be a realistic one that congregations could attain. I wondered how they knew God's mind when they finally set the budget and believed, "This is what God wants us to do." Nothing was said about stewardship digging and fertilizing by teaching Biblical standards aggressively. I could not sleep that first night, for I had not realized that the leaders at the Synodical Fiscal Conference were shaving the Synodical budgets to the extent that they did not tell the people all that was needed, but all that they thought the people would raise. The inconsistency bothered me, together with the failure to tie the budget with a strong educational program in giving.

In 1956 when I accepted the stewardship position in the Southern Nebraska District, there were already a number of District Stewardship Executives at work. First five men, then seven, then nine attempted together to encourage the Synod seriously to adopt the grace approach in Christian stewardship and use educational materials in the congregation to enlarge Synod's missions.

The 1956 St. Paul Convention and especially the 1959 San Francisco Convention were the first conventions when District Stewardship Executives tried to exert influence to wean the Synod's giving away from institutional needs to teaching Biblical standards. The 1962 Cleveland Convention was the scene of a major attempt on the part of at least a dozen District Stewardship Executives to consider a major campaign based on Biblical standards for teaching people to give firstfruit, proportionate gifts; however, Synodical leaders worked strongly to have a big collection, which ultimately was changed to what was termed, "Forward in Faith," a hybrid form of a big collection which was to take place over a period of years through teaching Biblical stewardship. When the program finally came out, the Synodical leaders had changed it into basically an appeal for mission needs which diffused the focus on the Biblical standards. Instead of a Synod-wide Grace System, a Proposal System was developed by Synodical leaders. There are several file folders which show materials and letters that a number of us District Stewardship Executives had developed, for whom I was spokesman, to try to get the Synod to take seriously Biblical grace and an educational approach in the stewardship of giving. Some District Stewardship Executives, the Praesidium of the Synod and selected faculty members of the St. Louis Seminary were involved in consideration of this issue. Finally, Pres. Oliver Harms arranged a meeting for some stewardship executives, again for whom I was spokesman, to meet with several Vice Presidents of the Synod and also several S. L. faculty members on Nov. 22, 1963 at the Statler Hotel in St. Louis. At that time, I presented a 25-page single-spaced essay titled, "THE PROPOSAL PLAN IN RELATION TO NEW TESTAMENT THEOLOGY."

Paul Lindemann — 1925

Biblical issues which were presented in that essay are still relevant today, so a summary will be produced for your consideration. Strategic in that presentation was this classical quotation from Dr. Paul Lindemann's 1925 book, "Christian Stewardship and Its Modern Implications," [37] in which he pointed out some of the organizational inconsistencies in stewardship.

He wrote, "Systematization is not stewardship...the contention has been made that the dearth of funds necessary to carry on our work successfully was due to the lack of proper machinery...we have preached systematization with laudable persistence...we have manipulated extensively with apportionments and quotas and tabulations. We have furnished reams of statistics. We have sought to set the official machinery of our Synodical body into operation in an effort to introduce effective methods of collecting the gifts for the Kingdom of God...others again contended that we embark upon a campaign of education. Under the term **education** we meant a systematic location, number, and extent of our various mission fields, with the financial needs represented by our wide-flung educational institutions and the money necessary to operate efficiently our Synodical machinery. Why is it that the earnestly applied remedies of systematizing our finances and of educating (mission information) our people have not brought the expected and desired results? These two measures are more or less mechanical in character.

Lindemann continues, "Christian giving needs a **heart stimulus**. It is animated not by a logic and reason and Synodical patriotism and pride of achievement or even by a sense of duty, but its actuating impulse must be love. The most meticulous systematization and the most thorough and factual education can never stimulate love...a church may be thoroughly informed regarding the various Synodical endeavors. It may be thoroughly conversant with detailed tabulations of Synod's financial needs. And yet the individual church member finds it difficult to realize that these needs have any relationship to him personally. We are convinced that all our Synodical and congregational problems are due to the fact that our people are not applying the principles of stewardship to their own lives...in presenting the cause of Jesus Christ, there has been entirely too much coaxing and wheedling, and pleading and scolding and threatening...it is high time that we take the church out of the beggar class. It is high time that we come to our people boldly, asking not for a congregational and personal handout of the driblets of what they have left after they have satisfied all their own personal needs and luxuries, but **that we come to them with the philosophy of life which the Holy Scriptures proclaim as the only logical reason why God has given us life**...it seems to us that what we need is a persistent, continuous campaign of **stewardship education**, and a patient inculcation of stewardship principles." What a penetrating analysis and solution written 66 years ago, but the bureaucracy could not comprehend. Nothing changed 28 years ago either after the Nov. 22, 1963 meeting in St. Louis.

1963 Stewardship Essay To Synod's Leaders

Besides the Lindemann quotation, the 1963 essay included 29 stewardship theses, of which we share 8:

"12. God deals with His people in terms of **promise** rather than **demand** (Rom. 9-11).

13. Christianity does not present a set of rules or a code of conduct which people are to follow in order to be Christians; Human suggestions and legalistic measurements or standards are not to be equated with God's will for the Christian.

19. 'Seek the Lord first' in the use of time, talents and money (Spiritual priorities and values) is the New Testament principle of living (Mt. 6:33).

20. All Christians need the nourishment of a living church fellowship if they are to grow into maturity and fruitfulness (Each Christian is called into the fellowship of the church for mutual edification within the church, all gifts given for the equipping each saint for his task.)

21. Hold to a concept of the church that indicates its nature and functions **as the Body of Christ**, not emphasizing the organizational and institutional image (not equate church membership with Christianity, nor church routines with God's mission **per se**).

22. The church is to help 'move people in the direction which **God** wants them to go,' (R. R. Caemmerer) challenging the whole man by sharing the **whole counsel** of God, not by **partial organizational goals.**

28. 'Busyness' or financial achievements that meet human goals do not prove the vitality of a congregation.

29. The church is not the guardian of forms and methods of the past, but a living organism of the Holy Spirit."

The essay then presented "A Short History of Giving": "Our European background has had its effect on our stewardship habits for many years. Coming from a state church which was tax supported and where there were no regular offerings, our church in America for may years did not concern itself with a Biblical study of Christian giving. Lutheran theologians, both in Europe and in America, were little concerned about the study of Christian giving and its Biblical theology. Consequently, pastors and leaders of congregations adopted the best methods of giving that they knew. Often, they adopted practices which were carried on in other Protestant denominations. The need for giving was very apparent in salaries that had to be paid and churches that had to be built. Bills for communion supplies and for heat had to be paid. Appeals were made to all members to do their share in order to meet all expenses. When needs arose, people were faced with them. Thus, generally, the local and Synodical needs were told, and then individuals would give or pledge a certain amount to try to help cover the needs.

"The needs were covered by pledges and payment of 'dues.' Everyone was to do his 'share.' Much of this was arbitrary and many times it was left to the emotions: Do we reach for another dollar for the poor heathen when the mission preacher touches a responsive chord? Do we give another $10 when the Voter's Assembly has not underwritten the local budget and everyone is asked to raise his pledge a little? Averages and fair shares were stressed.

'The Lord hath need' was the favorite chorus to get just a little more money, forgetting that in the Bible the man's colt may have been the only colt he had and that this was **Jesus** Himself asking and evaluating the immediate need.

"Usually, our financial policies have been geared to a **'starvation' policy**: there are so many dollars people will give, and each interest group must inspire for their own cause or it will not be given. Those who send out the best leaders and the best materials would get the most dollars; actually, each cause had to vie against each other — missions against home, home against charities, church charities against public charities, building funds against missions — and each against each other."

The next section of the essay was headed, "Rules and Regulations Confuse The Matter." It quoted T. A. Kantenon in his book, "Resurgence of the Gospel" [38]: "The enthusiasms which are drawn from man's emotional resources are soon used up. Weariness and exhaustion set in. The only alternative then left is the legalistic, 'You must.' The obstreperous will is flogged with exhortations: 'You must do better;' 'You must try harder.' Sensitive consciences are thus led to despondency, the less sensitive to self-righteousness. With the Gospel of grace the case is entirely different. It is in the indicative, a narrative of what God has done and is doing, not in the imperative, a demand to man to do something."

Our essay continued, "Healthy Christian growth is made difficult when leaders attempt to make rules that apply to all possible situations, thus narrowing the range of the congregation's and individual's choices and their independent action." K. Kuntz in *Wooden Chalices* [39] writes, "The terrible limitation of giving to meet need rests in the fact that once a particular need is met, the giver has no larger motivation for his stewardship." Werner Elert states in *The Christian Ethos* [40], "We dare never lose sight of the fact that in our relationship with God grace and legal order are mutually exclusive."

The 1963 essay continues, "It is necessary to clarify afresh what we as the 'people of God' are to be and do in the light of the teachings of Scripture. The patterns of the past, the traditions of men, nor the cry, 'Let's be practical,' must not thwart this fundamental quest. To say that the principles of New Testament theology alone are unrealistic may simply be an indication of how far down the road towards institutionalism the church has traveled. Methods and organization never go deep enough to change or inspire the deepest spiritual dimensions of human life. We organize when we fail to redeem: many churches can organize 600 people without changing any of them. Organization and programs are a quick way of deceiving ourselves into thinking that we've done something. Before we know it, we have organized far beyond the point of sustaining life, and many of our organizational enthusiasms actually exhaust life. Rachel Henderlite has said, 'The church is called to be the people of God, and the terms of the call are God's, not man's.' " [41]

Institutional Stewardship

The essay proceeded with asking why we need to continue with financial crutches and why we could not get back to a Biblical basis. The essay told that no "needs" program or legalistic system relieves us from the responsibility to confront God's people with God's proposals. Human proposals tend to view Christianity in terms of institutional relationships and loyalties. It reminded, "It is essential that we consider carefully the question: 'When God calls a person to be Christian, what does He call him to be and do?' Church members can easily evade the difficult and radical demands of God for total commitment by substituting loyalty to the church as an institution and by merely attempting to reach the church's goals. Then an achievement of these organizational goals becomes a substitute for real commitment on the part of most members."

D. M. Baillie reminds us of God's grace operative in stewardship in his book *God Was In Christ* [42]: "It means the One who **at the same time makes absolute demands upon us and offers freely to give us all that He demands**. It means the One who requires of us unlimited obedience then supplies the obedience Himself...**Giving** in response **to human obedience** is a sub-Christian idea, alien to the New Testament; and, indeed, if God's grace had to wait for man's obedience, it would be kept waiting forever." The temptation is always overwhelming to be satisfied with external evidences of success, hoping that somehow spiritual transformation will come. External success easily hides inner weaknesses.

F. B. Edge in *A Quest for Vitality in Religion* [43] states: "Institutions and organizations which were designed and intended to be used as a means of serving people may become ends, and the **loyalty of people is determined by their service to the institution.**"

The essay states, "Building the church as an institution does not correspondingly increase its power to minister in and to the world. It is not enough simply to do better than what we are already doing. No program or approach is proper unless it is culminated in terms of God's call through Word and Sacrament to mission. Institutionalism has weakened us to the extent that when we seek a greater sanctified membership, the first thing that comes to us is a fear of offending some or disrupting some program. Those misunderstand the Gospel message who set up stewardship requirements and goals to achieve the church's purpose or measure its success. God's call is greater than defining our mission responsibilities in little manageable terms that are acceptable to church members."

Under a section titled, "God's Priests at Work," the essay presented: "**Christians are called to be the priests of God** rather than just good 'church members.' As each believer sees himself as a priest **of Christ**, he realizes that he is responsible, not to church leaders first, but to God Himself. If the believers are not led to measure their primary privilege as **God's people**, neither can they hope to measure their responsibility **to God** and **His church**.

"How can we continue to use financial goals and budgets as the measure that should determine the offerings of God's people? What is a person supposed to do when he moves from a District that has World Mission goals that average $25 per communicant to a District where the average is $40? Or say that he moves from a congregation whose average 'needs' are about $250 per communicant and he transfers to one whose 'needs' are $470 per communicant — why should he change giving habits because of his change of residence and he faces a different Proposal? Has God's love for him changed or are the stated needs the motivation? The world need is so great and so demanding that only the challenge of firstfruit proportionate giving by every Christian will be an effective answer.

"Could we imagine St. Paul recasting 1 Cor. 16:2 into a message for organizational goals and so writing, 'Now concerning the collection, let everyone give generously and give 480 shekels for the Corinth Proposal to help the Northwest Asia Minor District meet its Mission Program of 3600 shekels.' Even amidst a particular need that dealt with only a specific **number** of Jerusalem saints, he indicated no organizational goal but faced each members of the Corinth Church with the 'individual goal' of giving as God had given to them while the leaders would spend the money wisely.

"What are we really communicating to God's priests? What do they hear as they sit in the pews and in meetings? To what extent do we truly interpret the Christian Vocation accurately without flavoring it with all kinds of institutional concerns and human goals? Do we give the impression that the essence of the church is its buildings, its machinery, its programs, its stated needs and its budgets? We may think we are presenting the priesthood doctrine clearly but the people may hear little more than the call for a 'crusade of good church members' to **march together** in a great **church campaign**. Have we shown more interest in the member in his relationship to his church body than we have in the man in his relationship with his Savior?

"As we communicate a relevant message of sin and grace, we will encourage all members to place the big offering on the Lord's altar: the truly repentant heart. For some, it may be more important at the moment that they repent of wicked words in their mouths and of the lovelessness in their hearts and of the little 'hates' in their lives than of repenting of congregational and synodical budget shortages. Congregations will seek to attack their besetting sins and to be helpful to members in their faltering ways, sharing the forgiving love of Christ and the empowering grace of His Spirit for a renewed life in Christ."

New Testament Theology

Under a section titled, "Teach The Word," we read: "What are the **means** to gain adequate financial gifts? What are the **goals** for faith? Spiritual growth does not come from a pre-cut, pre-fab program such as a work program and its proposals, but from the Word by the Spirit. Only the Word can make a man more spiritual. **Man's** word reaches the **ear** only. **God's** Word reaches the **heart**. Man's word divides. God's Word unites.

" 'Make full proof of your ministry.' What is our true ministry? It is a life-time encounter, not an annual battle. We are in this with everything we have for a thorough, all-absorbing ministry. Are we trying to secure adequate pledges annually or trying to encourage congregations and members to fulfill their ministry and grow towards that ministry? Our ministry is one of God's Word, not of man's word.

"It is the responsibility of the church to open the Bible for its members in such a way that they may come to it in faith, ready to hear God speak and in speaking to lead them into greater commitment. For the people of God must listen again and again to the story of their lives, how God took them when they were no people and made them His people. And as they listen, they become more mature in their witness and service to Him. Thus, the church body, too, needs to arouse the heart to a sensitiveness and willingness to listen for God's Word and to respond to His will.

"The man who declares 'I a servant of God declare unto you' should not after leaving the altar and the pulpit become a delivery man for promotional packets and for institutional goals that aim to meet limited goals of the organization.

"If there is to be a continuing reformation, the church must look at its stewardship habits and at its words of motivation that are designed to direct its members to give as God has given to them. We finally face the question of whether the New Testament theology of stewardship remains mere theory or not. Do we say that the Word with the Atonement is the all-embracing power and motivation, but them proceed to forget or violate to some degree both in our messages and materials to our members when we want to get Synodical and congregational support?

"When the church neglects the teaching of a true New Testament theology in relation to its practical activities, it has lost something that is indispensable to its truest nature. There is a need for a theological assessment of our programs and methods to study this theological gap, the dichotomy between theology and practice, aspiration and actuality, message and method. There should be a dramatic and creative attempt to place the educational process and the cutting edge of the Word into the very center and core of the life of the church and each congregation."

Under the heading, "Give Attention To The Educational Program," the essay presented: "In the grace approach, it appears that the position of the District is not to make proposals for the congregation's **financial pledge**, but to make proposals for the congregation's **educational program** where it is weak or lacking. District and Circuit leaders should be God's 'County Agents' who indicate what seed, fertilizer and cultivation methods are worthy of consideration. They do not come to make an appeal for increase of production at a specific level. The 'County Agents' show how production can be increased rather than telling exactly **how much more** fruit is expected. If congregations fail to plan properly and grow, then they should be visited. Problem congregations, then, should be given special attention by District and Circuit leaders so that they might be **led to evaluate their problems and needs and to seek adequate Biblical solutions.**

"Thus the 'giving potential' of God and the faithfulness of His promises is the big concern, **not** the 'giving potential' **of people** or the challenge to **their** faithfulness. The church's task is not to open the billfold, but to open the heart through the Word. The budget is not to be used to fill the treasury but merely to empty it. We do not appeal to the love of man for soon he will be out of love, but we appeal to God's love for man through the Means of Grace."

The 1963 essay to the Synodical leaders concluded under the heading, "Christians and Congregations Set The Pace In World Missions." We said, "Why not come clean and go all the way? Why not take away the human props and organizational goals as devices to get adequate support, but take members to the only place they should go — to God's Word? Why not ask for the **whole man** instead of the things he can afford? Why not force him to look **to no man** when he asks, 'What shall I do?', but look only **to Christ and His Cross** and at the Word itself?

"Synod through its Board of Directors and District leaders should adopt a World Mission 'Work Program' that finds meaning only as the members of Synod resolve to give generously for these tasks. Districts adopt their own Work Program that includes both Synodical and District tasks. Congregations and their members are to be thoroughly informed of the World Mission Program as seen by their leaders. Members are taught firstfruit proportionate giving and then are given an opportunity for full discussion of congregational and worldwide missions. The congregation then sets a Faith Goal for its world work and informs the officers of Synod what this goal is. After this, Synod's actual budget is set on the basis of the sum total of the Faith Goals of congregations.

"The method of determining Synod's budget or spending guide actually is designed to tell the members of each congregation, 'God's priests, it's up to you! By your offerings and goals you are setting the total work your church will do.' This goal is not to be used as a weapon or a prying device of Synod against congregations and members to get adequate funds. The Holy Spirit, not budget pressures, should direct God's priests in their giving!

"Our appeal is for the acceptance of scriptural and theological considerations that will help minimize the place of self and that will magnify Christ. Our appeal is for a theological use in stewardship that begins and ends with the receiving of God's forgiving grace, always telling how one must receive first the grace of God before he can express gratitude and respond and give. We look not for spurts of enthusiasm generated by men's promotional abilities but for growing and maturing Christians at work in their priestly functions by the power of the Word.

"**Partial** commitment by Christians as a result of **partial** Gospel challenges will not solve our dilemma. The church's 'long haul' task of world evangelism requires a 'long haul' program of education in the Word — anything less is a dubious 'stop-gap' approach. Through effective use of the Word our stewardship should be marked by the presence and activity of the Holy Spirit to produce maturing Christians that are true witnesses in their own Jerusalem, Judea, Samaria and unto the ends of the earth."

There has always been some generous giving on the part of the members of the LCMS. Certainly, there have been many inspiring examples of generous giving on the part of a strong corps of our members. The giving problem lies with the 70% who have never been effectively reached with the Biblical message of giving. This group provides a great potential for the future if we leave budget and needs-centered giving behind and concentrate on teaching New Testament principles of giving. There can be no question about the generosity on the part of a minority who have provided very generous gifts through special offerings such as through *Ebenezer, Forward in Remembrance,* and *Alive in Christ.*

Grace System

Since 1963 when the quoted essay was presented to Synodical leaders, a growing number of District Stewardship Executives have tried to influence the Synod toward basic year-round Biblical giving, rather than budget approaches. Unfortunately, the church bureaucracy which always exists is a deterrent to the LCMS entering a new and creative day of New Testament grace giving. Regarding fund-raising efforts in Synod, many District Stewardship Executives have encouraged the Synod to use the same manpower, effort, and time to introduce a massive program of firstfruit-proportionate giving as a challenge to all members.

At the June 1984 Synodical District Stewardship Executive COnference, I presented the **grace concept**, which a majority of the District Stewardship leaders have supported, in a presentation, "Supply-Side Stewardship Vs. Maintenance Stewardship." I suggested how such an educational process could have revolutionary financial results, also for the "Alive in Christ" large offering. Many District Stewardship Executives asked me to share a printed copy and also to send it to President Ralph Bohlmann, who responded very favorably. Leaders of some Districts said that they simply could not get support for "Alive in Christ" no matter how much the money is needed, for their leaders wanted a sound stewardship educational approach such as I presented. Some Districts reported a negative factor from 60% to 80% of the pastors, and some District Board of Directors told the Synodical leaders and the "Alive in Christ" fund-raising organization leaders that they could not support a big collection, but would support a thorough educational program in firstfruit, proportionate giving. Despite this fact, it was claimed by the organization that its feasibility study showed almost unanimous support for a big collection. When leaders give examples of big collections both in the Old and New Testaments, it must be remembered that these offerings were given by people who were **already** following God's plan of proportionate giving or tithing! Our Synod's big collections are planned to get larger offerings from some people whose giving habits are bad, and the big offering is intended to help them catch up a bit. I believe that our big offerings should provide an opportunity to teach all donors first to adopt Biblical principles of giving, then to add a special offering as God motivates them.

The problem with the big collections is that a small percentage of members actually give, while considerable manpower and time are used in the machinery for the campaign. The Forward in Remembrance campaign ended with 18% of the people participating, while 82% did not. Many of us agree that we need to look for an alternative in which we use all this machinery to focus on the responsibility to teach all members Biblical principles of giving, like my proposal, "Plus 1," involves. "Plus 1" [44] proposes a presentation that challenges people to give to God first, give a planned and generous percentage of their income to God, make it a generous percentage, and do it on the basis of God's grace. Every member is encouraged to pray for faith to increase their giving by 1% of their total income annually until at least they reach 10%. Such an effort would benefit the local congregation as well as the Synod.

At the suggestion of President Bohlmann, I was invited by the leaders of the "Alive In Christ" program to meet with them. When I completed my presentation in St. Louis,

I was told that this would not be part of the plan. Hearing that conclusion, without having any discussion, I summarized the plan again. Then, the leaders requested me to give them a formal document on the "Plus 1" approach, which I did. That is the last I heard from them.

New Testament Theology

Several years later while visiting with the Synod's Stewardship Executive at the Kansas City LLL COnvention, he invited me to give a presentation on the grace system to the Synod's Board of Stewardship, which I did a year later in Orlando. After portraying what I believed was a realistic appraisal of the Synod's stewardship and financial situation and what needs to be done, the Executive's comment was, "That is very depressing." However, no changes were made.

The Nov. 1990 *Lutheran Witness* carried an article by the Executive Director of the Department of Stewardship entitled, "How Is The Synod Funded?" The entire article presented only budget considerations, and did not provide leadership for Biblical principles for giving. I responded to that article in a Nov. 15, 1990 letter to the *Lutheran Witness*, which the *L. W.* did not print:

"Dear Co-Worker in Christ:

"The author of 'How Is The Synod Funded' in the Nov. 1990 *Lutheran Witness* states, 'The Bible remains silent regarding one funding model as compared to another. Just as our Lord avoids giving commands on how a congregation should organize itself, neither does He indicate a preferred model of funding the mission.' As one reads the Bible, one finds that this simply is not true. Unfortunately, only two human models are proposed by the author, one for appealing for unrestricted and the other for restricted funds. To reduce Christian stewardship of giving to making appeals is a disservice to our Lord's teaching. Some methods which have become popular today, such as mail and telephone campaigns, or the stale and tired bazaars and sales for restricted and unrestricted gifts, cannot be deduced from Biblical stewardship teachings. Neither are we told to give to the church, but to the Lord through the church.

"Nothing is said in this article about the Biblical emphasis of firstfruit giving (both the Old Testament and Jesus in Matthew 6:33) and generous proportionate giving which is a result of God's grace (2 Cor. 8 and 9). The article talks only about collecting money for the church. Jesus did not say, 'Go...collect money,' but He said, 'Go...teach,' and part of that teaching points to the Biblical principles of firstfruit generous proportionate giving.

"In view of the Biblical truths of giving from what God has given as an expression of personal faith, it is tragic that the author holds out no more hope for the Synod than generosity and response to appeals for either restricted or unrestricted funds. Such appeals raise more defense mechanisms, complaints, and excuses in a church body that corporately through congregations gives less than 2-1/2 cents out of each dollar the members receive in income.

"Which will we have? Continue with the dismal, failed system of budgetitis, needs and appeals limited to maintenance where giving has been based on the argument about the abundance and prosperity of the people, or the dynamic grace system which taps God's rich supply and divides it based on Biblical principles and empowered by grace? The first has no Biblical sanction, while the second is what the Bible teaches. The Bible is not silent. Let us reject the failed appeal system and adopt a dynamic grace system. Let's give more than lip service to grace, and stop using Bible verses only as a slogan for giving.

"J. Hudson Taylor was right, 'God's work done in God's way will never lack God's

321

supply? God has given His people all the spiritual and material resources required to get the saving Gospel of Jesus Christ to all people in the world in our lifetime. It's in our people's hands, and we will never extricate that money from them sufficiently to make our budgets by making appeals for restricted or unrestricted budgets. When will we stop going to man's poorhouse and learn to go to God's rich storehouse?

"Money and finances are not the problem, as we are not to talk people out of their money by telling them of church needs. The budget is not a means to get money, but a spending guide. The budget is not to be used to fill the treasury, but to empty it. God's Word properly taught will fill church treasuries.

"Our stewardship and fund-raising efforts are built upon the Biblical premise that generous offerings will result by God's grace as the whole church is mobilized by discipling the leaders, who in turn will teach all the members by a thorough method of contact to provide Biblical principles from God's Word for growing in knowledge, grace, faith and stewardship commitment. God's method to make healthy branches to bear abundant fruit for fulfilling the Great Commission locally and worldwide is through the Word by the Holy Spirit. The right stewardship of our God-given life, time, abilities and money is what life is all about. The textbook for proper stewardship is the Bible. The school for instruction is the church. The God-appointed agents or leaders for good stewardship education in the church are the pastor, the elders and the elected or appointed stewardship leaders.

"Let our appeal to the people be to change the focus **from** giving to church needs **towards** individual giving based on Biblical principles of firstfruit generous proportionate giving. God has taught this in His Word. Yours in Christ, Waldo J. Werning"

*　　　　　*　　　　　*　　　　　*　　　　　*

People do want a more direct role in supporting and expanding their church's mission, but a more basic stewardship plan is required than the special report in the June 1991 *Lutheran Witness* in the article, "Expanding the Circle." This is another new funding formula which will gain a little more mission support, but it does not attack the basic weaknesses of our stewardship approach. The failure to adopt an aggressive Biblical stewardship plan has resulted in great financial distress in the Synodical mission program, so much so that the July 1991 *Lutheran Witness* carried the article, "Tightening the Belt." It stated, "Due to changing priorities, congregations are keeping more of their money for local mission opportunities. This trend, resulting in less money for the national budget, is forcing the Synod to cut back services it has traditionally provided." The basic premise of the article is that there is only so much money and the pie cannot be enlarged, and so it is a question of how better to divide each piece in the pie. The Synod Stewardship Executive states that "the current financial problems are a 'no-fault' situation." We certainly do not have to give excuses for our people, for they are perfectly able to do that for themselves. There is plenty of fault to pass around. What is missing is an aggressive and extensive stewardship education program which utilizes manpower and time such as our big collections have in the past but teaches Biblical principles of giving.

While "His Love-Our Response" was helpful to a minority of congregations, it should have reached many more churches and people. A number of Districts have produced some good materials which have been used regionally with good effect. However, I believe that what is required is a major effort in stewardship education and giving which the LCMS Michigan District has produced with direction by Resources Services Inc. of Dallas, TX. The "Growing in Vision and Mission" program was written and developed under the leadership of RSI and the Michigan District staff, Stewardship Board and a special committee. Several large committees were responsible for editing and making suggestions, which resulted in final adoption of the program. The unambiguous goal in Christian giving was to challenge every member to increase their giving by 2% of their income annually.

Having been able to observe the Michigan Plan closely since I was contracted to write many of the materials (which were edited by their District Committees), I believe that the Synod's Board of Directors should study this approach carefully in order to ascertain the feasibility of a similar Synod-wide giving campaign for three years, which focuses on firstfruit, generous, proportionate giving with the encouragement to add at least 1% of income for the church each year. The Michigan District leaders and Resource Services Inc. are a primary resource for gaining information and leadership for such a major program which I believe would produce a permanent change in congregational and Synodical funding. This would exchange institutional giving for Biblical giving.

I have accepted an invitation to write and direct a major Stewardship-Renewal-Giving program for the Lutheran Church of Nigeria, similar to the one conducted by the Michigan District. Entitled "The Big Step Forward In Faith," this educational effort involves sermons and Bible studies every week during May and June of this year. A major planning session was held last November, and a training meeting of over 200 pastors, evangelists, some lay preachers, and seminary students for four days in February 1992 in preparation for the use of these Biblical materials and to meet weekly during those two months to help and encourage one another to be fully prepared for their ministry. A similar invitation for the same "Big Step Forward In Faith" program has been received from the India Evangelical Lutheran Church for a planning meeting in June, a training meeting in Sept. and for them to conduct the program in October and November, 1992. Our Lutheran Church in Ghana has shown some interest in the same effort. This is the first time that some of our partner churches overseas have committed themselves to an intensive Biblical, educational stewardship/renewal program which changes their focus from maintenance-survival to nurture-mission.

Stewardship is to change from the inside to the outside. This means changing our giving and fund-raising approach: not **to** budgets or needs, but **from** what God gives; not our share of the budget, but God's share of our income; not leftovers, but firstfruits.

Are LCMS leaders, especially the Board of Directors, ready to launch a Synod-wide, year-long **Big Step Forward in Faith** or **Growing in Vision and Mission**? Certainly our new Synodical Stewardship Executive, Rev. David P. Schmidt, and most District Stewardship Executives, are eager to experience a Biblical program of firstfruit, generous, proportionate giving now.

CHAPTER 10

COME WITH ME ON A GREAT ADVENTURE

Forty-seven years ago when I was ordained, I saw the Christian life and the pastoral ministry as a **Great Adventure**. I saw living in the fellowship of The Lutheran Church-Missouri Synod as a Great Adventure. Since then, this adventure at various times seemed distant, a bit tainted or even shattered. Thirty years of spiritual-political battles which were not expected or desired have affected mission dreams and hopes of most of us in one way or another.

The only purpose of this book is to try to restore our vision of the Great Adventure by identifying our sinful ways which are barriers to any normal Christian life together in our Synod. Unless and until Biblical procedures are re-introduced into our fellowship as a church, we will all be driven into an individualism which isolates individuals or congregations without the joyous, adventurous work together as God intended.

My prayer is that this book will give courage to ordinary Synod members and to a large number of leaders of the Synod and Districts, together with Pittsburgh Convention delegates, that a new spirit of Biblical integrity will arise from the weary fields of political battle, and that by the Holy Spirit we will be determined to close ranks, speak the truth in love, set new goals, and make the next three years a Great Adventure of building the body of Christ and aggressively sharing the saving Gospel of Jesus Christ with the entire world.

It's Friday, Sunday's Coming

My book asks you to leave behind the painful and disastrous problems which have been inflicted upon us through political action, and it proposes Biblical solutions, too. Even so, some readers may be quite depressed and wonder if we will soon see better days. I am reminded of the sermon topic which I heard on radio several years ago, "It's Friday, Sunday's Coming." The preacher gave a graphic description of how the disciples and followers of Christ must have felt on Good Friday after the Savior's crucifixion. On Sunday, the reality of spiritual hope unraveled as the Resurrected Christ victoriously arose to bring healing to the worried and distressed. The situation looks very bleak and dismal because of political campaigns which have inflicted much suffering in the Synod, but the Resurrected Christ rules and desires to restore health to our beleaguered and harassed fellowship. It all depends upon whether we have a humility which is manifested in true contrition and repentance — crucifying the flesh, as Paul says — and allow the New Man to stand strong by the power of the Spirit alive and well.

Cure Your Children's Warring Madness

"God of grace and God of glory" [45] offers a fitting petition at this time, "Cure Your children's warring madness, bend our pride to Your control; shame our wanton, selfish gladness, rich in things and poor in soul. Grant us wisdom, grant us courage lest we miss Your kingdom's goal." Looking forward to the Sunday of new life, we will also pray, "From the fears that long have bound us, free our hearts to faith and praise. Grant us wisdom, grant us courage for the living of these days."

A Christ-centered theology of hope directs us toward a Spirit-powered commitment, "Save us from weak resignation to the evils we deplore; let the gift of Your salvation be our glory evermore, grant us wisdom, grant us courage, serving You whom we adore." It's Friday, Sunday's coming!

A Great Adventure

Songwriter and musician Ken Medema offered an exciting invitation at a leadership conference in Garden Grove, CA, in January, 1992 which I am eager to share with you: "Come with me on a Great Adventure, come with me on a journey long, come with me and we'll hear the music, come with me and we'll sing the song."

The Great Adventure is not a jet-age, first-class flight, but is a marching through the difficult jungles of life. It presents a task which requires praying and working together, not devouring one another. I have attempted to outline some of the basics of this adventure in Chapters 1-4 of this book. Are you excited about our future together under grace? Do you blame others for your problems? Are you ready to get rid of excess baggage through repentance? Are you prepared to live in creative risk to pursue the divine plan — the Great Adventure?

It is much easier and safer to continue to maintain institutional security than to build relationships in the body of Christ. It's a long journey, and the Gospel "music" is powerful and glorious. The question is whether those with the shrill voices of public condemnation will learn the ways of Christ and be obedient to the Word which our Savior gives us for our mutual life together.

The Great Adventure for Christian soldiers is not merely showing up for dress parade with everything polished, or sitting in bunks eating junk food when we should be partaking of nourishment in the Dining Hall. Rather, it requires being present for all exercises in preparation, and being prepared for the Great Adventure, no matter what the cost. This adventure is not merely a Sunday affair. It is not one for which we write the script, but for which we follow the divine plan. The Word has given us the ingredients, components, and factors for stopping our "warring madness," and to build a model for regaining our spiritual health and to go forward in mission strength on a Great Adventure.

Issues That Require Solutions

Individual matters to consider for becoming healthy and functional again are summarized in this final chapter. As we weigh the baggage of institutionalism and some traditional habits, it is obvious that some of this must be dumped immediately through the act of repentance and forgiveness in Christ. Unresolved problems and harmful impediments must be discarded if there is to be any hope to go on a Great Adventure. Here is a summary of the issues which I believe require immediate attention:

1. The Eighth Commandment

LCMS members whose ears are sensitive to the full ramifications of the Gospel in their lives are experiencing earache and heartache from shrill voices which attack people callously and dishonestly through organized political campaigns that disregard Bible polity. Those who are attempting to be obedient to God's will related to building the body of Christ into a Christian community are gravely offended at the intemperate attacks on God's people who communicate differently than the cathedral people in the Synod and in congregations: Gossip and rumor-mongering is epidemic; we are living in an age of allegation churchmanship — allegation church procedures, allegation journalism and allegation scholarship; generalizations and gross misrepresentation to ridicule and smear anyone with whom we do not agree. Half-truths, begging the question, false analogies, related items that are made to appear contradictory, and false reasoning are utilized to attack people and tear them apart, instead of utilizing proper apologetics to make a valid point. This continued presence and activities of political groups with bombardment by publications finds the entire Synod immobilized by an intolerable spiritual barbarism. My book is filled with considerable documentation of this kind of behavior in the Missouri Synod which must be stopped immediately if we are really serious about God's Word and want to experience the Great Adventure.

But who will minister to our brothers who are carrying this "excess baggage" and creating great conflict in our church? Do not expect Synodical officials who are under constant assault from the torrent of accusation journalism to act **alone**, for that will only invite further attacks. Do not expect another victim to write a book and say, "We will not tolerate any of this any more." **Each LCMS member** must see his or her responsibility to arise and express individually and join others to stop this character destruction and carnage which is of Satan, not of God.

There will be no Great Adventure in our Synod until we recognize the difference between allegation and documentation, between public trials and Matthew 18. Our church will be hopelessly dysfunctional as long as tongues, pens and word processors are allowed indiscriminately to pour out blazing fires without following Biblical procedures: "So also the tongue is a small part, but it can boast of big things. You know how a large forest can be set on fire by just a little spark. The tongue is also a fire. It stands among the members of our body as a world of wickedness; it soils the whole body, it sets on fire the whole course of our life, and it is set on fire by hell. A human being can tame and has tamed all kinds of animals, birds, reptiles, and creatures in the sea. but not one person can tame the tongue — a restless evil full of deadly poison...Stop talking against one another, my fellow Christians...Who are you to judge your neighbor?" (Jas. 3:5-8, 11, 12 NET).

We pastors find it easy to translate these Scriptures from Greek into English, but all of us have a problem translating them from English into life situations. It is time for pastors and laity alike to transfer Biblical standards to personal relations. Let us not wait for someone else to act, or think, "We cannot answer every charge or deal with all the slander that is heard and read."

Can enough of us agree and declare privately and publicly that corporately the breaking of the 8th Commandment **will stop now**? Will we pray about it fervently until God gives us the courage so that we will no longer acquiesce?

Can we who are the majority in Synod arise as one and stop this slander and ungodly conflict so that after the Pittsburgh Convention we can dream, plan, and go on our Great Adventure for God? Will we refuse to tolerate any longer **unreasonable and unChristian treatment** not only of the innocent but also of those who need correction? Most members of the Synod do not read *Christian News* and *Affirm*, and very few read the *FORUM LETTER*. Yet **we are all affected** by these magazines which are vehicles by which the Synod's party of the right continues to fuel the scandalous treatment of brothers who are innocent or those who should be given due process by Biblical standards. When will we learn that ignoring these instigators of slander is allowing the spiritual cancer to go untreated while the "Confessional Lutheran" faithful troops are aroused for continuing the battle for the king who wears no clothes? If the story about the king without the clothes ever has had validity, it certainly does in the current situation in which the documentation regarding the "greatest Lutheran theologian of our times" is involved.

If you are not a reader of one of these magazines or a District "Confessional Lutheran Reporter," please be reminded that what you do not read can affect you tremendously because there is a political party in the Synod that takes its direction from them. If you are a reader of one of these deceptive journals, will you stop supporting them and begin to utilize the Synodical structures to get your views across and help our Synod get back on track? Let each ask, "Am I part of the problem or part of the solution?" With true repentance and forgiveness, let us join Paul, "Forgetting what is behind and straining toward what is ahead, I press on toward the goal to win the prize for which God has called me heavenward in Christ Jesus. All of us who are mature should take such a view of things. If on some point you think differently, that, too, God will make clear to you" (Phil. 3:13-15). There will be no Great Adventure until the Eighth Commandment is honored again in the LCMS.

2. Biblical Standards in Personal Relations

This is an essential topic which was covered extensively in Chapter 3 on Building Christian Community. All unhealthy individualism and "lone-ranger" tactics are unhealthy for a properly functioning Synod. We will be as sick as our individual or small group secrets when these secrets indicate our failure to deal with our spiritual diseases. Instead of public charges and complaints, we need to minister lovingly by speaking the truth to our brother, friend, our own group, congregation, Circuit, District, Synodical board, whatever the place, person or situation. If the Board of Regents or Commission on Appeals has conflict, we dare not let this invade the Synod to encourage choosing sides and utilizing gang warfare tactics, but these matters must at all times be settled **Biblically** within the group that is involved.

We cannot any longer tolerate an attitude of "Don't rock the boat," or "This, too, will pass," but rather exercise tough Biblical love and intervention whenever and wherever it is appropriate. To allow anyone to break the 8th Commandment without correction under any circumstance, no matter what level in Synod, will create confusion, hurt, and increasing cynicism about our ability to practice Christian doctrine and also about our willingness to be obedient to God's Word. When leaders fail, then members find themselves in an emotional and spiritual bind.

The steps of evangelical church discipline were outlined in Chapter 3 so that we might seriously consider putting an end to the wrangling, charges, and counter-charges which are occurring in many congregations and in the Synod. Until we are willing to say that evangelical church discipline has generally and basically broken down in the Missouri Synod, including many congregations, there is no chance to change our current destructive ways.

No one is too great or too small to repent and receive forgiveness, and to exhibit the fruits of true repentance. Only such a true change of heart will lead to the integrity of our fellowship and to full and complete reconciliation of brothers in Christ who have sinned publicly, including those who have slandered in any way. I pray that we have all come to the point that we are no longer willing to live with the denials and lies which we have allowed to exist in our Synod. Then Christian community building will lead to "exhorting one another," and "holding one another accountable to each other," and all the other responsibilities for edifying which God gives us through Paul's epistles.

At this date, it is not known what the Task Force on Conflict will propose to the Pittsburgh Convention for making the Adjudication process more effective. My observation is that there is little wrong with the system, but the people who are responsible for making the system work are sometimes perverting it. The work of the Commission on Appeals in the Robert Preus case has shown the Commission to have corrupted the system through untruths and has betrayed its trust. If they are a "supreme court," as trumpeted by *CN* and "Confessional Lutherans," they ought to be impeached on Biblical grounds. Whatever the Pittsburgh delegates decide, let the adjudication process be Biblical without pragmatic shortcuts or any human sidetracking of the simple Scriptural plan.

What about the continuation of *CN*, "Confessional Lutheran Reporters," *Affirm*, and private "Confessional Lutheran" organization meetings throughout the Synod in the future? It would be a great blessing if a place could be found where Rev. Herman Otten could use his tremendous abilities for the edifying of the church to the glory of God by use of Apologetics Biblically. But he must first be faced with his sinful slander of fellow Christians during the past few years, and made to cease and desist if he desires to remain a member of a congregation of The LC-MS. *CN* has no useful purpose from a Biblical perspective unless Otten decides to make it a helpful and productive publication for Apologetics with no rancor. Writers who make reckless charges against others through articles and letters, together with "Calvary Contenders," should be given the permanent "blue pencil" by the editor. The "Confessional Lutheran Reporters" are very divisive instruments in the hands of people and organizations which refuse to use Biblical and Synodical channels to make their charges.

Conducting separate meetings destroys community and trust, while it hardens misconceptions about others. If meetings are held by a political party, then the ones who are criticized should be present, or there should be no meeting! Minnesota South District President Lane Seitz in the April 1992 District *Lutheran Witness* quotes a newsletter article of Rev. Ronald Dommer of Winona, which provides counsel we all need to heed:

"Recently, at a Circuit Pastors' meeting, an announcement was made concerning forming 'A Confessional Laymen's Group' in this area. We were asked to publicize this and encourage our lay people to attend. My response was that I would not encourage this; in fact, I strongly discouraged it.

"While the intent sounds good, 'to study issues and doctrines, and to discuss what members view as positive and negative in our district and Synod,' this is not the proper forum or composition for this to be done as it should be. We are told 'one or more pastors' will be present. Were these pastors elected by the Minnesota South District convention to such a position? No. Were they appointed to this by the District President? No.

"We are pastors to the congregation to which we are 'called' and have no authority and license beyond that, unless duly elected to an auxiliary position or appointed as such by our elected officials. We don't need 'rump' sessions and groups. This discussion should properly take place in the structure already established; circuit meetings, pastoral conferences and district conventions.

"I have been invited to groups like this in the past, both from the right and left. I attended a few of each, although none here in Minnesota. Neither was truly informative, edifying, or positive. Both were on the extreme end of the scale and did not fairly represent the confessional or 'official' doctrine and LCMS position.

"In general it was like-minded and people gathering because they already knew they were like-minded and simply wanted to chart strategy to ramrod their positions and candidates in later conferences and conventions. We don't need power politics. We have too much of that already. Both groups would have profited themselves and their church better had they met in the same room at the same time and really studied the issues together without acrimony and recrimination...The problem arises when either sees themselves as the center, the gauge and limit of what is right and true, against which all others must be compared and censored. Both need to talk and study together as a check and balance against themselves.

"For these reasons among others, I find the forming of such a group more disturbing than satisfying. It is not in the best interest of the Church or the individual."

Can we corporately agree that none of us will tolerate accusations or political interference by journals or groups in our Synod? Can we make a mutual commitment that we will insist that contending parties face each other under "conflict management" conditions, if necessary, in order to gain a Biblical solution? Will each of us pursue the principle, "Talk to people, not about people"? Do we have the motivation to start in our own congregations and our own Circuits?

3. Synodical And District Leaders Supervising Doctrine And Practice.

Chapter 4 of this book presents adequate insights on the necessity of true Biblical and confessional practice. The Synod will be tested in the next three years to see whether we honestly intend to be faithful to our mutual commitment in such matters as ordination of women, ecumenical policies, close(d) communion and lodge practices. Chapter 8 already urged faithfulness to our tradition on ordination, which is consistent with the Bible. The disagreements on the general question of which activities we may participate in should be clarified in view of the misunderstandings and distortions by those who read more into New Testament texts than what they say.

Dr. Jean Garton, who chairs the President's Commission on Women told the *Reporter* in her conversations with women throughout the Synod, she finds "no great interest in ordination" to the pastoral office. But she added that in some LCMS congregations, women are being denied opportunities for service that should be theirs as members of the priesthood of all believers. Garton said, "We're losing women, not because of ordination but because no one is answering their questions" about some limitations placed in recent years on their service as lay people. As an example, she told about a Bible study prepared by women for a presentation to a women's group, but which a pastoral advisor forbad them to use without his approval. In view of the untenable narrow interpretations which are held by some "Confessional Lutheran" pastors, we look to the CTCR to clarify this issue and help be united in Biblical practice to women to serve freely in those areas which the Scriptures suggest.

Regarding fellowship and ecumenism, we look forward to an unambiguous document on "Inter-Christian Relationships" from the CTCR, which will be presented in a way to unify us, not to encourage discordant voices and keep controversy alive. The Synod's Praesidium and District Presidents should be expected to make a commitment to the Synod to honor our Synodical practice in this regard.

Regarding leadership by the Synod's Praesidium and District Presidents, a spirit of toleration or procrastination will not only allow the continuation of our present dysfunctions, but will ultimately result in the disintegration of the Synod. It takes no prophet to recognize that. If we are to realize the Great Adventure, then the Synodical President and Vice Presidents, and Districts Presidents, and all boards and commissions must have a commitment that their work will be consistent with Biblical and Synodical expectations. This means that we stand firm and unmovable, kindly, graciously, and lovingly.

We members should make certain that Synod's leadership, boards and commissions function effectively in order to bring the LCMS back to Lutheran and Biblical orthodoxy in doctrine and practice. We should make certain that all of us work in and through the system with integrity, and that the system welcomes a legitimate concern.

Only cases involving pastors and congregations which have a legitimate complaint against a District President for his inaction should be processed in the Council of Presidents (COP). Such matters ought to be placed on the COP agenda regardless of the number of District Presidents who will or will not support the Biblical and Synodical standard. The day of "Lone Ranger" Districts with the concurrence of a "Lone Ranger" District President who refuses or fails to abide by the Synod's position should end after the Pittsburgh Convention! No case should ever be allowed to come to public trial, and none should be delayed in any way. There are some identifiable crises in belief and practice which require more than public assurances that something is being done. Let us never allow anyone to deal under the table, but all "cards" should be face up in the proper forum and between those who are involved or responsible. If any District President fails to stand and act where the Synod which elected him through the District stands and acts, then ask him to resign and make place for a man who will be obedient to the will of God and the Synod.

In order to have consistent and dependable practice in congregations and between congregations for people who transfer, the level of leadership which requires considerable attention is the office of the Circuit Counselor. Some basic criticisms were heard about the August 1991 Circuit Counselor Conference in St. Charles, Illinois. Some thought that there was no adequate direction from Synod's leaders related to existing doctrine and practice. Much of the meeting centered on, "What do you think?" There appeared to be legitimate complaints about not being fed, but mostly sitting in buzz groups with considerable discussion with no Biblical direction. There were many conflicting viewpoints, which revealed disagreement in doctrine and practice. So why did the Circuit Counselors meet and why was the time and money spent? Are we really back to the "diversity and unity" confusion of twenty years ago? Doesn't God's Word really have anything to offer for directing and unifying our Circuit Counselors so that they can provide Biblical leadership in our Circuits?

There obviously are still deep rifts in the understanding of God's plan for the church, coming from political ideologies or a blurred theological mission vision which is not totally consistent with the Word of God. The Great Adventure should lead us to hold firm to theological orthodoxy and to shun any and all compromises, because it is not of God.

4. Godly Elections

At a minimum in Synodical elections, can we walk together in agreeing that the "Ministry of Influence" document of the Council of Presidents provides godly outlines for each of us to follow? Can we expect the members of the COP who are uncomfortable with the historic position of The LCMS in its doctrine and practice not to become agents for any particular candidates, including President? May we all expect *Affirm* and "Confessional Lutherans" to dispense with their disgusting public list and use their ministry of influence through legitimate private contacts? *Affirm* has promoted some very faithful, able and loyal members for election, but looking at past performances, the only qualification that several of the nominees proposed had was that they were **faithful functionaries of their own group**. That is not a harsh judgment, merely a **reality**. If any of the nominees cannot separate themselves from a political group which backs them and also do not have the courage to correct the poor conduct of their backers, then I see no reason why one should consider voting for them. This includes the Presidency of The LC-MS. We want Biblical Lutherans, not political Lutherans, to lead us during the next triennium on a Great Adventure.

5. Liturgy-Worship Issues

Hopefully, our Synod's Commission on Worship and our Seminaries will provide our Synod with creative leadership so that we as Lutherans will have rich Biblical resources with a variety of liturgies and hymns that reflect the best in communication of God's Word to various cultural and ethnic groups in our Synod. Lutherans are true to their Biblical heritage in providing such resources and encouraging such rich variety of worship without critics confusing style and substance or fusing style with substance.

6. The Doctrine of the Call and Ministry Issues

I am sure that many join me in saying that this is another issue that should be settled in the next three years so that we can go united on our Great Adventure. There is no reason or good in continually confusing this issue by failure to distinguish between plain Biblical doctrine and interpretation. This issue, like a few other major ones, might well be settled by requesting at least five more members of each Seminary faculty, together with five members of the Council of Presidents to work with the CTCR to allow the CTCR to release a document which will bring us together on the doctrine of the Call, and help all understand that the word "ministry" has broad application without confusing or becoming indistinct from the Office of the Pastoral Ministry.

7. The Seminaries, the Curriculum and Direction.

Does the Seminary have anything to do with effective evangelism, productive stewardship, building Christian community, spiritual formation, or is its only responsibility to give doctrinal content for a "cathedral chaplain" type of pastors? Is the theological seminary geared to God's priorities, and is it balanced between doctrine and practice? Should the theological seminary communicate to the church only correct views and doctrines of the Bible, or also inculcate profound understanding and ability related to Christian education, evangelism, stewardship and social ministries? How can we get rid of the maintenance mentality in our curriculum and commit ourselves to a balanced preparation of men for the "real world"?

In preparing effective pastors, our seminaries should pay considerably more attention to how correct doctrines can be implemented in order to carry out Christ's Great Commission. There is a need for a pastor to be able to preach and teach the Word and offer a Biblical theology which builds Christian community, helps members discover and use their spiritual gifts, teach, evangelize, and give money by Biblical principles, and to be able to plant new congregations.

Some seminaries, taking their direction from the Scriptures, have introduced a Department of Prayer and Spiritual Life in the seminary in order to: "1) train pastors to pray and establish a sound personal devotional life; 2) promote a life of prayer and spiritual growth for the seminary family; 3) be a spiritual arm of the seminary for a spiritual ministry to the surrounding community and to visitors; 4) prepare students to impart principles of prayer and spiritual life to the people of their congregations; 5) integrate the doctrinal matters and the highly academic subjects of the seminary into prayer and spiritual life; 6) witness to the Synod and to all the world that the seminary recognizes the necessity for New Testament spirituality and prayer as an integral part of Christianity." We may not need such a Department, but we need the emphasis and activity!

Our Synod can ill afford a pastoral training program which allows students to major in Systematics, History or Exegesis **without an adequate context in pastoral ministry and in missions with spiritual formation undergirding it all**. If this does not become our immediate goal, we will to that extent be irrelevant to the world of the 21st Century and learn too late that our pastors have become the "theological elite" who can relate to doctrine, but not to people. It is not trite to say that Jesus did not die for doctrine, but He died to save people in the context of their misery and suffering, which is what the Gospel is all about. The congregations of the Synod will not be served well if our future pastors are not learning to be functional educators in the context of human distress and grief, inculcating a vision of the kingdom of God that gives meaning to life. The Seminary Faculties should determine Biblically what an effective curriculum should be that serves the Synod well. The Board of Regents should be expected to have a hands-on attitude in communication with the faculties. We would encourage the Task Force on Pastoral Ministry to offer creative insights into preparing pastors confidently for our Great Adventure together.

Concordia Theological Seminary of Fort Wayne has had difficulties in recruitment and placement acceptance. The source of the problem is obviously the pro-active Preus party professors who are enablers in influencing a certain percentage of students to join their camp of "theological elites." While this has negatively influenced a certain amount of students, it has not taken this great Seminary too far off course, and we can expect that its mission can and should during the next several months get back on track under the direction of the Faculty **no longer under the influence of the Robert Preus party line.**

It is unfortunate that many of the congregations calling pastoral candidates from the seminaries made the stipulation that they wanted St. Louis candidates or refused to accept a Fort Wayne student. As one who has shared the documentation in this book, I want to assure the congregations of the Synod that there are a good number of Faculty and Seminary officials who believe strongly that there will be a new commitment and fresh spirit of Biblical Christianity and of wholesome Lutheran doctrine and practice here to the extent that we **urge all potential students** to consider seriously **to register** at Fort Wayne if they have not already done so. Synod needs two strong and healthy seminaries. Many of us believe that with new leadership this Seminary will quickly regain its previous stature and quality, and merit total support. As a regular Adjunct Professor and retiree, I urge all potential students and financial supporters to come along with us at Fort Wayne on a Great Adventure!

8. New Testament Stewardship

The Planned Giving Unit of Synod's Stewardship Department must be commended for doing a tremendous job in acquiring deferred and current gifts for the World Mission of our Synod, offering resources for our congregations, Districts, Synodical educational institutions, World Mission Program, and charitable work. Their work is making possible many new thrusts for our Great Adventure.

Chapter 9 of this book depicts the stewardship slavery to institutional, maintenance and bureaucratic needs. Let us ask our Synod's Board of Directors to move away from budget and fund-raising approaches, and give our Synodical Stewardship Counselor, Rev. David. P. Schmidt, encouragement and support, together with all of the District Stewardship Executives and their boards to proceed with a *Grace Stewardship Plan*. Full research and study should be made of the "Growing in Vision and Mission" Michigan program through consultation with the Michigan leaders and representatives of Resource Services Inc. A New Testament *Grace Stewardship Plan* will by the Holy Spirit's power provide growing financial resources for annual budgets which we have never dreamed possible under our present legalistic systems, and find us on a Great Stewardship Adventure.

9. Mission Services, Parish Education, and Ministry Challenges

It is vital that Synod leaders establish budget priorities which help fulfill the congregations' needs in Christian education and world missions more than in public relations and media for the Synod itself. I believe that it is tragic that the staff of the Board for Parish Education Services has been allowed to be decimated with a minimum number of writers and administrators. In my several presentations to the staff in behalf of the *21st Century Discipling* course, I found an able and faithful staff, which is overworked and understaffed to the extent that it is not possible for them to provide all the educational resources required by our congregations. The unique *21st Century* discipling course focuses on members who are helped to gain greater maturity through self-discovery and group-discovery with applicational and relational teaching, and should have been available to congregations and the Synod before this time. The staff has no time available to produce materials on this mature level, and hardly had time to read or study the manuscripts of the Basic Text, the Student's Workbook and the Teacher's Guide of this course.

One of the priorities of our Synodical budget should be to finance adequately the maintenance of a bigger, well-qualified staff so the unmet needs can be satisfied. The BPES staff should remain a part of Synod, and under no condition become employees of Concordia Publishing House. Dr. H. James Boldt and his staff should have the full financial support of the Synod so that they can help us forward on our Great Adventure in Christian education.

Synod members should be grateful for the excellent work done by leaders of Concordia Publishing House in producing more new and creative materials for the continuing education of pastors and relevant materials for congregations. CPH President Jack Gerber, Dr. Steve Carter, Rev. David Koch, Dr. Wil Rosin and others should receive our full support in developing and producing the materials we need to go on this Great Adventure together.

We are not keeping pace with the mission efforts of others with whom we disagree doctrinally: The Assemblies of God, a younger church than ours, has 2.5 million U.S. members in 1,123 churches and a worldwide membership of 18 million in 120 countries; Campus Crusade for Christ last year produced a ten-lesson curriculum designed to help lay a Christian foundation for ethics and morality for Russian teachers to use in their schools. For starters, each school received a video copy of a "Jesus" film, and each teacher received a New Testament, two books, the curriculum, and a set of materials for 300 school libraries. A 20-member teaching team trained teachers in three different major areas, including 220 teachers and principals representing 112 schools from the Moscow area, and in Vologda, almost 400 educators came from 23 of the 26 regions. Already 2.3 million Soviets have viewed the "Jesus" film. The annual mission report of Campus Crusade for Christ showed an incredible number of workers worldwide reaching millions of students and leaders through training programs. Two non-Christian groups, the Mormons and the Jehovah's Witnesses, certainly put us to shame.

The Board for Mission Services which has been hampered and hurt considerably in its responsibility to reach into the whole world for us. Dr. Glenn O' Shoney and his very able and faithful staff are doing a terrific job. It is our work that they are administering. Every congregation and every member should support them prayerfully and financially in a greater way than in the past. The weak stewardship in various places and the withholding of funds by a few has been very destructive to our World Mission program. There are many open doors which are being entered feebly or not at all. Our excellent staff members are providing creative solutions to past problems, but they need the encouragement and participation on the part of of us all so that we can enter a new era of mission explosion during the next three years after 30 years of political battles. We should take extraordinary measures to assure that greatly enlarged funds will be available for our world mission program already in 1992 in a Great Adventure of world mission outreach.

10. Function and Form Issues

The Synod has been informed through the Reporter that the Task Force on Structure and the Board of Directors are proposing some major changes in structure at the Pittsburgh Convention. It should be obvious that the Synod's first need is to be agreed in its theology of ministry and mission, and the concepts, principles, and functions required to carry out our beliefs. The Task Force on Structure has proposed various structural changes for a number of conventions already, and while some of them have been adopted, a number of them have been rejected. If we are to go on a Great Adventure, we need **first** to find ourself, our true identity. Planning procedures and structures should not be our primary concern now, but rather the recapturing of a living Lutheran faith. Our priority should be a reshaping of our sanctified life corporately and individually in a united walk together, not the remodeling of church form. That can wait for three years.

We certainly do not need the practice of the corporate model with a number of Vice-Presidents in charge of various Synodical divisions. Rather, we should utilize or even strengthen the positions of the present Vice-Presidents in their ecclesiastical responsibilities. Not having the Convention Workbook at hand, and having heard only a summary of a few of the proposals, it appears to be a good idea to make the Synodical President the chief Ecclesial Officer of the Synod, not its CEO. The Synod Vice-Presidents should support the President in the spiritual leadership of the Synod. That follows the Biblical approach.

The proposed Mission and Ministry Council with 28 voting members, and 14 non-voting members, which would meet twice a year, raises too many questions and uneasiness in view of a very unstable Synod which needs agreement on what our adventure is and how to achieve it. An important question: How many of these proposals were resurrected from previous suggestions by the Task Force on Structure which were defeated at another convention? We want to avoid at all cost anything unwieldy, unrealistic, and unworkable. There has been some word that there are some members of the Synod's Board of Directors who disagree quite strongly with some of the proposals. It is important for the delegates and the Synod to hear what their observations are and what their alternate proposals may be.

Regarding structure, we cannot afford at this time to rearrange the boxes on the organizational chart, but recognize that our problems lie deeper than Synod's structure, image or planning procedures. We want no actions which will further polarize or fracture our tender Synodical fellowship. Our consciences have been de-sensitized because of years of political battle while cultural values have entered our fellowship. We are drowning in a super-abundance of administrative efforts and legal advisors which have replaced pastoral leadership and practice! It is not the business of the Synod to confuse and disturb people by allowing non-Biblical approaches to prevail. What we need is to catch a vision of the total task, discuss new initiatives that will later lead to development of a better model, and test them to see if they are of God.

What we most need is theological and mission revitalization that finds us a caring, courageous, evangelical, pastoral, prophetic, locally and globally involved church which has the integrity to be an authentic first Century Biblical church. We will not achieve that at the Pittsburgh Convention or during the next three years, but we can build the foundation for such a Great Adventure.

Some disenchanted members of the ELCA with their deep problems in doctrine and practice are looking for a viable alternative, but find the LCMS very unattractive at this time. The battles waged against the Missouri Synod through organizations and publications by political parties on the left and on the right should end. Now we should put a sign out to anyone who insists on propagandizing with political agendas instead of a Biblical one: "Not accepted or welcome here!"

Do We Have the Will?

We have the Word, the Promise, the Resurrection Power, and have been given the Divine Plan. Do we have the will? Without the will **empowered by the Holy Spirit**, we face a bleak future with more chaos and more political battles. Our vision for a functional Missouri Synod can be a reality. The question is whether we are willing to pay the price of showing humility, of repenting in areas and at times when we don't want to, and of receiving the forgiveness of Christ which frees us to go on the Great Adventure.

Are we refusing to take new steps of faith for fear that we may fail? A few failures are no good reason to neglect the great mission challenges that God places before us. The Great Adventure begins in the mind of God. He plants it in our lives through His Word by the Holy Spirit. We are the adventurers whom God matches with the Great Adventure. God times the process of the Great Adventure. I am convinced that He will hear the cries of His people who are walking in the wilderness of dysfunction, and desire it to be a healthy church on a great adventure. There will be setbacks and frustrations, and a need for course corrections. We will be surprised to gain support from unexpected sources. We will continue to see an explosion of change, but we will not be fearful. We have asked God for the power and the will to be faithful in the Great Adventure.

Not Man's Word, But A Word From God

Many words have been spoken and written during the past three years to try to influence members of Synod toward one viewpoint or another. Much has been good, but some of it very political and bad. The farther we get away from the Word, we will find the necessity of man's words and administrative tactics. It is not too harsh a suggestion to make that whenever anyone speaks at the Convention or speaks at different forums of the Synod, we ask, "Who says so?" Is this the viewpoint of a political group, of the theological elite, or of one who has a personal agenda? If we want to be truly Biblical, we will listen only to the Word of God. At all times and places, we will ask for a Word from God, and settle for nothing less.

I pray that God will give us leaders now who will not be afraid to give us hard Words from God (Jn. 6), who ask us, "Now that you know, do you still want it?" Renewal of the Missouri Synod must come as an outpouring of the Holy Spirit in God's way and in God's time by people who are eager to hear a Word from God, and will tolerate nothing less. Renewal of a church is God stirring, shaking and changing His people from apathy, selfishness, self-promotion, and personal agendas to deep repentance and openness in receiving the freeing forgiveness and joy in Jesus Christ.

At the beginning I said that I come only as a wounded healer and a seeking servant. Where my words have not fulfilled that role, please forgive me. Where they spoke the things of God, may the Holy Spirit make them productive in your life. We are surrounded by wounders who take and grasp, manipulate and control. What we desperately need is for all those who have been wounded to become wounded healers. From Jesus' wounds flow forgiveness and healing for the wounders. Our repentant lives and forgiven spirits by Jesus' love and power comes from the healing Gospel.

It is time to pray: **"God of grace and God of glory, on Your people pour Your power; crown Your ancient church's story, bring its bud to glorious flower. Grant us wisdom, grant us courage for the facing of this hour."** [46]

"COME WITH ME ON A GREAT ADVENTURE.
COME WITH ME ON A JOURNEY LONG.
COME WITH ME AND WE'LL HEAR THE MUSIC.
COME WITH ME AND WE'LL SING THE SONG." [47]

ENDNOTES

[1] Neighbour's materials and books are named in his promotional pamphlet, "Cell Group Churches," Touch Outreach Ministries, P. O. Box 19888, Houston, TX 77079.

[2] Kennon L. Callahan, *Twelve Keys to an Effective Church* (New York: Harper & Row, 1983), pg. xii.

[3] Ibid., pgs. xii-xiii.

[4] Ibid., pg. xiii.

[5] Ibid., pg. xiv.

[6] Adolf Koeberle, *The Quest For Holiness* (Minneapolis: Augsburg Publishing House, 1938), 150-151.

[7] Ibid., 246.

[8] Available from Biblical Renewal Publications, 1914 Wendmere Lane, Fort Wayne, IN 46825.

[9] At this time, this course is available from the Discipling/Stewardship Center, 5729 St. Joe Rd, Fort Wayne IN 46835 for field testing with computer print quality. Sets may be ordered for study.

[10] Norman L. Geisler, *Christ: The Theme of the Bible* (Chicago: Moody Press, 1968).

[11] Ibid., 11.

[12] O. H. Pannkoke, *A Great Church Finds Itself* (Quitman: O. H. Pannkoke, 1966), 239-243.

[13] Frederick W. Danker, *NO ROOM IN THE BROTHERHOOD, The Preus-Otten Purge of Missouri* (St. Louis: Clayton Publishing House. 1977).

[14] Ibid., 55

[15] Ibid., 75.

[16] Ibid., 95

[17] Ibid., 132-133.

[18] Ibid., 96

[19] Ibid., 188.

[20] Ibid., 233.

[21] John Tietjen, *MEMOIRS IN EXILE, Confessional Hope and Institutional Conflict* (Minneapolis: Augsburg Press, 1990).

[22] Ibid., 6.

[23] Ibid., 55.

[24] Ibid., 72.

[25] Ibid., 109.

[26] Ibid., 112.

[27] Ibid., 117.

[28] Ibid., 129.

[29] Ibid., 140.

[30] Ibid., 169-170.

[31] *Evangelical Directions for the Lutheran Church*, edited by Erich Kiehl and Waldo J. Werning, (Produced for the Lutheran Congress in Chicago, 1970). Available from Biblical Renewal Publications, 1914 Wendmere Lane, Fort Wayne IN 46825.

[32] Ibid., 79-80.

[33] Kenneth Woodward, "The Missouri Synod Lutheran Civil War," *Christian Herald* (January, 1971).

[34] *Christianity Today* (August 7, 1981), 42.

[35] Herman Sasse, "Selective Fellowship," *The Australian Theological Review* (September, 1957) Volume XXVIII, No. 3).

[36] The Mission Affirmations are printed in the Proceedings of the 1965 Detroit Convention-46th Regular Convention of The Lutheran Church-Missouri Synod.

[37] Paul Lindemann, *Christian Stewardship and Its Modern Implications* (St. Louis: Concordia Publishing House, 1925), 32-38.

[38] T. A. Kantonen, *Resurgence of the Gospel* (Philadelphia: Muhlenberg Press, 1956), 214.

[39] Kenneth Kuntz, *Wooden Chalices* (St. Louis: Bethany Press, 1963), 85.

[40] Werner Elert, *The Christian Ethos*, trans. Carl J. Schindler (Philadelphia: Muhlenberg Press, 1957), 208.

[41] Rachel Henderlite, *Forgiveness and Hope* (Richmond: John Knox Press, 1961). 40.

[42] D. M. Baillie, *God Was In Christ* (London: Faber and Faber Ltd., 1961), 121.

[43] Findley B. Edge, *A Quest For Vitality In Religion* (Nashville: Broadman Press, 1963), 25.

[44] Waldo J. Werning, *Supply-Side Stewardship* (St. Louis: Concordia Publishing House, 1986), 90-93. Also see *Christian Stewards — Confronted and Committed* by Waldo J. Werning (St. Louis: Concordia Publishing House, 1982)

[45] Harry E. Fosdick, "God of Grace and God of Glory," *Lutheran Worship*, #398.

[46] Ibid., verse 1.

[47] Unpublished song by Ken Medema, 3825 Meadow Wood Lane, Grandville, MI 49418.

BOOKS WRITTEN BY THE AUTHOR

EVANGELICAL DIRECTIONS FOR THE LUTHERAN CHURCH (Erich Kiehl and Waldo Werning, Editors)

Essays of the Aug. 31-Sept. 2, 1970 Congress in Chicago. Twenty-two stimulating studies on the Nature of Scriptural Truths by Dr. Paul Zimmerman, Dr. Martim Warth, Dr. Francis A. Schaeffer, Dr. Richard Klann, Dr. Manfred Roensch, Dr. Robert Preus, Dr. George Wollenburg, Dr. Waldo Werning, Dr. Ralph Bohlmann, Dr. Lowell Green, Dr. Erich Kiehl, Dr. Edwin Weber, Rev. Elmer Reimnitz, Dr. Eugene Bertermann, Dr. Herman Sasse, and Dr. Wilbert Sohns. Only 200 copies remaining — orders will be filled as they come.

RENEWAL FOR THE 21ST CENTURY CHURCH

Calling for full Christianity for an empty world which goes beyond cultural preoccupation and individualism, this book proposes communication of repentance-forgiveness and Law-Gospel instead of self-sufficiency and centrality of man. It calls for a wholistic Christianity for a segmented and compartmentalized world. The problems of Christianity are not so much a matter of lack of resources as of misplaced priorities. Calling for a radical world view adjustment and renewal, the book proposes many valid ideas on how to overcome the major roadblocks on the path to world evangelization.

CHRISTIAN STEWARDS — CONFRONTED AND COMMITTED

Most needed and popular stewardship book...total basic resource, Grace, Law-Gospel, New Man's victory over the Old Man. Presents money management, stewardship of abilities, giving, body and health. Presents theology, principles and messages for total stewardship, including organizing the congregation's stewardship task. The basic stewardship tool which every congregation needs.

SUPPLY-SIDE STEWARDSHIP: A CALL TO BIBLICAL PRIORITIES

Contrasts a maintenance stewardship mentality with the abundant supply which God offers. Far too often we concentrate on keeping things running while ignoring the primary Biblical mandates for Christ's mission. Offers model, charts and steps to follow the Biblical direction. Emphasis is on spiritual growth rather than on fund-raising. Proposes giving from God's supply rather than to the church's needs.

THE RADICAL NATURE OF CHRISTIANITY

A refreshing change in its theological orientation from much literature on stewardship, missions, and church growth. Presents a practical strategy for continuing change and reform in individual lives and church structures. Shows the tie between pure doctrine and aggressive mission.

VISION AND STRATEGY FOR CHURCH GROWTH

Refreshing, incisive, and practical, this book will not overwhelm the busy pastor or intimidate lay leaders. Churches are challenged to take the mission of Christ seriously, to recognize that the foundations and resources of grace rather than human manipulation are fundamental to a growing dynamic church. Helpful section on reclaiming inactive members, evangelical discipline, spiritual formation and goal-setting.

DATE DUE